Readings in Early Indian History

Readings in Early Indian History

Romila Thapar

OXFORD
UNIVERSITY PRESS

OXFORD
UNIVERSITY PRESS

Oxford University Press is a department of the University of Oxford. It furthers the University's objective of excellence in research, scholarship, and education by publishing worldwide. Oxford is a registered trademark of Oxford University Press in the UK and in certain other countries

Published in India by
Oxford University Press
YMCA Library Building, 1 Jai Singh Road, New Delhi 110 001, India

First published in 2013

ISBN-13: 978-0-19-808376-4
ISBN-10: 0-19-808376-9

Typeset in 11.5/13.8 Adobe Garamond Pro
by The Graphics Solution, New Delhi 110 092
Printed in India at Akash Press, New Delhi 110 020

Contents

Preface

The essays selected for this Reader were written by me over the last half century and at different points of time. They reflect some of the changes in the writing of early Indian history during this period. Such changes were due both to the discovery of new evidence—largely through archaeological excavation—and from asking new questions of existing data. The answers to the questions provided fresh explanations for historical events. The perspective of history as a social science introduced the potential of a larger range of historical explanations.

Some reflections on these changes are mentioned in the opening essay in the section 'Historiography'. This section in itself points up the interest in historiography that has developed substantially in the last few decades. The first essay attempts an overview of the change among modern historians writing on the early past, moving from the views of colonial historians to those of a nationalist bent, to those underlining the importance of social and economic history. These last were influenced by the debate on historical materialism as a method and as a theory of historical explanation, which began to be widely discussed from the 1960s. The essay on D.D. Kosambi implicitly touches on this debate.

This section incorporates an initial foray into the question of the forms that the expression of a sense of history might have taken in the early period. I have argued for there having been various historical traditions with diverse representations of the past. I have differentiated between what I call 'embedded history', where narratives are folded into texts that acquired a religious orientation, such as the epics and *Purāṇas*, and to some extent the histories of Buddhist Saṅghas, and a more familiar kind of history, which I have called 'externalized history', written as independent historical genres such as biographies, inscriptions, and chronicles.

The section 'Economy and Society' begins with a suggested reconstruction of the post-Harappan phase of Indian society. It is a deflection from the usual focus limited to considerations of what constituted 'Aryan' culture. It looks at the history of northern India in the late second and early first millennium BC in terms of the emergence of a dominant culture in a multi-cultural situation. The fundamental question is that of the prevalence and status of a language, namely Indo-Aryan. Although the archaeological evidence for this period has been much enlarged through recent excavations, I have not referred to these in this essay because I believe that the thrust of the original questions is still relevant, and these questions can continue to be posed even with new evidence. The society under discussion conforms broadly to what I have called a lineage society. This, I have tried to discuss in the next essay, which is part of a larger work on defining lineage societies and kingdoms.

The formation of the state and the emergence of kingdoms is now a recognized process in the evolution of some historical societies. I have described this process for the Ganges plain in the mid-first millennium BC. My argument is that in this region the process was initially dependent on the cultivation of rice which enhanced production, and on the adoption of new technologies. By way of contrast, the emergence of kingdoms in southern coastal regions drew more heavily on trade as a resource for change. Initially this was the maritime trade with the eastern Mediterranean as has been discussed in the next essay.

The section 'Changing Political Formations' attempts to define an empire as a further stage in the formation of states, indicating the difference between the two through analysing the emergence and functioning of the Mauryan Empire. It also has a chapter from my first publication on the Mauryas where I was trying to sketch the historical background of the society that gave rise to an imperial form. This is contrasted with a more recent study of one segment of this background, that of caste, as described in one major source. In later years different questions were asked of the same source. I have tried to show how the original statement from Megasthenes, when referred to in subsequent Greek writing, carries somewhat diverse interpretations. These contribute to showing the complexities of a theme that was once thought to be an unambiguous statement. The essay on Aśoka tries to bring together the many facets of this ruler as have been variously discussed at different times.

The essays in the section 'Religion, Philosophy, and Society' relate to three topics. One is the need to examine the historical context of ideas and ideologies where they have a social role. The new philosophical concepts and discussions recorded in the *Upaniṣad*s are shown as emerging in part from historical changes of the mid-first millennium BC. The contrast between the life of the householder and of the renouncer, which is a common thread in many texts of the late first millennium, is concerned not only with religious perceptions but also reflects the social conditions of the time. Religious sects that build monuments such as Buddhist *stūpa*s and Hindu temples as places of worship require the material support of the community for which such places are constructed, and even better the more substantial support of royalty. Patronage therefore, both from royalty and from lay-followers, becomes an essential feature of the requirements of religious sects that have a community following.

The last section has two essays that are different from the previous ones (except those on historiography). They discuss two themes that are rooted in descriptions first written about in earlier times but with continuity to contemporary times. The story of Śakuntalā was fiction, yet the story was repeated with some change of character and event in later times, and these changes reflect a different historical context. Observing these changes provides a glimpse of how historical change affected the story.

The essay on Somanātha argues that we have relied largely on the chronicles of the Sultanate courts for accounts of Maḥmūd of Ghazni's raid on the Somanātha temple. The accounts are not uniform in what they state and yet we have accepted them as such. This has limited our comprehension of the history of Somanātha. Many other groups of people were involved with events at Somanātha in various ways, and have left evidence that differs from the narratives of the chroniclers. If we read the Sanskrit inscriptions, the Jaina chronicles of the dynasties of Gujarat, and popular ballads from the neighbourhood, we get quite another picture of the history of the temple and the people involved in that history. We also have to question colonial scholarship which relied on only one group of texts in their rather erroneous reconstruction of the event.

In sum, the essays touch on facets of the historiography of the last few decades, suggesting a directional change, and situate the change in its contemporary context.

Romila Thapar
New Delhi, 2013

Section I

Historiography

CHAPTER 1

Decolonizing the Past*

Fifty years ago, at the time of independence, we had inherited a history of the subcontinent which incorporated two substantial views of the past: the colonial and the nationalist. Both claimed to be based on contemporary techniques of historical research. The claim was reasonably correct to the extent that they were primarily concerned with chronology and sequential narratives about ruling powers. The initial colonial view going back to the early nineteenth century was a departure from any earlier Indian historical traditions and drew on European preconceptions of Indian history.

It had three foundational arguments. The first was the periodization of Indian history, a periodization that was to have consequences not only for the writing of history but in a major political fallout effect in the twentieth century. Indian history was divided into the Hindu and the Muslim civilization and the British period, formulated by James Mill in *The History of British India* written in the early nineteenth century. These labels were taken from the religions of the ruling dynasties—Hindu and Muslim. The divisions were endorsed by the assumption that the units of Indian society were mutually hostile, monolithic and uniform religious communities, primarily the Hindu and the Muslim. The Hindus came to be called the majority community, and the Muslims and others were the minority communities on the basis of their numbers in the census returns. This periodization

* An earlier version of this essay was published as 'Decolonising the Past: Historical Writing in the Time of Sachin—and Beyond', *Economic and Political Weekly*, vol. 40, no. 14, 2 April 2005, pp. 1442–8.

projected an obsession with an absence of historical change in India and further, it presumed that religion superseded all other authority. That we still cling to it or to its shadow almost two hundred years later indicates our willingness to deny historical change in our past.

The second assertion was that the pre-colonial political economy conformed to the model of Oriental Despotism, which assumed a static society characterized by an absence of private property in land, despotic and oppressive rulers and therefore endemic poverty. This pattern did not envisage any marked economic change and was characteristic of backward societies.

The third aspect was the argument that society was divided into castes—the four *varṇas*—and these formed a frozen social structure, again unchanging through history. Those that had some admiration for the Indian past, such as Max Mueller and a few other Orientalists, derived it largely from what they saw as the Aryan imprint on Indian civilization both as a race and a language, and caste was said to be rooted in these foundations. The dominant language of the civilization was Sanskrit and the paramount religion was Vedic Brahmanism. This was seen as characteristic of Aryan culture and there was a concern to identify and segregate the Aryan from the non-Aryan. Aryan was seen as superior in part because of a supposed link with Europe.

These preconceptions governed routine history focusing on chronology and the narrative of dynasties. Indian historians, by and large continued this routine. Nevertheless, there was also some concern especially among historians influenced by nationalist ideas about some of these preconceptions. Most accepted the colonial periodization. Others changed the nomenclature to ancient, medieval, and modern, borrowed from Europe and thought to be more secular, although the markers remained the same. Thus, there was no effective change in periodization.

The theory of Oriental Despotism was rejected. Curiously however, there was little interest in providing carefully thought-out alternative hypotheses on the Indian political economy and society. Social history in standard works largely reiterated the description of the four *varṇas*, registering little recognition of deviations, leave alone explaining them. Although there were exceptions pointing to other ways, these exceptions were not at the forefront.

Parallel to the above—what has been described as mainstream, secular nationalism—were the two religious nationalisms, Hindu and Muslim. These were systematized into ideologies of political mobilization in the early twentieth century. For them the interest was less in researching alternate paradigms and more in seeking to use history to legitimize current political ideology and mobilization. An example of this was the insistence that a religious identity was the seminal identity in the past and continued to be so in the present. This was a justification for separate nation states in contemporary times. These historical views were based on the colonial interpretations of Indian history which were reincarnated, as it were, to serve the political intentions of the present.

The past is inevitably part of the present. But the relationship between the two, which includes continuities and disjunctures, becomes more meaningful if the past can be explained and understood, with all its features both agreeable and disagreeable, rather than being used arbitrarily to validate the agendas of the present.

Re-examining History: Early Trends

The need to examine history in terms of a different set of parameters was, at this point, a somewhat premature thought among mainstream historians. However, such parameters were being suggested by other writing. The prehistory of the social sciences, as it were, had begun in discussions around the nature of Indian society and the cause of economic poverty. Dadabhai Naoroji had maintained that the colonial economy drained the wealth of India and was the source of Indian poverty. Analysing the colonial economy was the first step for those who either supported or contested this theory. Rajni Palme Dutt's indictment of colonial policy made a substantial contribution to the debate.

The teasing out of the strands of the caste structure and its social implications was evident in the writings of D.P. Mukherjee and N.K. Bose who were unfreezing the theoretical pattern. By describing the ground reality of caste and underlining what differentiated it from the norms set out in the dharma-shastras, new research on caste was initiated. The point was not easily taken by most historians. The normative view was implicit to the then vision of Indian civilization where caste, tied to the conventional reading of religion, was seen as the enduring feature. B.R. Ambedkar's writings on the history of the *śūdra*s and dalits were not cited in studies of social history, nevertheless, they had an indirect impact. Caste was not merely a social hierarchy but was inherently linked to issues of domination and subordination. The interlinking of higher and lower through intermediate categories in the hierarchy prevented a confrontation between the dominant and the subordinated.

Among the more influential colonial representations of the world at that time was its division into discrete civilizations. Each was demarcated territorially and associated with a single language and religion. The implicit counterpart to the civilized was the presence of the non-civilized, the lesser breeds without the law. The implications of this superiority had not been questioned at the time. (I might add as an aside, that even now, although questioned by many, nevertheless Arnold Toynbee's twenty-six civilizations have merely been overlaid by Samuel Huntington's eight.) Colonial perception identified caste Hindus as the civilized and the others less so and labelled some of the latter as primitive, a label that persists at the popular level.

Cultural nationalism came to be formulated from colonial notions of civilization, much discussed by the Indian middle-class. Few attempted to ascertain pre-colonial definitions of culture with its multiple variations. It was easier to stay with the colonial reading. The powerful intellectual controversies of earlier times, authored by *brāhmaṇa*s and non-*brāhmaṇa*s, tended to be projected as religious sectarian discourses by both colonial and nationalist interpreters. That these earlier discussions had drawn on dialectics incorporating rational and logical reasoning and had recorded dissent, was hardly conceded and rarely explored. There was a preference for viewing them as minor disagreements within a centrally agreed philosophy. Early scientific knowledge was described but its social implications were seldom part of a historical discourse. Given the separation between history and philosophy as disciplines it was not thought necessary to locate ideas in a historical background. Cultural nationalism was confined to contours dictated by colonial preconceptions. The current claims to authentic, indigenous identities, unchanging and eternal, pose immense problems to historians. Identities are neither timeless and unchanging, nor homogeneous, nor singular as maintained in the nineteenth century notion of civilization. Even concepts of cultural nationalism have to be located in the historical circumstances that fashion them.

The questioning of existing theories about the past gradually altered the criteria of analyses among historians and the asking of new questions also widened the range of sources. This led to some distancing from both the colonial and the nationalist interpretations of Indian history. Since knowledge is not chronos-free, it has to be related to a specific situation and time. This is all the more so where a shift in paradigm is involved, where the frame of reference is being realigned. In part this shift had to do with questions related to the broader issues concerning the Indian nation state in the 1950s. This was not an attempt at imposing the present on the past, but at trying to understand the present by more insightful explanations of the past.

Emerging from a colonial situation, the initial question was how the new nation was to be shaped. This required understanding the components of the nation and the form they had taken in the past. A better understanding of this provided a prelude to current concerns. These included discussions on economic growth, the establishing of a greater degree of social equality and comprehending the potential of a variegated cultural heritage. These were issues that were being discussed in *The Economic Weekly* and the discussions were to continue in the *EPW*. Inevitably this also led to questioning the view of history that had been constructed in the last two hundred years, apart from obtaining information about aspects of the past that had not been researched earlier. The questions were not limited to politics and the economy but extended to social forms, cultural and religious expression and the formulation of identities and traditions. Historiography, the history and philosophy of historical writing, and seeing the historian as part of a historical process began to surface in historical writing. This was to become a significant aspect of historical exploration. Earlier historical writing came to be re-assessed in the light of new kinds of evidence and of theories explaining the past.

In the questioning of existing explanations the validity of periodizing history as Hindu, Muslim and British was increasingly doubted. It posited two thousand years of a golden age for the first, eight hundred years of despotic tyranny for the second, and a supposed modernization under the British. Such divisions set aside the relevance of significant changes within these periods. That any such age can be described as consistently glorious or tyrannical was questioned as also the characterization of an age merely by the behaviour of rulers or by their religion. The doubt was encouraged when history became more than just the study of dynasties, and also from the realization that communities and religions are not monolithic, but are segmented, and segments had their own varying relationships with each other.

Dialogue with Other Disciplines

Alternate notions of periodization were in part a reaction to the opening up of a dialogue between history and other disciplines, in ways that were different from earlier attempts at introducing diverse facets of the past. Conventional history juxtaposed the succession of dynasties—one more glorious than the next—with economic history, social history, and the history of religion and the arts. These were all included within the same chronological brackets but were segregated. However, by relating them more closely to each other and to a historical context they formed a network of interconnected features and gave greater depth to historical argument. The interface between the past and the present encouraged the notion of exploring some themes even in other disciplines through looking at their historical past. Some familiarity with earlier historical experience could provide insights into contemporary phenomena. This also introduced the idea of comparative history. The intention was not to apply the patterns of other societies to India but to use the information in a comparative manner to ask further questions of one's own society.

I would like to consider some examples of the kind of history that emerged from these dialogues. Discussion on these went through two phases. Initially history was opened up to interdisciplinary perspectives and to new analytical methods in the 1950s and 1960s. Consequently extensive explanations of the past followed. Some were based on hitherto unknown evidence but, more generally, they arose from new enquiries. To pinpoint the precise time when these interpretations came to be established is difficult since it is an ongoing process. I shall, therefore, also be touching on more recent work that has followed the initial paradigm shift, referring, where possible, to the earlier and later phases.

The concept of the nation had run into confusion with the two-nation theory. The clarification did not lie in taking it back to earlier times but in differentiating between nation and state, with the state being the primary entity in early times. The state had earlier been associated with a patriarchal society whereas in the theories of state-formation in the 1960s various other features were given priority, ranging from environment to the nature of political control. A centrally administered kingdom had been assumed to be the basis of all states in the past. The break-up of large kingdoms into smaller ones was equated with political decline and read as a fragmentation of a polity accompanied by an absence of consolidated power. But this was not invariably so.

The likelihood of variation in patterns of power gradually led to the demarcation between forms of political organization. Clan-based societies with chiefs, generally agro-pastoral, are thought by some historians as being prior to the existence of a state, although not all would agree. Kingdoms demonstrated greater complexity reflecting more clearly the emergence of the state. The change has been seen as seminal to the societies described in the Vedas, the Mahābhārata and the Rāmāyaṇa, and the early Buddhist canon. These studies will hopefully shift the obsessive discussion on the origin and identity of 'the Aryans' and the Aryan foundations of Indian civilization to broader questions such as those being currently considered on the nature of social change, on the interface between multiple cultures, and on mechanisms of legitimizing power; all questions germane to enquiries into the early Indian past. Historical analyses are of course complicated by the fact that these variant forms have coexisted as they still do and their complexities are reflected in historical sources.

When the structure of the state began to be discussed it led to a focus on the typology of state systems. How a state comes into existence at different times has now become a focused study in which the state is not something distinct from society. The nature of the formation of states suggested variables that were different from earlier to later times. The Mauryan state was not identical with that of the Guptas. The discussion on varied forms had implications for the definition of empire as well, as is evident in the study of imperial administrations. Thus it can be asked whether the Mauryan empire was a highly centralized bureaucratic system as most of us had argued in our earlier writing or can it be seen as a more diversified system as some of us began arguing in our later writings. The tension between control from the centre and assertion of local autonomy has been a recurring feature and is now being commented upon. The regular use of the term 'empire' for all kingdoms has come in for questioning with kingdom being differentiated from empire. Religion was an unlikely primary factor in the initial emergence of the state which required more utilitarian resources. But in the welding of segments into empire, as in the policies of Aśoka and Akbar, there was recourse to certain facets of religion.

In the colonial view, the village was the economic unit of Indian society and towns received less attention. The trend towards what were to become urban centres of the historical period in the Ganga plain dates to about the sixth century BC. The presence of towns becomes gradually more marked in subsequent centuries. Cities were linked to state systems, not just as capitals but also as centres for the exchange of goods. The recognition of urban sites on the ground also led to broader definitions of urbanization. As a process it was investigated in terms of the environment and resources of its location, its demography, and its potential as a centre for exchange. This was partially influenced by the focused research on Harappan cities both in tracing their emergence as urban centres and the causes of their decline.

The ideological confrontation between the '*gaṇa-saṅghas*'—the oligarchies or chiefdoms, and the '*rājyas*'—kingdoms, earlier referred to in passing, is now eliciting greater interest. The texts present divergent views on social ethics, as for example, on *ahiṃsā*/non-violence, in the Pali Buddhist canon and the *Bhagavad Gītā*. Arguments and counter-arguments among the intellectuals of those times were an intrinsic part of the urban experience. Earlier studies noted that orthodox views were challenged by the heterodox, whom the *brāhmaṇas* referred to as the '*nāstika*' and the '*pāṣaṇḍa*'; and the latter used similar terms for the former. Relating these ideas to a historical context had only a small beginning in historical studies, the trend being to treat them non-historically.

Exchange in varying forms, from barter to commerce, for which there is a spurt of evidence from the post-Mauryan period, provided an additional economic dimension. Numismatics or the study of coins was not limited to honing the chronology of rulers but introduced the preliminaries of money and markets at exchange centres. Closeness to other parts of Asia was known through overland routes. Maritime connections have now come to the forefront, underlining further cultural and intellectual cross-currents. The dialogue between Indian astronomers and those of Alexandria in the early centuries AD, was but one aspect of this. More recently evidence of what seems to have been bilingualism in Greek and Prakrit, and probably Sanskrit, suggests a need to re-examine the cross-currents in the many cultures of the north-western areas. The role of commerce in a range of Asian economies was once limited to the listing of archaeological and textual evidence. Now the questions relate to the complexities of commercial arrangements. The orbit ran from Tunis to Canton in the period prior to European expansion. Half-serious comments are being made on globalization before globalization. Serious observation questions the validity of discrete, self-sufficient civilizations.

Theories of Explaining the Past

In the 1960s and in many parts of the world, historical research had become an attempt to explain the past. Consequently, theories of explanation came in for intense discussion. These incorporated commentaries on the writing of Karl Marx, Max Weber, the French sociologists, and historians of the Annales School, and more recently on Michel Foucault. The 'Otherness' of India, sometimes projected as the absence of features leading up to capitalism, can be seen, for example, in Karl Marx's construction of the Asiatic Mode of Production and in Max Weber's projection of the religion of India. Their explanations were not always applicable to Indian history in a literal sense, nevertheless, even in rejecting these, questions were raised that led to exploring new themes, as did their methods of analyses.

Explanations of Indian society were debated, particularly those drawing on Marxist thought. The explanations were not definitive and permanent although the fervour of the discussion suggested that they might be so. They introduced the historian to aspects of the past that had earlier seemed closed and brought the peripheral into the mainstream in a meaningful way.

The centrality of social and economic history was evident in all these theories. Methods of analysis influenced by historical materialism were adapted by some but with the caveat that the Indian data might suggest variant patterns. The work of D.D. Kosambi was a paradigm shift and whether or not one agrees with his generalizations, his writings were impressively wide-ranging and catalytic. He was able, authoritatively, to open to wide scholarly discussion in what was often regarded as the closed preserve of Indologists.

Marxist historical writing introduced the idea of modes of production which further altered periodization. Marx's notion of an Asiatic Mode of Production was set aside. However, the possibility of a feudal mode of production and the debate on the transition to capitalism captured historical interest. The notion of feudalism had initially drawn on European parallels but now the discussion was of the more extensive Marxist model. Significantly, the critiquing of the feudal mode for India was also initiated by Marxist historians and when joined by others became an even more vigorous debate.

The argument was based on changes in land relations in the latter half of the first millennium AD. The transition to feudalism lay in the system of granting land or villages, primarily to *brāhmaṇas*, to temples, to Buddhist monasteries and to a few who had served the state. Since the granting of land became a focal point of the political economy, it brought about a tangible change in agrarian relations. This change played a significant role particularly after about the eighth–ninth centuries AD. The discussion for and against the feudal mode opened up new perceptions about the state, the economy and society, religious activities, and other potential areas of investigation, as well as other theories of explanation.

Grants of land to religious beneficiaries led predictably to innovations in their activities and beliefs. They established institutions and became powerful property holders. Inscriptions recording these grants are a telling example of how a historical record is used only minimally until a new set of questions are asked. The inscriptions had been read since the nineteenth century but largely for data on chronology and on dynasties. Only in the last fifty years did they begin to be examined in-depth for data on agrarian relations and for assessing elite patronage to religious groups.

Some religious cults became a network of support for particular dynasties, a process that was more visible at the local level. The Yadavas, for instance, were both devotees and patrons of the emerging cult of Viṭṭhala, and the geographical distribution of the cult could also be seen as the area of support for the patron. Religious institutions such as the '*vihāra*' and the '*maṭha*', have been studied as agencies of intervention, often in association with the ruling powers, quite apart from their fostering formal religions.

Sifting the activities covered by the all-inclusive label of 'religion', and attempting to unravel their social functions helps to clarify the links between social roles and religious beliefs. At the same time popular religious movements, some known to contradict or deviate from the orthodox, occupied a prominent place on the historical canvas. The contours of popular religions—the Bhakti and Śākta sects in particular and later the *gurus* and *pirs*—are being mapped through finding out who their followers were and their patrons, as well as through the manner in which they either distanced themselves from or accommodated conventional religious teachings. Such intersections are of historical interest, particularly in the current ambience when political groups are muscling in and claiming to be defending this or that religion. The interaction between religious sects and social groups are often lost in the rigidities of formal religion. The relationship between the worshipper and his deity in the *bhakti* tradition has been compared to that of the peasant and his feudal lord. This remains a continuing argument but the discussion it has provoked enables us to know more about the intricacies of both relationships.

Anthropological studies used in a comparative manner have pointed to further directions in social history. Thus the analysis of kinship connections is helping to trace diverse genealogical patterns in the lengthy ancestral lists of the Kurus and the Pāṇḍavas in the Mahābhārata. The earlier presumed uniformity is being replaced by seeing these lists as incorporating varied social groups. Ritual is inherently an act of worship but when encrusted with social meaning it could also become a way of legitimizing power and status. The discrepancies between statements in narrative sources and the regulations of the *dharma-śāstras*, pointed up the fact that the latter were indeed normative texts and did not necessarily describe actual society as had been assumed earlier. Nor were claims to opulence and grandeur to be taken literally without other supporting evidence. The point was brought home more visibly through excavations of simple mud and mud-brick structures at places believed to be those mentioned in the *Mahābhārata*. Epic poetry is more often the capturing of an illusion rather than the mirroring of reality.

The supposedly immobile character of caste gave way to realizing that there were degrees of caste mobility. The sociological theory of sanskritization—that lower castes sometimes sought upward mobility by imitating the mores of upper castes—was applied to certain historical situations but it had its limitations. It was more appropriate to assertions of status among the *brāhmaṇa*s and *kṣatriya*s who were sometimes recruited from lesser castes. Ritual specialists of various kinds could end up as temple priests when cult shrines evolved into temples. Politics was an open arena and claims to *kṣatriya* identities are among the more ambiguous. The process was not always one of osmosis. Imitating lifestyles can be the cause of some friction if not confrontation.

These re-orientations in the study of early Indian history were anticipated as a consequence of interdisciplinary trends, of theories of explanation, and of methodological change. The later themes emerged from these discussions although some also touch contemporary concerns.

For instance, gender studies have not been just the accumulation of more data on the history of women but garnering the views and activities of women and observing how these conditioned society. Particular social forms became patterns of control over women, and resistance to these is significant to social history. Earlier, popular belief held that Gārgi asking philosophical questions, or the official recording of the donations of Aśoka's queen, Kāruvākī, were proof of women generally being held in respect. But when such references were placed alongside the evidence of a subordinate status, the assessment required reconsideration. Historically women were as central to the creation of communities and identities as were men.

The mutation implied in the phrase, from *jana* to *jāti*, from clan to caste, suggested new modalities in the history of social change. For example, it was perhaps possible to trace the origins of certain *jāti*s to non-caste groups such as forest dwellers. The chiefly families aspired to become *kṣatriya*s and other clansmen were relegated to being *śudra* peasants and providing labour. A vignette of this process is given in the *Harṣacarita* of Bānabhaṭṭa, a seventh century biography of the king Harṣa. The mutation required an alteration in the immediate economy, often converting forest into fields, and an acceptance by an erstwhile relatively more egalitarian society of the hierarchies essential to caste.

Descriptions of the *Niṣāda*, *Bhil* and *Śabara* overlap at times with those of the *rākṣasas*/demons. One wonders whether the *rākṣasas* were figures of fantasy as was thought earlier, or whether some at least represent a demonizing of the culturally alien as is being thought now. The initial systematic study of collecting references to the *caṇḍāla* needs now to be related to delineating alternate social forms, to whatever degree the references allow. Seeing the change as a historical process involves the need to integrate the contribution of such groups to the making of Indian history, a contribution still waiting for recognition.

Shifts in Understanding

Subba Rao's work in the late 1950s suggested connections between geographical regions, the environment and historical perspectives. These were causal factors in history and sometimes became problematic. Awareness of the environment reflected on historical causation. The range included the silting up of deltas as observed by ancient Greek navigators requiring the relocation of ports; changing river courses leading to migrations and shifting settlements, as happened with the late Harappan settlements on the Hakra river; or deforestation changing the landscape, the economy, and much more.

The interest in regional history grew by degrees, assisted to some extent by the creation of linguistic states from the 1950s superseding the more arbitrary boundaries of the erstwhile provinces. The new states were treated as sub-national territorial units. Texts in the regional languages provide abundant information, some from early periods as in south India and more generally with a marked increase after about AD 1000. The standpoint of subcontinental history, conventionally viewed from the Ganga plain, has had to change with the emergence of regional perspectives. For example, when kingdoms were no longer seen invariably as centralized bureaucratic systems then the region as part of larger polities had a more defined role.

Regional histories form patterns that sometimes vary and the variations have a historical base. For example, the model of the four *varṇas* was not the caste pattern in the entire subcontinent as was maintained earlier. Why did *brāhmaṇas* and *vellāla* peasants give shape to the history of Tamil Nadu whereas *khatri* traders dominated the Punjab? Differences are not just diversities in regional styles. They are expressions of multiple cultural norms that cut across monolithic, uniform identities. This requires a reconsideration of what constitutes the identities that have come to us from the past.

This also requires the historian to juxtapose a diversity of sources from artifacts to texts. It was thought that whereas artifacts, being material and tangible, can be examined from multiple perspectives, this was not possible with texts. But gradually texts are also being examined from various perspectives. Indological studies, and especially philology, were extensive investigations into the structure of the languages which also helped to date the texts. These studies are now being further facilitated by computer analyses of the literary styles of a text, the constructing of concordances of words/signs, and locating the occurrences of words, although such studies are sporadic. Individual words have a history and their meaning may change in a changed historical context. The word *pāṣaṇḍa*, initially used in the sense of any doctrine, was in later centuries, used for heresy.

However, a different kind of investigation of placing the text in its context has widened the possible range of meanings and intentions. We know that texts cannot be taken literally. Their authors, audiences and agendas have to be scrutinised. Thus intention and agency become significant and have to be differentiated for each text. For example, inscriptions are often the official version issued by the ruler. They have to be distinguished from narratives claiming historicity, the '*vaṃśāvalīs*', of which the *Rājataraṅgiṇī*—the history of Kashmir, written in the twelfth century by Kalhaṇa is the finest example. These again are different from the '*caritas*'—the biographies of rulers, such as the *Ramacaritam* of Sandhyākara Nandin, a biography of the Pāla king Rāmapāla. Where court poets pursued literary style at the expense of veracity, rhetoric has to be separated from fact.

The texts that have survived from the early period are generally those of elite groups. There are hardly any written sources from those marginalized by mainstream society—women, dalits, forest dwellers, lower castes. This realization has led to a re-reading of texts in search of even oblique references to the perspectives of such groups. In earlier historical studies creative literature was used largely only as a source of information. In recent times literary texts are beginning to be used as articulations of time, place and people, visualizing a glimpse of a historical moment. Resort to the more influential 'literary turn' as it has been called, is apparent in some of the writing of the subaltern historians, but this is restricted so far to analyses of modern times.

The decades of the 1950s and 1960s therefore were a watershed in the writing of history. Narratives of the past continued to be written as they are to this day, and there continues to be a valuable gathering of new evidence. But the more challenging trend has been to pursue answers to questions that relate to why and how something happened rather than merely when and where. Actions and events had multiple causes and the priorities among these have to be justified by the evidence as well as logical argument. There is also the need to integrate a variety of facets in constructing a historical context—the nature of the state and the economy; the pattern of caste and gender relationships; religious sects, icons, monuments and institutions as forms of social expression; the impact of the environment; and many more still awaiting exploration. History was an explanation of what happened in the past, an attempt to understand the past, and of basing this understanding on what was recognized as the necessary critical enquiry, incorporated into what is also called the historical method. The understanding is not confined to just a moment in time, to a particular context, since it has also to be viewed as a process in time.

History Today

This was not something that we were taught as students, but it is an essential part of what we teach our students today. It is a training that begins with a careful assessment of the reliability of the evidence and an insistence that all possible evidence pertaining to a subject be used. The analysis of the evidence revolves around issues of causality and objectivity and centres the argument on logic. An initial hypothesis is tested at various stages as the research proceeds. Where necessary it is modified or changed. The generalization that emerges is an explanation of the theme being researched and hopefully provides an understanding of a segment of the past. Even where the explanation requires a small leap of the imagination, the leap takes off from critical enquiry. This is the historian's contribution to knowledge but it is also an essential process in human sciences. And in making this contribution the historian is aware that other evidence may surface, fresh generalizations may emerge and knowledge be further advanced. But claim to an advance receives consideration only if it fulfils the requirements of the historical method.

My attempt at an overview of the directions taken by recent interpretations of early Indian history would be incomplete if I did not comment on the recent controversy over historical writing. The comment is necessary because an attempt is being made mainly through the propagation of what some are now calling the Hindutva view of history, to dismantle the history and the historical method that I have been discussing. It uses history as the bedrock of legitimizing a particular identity and a particular self-perception projected as Hindu nationalism. In the claim to propagating an indigenous view of history it effectively endorses the 19th century colonial frames of interpreting Indian history—in fact precisely the kind of history that has now been critiqued and sloughed off.

It insists, for example, on exclusive 'Aryan' foundations of Indian civilization. This is taken back to the Harappa culture by stating that the creators of the Indus cities were 'Aryans'. It is taken forward by asserting that Hindus are Aryans and the ancient period was the age of Hindu glory brought to an abrupt end by Muslim invasions. The medieval period is characterized by continuous Muslim conquests with their counterpart of continuous Hindu resistance. Colonial preconceptions are re-incarnated in this view through returning to the periodization of Indian history into Hindu, Muslim and British; through the theory of Oriental Despotism which is sought to be applied to governance in the Muslim period; and through the assertion that

Indian society throughout the Hindu period conformed to the ideals of caste society as laid out in the '*varṇāśramadharma*' and therefore did not need to change. There is a refusal to concede social and economic change, nor the interface between many cultures with varied relationships, nor the pluralities of Hindu, Muslim and other societies.

Obviously there is always an element of ideology—conscious or subconscious—in the exploration of knowledge, but this is not the same as the induction of arbitrary preconceptions into knowledge: and the more so if they are intended for political mobilization and sectarian ambitions. A differentiation has to be made between a history based on the critical enquiry that governs historical method, and a history put together from preferred preconceptions.

If the history of the subcontinent is to be written as a sensitive and thoughtful understanding of the past, the analyses have to draw on critical enquiry. Should this be abandoned, then that which is labelled as 'history' becomes a free-for-all, accompanied by public abuse and physical force (as we witnessed in recent years), in order to silence those that still respect the procedures inherent in advancing knowledge. Such silence is not just a censoring of history but a censoring of knowledge. These assaults will continue to be possible until critical enquiry is given the centrality that it should have in our academic and intellectual discourse.

CHAPTER 2

The Contribution of D.D. Kosambi to Indology*

It has recently been argued that a revolution in scientific knowledge comes about not through the accumulation of data alone but through a change in the paradigm.[1] When the framework of explanation or the hypothesis is altered or a new set of questions is posed only then can there be a breakthrough in scientific knowledge. This applies as much to the social sciences such as history. The accumulation of data is, of course, a necessary first step and includes the deriving of fresh data from new sources, but an advance in knowledge is dependent on using the data to present new formulations.

Histories of the Indian subcontinent, such as were to become germane to the perception on the Indian past, have subscribed to three major changes of paradigm. The first comprehensive history was James Mill's *History of British India*[2] published in the early nineteenth century, where he set out his theory of Indian history evolving out of three civilizations, the Hindu, the Muslim, and the British. The first two of these he described as backward, stagnant, and ahistoric. His theory was to become axiomatic to the periodization of Indian history and is with us still, though sometimes in a disguised form. A change came about with Vincent Smith's *History of India*[3] published in 1919, which tried to avoid the sharpness of Mill's value judgements. Smith concentrated more on a chronological overview which was in any case less

* Lecture delivered at the Asiatic Society, Bombay. Published in *Journal of the Asiatic Society of Bombay*, 1977–8, n.s., vols 52–3, pp. 365–84.

charged with colonial and anti-colonial sentiment and argued for the rise and fall of dynasties as being crucial to the study of Indian history. By the early twentieth century, chronological data had accumulated to the point where such a treatment of history was possible. Where Mill's assessment was seeking to justify the British conquest of India, Smith was justifying colonial rule. The infrequency of explicitly negative value judgements on the pre-British period was largely an indication of his awareness of Indian national sentiment in the matter. Nationalist historians writing on early India reversed some value judgements but adhered to the paradigm of dynastic and chronological concerns.

Kosambi's first book, *An Introduction to the Study of Indian History*[4] published in 1956, was a major shift in the paradigm. He had little use for a chronological narrative since he argued that chronology for the early period was too obscure to be meaningful. For him history was the presentation in chronological order of successive developments in the means and relations of production.[5] Because of the absence of reliable historical records he argued that Indian history would have to use the comparative method.[6] This meant a familiarity with a wide range of historical work and his own familiarity with classical European history is evident in his writing; it also meant the use of various disciplines and interdisciplinary techniques to enable the historian to understand the pattern of social formations. His definition of the comparative method required the historian to be an interdisciplinary creature in himself with the ability to use a large number of investigative techniques. This ability he demonstrated to the full in his writings on Indology. Added to this was his conviction that the historian in India was in a particularly happy position since so much of the past survives in the present. As he puts it, '. . . the country has one tremendous advantage that was not utilized till recently by the historians: the survival within different social layers of many forms that allow the reconstruction of totally diverse earlier stages.'[7] For him, this amply made up for the absence of reliable historical records.

Kosambi's acknowledged status as an Indologist was all the more remarkable, in that by profession he was a mathematician.

Indology to begin with was a subsidiary interest, perhaps inherited from his father, a scholar of Pāli and Buddhism who taught at various centres in India, apart from a period at Harvard. The older Kosambi walked the countryside in an effort to relate the texts to their original milieu, an approach which was followed by his son. A quick perusal of the younger Kosambi's many publications points to a telling trend. His earliest papers in the 1930s are mainly on various aspects of mathematics. In the 1940s, his interest in Indology become apparent in the form of occasional papers. (This was also the period when he wrote on Soviet contributions to mathematics and genetics and was enthusiastic about the Soviet attempt to build a socialist society.) He was appointed to a Mathematics Chair at the Tata Institute of Fundamental Research in Bombay in 1946. During the 1950s however, and until his death in 1966, most of his publications were on Indology and early Indian history although his mathematical interests remained constant.

Given that Indology is now seen as essentially rooted in a colonial perception of the past, and since Kosambi's writing challenged this perception, it would be more appropriate to refer to him as a historian, the field in which his was a major contribution. But he was prolific and researched into other related areas as well, hence the continuing use of the label, Indologist. His first venture into early Indian sources was a critical assessment of Bhartṛhari which can be regarded as a model for such analysis.[8] At a later stage he edited, jointly with V.V. Gokhale, the Vidyākara *Subhāṣita-ratna-kośa* for the Harvard Oriental Series.[9] Apart from applying the norms of higher criticism to such texts he also tried to place them in historical context not merely through a chronological analysis, but by referring them to the society from which they emanated. He argued that from the first millennium AD Sanskrit should be seen as a measure and expression of upper-class unity when it replaced Prākrit in the royal courts and was patronized, particularly in the initial stages, by foreign rulers. This is of course evident in the change from Prākrit to Sanskrit as the language of royal inscriptions between the Mauryan and the Gupta periods. He stressed the feudal background of many Sanskrit texts which brought him into a lively controversy with one of his closest friends, the Harvard Sanskritist, Daniel Ingalls. Kosambi maintained that Sanskrit was deliberately kept restricted to a small number of people, even though the excellent early grammar of the language by Pāṇini, commented upon by Patañjali, converted it into an orderly and systematic language, open to anyone who was taught it properly. However, he felt that it froze in the hands of what he called 'a disdainful priest class',[10] and much of the real world was by-passed in the courtly literature.

The relation of text to context was examined at greater length in his papers on the *Bhagavad Gītā* where he attempted to relate ideology to society.[11] He argued that the *Gītā* in propounding the concept of *bhakti* laid emphasis on unquestioning faith in, and personal loyalty and devotion to, a deity, and these values were in conformity with the ideology of feudalism, which also required a chain of unquestioning loyalties. The text emphasized caste functions and the requirement to do one's ordained duty as a member of a particular caste, which he saw as a message in support of caste society and the conservatism which such a society entails; a message propounded by the upper castes to keep the rest of society passive. He further suggests that religious sects supporting a synthesis of gods and of tolerance are expressions of a period of a social surplus, when wealth was more widely distributed; whereas the ideology *of bhakti* is more frequent in periods of crisis, but that it nevertheless acted as a means of interrelating the scattered religious beliefs of a region. It could be argued however that the *bhakti* endorsed by the *Gītā* is not identical with that which was taught by later *bhakti* teachers. Whereas the single-minded devotion to a deity is retained, the social content changes substantially and is expressed in a concern with a universal ethic which echoes that of the Buddhists and Jainas and which permits the *bhakti* movements to become powerful mobilizers of various social groups. There is an almost apparent contradiction between the emphasis on caste-duty in the *Gītā* and the universal ethic of the later *bhakti* movement.

Kosambi uses Buddhist texts mainly to draw out data on social and economic life and much of his discussion on early trade, for instance, is based on these sources. This was not new as such data had earlier been extracted from these sources by scholars of Buddhism such as Rhys Davids[12] and Fick.[13] Kosambi co-related this data with evidence from Sanskrit sources but also from archaeological excavations and contemporary inscriptions and brought the Buddhist material into the wider orbit of reconstructing the history of the late first millennium BC. The fact that the Buddhist sources do at times contradict the brahmanical tradition was for him a particularly important aspect of the Pāli texts and invested them with the kind of authenticity which he found invaluable. The recognition of this feature he owed to his father's work on the Buddhist texts.[14]

His knowledge of Sanskrit led Kosambi to a series of etymological analyses which he used to great effect in reconstructing the social background, particularly of the Vedic period.[15] Thus he argued that the names of many of the established *brāhmaṇa*s in Vedic literature and the Purāṇic tradition clearly pointed to their being of non-Aryan origin. Some were given the epithet, *dāsyāḥ-putraḥ* (such as Dīrghatamas) or else their names suggested totems, as for instance, Ajigarta or Kaśyapa. Further, that the original seven *gotra*s of the *brāhmaṇa*s were of mixed Aryan and non-Aryan priests. His analysis of the *gotra*s led him into a debate with John Brough.[16] From the study of the *gotra*s he went on to the logical point that the language of the Vedic texts could not have been pure Aryan and must have had an admixture of non-Aryan elements reflecting the inclusion of non-Aryans as *brāhmaṇa*s. This theory is now more acceptable to those who have worked on Indo-Aryan linguistics, on the basis of the linguistic analyses of the texts and language which clearly indicates non-Aryan structures and forms both in syntax and vocabulary.[17] Kosambi's own use of linguistic analyses bears the stamp of philology and he was evidently less familiar with the changes in linguistic practices of the mid-twentieth century. His etymological reconstruction of Sāta-karṇi as Indo-Austric is an example of this where he makes no attempt to support his argument by providing other Austric links.[18] The same problem arises with his attempt to equate the Hittite *khatti* with the Sanskrit *kṣatriya* and the Pāli *khettiyo*.[19]

An area in which he successfully utilized his mathematical knowledge was Indian numismatics and more especially in the one coinage system on which he worked in great detail, namely, the punch-marked coins which were in circulation between c. 500–100 BC. These were coins cut from a sheet of silver, each coin bearing a set of symbols but generally with no legend. Hence their chronology and the agency which issued them was an enigma. Kosambi wished to demonstrate the application of scientific methods for obtaining information from numismatic evidence. He worked initially on a statistical analysis from one hoard with a meticulous weighing of each coin to ascertain loss of weight by wear and tear and with a careful analysis of their fabric and alloy. By arranging the coins in accordance with their weight and their set of symbols, he hoped to provide a chronological sequence of the coins and believed that this would in turn provide a clue as to the source of their issue.[20] For the method to be ultimately successful, the coins to be used as control had to come from stratified excavations. These could be tested against coins from hoards provided they were free from encrustations. His analyses revealed that the average weight decreases when the symbols on the reverse increase. From this he argued that coins in constant circulation would also be the ones to be weighed and valued more frequently. He maintained that they were originally issued by traders but were ratified by the kings' valuers and marked with the kings' symbols. The next step was the identifying of particular symbols as the marks of particular kings. Whereas the statistical analyses of the coins is generally accepted, the identifications of certain symbols with royalty remain controversial with some numismatists still arguing that the coins may not bear any royal marks. It does seem curious that with major changes in the nature of the state and of royalty during this period, the coins, if connected with royalty, should have remained without any appreciable change in style. It seems implausible that the Mauryan kings would not have issued special coins and would have been content to merely ratify those issued by traders, for, if nothing else, they would at least have imitated the Persian and Greek coins which were circulating in West Asia and with which area Indian kings and traders were in contact. It seems more likely that the coins continued to be issued and ratified by guilds as legal tender, a suggestion which has been linked to the occasional legend of *negama* (from *nigama?*) on some issues from Taxila. The evaluation of coins by the king's valuer, as described in the *Arthaśāstra*, would doubtless have applied to all coins irrespective of where they were issued.

Kosambi's use of archaeology was in part to reconstruct the prehistoric period where he literally walked the stretch around Pune in an effort to record the archaeological data. On the basis of his extensive fieldwork on microlithic sites and through his typology of microlithic artefacts he was able to suggest the routes which herders, pastoralists, and incipient traders would have taken across the western Deccan in the prehistoric period.[21] Relating to a more developed culture, he looked for continuities of archaic artefacts and sought to explain these in their fullest function, for example, the function of the saddle-quern, which he explained both with reference to those found in archaeological excavations as well as those in current use.[22] By the term 'use' he meant not merely the technological function but also the role of the object in religious ritual. He was also among the earliest scholars to recognize the significance of the megalithic material and the potentialities which it held in the discussion on the origins of many institutions.

Added to the fieldwork was an intelligent understanding of geomorphology and topography. In many cases his assessment of the historical importance of a site was based on the logic of geography. This he felt should indicate to the historian where to look for sites and the likely nature of the sites. This approach is demonstrated in what can only be called a brilliantly insightful discussion of the trade routes from the west coast up to the plateau and across the *ghat*s in the western Deccan.[23] Geographical considerations were partially responsible for the location of urban centres and Buddhist monasteries in this area during the first millennium AD with a continuity of Maratha forts and British railway links in the second millennium.

It was the recognition of cultural survival which led Kosambi to weave so much material from ethnology and anthropology into his historical narrative. This is perhaps best demonstrated in the pages of his *Introduction to the Study of Indian History,* where he describes what he sees in the vicinity of his house in Pune.[24] Here we have history virtually on the doorstep, what with the encampment of a nomadic group, the presence of a tribe which had once given rise to a *jāti,* and of another which became a quasi-guild. He noticed trees and sacred groves, stones marking a sacrificial ritual, caves and rock shelters which may have been occupied successively by prehistoric men, by Buddhist monks and later by practitioners of Hindu cults. Such places have a remarkable continuity as sacred centres and often provided a greater historical continuity both in object and ritual than many written texts. These for him were primary areas for archaeological and historical investigation. It is important to clarify that Kosambi was not arguing that religion played a more significant part in Indian culture than has been the case in other cultures, as has been the stand of those who maintain the greater spirituality of the Indian past; but rather, Kosambi's position is that there was a greater survival of the archaic in religious ritual than in other areas of Indian life suggesting a certain conservatism, but which at the same time makes it worth investigating historically. This perspective on culture is again demonstrated in the discussion on the probable Harappan religious forms and their continuity into later periods.

Kosambi had little use for physical anthropology. For him, both the measuring of nasal indexes and the theories on the racial identities of India derived therefrom, were worthless.[25] At a wider anthropological level, he maintained that one of the clues to understanding the Indian past was the basic factor of the transition from tribe to caste, from small, localized groups to a generalized society.[26] This transition was largely the result of the introduction of plough agriculture in various regions which changed the system of production, broke the structure of tribes and clans and made caste the alternative form of social organization. This process he traced in part from the evolution of clan totems into clan names and then into caste names. The agency through which plough agriculture was introduced would, therefore, become the major factor of control in caste society. This agency he saw as the brahmanical settlements in various parts of the country. These led to an assimilation of local cults into the brahmanical tradition as is evident from the various *Purāṇas* and *Māhātmyas*. But equally important it led to the sanskritization of local folk cults with the incorporation of *brāhmaṇa* priests and rituals, the association of epic heroes and heroines, and by the inclusion of such cults in Sanskrit mythology.

The interpretation of myths is essential to any study of early cultures and Kosambi's work is peppered with such interpretations. In a detailed discussion of the story of Purūravas and Urvaśī, which he traces through its many variants in the texts,[27] he dismisses the simplistic nature-myth interpretation of Max Müller and his contemporaries who saw the disappearance of Urvaśī as symbolic of the vanishing dawn on the rising of the sun. Kosambi attempts a functional anthropological analysis in which he argues that it reflects the institution of sacred marriage in prehistoric societies as well as the ritual sacrifice of the hero by the mother goddess.[28] One of the frequent strands in his explanations of myths was related to his belief that societies were matriarchal in origin and many gradually changed to patriliny and that myths, therefore, reflect the transition from the one to the other. This view was largely derived from the writings of F. Engels[29] and what one might call the 'mother-right school of anthropology'.[30] He applied the same argument to explain the *kumbha* symbol or birth from a jar of certain *brāhmaṇa gotras* and of the Kauravas in the *Mahābhārata* where the jar has an obvious symbolic equation with the womb. Bride-price is also for him a survival of matriliny.[31] The insistence on a transition from matriarchy to patriliny in every case is not now acceptable since many societies are known to have been patrilineal from the beginning. It is curious that the structural study of myths was known at that time but Kosambi shows little interest in it.

I have tried to indicate the various ways in which Kosambi contributed to Indological studies in his handling of the various sources and data. That his scholarship ranged over a variety of aspects was in conformity with the best Indological tradition, which required a many-faceted scholar who could claim familiarity with different source materials. What distinguished Kosambi from other scholars was that his ultimate concern was with an overall theoretical framework into which not only was his scattered research directed, but which he propounded as an attempt to comprehend the totality of Indian history. His first book, *An Introduction to the Study of Indian History*, drew together the many themes on which he had researched in earlier years and which he had published as papers in various journals of Oriental Studies. This book was to prove his claim not merely to being a historian but to changing the paradigm for early Indian history.

For Kosambi, Marxism provided the clue to understanding the past and he identified his method unambiguously with Marxism. Kosambi would doubtless have accepted the judgement of Jean Paul Sartre that Marxism is the 'necessary' philosophy of our time, by which Sartre meant that even if Marx's particular conclusions are unacceptable, the method of analysis which he had worked out is virtually unavoidable in the social sciences. Many among the non-Marxist and anti-Marxist historians in this country tried to dismiss the book with the predictable critique of all Marxist histories, that the author was forcing the facts to fit a preconceived theory: a critique which is applied *ad nauseam* to many versions of knowledge which are intellectually uncomfortable for those who are incapable of changing the paradigm and who are fearful of scholars attempting to do so. A few among the more intellectually gifted realized that what Kosambi was doing was not forcing the facts to fit the received Marxist pattern on Indian history, but was instead using a Marxist methodology to investigate a possible pattern and suggest a new framework; that, in fact, he was using the method creatively. As he himself states elsewhere, Marxism was not being 'proved' or 'justified', but simply being used as a tool of professional investigation. And this was also part of the reason why he was regarded with suspicion by the then Marxist political establishment in this country, the people whom he has referred to in his writings as the OM—the Official Marxists![32] Enthusiastic support came to him from intellectuals interested in Marxism and in history and from liberal intellectuals in Europe and America. It is significant that Kosambi was invited to give a series of lectures on the history of Hinduism at London University and to lecture at the Oriental Institute in Moscow in 1955, and this was before any Indian university took such a step.

I would like now to consider his approach to early Indian history with which he was centrally concerned. In the context of his general argument of the transition from tribe to caste, socio-economic formations were his primary interest. He draws his evidence on tribal forms both from literary sources as well as from the survival of such groups into recent centuries and from their interaction with peasant groups. The earliest of such transitions occurred in the Indus valley; hence Kosambi's concern with agrarian technology at that time.[33] He assumed that it was a culture without the plough, that the river bank was cultivated with a harrow and that the seasonal flood water was utilized for irrigation with dams and embankments helping in retaining this water and the river silt for a longer period. The decline of the Indus civilization is attributed to the Aryans who destroyed the agricultural system by breaking the embankments, which action he maintains, is symbolically referred to in the Ṛgvedic descriptions of Indra destroying Vṛtra, and releasing the waters. Kosambi was of the opinion that the plough was brought by the Aryans (that is, the speakers of Indo-Aryan) who thereby changed agricultural technology. Recent evidence on the Indus civilization makes it clear that plough agriculture was practised even as early as the pre-Harappan period and that the plough was known to the non-Aryan since the more commonly used word for the plough in Vedic literature is of non-Aryan etymology.[34] The theory of the destruction of the embankments is conjectural and may have greater application to dams built to prevent the flooding of the cities rather than for agricultural purposes. Nevertheless the question posed by Kosambi as to why the agrarian base of the Harappan culture declined and was unable to support an urban civilization in the later stages still remains a valid one and is now sought to be answered by evidence of a far-reaching ecological change with which Harappan technology could not cope and which at a later time resulted in the location of new urban centres in the Ganga valley.

Although he had no use for any theory of an Aryan race, Kosambi did support the idea of the Aryan-speaking peoples having settled in northwestern India and spreading gradually into the Ganges valley, in both cases initially as conquerors.[35] Such a theory of conquest had been questioned by those working in Indo-Aryan linguistics and it is now being proposed that conquest should be replaced by considering the possibility of migrations and technological changes being responsible for the arrival and the dominance of the Aryan speakers, the resulting long period of co-existence between them and the indigenous peoples being suggested by the evidence of bi-lingualism. Even the archaeological data, which was once put forward to support the destruction of the Harappan cities by invaders is now discounted.[36] The new evidence however tends to strengthen the more important point made by Kosambi that much of the Indian tradition from the earliest Vedic texts is already an amalgam of Aryan and non-Aryan as indeed are even those of the highest caste.

Plough agriculture and iron technology, when they were introduced into the Ganges valley, led ultimately to the growth of urban centres as well as the recognizable forms of caste. Recent views would include as causal factors in this development, the role of a change in crop patterns with a dependence on rice agriculture, the diversity of irrigation systems, the use of labour in the new technologies, and the range of control over these factors by different social groups. This is a fleshing out, as it were, of Kosambi's argument by extending the span of causal factors. Analyses of the structure of caste at this time in terms of the theoretical form given to the actuality, gives further rein to the question implicitly raised by Kosambi, namely, the degree to which ideology and social structure are interconnected.

The Mauryan monarchy which controlled the Indian subcontinent was a feasible political system according to Kosambi because of the expansion of the village economy through *śūdra* agriculturalists being settled on state lands and by the deportation of prisoners-of-war who were used for the same purpose.[37] He argues against the use of slavery in production in early India and prefers the theory of *śūdra* helotage, although he does not develop this theory in detail. The decline of the Mauryan empire is attributed to an economic crisis, the details of which are debatable. His argument that the currency was debased devolves from his own chronological interpretation of the coins, which as we have seen, is not entirely acceptable, as also the argument that double cropping indicated an economic crisis, for we now know from archaeological sources that double cropping was an established practice even in earlier centuries.[38] However, that the inability of the Mauryan polity to survive must be attributed to causes which in part were economic, cannot be doubted. A more plausible analysis would be to examine the nature of the Mauryan polity in terms of whether the existing manpower and agricultural resources were conducive to such a system. Equally important is the question of whether the polity was as centralized as has been made out in historical studies.

Kosambi's treatment of the rise of the Buddhist, Jaina, and other sects of that time links them to major technological changes and to urbanism. But above all he maintains that they reflect a situation of detribalization in which they attempt to reach out across castes to a wider social range through their universal ethic. He argues forcefully in support of a mercantile patronage extended to these sects which rooted them in society more firmly than did the help they received from royal patronage. The punch-marked coins are for him an indication of developed commodity production[39] which provided a high status for artisans and traders as members of urban society and their link with religions propagating a universal ethic would not be surprising. This link was demonstrated in his discussion of the post-Maurya period where he examines the role of guilds and artisans as donors to the Buddhist *saṅgha* in the light of the expansion and diffusion of trade. The emergence of occupational *jātis* in urban areas can frequently be associated with this development.

An evident departure from the orthodox Marxist pattern of historical periodization is Kosambi's refusal to apply either the Asiatic Mode of Production or the Slave Mode of Production to early Indian history without modifications of a major kind. For Karl Marx the Indian past conformed, by and large, to what he called the Asiatic Mode of Production characterized by a static society, an absence of private property in land, self-sufficient villages, a lack of a commercial economy, and by state control over the irrigation system. Although he and Engels recognized deviations from this pattern, they saw this pattern as a contrast to that prevalent in Europe and argued that historical stagnancy in India was broken by the coming of colonialism. This was not altogether acceptable to Kosambi for whom the key to the Indian past in the advance of plough agriculture over tribal society made a static history impossible. Of the notion of the self-sufficient village economy he writes, '. . . acute and brilliant as these remarks are, they remain misleading nevertheless . . .'.[40] The dependence of the village on external sources for salt and metals would automatically preclude self-sufficiency. Elsewhere he has argued for the existence of the tenant and of the landowning peasant.[41] He did however concede that from the end of the Gupta period, there was a relative increase in self-sufficiency and this brought with it a static mode of production which was not the Asiatic mode for it came about during a period of feudalism.[42] He also argued that the lack of a sense of history and the power of myth further reduced individuality. A static mode of production could not have co-existed with a form of feudalism since the latter breeds its own contradictions. Perhaps if he had been questioned on this ambiguity he may have modified his position to argue that the degree of self-sufficiency increased, but not to the extent of the static mode of production becoming the dominant feature.

Elaborating his views on the Asiatic Mode of Production he wrote:

> The real difficulty here (not in China) is the misleading documentation. Ancient Indian records derive from the brahman caste and those who read them pay no attention to the function of caste in ancient—(as well as modern and feudal) Indian society. Indian history is, to me, a very fine example of Marxist theory working very well in practice. Unfortunately, Marx had only the solitary report of Buchanan-Hamilton on Karnatak villages, not even the *Foral* of 1640 by the king of Portugal guaranteeing the rights of Goa village communities, which existed in a much more primitive form, and which could not

be called 'hydraulic', in view of the torrential rainfall. The Goan organisation (which I have studied elsewhere, *Myth and Reality*, Chapter V) was actually the model for the Karnatak settlement, and survived almost to this day.

It follows that 'Oriental Despotism' has to be looked at from some other points of view than Wittfogel's hydraulic social aberrations. It seems to me that the two main Marxist considerations are: (1) The incidence of commodity production (per head) with the relative ease of food-gathering. This becomes vital when you consider Africa. By the way, the Pharoah's main function was not regulation of water or irrigation, but distribution of the numerous materials which had all to be imported from a long distance, including wood, metals, and so on. Henri Frankfort has a very neat answer to Toynbee, where he brings this out, in contrast to Mesopotamian development of numerous warring cities. (2) The need to use overriding force to compel the people (in an environment where food-gathering was, however irregular, always possible) to change over to food-production i.e. agriculture with the plough. In Egypt food-gathering was different except in the delta, but the cultivator had to be kept at his work. You will find that the British had to impose a poll-tax in Africa in order to get cheap labour for the mines and the white man's farms.

If you grant this, then, it follows that despotism, even of the so-called oriental type, was a tool (however disgusting) used to bring a more productive form of society into existence. But during this very process, there came into being a class of state servants, state nobility or administrators—at times priests, who reduced the need for violence and helped develop the back-lands (as did my own ancestors in Goa and the Buddhist monasteries in China as well as in the Deccan). This class then used the absolute, despotic monarchy and the more or less passive substratum for its own purposes. Hence the changeless appearance of the country, seeing that the actual tools of production need not become more efficient. Under such circumstances, feudalism is a special development used to keep the rule in the hands of a ruling warrior caste-class, often conquerors. Don't be misled by the supposed Indian *kshatriya* caste, which was oftener than not a brahmanical fiction . . . .[43]

His rejection of the Slave Mode of Production as applicable to the Indian past arose from a hesitation in applying the accepted Marxist periodization of European history. Marx had suggested that primitive communism gave way to a Slave Mode of Production predominant in Greco-Roman antiquity and this in turn gave rise to feudalism in Europe from which evolved the capitalist mode of production. Kosambi was averse to the mechanical application of this model to India as had been done by various historians in Soviet Russia and in India, as for example, by S.A. Dange. Kosambi was caustic in his evaluation of Dange's book, *From Primitive Communism to Slavery,* which he said followed the Russian analysis and which analysis, ' . . . saves a certain type of "left intellectual" the trouble of reading anything else or thinking for himself.'[44] Kosambi's analysis differed from any existing model. He maintains that the statement of the Greek ambassador Megasthenes (of the fourth century BC) that there was an absence of slavery in India was correct because Megasthenes makes a comparison with Sparta which suggests helots instead of slaves.[45] Kosambi states that at this period the *śūdra*s were essentially helots. He does not, however, discuss in greater detail the nature of *śūdra* helotage. Whereas the origin of the *śūdra* caste could perhaps be traced to a form of helotage, the classification cannot hold for the entire past. At the ideological level it would be clearly contradicted by the early *Dharmaśāstra* exposition of the *varṇa* theory where the origin of the *śūdra* is attributed to mixed caste marriages including those involving the upper castes. Such a theory even if not based on actuality would have undermined the notion of helotage. The possibility of a Slave Mode of Production in early India is problematical since it is difficult to assess the ratio of slaves to other forms of labouring men nor is there a clear distinction between slaves in domestic employ or in agricultural and craft production. Doubtless, these numbers would also have varied in the *gaṇa-saṅgha* chiefships where they were probably higher and in the kingdoms where with a diversity of labour, slavery for production may have been smaller. It would also be important to consider the degree of unfreedom of the *dāsa* in relation to the *karmakāra, bhṛitaka,* and *śūdra,* which would involve questions of the legal status of these categories.

Kosambi accepts the Feudal Mode of Production as relevant to pre-modern Indian history, although even here he makes his own distinction between what he calls, 'feudalism from above' and 'feudalism from below', and which he regards as the peculiar feature of Indian feudalism. 'Feudalism from above' was his characterization of the changes which came about in the late first millennium AD subsequent to the Gupta period.[46] Incidentally, he has little time for the Gupta period and is justifiably contemptuous of the nationalist historians who described it as the golden age of Hindu revivalism. His contempt is summed up in the sentence, 'Far from the Guptas reviving nationalism, it was nationalism that revived the Guptas.'[47] Recent research has not only tarnished some of the golden quality of this age, but has on occasion even revealed that a part of it was mere tinsel. The changes noticeable in the post-Gupta period were mainly those of an increase in the granting of land with a greater frequency of transition from tribe to caste through the introduction of plough agriculture, a decline in trade and commodity production which adversely affected the growth of urban centres, the decentralization of the army, and a concentration of wealth at local courts. With this was associated the spread of *bhakti* cults whose emphasis on loyalty and devotion he saw as a characteristic feature of feudal society. In a discussion on private property in land, central to the concept of the Asiatic Mode of Production, he argues that it should be viewed in the Indian context which implies, firstly, that actual cultivators were ex-tribals who still regarded land as territory deriving from kinship rights, and secondly, the holding of a field was proof of membership of a community rather than ownership of land and thirdly, that in a non-commodity producing village or one located near waste land, land would have no sale value. The only conditions were the regular payment of taxes to either the grantee or the king. These arguments read more like an attempt to somehow salvage the notion of the absence of private property without a willingness to admit the pattern of the Asiatic Mode of Production as an explanatory model. Nor are these arguments wholly convincing because although in some areas the cultivators were recent converts to peasantry in others they were peasants of long standing since many of the grants of land were made in villages of well-established cultivators. The statement that land had no sale value in newly settled areas is contradicted by inscriptional evidence in some areas where, in Bengal for example, land is sold and the price is stated in districts which were regarded as being on the edge of waste land.[48] Part of the problem with his analysis of the two phases of feudalism, and this is a problem of which he is well aware, is that no generalization can cover the entire subcontinent since the changes varied from region to region.[49]

In his discussion on 'feudalism from below', he draws his evidence mainly from Kashmir and Rajasthan and depicts a more clearly recognizable form of feudalism but with specific Indian features.[50] This phase is characterized by political decentralization accompanied by a low level of technology with production for the household and the village and not for a market, and the holding of land by lords on a service tenure who also have judicial or quasi-judicial functions in relation to the dependent population. The Indian features were the absence of demesne farming on the lord's estate by forced labour where in many cases, slaves were used instead, leading to an increase in slaves; there was also an absence of guilds and of any organized church. The backwardness of technology allowed for an easy conquest of northern India by those with a more advanced military technology. Changes in the ruling class did not substantially affect the nature of feudalism in India and it continued until the coming of colonialism.

Kosambi's definition of feudalism would today find its critics and its general applicability to the subcontinent would be debated. On the latter point one would have to consider whether other systems prevalent in other parts of the subcontinent would seriously subtract from the generalization.[51] The nature of control over land was different in parts of the peninsula as also was the condition of trade, where the rise of powerful guilds was characteristic of this period. The increase in the number of slaves was not such as to constitute a Slave Mode of Production and as Kosambi maintains quite correctly, there was no slave economy of the Roman kind to initiate the institution of the manor. The existence of serfdom has also been suggested for many areas. Although there was no organized church nevertheless, there is what Max Weber has called 'monastic landlordism' both among Buddhist and Hindu sects, which at some levels was a parallel system to that of church lands in Europe. The monastic centres of this period were opulent and powerful. Kosambi argues that religious sects frequently failed to provide the ethical and religious values by which they had once held the society, but he does not consider the monastic institution as the foci of political and economic control, a role which it often played at this time.[52]

It is curious that Kosambi takes as his model feudalism in England and shows no familiarity with the classic work on feudal society by Marc Bloch which would have been far more pertinent to his analyses. (His facility in French would have enabled him to have read Marc Bloch in the original.) In a sense, this points to something of a narrowness in his wider historical reading. Although far from being an orthodox Marxist, he nevertheless showed little interest in schools of analyses other than the Marxist as far as interpreting early societies was concerned. He does not, for example, indicate any familiarity with the works of those who were critical of Lewis Morgan and Frederick Engels in spite of using Marxist analyses as a starting point for the study of early societies, such as Karl Polanyi. It is also curious that in spite of his interest in French scholarship (arising out of a concern with French colonial activities in Vietnam and North Africa) he was not introduced to the writings of French historians such as Fernand Braudel with which, one suspects, he would have found a rapport. Whereas his respect for the works of Gordon Childe and George Thomson is evident in his own studies, his acquaintance with Moses Finley's work on the Greeks came later[53] and one wonders whether he would have analysed the Indian epics in a manner similar to Finley's analysis of the Greek epics. Convinced as he was of the correctness of one methodology, Kosambi seems to have found the debate on methodology unnecessary. His utilization of Indian anthropological literature was more as a source of ethnology and a study of survivals and indigenous forms rather than as a means of examining the validity of any anthropological method. Possibly this limitation may also have been due to the tendency among Indian Marxists at that time to confine themselves to the writings of British Marxists, which can perhaps be explained as a curious reflection on the limitations of colonial scholarship where, even in radical circles the intellectual metropolis remained British with occasional forays into the writings of Soviet scholars. This is in striking contrast to more recent years in which the translations of European Marxist writing and that from other parts of the world are as widely read as the works of British Marxists.[54] A more mundane explanation may be the paucity of new books at that time and Kosambi was very conscious of this lack of availability of up-to-date research. In his personal correspondence with scholars in fields other than Indology he makes repeated requests to be kept informed of new studies since such information was not available in India. Where he could obtain such works he read them with great thoroughness and commented at length on them, as for example, on Maurice Godelier's views on early societies, many of which views he endorsed. That the deepest intellectual influence on Kosambi came from the writings of Frederick Engels is evident from both his books on Indian history.[55]

Such limitations, as these may be, are marginal to the serious quality of Kosambi's work, a quality which is enhanced by the intellectual honesty with which he justifies his use of Marxist methodolgy. His was a mind which by any standards would be considered outstanding. He combined in himself the best of a rigorous Indian intellectual tradition and rejected the facile revivalism and cultural chauvinism which in recent decades have emasculated Indian thinking. In changing the paradigm Kosambi presented a view of Indian history which sought answers to the fundamental questions of how and why Indian society is what it is today. He provided a new theoretical framework which was not a mechanical application of theories derived from elsewhere but was hammered out by his proficiency in handling a variety of sources and the intellectual perceptions and originality of thought which he brought to bear on his explanations. Fresh evidence may well lead to a reconsideration of the answers which he gave to these questions but his questions and his concerns still remain valid. Even in this reconsideration we are often dependent on the leads which he initially gave and which he indicated were worth pursuing. Kosambi raised the debate on early Indian history from variations in narrative to contending theoretical formulations.

Above all, he was concerned with the contemporary relevance of his understanding of the past. But he insisted that the relevance was never to serve any doctrinaire purpose;[56] rather, it should stem from what he thought was the natural function of the historian. I can only conclude with what he himself quoted as the summation of the role of the historian. E.H. Carr writes: 'The function of the historian is neither to love the past nor to emancipate himself from the past, but to master and understand it as the key to the understanding of the present. Great history is written precisely when the historian's vision of the past is illuminated by insight into problems of the present . . . . The function of history is to promote a profounder understanding of both past and present through the interrelation between them.'[57]

Notes and References

1. T. Kuhn, *The Structure of Scientific Revolutions,* Chicago, 1970.
2. J. Mill, *History of British India,* London, 1918–23.
3. V. Smith, *The Oxford History of India,* Oxford, 1919.
4. D.D. Kosambi, *An Introduction to the Study of Indian History,* Bombay, 1956. Henceforth *ISIH.*
5. Ibid., pp. 1ff.
6. Ibid., pp. 5ff; 'Combined Methods in Indology', *Indo-Iranian Journal,* 1963, VI, pp. 177–202.
7. D.D. Kosambi, *The Culture and Civilisation of Ancient India in Historical Outline,* London, 1965. Henceforth *CCAIHO.*
8. 'Some Extant Versions of Bhartṛhari's *Śatakas*', *JBBRAS,* 1945, XXI, pp. 17–32; *The Śatakatrayam of Bhartṛhari with the Commentary of Rāmarṣi,* ed. in collaboration with Pt. K.V. Krishnamoorthi Sharma, Anandāsrama Sanskrit Series No. 127, Poona, 1947; *The Southern Archetype of Epigrams Ascribed to Bhartṛhari,* Bharatiya Vidya Series, 9, Bombay, 1946; 'The Quality of Renunciation in Bhartṛhari's Poetry', in *Exasperating Essays,* Poona, 1857, pp. 72ff.
9. Harvard Oriental Series No. 44, Cambridge, Mass., 1956.
10. *ISIH,* p. 266.
11. 'The Avatāra Syncretism and Possible Sources of the Bhagavad Gītā', *JBBRAS,* 1948–9, XXIV–XXV, pp. 121–34; 'Social and Economic Aspects of the Bhagavad Gītā', in *Myth and Reality,* Bombay, 1962, pp. 12ff.

12. *Buddhist India,* London, 1903.

13. *The Social Organisation in North East India in Buddha's Time,* Calcutta, 1920.

14. *ISIH,* p. 174, f.n.1.

15. 'Early Brahmans and Brahmanism', *JBBRAS,* 1947, xxiii, pp. 39–46; 'On the Origin of the Brahman Gotra', *JBBRAS,* 1950, xxvi, pp. 21–80. 'Brahman Clans', *JAOS,* 1953, 73, pp. 202–8.

16. J. Brough, *The Early Brahmanical System of Gotra and Pravara,* Cambridge, 1953; D.D. Kosambi, 'Brahman Clans', *JAOS,* 1953, 73, pp. 202–8.

17. T. Burrow, *The Sanskrit Language,* London, 1965; B.M. Emeneau, *Collected Papers,* Annamalai University, 1967; M.N. Deshpande and P. Hook, *Aryan and Non-Aryan in India,* Ann Arbor, 1979.

18. *ISIH,* pp. 229–30.

19. *CCAIHO,* p. 77.

20. 'Study and Methodology of Silver Punch-Marked Coins', *New Indian Antiquary,* 1941, 4, pp. 1–35 and 49–76; 'The Effect of Circulation upon Weight of Metallic Currency', *Current Science,* 1942, xi, pp. 227–30; *ISIH,* pp. 162ff.

21. 'Pilgrim's Progress: A Contribution to the Prehistory of the Western Deccan', in *Myth and Reality,* pp. 110ff.

22. *ISIH,* pp. 43ff.

23. Ibid., pp. 246ff.

24. Ibid., pp. 24ff.

25. *Sovetskaya Etnografia,* Ak. Nauk USSR, No. 1, 1958, pp. 39–57.

26. *ISIH,* pp. 24ff.

27. 'Urvaśī and Purūravas', in *Myth and Reality,* pp. 42ff.

28. 'At the Crossroads: A Study of Mother Goddess Cult Sites', in *Myth and Reality,* pp. 82ff.

29. *The Origin of the Family, Private Property and the State,* London, 1946.

30. For example, R. Briffault, *The Mothers,* New York, 1927; O.R. Ehrenfels, *Mother Right in India,* London, 1941.

31. *ISIH,* p. 27. In his letters to Professor Pierre Vidal-Naquet dated 18 September 1965 and 27 September 1965 he provides further examples of this in the wealth paid by Bhīṣma for the marriage of Pāṇḍu to Mādrī, the Madra princess, *Mahābhārata,* I.105.1. and also in the form of the marriage of Arjuna to Subhadrā of the Yadu tribe. I am grateful to Professor Vidal-Naquet for showing me this correspondence.

32. In the introduction to *Exasperating Essays,* Poona, 1957, pp. 3–4 and on p. 18. He says of them, 'These form a decidedly mixed category, indescribable because of the rapidly shifting views and even more rapid

political permutations and combinations. The OM included at various times several factions of the CPI, the Congress Socialists, the Royists and numerous left splinter groups . . . The OM Marxism has too often consisted of theological emphasis on the inviolable sanctity of the current party line, or irrelevant quotations from the classics.'

33. Ibid., pp. 62ff.

34. Romila Thapar, 'The Study of Society in Ancient India', in *Ancient Indian Social History: Some Interpretations,* New Delhi, 1978, pp. 211ff.

35. *CCAIHO,* p. 41.

36. Romila Thapar, 'Study of Society.'

37 *ISIH,* pp. 176ff.

38. K.A. Chaudhuri, *Ancient Agriculture and Forestry in Northern India,* Bombay, 1977.

39. *CCAIHO,* p. 125.

40. *ISIH,* p. 244.

41. *CCAIHO,* p. 101.

42. *ISIH,* pp. 244ff.

43. Letter to Pierre Vidal-Naquet dated 4.7.1964.

44. Ibid., p. 6; see also, 'Marxism and Ancient Indian Culture', *ABORI*, 1949, 29, pp. 271–7. Kosambi's views on his relations with the Communist Party of India over his review of Dange's book and his relations with Dange are described in his letters to Vidal-Naquet dated 22 November 1963 and 4 December 1963.

45. *ISIH,* p. 187.

46. Ibid., p. 275.

47. Ibid., p. 291.

48. B. Morrison, *Political Centres and Culture Regions in Early Bengal,* Tucson, 1970.

49. *CCAIHO,* pp. 177ff.

50. *ISIH,* pp. 326ff.

51. R.S. Sharma had argued for a substantial similarity in many parts of northern India, *Indian Feudalism,* Calcutta, 1965.

52. An example of the analysis of this role can be found in H. Kulke, *Jagannatha Kult und Gajapati Konigtam,* Wiesbaden, 1979.

53. M. Finley, *The World of Odysseus,* was first published in 1954. The fact that he was initially working in the United States would at that time have made his books less easily available in India. Kosambi refers to his study *Ancient Greeks* as being most stimulating, but not to his more acclaimed work on the Greek epics.

54. The easy availability of English translations has helped in this, such translations resulting mainly from the interest in Neo-Marxism on the part of American radicals and academics. It is significant that some of the most

stimulating debates on precapitalist societies emanating from new Marxist writing are to be found in the issues of the last fifteen years of *Current Anthropology* and *American Anthropologist.*

55. A view put forward in the course of a conversation by Charles Malamoud (who translated *CCAIHO* into French) and with which view I am in agreement. In a letter to Vidal-Naquet dated 4 June 1964 Kosambi writes, 'I learned from these two great men [Marx and Engels] what questions to ask and then went to fieldwork to find the answers, because the material did not exist in published books'.

56. *CCAIHO,* p. 24.

57. *What Is History?,* pp. 20, 31, 62.

CHAPTER 3

Society and Historical Consciousness

The Itihāsa-purāṇa *Tradition**

The expression of historical consciousness, it has often been assumed, takes the form of historical writing, clearly recognizable as a genre of literature. More frequently, however, the geological analogy of a particular vein embedded in rock seems more apposite, in that such consciousness is not always visible and has to be prised from sources which tend to conceal it. Within the vein lies information purporting to relate to events of the past, and enveloping this vein is the commentary which arises from concerns of the present. The form it takes tends to reflect the kind of society from which it emanates.

Historical consciousness, therefore, can change over time. Historians tend to view historical writing as conforming almost entirely to the format and pattern familiar from the last couple of centuries, or from models borrowed from particular societies such as ancient Greece and China. The more important but neglected aspect is the search for historical consciousness, irrespective of how immediately recognizable or evident it may be, in its literary form. This perhaps requires a distinction between what might be termed 'embedded history'—forms in which historical consciousness has to be prised out—and its opposite, 'externalized history'—which

* This essay was previously published in S. Bhattacharya and R. Thapar (eds), *Situating Indian History*, Delhi, Oxford University Press, 1986, pp. 353–83.

I am grateful to my colleagues Satish Saberwal and B.D. Chattopadhyaya for comments on an earlier draft of this essay.

tends to bring embedded consciousness into the open, as it were, and to be more aware of its deliberate use of the past. The need for such a deliberate use suggests a changed historical situation. This distinction can be apparent not only between societies but also within the same society as it undergoes change. The attempt in this essay is not to analyse historical consciousness in relation to society as a whole, but in relation to a more restricted view of its expression among those who successfully aspired to power. It relates, therefore, only to historical writing in terms of changing forms in the perception of power.

Each version of the past which has been deliberately transmitted has a significance for the present, and this accounts for its legitimacy and its continuity. The record may be one in which historical consciousness is embedded: as in myth, epic and genealogy; or alternatively it may refer to the more externalized forms: chronicles of families, institutions and regions, and biographies of persons in authority. There is no evolutionary or determined continuum from one form to the other and facets of the embedded consciousness can be seen as a part of the latter, whether introduced deliberately or subconsciously. The degree to which forms change or overlap has a bearing on dominant social formations. Similarly, major social and political changes influence the form of historical consciousness even though there is no mechanical correlation between the two.

Evident historical texts such as chronicles of families, institutions and regions often incorporate mythical beginnings which act as charters of validation. The tracing of links with established lineages through genealogical connections, and frequently with epic heroes, plays the same role of drawing upon embedded history. I shall consider some forms of embedded history, such as the prevalent myths in the *itihāsa-purāṇa* tradition, which encapsulate features of what might be seen as historical experience; the eulogies and hero-lauds which were gradually expanded into epic literature; the genealogical sections or *vaṃśānucarita* of the Puranic texts which, by implication, carry a commentary on the social status of ruling families.

In contrast to these the more externalized forms draw upon the embedded but have other primary concerns and carry a different type of historical information. Thus historical biography or the *carita* literature has as its germ the hero-laud and the epic hero. Family chronicles and *vaṃśāvalīs* assimilate myth and genealogy to other events. Chronicles of institutions and regions maintain a variant form of mythology and genealogy, and are aimed at recording the history of the institution or the area. The distinction made between the two forms is not arbitrary; I am arguing that the embedded form is closer to what have been called lineage-based societies and the externalized form to state systems incorporated in monarchies. Or, to put it in another way, the existence of the state requiring its own validation encourages the creation of an externalized historical consciousness.

In the articulation of historical consciousness in early north Indian society, the truly embedded forms are evident in the literature of the lineage-based society characterized by an absence of state formation, and the more free-standing or externalized forms emerge with the transition to state systems. The terms 'lineage society' and 'state systems', used here as a short-hand, represent not merely a change in political forms but a multiple social change. Thus the term 'state' would refer to a society registering political polarities, an increasingly vertical hierarchy of authority, social inequalities, differentiated economies and distinct ideological identities; not that these characteristics are completely absent in lineage societies, but there are endemic differences between the two. Sometimes these differences are blurred in the texts. Lineage society derives its validity from different sources of authority as compared to state systems, with which we are in any case more familiar.[1] The central role of lineage in the earlier society has reference to more than just the ordering of kinship for it dominates virtually every aspect of activity.

I

The deepest layer of the embedded form is myth. Events are assumed to have happened, and time is almost proto-chronos since it involves gods and the supernatural in an active role with humans and animals. The significance of myth to the historian lies more in its being the self-image of a given culture, expressing its social assumptions. The role of myth in this context is often explanatory. Origin myths are concerned with cosmogony and the start of events such as the Flood myth.[2] The *Śatapatha Brāhmaṇa* version of the Flood myth carries obvious traces of association with the Mesopotamian Flood myth. Manu, when performing his morning ablutions, finds a fish in his cupped hands and rears the fish until it reaches an enormous size. The fish explains the intention of the gods to drown the earth in a deluge and, wishing to save Manu and the seven *ṛṣis* (in whom vests all knowledge) from this disaster, it orders Manu to build a boat for this purpose. This is tied to its horn and it swims through the deluge. The boat and its passengers remain safely on a mountain until the flood subsides, after which they return. By means of sacrifical rites Manu creates a series of sons for himself and one androgynous daughter, his children being the founders of the various lineages. The eldest son, Ikṣvāku, establishes the Sūryavaṃśa or Solar lineage, and the androgynous daughter, Iḷā, establishes the Candravaṃśa or Lunar lineage.

The *Matsya Purāṇa* version links the fish with the incarnation of Viṣṇu, thus bringing the gods more directly into the story, and at the same time using what was obviously a familiar myth to demonstrate the power of the new god, Viṣṇu. Manu, as the name suggests in its association with *mānava* (mankind), is the primeval, archetypal man who is the eponymous ancestor of all the lineages. The emphasis on origins is again stressed in the deluge, where the flood is seen as a time-marker. Floods tend to wipe away earlier conditions and society can start afresh.[3] The survival of Manu and the *ṛṣis* links the new creation with the old, in spite of the deluge washing away the old, since Manu is the seventh in a succession of pre-Flood Manus. The link is important to the genealogical records. The status of the earlier Manus is conveyed through it to the new lineages. All the eponymous ancestors of the lineages are the children of Manu.

Other myths provide social sanctions, one such being the Puruṣasūkta story in the *Ṛg Veda* describing the origin of the four castes.[4] The Puruṣasūkta hymn occurs in a late section of the *Ṛg*

Veda and describes the sacrifice of the god Prajāpati, from whose body the four *varṇa*s are said to have sprung: the *brāhmaṇa*s from his mouth, the *kṣatriya*s from his arms, the *vaiśya*s from his thighs and the *śūdra*s from his feet. The symbolism of each bodily part relates to the ritual status and function of the particular *varṇa*. That the origin and hierarchy go back to a ritual occasion underlines the nature of the ranking. The evolution of *varṇa* stratification is rooted in the lineage-based society of Vedic times. In a sense the *brāhmaṇa* and the *kṣatriya varṇa*s were to evolve as distinct lineages with their separate rules of marriage and descent: exogamy in the *brāhmaṇa gotra*s and the more frequent endogamy of the *kṣatriya*s. The *śūdra varṇa* is excluded by its very origin, which is a denial of lineage since it is said more often to include groups identified by the status of the two parents.

Some myths legitimize a changed social and political condition, as is apparent from the much repeated story of Pṛthu.[5] The various versions of this story begin by referring to the wickedness of Veṇa who had to be killed by the *ṛṣi*s because of his unrighteous rule. From his left thigh they churned a successor, Niṣāda, who was inadequate and was expelled to the forest as a hunter-gatherer. From the right arm of Veṇa they churned another successor, the righteous *rājā* Pṛthu, who introduced cattle-keeping and agriculture and bestowed so many benefits on the earth that she in gratitude took his name Pṛthivī. Veṇa was wicked because he ceased to perform the sacrificial ritual and had to be killed by the *ṛṣi*s (and not expelled by his subjects), who alone had the right to depose a ruler. The dark, short, ugly Niṣāda became the prototype of all forest-dwelling people. The myth sought to legitimize the expulsion of such groups when land was cleared and settled by agriculturists.

In each of such cases an attempt is made to explain social origins and assumptions which are significant to historical reconstruction. Myth was transmitted orally in its earliest phase. With the evolution of a more heterogeneous and stratified society, myths were questioned and explanations sought. Some myths were replaced with new or different versions and others added to and embellished, often to such a degree that the original myth became almost opaque. That myths in some ways mirrored society was not their sole function, but for our purposes this aspect is significant.

Myths of descent often serve to integrate diverse groups by providing common origins. Among competing groups a myth can be used for the reverse process of distinguishing one from the other. Origin myths posit beginnings authoritatively and are therefore central to embedded history. The degree to which myths reflect different social assumptions can be demonstrated by a comparison of origin myths from the *Ṛg Veda* and from Buddhist sources, a comparison which also demonstrates the degree to which historical consciousness is embedded in myth.[6] The origins of the Śākyas, Licchavis, Mallas and Koliyas are all described in stories which have a common format, which format suggests a tradition deviant from the brahmanical origin myths. The clans of the Ikṣvāku lineage, are said to be of the families of *rājā*s (which could mean royal descent but more likely refers to families of lineage chiefs) and are often the exiled children of such families, thus suggesting a lineage migration or fission. The new settlement is in a forest clearing with a town as its nucleus. The name of the lineage is frequently associated with an object such as the *kol* or *śaka* tree. More interestingly, the original founders have a system of sibling marriages and in each case sixteen pairs of twin children are born: it is from these that the lineage expands. Sibling incest, since it is never actually referred to as prevalent, would point to a symbolic concern with purity of lineage, a demarcation between the families of the *rājā*s who owned land and the rest of the people, by the assertion of origins otherwise taboo; or perhaps an endorsement of cross-cousin marriage, which, because it was prohibited by brahmanical codes referring to northern India, may have been seen as a form of sibling incest. That the origin myth was of some consequence is evident from its inclusion in the history of every lineage and by the considerable emphasis given to it in the biographies of the Buddha. There is an absence of any reference to ritual status.

II

Apart from myth, other embedded forms are associated with various fragments of literature moving towards the emergence of the epic. The evolution is traceable via the *dāna-stuti* (eulogies on gift-giving), *gāthā, nārāśamsī* (eulogies on heroes) to the *ākhyāna*, and the *kathā* (cycles of stories generally involving heroes). The *dāna-stuti* hymns scattered throughout the *Ṛg Veda* are eulogies on chiefs and deities who act as would chiefs bestowing generous gifts on grateful bards and priests.[7] The prototype of the gift-giver was the god Indra. The Indra-*gāthā*s express the gratitude of the *jana* (tribe) whom he has led successfully in a cattle-raid and subsequently in distributing the wealth bestowed, much of it on the priests. The same was expected from the ideal *rājā* (chief) in a society where raids were a major access to property and where wealth was computed in heads of cattle and horse, in chariots, gold, and slave girls. The *dāna-stuti*s mentioned the names of their patrons, who were doubtless actual chiefs, but, equally important, the hymns indicated the purpose of the gift and the items of wealth. They were not only eulogies of past actions but also indicators of what was expected from the chiefs.

The *ākhyāna*s, commemorating *rājā*s and heroes, were the cycles of stories recited at the time of the *yajña*s (sacrificial rituals).[8] Some heroes underwent a metamorphosis in time and came to be remembered for reasons quite different from those of the earliest stories. Thus Purūravas in the *Ṛg Veda* is a mortal who loves a celestial woman, Urvaśī; in the *Śatapatha Brāhmaṇa* he is shown as aspiring to become a celestial being himself in pursuit of his love; and finally in the *Mahābhārata* he is not only a celestial being but is among the more important ancestors of the Candravaṃśa lineage.[9] The protagonists in these stories are members of the chiefly families (*rājanya*s and *kṣatriya*s); the stories narrate their lives and activities and incidentally provide information on the lineages as well. An example of the latter is the transformation of single lineages into confederacies of tribes—the Bharatas and the Pūrus of the *Ṛg Veda* confederating with others into the Kurus of later times. The genealogies tend to be shallow and activities centre around the lineages rather than the succession of hereditary status.

A common feature of these many embedded forms is that they are linked to the ritual of sacrifice, the *yajña*. This imparts sanctity to the story and ensures it a continuity coeval with the performance of the ritual; it also imbues it with what were believed to be transcendental powers associated with the accurate and precise performance of the ritual. Even if the events were limited to the activities of the *kṣatriya*s, the audience was much wider and incorporated the entire clan. Apart from the obvious ritual and religious function of the *yajña*, its relevance also lay in its being the occasion for the redistribution of wealth, both from cattle raids and from agricultural production. Up to a point certain rituals had elements of a potlatch in which wealth was not merely redistributed but was also consumed. Both the redistribution as well as the destruction of wealth were directly concerned with claims to status.[10]. When the ritual was enlarged to include representation from other *jana*s, either in the form of honoured guests or as tribute bearers, its function as a potlatch gradually gave way to its symbolizing status on a grander scale. The claims of individual lineages or their segments as descent groups could be established on such occasions, as for example the famous *rājasūya* sacrifice of Yudhiṣṭhira,[11] which raises a complex set of problems concerning the status of various lineages, not least among them that of Kṛṣṇa as the chief of the Vṛṣṇis. The *yajña* therefore stated, as it were, the ranking order of the lineages. The stories which related to these lineages became social charters recording status *vis-à-vis* other lineages, or changes of status, as for example from segment to confederacy, or the migration and fissioning off of a segment from a lineage, as in the case of the Cedis migrating from the western Ganga valley to central India.[12] The record of such migrations was crucial not only to territorial claims but also to genealogical links with established lineages by those newly formed. The *yajña* was a conduit of gift-exchange as well where the wealth of the lineage brought as *bali* or tribute (initially voluntary and later less so) by the *viś* (clan) to the *kṣatriya* or the *rājā*, or else the wealth captured in a raid would be ceremonially used in the ritual and what remained of it would be gifted to the *brāhmaṇas* performing the *yajña*. The exchange was at many levels. Wealth was offered to the gods in return for the success and well-being both of the *kṣatriya* and the *viś*, the well-being guaranteed by the *brāhmaṇas*. Tangible wealth moved from the household of the *kṣatriya* to that of the *brāhmaṇa*. Such a limited exchange was economically non-productive in the sense that it was self-perpetuating with little chance of breaking through to new social forms. But its actual significance lay in its being an operative process in maintaining the lineage society.

III

It was doubtless these fragments of eulogies (*praśastis*) on the heroes and the cycles of stories which led to the first gropings towards epic forms in India, referred to as the *kathā*. Both the *Mahābhārata* and the *Rāmāyaṇa* had their earlier and perhaps more truly epic versions in what have been referred to as the *Rāma-kathā* and the *Bhārata*[13] or *Jaya*. In their later forms, as we have them now, each of the two epics has a distinct locale and the narrative is woven around one of the two main lineages. Thus the *Mahābhārata* focuses on the western Ganga valley, referred to as *madhya-deśa* in the literature, and is concerned with the Aila lineage. The *Rāmāyaṇa* as the epic of the Ikṣvāku lineage has its nucleus in the middle Ganga valley, in Kośala and Videha, and is concerned with migrations southwards into the Vindhyan region, with Daksina Kośala perhaps providing the clue to the area of exile.

The epic continued to be recited, initially on ritual occasions; the *Mahābhārata* is said to have been recited at the *yajña* in the Naimiśa forest and the *sarpa-yajña* of Janamejaya, the *Rāmāyaṇa* by Lava and Kuśa at the *aśvamedha* at Ayodhyā. But it also became the stock for court poetry, the *kāvya*, in the newly emerging courts of the monarchies of the late first millennium BC, or for that matter in more elaborate literary fashions in the courts of the various kingdoms of the first millennium AD.

The epic form carries within it the germs of a more conscious and less embedded historical tradition.[14] Its historicity lies in the fact that it is a later age reflecting on an earlier one, the reflections frequently taking the form of interpolations interleaved among the fragments of the oral, bardic tradition. When epic literature ceases to be a part of the oral tradition and is frozen into a written form, reflections begin to tail off. The pastoral-agricultural society of the world of the heroes structured around lineage gives way to the more clearly agrarian societies and to the rise of urban centres controlled by what is visibly emerging as a state system—which in the Ganga valley at this time was mainly monarchical.

Many of the seeming contradictions in the stances and configurations characterizing the epics can perhaps be explained by these texts (and particularly the *Mahābhārata*), reflecting something of a transitional condition between two rather different structures, the societies of the lineage-based system and that of the monarchical state. Idealized characters are seldom the gods but rather the heroes who occupy the centre of the stage and the gods remain in the wings. Sometimes the earlier deities even come in for a drubbing.[15] The importance of the heroes is further endorsed by their being almost the terminal descendants in the major lineages of the past, a matter of some despair for their death is seen as the wrapping up and putting away of the lineage society, which, in certain areas, was being replaced by monarchies. However, some elements of the lineage society did persist and among them was the continuation of *varṇa* ranking. In many areas outside the *madhya-deśa*, lineage society continued for longer periods and the transition to monarchical states was a gradual process. Nevertheless the change to monarchy meant a substantial alteration of social configurations.

Unlike myth, epic does not attempt to explain the universe or society. It is sufficient that the problems of society are laid bare, and even solutions are not sought since the ultimate solution is the dissolution of the system. Societies experiencing greater stratification require an overall authority to maintain the cohesion of lineage and strata. When such an authority comes into being and is eulogized, that eulogy becomes the dirge of a truly epic society. In laying bare the conditions in the transition from lineage society to state systems, a number of bi-polarities are reflected in the literature which give an added edge to the image of the past and the contours of the present. Thus *grāma* (settlement) is contrasted with *araṇya* (forest), the kingdom with exile; the orderliness of the *grāma* is opposed to the disorder of the *araṇya*; the kingly ethic arises out of governing a people and claiming land, the heroic ethic emerges from war and confrontation. The monarchical state is seen as the superior and is the successor to lineage society, irrespective of whether this is clearly spelt out—as in the conflict between the kingdom of Kosala and the *rākṣasa*s in the *Rāmāyaṇa*—or whether it is left more ambiguous—as in the diverse assumptions of the narrative and didactic sections of the *Mahābhārata* where the Sabhāparvan, encapsulating the essence of a lineage society, stands in contrast to the Śāntiparvan with its rhetoric on the monarchical state. The new ethic is sustained in part by the popularizing of new sources of authority. Among them and significant to the political arena were the king, the *brāhmaṇa* and the *ṛṣi*. None of these were entirely new in that the chief, the priest and the shaman were dominant figures in lineage society. But it is the tangible authority of the king based on land as the source of revenue, or of the *brāhmaṇa* as the sole performer of and manual on rituals, and of the *ṛṣi* and *saṃnyāsi* as symbolizing an intangible moral authority almost as a counterweight to that of the first two, which gives a fresh dimension to their role and their interrelations. The changed situation is reflected in a shift in the kind of authority exercised. From a more diffused, equitable authority there is a movement towards a hierarchical, vertical authority.[16] This was mitigated somewhat by the countervailing presence of the renouncer and the charisma attached to renunciation.

The epic as the literature of one age looking back nostalgically on another can become a literature of legitimation. Interpolations are often the legitimation of the present but are attributed to the heroes of the past. The bards were perhaps providing the models of what patrons should be like. But, more important, it is the kingdoms looking back on an age of chiefships: where recently founded dynasties were seeking ancestry from the *kṣatriya* lineages through actual or, more often, imagined genealogical links; where such ancestry would also bestow social legitimacy and validate kingship. That legitimacy and validation are essential to the epic is clear from the central event of the narrative, namely the legitimacy of succession, involving elder and younger sons and the problems of disqualification.[17] Legitimacy also relates to using the past to explain the present. Perhaps the most dramatic example of this is the series of explanations in favour of accepting the strangeness of Draupadī marrying five brothers, fraternal polyandry not being a commonly practised form of marriage. Among the explanations is predictably a reference to an earlier birth of Draupadī.[18] Fortunately the doctrine of transmigration, referring to events and situations in a previous birth, makes the use of the past more plausible. The interplay of the past and the present is thus not only part of the implicit epic idiom but is made more explicit by recourse to the theory of transmigration. At another level, the past validates the present in the long discourses on what constitutes good government or the correct functioning of the *kṣatriya* as king: perhaps best exemplified in the dying Bhīṣma delivering the lengthy *mokṣadharma* perorations, lying on his bed of arrows. Legitimacy makes the claim to historicity more feasible and the association with myth is weakened.[19]

IV

The gradual prising of historical consciousness becomes visible in the compilation of what came to be called the *itihāsa-purāṇa*.[20] The phrase remains difficult to define, veering between the perceived past and historicity. It is described as the fifth Veda but was an oral tradition for many centuries until it was compiled in the form of the *Purāṇa*s in the mid first millennium AD. The genealogical sections of the *Purāṇa*s were a reordering of the earlier material in a new format. The lesser and multiple *Purāṇa*s borrowed the format of the earlier major *Purāṇa*s, although their contents differed. The *Purāṇa* was to become a recognized literary form. To the extent that it recorded history, it was initially transitional from embedded to externalized history, It was linked to the bardic tradition, where the *sūta* and the *māgadha* are said to have been its earliest authors.[21] In the

Vedic texts the *sūta* has a close relation with the *rājā* and was of high status, but by the time of the Manu *Dharmaśāstra*, the *sūta* had been reduced to the level of a *sankīrṇajāti* or mixed caste. Doubtless by now the tradition had been appropriated by the literate *brāhmaṇa*s who had also seen the potential value of controlling oral information on the past and recording it in a literary form relevant to emergent contemporary requirements.

There is evidence to suggest that the Purāṇic texts were translated from the oral Prākrit to the literate Sanskrit.[22] The structure of the *Purāṇa*s was an attempt to provide an integrated world view of the past and present, linking events to the emergence of a deity or a sect, since each *Purāṇa* was dedicated to such a one, the *Viṣṇu Purāṇa* being regarded as the model. The historical epicentre of the *itihāsa* tradition was the *vaṃśānucarita*, which, as the name suggests, was the genealogy of all the known lineages and dynasties up to the mid-first millennium AD. It was not a parallel tradition to the earlier *kathā*s and *ākhyāna*s since it incorporated many of these forms of embedded history. The genealogical core pertaining to those who were believed to have held power in the past was carefully preserved after it had been worked out into a systematic pattern. This was because it not only purported to record the past but was also later to become essential to future claims to lineage status, and was therefore linked with historical writing. Evidently there was a need for a recognizable historical tradition at this time. In the transition from lineage to state, which was occurring in many parts of north India, monarchy had emerged as the viable political form.

The major dynasties recorded in the *Purāṇa*s up to the mid-first millennium AD start with descendants of recognized *kṣatriya* lineages, but by the mid-first millennium BC begin to refer to families of non-*kṣatriya* origin. Some are specifically said to be *śūdra*s, such as the Nandas and possibly the Mauryas. Others, judging by their names, were *brāhmaṇa*, such as the Śuṅgas and Kāṇvas. The lesser dynasties dating to the early centuries AD are stated to be *vrātya-dvija*, *śūdra*, and *mleccha*, and this is explained as resulting from the inevitable degeneration of all norms in the Kaliyuga. Successor dynasties are frequently referred to as the *bhṛtya*s or servants of the previous ones, suggesting that the founders of dynasties may often have been administrators, high in the hierarchy of office who overthrew weak kings. This may well account for the rise of *brāhmaṇa* dynasties. The gradual increase in references to *śūdra* rulers would indicate that political power, although in theory restricted to *kṣatriyas*, was infact open to any *varṇa*. It required force and administrative control to establish a dynasty. Claims to territory were established through strength of arms. Legitimation through brahmanical ritual was evidently not required since some dynasties are described as not conforming to Vedic rites. This may well have been due to the influence of Buddhism and Jainism at this time. The brahmanical refusal to bestow *kṣatriya* status on such families may have been in part due to their being patrons of non-brahmanical religious sects. Buddhist and Jaina literature on the other hand insists on the *kṣatriya* status of some of these dynasties. Thus the Mauryas are not only listed as *kṣatriyas* but are linked to the clan of the Buddha, the Śākyas, which would automatically have related them to the prestigious Sūryavaṃśa as well.[23] The absence of proper status in the brahmanical sources did not detract from the importance of these families. If anything it points to the relative independence of the state as a political form from the clutches of traditional validation during this period. The need for legitimation through lineage status was apparently not required at this time.

The encroachment of foreign rulers in the post-Mauryan period led to some indigenous families having to recede into the background. Claims to power and to actual status were conceded to the Indo-Greeks, Śakas, Parthians, and Kuṣāṇas, but claim to *varṇa* status was denied them and they continued to be called *vrātya-kṣatriyas* (degenerate), having no indigenous land-base in the subcontinent nor being able to claim kinship links with earlier established lineages.[24] This was despite the fact that some among them did claim *kṣatriya* status in their own inscriptions.[25] The lack of genealogical connections was a form of exclusion, effective in a society where ritual status still drew heavily on the values of a lineage-based social organization and where genealogical links had played a crucial role.

Although dynastic status was not confined to any particular *varṇa*, those who succeeded to kingship from the mid-first millennium and onwards often observed the formality of claiming *kṣatriya* status, or at least of participating in a common *kṣatriya* past, as embodied in the *itihāsa-purāṇa* tradition. The question may well be asked as to why such a practice becomes more necessary during this period, and the answer covers a range of possibilities. The making of land grants to *brāhmaṇa*s and the consequent spread of Sanskritic culture provides an obvious reason. But it would be as well not to overlook the reality on the ground, as it were, and examine the actual process of state formation at a time when it related to secondary (if not tertiary) states, or new states emerging from association with established states. Land grants of a substantial size to non-religious grantees would have provided the base for the grantee establishing a network of political control over the area through his lineage connections.[26] The partial *brāhmaṇa* ancestry of some ruling families as given in their genealogies would suggest that even *brāhmaṇa* grantees were not averse to participating in this process. Where unoccupied land was still available and the migration of peasants feared, political control would be less effective if dependent on force and more effective if drawing its strength from legitimacy. The expression of power in the sense of controlling resources and seeking compliance through persuasion, influence and support[27] would be better achieved by legitimacy than by force. The legitimation of lineage origins therefore became a necessity.

The granting of land, apart from its other functions, served also to incorporate areas under lineage systems into the society dominated by the state. Lineage-based agrarian activity was assimilated into the new economy and erstwhile clansmen or else their chiefs were converted into tax-paying peasants. Lineage traditions continued up to a point and could be adjusted to the *varṇa* framework, which acted as a bridge between the earlier society and its later form.

It would be worth investigating whether the process of state formation in the late first millennium AD provided a different emphasis from that of the earlier period. The overlap between lineage and state continued, but the political form was perhaps not so reliant on institutions of the state and included a more substantial dependence on lineage. Would it then be correct to argue that the post-Gupta state did not attempt to uproot the *kṣatriyas* (to use the phrase of the *Purāṇas*) and reduce the importance of lineage societies, but rather that it attempted to encourage the emergence of a new role for lineages through which it sought to extend its control?

With the kaleidoscopic formation of states in the post-Gupta period, new ruling families relied heavily on genealogical links, fabricated genealogies providing them with claims to being *kṣatriyas*: claims which were carefully stated in the then legal charters, that is, the inscriptions recording the grants of land by these families to *brāhmaṇas* and other grantees. Such claims became even more crucial in a situation of competition for status by horizontal marriage alliances among the 'new' *kṣatriyas*. Matrimonial links sealed the claims to status. Thus the possible tribal Gond and Bhil associations of the Candella and Guhilot ruling families did not eventually stand in the way of their claims to *kṣatriya* status, which were backed not merely by land-ownership but also by claims to genealogical links with the Candravaṃśa and the Sūryavaṃśa: the claim being recognized with marriage into other established *kṣatriya* families.[28] The sixteenth-century marriage of a Gond *rājā* into the Candella family is an interesting example of how the system worked. The acceptance by other competing families of the origin myth and of the genealogy of the family successfully installed in power was largely because political power was relatively open and individual families were concerned with succeeding to power, not with altering the framework within which status was conferred. The narrowing down of legitimation to one family meant that others could aspire to the same power in changed circumstances.

The earlier states from the Mauryan to the Kuṣāṇa tended to develop administrative structures in which local regions were left relatively untampered, as long as they provided the required revenue.[29] When revenue requirements became oppressive, peasants could threaten to migrate from the state and establish new clearings in the forest and on waste land. Migration was the alternative to peasant revolt and kings are cautioned against oppressive taxes lest peasants migrate. From the Gupta period onwards there was a gradual and increasing tendency to intensify the revenue demands and tie down the peasantry.[30] The economic restructuring of the local region was regarded as part of the state's legitimate right to revenue. The ability of the peasant to migrate was hampered, and even though there is little apparent evidence of peasant revolts the earlier flexible relationship between peasants and the state would have changed—with the intermediate grantees playing the difficult role of keeping the peasants tied since it was not only the revenue demands of the state but also their own revenue rights which were at stake. This points towards an urgent need on the part of grantees and landowners and clan chiefs, the potential ruling families, to not only insist on their high status but to be able to prove it whenever necessary. An emphasis on status, with the insistence on service by the lower orders inherent in the formulation of *varṇa*, became in some areas an adjunct to coercion by those who had succeeded in rising to higher levels of political power. The *itihāsa-purāṇa* tradition became one of the means of legitimizing status and the *vaṃśānucarita* sections had to be carefully preserved.

Lists of succession (*vaṃśa*)—whether of teachers as in the Vedic texts, or of elders in the *saṅgha*, or of descent groups as in the case of the Sūryavaṃśa and the Candravaṃśa, or of dynasties—encapsulate perceptions of the past. Genealogy as a record of succession lay at the core of the epic tradition and linked epic to embedded history as well as to the *itihāsa-purāṇa* and later historical forms. Genealogy is used by new groups in the ascendant to legitimize their power and claim connections with those who were earlier in power. Links were therefore sought in the post-Gupta period by new ruling families with the Sūryavaṃśa and the Candravaṃśa. The epics embodying the stories of these lineages were thus assured continuity, quite apart from the infusion of a religious dimension through the theory of epic heroes being *avatāras* of Viṣṇu. The less obvious information from genealogical data indicates kinship patterns, marriage forms, geographical settlements, and migration.[31]

The pattern or structure of a genealogy is often indicative of social integration where competing groups are shown through a listing of descent. Among these the successful ones claim a larger share of the genealogical structure, parallel to their claim to inheritance and power. In the Aila genealogy, for example, the Pūrus and the Yādavas claim the major part of the genealogy and the lines of Turvaśa, Anu, and Druhyu peter out fairly soon. The ideological function of the genealogy is to legitimate those who have succeeded to power or to subvert the claims of those who for various reasons are unacceptable. That genealogy was of considerable consequence is indicated not only by the *Purāṇa*s but also by other sources.[32]

The *vaṃśānucarita* section has three distinct constituent parts.[33] The first is the mythical section of the rule of the seven Manus, which is wiped away by the action of the Flood. This is followed by the detailed listing of the generations in each of the two major lineages. The Ikṣvāku is the senior and more cohesive. Descent is recorded only from eldest son to eldest son with a tight control over a well demarcated territory, indicative of a stronger tendency towards monarchy and primogeniture. The Aila lineage is more akin to the pattern of a segmentary system with a wide geographical distribution involving northern, western, and central India. Possibly it reflects a more assimiliative system in which the segments are less the result of branching off or migrating away from the main lineage and more a record of alliances with existing clans. The spread of the Haihaya group in central India would suggest this. It might also be the result of an element of the 'tidying up' of lineages by the authors of the Purāṇas. Two sub-lineages among the Candravaṃśa are given pre-eminence, those of the Pūrus controlling the western Ganga valley and the more diffused Yādavas migrating to western and central India. The segments are all treated as *kṣatriya*s, even though at times this status conflicts with the status assigned to some of them in other sources.[34] Thus the genealogy was a method of legitimizing all those who had held power. However, they had to have performed the brahmanical sacrificial ritual in order to be included in the *itihāsa-purāṇa*, for those who were lax in this matter were either dropped altogether, such as the Licchavis, or like the Śākyas were merely mentioned *en passant*.[35]

The *Mahābhārata* war acts as another time-marker and brings to the battlefield virtually all the lineages of the Candravaṃśa, and a few others as well, and marks the death of the lineages. That it was a terminal event is reflected in the switch to the future tense after the war, suggesting a prophetic form, and is followed by details on dynastic succession in the kingdom of Magadha, an area which emerged in fact as the most powerful kingdom of the Ganga valley. Descent lists now become king lists mentioning historically attested dynasties—Nandas, Mauryas, Śuṇgas, Kāṇvas, Āndhras, and so on, as well as the regnal years of kings. The genealogical record thus indicates a change to monarchies during this period, a change which was of considerable historical importance. Those dynasties which did not claim links with earlier descent groups such as the Indo-Greeks, Śakas, Kuṣāṇas, and Kṣatrapas receive short shrift at the hands of the genealogists. The Yavanas as a generalized term are described as the descendants of the Turvaśa, who, as a segment of the Candravaṃśa, become relatively insignificant fairly early in the genealogical listing.[36] The entry of *śūdra*s as kings, be they Indian or foreign, was of course seen as the inevitable consequence of social imbalances foretold for the Kaliyuga. The *vaṃśānucarita* section therefore becomes a preservation of the record of social and political relations as perceived at a crucial historical moment, and incorporates much of what was believed to be historically accurate. This is put together in a distinctive structure which not only gives form to the past but also becomes a charter of sanction for existing social institutions as well as a potential charter for future claims to legitimacy and status.

Purāṇic literature, in the sections other than the *vaṃśānucarita*, reflects facets of change which impinged upon the historical tradition. It comprises essentially assimilative texts where the Sanskritic tradition and the local tradition are sought to be intermeshed. This was inevitable in a situation where those of a Sanskritic cultural milieu received grants of land and settled in areas where the exposure to Sanskritic culture had been relatively sparse, if at all. Some degree of mutual interchange was required, even if for no other purpose than that of establishing dominance. The Purāṇic texts with their various sub-categories are facets of this development. The culture of the dominant and of the subordinate remained distinct, but proximity and some degree of absorption smoothened the edges of an otherwise angular relationship in many areas. The rhetoric of the Great Tradition and the systematizing of substratum cultures, both of which are reflected in the *Purāṇas*, made the literature acceptable to the audience and useful in mobilizing social and political action.[37]

V

A more clearly recognizable historical tradition is evident in the post-Gupta period, linked in part to the historical changes of the early and mid-first millennium AD. The states of this period were territorially not as large as the Mauryan and the Kuṣāṇa, for example. There was a multiplicity of state formation, particularly in areas hitherto regarded as peripheral or marginal and often characterized by a lineage society. Many of these new states emerged as a consequence of the changes in agrarian relations in the earlier established states, when the system of making grants of land became current. These changes required new processes of authority, law and revenue collection in areas which earlier were either outside the state system or on the edge of it. The change was not limited to the political arena but also introduced new forms of a wider social mobility. There was a growth of sectarian religious groups, some of which professed a doctrinal cult (*bhakti*, narrowing in on an individual's devotion to a particular deity); others which attempted to systematize more earthly cults of fertility and magic; and still others which remained loyal lay supporters of the Buddhist and Jaina *saṅgha*. It was also perhaps in part a reaction to this last group which motivated the increasing interest in an *itihāsa-purāṇa*. Both the Buddhists and the Jainas had shown a sense of centring their sects in avowedly historical events which imparted a certain historicity and added to the intellectual strength of their institutions. The historicity of the Buddha and Mahāvīra was emphasized, major events in the history of the respective *saṅgha*s were linked to political events and personalities, chronology was often calculated on the basis of the date of the death of the Buddha and of Mahāvīra. This point was not missed by other groups and in the latter half of the first millennium AD when Vaiṣṇava and Śaiva sects competed for royal patronage, they not only established monastic institutions but also introduced a historical dimension into the discussion on the evolution of the sect. It can be argued that Buddhist and Jaina sects arose as a part of a counter-culture and therefore as groups in dissent had a clearer sense of their historical purpose.[38] This is a partial explanation of a far more complex question: why Buddhism has a more recognizable sense of externalized history—a question which cannot be discussed in this brief essay. Be it said in passing that apart from considerations of eschatology and epistemology, all of which have their own significance, it is as well to consider also that Buddhism and Jainism were quite early on institutionally based and moved fairly soon to becoming property-holders on a considerable scale. As such the records of their evolution did not merely narrate the life of the Buddha and the history of the *saṅgha* (with its various divergent sects, each claiming status and authenticity), but also described the building of monasteries, the amassing of property and the rights to controlling these—rights which became complex and competitive with the fissioning off of sects from the main stems. The sense of the historicity of the sect becomes evident even in Śaiva and Vaiṣṇava sects when they begin to locate themselves in *āśrama*s and *maṭha*s and become immensely wealthy property-holders, and when intensified competition for patronage has to be supported by claims to legitimacy—which require a substantial input of historically phrased argument.

Implicit in the genealogical form is the notion of time and chronology. The arrangement of events in a chronological order is less precise for earlier times and only when sequential causation becomes important does chronological precision enter the focus of history. Genealogical generations indicate time periods, as also do regnal years. The latter move from fanciful figures to more credible ones as the dynastic lists approach historically attested time. Thus the chronology given for the

Śiśunaga, Nandas, Mauryas and other dynasties is feasible. The arrangement of chronological order becomes more important as historical memory becomes less embedded. The cosmological time of the *mahāyuga* and the start of the Kaliyuga gives way to historical time.[39] The accuracy of historical time increases by the reference to dateable eras—the Kṛta (c. 58 BC), Śaka (AD 78), Gupta (AD 319–20), Cedi (c. AD 249), Harṣa (AD 606), and so on: and by the very precise dates recorded in era, regnal year, season, month, lunar fortnight and day in the inscriptions. The era, apart from commemorating an event, can also be seen as a capturing of time, symbolic of an articulation of power in a context where time is viewed as part of an eventual point of destruction. The word for time is *kāla* from the root *kal* 'to calculate', which suggests a meaning indicative of measurement. Perhaps because of the cyclical theory it was also associated with destruction in the sense of the end of time.

The inevitability of time is strengthened by the use of prophecies in genealogies, for time is the ultimate destroyer, *mahākāla*. Cosmological time is distinct from historical time not only by its mathematical pattern and the spatial form in its description, but also by its total orderliness, an orderliness which emphasizes its unreality. This in part might also explain the marginality of chiliastic and millenarian movements in such a pattern as compared to the Judaeo-Christian tradition in which they play a distinctive role. The coming of Viṣṇu as Kalkin arises out of an anxiety relating to the present—the wish to terminate the inequities of the Kaliyuga through Viṣṇu yet again being incarnated as a saviour figure. But such a termination is predetermined by the length of the cycle and will in any case lead to the ultimate ending of the cycle. It is more to the weakness of the eschatology that the marginality of millenarian movements can be attributed. The interplay of cosmological and historical time in the brahmanical tradition can perhaps be explained partially by the *yajña* and *varṇa* requirements which were part of the process of legitimizing families and cults. Cyclical time it has been argued, goes counter to an eschatology which would point to a historical change towards a directed goal.[40] Yet within the *mahāyuga* there is an emphasis on change. It is change rather than repetition which is inherent in the concept, and within this the explanation of change is also implicit.[41]

The notion of change is even more central to the Buddhist concept of time.[42] Because of the claim to the historicity of the Buddha there is a single, central point to which all events relate chronologically, namely the Mahāparinirvāṇa, the death of the Buddha. Buddhist eschatology envisages the extinction of consciousness in *nirvāṇa*, which, although seemingly negative, is the aim of human endeavour since it is a release from rebirth. Change within cosmological time is emphasized further by the cyclic movement of time taking the form of a spiral, in that the cycle never returns to its point of origin: and a spiral if fully stretched can become a wave, if not a linear form. The rise and fall within the cycle purports constant change and even the fall carries within it the eventual upward swing of the cycle, and this is conducive to the idea of a coming millennium, an idea envisaged in the Buddha Maitreya. This in turn is paralleled by decay carrying within it the seeds of regeneration.

The precision of historical time as recorded in inscriptions probably derived from the more widespread use of the solar calendar from the first millennium AD. But it also had to do with the legitimacy of the individual in authority, for the inscription was frequently a legal charter. Not only was the authority of the king time-bound in such charters, but so also was his claim to the property which he was donating in as much as later kings could revoke these grants in spite of the insistence in the inscriptions that they were given in perpetuity. An additional factor was the influence of the idea that all actions are conditioned by the auspiciousness of the moment when they are carried out, and in the case of donations and grants, this would be particularly apposite.[43] The multiple use of historical time focused on the individual and gave sharper definition to the individual as a figure of authority: an idea by no means unfamiliar by now in the historical consciousness of the period. A fuller exposition of this idea had come from Buddhist sources. Aśoka Maurya, as a patron of Buddhism, acquired an accretion of legends, some of which were gathered in the *Aśokāvadāna*. The attempt was to give historicity to the

Buddhist *saṅgha* by linking it to a powerful political personality, a notion which was not alien to the emergence of much of the other non-Buddhist *carita* literature. The need to write the biography of the Buddha, *Buddha-carita*, had been felt since the time of the early monastic movement, and the first missions. It changed from being a part of the canonical texts to a separate genre of literature.[44] Gradually the idea of biography was extended to the 'hero' in a wider context. A historical background is also helpful to organized missionary activity in new areas where antecedents have to be explained; this was useful to the entry of Buddhism into Asia, as indeed it was useful to brahmanical centres in the more remote parts of the Indian subcontinent. The *carita* tradition doubtless also drew on the *praśasti*s incorporated in a number of early inscriptions, such as that of Khāravela at Hāthigumphā and Rudradāman at Junagadh; a style which became more elaborate in time as evidenced by the Udaipur *rāj-praśasti*.[45]

VI

Those in authority seek validation from the past, and this validation was the starting point of a new category of texts, the *vaṃśāvalī*s and the *carita*s of the post-Gupta period. The *vaṃśāvalī*s were the histories of the ruling families in specific geographical regions, the latter often coinciding with the new kingdoms and states in areas previously either unoccupied or settled by groups of tribes. As a genre they lay between the lineage lists of the *Purāṇa*s and the historical biographies of individual rulers. The *carita* or historical biography was a complement to the *vaṃśāvalī* and focused on the king, who was seen as the centre of authority in a more radial state system. Bāṇabhaṭṭa's *Harṣacarita* led off the biographical form and was followed by a large number of others.[46] Most of the better known ones were written between the eighth and twelfth centuries AD, but as a form, *carita* literature continued into later times, in each case commemorating the rise of new kings. The *carita* was unashamedly the eulogy of the patron, but the persons chosen were those who had a special status and function in the ruling family and were contributors of a more than ordinary kind, not only to their own families but also to the consolidation of kingdoms and kingship. The rhetoric of eulogy when deconstructed would doubtless reveal multiple relationships within a courtly edifice of norms and actions, and despite the ambiguity in presenting hard historical data, much of the subtlety of historical nuance can be gathered from these biographies. *Carita* literature also focuses on other aspects of the individual in society. Cyclic time carries a certain inevitability but the individual can opt out of it, and on a lesser level this is demonstrated in biographies where the *karma* of the individual may play a larger role than the inevitability of the time cycle: and the individual *karma* and its historic role was central to the doctrine of Buddhism as well as the ideology of the *bhakti* tradition.

On occasion the subjects of the biographies were younger brothers who had come to rule (as for example, Harṣavardhana and Vikramāditya VI), and their legitimacy over other claimants had to be established. The royal patron was linked with the major lineages of the *itihāsa-purāṇa* or with a new lineage which had acquired status since then, such as the Agni-kula among Rajputs or the Nāgavaṃśa among certain central Indian dynasties. The *carita* was essentially a literary form in origin and thus a far cry from the bardic fragments of epic times. The most sophisticated courtly tradition found expression in this literature and the courtly values of chivalry, heroism, and loyalty were at a premium.[47] Two obvious characteristics of this form were the depiction of the king as the focus of the court and a clear awareness of a well-defined geographical area which constituted the kingdom and was identified with the dynasty. Obeisance is made to the lineage but it plays a secondary role in relation to the king who is now most clearly the figure of formal political authority in both state and society.

Political decentralization inherent in the granting of land on a large scale encouraged a competition among families aspiring to dynastic status. Dynasties survived through an assertion of power, legitimacy, and recourse to marriage alliances with ambitious feudatories. Attempts to restructure the economic potential within certain areas of the state and to balance the intricate relationship between royal power, brahmanical authority, and the dominant religious cults of the region become a further support to power. The emphasis on territory had again to do with the jostling of new states and with the legitimizing of the economic and administrative changes which the system of land grants introduced into the kingdoms.

The *vaṃśāvalī* was the chronicle of a dynasty, and inevitably also the chronicle of the territory controlled by the dynasty. The *vaṃśāvalī* therefore used as source material the various local *Purāṇa*s as well as the oral tradition.[48] It became associated with some new states in various parts of the subcontinent in the early second millennium AD. This is indicative of elements of similarity in historical change, which in turn reflects a degree of cultural uniformity. These elements do not indicate the influence of one dominant regional culture over the others, but rather the expression of a similar historical situation, which, formulated in a certain kind of literature, was common to many regions.

The structure of the *vaṃśāvalī* was almost identical in all these regions. The earliest section narrated the origin myths pertaining to the region and the dynasty. In this there was a recording of local lore as well as a borrowing from the *itihāsa-purāṇa* tradition. Attempts were made to link local history with themes from the *Purāṇa*s incorporating the myths and the genealogies of the Great Tradition with local persons and places. The *Purāṇa*s were the prototypes and local personalities were the protagonists. This required the continued availability of the *Purāṇa*s as sources from which the *vaṃśāvalī* could draw. The major part of the text, however, dealt with more contemporary events, and a history of the ruling dynasty was narrated giving its genealogy and referring to important events associated with the dynasty. The veracity of this information can often be ascertained by comparing it with the evidence of inscriptions, since many of the grants of land were recorded on copper plates or on temple walls. Whereas the need for a *vaṃśāvalī* was motivated by the acquisition of power, the historically authenticated section would appear to coincide with the constitution of power, often articulated in the taking of royal titles such as *mahārājādhirāja*. Concomitant with this was the acceptance of responsibilities of power by the family. The authors of the *vaṃśāvalīs* were court poets and officials and were therefore familiar with political and administrative concerns. The *vaṃśāvalīs* would also be important to those who received grants of land in vouching for the legitimacy of the granting authority.

The *vaṃśāvalī* differs from the earlier tradition in that it legitimates a particular family and not an entire lineage, and to that extent the legitimation of lineage is indirect. The family was not seen merely as a household of agnatic and affinal kinsfolk but was the hub of power. It drew its strength both from claims to high descent as well as to property. Marriage alliances were controlled because dowry and inheritance were a part of the property structure. Such forms of the legitimation of families in power and of regions were of more immediate necessity to newly risen families in small states. The *vaṃśāvalī* therefore was by its very nature not a record of expansionist states. The major dynasties of the past, such as the Nandas and Mauryas, were not the models and only the very early lineages were considered possible sources of status. The appeal was not to the political system of the state but to sources of power which could back up the economic reality of aristocratic families with visions of dynastic ambition. It is significant that the *caritas* and the *vaṃśāvalīs* take up the narrative, as it were, from where the major *Purāṇas* leave off. The Purāṇic accounts of the ruling dynasties come to a close soon after the Guptas. The dynasties listed prior to these are mainly of the core regions of the Ganga valley and western and northern India. That the account was not continued in these *Purāṇas* was probably because there was a bigger distribution of centres of power in the post-Gupta period, and in each of such areas, local *Purāṇas* and chronicles of various kinds began to be maintained. These texts often incorporate both the Purāṇic tradition and the local tradition, as is exemplified in those cases where legitimation is sought by reference to local myths of descent—as in the case of the Agni-kula Rajputs and the Nāgavaṃśis of central India.

As a form, the *vaṃśāvalī* was not restricted to dynastic chronicles and was adapted to the history of other institutions as well. Some of these were monastic institutions where not only was the succession of elders chronicled but also their relations with political authority. This dynastic and political information pertained either to royal patrons of the institution or recorded relations between the institution and political authority, generally in the context of the institution establishing its own legitimacy. An early expression of this relationship is evident from the Buddhist tradition where monastic chronicles were a regular part of the historical tradition.[49]

In attempting to establish the legitimacy of the dynasties or institutions whose history they are recording, chronicles stress the uniqueness of historical events relating to the origin and history of the subject of the chronicle, with indications of its growth and change. Actions are directed towards a goal, often resulting in the success of the subject. Chronicles are, therefore, compiled when a dynasty or institution has established itself and is recognized as powerful. The chronicle helps to establish its claims to authority over competing groups, especially those which are politically important. The borrowing from the *itihāsa-purāṇa* tradition suggests continuity and also stresses legitimacy for the new group. This is seen as being related to those who were in power in the past and can also claim antiquity by maintaining these connections with earlier lineages. The chronicle is again the statement of the successful group and manages to deflect if not erase the presence of competitors. This becomes a particularly useful aspect of the chronicle in a society where not only dissent but even protest often takes the form of opting out or migration away, in preference to confrontation.[50]

If changing forms in the expression of historical consciousness symbolize historical change, and if changes in the political forms of society are reflected in the nature of historical expression, then the *itihāsa-purāṇa* tradition would point to three phases in the unfolding of early Indian history. Initially, in lineage societies, historical consciousness was embedded, and it recorded the perception of the ordering of lineages. With the evolution of states in northern India the second phase was inaugurated, focusing on dynastic power and the supremacy of the state as a system, which in the political arena seems to have overridden caste ordering. The post-Gupta period saw a change in the structure of the state, accompanied by the need in many cases for the legitimation of status of ruling families.

Historical consciousness in early India took a form which grew out of embedded history. Part of the explanation for this may lie in the fact that the *varṇa* ordering of society, which never fully coincided with a clearly defined socio-economic stratification, carried a large element of the lineage-based structure and therefore also the embedded history of that structure. Where *kṣatriya* legitimation became necessary, the *itihāsa-purāṇa* tradition was strengthened with a drawing upon embedded history for origins. In such cases the past in relation to political power became a *kṣatriya* past. But at the same time it did not remain embedded. Although the origin myths of the dynasties recorded in the *vaṃśāvalīs* become something of a mantra or a formula, this should not hide the fact that despite the continuing idiom from the past there is a substantial historical core in the *vaṃśāvalī* which is distinguished from the embedded section, and which is, therefore, a break from the past and takes the form of historical consciousness expressed as externalized history.

Notes and References

1. I have discussed these differences as they pertain to early Indian society, specifically to Vedic and post-Vedic times prior to the rise of the Mauryan state, in *From Lineage to State,* Delhi, 1984. The term 'lineage' is used in preference to the more commonly employed term 'tribe', as lineage, whether fictive or real, is central to such societies, is more precise, and points to the crux of such societies where descent and birth are, in fact, the major focus of social ordering.

2. *Śatapatha Brāhmaṇa* I.8.1.1–10; *Mahābhārata*, Sabhāparvan, 185; *Matsya Purāṇa*, I.11–34; Romila Thapar, 'Puranic Lineages and Archaeological Cultures', in *Ancient Indian Social History: Some Interpretations,* New Delhi, 1978 (hereafter referred to as *AISH*), pp. 240ff.

3. M. Eliade, *The Myth of the Eternal Return,* Princeton, 1971.

4. *Ṛg Veda,* x.97.

5. *Mahābhārata*, Śāntiparvan, 59; *Viṣṇu Purāṇa*, I.13; *Matsya Purāṇa*, x.4–10.

6. *Sutta Nipāta*, 420ff; *Sutta Nipāta Commentary*, I.352ff; *Sumaṅ gala-vilāsinī,* 1, pp. 258–60; Romila Thapar, 'Origin Myths and the Historical Tradition', *AISH*, pp. 294ff.

7. *Ṛg Veda*, VI.63; V.27; V.30; VI.47; VIII.1; VIII.5; VIII.6.

8. Both the terms *ākhyāna* and *kathā* have the meaning of recitation or oral narration, and the purpose of the form is clear from these words. Some of the bardic fragments in the form of stories are also to be found in the *Jātaka* literature.

9. *Ṛg Veda,* X.95; *Śatapatha Brāhma*, XI.5.1.1ff; *Mahābhārata*, Ādiparvan, VII.70–1.

10. Romila Thapar, '*Dāna* and *Dakṣiṇā* as Forms of Exchange', in *AISH*, pp. 105ff.

11. *Mahābhārata*, Sabhāparvan, 30ff; 34ff.

12. *Mahābhārata*, Ādiparvan, 57.

13. V.S. Sukthankar, *On the Meaning of the Mahābhārata*, Bombay, 1957; 'Epic Studies', *ABORI*, XVIII, pp. 1–76; C. Bulke, *Rāma-kathā*, Allahabad, 1972; H. Jacobi, *The Ramayana* (trans. S.N. Ghoshal), Baroda, 1960. It is a moot question as to how much of the original epic persists in the now heavily inflated and interpolated versions, which, despite the critical editions of both texts, still require substantial pruning to be brought anywhere near the original: The interpolations have been both of substance and form: hence the reference to the *Rāmāyaṇa* as a *kāvya* or literary poem and to the *Mahābhārata* as *itihāsa*, more closely approximating history although the historical content remains difficult of access.

14. This is in part reflected in the perennial search by archaeologists for 'epic ages'. The financially flourishing 'Ramayana archaeology', even though without any tangible results, continues to be discussed seriously in some archaeological and historical circles, despite the idea being discarded by most scholars. That epic archaeology is an almost non-existent category becomes clear from a discussion of the encrustations which go into the making of an epic. E.W. Hopkins, *The Great Epic of India: Its Character and Origin*, New York, 1901; V.S. Sukthankar, Prolegomena to the *Critical Edition of Adi Parvan*, Poona, 1933; Romila Thapar, *Exile and the Kingdom: Some Thoughts on the Rāmāyaṇa*, Bangalore, 1978; 'The Historian and the Epic', *Annals of the Bhandarkar Oriental Research Institute*, 1979, vol. LX, pp. 199–213; B.D. Chattopadhyaya, 'Indian Archaeology and the Epic Tradition', *Puratattva*, VIII, 1975–6, pp. 67–71.

15. The treatment of Indra in the epics, for example, records a change from the Indra-*gāthās* of the *Ṛg Veda*. Indra is now subservient not only to the rising status of Viṣṇu but is unequal even to the superior power of the *ṛṣis*. Leaving aside the deliberate incarnating of Viṣṇu as the epic heroes Rāma and Kṛṣṇa, there is little doubt that the epic heroes are now more central than the Vedic gods.

16. Cf. W.B. Miller, 'Two Concepts of Authority', *American Anthropologist*, April 1955, vol. 57, pp. 271–89.

17. J.A.B. van Buitenan refers to the problem of the 'disqualified eldest' in his introduction to the translation of the Ādiparvan. The *Mahābhārata: The Book of the Beginning*, Chicago, 1973, p. xviii. The problem goes back to earlier antecedents. Thus the Candravaṃśa lineage starts with the replacement of Yadu, the eldest son of Yayāti, by his youngest son, Pūru. The *Mahābhārata* war, which involves virtually all the *kṣatriya* lineages and becomes the last heroic act of a lineage society, is again motivated by the problem of succession where physical ailments further complicate the question. The exile of Rāma is over the issue of succession, which, in spite of the heavier emphasis on primogeniture, is still subject to the whims and wishes of the parents.

18. *Mahābhārata*, Ādiparvan, 189.

19. Romila Thapar, 'The *Rāmāyaṇa*: Theme and Variation', in S.N. Mukherjee (ed.), India: *History and Thought*, Calcutta, 1982, pp. 221–53.

20. The *itihāsa-purāṇa* is referred to in the *Arthaśāstra*, 1.5. Its literal meaning is 'thus it was'—*iti-ha-āsa*. The events of the past were to be so related as to link them with the goals and purposes of the tradition which was being historicized.

21. The *sūta* and the *māgadha* are said to have arisen from the sacrifice of Pṛthu, and immediately on appearing began a *praśasti* of the *rājā*. *Atharvaveda*, 3.5.7; *Taittirīya Brāhmaṇa*, II.4.1. In texts such as *Gautama*, IV.15; *Manu*, X.11, 26; *Nārada*, 110, the status of the *sūta* has changed. This change is made explicit in the *Mahābhārata*, Ādiparvan, 122.4ff and 126.15ff, in which the *sūta* is inferior to the *kṣatriya*.

22. F.E. Pargiter, *The Ancient Indian Historical Tradition*, London, 1922, pp. 77ff; *Dynasties of the Kali Age*. . . , 1913 (reprint, Delhi, 1975), pp. 77ff.

23. *Mahāvaṃsaṭīkā*, pp. 180ff.

24. *Viṣṇu Purāṇa*, IV.21–4: *Manu*, X.43–5.

25. *Epigraphia Indica*, VIII, pp. 59, 86; E.J. Rapson (ed.), *The Cambridge History of India*, vol. I, *Ancient India*, Cambridge, 1935, p. 577.

26. For a later period, cf. R.G. Fox, *Kin, Clan, Raja and Rule*, Berkeley, 1971.

27. Miller, 'Two Concepts of Authority'.

28. J.N. Asopa, *Origin of the Rajputs*, Delhi, 1976, pp. 102ff, 208ff; J. Tod, *Annals and Antiquities of Rajasthan*, vol. I, London, 1960, pp. 173ff. Asopa argues that 'Guhila' means a forest and that it is to be located in the area between Guhila-bala and the Mahi river. See also B.D. Chattopadhyaya, 'Origin of the Rajputs: The Political, Economic and Social Processes in Early Medieval Rajasthan', *The Indian Historical Review*, July, 1976, vol. III, no. 1, pp. 59–82. Claims to *kṣatriya* status were also made by ruling families and politically powerful groups in south India. Thus the Colas claimed to be Sūryavaṃśi, the Pāṇḍyas Candravaṃśi, and the *vel* chieftains sought Yādava descent.

29. Romila Thapar, 'The State as Empire', in H. Claessen and P. Skalnik, *The Study of the State*, The Hague, 1981, pp. 409ff.

30. R.S. Sharma, *Indian Feudalism*, Delhi, 1980.

31. Romila Thapar, 'Genealogy as a Source of Social History', in *AISH*, pp. 326ff.

32. Pliny in *Natural History*, VI. 21.4–5, quotes Megathenes as stating that the Indians count 154 kings upto the time of Alexander. Genealogical data is also contained in the seals and in most land-grant inscriptions from the Gupta period onwards, e.g. the Sonpat Copper Seal of Harshavardhana, in J.F. Fleet (ed.), *C.I.I.,* vol. III, Inscriptions of the Early Gupta Kings, Varanasi, 1970, p. 231: Ratanpur Stone Inscription of Jajalladeva I, V.V. Mirashi (ed.), *C.I.I.,* vol. IV, Inscriptions of the Kalacuri-Cedi Era, Ootacamund, 1955, p. 409; the Lakhamandala inscription, *Epigraphia Indica*, I, 1892, pp. 10ff.

33. Romila Thapar, op. cit.

34. Pargiter, *The Ancient Indian Historical Tradition,* pp. 109ff; *Manu,* X.8, X.23 refers to the Āndhras and Sātvats as *śūdras*. The Āndhras are identified with the Andhaka of the Andhaka-Vṛṣṇi group and the Vṛṣṇis married the Sātvats. Pāṇini, II.2.95 and VI.2, 34, refers to the Andhaka and the Vṛṣṇis as being *kṣatriya gotras*. The events of the *Mahābhārata* suggest that the Vṛṣṇis were of a lower status, judging by the objection of some of the *kṣatriyas* present to giving Kṛṣna the status of the honoured guest. Sabhāparvan, pp. 33.26ff; 34.1ff.

35. *Viṣṇu Purāṇa*, IV.22.

36. *Mahābhārata*, Ādiparvan, 80.1ff.

37. Examples of such adjustments extend even to the literal Sanskritization of non-Sanskrit names, and to the story which relates the event, e.g. the Śailodbhava dynasty in its origin myth relates the story of how a *brāhmaṇa* was requested to create a man out of chips of rock, and thus the ancestor of the Śailodbhavas was created, the story evidently explaining the Sanskritization of a non-Sanskrit name. R.G. Basak, *History of North-eastern India*, Calcutta, 1967, pp. 211ff.

38. Romila Thapar, 'Renunciation: The Making of a Counter-culture?', in *AISH*, pp. 63ff.

39. Cosmological time moves in the Mahāyuga of 4,320,000 years and the complete cycle is then divided into four *yugas*: the Kṛta of 1,728,000 years; the Tretā of 1,296,000 years, the Dvāpara of 864,000 years and the Kaliyuga of 432,000 years, the size of the *yugas* declining in arithmetical progression. The Kaliyuga is crucial and there is a regular reduction by subtracting the length of the Kaliyuga from each preceding *yuga*, an orderliness which is basic to the concept. The numbers used are quasi-mathematical, a mixture of magic and astronomy. Numbers such as 3, 7, 12 and 72 are considered magical

and constitute the fractions in the figures. Thus 432,000 = 60 × 7200, and this further introduces the sexagesimal unit of 60, frequently used in ancient West Asia as well as in south Indian astrology. The Babylonian tradition also uses 72,1,200 and 432,000 for its chronology (J. Campbell, *The Masks of the Gods,* vol. II, New York, 1959, pp. 128ff) and the *Jyotiṣa-vedāṇga* shows a familiarity with Babylonian astronomy and mathematics. (D. Pingree, 'The Mesopotamian Origin of Early Indian Mathematical Astronomy', *Journal for the History of Astronomy*, 1973, IV, pp. 1–12). The figure of 72 years is taken to calculate the processional lag moving over one degree and 432,000 is the basis of calculating the epicycle. Was cosmological time the earlier and more popular astronomical knowledge which was deliberately preserved in this manner, as distinct from the mathematics and the solar-based astronomy of the period, reflected in the more formal writings of astronomers and mathematicians? As a contrast to these majuscule dimensions there are also the minuscule fractional parts of time listed in Jaina texts of the late first and the early second millennia AD. Interestingly, the description of the *yugas* and *kalpas* is spatial, e.g. *Saṃyutta Nikāya*, XV.1.5–8.

40. M. Eliade, *Cosmos and History*, New York, 1959.

41. Kalhaṇa, *Rājataraṅgiṇī*, V.21.

42. A.L. Basham, *The Wonder That Was India, London*, 1964, pp. 272–3; *Digha Nikāya*, III, pp. 75ff.

43. Some of the dates for inscriptions were provided by astrologers, and these include astronomical details. However, they are not always correct. D.C. Sircar, *Studies in Society and Administration of Ancient and Medieval India,* vol. I, Calcutta, 1967, pp. 171–2. It is worth noting that apart from the legal charters, another sphere of life in which time was very precisely recorded was the horoscope. As a corollary to this it is interesting that an almost exact counterpart to the careful record of time in inscriptions is to be found in discussions on the precise time for conducting a *yajña*, where the time is again indicated in terms of the year, season, month, lunar fortnight, constellation, date and time of day.

44. This change is reflected in the difference between the *Suttas* and the *Vinaya*, where the life of the Buddha is part of canonical scripture, and Aśvaghosa's *Buddhacarita*, which is a biography per se.

45. D.C. Sircar, *Select Inscriptions*, second edition, Calcutta, 1965, pp. 213–19, 175–80; *Epigraphia Indica*, vol. XXIX, 1951–2, parts 1–5, pp. 1–90.

46. Such as Vākapati's *Gauḍavāho* on Yaśovarman of Kannauj; Bilhaṇa's *Vikrāmankadevacarita* on Vikramāditya VI, the Cālukya king; Sandhyā-karanandin's *Rāmacarita* on Rāmapāla; Jayānaka's *Pṛthvīrājavijaya*; Nayacandra Sūri's *Hammīra-mahākāvya*; Somesvaradeva's *Kirti-kaumudi,* a biography of Vastupāla, who, although not a king, was a person of great political importance; and Hemacandra's *Kumāra-pālacarita.*

47. V.S. Pathak, *Ancient Historians of India,* Bombay, 1966, pp. 21ff.

48. The sources drawn upon by the authors of the *vaṃśāvalīs* included the *sthala-purāṇas, upa-purāṇas, tīrtha-purāṇas,* caste *purāṇas* and *māhātmyas*, all of which were texts recording the past and the evolution of places, sects and deities, locations of pilgrimage, dominant castes and local history. Such texts were part of the larger Purāṇic tradition and, although conforming to the major *Purāṇas* in spirit if not in form, included a large amount of local and regional data. The oral sources consisted of bardic fragments and ballads on local heroes and events of significance, not to mention the genealogies and marriage alliances of land-owning families, for the bardic tradition was still alive, as it remains to this day. It has been argued that Kalhaṇa's *Rājataraṅginī,* a fine example of a *vaṃśāvalī,* was a unique document in that it was the only genuine piece of historical writing from India (A.L. Basham, 'The Kashmir Chronicle', in C.H. Philips, *Historians of India, Pakistan and Ceylon,* Oxford, 1961, pp. 57ff). Yet the *vaṃśāvalī* form occurs in various parts of the country—from the neighbouring Chamba *vaṃśāvalī* (Vogel, *The Antiquities of Chamba State,* Calcutta, 1911, ASI, vol. 36 to the most distant *Mūṣakavaṃśa* or chronicle of the Ay dynasty in Kerala. Gopinath Rao, 'Extracts from the Mūṣakavaṃśam . . .', *Travancore Archaeological Series,* 1916, II.1, no. 10, pp. 87–113; See also M.G.S. Narayanan, 'History from Mūṣakavaṃśa-kāvya of Atula', *PAIOC,* Jadavpur, 1969. Curiously, in both cases the founder is born in a cave (*guhā*) and is associated with a *Mūṣaka-vaṃśa* (literally: 'mouse lineage'). A better known cave association is of course that of the Guhilots of Mewar (J. Tod, I, pp. 173ff). For further lists of *vaṃśāvalīs* see A.K. Warder, *Introduction to Indian Historiography,* Bombay, 1972, and J.P. de Souza and CM. Kulkarni (eds), *Historiography in Indian Languages,* Delhi, 1972.

49. The *Mahāvaṃsa,* as the chronicle of the Mahāvihāra monastery in Sri Lanka composed in the mid-first millennium AD, is primarily concerned with establishing its legitimacy both as the fount of the pristine teaching of the Buddha as well as in its interaction with political authority. Thus the Theravada sect, which was established in the Mahāvihāra monastery, is said to have originated from the schism at the Council of Pāṭaliputra, called at the initiative of Aśoka Maurya, and was established in Sri Lanka largely through the patronage of Devānampiya Tissa. Buddhist chronicles do tend to show a greater degree of historical determinism. Sri Lanka is predestined for the establishment of Buddhism. Events move towards proclaiming the primacy of the *saṅgha*. L.S. Perera, 'The Pali Chronicles of Ceylon', in C.H. Philips, pp. 29ff. This is further emphasized by the notion of causality and contract so central to Buddhist ethics, and by the historical role of the missionaries who propagate Buddhism in new areas.

50. Romila Thapar, 'Dissent and Protest in the Early Indian Tradition', *Studies in History,* 1979, vol. I, no. 2, pp. 177–95.

Section II

Economy and Society

CHAPTER 4

Society in Ancient India

*The Formative Period**

I would like to take as my theme an exploration in the study of society in ancient India and to deal with the period from *circa* 2500 BC to 500 BC in northern India, treating it principally as an occasion to demonstrate what I mean by a reorientation of perspectives.

The beginnings of Indian history have been projected for decades now in the supposed invasion of northern India by the Aryans and the establishment of Aryan culture as a result of this conquest. The projection was that of a racially superior people. The study of both the Sanskrit texts and of ethnology went into the making of this theory.[1] Let me say at the outset that I am not concerned with 'the Aryan problem' *per se.* It is perhaps the biggest red herring that was dragged across the path of historians of India.[2] What I am concerned with is the need to understand the evolution of society at this time. This is a crucial period not only because it saw the initial pattern of Indian culture take shape, but also because it can provide clues to a more analytical understanding of subsequent periods of Indian history. As it happens, the more important and controversial announcements pertaining to ancient Indian studies made during the year also relate to this

* Presidential Address, Ancient Indian History Section, XXXI Indian History Congress, 1969, Varanasi. Published in *Proceedings of the Indian History Congress*, 1970, pp. 15–39. The archaeological evidence quoted here needs updating but my concern is more with the methods of analysing and integrating various data, and the ones discussed here are still valid.

period. The most serious of the many claims to have deciphered the Harappa script, in terms of the methodology used and the discussion it has provoked, is that of the Finnish scholars, who read the script as proto-Dravidian.[3] An interesting facet of the controversy has been the vehemence of the loyalty to the respective Indo-Aryan and Dravidian language groups, with undertones almost of an Aryan and a Dravidian nationalism! This, in spite of the fact that specialists in both languages have for many years been suggesting that although linguistically distinct, at the cultural level at least this dichotomy is false.[4]

Our starting point could be the fact that we have two types of evidence, archaeological and literary. The literary sources are well-known and comprise the corpus of Vedic literature. The archaeological evidence consists of a number of cultures, most of them seemingly disparate. The earliest are the pre-Harappan cultures; the Sothi culture[5] of the Sarasvati valley and the Chalcolithic village sites of Baluchistan and Sind. These were the precursors of the Harappa culture (*c.* 2300–1750 BC) which extended from southern Punjab and Sind to the Narmada delta largely following the coastal region, and eastwards as far as the upper Ganga–Yamuna Doāb.[6] Of the post-Harappan cultures there is evidence from both the Indus and Ganga valleys. In northern Punjab the Gandhara Grave culture[7] (*c.* 1500–500 BC), using a red ware and a plain grey ware, shows evidence of copper in the early stages and later an iron technology, and contacts with Iran and central Asia. The Banas culture of southern Rajasthan (*c.* 2000–1200 BC, with possible extensions in the Ganga valley coming down to 800 BC) with its characteristic white-painted black-and-red pottery and its probable internalizing of certain Harappan forms, possibly acted as a bridge between the Harappan and post-Harappan cultures.[8] In the upper Ganga valley, the earliest remains belong to the culture represented by the Ochre Colour Pottery which is post-Harappan in time range (*c.* 1400–1200 BC). This has been associated sometimes with the Copper Hoard Culture[9] found both in the Doāb and in southern Bihar and West Bengal, and whose authors were perhaps the Munda-speaking peoples. At some sites in Bihar there is evidence of the black-and-red ware (occasionally white-painted and similar to that of the Banas culture) forming the earliest level. In parts of the Doāb it succeeds the Ochre Colour Pottery and precedes the predominant culture of the region. The latter is the Painted Grey Ware[10] (*c.* 1100–400 BC), an initially agrarian culture familiar with iron technology and the horse. Finally, the Northern Black Polished Ware culture (*c.* 500–100 BC) is associated with urbanization in the Ganga valley.

The archaeological picture, therefore, shows a large variety of cultures, none of which can be identified as specifically Aryan.[11] Nor does the evidence suggest that there was a single dominating culture which slowly spread throughout northern India bringing the various diverse cultures into its fold, which is what one would expect if the popular notion of the spread of Aryan culture be accepted. In comparing the Indian and West Asian material there is again little consistent evidence of a dominant culture recognizably coming from West Asia to India, or for that matter going from India to West Asia, though there are certain similarities of techniques, such as the socketed axe and in ceramics. This would suggest migrants carrying aspects of technology and probably the language in both directions.

In comparing literary and archaeological evidence, it is important to determine the nature of the society concerned. In the case of the *Ṛg Veda* the geographical focus is that of the *sapta sindhava* roughly from the Kabul river to the Sarasvati river.[12] Ṛgvedic society is essentially a pre-urban society with a copper and possibly iron technology.[13] It is evolving from nomadic pastoralism dependent on cattle to an agrarian form with more settled communities. Barley (*yava*) appears to have been the staple food. There is a strong sense of tribal identity and the basic social unit is the patriarchal family. Close linguistic connections with Iran are evident. The important deities are Indra, Mitra, Varuṇa, Savitṛ, Soma, and Agni. There is a distinct feeling of cultural exclusiveness and separation from some local people who are both feared and disliked and with whom relations are frequently hostile (for example, the Dasyus and the Paṇis).

The Later Vedic literature depicts a recognizable change in material culture. The geographical focus includes the Punjab and the middle Ganga valley in the main, with a more marginal familiarity with the Indus area, western and eastern India, and the Vindhyas. The society is essentially agrarian, culminating in a series of urban centres. There is a considerable acquaintance with iron technology. Frequent mention is made of rice (*vrīhi*), which is not mentioned in the *Ṛg Veda.* The clan identity continues and in many cases is extended to territorial identity. The Ṛgvedic deities do not have the pre-eminent position which they had had earlier since equal importance is now given to more recently incorporated deities. The fourfold *varṇa* structure mentioned only once in the *Ṛg Veda* is now a recognized feature. The geographical and philosophical connections with West Asia have weakened. There appears to be a greater assimilation with local cultures. In comparing the early and late Vedic literature it would seem that the major characteristic of continuity remains the language, Sanskrit.

Whatever our cherished notions about the Aryans may be, the archaeological evidence does not suggest a massive invasion or a massive migration.[14] Even if it be conceded that the presence of the Indo-Aryan language in the *sapta sindhava* region can be attributed to invasion, which is at times hinted at in the *Ṛg Veda,* the same reason cannot be given for its presence in other parts of northern India. At most it can be said that the Indo-Aryan speakers were small groups of migrants with a strong adherence to a linguistic equipment deriving from the Indo-European. Both linguistic evidence and the literature point to the Indo-Aryan speakers living in the vicinity of those who spoke an alien language (*mṛdhra vāc*) and those later called the *mlecchas*.[15] Were these the Munda or Dravidian speakers? Were they also the authors of pre-iron Chalcolithic cultures? In the Ganga valley, archaeological evidence does not suggest that the earlier inhabitants fled or migrated. Therefore, their continued presence must have necessitated a process of acculturation. What then was the nature of the impact of these Indo-Aryan speakers? Perhaps it would make greater historical sense if we see it not as the imposition of Aryan culture on the existing Indian cultures, but rather, as the diffusion of Indo-Aryan. The new language could have been accepted for various reasons without necessitating the imposition of a totally new culture.[16]

In the study of the interaction of cultures there are many facets which require investigation. Let me start with the most primary, the question of the numbers of people involved. This would imply demographic studies of various sites and settlements. Comparative assessments of population figures from the sites of varying cultures could be helpful, as also the detailed charting of the location of sites—whether they are superimposed or adjacent. Would there be a greater possibility of cross-cultural assimilation if the numbers are consistently small and equally matched?[17] A demographic analysis, even if impressionistic, studied together with the nature of the terrain and technology and facilities for transportation would provide indications of the pace and flow of migration. The Painted Grey Ware settlements being generally small, the nature of the terrain being thick jungle, the pace of migration would be slow even if the river was used as the main channel of communication. It should not be forgotten that in spite of a time-span of about six hundred years the geographical distribution of the Painted Grey Ware remains broadly the Ganga–Yamunā Doāb and the Sarasvati valley. However, acceleration in the pace of communication seems to accompany the development of an urban culture as it would appear from the distribution of the Northern Black Polished Ware.

Even a rough demographic picture will introduce an element of reality into the study. If the settlements of a particular culture are small then production is also likely to be small. A comparison between such data and literary descriptions of extravagant wealth may lead to a correcting of the poetic license implicit in great works of literature. Estimates of production are relevant to the study of towns owing to the interdependence of towns and villages.[18] More mundane factors such as food habits have their own significance. The Ṛgvedic people had a diet substantially of barley and wheat, and the Later Vedic literature introduces rice. From the archaeological evidence we know that the Harappans were mainly barley and wheat eating, whereas the Ganga valley, the Banas valley, and probably a part of western India, was predominantly rice eating.[19] This points to a major difference of staple diet between the Ṛgvedic and Later Vedic people. If they were the same ethnically then they must have rapidly adjusted to a change of diet. However the Painted Grey Ware levels in the Doāb suggest a people long accustomed to rice. It is interesting that in later Sanskrit literature, wheat is sometimes referred to as *mleccha-bhojana.*[20]

Another aspect in the process of acculturation is the role of technology. A language which is associated with an advanced technology can often make a very effective impact. The use of the horse and of iron would point to an advanced technology. The acceptance of the Indo-Aryan language would, therefore, not require the physical conquest of the areas where it came to be spoken but rather the control of the advanced technology by the speakers of Indo-Aryan.[21] The horse-drawn chariot seems to have swung the balance militarily in favour of the Indo-Aryan speakers, judging from the hymns of the *Ṛg Veda.* The horse as compared to the ox was a swifter means of transportation as also was the chariot as compared with the cart.[22] The introduction of iron did not mean totally new technological implements. It was more a qualitative improvement of existing forms particularly in relation to the ecological conditions of the region. The hafted copper axe gave way to the socketed iron axe, the wooden plough had an iron tip added to it, and the stone hoe was replaced by the iron hoe (or it was introduced where the hoe was not known before), not to mention adzes, arrow-heads, spear-heads, knives, daggers, nails, etc.[23] The technology of the Painted Grey Ware culture seems to support this assessment. The question of who first used iron technology in India has its own importance, but for our purposes it is more relevant to enquire as to whether the speakers of Indo-Aryan exploited the knowledge of iron technology to their advantage. That the new technology was essentially the improvement of existing forms is supported by the use of certain significant words in Vedic literature which appear to have a non-Indo-Aryan origin. Thus the most frequently used word for plough is *lāṅgala,* which is of Munda origin, and the word for rice *vrīhi* is believed to be of Dravidian origin.[24] Could there have been a correlation between the degree of technological change and the utilization of Indo-Aryan? That the caste status of iron smiths ultimately became low would accord with the probability that as long as the control of the technology lay with the higher-status groups, the actual working of the technology could remain with low-status groups.[25]

In ancient agricultural societies, apart from agricultural technology, another factor of some consequence would be the knowledge of the calendar. It is thought that the earliest calendar used in India was the lunar calendar. Yet the solar calendar was more efficient in its application to agriculture and astronomy (and thereby to astrology). The discovery and use of the solar calendar would require more advanced knowledge in mathematics and astronomy. A basis of mathematical knowledge must be assumed in order to explain the construction of the Harappan cities. Was this knowledge continued in some tradition? If the Harappans had used a binary system (by and large), then the decimal system referred to in the Vedic literature would have been an improvement.[26] The essential geometrical knowledge necessary for evolving a solar calendar may have been inherent in the geometry required for the construction of complex sacrificial altars.[27] There appears to be a groping towards understanding the principles of the solar calendar in the Vedic literature. The year of 360 days (30 × 12 months) was known to be defective and attempts were made at intercalation in which the 366-day year was not excluded.[28] It is true that the widespread knowledge of the solar calendar is associated with Greek contacts at a later period. It is not to be ruled out, however, that a secret knowledge or a restricted knowledge of it may have existed earlier. The appropriation of such knowledge by certain groups may well have given them access to power and influence. A scientific study of the application of astronomy and mathematics to activities such as agriculture and astrology within the context of contemporary society might be revealing: as also the transmission of mathematical ideas between Babylon and India.

In the post-Harappa period, the centre of historical activity moved away from the Indus valley towards other directions: to the Ganga valley with Magadha eventually emerging as a nuclear region, to western India, and later, to the coastal regions of the peninsula. Part of the reason for the movement away from the Indus valley was the break-down in the Harappan economic system.[29] The post-Harappan sites in western India appear to have re-introduced the earlier maritime contacts with Mesopotamia, from at least the first millennium BC. As such, western India would have acted as a point of communication for goods and ideas between India and West Asia. A further archaeological investigation of the west coast and routes from here to the Ganga valley may prove worthwhile.[30]

Another aspect worth considering in assessing the reasons for the spread of Indo-Aryan is the interrelationship between language and society. The fact that the earliest Sanskrit grammars were written in the north points to a greater use or longer tradition of the language in this region. By contrast the lower Ganga valley retains a Prākṛt tradition for a longer period.[31] Was this distinction due to the linguistic differences in Indo-Aryan itself or was it due to a greater influence of non-Indo-Aryan languages in eastern India? Magadha is described as an impure land and the people of Aṇga, Vaṇga and Kaliṇga are referred to as *mleccha*.[32] It is also worth examining why certain important words relating to technology were introduced from non-Indo-Aryan sources and retained in Indo-Aryan. We have already noticed the case of *lāṇgala* and *vrīhi*. The Indo-Aryan for horse is *aśva*, yet *aśva* was never as commonly used in the Late Indo-Aryan languages as *ghoṭa* and its derivatives. That this could happen with items as important as the plough, rice, and the horse, makes one wonder whether the question of loan words from Munda and Dravidian does not call for a coordinated study by the specialist in linguistics and the historian, which would not merely trace the loan or the etymology of words, but would also throw light on the cultural context of their incorporation. The etymology of technical and professional words in their historical context would alone be worth a study.

It is historically well-known that in the spread of a language associated with an advanced technology it is often the dominant groups in the existing society which take up the new language first. This would be easier to understand in our period if we had some concrete evidence on the origin of the caste structure. It is curious that although the origin of the caste structure is frequently associated with the Aryan-speakers it occurs only in India and not in other societies which were also recipients of Aryan culture. It may, therefore, have been a pre-Aryan system which was reconstituted somewhat, and described in Later Vedic literature. To see caste as the distinction between fair Aryans and dark-non-Aryans is to over-simplify a very complex system. In the study of social structure the historian of ancient India must of necessity now take the help of social anthropology. The essentials of a caste society are, firstly, marriage and lineage functioning through exogamous and endogamous kinship relations (*jāti*); secondly, the integration of the division of labour into a hierarchical system which eventually takes the form of service relationships; thirdly, the idea of pollution where some groups are seen as ritually pure, others less so and yet others totally impure or polluting; and finally the association of castes with particular geographical locations. All these factors could have been present in the Harappa culture where social stratification can at least be surmised.[34] If a similar system prevailed in the Banas culture and those of the Ganga valley, then the spread of a new language could be achieved through influencing the groups which held high status and by rearrangement of endogamous groups.[35]

Ascribing caste status did not merely depend on the occupation of a group. In some cases, an entire tribe was ascribed a particular rank. Those speaking a non-Indo-Aryan language were frequently given a low rank and described as *mleccha*. In the case of the *caṇḍāla*s there is reference to a *caṇḍāla-bhāṣā*.[36] Some of these tribes remained consistently of low status over many centuries, such as the Kirāta and the Pulinda;[37] others acquired political power and thereby higher status. Even today there are pockets of Munda and Dravidian-speaking people in areas of Indo-Aryan languages. This is not due to any historical oversight. The Munda-speaking groups until recently were hunters and pastoralists with, at most, digging-stick agriculture. In contrast to this the Indo-Aryan-speaking people are, by and large, plough- and hoe-using agriculturalists. Were the *śūdra* tribes those who in the initial stages either did not accept the new agricultural technology or did not apply it? Did the Aryanization of language accompany the expansion of the iron-using agrarian village?

This village was not the neolithic village growing essentially in isolation, nor the Chalcolithic village with restricted trade interrelationships. It was the prosperous iron-using village whose prosperity increased with easier access to both iron ore and more land for cultivation. This prosperity could not only give these villages a political edge over the others but also provide a larger surplus for those in control. At one level this became the stable base for the growth of towns;[38] at another level it strengthened the language, Indo-Aryan.

With the change from nomadic pastoralism to settled agrarian villages, tribal identity was extended to territorial identity, as is reflected in tribal names being given to geographical areas. This in turn gave rise to the concept of the state with both monarchical and non-monarchical forms of government. Woven into this concept were the institutions of caste and private property.[39]

Even among those tribes who had accepted the new technology and language, the priests—the ritually pure groups—would have resisted the new culture unless their own status was safeguarded. Was this done by allowing them to preserve their ritual purity through the caste structure and by their continuing to hold a priestly status, and also by incorporating much of their religion into the new culture? The assimilation of a tribe into the caste structure would also require some assimilation of its religion. The religious aspects of Later Vedic literature, inasmuch as they differ from the *Ṛg Veda,* include a large amount of non-Aryan practice and belief—both at the level of ritual and of deities.[40] It is indeed a moot point whether this literature can be called the religious literature of the Aryans alone.

Every society has a method of remembering what it regards as the important aspects of its past and this is woven into its historical tradition. For our period it is the *itihāsa-purāṇa* tradition which sets out to record the past. The most significant section of this tradition is the preservation of the royal genealogies and the myths associated with them. The royal genealogies (*vaṃśāvalī*) may not be historically correct but when studied carefully they indicate the pattern of the migration and spread of various peoples. Such an analysis can be more useful than the repeated but so far unsuccessful attempts to identify the tribes as either Aryan or non-Aryan. Genealogies have played a noticeably important part in the Indian historical tradition, even when they are known to be fabricated. This is surely the clue to understanding the role of the genealogy, not necessarily as an authentic dynastic chronicle but rather as a social document. Similarly, what is important about the myths is not whether they are historically authentic, but the cultural assumptions of the society which are implicit in the myth.[41]

The questions which arise in the study of the proto-historic period have a relevance to later history. It would seem that in northern India, the expansion of the village economy based on iron technology accompanied the diffusion of Indo-Aryan, judging by the archaeological evidence for the distribution of iron in association with literary evidence for Indo-Aryan. Indo-Aryan, therefore, would not be widely accepted in those areas where iron technology was already known. In the peninsula the area covered by the iron-using Megalithic settlements roughly coincides with the area of the widespread use of Dravidian languages.

If we can explain the reasons for the shift in focus from the Indus valley to the Ganga valley in proto-historic times, then we can also throw some light on one of the more interesting facets of ancient Indian history, namely, the geographical shift in the nuclear regions: which were the matrices of large states and empires. At least three regions come immediately to mind: Magadha, the Raichur-Bijapur districts, and the area between Kanchipuram and Tanjore. Why did these regions give rise to a series of politically dominant states and then go into quiescence?[42] Was it due to the fertility of the region yielding large revenues, or the abundant availability of iron, or access to trade routes, or the exploitation of a new technology or the rise of ideologies motivating political action? Or was it merely the strange but happy coincidence of a series of strong rulers, which is the explanation generally offered?

In the analysis of social structure there is a need for redefining social relationships. To see caste only in terms of the four-fold *varṇa* does not take us very far. One would like to know how tribes and social groups were adjusted into the caste hierarchy and assigned a caste status. The theory that the caste-structure was initially flexible but gradually became rigid and allowed of little mobility, is now open to question. There is enough evidence to suggest that there have been in all periods deviations from the theoretical concept of caste.[43] We also know that there was a continual emergence of new castes for a variety of reasons. Furthermore, social change presupposes social tension and at times even conflicts between groups, and these are referred to in the sources. The origin, nature, and consequences of these tensions constitutes another significant area of study.

The history of religion, apart from its theological, philosophical, and iconographical aspects, also has a social aspect, since religion has to be practised by people in order to be viable. The interrelation therefore of religious cults and movements with social groups is very close. What were the social roots of Buddhism and Jainism? Why were certain cults assimilated and others left out in what later came to be called Hinduism? What accounts for the remarkable popularity of the mother-goddess cults in various forms in the post-Gupta period? More precise answers to such questions would help us ascertain with greater accuracy the nature of the 'brahmanical renaissance' as it has been called in the Gupta and post-Gupta periods.

It will be evident that I am making a plea for more intensive studies of the nature of society in ancient India, and by this I mean an integrated understanding of the many facets which go into the functioning of a society. Such a study involves not merely additional dimensions in terms of methods and sources, it also means, if need be, altering the perspective from which we view the past. New perspectives, although they may initially appear whimsical, often provide new insights. The immense labour and scholarship of our predecessors has provided us with a firm foundation on which to base our studies of ancient Indian history. We can with confidence, therefore, explore new perspectives. Ultimately, as historians we are concerned not merely with attempting to discover the past, but with trying to understand it.

Notes and References

1. T.R. Trautmann, *The Aryans and British India,* Delhi, 1997.

2. The Aryan problem arose out of a series of philological studies in the eighteenth and nineteenth centuries which recorded the similarities

between a number of languages of Asia and Europe and postulated a common ancestry in Indo-European languages (T.R. Trautmann, *The Aryans and British India,* Delhi, 1997). Max Müller's statement about the Aryan nation as the physical manifestation of Aryan culture lent support to the search for the Aryan race. His later repeated attempts to deny the existence of an Aryan race were often ignored (*Biographies of Words and the Home of the Vedas,* 1887, p. 90). Incidentally, it is conceivable that Max Müller's Aryan–Semitic dichotomy may well have influenced the Aryan–Dravidian dichotomy. The real damage was caused by his assertion of the superiority of Aryan culture over all other cultures, which has been made axiomatic to the study of the Indian past (*Chips from a German Workshop,* 1867, I, p. 63. '. . . In continual struggle with each other and with Semitic and Turanian races, these Aryan nations have become the rulers of history, and it seems to be their mission to link all parts of the world together by chains of civilisation, commerce and religion . . .') Aryan culture is often taken as the starting point of Indian culture and is projected both backwards (in attempts to prove the Aryan basis of the Harappa culture) and forwards in time. It is also sought to be associated with every worthwhile achievement in early India.

In his enthusiasm for the Aryan way of life (as he saw it), Max Müller further depicted Aryan society as an idyllic society of village communities where people were concerned not with the mundane things of everyday living but with other-worldly thoughts and values (*India, What Can It Teach Us?* pp. 101ff). This has also acted as a check on the more realistic study of the actual conditions of life in the Vedic period. That the motives of Max Müller and other Indologists of his views in acclaiming Aryan culture derived from a genuine admiration for Aryan society as they saw it, has to be conceded, but this does not exonerate them from gilding the lily. Max Müller's attempt to link India and Europe via the Aryans was in part to connect the origins of Indian culture with the founders of European culture. Thus Indian culture could acquire status in the eyes of Europe and, at the same time, early Indian nationalism could exploit this connection to combat the cultural inferiority complex generated among Indians as a result of British rule. In fact, early Indian nationalism gave greater attention to extolling the Aryans in India rather than to the connection with Europe. Historical scholarship has now moved beyond the needs and confines of nineteenth-century nationalism and a re-evaluation of Max Müller's theories is necessary.

Even some modern sociological theorists have made sweeping generalizations on contemporary India and Indian society on the basis of the nineteenth-century understanding of Indian history. Max Weber in his study, *The Religion of India* (New York, 1967 reprint) used fairly uncritically much of the writing of Orientalists such as Max Müller. A more recent example of the acceptance of this tradition, without a sufficient investigation of the alternatives, is Louis Dumont's *Homo Hierarchicus* (1967). That the influence of such thinking, stressing the other-worldly character of Indian society, is apparent even on economic historians is evident from Gunnar Myrdal, *Asian Drama* (1969), where the Weberian thesis is given considerable emphasis to explain the failure of the development of capitalism in India. My use of the term 'Aryan' is a short-hand for 'the Indo-Aryan speaking people', which is the more correct form.

3. Asko Parpola et al., *Decipherment of the Proto-Dravidian Inscriptions of the Indus Civilisation,* The Scandinavian Institute of Asian Studies, Copenhagen, 1969.

Asko Parpola, *Progress in the Decipherment of the Proto-Dravidian Indus Script,* 1969.

Asko Parpola, *Further Progress in the Decipherment of the Proto-Indus Script,* 1969.

A less publicized attempt was made by a number of Russian scholars. Y. Knorozov, *Proto-Indica,* 1968. Two other recent attempts, those of Dr Fateh Singh and Mr Krishna Rao, are generally not acceptable to scholars.

Owing to a lack of bi-lingual inscriptions most attempts so far have used a system of intelligent (and in some cases not so intelligent) guesswork. Using the inconographic representation as the starting point, attempts have been made to try and read the script as that of an Indo-Aryan language (Wadell, S.K. Ray, Krishna Rao). Those who have used the script as their starting point have more often arrived at Proto-Dravidian (Hunter, Heras, the Russians and the Finns). Parpola et al. read it as a largely logographic script based on the principles of homophony. The advance made by the Finnish scholars and to some extent, the earlier Russian studies, is that they have placed greater reliance on linguistic and mathematical techniques rather than on historical guesswork. Any claims to decipherment must satisfy certain preconditions. The decipherment must conform to a grammatical and linguistic system and cannot be arbitrary (this being the major objection to the attempt by Krishna Rao); it must conform to the archaeological evidence of the culture and to the chronological span of the Harappa culture; the reading of the inscriptions must make sense in terms of the context of the culture. Of the recent attempts, the Russian and the Finnish conform most to these preconditions. However, even their readings present problems which they have not satisfactorily overcome. As to whether the Finnish claim is justified will depend on the publication of their readings of complete texts, which are still awaited.

4. As for example in the essays of Sylvain Levi, Jean Przyluski, and Jules Bloch, translated and published by P.C. Bagchi in *Pre-Aryan and Pre-Dravidian in India,* 1929, and more recently in the writings of S.K. Chatterjee, T. Burrow, and M.B. Emeneau.

5. A. Ghosh, 'The Indus Civilisation—Its Origins, Authors, Extent and Chronology', in V.N. Misra and N.S. Mate (eds), *Indian Pre-history*, 1964. An attempt has been made to try and identify the Sothi Culture with the Ṛgvedic people by A.D. Pusalkar, 'Pre-Harappan, Harappan and Post-Harappan Culture and the Aryan Problem', *The Quarterly Review of Historical Studies*, VII, no. 4, 1967–68, pp. 233ff. Apart from the problem that the geographical extent does not coincide since the Ṛgvedic culture included northern Punjab and excluded Sind and western India, there is also the problem of chronology. Attempts to date the *Ṛg Veda* to the fourth and fifth millennia BC are based mainly on references to astronomical positions mentioned in the texts, for example, Tilak, *The Orion* . . . ; Jacobi, 'On the Date of the *Ṛg Veda*', *Indian Antiquary*, June 1894; *and Buhler, Indian Antiquary*, September 1894. Such evidence is not conclusive, since references to astronomy could have been incorporated from the traditions of an earlier people. The parallels with Gathic Avestan and with Kassite and Mitanni inscriptions which are very close, would date the *Ṛg Veda* to the middle of the second millennium BC.

6. The attempted identification of the Harappa culture with the later Vedic society on the basis of both being agro-urban societies is again controverted by the differences not only in the total culture but also in the geographical nuclei. The Harappa culture is located in the Indus valley and western India and its urbanization is based on a chalcolithic system with an absence of iron. Later Vedic society, centring on the Ganga valley from which the Harappa culture is largely absent (except for a few minor sites in the upper Doāb), owes its gradual urbanization to iron technology. The technology of the two cultures is different. The pre-eminent role of the fertility cult among the Harappans is absent in Vedic society. The Harappans buried their dead, the Vedic people largely cremated their dead. (It is interesting that so far no graves have been found in association with the Painted Grey Ware cultures, which may suggest that they cremated their dead.) The horse so characteristic of Vedic society is not associated with the Harappans. The Harappa culture from the very beginning used a script whereas references to writing in Vedic society come at a later stage. If, finally, the Harappan script is read as Proto-Dravidian then there will be hardly any possibility of identifying the Harappa culture with Indo-Aryan speakers.

7. A.H. Dani, 'Gandhara Grave Culture', *Ancient Pakistan*, III, 1967.

8. B.B. Lal, *Indian Archaeology—A Review*, 1959–60 (for the site of Gilund); D.P. Agarwal, 'C-14 Dates, Banas Culture and the Aryans', *Current Science*, 5 March 1966, pp. 114ff; H.D. Sankalia, 'New Light on the Indo-Iranian or Western Asiatic Relations between 1700–1200 BC', *Artibus Asiae*, XXVI, 1963; H.D. Sankalia, S.B. Deo, Z.D. Ansari, *Excavations at Ahar*, 1969.

9. B.B. Lal, 'Further Copper Hoards from the Gangetic Basin and a Review of the Problem', *Ancient India,* no. 7, 1951, pp. 20ff; S.P. Gupta, Indian Copper Hoards', *Journal of the Bihar Research Society,* 49, 1963, pp. 147ff.

10. B.B. Lal, 'Excavations at Hastinapur', *Ancient India,* nos 10 and 11, 1954–55, pp. 5ff; T.N. Roy, 'Stratigraphical Position of the Painted Grey Ware in the Gangetic Valley', *Bharati,* no. 8, II, 1964–65, pp. 64ff.

11. A recent summary of attempts to identify the Aryans with archaeological evidence is that of Dilip K. Chakrabarti, 'The Aryan Hypothesis in Indian Archaeology', *Indian Studies,* IX, no. 4, July–Sept. 1968, pp. 343ff. The more recent evidence of the Gandhara Grave Culture has been interpreted by Dani as representing perhaps, the early Indo-Aryan migration identified with the Ṛg Vedic literature. The linguistic theories of Hoernle and Grierson, suggesting that there were two bands of migration and therefore of language, have been used in the argument that the first band settled in the *sapta sindhava* region, and the second, skirting round the Indus, perhaps settled in the Banas valley. From here there was a movement both along the northern slopes of the Vindhyas to Bihar and also into the Doāb. Incidentally, in the latter case it would have followed a route which was frequently used in historical times to connect the Doāb with the west coast.

12. There are incidental references to migration in the *Ṛg Veda,* in verses such as I.30.9; I.36.18; and they read clearly as, for example, VI.45.1, '... *ya ānayat parāvataḥ sunītī turvaśam yaduṁ indraḥ sa no yuvā sakhā* ...' Furthermore, it must be remembered that the *nadi stutī* hymn, which is often quoted to contradict the theory of migration, is in fact from the tenth *maṇḍala* of the *Ṛg Veda* which is later than the other sections.

13. The element of doubt arises because of the meaning of the word *ayas.* It is possible that it originally meant copper, as it seems to in some contexts, but later, with the introduction of iron, it was qualified by the terms *kṛṣṇa ayas* and *śyāma ayas.* When the association of *tāmra* with copper became common, then *ayas* may have been reserved for iron. It has, however, been argued that *ayas* originally meant iron and that the earliest knowledge of iron in India has therefore to be associated with the Ṛgvedic people. L. Gopal, *Uttar Bharati,* IV, no. 3, pp. 71ff and N.R. Banerjee, *The Iron Age in India,* pp. 158ff. The Indo-European root of *ayas* and its consistent use as iron in other Indo-European languages (*aes, ais, aisa, eisarn*) is a strong argument in favour of this view.

14. The migration theory would seem more acceptable than the invasion theory. The association of the Cemetry H evidence with the Aryans and the supposed massacre at Mohenjo-daro has been doubted. B.B. Lal, 'Protohistoric Investigations', *Ancient India,* no. 9, 1953, p. 88; G.F. Dales, 'The Mythical Massacre at Mohenjo-daro', *Expedition,* VI, no. 3, 1964, pp. 36ff;

A. Ghosh, 'The Archaeological Background', *MASI,* no. 9, 1962, p. 1; G.F. Dales, 'The Decline of the Harappans', *Scientific American,* vol. 214, no. 5, 1966. There is no evidence of Kalibangan having been attacked and it is unlikely that it would have been spared, being so close, if Harappa had been attacked. Post-Harappan cultures rarely build directly on the debris of Harappan sites except at Rupar and Alamgirpur. The extremely interesting discussion by Burrow on the significance of the terms *arma* and *armaka* in the Vedic literature and Pāṇini (*Journal of Indian History,* XLI, 1963, part 1, pp. 159ff) suggests that the references to ruins were to the Indus civilization cities. What is curious, however, is that in some cases it would appear that Indra and Agni were responsible for the destruction of these cities, whereas in other cases they appear already to have been in ruins. It would seem that most of these cities were in the Sarasvati and Punjab region. It is stated that the dark inhabitants fled and migrated. This would agree with the archaeological evidence that the cities were deserted and not occupied by the new arrivals. They were regarded as places of evil and the haunt of sorceresses (*yātumatī*) and therefore to be avoided. This would hardly be the attitude of a conquering people who had actually destroyed the cities. Could the cities have been deserted owing to a natural calamity before the arrival of the Indo-Aryan speakers, who associated the ruins of cities with evil, perhaps set fire to the remaining ruins and ultimately attributed the destruction of the cities to Indra and Agni? This would also explain the chronological gap, that is, the Harappa culture having declined by 1750 BC and the Ṛgvedic Aryans being dated to *circa* 1500 BC.

Recent skeleton analysis of the Harappa culture sites are tending to puncture the theory of the Indo-Aryan speakers representing a large and separate racial group. Dr K. Sen, 'Ancient Races of India and Pakistan, a Study of Methods', *Ancient India,* nos 20 and 21, 1964–65, pp. 178ff, has suggested that the ethnic stock of Cemetry R 37 and Cemetry H appears to have been the same although there are cultural differences.

15. In describing the *dāsa* the references to their being conquered in battle are only a few among a large number of other references to the differences between the *ārya* and the *dāsa.* These differences emphasize the fact of the latter having an alien culture. Thus the *dāsa* are described in the *Ṛg Veda* as *hatvī dasyūn pura āyasīrni tārit* (II, 20.8); *yo dāsam varṇam* (II.12.4); *hatvī dasyūn prāryan varṇam āvat* (III, 34.9); *ayajvānah* (I.33.4); *māyāvān abrahmā dasyurarta* (IV.16.9); *anāsa* (V.29.10); *akarmā dasyūr abhi no amantur anyavrato amānuṣah tvam tasyāmitrahan vadhar dāsasya dambhaya* (X.22.8); *mṛdhra-vāc* (V.29.10), etc.

The word *mleccha* occurs in Later Vedic literature, for example, in the *Śatapatha Brāhmaṇa,* III.2.1.23–24, and is essentially a term of contempt for those who cannot speak the Aryan language and only gradually comes to acquire the meaning of a barbarian in a cultural sense. The etymology of the word is uncertain and does not appear to be Indo-Aryan, although it is said to derive from *vāc.* It is also said to be onomatopoeic, based on the strange sounds of an alien tongue. A reference to *milakhuka* (from Pali *milakkhu,* Sanskrit *mleccha*) in the *Vinaya Piṭaka,* III.28 is explained by Buddhaghoṣa as *Andha-Damil ādi.*

16. It is not surprising that elsewhere too where Indo-European speakers have migrated and settled, the evidence for their presence is largely the Indo-European base of some of the languages of those areas. Greek contains elements of pre-Greek languages and the culture of classical Greece is rooted more in the pre-existing cultures of the region than in Indo-European culture (Luigi Pareti, *The Ancient World,* part I; Moses Finlay, *The Ancient Greeks*; George Thompson, *Studies in Ancient Greek Society*). The culture of the Hittites is derived from the Hattians and only the language is Indo-European. The Mitannis worshipped 'Aryan' gods and used technical terms for chariotry which are Indo-European, but their language, Hurrian, is not included in the Indo-European group. Similarly some Kassites had Aryan-sounding names but only their ruling class seems to have been familiar with the Indo-European language. The idea of a common culture of the Indo-European speakers grew out of philological evidence. Archaeological evidence does not support such an idea. It might be worthwhile for philologists to reconsider the question of how common in fact was the culture of the Indo-European speakers. Clearly there was an early stage when certain ideas and perhaps some institutions were common to the Indo-European speakers. This stage is reflected in, for example, parts of the *Ṛg Veda,* the Avestan *Gāthās*, and the Mitanni-Hittite treaty inscription. This forms the starting point of the ideas on comparative mythology developed for instance in the Kuhn–Müller theory and more recently in the writings of George Dumezil and Paul Thieme, which theories were applied to other areas on the basis of philological evidence. Had the spread of the language also resulted in the spread of similar ideas and institutions then there would have been a far greater identity in the subsequent development of the cultures of the regions where Indo-European languages were spoken. S.C. Malik in *Indian Civilisation, The Formative Period* (1969), p. 144, refers to the Aryan superstructure of ideology being imposed upon the earlier socio-economic organization. 'Hence, it was contrary to the general opinion, not the Aryanisation of India, but rather the Indianisation of the Aryan nomadic pastoralist hordes.'

17. The large concentration of people in the Harappan towns immediately indicates a different type of organization from the smaller settlements of the Painted Grey Ware. Even when describing the Harappan cities, it is sobering to remember that Kalibangan, for instance, could hardly have

had a population larger than 5,000. In cases where a series of trenches have been cut across a mound it is possible to assess the increase or decrease of population in an area of habitation at particular periods by comparing the stratigraphy. For example, a comparative study on these lines of PG Ware levels and NBP levels could provide considerable information. Population estimates are, of course, best carried out from the evidence of burials and of habitation sites uncovered in a horizontal excavation. Where the latter is not possible, a controlled series of soundings may help. Palaeo-demography has already attracted the attention of scholars after the pioneering work of Matiga half a century ago. Attempts have been made to compute population by studying the relative density of remains, by estimating the mean number of individuals in a village site through the habitations and the burials, the land–man ratio in the context of the technology of the period, the estimated number of persons required for a cooperative effort, the setting-up of menhirs, and by a variety of statistical methods.

18. Attempts can be made to estimate the nature of food production by calculating the area of land required to feed a given number of people on the basis of the agricultural technology and possible soil conditions of the time. The interrelation of town and village raises the question of the precise use of the term 'urban'. Does it refer to a fortified village, a town, or a city? The Indo-European root of *pur* means a wall or a rampart, therefore, although in later periods the word *pura* referred to a town, in the early period it could have been a fortified village. A distinction has also to be maintained between the village which becomes an important market and thus the focus of the region, and the town. These distinctions in the degrees of urbanization are relevant not only to the study of prehistory but also in historical periods.

19. The words *dhānya* meaning corn or grain, and *yava* barley or grain, occur in the *Ṛg Veda* and in Later Vedic literature. Specific words for rice, of which the most frequent is *vrīhi* and others are *taṇḍula* and *śāli* occur only in the Later Vedic literature, for example, *Atharvaveda,* VI.140.2, etc.; S.K. Chatterjee suggests a possible Dravidian origin for *vrīhi* in *arichi* (History and Culture of the Indian People, vol. I, *The Vedic Age*, p. 1449). Wheat is referred to as *godhuma* in Later Vedic literature. It is still not certain whether the rice remains at Lothal indicate rice cultivation or merely a wild variety growing in the marshes (Visnu Mittre, unpublished paper read at Patna 1969, 'Environmental Background to the Neolithic–Chalcolithic Complex in North-Western India'). Archaeological evidence suggests that rice was the staple food in a major part of the subcontinent during this period. The use of the word *dhanya* for paddy is late.

20. As for example in the *Trikāṇḍaśeṣa,* a supplement to the *Nāmaliṅg-ānuśāsana* of Amarsiṃha, by Puruṣottamadeva, who is said to have flourished in the court of Lakṣmaṇasena in the twelfth century AD.

21. It is not entirely coincidental that the spread of Indo-European elsewhere is frequently associated with the arrival of the horse-drawn chariot and on occasion, with iron technology.

22. It is curious that there should be no substantial remains of at least the metal parts of the chariot in various excavations, and particularly at Harappa and Mohenjo-daro if we are to accept the theory that these cities were invaded by the Ṛgvedic people. This is in striking contrast to the evidence from Egypt where the new arrivals in their horse-drawn chariots are depicted clearly in reliefs and engravings on stone. The Aryan chariot was lighter, had spoked wheels, could accommodate three persons and was horse-drawn. It was therefore speedier, had greater manoeuvrability and consequently, the two combatants had a vantage position (O.R. Gurney, *The Hittites,* pp. 104ff and S. Piggott, *Prehistoric India,* pp. 273ff).

23. The significance of these improvements is that the socketed iron axe is more efficient in a heavily forested region; the iron hoe makes a substantial difference in rice cultivation where more continual weeding is necessary than in other crops. This is also suggested in one of the frequently used words for 'hoe' in Vedic literature, *stambhaghna,* literally that which destroys clumps. The importance of the iron hoe has not received sufficient attention in the evaluation of technological change during this period.

24. The Munda derivation of *lāṅgala* is discussed by J. Przyluski in Bagchi (ed.), *Pre-Aryan* and *Pre-Dravidian in India,* pp. 8ff; also in T. Burrow, *The Sanskrit Language,* p. 379. It occurs as *nāṅgal* in Dravidian (Dravidian Etymological Dictionary, No. 2368). An attempt to associate it with the Indo-European *leg/leng* as in J. Pokorny, *Vergleichens des Worterbuch der Indo-Germanischen Sprachen* and thereby to link it with *Nirukta,* VI.26 of Yāska has not been accepted for linguistic reasons (S.K. Chatterjee, 'Non-Aryan Elements in Indo-Aryan', *JGIS,* III.42). It could be added that even from the point of view of the technology of the plough, the ploughshare is the central object and not an attachment.

The early occurrence of the word for 'plough' in non-Indo-Aryan languages would invalidate the suggestion that the Aryan-speakers introduced the plough. The possibility that the plough may have been known to the Harappans on the basis of a particular sign in the script resembling the Sumerian sign for plough has now been confirmed by the last season's excavations at Kalibangan, which uncovered the furrow marks in a field outside the city's fortification which date to the pre-Harappan period. On a purely impressionistic view it seems unlikely that a sufficient food surplus could have been produced to maintain the cities without plough agriculture.

25. In the *Saṃhitā* literature the *karmāra* is respected, but gradually his status becomes low. *Ṛg Veda,* X.72.2; IX.112.2, *Atharvaveda,* III.5.6. Ultimately the *karmāra* is ranked with the *Niṣāda* and the *kulāla. Manu,* IV.215;

Kane, *History of the Dharmashastras,* II, p. 73. The lowering of the status may have had to do with the fact that the smiths were possibly non-tribal artisans, (it has been suggested that the coppersmiths were itinerant smiths) who would be allowed commensality and participation in the ritual, but not marriage relationships with the tribe. The social rights and obligations of such professional groups would be worth examining.

26. The Harappan system of weights has been described as binary in the lower weights—1, 2, 8/3, 16, 32, 64 . . . and decimal in the higher weights. The decimal basis of counting is referred to in the *Taittirīya Saṁhitā,* IV.40.11.4; *Maitrāyāṇīya Sam.,* II.8.14; *Kāṭhaka Sam.,* XVII.10 and XXXIX.6; *Vājasaneyi Sam.,* XVII.2. There are references to ten raised to the power of twelve. The existence of the earlier binary system suggests that calculations may have been on the basis of the square. The commonly used cosmology of the Babylonians and Sumerians is believed to have had the mathematical base of the square. The use of both the square and circular cosmology in Indian sources at this time does suggest that new ideas on astronomy may have been in the air. There is a great likelihood that the circular theory was first developed among navigators, perhaps the Phoenicians, and would have then travelled to those in contact with the Phoenicians. C.P.S. Menon, *Early Astronomy and Cosmology,* pp. 36ff, makes an interesting correlation between the prevalence of the square cosmology and the circular cosmology in early India.

27. The need for exact geometrical knowledge arose in part because, although there were a variety of shapes permitted for altars such as the falcon, the chariot-wheel, the tortoise, the triangle, etc., their area had to be identical. The number of bricks was also prescribed. The geometrical principles involved in both creating precisely measured forms and converting one form into another are described in detail in the *Śulva Sūtras.* Admittedly most of these texts belong to the end of the Vedic period or even to the immediately post-Vedic period. Nevertheless they contain the developed and classified knowledge of geometry which must certainly have had earlier beginnings. This geometrical knowledge would be of use in other spheres of life as well, as for example, in measuring land.

28. One year of twelve months comprising 360 days is frequently referred to in the *Ṛg Veda,* I.164.11; I.164.48. A year of 366 days has been suggested on the basis of the Ribhus in *Ṛg Veda,* IV.33.7. An intercalary month in a five-year circle finds mention in a late section of the *Ṛg Veda,* X.85.13. An intercalary thirteenth month of thirty days in a five-year circle occurs in the *Atharvaveda,* IX.9.19.

A primaeval element in Vedic society is indicated by the fact that magic is a substantial feature in both religious and technological concepts. It would be expected, therefore, that mathematical and astronomical knowledge would tend to be hidden' in a mesh of symbolism and magic. That this element persists is apparent from the consultations with the village pandit which are still a part of the rural scene for determining the 'right day' for important agricultural activities such as sowing and harvesting. This has implications relating to the calendar as well as the notion of the auspicious day. The latter almost certainly derives its sanctity from the former.

29. In the Indus valley this would be caused by any or all of the following factors: the geological uplift at Sehwan resulting in the excessive flooding of the Indus near Mohenjo-daro, the salination of the soil, deforestation causing soil erosion and decrease in natural irrigation and thereby rendering agriculture difficult, and finally, the termination specifically of the Harappan trade with Sumer in the eighteenth century BC; apart from a possible attack on the cities of Harappa and Mohenjo-daro. Some of these factors are discussed by R.L. Raikes, 'The End of the Ancient Cities of the Indus'. *American Anthropology,* 1964 and 'The Mohenjo-daro Floods', *Antiquity,* 40; G.F. Dales, 'New Investigations at Mohenjo-daro', *Archaeology,* 18,1965; H.T. Lambrick, 'The Indus Flood Plain and the Indus Civilisation', *Geographical Journal,* 133, 1967. Detailed discussion of the Sumerian trade is available in L. Oppenheim, *Ancient Mesopotamia* and W.F. Leemans, *Foreign Trade in the* Old *Babylonian Period.* The breakdown in trade is supported by the fact that the dockyard at Lothal had fallen into disuse by *circa* 1800 BC (*Ancient India,* nos 18 and 19, 1962–63, p. 213).

30. The trade with Ophira during the reign of Solomon, the obelisk of Shalmanesar III depicting Indian elephants, the evidence of Indian teak at Mugheir and in the palace of Nebuchadnezzar and a variety of linguistic evidence (some of which is discussed in Rawlinson, *Intercourse between India and the Western World*) would attest to trading contacts between India and the Near East. The *brāhmī* script may have originated in western India as a kind of merchant's code partially associated with the Semitic script and in course of time and use in commerce travelled to the Ganga valley and to north India where it was perfected for use with Sanskrit and Prākrit. The *aramaic* adaptations in *kharoṣṭhī* clearly arose from commercial and administrative needs.

31. In the *Śatapatha Brāhmaṇa,* III.2.3.15 and the *Kauṣītaki Brāh.,* VII.6, the speech of the Kuru Pañcālas and the north generally is extolled and made a model for study. This ties in with the fact that Pāṇini is associated with the north. Yet the Punjab had been relegated to the status of a *mleccha-deśa* in the *Atharvaveda,* V.22.14.

The linguistic differences between the Punjab and the middle Ganga valley were earlier sought to be explained on the basis of the theory that there were two bands of Aryan-speakers and this theory was developed by Hoernle, *A Grammar of the Eastern Hindi Compared with the Other*

Gaudian Languages, 1880, and by G. Grierson, *Languages,* IGI, vol. 1, 1907. More recently, S.K. Chatterjee and S.M. Katre in *Languages,* GI 1965, have preferred the argument that the differences are due to many more groups mutually interacting. What is perhaps called for at this stage is a comparative study of the linguistic structure of the various Prākrits and the pre-Aryan languages.

32. *Atharvaveda,* V.22.14; *Gopatha Brāhamaṇa,* II.9; *Vājasaneyi Sam.,* XXX.5.22; *Taittirīya Brāh.,* III.4.1.1; *Baudhāyana Dharma Sūtra,* I.1.14.

33. Jules Bloch, 'Sanskrit and Dravidian', in Bagchi (ed.), *Pre-Aryan and Pre-Dravidian in India,* pp. 46ff. The use of the word *ghota* in Sanskrit is late occurring in such texts as the *Āpastamba Śrauta Sūtra,* XV.3.12; *ghoṭaka* in *Pañcatantra,* V.10.4; *Vikramādityacarita,* etc. An early use of *ghoṭaka* in Pāli occurs in *Jātaka,* VI.452.

A micro-study of the etymology of place-names, even contemporary place-names, would be revealing, particularly in the context of early Munda and Dravidian settlement in northern India. Names such as Ganga, Kaliṇga, Aṇga, Vaṇga, etc., have already been discussed as probable Munda names, Bagchi, *Pre-Aryan and Pre-Dravidian in India,* pp. 72ff.

34. The pattern of settlement at Harappa, Mohenjo-daro, Kalibangan suggests an elite in residence on the citadel mound; the large and separate residential area to the east of the citadel occupied by lesser status groups; and the single or double-roomed 'workmen's quarters' indicating a third-level of stratification. The question has often been asked as to who was in authority in the Harappa culture and how was authority maintained? The answer could lie in the existence of a kind of caste structure, where a small group preserving itself through strict endogamous marriage and organizing its authority through a hierarchy of service relationships in which it was assigned a high status, and stressing its ritual purity, could have held power. The Great Bath at Mohenjo-daro is now almost universally recognized as being indicative of an ablution ritual which could have been central to a notion of ritual purity.

35. All tribal societies have a social organization based on kinship relations deriving from rules of exogamy and endogamy. Family structure, whether matrilineal or patriarchal, lineage, and tribal identity are some of the features which might be ferreted out of the references to the earlier populations. Chalcolithic cultures invariably indicate a division of labour, and where there is trading activity as well, the division of labour is intensified. Nor would identity with a particular geographical location be precluded. The evidence of the notion of pollution in non-Aryanized societies has been noticed by anthropologists and some would regard it as essential to the development of religion and society in India (e.g. M.N. Srinivas, *Religion and Society among the Coorgs*). Thus the pre-requisites for a caste structure

were available. It could be suggested that a rudimentary form of the caste structure existed in the pre-Aryan Ganga valley cultures and perhaps a better defined form in the Harappa culture. The Ṛgvedic people show an unfamiliarity with this structure, which is not surprising if they regarded the non-Aryan culture as alien. The division of society into four groups has a single reference in the Puruṣasūkta hymn in the late tenth *maṇḍala* of the *Ṛg Veda* (X.90.12). The logic implicit in this particular myth regarding the origin of the castes would in itself suggest the re-arranging of endogamous groups into a carefully worked-out pattern. The word *varṇa* with the connotation of caste is used in the *Ṛg Veda* to differentiate between two groups, the *ārya* and the *dāsa*. The later literature clearly refers to the *catvāro varṇāḥ* (*Śatapatha Brāh.*, V.5.4.9; VI.4.4.13). The expansion to four categories would be necessary once society became more complex and endogamous groups were incorporated and had to be arranged in a pattern. The *jāti* structure may well reflect a pre-Aryan aspect of the caste structure.

36. For example, *Chāndogya Upaniṣad*, V.10.7; Manu (X.45) makes a distinction between the Dasyus who speak the Aryan language and those who do not.

37. The Kirāta are referred to as low-status tribes in the *Vājasaneyi Sam.*, XXX.16; *Taittirīya Brāh.*, III.4.12.1; *Atharvaveda*, X.4.14; *Manu*, X.44; *Raghuvaṁśa*, XVI.57. The Pulinda are similarly referred to in the *Aitareya Brāhmaṇa*, 7.18; Aśoka's Thirteenth Major Rock Edict.

38. The urbanization of the Ganga valley in the first millennium BC is often referred to as the second urbanization. A crucial factor in this urbanization was iron technology as is evident when one compares the NBP levels with PGW levels or black-and-red ware levels. Surplus produce and the specialization of crafts both utilizing the *dāsa-bhṛtaka*, increase in trade based on production as well as improved communication (both by land and through the use of river navigation) all combined to make urbanization possible. This in turn produced the characteristics associated with urban culture—the building of fortified cities, the introduction of a script (*brāhmī*), the use of coinage (punch-marked coins for example), a wide range of intellectual and metaphysical speculation (from the Cārvākas to the Ājīvikas), some of which reflected the requirements and aspirations of the new urban groups—the artisans and the merchants and traders.

Unlike the first urbanization in the Indus valley, we have for the Ganga valley enough evidence to be able to trace its gradual evolution. The quality of the early urbanization of the Ganga valley as compared to that of the Indus valley was less impressive in terms of material culture. But there seems to have been a more even distribution of the characteristics of urbanization, suggesting perhaps that the perquisites of urban living were concentrated and centralized to a lesser degree than in the Indus civilization.

39. The origin of the state is ascribed to a number of intersecting factors in early literary sources. We are told, for example, that the surplus production of rice led to the emergence of the institution of family and private property (initially connoting fields). The state arose because both of these had to be protected as also because of the need to prevent conflict between castes (*Vāyu Purāṇa,* VIII, 128–61; *Mahāvastu,* I, 342ff; *Mārkaṇḍeya Purāṇa,* 49, 74ff). The literature of the mid-first millennium BC indicates the beginning of political concepts. This is in contrast to the Ṛgvedic period where loyalty is primarily to the clan and where, therefore, government is seen in more simplistic terms, namely, authority invested in the chief or leader whose main function is to protect the clan. This concept is assumed in the various stories regarding the appointment of Indra as the *rājā,* which stories are elaborated upon with the growth of the contractual element in the notion of the state in Later Vedic literature (*Ṛg Veda,* VIII, 35, 86; *Aitareya Brāh.,* I.14; *Śatapatha Brāh.,* III.4.2.1–3). The purpose of the contract gradually changes from protecting the clan militarily, to the king maintaining the order of the castes and also protecting private property (*Arthaśāstra,* III.1; *Manu,* VII.17–35; *Śānti Parva,* 75.10; *Manu,* X.115). The contract is complete when the *rājā* is paid one-sixth in tax as his wage for services to the people (*ṣadbhāgbhṛto rājā rakṣet prajām, Baudhāyana Dharma Sūtra,* I.10.6). The *rājā* is associated with divinity which permits of a different perspective on the notion of contract.

Buddhist texts, however, indicate the contractual basis of the concept of the state, more clearly as the association with divinity is absent (*Dīgha Nikāya,* III, 84–96; *Mahāvastu,* I.338–48). It was more suited to the context of the non-monarchical systems of government.

40. At the level of ritual there was the incorporation of prayers, spells, and magic, as for example in the *Atharvaveda* and the *Yajurveda.* At the level of deities the acceptance of the erstwhile distant Rudra and the growth of the Rudra-Śiva concept for instance. The recruitment of local priests into the *brāhmaṇa* fold can be seen not only in the various purification rites for those of degenerate castes, such as the *Vrātyastoma,* but is also perhaps reflected in the mysterious origin of many *brāhmaṇa gotras.* The concession to the worship of the mother goddess, to any appreciable extent, is a later phenomenon as also the acceptance of phallic worship.

41. Pargiter's attempt to sort out the genealogies on the basis of Aryan and non-Aryan has been criticized. It is possible that, eventually, the Purāṇic genealogies will be found to be more true to the essence of the history of this period since they are not concerned with the Aryan problem as such but with the activities of a large number of clans and kings in northern India. It is interesting that the two royal lineages, the Ailas and Ikṣvākus are both based in the Ganga valley, from where various lineages move in various directions.

The *vaṃśāvali* tradition has as its genesis the myth of the Flood and this agrees in many particulars with the Sumerian Flood legend. Indeed it is the agreement in details which is so striking. What is even more interesting is that the traditional date of the Kaliyuga according to the astronomical tradition of Āryabhaṭa works out to about 3102 BC, which agrees with the archaeological date ascribed to the flooding of Shuruppak in Sumer which is probably the genesis of the Sumerian Flood legend (C. Leonard Woolley, *The Early Periods—Ur Excavations,* vol. IV, 1956; M. Mallowan, 'Noah's Flood Reconsidered', *Iraq,* XXVI, 1964). The reference to this legend in Vedic literature is late, in the *Śatapatha Brāh.,* I.8.1.1 and the *Kāṭhaka Sam.,* XI.2. Had the legend been of Aryan origin, one would expect it to occur in the *Ṛg Veda* or be associated with the Avestan tradition rather than the Sumerian. The legend relating to the genesis of a people is after all of prime importance. Considering the close contacts between the Harappa culture and the Sumerians, it is possible that the same legend may have been used as a genesis in both cultures and the Purāṇic genealogies may therefore contain a pre-Aryan tradition. R.C. Hazra's very able studies of the Purāṇic sources point to some non-Vedic religious contents in the *Purāṇas.*

As regards the mythological sections, the initial legend alone raises a host of interesting ideas: the concept of the Flood as genesis, the use of the sun and the moon as the symbol of the two royal lineages (*Sūryavamsi* and *Candravaṃśi*) and the association of these in the tribal mythology of India and elsewhere; the fact that the Aila lineage derives its name from the sole daughter of Manu, Ilā who married the son of the moon deity (Soma), may suggest a matrilineal-cum-mother goddess tradition.

42. Magadha in the period from 400 BC to AD 400 saw the rise of the Mauryas and the Guptas; the Raichur–Bijapur region in the period from 500 to 1200 was the nucleus of Cālukya and Rāṣṭrakūṭa power and the Kanchi–Tanjore region in the same period was the homeland of the Pallavas and Colas. Other areas also gave rise to important dynasties, but generally to only a single dynasty in a shorter period, e.g. Kannauj under Harṣa, Bengal under the Pālas, etc.

43. We know that various groups were recruited to the *brāhmaṇa varṇa* and that their status within the *varṇa* could change; thus the Kuru-Pañcāla *brāhmaṇas* looked down upon the Magadha *brāhmaṇas (Jātaka,* I.324, II.83; *Aitareya Brāh.,* VIII.14), the Gandhara *brāhmaṇas* are described with contempt in the *Rājataraṅgiṇī* (I.306ff) yet are regarded as respectable in the *Bhaviṣya Purāna.* It is also evident that families of non-kṣatriya origin became rulers or were given *kṣatriya* status through fabricated genealogies. Thus the Nandas are described as *śūdras* in the Purāṇas. The Candella kings claimed Candravaṃśi lineage and *kṣatriya* status in spite of obscure origins and having acquired the status continued to marry into the local Gond

families. There is an absence of any reference to the *vaiśya varṇa* in certain parts of India. The composition of the *śūdra varṇa* varied from region to region and its role was different in south India as compared to the Ganga valley. When we cease to look at early Indian society as a static, rigid structure stratified into immobile castes, we then begin to see considerable evidence to suggest the contrary.

CHAPTER 5

Lineage Society*

The archaeology of the Indo-Gangetic divide and the western Ganga valley indicates that the settlement of this area goes back to the second millennium BC. The upper Doāb in particular receives the stragglers of the Late Harappan culture and is the hub of a possibly unrelated people of the Ochre-Colour Pottery culture. Ultimately the much more impressive sites of the Painted Grey Ware[1] culture come to dominate the region. This culture seems to have spread from northern Rajasthan and southern Punjab in the late second millennium, BC. into the western Ganga valley with a heavier settlement in the upper Doāb. Recent excavations in the Beas-Sutlej *doāb* indicate an overlap between the Late Harappan[2] and the Painted Grey Ware cultures which, if correct would point to some continuity of Harappan traditions, albeit indirect and probably diluted, into the first millennium BC.

The changing of river courses in southern Punjab and northern Rajasthan where the Painted Grey Ware is found in abundance, may have necessitated a movement southeastwards to avoid the ensuing ecological uncertainties.[3] Sometimes the sites are located on dry river beds, suggesting hydraulic changes. The Sutlej, described in post-Vedic sources as the river with a hundred channels has been known constantly to change its course. The Sarasvatī, the river of many pools, disappeared into the desert near Sirsa leaving only traces of its original bed. It has been argued that a change in the course of the Yamuna drew off the waters of the Sarasvatī

* This chapter was originally published in Romila Thapar, *From Lineage to State: Social Formations in the Mid-first Millenium BC in the Ganga Valley*, New Delhi, Oxford University Press, 1984.

and other rivers of the Indo-Gangetic divide. Added to this is the possibility of climatic changes with increasing aridity in northern Rajasthan.[4] Given the increase in the size of sites of the Painted Grey Ware, it is equally plausible that there was a demographic rise which led to a search, in a literal sense, for fresh fields and pastures new. The argument that a profusion of closely spaced settlements may point to shifting cultivation requiring new sites every few years would probably not apply in this case since the archaeological evidence suggests a more sophisticated agricultural activity. The Painted Grey Ware culture marks an assertive society, richer than its immediate predecessors. There is evidence of pastoralism and agriculture with the noticeable presence of a new animal, the horse, and with minimal use of iron (almost restricted to weapons) in the early part of the first millennium BC. The finely made wheel-thrown grey pottery with its floral and geometric designs provided a further distinction to the culture.

The *Ṛg Veda* refers to various tribes settled in the region between the Indus, the rivers of the Punjab and the now extinct Sarasvatī, an area described in the text as the *sapta sindhava.*[5] The major concentration of settlements from archaeological data points to the lower *doābs* of the Punjab and it is possible that the text may have been referring to the five rivers at their points of confluence rather than to their upper reaches. The Sarasvatī is described as eventually joining the ocean,[6] which it has since ceased to do, if it ever did. The possibility of hydraulic changes in this area would date to the latter half of the second millennium BC, a date which would not conflict with the generally accepted chronology for much of the *Ṛg Veda.* Hydraulic changes in northern Rajasthan and the watershed may well have required migrations of a scale such as are suggested in the movement of the Bharatas and the Pūrus from southern Punjab and northern Rajasthan to Haryana and the upper Doāb or the wanderings of the Yadus to Mathura and Saurashtra. Desiccation and changes in river courses would have caused major population movements.

Ṛg Vedic society was essentially pastoral. This did not preclude agriculture although agrarian activities are more frequently described in the later section of the text. The pastoralists may well have controlled the agricultural niches without being economically dependent on them, particularly if the cultivated areas were worked by people other than those who belonged to the pastoral clans. The society of the Ganga–Yamuna Doāb as reflected in the Later Vedic texts was more dependent on agriculture although cattle-rearing remained a significant activity. Historically the west bank of the Yamuna has been associated with continuing pastoralism whereas the Doāb itself became prime agricultural land fairly early. Sedentary settlements become characteristic of the increasing emphasis on agriculture, although here again the change was evidently not rapid. Settlements in the Doāb would have had to adjust with the smaller settlements of earlier populations indicated by the Ochre Colour Pottery and the Copper Hoard cultures,[7] which may well have been assimilated by the more dominant culture. The existence of earlier agricultural communities in the region may have formed the nucleii of the larger communities as is suggested by the evidence from those sites where settlements of the Ochre Colour Pottery culture are succeeded by the Painted Grey Ware. It is not surprising then that both the Kurus and the Pañcālas are in origin confederations of earlier clans some of which were known to the *Ṛg Veda.* Neither the Kurus nor the Pañcālas as such are referred to in the *Ṛg Veda.* Whereas the Kurus emerged after the confederation of the Pūrus and the Bharatas in the main, the Pañcālas, as the name suggests, were an amalgam of five clans.[8] It would be reasonable to expect that this confederation was the result of a re-alignment arising out of new settlements and some degree of conquest and subordination. In the case of the Kurus it is the Pūru lineage which is listed as the dominant one.[9] The subordination was not necessarily of non-aryans by aryans (whoever the latter may have been!) but equally of various weak clans by the strong, all of whom could have called themselves aryans. The emergence of what came to be identified as the Kuru-Pañcāla region was clearly important as it is called *madhya-deśa* and *āryavarta,* the land of the *āryas* in later tradition,[10] and is regarded as the epitome of *āryan* society. However, the assimilation of earlier populations would also have resulted in the inclusion (in later texts and rituals) of earlier traditions surviving among indigenous groups.

The pastoralism of Ṛg Vedic society made livestock breeding, and more specially, cattle herding the major activity. Pastoralism is dependent on assured grazing grounds and the ability to accumulate and increase the herd, this being the primary source of wealth. It required what the *Ṛg Veda* describes as 'meadows rich in grass'.[11] Its political implications demanded that grazing grounds be demarcated and a constant watch kept to exclude trespassers. The accumulation of cattle, *gāviṣṭhi,* comes through breeding as well as capturing other herds.[12] Cattle raids are therefore a form of acquiring fresh stock and the same word is used for such raids. The winner of cows, *gojit,* is an epithet for hero.[13] The Kuru-Pañcāla *rājā*s we are told, raided in the season when the dew falls.[14] Inevitably the worst enemies are the Paṇis, given to cattle lifting.[15] Cattle raiding is often accompanied by the capture of herders who are often enslaved. Leadership in this situation requires the ability to protect not only the herd, since cattle are the chief form of wealth, but also one's clan, and to defend the claim to ownership of cattle and control over the grazing ground or *vraja.* Hence the synonyms of *gopa, gopati,* and *janasya gopati* for the *rājā,*[16] as against the later terms *nṛpati* and *nareśvara,*[17] the lord of the herd eventually giving way to the lord of men. Leadership in the context of cattle raids and protection also became the incentive for winning loyalties and establishing the rights of lineages.

Grazing lands are liable to change since the same pastures may not remain constant year after year and cattle herders have to be mobile. Since the economy is dependent on the increase of the herd, identification with land plays a peripheral role and the search for pastures remains crucial. Thus the Pūrus are earlier said to be settled along the grassy banks of the Sarasvatī,[18] but later become the core of the Kuru lineage in the Ganga–Yamuna Doāb.

Wealth is frequently computed in heads of cattle and in this the cow has a special status. The *gomat* is the man of wealth.[19] The cow is a unit of value, a man's life being calculated to be worth a hundred cows (*śatadeya*). It gains religious sanctity and is sacrified on the more auspicious occasions.[20] It acquires the sanction of a totem animal in that its flesh is eaten on specified occasions in association with rituals,[21] or equally specially when welcoming a guest. The condemnation of the arbitrary killing of cows would point to their ritual importance.[22] Wealth is also computed in heads of horse, crucial to cattle raids and migrations. The horse too acquires religious sanction but less so than the cow. Its sacrifice is symbolic of fertility and power but its flesh is not eaten. The horse appears to have been more valuable than the cow.[23] In the enumeration of wealth the numbers of cattle are invariably much larger than those of horses. The latter is not ritually sacrificed in the same number as cattle. This may well have to do with the necessity of importing horses into India. Apart from the northwestern borders the Indian ecology was not generally conducive to breeding horses of quality.

The *rājā* or chief was the successful leader of a raid and by extension, of a battle.[24] The booty thus acquired was distributed among the clan, but the distribution was already unequal. Some of it was retained by the *rājā,* but a substantial amount was also claimed by priestly families on the grounds that their rituals ensured success in battle and they were the bestowers of praise and therefore of immortality on the hero. The heroic ideal, apart from bravery, included generosity in gift-giving and thus, implicitly, access to wealth. The *dāna-stuti* hymns of the *Ṛg Veda*[25] refer to the established heroes as gift-givers in extravagant terms. Cattle, horses, gold, chariots, and female slaves are said to have been bestowed in their hundreds and thousands on enthusiastic bards and priests. The wealth is as mobile as the chiefs from whom it comes and its recipients. The figures may be exaggerated but wealth was distributed at least among the families of the priests and the chiefs, a redistribution which increasingly neglected the rest of the clan. The ability to conduct a successful raid was in part motivated by the capacity to acquire wealth in order that it be distributed or even destroyed in a potlatch type ceremony; this is reflected in increasing references to the bestowal of wealth on ritual occasions, particularly to priests.[26]

The reciprocal relationship between chief and priest undergoes its first change in the period after that of the *Ṛg Veda* as is reflected in the other Vedic texts. Pastoralism, even in the earlier period did not exclude agriculture but the balance between the two gradually shifted in favour of agriculture. The more elaborate ceremonial sacrifices of the later period such as the *rājasūya* include offerings made of grain together with milk, *ghī* and animals.[27] Plough agriculture is referred to in the *Ṛg Veda*,[28] generally in the later *maṇḍala*s, but curiously some of the major agricultural implements carry names which are linguistically non-Aryan, such as *lāṅgala*.[29] That there were sedentary agriculturalists in this region prior to the Ṛg Vedic period is evident from archaeology. The Asuras, for example, are said to have had a correct knowledge of the seasons for agricultural activities.[30] The subordination of such groups to pastorally based power is not unknown and could be explained in terms of environmental circumscription, where, in favourable areas cultivators prefer not to migrate when encroached upon by pastoralists.[31] Alternatively, the close proximity of herders to agriculturalists may well have led to a symbiotic relationship of mutual dependence. Thus herders might graze their animals on the stubble of fields or be provided with fodder in return for protection. Such agriculturalists would then accept the authority of the herder chiefs without necessarily being conquered by them. At the individual level this would require a relationship simultaneously drawing on notions of alienness and friendship which is perhaps what is reflected in the complex meaning of the word *ari*. Such symbiotic relationships could encourage circuits of exchange of a simple and direct kind, should the herders practise transhumance. They would also presuppose a situation of bilingualism should the two groups be speaking different languages. It has been suggested that the presence of non-Aryan features, particularly Proto-Dravidian and Austro-Asiatic, in Vedic Sanskrit may have resulted from situations of bilingualism between speakers of Indo-Aryan and other languages.[32]

The migration into the Doāb carries few references to the conquest of or battles against local populations. Most of the celebrated battles were among the major clans and conflicts involved claims to territorial control and rights of succession to these territories. Apart from the famous *dāśarājña*[33] when the Bharatas fought against a confederacy of ten clans, the best known of which were the group of five, the Pūru, Druhyu, Anu, Turvaśa and Yakṣa/Yadu; the Bharatas were also involved in battles against the well-established *dāsa* chief Śambara and raids against the cattle-lifting

Paṇis.[34] The Turvaśa and the Yadu fought against the Bharata Divodāsa and were defeated by his son Sudās,[35] the Srinjayas were victorious against[36] the Turvaśa and Vṛṣivant as also against the Bharatas and the Satvant.[37] Such references come from the *Ṛg Veda* or refer to earlier events in the later texts and the location of such hostilities was in areas to the northwest of the Doāb and prior to the migration into the Doāb. There appears to have been systematic settlement on the new lands with the indigenous population either being absorbed, or being pushed to the margins of the settlement. Such settlements would have been clearings in the monsoon forests which covered the Ganga valley at the time. The proximity of the forests is always present in the consciousness of the settlers as is evident from the contrasting images of *grāma* and *araṇya,* where the forest is the place of exile, of demons and *rākṣasas,* but also where the hermitages of *ṛṣis* were situated. The latter were in a sense the vanguard of the new society and the hermitages could act as the nucleii of new settlements. This might also explain why there was such hostility towards these hermitages from those who regarded the forests as their hunting grounds.[38]

The story of Pṛthu Vainya, the first righteous ruler according to tradition, is pertinent in that Niṣāda, the original chief created by the *ṛṣis,* whose name becomes synonymous with hunting and gathering tribes, is expelled to the forest to become a hunter and gatherer. Pṛthu Vainya, who is created subsequently, introduces cattle-rearing and the plough, an action for which the grateful earth goddess Pṛthivī bestowes her name on him.[39] The entire process would not have been too difficult for those acquainted with the superior technology of iron weapons, with the horse and chariot, and no longer pastoralists but familiar also with the advantages of agriculture. That land was now recognized as an item of wealth is evident from its ownership being vested in the clan. The *rājā* Viśvakarma Bhauvana was rebuked by the earth, Pṛthivī, when he tried to make a grant of land and it is also stated that the *rājan* cannot settle people on land without the consent of the clans (*viś*).[40] There is no reference to the sale of land in the Vedic texts.

In the initial stages of settled agriculture pastoralism retained its importance. Apart from the milk provided by cattle, the grazing of cattle in fallow fields resulted in the manuring of these fields not to mention the use of cattle in providing power, for traction. This was known to the earlier people of the *Ṛg Veda*[41] and doubtless intensified as agriculture began to take precedence over pastoralism. Not only does agriculture become more important than cattle rearing in the Doāb but it may also have been the utopian land yielding two crops a year. Reference is made in later sources to harvests of barley in summer and rice in autumn and to the best fields yielding two crops.[42] It has recently been argued from archaeological evidence that double cropping in the Doāb appears to have been regular at this time.[43] Whether it was a system of double cropping or one of rotation remains uncertain, but of the increasing importance of agriculture there can be no doubt. The *Ṛg Veda* refers to the cultivation of *yava* (barley).[44] The later texts mention *vṛhi* (rice).[45] The cultivation of both was possible in the lower Doāb, as for example, at Atranjikhera (Etah distrct). The sites from which rice remains are available are located in the more elevated areas of the Doāb and its environs, and this was clearly not wet rice cultivation. Since it was grown in rotation with barley and wheat its cultivation was neither as labour intensive nor as demanding of irrigation as was the cultivation of rice in the middle Ganga valley. It is equally possible that some of the rice was not locally cultivated but brought from the area to the east of the upper Doāb where it was more widely grown and where wheat and barley played a lesser role. In the later texts there are references to heavy ploughs drawn by anywhere between six to twenty-four oxen,[46] which would be indicative of the heavier wetter soil east of the Doāb. The *Ṛg Veda* mentions wells and doubtless these were used for irrigation as well in the watershed area and the western Ganga valley.[47] Given the obsession with the theme of release of waters in the frequent references to the conflict between Indra and Vṛtra, it is tempting to think that agriculture was primarily dependent on rainfall.

The gradual transition to agriculture made an impact, perhaps indirectly, on other aspects of Vedic life. Among these was the pattern of change in different sections of society. The vedic *jana* (tribe) incorporated a number of *viś* (clans). These may in origin have been more egalitarian but by the time of the *Ṛg Veda* were bifurcated into the *viś* and the *rājanya,* the latter constituting the ruling families. The description of the *rājanya* even in the Later Vedic literature depicts him as sporting a bow, shooting arrows with accuracy, running chariot races, drinking *surā* and being in effect the epitome of the hero. It was from among these families that the *rājā* was chosen. In one place it is said that those who successfully complete the *aśvamedha* sacifice will share in *rāṣṭra* and become *rājā*s worthy of consecration whereas those who fail to do so will remain members of the *rājanya* and the *viś*.[48] The original relationship between the *viś* and the *rājanya* must have been close.

The bifurcation of Ṛg Vedic times suggests a division into the senior lineages of the *rājanya*s and the lesser, junior or cadet lineages which continued to be called *viś*. Clan lands were held in common by both lineages but worked by the lesser lineage, since the permission of the *viś* was necessary before the *rājā* could settle people on the land. The clans were the original settlers which is the literal meaning of the word *viś* and when land was converted to agricultural use or agricultural land was incorporated into the territory over which the *viś* claimed usage, it belonged jointly to the *viś*. In the past *viś* has been translated as peasantry.[49] This has led to some ambiguity in determining the beginnings of a peasant economy in the Ganga valley. ('Peasant economy' is here differentiated from 'peasant society' since the former entails specific obligations and dues which may be absent in the latter where the emphasis is on the presence of cultivators.) That *viś* means a clan is generally accepted and it is used as such for *dāsa*s and *āryas*. The *viśpati* is in some contexts the chief of the clan and in others the head of the household.[50] Rights on land were probably of usage since ownership is not recorded. The demarcation and measurements of fields mentioned in the late books of the *Ṛg Veda*[51] may well have been lineage and family allotments rather than indications of ownership. Pastoral land raises no problems, remaining common to the village as *vraja* and most animal grazing took place on waste land and forest, of which there was plenty at that time. The allocation of holdings was probably made by lots; hence the symbolic significance of dicing and its association with wealth. Cultivation could also have been carried out by rotation with no claims to ownership.

The bifurcation of clans into those of higher status and others is not unusal. It often comes about through a claim to differentiation between elder sons and younger sons or the ability of some to lead in cattle raids, to protect the clan, to establish new settlements as also through the control of alliances with other clans. In the Ṛg Vedic case there was a distinction between the chariot-riding warriors who were pre-eminently the guardians and protectors of the *viś* and the latter who were more sedentary and were the producers of both pastoral and agricultural items. The *viś* as the junior lineage provided prestations, informally extracted on special occasions, to the *rājanya*s who redistributed these among a limited group with *dāna* and *dakṣinā* given to *brāhmaṇa*s and bards and oblations offered at the *yajña* rituals. The link between the *rājanya* and the *viś*, suggesting an earlier, closer relationship, is referred to obliquely, for example, in the statement that the *kṣatra* and the *viś* might eat from the same vessel,[52] which in a society placing a high value on commensality was a substantial statement of relatively equal status. It is also said that the *kṣatra* is created out of the *viś*, the analogy being to *soma* the ritual drink which when purified leaves the substance for the more common inebriant, *surā*.[53] A comparison is also made then in terms of one being *soma* and the other various plants or of Varuna and the Maruts or Indra and the Maruts or Yama and the Pitṛs.[54] It is interesting that these comparisons are to superior and inferior statuses in the same species. Had the *viś* in origin been commoners with no lineage status or links with *rājanya*s it is unlikely that so much effort would have gone into stating the obvious, that the *viś* was inferior to the *rājanya* and the less powerful.[55] That some awareness of the earlier relationship of common origins persisted is indirectly suggested by the statement that those who seek to equate the two produce chaos.[56] The *rājanya*s as the senior lineages doubtless kept a larger share of the booty from raids but as long as the wealth came from pastoralism in the main it had a relatively more equitable distribution. The relationship between the *rājanya* and the *viś* in the *Ṛg Veda* is not as distant as it was to become in the Later Vedic period. The *viś* brought its prestations in the form of *bali* to the *rājā* or the chief[57] and the relationship is a subordinate one since the *rājā* is generally chosen by other *rājā*s and the *viś* is essentially the provider of tribute. It is this which sustains the families of the *rājanya*s, together of course with the booty from raids.

Within the broad framework of this dual division there is a further expansion of both those who utilized this wealth and those who produced it. The redistribution expanded from the *rājanya*s to include the priests who legitimized them through the performance of rituals. This in turn required a larger amount of wealth and when booty could not provide enough then the *viś* had to increase its agricultural output. Sacrificial rituals drew off a large proportion of extra wealth and in this process the status of the *rājanya* was not only ensured but gradually raised through priestly legitimation and eventual association with deities. The redistribution at the sacrificial ritual became a fee for the priest. The *viś* was involved as the provider of items to be used as oblations and as the gifts bestowed by the *rājanya* on the *brāhmaṇa*. The *rājanya* of the *Ṛg Veda* was gradually replaced by the *kṣatriya* of the later Vedic period, the term deriving from *kṣatra* meaning power. The power was based on a greater control over the *jana* and its territory which is partly expressed by the territory being named after the *kṣatriya* lineage; to this was added the increasing investment of the ruling chief with attributes to deities by the *brāhmaṇa*s as also the demands made by the *kṣatriya* on the *viś*. The latter is succinctly summarized in the sentiment that the *yajamāna* ensures cattle to the *vaiśya* which leads to the subordination of the *vaiśya*, and the *kṣatriya* then requires that the *vaiśya* bring out what he has stored away.[58] That the demands were met was because the *kṣatriya* led the settlement in new lands and protected those already in existence. The advantage of an increasing emphasis on agriculture was that wealth could be augmented without resorting to many cattle raids and this was encouraged by the *kṣatriya*s asserting their superiority. Cattle raids did not cease but began to play a more marginal role in the access to wealth.

The distance between the *kṣatriya* and the *viś* brought about a certain tension and ultimately took the form of the *kṣatriya* claiming more rights of appropriation and the *viś* being reduced to subordination.[59] The tension between the two is indicated in remarks, such as the *kṣatra* eats the *viś*,[60] the simile being that of the deer eating grain, or the repeated reference to the *rājā* as the *viśāmattā*,[61] 'the eater of the *viś*' and the *kṣatriya* being more powerful than the *viś*. The *viś* sets apart a share for the *kṣatriya*,[62] the latter having a share in whatever belongs to the former; suggestive of the germinal idea of what later became a tax and where terms for taxes in later periods such as *bhāga* (a share) and *bali* (a voluntary tribute) can be traced back to these times. In all accounts the *viś* is made obedient to the *kṣatriya*. Despite the distancing between the *kṣatriya* and the *viś* there is no ritual and social exclusion as there was with the *śūdra*s who were not even allowed to enter the sacrificial enclosure (*śālā*) to which only *brāhmaṇa*s, *rājanya*s and *vaiśya*s had access.[63] But the *vaiśya* was treading a tight rope for those with wealth could associate with senior lineages whereas those who were impoverished were doubtless treated on par with the *śūdra*s. The difference begins to be evident in occasional statements; for on the whole the *viś* was still included in with the *brāhmaṇa*s and the *kṣatriya*s.

The necessity for the *viś* to increase their production to meet these new needs was met partly by new settlements and more land coming under cultivation and partly by incorporating the services of those who were outside the lineage system and could be employed. In this situation the *śūdra*s and *dāsa*s would be the ones available for such work. This ultimately brought about a householding economy in which the extended family constituted the household and employed labour in a series of service relationships. The overall lineage structure did not require a radical change since the flow of wealth still pertained essentially to the requirements of prestations which were consumed in sacrificial rituals and gift-giving. The word for wealth, *rayi*, has its origin in the root **rā*, to give.[64] The prestations made by the *viś* to the *kṣatriya*s and the labour provided by the *śūdra*s was a sufficient basis for stratification although the maintenance of stratification did not require the machinery of a state, the importance of lineage still being central and adequate for asserting authority. It is perhaps in this context that the *viś* and the *prajā* are said to go down before the *kṣatriya.*[65] *Prajā* is a new concept and presumably includes the non-kin groups as well as the non-lineage groups such as the *śūdras*. A further exclusion of the *viś* from their original status lies in the statement that the *viś* cannot eat the offerings at the sacrifice.[66]

A group of clans constituted a *jana* and the territory where they settled was referred to as the *janapada,* literally where the tribe places its feet. Since the economy of the *jana* included hunting and pastoralism, large forested areas adjoined the settlements and could even carry the name of the *jana,* as for example, the Kuruvana. Actual control over territory was limited to smaller areas of cultivated land. As long as the settlements were comparatively small (as is suggested by archaeological evidence), lineage authority was sufficient as a mechanism of control. This is in part indicated by the fact of the *janapada*s being named after the *kṣatriya* lineages which had established their control in the area. Thus apart from the Kuru and Pañcāla, mention is made of Kekaya, Madra, Matsya, among others.

The *kṣatriya* lineages claimed control over the territory of the *janapada* but the notion of a well-defined territory was uncertain at this time. The boundaries between *janapada*s tend to be topographical features such as forests, rivers and streams, and hills. Territory was seen as the clearly indentifiable settlements and the more liminal areas of forests and waste land between settlements. The term which in the post-Vedic period is used for territory, *rāṣṭra,* is mentioned at this time, but its meaning does not seem to be that of a well-defined area over which absolute control is claimed. *Rāṣṭra* from the root **rāj,* to shine, is used more in the sense of realm, sphere, or authority. Both in the *Ṛg Veda* and later Vedic texts it is the sustaining of the *rāṣṭra, rāṣṭrabhṛt*, which is crucial.[67] In the reference to the *rāṣṭrabhṛt* oblations the idea of nourishing is further endorsed by the oblations being of *ghī* (clarified butter).[68] This would hardly suggest territory in a literal sense. It is also stated that the *rājā*s are the *rāṣṭrabhṛt* and because of their association with the deities they are permitted by the gods to offer the *rāṣṭrabhṛt* oblations. Even more important is the statement that only he becomes a *rājā* who is allowed by other *rājās* to assume the title. This suggests a strengthening of the demarcation between lineages to which the *rājās* belonged and the lower status lineages which played little or no role in the choice of the *rājā*.

There is some controversy as to whether the *rājā* was elected by the clans or was the choice of a more select group. In one hymn of the *Ṛg Veda* it is clear that those who chose the *rājā* are distinct from the *viś*.[69] The nature of the bifurcation between the senior and junior lineages would support the former selecting the *rājā* if only to further curb the power of the *viś*. The demand of *bali* would have been weakened if the *viś* had the right to elect a *rājā*. The *Śatapatha Brāhmaṇa* asserts that ruling power and social distinction are attached to a single person and multiplicity is the characteristic of the clan.[70] Yet in another hymn of the *Ṛg Veda*, again of a late section of the collection, there is a reference to the *viś* choosing a *rājā*.[71] Possibly this was the earlier custom which was later discontinued when the *rājanyas* became more powerful.

The title *rājā* has frequently been translated as king rather than chief. In many cases the later meaning of the term is applied to these early sources. Yet even in later periods the connotation of *rājā* has varied from landholder to king. The office of *rājā* in the Vedic sources was primarily that of a leader in battle and the protector of the settlements. This is evident both from the functions of the office and the association of *rājā* with Indra. Gradually, the notion of the *rājā* as the nourisher and as the symbol of prosperity and fertility took precedence and the deities associated with the office were suitably enlarged. Reference to *rājās* as in an assembly[72] would suggest members of the *rājanya* lineages or an assembly of chiefs. Later references even when the role of the *rājā* had changed still occur, often in the plural, and suggest persons belonging to a superior social group rather than individual kings, for example, the *rājās* sharing the wealth among themselves and offering a sixteenth share at the *yajña* or the prayer for the prosperity of the *rājās*.[73] It was at these assemblies that one among the *rājās* was chosen to preside and to protect. The office was not hereditary to begin with and the choice and the consecration of the *rājā* would have occurred with every vacancy. It is curious that of the many close associates listed as the *ratnins*, there is no mention of any heir-apparent as would be expected in a system of kingship with hereditary succession. In the later Vedic period the consecration of the *rājā* became more elaborate with claims to *kṣatra* and consecration became an avenue to power. Claims to sovereignty and increasing demands of prestations were sought to be justified through consecration rituals. The absolute, secular authority associated with kingship appears to be absent in these sources and the income from prestations is poured into the rituals and given to those who perform the rituals. This also led to the greater interdependence of the *kṣatriya* and the *brāhmaṇa*, a relationship which is pointed to in the *Śatapatha Brāhmaṇa*. It is said that the *brāhmaṇa* was the god Mitra and therefore the conceiver and the *kṣatriya* was Varuṇa the doer. At first they were separate and thus undermined each other's power. Then Varuṇa called for unity with Mitra and conceded pre-eminence to him, after which both prospered.[74] Thus the *kṣatriya* must always have a *brāhmaṇa* (the reverse is too obvious and is left unsaid!). In the absence of both the hereditary principle and primogeniture, the consecratory rituals had special significance to legitimation. In the search for power, consecration became the hallmark of the *rājā* backed by senior lineages of the *kṣatriyas* and the cultivation of land was left to the householding families of the *viś*.

The inclusion of the householding system in the lineage structure was probably a marginal change to begin with. Gradually it became the thin end of the wedge which was partially responsible for erosion of the lineage system with the eventual arrival of the notion of private ownership of land and of the development of commerce as more than just exchange. The significance of non-kin labour in the householding economy can be seen at the point where in some areas lineage society underwent a change and the householding economy emerged but in a different framework incorporating a peasant economy and commerce.

Initially the householding system was probably common to both the *rājanyas* and the *viś*. Hence the *gṛhapati* or the head of the household could be from either and is mentioned with respect in the texts. In the late sections of the *Ṛg Veda* and in the *Atharvaveda* the *gṛhapati* appears to be of the higher lineage since the term is brought in when describing the nuptials of the daughter of Sūrya the sun god.[75] Elsewhere in the *Ṛg Veda* Agni is called the *gṛhapati* and the sacred household fire is the *gārhapatya.*[76] That the *gṛhapati*s are associated with wealth is indicated by a hymn in which Pūṣan is urged to make them generous in their gifts.[77] In the later Vedic literature there are references to *gṛhapati*s and *yajamāna*s which suggest *kṣatriya*s but do not preclude *vaiśya*s. The principal ritual role of the *gṛhapati* was that of the *yajamāna* (he who orders the sacrifice) and it is possible to trace the growing importance of the *gṛhapati* through the rituals. The *vaiśya gṛhapati* occurs in the later Vedic literature but more often in the context of the *grāmaṇī.* It is said that all *vaiśya*s wish to become *grāmaṇī*s, probably because *grāmaṇī*s were thought to be wealthy.[78] That the *grāmaṇī* was from the *viś* is clear from the ceremony when the *rājā* visits the home of the *grāmaṇī* and offers oblations to the Maruts and it is said that the Maruts are the *viś,* a connection which is frequently mentioned, and that the *grāmaṇī* is also the *viś.*[19] The *grāmaṇī* was among the lineage heads and important families of the *viś* who had both power and wealth. Their wealth did not come from prestations but was produced by their own efforts, its abundance dependent on an economy which may be termed householding.

With the increasing shift to agriculture and the decreasing interest in pastoralism the role of the *rājanya*s as chariot-riding chiefs carrying out cattle raids and bringing in booty was not as conducive to producing wealth as it had been earlier. When the *rājanya*s were converted into *kṣatriya*s and they acquired power and became the hub of the redistributive system, they came to depend more on the agricultural activities of the *viś* and the prestations which the *viś* could provide. Since numerically the *kṣatriya*s as chiefs would have been considerably smaller than the members of the *viś* such a dependence was not impossible. Gradually, therefore, the householding economy came to be associated with the lineages of the *viś* rather than with those of the *kṣatriya*s. In a more sedentary phase the household became the unit of agricultural production and doubtless began to claim permanent usage over the land which it worked and in which it invested its labour, a permanency which was acceded to by the community when it saw that it was necessary to agriculture and that it ensured a predictability in prestations. With the weakening of clan control over agriculture and probably more so in new areas of settlement the permanency of usage was likely ultimately to be transmuted into family ownership. This was probably aided by a greater concern on the part of the *kṣatriya* lineages with demanding prestations than on asserting ownership over clan lands. Prestations were stored in the *kṣatriya* household for consumption in rituals, for using in gift-giving and to furnish the basis for the generous hospitality expected of the *kṣatriya* household. However the storage seems to have been shortlived as the references to such 'treasuries' are few and far between.[80] The households of the *viś* also began to maintain a minimal storage in cases where the *gṛhapati*s of the *viś* are described as *yajamāna*s. The eventual emergence of the *gṛhapati* as a social category was in relationship to the *viś*. When *viś* is replaced by *vaiśya* it suggests an altered status, the clan element decreasing and the individual status becoming more apparent. At this stage the *śūdra* is also mentioned more frequently and a distinction made between the *vaiśya* and the *śūdra,* as in the famous passage which states that the *vaiśya* can be oppressed but the *śūdra* can be beaten or slain.[81] This raises the question of whether the actual cultivation was done by the *vaiśya*s or the *śūdra*s.

The cultivator in the technical sense of the word was the *kīnāśa* of the *Ṛg Veda*[82] and is referred to as the *karṣaka/kassaka, kṣetraka* and *śūdra* in post-Vedic literature. *Vaiśya* is not used for the cultivator although the *vaiśya* may have derived his wealth from agriculture. The explanation for this may lie in the need to differentiate between three categories of cultivators: the primitive cultivator, the cultivator in a system which has been called the householding economy and the cultivator in a peasant economy. Primitive cultivation is almost limited to swidden and subsistence agriculture and is outside our context. In the second category the household is the unit of production and consumption based on agriculture and livestock breeding. In borrowing the term 'householding' from Polanyi[83] an attempt is made here to use it with reference to a pre-state society. Although in the Vedic period householding does not emerge as an independent social formation in the terms in which Polanyi describes it, certain attributes of the form can however be usefully extracted from Polanyi's model and can perhaps elucidate Vedic data.

Polanyi describes the household as consisting of agnatically related men and their families claiming membership of a patrilineal lineage. The household as a unit is often made up of smaller houses functioning as an entity. Inheritance remains within the kin group and alienation of neither house nor land is permitted. The cult of the ancestor is the focus of the household and is maintained by hereditary priests. To this may be added other features: the household utilizes family labour as well as some specialists—herders and craftsmen for example—who are not kinsmen and are more in the nature of retainers except that they are not paid a wage but maintained by the household and paid in kind. Presumably such labour could be extended to cultivators helping in the fields. Slaves would be attached to the families of chiefs and they would be mainly domestic slaves. The household consumes much of what it produces but the excess is taken by those to whom it is politically subordinate in the form of prestations and gifts. This system is marked by the absence of two factors which distinguish it from a peasant economy. Firstly, the family exercises rights over the land which it cultivates and there are no tenants since cultivation is carried out by family labour and by those who are attached to the household in various occupational capacities. Secondly, there is no regular contractual payment of rent or tax to the political authority or to the state since it does not presuppose the existence of a state. The point at which taxes start to be paid by the household is also the point at which cultivation through membership of a landowning lineage weakens and individual ownership is asserted, even though lineage ties would still be respected and often seen to be effective.

The *viś* was by now characterized by the householding system, with the *gṛhapati* as the patriarchal head, commanding both family labour and that of *śūdra*s and *dāsa*s. Neither of the latter were helots and could well have been impoverished members of the *dāsa-varṇa,* their subordination arising as much from their being aliens outside the lineages as from their impoverishment. It is difficult to describe the *śūdra*s or the *dāsa*s as helots in the strict sense as there were clans of each which co-existed with the *ārya*s and some of the chiefs of these clans are described as wealthy or are spoken of with respect in the earlier texts. In time, however, the terms *śūdra* and *dāsa* came to be used for those performing labour services. The interchangeability of *ārya* and *dāsa* status in the post-Vedic period and the fact that an *ārya* could become a *dāsa* for a temporary period precludes a system of helotage.

The mention of *bali, bhāga,* and *śūlka* has been interpreted as reference to taxes of various kinds. But none of these were collected at a specified time and regularly, nor were they of a precisely defined amount and there is no mention of specific occupational groups from whom they were collected or of designated persons who made the collection. All these conditions were fulfilled in the post-Vedic period when taxes were collected and these terms were used as terms for taxes. In Vedic literature their connotation would appear to differ. The *balihṛt* is clearly the tribute paid by a conquered tribe in one instance.[84] More frequently *bali* is a generalized offering made by the *viś* and may better be translated as tribute or a prestation rather than tax.[85] If there was any seasonality associated with the *bali* then it related to the performance of rituals or occasions of consecration. It may in origin have been the tribute of a defeated tribe but came to be extended to offerings brought by subordinate groups to those in authority. Terms such as *balihṛt* and *balikṛt*[86] can be rendered as the bearers and providers of tribute rather than as tax-paying groups, as in the case of the reference to the *vaiśya* as the *balikṛt.* This is further clarified by the request to the gods to distribute the wealth thus collected.[87] *Bali* therefore remained a prestation. *Bhāga,* in the sense of share relates to the distribution of spoils after a raid or the division of prestations on ritual occasions. Its origins may be traced to the offering of the first fruits as a token to the sanctity of the chief, an idea which is known to other early societies.[88] It is connected with *bhāgadugha* which because of the word *dugha* (milking) can be interpreted as the collector of the share or in the association of *bhagādugha* with Pūṣan, the distributor.[89] The share of the chief is not stipulated and this is in contrast to the later period when it is said that the king is to receive one-sixth of the share as a wage for protecting the people,[90] and still later when in the post-Mauryan period the designation *ṣaḍbhāgin* (the receiver of one-sixth share) comes to be used for the king.[91] The term *śūlka* in the *Ṛg Veda* does not mean a tax but is used in the sense of a measure of value and in the *Atharvaveda* the context is generally that of the weak paying a price to the strong.[92] In the *Dharmaśāstras* of the post-Vedic period and in Pāṇini there is the meaning of a tax but also the meaning of a nuptial gift or dower, suggesting that it might have been used for bride-price or dowry.[93] This meaning could well have gone back to the Vedic period when such gifts were a part of marriage alliances. The words *bali, bhāga,* and *śūlka* do change their meaning from tribute, distribution, and price (in the sense of value) in the *Ṛg Veda* to forms of taxes and dues in the later *Dharmaśāstra* literature. Whether they meant the former or the latter in the intermediate period of the later Vedic texts would depend largely on the context of their occurrence and the context suggests the greater likelihood of the former meaning. The change of meaning carried with it a major change in the relations between the chief and the clan. From voluntary giving with a pattern of mutual honouring it changed to compulsory giving with a pattern of unequal reciprocity. As long as status was based on genealogy the inequality was symbolic, when it was based on land it became substantial.[94]

The *vaiśya* as the *gṛhapati* was the source of wealth for the *kṣatriya* and the *brāhmaṇa* through prestations for the *kṣatriya,* and through *dakṣinā* as well as the items consumed in the course of the sacrificial rituals, for *brāhmaṇas*;[95] hence the statement that *vaiśya*s can be oppressed, presumably to extract further wealth.[96] The *vaiśya* was beholden to the *kṣatriya* for protection as well as the provision of lands to settle and cultivate. The prestations necessary for the sacrificial ritual precluded a completely self-sufficient village economy and established links across lineage segments and consequently a circuit of villages as well. With the disintegration of clan holdings, the *gṛhapati* who had earlier cultivated lands held jointly gradually came to exercise ownership, though perhaps still as the head of the family, over land cultivated by the family, since the *Dharmasūtra*s in the subsequent period invest him with the right to bequeath property to his eldest son or divide it among his sons.[97] The transition from clan ownership to family holdings was probably accelerated when clan settlements became more scattered in new clearings together with the establishment of the economic viability of the household as a unit. In such a situation voluntary prestations were perhaps less forthcoming and the need for protection in new areas was paid for by a regular contribution which was to assume the character of a tax in the post-Vedic period. This became feasible when, with the intensification of plough agriculture, such an economic surplus was possible. Ultimately, in the post-Vedic period the decline of the householding economy would lead to the rise of peasant tenures in which the *śūdra*s were to emerge as the major peasant group. This change is reflected in the statement in a *Gṛhya-sūtra* that the *gṛhapati* should have his fields ploughed, suggesting thereby not only the working of the land by another[98] but possibly also the individual ownership of land since the *gṛhapati* is not described as a member of a lineage.

The changing relationships wrought by agriculture and the new settlements in the western Ganga valley would also have required some readjustments within the *viś*. Those who were able to establish a household and farm would have aspired to *gṛhapati* status and constituted a part of what came to be the *vaiśya varṇa*. Others reduced to the condition of labourers and artisans would have moved increasingly to the edges of society to finally become part of the larger population of *śūdra*s. At a still further remove, *dāsa* came more frequently to mean a slave. Most references suggest domestic slavery as in the case of the hundreds and thousands of slaves employed in the household of Yudhiṣṭhira and who are listed as part of his wealth staked in the game of dice.[99] The figures are almost certainly exaggerated, for the functions which they performed would not have required such excessively large numbers.

These developments resulted in a series of contrasting status stratifications which were sought to be arranged into a system through the scheme of *varṇa*. The earlier texts speak of an *ārya-varṇa* and a *dāsa-varṇa*, suggesting a dual, division.[100] The words are traced to *ārya* and *dāha* in Iranian sources and *ārya* connotes a man of wealth and possessions,[101] a frequent association in Vedic sources too. A contemporary lexicon explains it as an owner or master[102] and Pāṇini glosses it with the statement, *aryaḥ svāmi vaiśyayoḥ,*[103] the wealth of the *vaiśya*s being an indication. The *dāha* of the early Iranian becomes *dāsa* in Vedic texts and means 'a male, man, a hero', in much the same sense as *manuṣa*. This is often the meaning of the names taken by tribal groups.[104] Tacitus refers to the Arios and the Dahas settled along the Indus river.[105] (That *ārya* was a term of respect is clear from Buddhist sources where *bhikkhus* are often addressed as *ārya* and where the *ārya* and the *dāsa* are juxtaposed to mean master and slave, especially with reference to lands beyond the Indus.)[106] The dichotomy is expressed in Vedic sources by regarding the *dāsa-varṇa* as of a different symbolic colour. In the *Ṛg Veda* they are associated with wealth, walled settlements, and with darkness or blackness.[107] But they were apparently not a helot group or slaves since their wealthier members are mentioned by name. These were evidently people of some substance and *dāsa* chiefs such as Balbūtha and Tarukṣa are eulogized by *brāhmaṇa*s for their munificence or else, as Śambara, are feared, for their strength.[108] Some *dāsa* chiefs are so powerful that Indra is said to have battled against them.[109] The *viś* of the *dāsa* are referred to in the *Ṛg Veda,*[110] indicating that they were distinct and separate. Possibly the *dāsa*s of the *Ṛg Veda* were agricultural communities of the Late Harappan or post-Harappan cultures of the area, perhaps even of the agricultural niches scattered in the region. That the word eventually came to mean 'slave' may initially have had more to do with the hostility towards them than with their actual subordination. The *Dasyu*[111] are noted for their variant religious beliefs and customs which the *ārya*s saw as the negation of their own and which appear to have been the chief distinguishing characteristic. The assimilation of these groups was facilitated by their being given subordinate status. Reference to *ārya-kṛita* in later texts indicate a status to which a person can be restored after having been a *dāsa*.[112] *Varṇa* was to become a system of putting together the structure of the society and the colour symbolism was retained. The four *varṇa*s were later associated with the colours white, yellow, red, and black.[113] In the dual division of *ārya* and *dāsa,* the *ārya* was distinguished by wealth and status. The *ārya*s would be those who either belonged to the senior or to the cadet lineages (*rājanya*s and the *viś*) as well as those who were included in the circuit of prestations and redistribution, that is, the *brāhmaṇa*s. The *dāsa*s were excluded from this circuit even when they were wealthy enough to bestow gifts on the *brāhmaṇa*s. With the sharpening of stratification and the beginnings of professional specialization, the constituents of the *ārya*s were more clearly demarcated into *brāhmaṇa, kṣatriya,* and *vaiśya,* with the *śūdra*s incorporating an amorphous group of excluded clans and low-status professions. The former described as *dvija* or twice born (the second birth being initiation) in later texts deepens the demarcation and underlines the connection between initiation and lineage customs.

Another contrast of a more broadly cultural kind but going back to Iranian sources was that between the *deva*s and the *asura*s. Among the Iranians the *deva*s were hostile and the *ahura/asura* god-like. In Vedic sources both are described as the progeny of Prajāpati[114] and the *asura*s in some cases are treated with respect but eventually come to represent evil, hostile forces. The *asura*s though feared are depicted as the more sophisticated of the two. They lived in permanent habitations whereas the *deva*s moved about in carts.[115] They were acquainted with the right seasons for agricultural activities[116] and associated with wheel-thrown pottery.[117] The *asura* form of marriage involved a bride-price[118] and they performed regular burial rites.[119] The magical power of the *asuras,* perhaps a subtle concession to their superiority, which plays a role in the narrative of the *Mahābhārata,* is mentioned in the *Ṛg Veda* in association with the bringing of rain.[120] The ambiguity towards the *asura*s revolving around common origins, power, and hostility, remains a constant feature in Vedic literature.[121]

To this list may be added a further social duality, recorded only in later Vedic literature. This essentially linguistic distinction to begin with, between the *ārya* and the *mlecchha,* separating the speakers of Indo-Aryan from others, takes on a social connotation as well, with *mleccha* meaning a barbarian or one outside the pale and ritually impure.[122] The recognition of basic differences in these dualities of *deva-asura* and *ārya-mleccha* is an indication of the recognition of heterogeneity and the need to juxtapose the differences within a working system.

The integration of groups through particular forms of kinship was a parallel process and is more often referred to in the concept of the *gotra,* literally meaning a stockade for cows, which was used to identify descent groups among the high status *varṇa*s. Initially it appears in more frequent association with the *brāhmaṇa*s and was to remain essential to *brāhmaṇa* identity. Later sources mention certain *kṣatriya*s (such as the Andhaka-Vṛṣṇi, Śakyas, and Licchavis) using *gotra* identities. But among them it was more a means of differentiating between families within the clan than for wider social identification. The *gotra* was an exogamous clan where exogamy was emphasized in the prohibition on marrying *sagotra*s, and marrying those related up to seven generations on the father's side and five on the mother's. The latter would preclude cross-cousin marriage, so a special exception had to be made in case of *brāhmaṇa*s from the south.[124] The exogamous basis of the *gotra* system doubtless facilitated the induction of outsiders of high or appropriate status; the insistence on marrying out meant the necessity of bestowing equal status on new groups and inducting such groups into the *varṇa.* This is reflected in the increase in the number of Brahmanical *gotra*s from seven to eighteen and forty-nine, and many more by the end of the first millennium AD. Doubtless the increase was partly due to segmentation among the main *gotra*s, although this generally took the form of a new *gaṇa* or *pravara,* a new sub-group. More likely this was also the result of co-option of new groups. This might account in part for *brāhmaṇas* of non-*brāhmaṇa* ancestry. The counterpart to exogamy was that inheritence of property was open only to members of the same *gotra.*

For the *kṣatriyas* to adopt the *gotra* system was something of an anomaly since they were identified by lineage or *vaṃśa,* preferred endogamy and are known to have made cross-cousin marriages as well as to have married into collateral lineages. There is a greater frequency of variation in the actual types of marriages among *kṣatriyas*. The classic example would be the implications of marriage alliances in the three generations of Pāṇḍavas from Pāṇḍu to his sons and grandsons who subscribe to endogamy, fraternal polyandry, and cross-cousin marriage, but all among lineages claiming *kṣatriya* status. Within the *vaṃśa* there was a differentiation between the senior lineages and the rest as is interestingly demonstrated by the story of Yayāti and the interchange of status between his eldest and youngest sons. Yadu and Pūru;[125] the inheritance having gone to the youngest, it became necessary to justify this action. Endogamy among the *kṣatriya vaṃśa*s was doubtless encouraged because land rights were vested in kinship links and birth. In the initial transition to agriculture, genealogical links would have acted as a means of narrowing access to status and resources; genealogies of increasing depth in later sources would perhaps point to wider mobilization, particularly among the Candravaṃśa lineages which tend to follow a segmentary pattern. There is evidence of a fairly widespread movement of peoples not only from the watershed to the Ganga valley, but also into the Vindhyan region. The assimilation of local populations must certainly have been part of the reason for the frequency of breaking away or a fissioning off from the main lineage, although migrations were also a form of easing tension and establishing new settlements.

The nuclear unit in such a society was the *kula,* the family, and a group of such families made up the *grāma* or village. *Grāma* by extension therefore also referred to a community. In some instances it conveyed the meaning of a body of men.[126] It was therefore a larger unit than the *kula* but smaller than the *viś*. The term *grāmaṇī* used for a village headman in many sources was also at this stage the chief of an aggregate of families or of a community settled in the same place. The larger unit *viś* or clan is recorded even among the *dāsa.* It counted in turn towards the identity of the tribe or *jana.* The word *jana* carries the notion of people as well as growth and fecundity.[127] A characteristic phrase of this literature is *pañca-janāḥ,* the precise meaning of which remains elusive.[128] It has been suggested that it may refer to five specific tribes whose eponymous ancestors are the founders of the clans, namely Yadu, Turvaśa, Druhyu, Anu, and Pūru, or that it may symbolize the totality of the people, the image deriving from the five fingers of the hand.[129] The notion of the *pañca-janāḥ* seems to have been basic to the pattern of one of the two major *kṣatriya* lineages, that of the Aila or Candravaṃśa as given in the *Purāṇa*s and the *Mahābhārata.*[130] The main lineages are described as descended from the five sons of Yayāti of which the Paurava and the Yādava are the most important and the descent lines close with the victory of the five sons of Pāṇḍu at the Kurukṣetra battle. At crucial points of geographical diffusion, the genealogies list a pattern of five brothers such as the reference to the five sons of Uparicara establishing themselves along the southern bank of the Yamuna as far as Magadha[131] or the five sons of Bali establishing themselves in eastern India.[132] At one level the concept of the *pañca-janāḥ,* could have referred to all the clans, but at another level it carried a symbolism which remains obscure.[133] If it is to be interpreted as the symbol of the totality then its derivation would probably be from the notion of the four on all sides and the one in the centre, thus reflecting the idea of the four quarters as well.

The *kula, viś,* and *jana* was a spatial distribution moving in widening circles from the nucleus to the rim. A vertical hierarchy was also evident in the *jana* with the distinction between the *rājanya* and the *viś,* where the *rājanya* was increasingly identified with the senior lineages aspiring to power and the *viś* represented the lesser lineages. Among the *rājanya* were those who had been consecrated as chiefs.[134] The *rājanya*s had access to power, *kṣatra,* and came to be called *kṣatriya*s, and the gradual displacement of the term *rājanya* by *kṣatriya* would indicate the emergence of a new focus of power among the ruling clans. The etymology of *rājā* remains uncertain and the later view that it derived from the verb 'to please' is unacceptable. The roots **raj, *rañj, *riñj,* suggest the connotation of the verb 'to glow' or 'to shine'. This could be extended to mean the one who shines and is resplendent and therefore the chief.[135] It has also been suggested that the Indo-European root **reĝ* for *rex* in Latin indicates the one who leads, directs, follows what is right, or proceeds in a line,[136] a meaning which would suit the idea of a head of a lineage. The increasing emphasis on the special status of the *rājanya/kṣatriya* had its counter-weight in the declining status of the lineages of the *viś*. The *viś* perhaps consoled themselves through a control of the householding economy in which they continued to have access to wealth as the *gṛhapatis*. Nevertheless the wealth of the *rājanya* was considerably greater since he was the recipient of prestations and doubtless also took a substantial share of the booty. Although much of this wealth went into the *yajña*s some of it would certainly have been temporarily stored since the *rājanya* was expected to use it to make gifts on frequent occasions.

The emergence of the *kṣatriya* was linked to clan rights over land as well as to the sanction given to the new status by the *brāhmaṇa*. In the definition of the *ārya*, three groups are mentioned, the *brāhmaṇa, kṣatriya,* and *viś*. Whether or not one subscribes to the theory of the tripartite function in viewing the relationship between the three,[137] or to the definition of these three which such a function assumes, it is clear that an attempt is made to link them. But gradually, this link is broken when the *vaiśya* is more often included with the *śūdra* and the two are regarded as of lower status than the *brāhmaṇa* and the *kṣatriya*. Kinship links between the *brāhmaṇa* and the *kṣatriya* are occasionally conceded but the formal systems remain quite distinct. The ranking order between *brāhmaṇa* and *kṣatriya* is ambivalent to begin with where the former is dependent on the latter for *dāna* and *dakṣinā* and the latter requires that his power be legitimized by the former.[138] In any case the two are superior to the rest of the community, a superiority which is clearly expressed in the formula that the *vaiśya* and the *śūdra* should be enclosed by the *brāhmaṇa* and the *kṣatriya* at the sacrifice in order to make the former submissive.[139] Even in burning wealth, so characteristic of the *yajña* ritual, the decision to do so is controlled by those who had access to the maximum wealth—the *kṣatriya* and the *brāhmaṇa*. The redistribution of wealth was therefore curtailed by the requirement of reciprocity between the *kṣatriya* and the *brāhmaṇa* where the reciprocal relationship enhanced the status of each. The *kṣatriya* provided the *brāhmaṇa* with what was essentially a sacrificial fee disguised as it may have been in ritual gift-giving. The *brāhmaṇa* not only bestowed legitimation on the *kṣatriya* but also gave him access to special skills and knowledge intermeshed with the ritual which inevitably augmented the power of the *kṣatriya.*

In addition to the first three the other distinctive unit included in the overall definition of a caste society was the *śūdra,* associated with servility in the earlier texts. The *śūdra*s were described in the later *Dharmasūtra*s as including *sankīrna* or mixed *jāti*s. Each *jāti* was born out of a hypergamous (*anuloma*) or a hypogamous (*pratiloma*) marriage from among the three *dvija* or upper castes, *brāhmaṇa, kṣatriya,* and *vaiśya* or their progeny. The number of *jāti*s could theoretically increase on each new intercaste marriage but in effect the increase occured whenever there were major changes in which new social groups and professions were established. The *śūdra* as a *varṇa* was clearly a category added onto the original structure at a time when artisans and cultivators had to be accommodated and when alien groups were assimilated into caste society and had to be assigned varying statuses. That the concept of the *sankīrna-jāti* was a later attempt at explaining a *de facto* situation is evident from the divergence in the texts regarding the particular combinations of castes producing *śūdra* offspring.[140] The elimination of kin-body in the case of *śūdra*s, by assigning them only the status of their parents, was a means of excluding them by denying them a lineage connection. In a strongly lineage-oriented society this would in itself place them outside the social pale. The occasional substitution of *śūdra* and *dāsa* would suggest that many of the groups included in the *śūdra* category may have earlier been *dāsa*s prior to the technical meaning of the word as slave. Etymologically *śūdra* could have been derived from *kṣudra* meaning small. Both these are known to have been the names of particular peoples at some stage. Latin sources mention the Oxydrakoi and the Sudracae and Sodroi as tribes of northwest India.[141] The Kṣudraka are linked with the powerful Mālava (the Malli/Malloi of the Greeks) almost as a compound to mean the small and the big. Mention is also made of the *gaṇas* of the śūdras and the Abhiras dwelling on the Sarasvatī [142] The sense of smallness was worked into that of lowliness, indicated in a statement that the *śūdra* is the servant of another, he can be made to work at the will of his master and even be beaten,[143] a sentiment endorsed in the later *Dharmaśāstra*s as well. The denial of a lineage and the insistence on mixed caste origins, if not the word *śūdra* itself, would also point to the members of this group coming from a floating population of those who had fallen out of lineage ties and were available to serve whomever could provide them with a livelihood. As such the labour of the *śūdra* was to become an important factor in eventually augmenting the wealth of those whom they served.

Distance between the *dvija* and the *śūdra* was also maintained through the notion of pollution. This was to influence yet another category that, designated by the adjective *vrātya* or degraded, applied to degradation from the three upper castes, resulting from the non-observance of the required rituals. Thus *vrātya-kṣatriya*s was to become a useful category in which to place those who were politically powerful but were obviously not *kṣatriya*s in the true sense. The ultimate in distance and separation was of course the untouchable who is referred to in the later period. Purity and pollution, central to the question of ritual status was expressed in terms of bodily contact, through ceremonies relating to rites of passage; through touch, the one among the five senses which was crucial in this matter; through food taboos and through sex by the regulation of marriage relations.

The theoretical construct of caste society was not the simple unfolding of a class society, nor the mechanical measurement of ritual status. It was an attempt at interlocking a series of social units based on diverse rules of functioning but all in the context of a lineage system. At least three formal structures were to evolve from this genesis: the exogamous *brāhmaṇa gotra*s, the preference for endogamy of the *kṣatriya*s and the *śūdra jāti*s identified by parental status in which lineage is negligible. The differentiation therefore includes the widest possible lineage system, the out-going *gotra,* as well as the narrowest social unit, the *śūdra jāti.* In its initial phase the notion of *varṇa* attempted to construct a complete social framework using differentiated lineage systems demarcated by distinctive kinship forms. Variations in marriage rules are sometimes indications of status where higher-status groups prefer exogamy and lower-status groups endogamy. Descent however lies at the heart of status.[144] At the theoretical level this would be one condition for working out a hierarchy, although the emphasis lies in each unit constituting its own method of comprehending lineage. Added to this was the notion of ritual status which was made explicit in the idea of purity and pollution where the hierarchy goes from the purest to the most polluting, and where, in an exchange of services, those not actively involved in production would claim higher status on the basis of intangible authority seeking justification from religious sanction through the performance of rituals. Yet implicit in this hierarchy is the attempt to define and limit the access of each group to economic resources by the gradually increasing insistence on occupational functions, accompanied by the channelizing and redistribution of wealth being limited to the castes claiming ownership of clan resources and higher ritual status. That the attempt was not entirely successful, would be suggested by economic stratification also taking place within each of these vertical *varṇa* groups. There are impoverished *brāhmaṇa*s[145] and there are wealthy *śūdras*.[146] The inequality implicit in the process of an exchange of services was to the advantage of those who were dominant, who had access to resources and used these to claim higher status. In terms of economic status the wealthier *brāhmaṇa*, the *rājanya*s and the *gṛhapati*s among the *viś* would constitute the upper level, their wealth being comparable. The initial attempt therefore, in the *varṇa* scheme, was not to reflect a class system but a lineage system and seek to integrate and reflect the reality of a lineage system. When eventually the lineage system declined, the structure of caste society also underwent a change, even though it carried with it elements of the lineage system.

With ritual status as a criterion of hierarchy, it was relatively easier to induct groups into higher *varṇa*s. *Brāhmaṇa*s of *kṣatriya* origin are met with in the earlier sections of many genealogies and may even reflect common origins in some cases. What are equally evident are *brāhmaṇa*s of non-Aryan origin. Agastya and Vasiṣṭha are said to have been born from jars.[147] Kavaṣa Ailūśa, the Ṛg Vedic seer appears to have been a *dāsiputrah* as was the well-known Kakṣīvant.[148] These may have been *dāsa* families of some standing who could have been profitably inducted into the *brāhmaṇa varṇa.* The associations of the early *brāhmaṇa gotras* are barely in conformity with orthodox tradition considering that the Bhṛgus were priests to the *daitya* kings,[149] and Pulastya was the ancestor of the *rākṣasas.*[150] Induction would also have been easier through exogamy. In later periods it was maintained that the *gotra* system was prevalent only among *brāhmaṇas*,[151] although it is conceded that *kṣatriyas* could take the *gotra* of their *purohitas.*[152] In the case of the *kṣatriyas*, recruitment to the *varṇa* meant latching onto one of the two major genealogies, Sūryavaṃśa or Candravaṃśa, which was done with considerable facility in the first millennium AD, when low status chiefs acquired power and aspired to the best lineage links.[153] Within the *varṇa* however, it often took economic reality to guarantee tangible status.

At the core of the *jana* the substantial division was the bifurcation of the *kṣatriya* and the *viś.* In the initial structure of the *varṇa* system, both the *brāhmaṇa* and the *śūdra* could have been, as it were, addenda. As priests attached to the clans, the ancestry of the *brāhmaṇas* went back to the shamans, mantics, and seers of earlier times (the *vipras* and the *ṛṣis*), to which were added the reciters of hymns and the living manuals on rituals. The latter may have required co-option of priests from the indigenous cultures since the continuance of ancient rituals is strongly endorsed. The more priestly function of the *brāhmaṇa* comes into its own in the rituals of the Later Vedic texts. His special status is underlined by his privilege of being allowed to consume the remains of the sacrifice and this included the flesh of the sacrificed animal.[154] In the analysis of rituals, elements of earlier cultures may be seen to have survived.[155] It has been argued that the notion of purity and pollution may have been a survival of Harappan times. If Harappan society was ruled by an aristocracy claiming power through ritual and religion then it would be tempting to suggest that the *brāhmaṇa–śūdra* dichotomy went back to Harappan times, constituting the equivalent of an *ārya* and *dāsa varṇa* and into which the *jana* with its dual division of *kṣatriya* and *viś* intruded, and had to be accommodated. This is not to suggest that there was a continuity from Harappan times, but that some elements of an earlier culture can be recognized as part of the new lineage system.

The *varṇa* framework therefore was visualized as a structure for the integration of varying sub-systems rather than merely a reflection of the socio-economic hierarchy. This would account for the seeming changelessness of the rules of social functioning, although within each sub-system change was clearly registered. That the *varṇa* system was a consciously worked out structure by the mid-first millennium BC. is apparent from the late hymn added onto the *Ṛg Veda,* the *puruṣasūkta,*[156] in which the origin of the four *varṇa*s from the body of Prajāpati is described: the symbolism being that of separate limbs performing different functions but co-ordinated in the unit of the body and listed in hierarchical order. The tying in of this description to a ritual event was perhaps an implicit emphasis on *varṇa* relating increasingly to ritual status.

Not only was the stratification rationalized in the concept of *varṇa,* but the function of each group was more clearly defined. The *brāhmaṇa* was now less of the seer and more of the expert on ritual. The more elaborate rituals such as the consecration sacrifices for the *rājā*s required an array of trained professional priests. The more simple *gṛhya* (domestic) rituals described in the *Gṛhya-sūtras,* mainly concerned with rites of passage, required a single *brāhmaṇa* in most cases. The increasing importance of both categories of rituals emphasized not only the political role of the *brāhmaṇa* as a source of legitimization for chiefs but also as the authority and sanction of cultural identity in relation to the *gṛhapatis,* as also for the assimilation of new groups. The emphasis on *vāc* and *mantra,* the correct recitation of the right formula required meticulous training and memorizing with a comprehension of the language of the texts, which in turn became, a criterion of *āryahood* together with the observance of *varṇa* rules. The Kuru-Pañcāla region was noted for the excellence of the language and the relative purity of the rituals, suggesting that it was in this area and this period that the norms were decided upon—a time and a place which had already seen a considerable assimilation of varying groups of people and observances. Many of the people further away such as those in the *janapadas* of the Punjab and the middle Ganga valley are castigated for having discarded the rituals,[157] a rebuke which had more to do with other changes in these areas.

The importance of political authority is highlighted in the substitution of *rājanya* by *kṣatriya*. The context of the *rājanya* was essentially status within the lineage. *Kṣatra* implied temporal authority and power which was based less on being a successful leader in battle and more on the tangible power of laying claim to sovereignty over territory, demanding prestations and also symbolizing ownership over clan lands. The status of the chief had been hedged around by his relationship to various clan-gatherings. Among these were the *gaṇa, vidatha, sabhā, samiti,* and *pariṣad,* some of which, as nomenclatures at least, survived into later periods although their functions changed.

The *gaṇa* is identified by the name of a common ancestor and is also reflected in the *gotra* system in which sub-groups are referred to by *gaṇas*. That it was at some stage a clan would seem evident from terms such as *gaṇapati, gaṇeṣa,* and *gaṇasya rājā,* which were synonyms for *rājā*.[158] It may have been a special body of selected members who held equal status and formed a peer group, as is suggested by the *kṣatriya gaṇas* of later sources, and by the compound of *gaṇa-saṅghas* for chiefdoms.[159] It may have been a cattle raiding peer group in origin since the leader is associated with cattle raids.[160]

The *vidatha* as its name suggests was probably a ritual occasion on which the distribution and sharing of wealth took place, among other things.[161] Booty being a major source of wealth, the *vidatha* would also be linked with cattle raids and heroic exploits.[162] The distribution doubtless had to carry the sanction of *brāhmaṇas* as well as their inclusion as recipients, hence their presence at these gatherings.[163] Sāyana's gloss that the *vidatha* be equated with the *yajña*[164] would be expected in a system where redistribution or exchange of wealth was a ritual occasion. This in turn would explain the need for Indra-Mitra-Varuna being the presiding deities of the *vidatha*.[165] That the *vidatha* declines in the later Vedic period would reinforce its original function as the ritual occasion for the redistribution of wealth for, when other forms of economic redistribution became prevalent, the *vidatha* would have become redundant. Although it has been argued that the *vidatha* was a folk assembly, a view which has been strongly opposed,[166] it was nevertheless of some consequence to Ṛg Vedic society judging by the frequency of reference to it. If it was an occasion for the distribution of wealth, then even its being a kin gathering rather than a folk assembly would be in keeping with such a function.

Indo-European cognates for *sabhā* mean the assembly of the kinsfolk which would make its membership exclusive.[167] In later periods the *sabhā* becomes an advisory body assisting the king. The association of the *sabhā* with gambling may have had antecedents in the division of grazing lands and arable lands by lot.[168] This would of course be a different function from sharing booty. This is indirectly supported at the symbolic level in the Sabhā Parvan of the *Mahābhārata*. The Pāṇḍavas lose their wealth and power in a game of dice which is held in the *sabhā* which was an assembly of kinsmen who not only witness the throw of dice but also discuss the question raised by Draupadī regarding the legal validity of Yudhiṣṭhira placing her as a stake when he himself had lost his freedom.

Dicing is not merely indicative of a weakness for gambling. The names used for the dice and the throws are heavily imbued with symbolic meaning. Dicing is not only associated with the *sabhā*, the most respected of the assemblies, but the one who throws the dice is on occasion referred to as the *sabhā-sthānu*,[169] literally, the pillar of the assembly hall. This gives dicing far greater importance than mere entertainment. Its significance may have derived from a time when the throw of dice determined the division of wealth. This can only be inferred from the frequent association of dicing with wealth and the notional significance of dicing with rituals conferring and legitimizing power. The inclusion of a simulated game of dice as part of the ritual of the *agnyādheya* and *rājasūya* sacrifices[170] would again point to its symbolic importance. Possibly lots were also transferred from one person to another by a throw of dice, an echo of which can be heard in the events of the Sabhā Parvan. Thus the association of wealth and loss of wealth with gambling need not be taken in a literal sense but may refer to a more complex activity involving an exchange of wealth conditioned by a throw of dice. The stake was referred to as *dhana,*[171] generally meaning wealth and rarely, booty. The earlier texts refer to *vibhīdaka* nuts used as dice and since these cannot carry numbers, a computation must have been essential to gambling.[172] Later there are references to throws—Kṛta, Tretā, Dvāpara, and Abhibhū or Kali—which suggest numbered surfaces of dice reading four, three, two, and one. These terms are ultimately transferred to the division of the *mahāyuga* into four *yugas* or periods of cosmic time, thus linking the throw of dice with time and fate. The association of a share or distribution of wealth with the notion of fate is also evident in the use of terms such as *bhāga* and *bhāgya.*

The terms *sabhā* and *samiti* occur more frequently in the late books of the *Ṛg Veda* and in the later Vedic literature. In the *Atharvaveda* they often occur together.[173] There is also an association of the *rājā*s (in the plural) with these assemblies suggesting that they were the gathering points of the senior lineages, those of the *rājanya*s. The infrequency of the presence of the *viś* in these assemblies may reflect its declining status. The presence of the *rājās* did not preclude the selection of one among them as the presiding *rājā.*[174] The *samiti* appears to have been a more open assembly than the *sabhā. The pariṣad* is mentioned even less frequently and appears to have had an even smaller membership.[175] If its later function is any clue to its origins then it may have been a body of specialized advisers, although such a body may not have been particularly relevant to the political needs of the time.

To the extent that some were plenary assemblies, and some limited to the *rājanya*s, they were essentially occasions for reiterating hierarchy and order; consultation was more a ritual function than an administrative necessity as it was to become in later periods. Over time, some of these gatherings declined in importance whilst others increased and even changed their function. To maintain that in the Vedic period different tribes used different forms of assembly is not indicated by the evidence as the gatherings are not differentiated in accordance with tribes.[176] What is certainly feasible is that some types of assembly were more central to the functioning of certain tribes than others.

Sharing of wealth was an intrinsic part of raids providing booty. Cattle-herding and agriculture provided the items required for the performance of rituals. The redistribution and consumption of this wealth was channelled through separate acitivities. Booty from raids was shared by general consent in the assemblies where the larger shares presumably went to the chief who led the raid as well as to the priest who had invoked the deities and who would be doubly blessed if he was also to perform the role of the bard eulogizing the chief, as he often did in the *dāna-stuti* hymns of the *Ṛg Veda.* This would serve to reinforce the status of the *kṣatriya* and the *brāhmaṇa* and further demarcate them from the lesser lineage of the *viś*. The wider distribution among other members of the *viś* who had participated in the raid was doubtless conducted in the assembly so that it would not be an arbitrary division. A decline in inter-tribal raids would lead to a corresponding decline in those assemblies where the wealth from such raids was allocated to the clan of those who were successful in the raid. The wealth listed in the *dāna-stuti* hymns, primarily cattle, horses, chariots, gold, and slave girls were all items which could have been picked up in a raid. Wealth obtained from herding and agriculture consisted of objects offered as prestations at the ritual of sacrifice and therefore included the best animals of the herd, milk, *ghī,* grain, cakes, and the like. The offering of these items had to be induced from the *viś* and the ritual occasion provided the incentive to part with wealth. The re-distributive aspect lay not only in the gifts made to the priests but also in the sacrificing of the animals and the burning up of the other items as part of the prayer for the well-being of the *yajamāna* and the *viś*. The destruction of wealth in this fashion was a method of underlining the status of the *yajamāna* (either a chief or a *gṛhapati*) but at the same time, a subtle means of preventing the *yajamāna* from amassing excessive wealth.

The specific and precise functions of each of the assemblies remains unclear. With a changing social system the interlocking of functions and overlapping between them also changed and varied. The curb on the concentration of power in the hands of the *rājā* was not a legal formality, but was born out of a society in which power was not completely restricted to a few. With the narrowing of kinship rights on land and an increase in prestation requirements, the more exclusive gatherings of kinsmen such as the *sabhā* became channels for the concentration of power and the more open assemblies were further diffused. The selection of the chief which was validated in the assemblies gradually gave way to more emphasis on succession being legitimized through ritual consecration by the priest.[177] The nature of these assemblies indicates that they relate to stratified societies and not to egalitarian clans.

The retinue of the *rājā* moves in inverse proportion to the concentration of power in his hands and includes widening circles of representation. This is reflected in his relationship with the *ratnins*,[178] frequently translated as 'recipients of treasure' but originally meaning 'recipients of a gift'. The list varies slightly from text to text but generally includes the *purohita*, *rājanya*, chief wife, favourite wife, discarded wife, *senāni*, *sūta*, *grāmaṇī*, *kṣattar*, *saṃgrahītar*, *bhāgadugha*, and *akṣavāpa*. Some texts include the *go-nikartana* which has been taken to mean a slayer of cows or a butcher and by extension probably a huntsman. In the course of the *rājasūya* ritual the *rājā* goes to the home of each offering an oblation to a particular deity. The deity is generally one that is associated with the function of the *ratnin* and relates to either protection, fertility and the evil eye or wealth and its distribution. This procedure is referred to as the *ratna-havis* and symbolizes the *rājā* making a gift to the *ratnins*. In a society characterized by the system of gift-giving this would be seen not merely as a symbol of the status of the *ratnins* but also as a sign of the *rājā*'s dependence on them. It is for this reason that they are referred to as the makers of the *rājā*. (The post-Vedic concept of the *ratnāni* reflects a reaching back to the idea of the *ratnins* since it consists of the seven elements which are said to constitute the 'treasures' of the king: the wife, the minister, the general, the wheel, the elephant, the horse, and the jewel. The inclusion of the latter four suggests a distancing of the king from his subjects, where each object provides an abstract concept associated with kingship.)

The *ratnins* are the support to the *rājā*'s office both at the symbolic and functional level. The *purohita* at this early stage rode in the *rājā*'s chariot and recited the appropriate *mantras* for his safety and well-being.[179] His role as domestic priest to the royal household evolved with the coming of monarchy. The *rājanya* was clearly an important member of the clan. The inclusion of the wives points to fertility rituals, the avoidance of the evil eye from the discarded wife and marriage alliances. The latter would be particularly important in a ritual such as the *rājasūya* where even if the *rājā* had made fresh alliances through marriage, the earlier links had to be restated. The rest of the twelve would be members of the *rājā*'s entourage but with a wider concern with economic and political functions. The *sūta* (bard) remained close to the *rājā* and ensured his immortality in the land of the living. As *saṃgrahītar* the charioteer had responsibility for the well-being of the *rājā*. In one of the variant lists the significance of the chariot is further emphasized by the inclusion of the *takṣa-rathakārau* (carpenter and chariot-maker) amongst the twelve.[180] The *senāni* as a designation was used in later times for the commander of the army. In this context the latter probably refers more to the head of a troop since there is no reference to any regularly constituted army or to professional soldiers. Raids and battles seemed to have been the business of members of the *viś*.[181] The *kṣattar* is taken as the door-keeper or as one who distributes. The *bhāgadugha* and the *akṣavāpa* were both involved in distributive functions in the lineage system. The emphasis in this group is on the centrality of the *rājā* in his chariot, presumably symbolic of the cattle raid and of skirmishes highlighting his role as protector; of the dependence on fertility for prosperity; and of the persons involved in the procedure relating to the distribution of wealth. The twelve *ratnins* represent the sanction of a wider circle but they remain essentially within the orbit of clan functioning. The extent to which they were regular office-bearers is limited since there is little reference to the periodic assesment and collection of taxes or to a separate armed force. It was, however, from the germinal functions of this group that the designations for some of the later offices were adopted. The *rājā* at this point remains the 'eater of the *viś*; the *viśāmattā*[182] and the *bhāgadugha*[183] assists him in this activity. Thus the *rājā* was surrounded by persons performing specific functions and some of them were even in a sense his retainers but there was no adminstrative machinery and no system of delegating powers. The existence of the *ratnin*s would point to two significant developments. One was the emergence of a group of non-kinsmen who ultimately took on the character of retainers to the *rājā* and who could contribute to the accumulation of power in the office of the *rājā*. It is also suggestive of a relationship between the *rājā* and others not based on kinship but on reciprocity.

Underlying the concept of *kṣatra* is that of *rājya*, temporal authority which is demarcated from sacred authority, and this is firmly stated at the time of the consecration when it is said that the *rājā* has authority over the people, *prajā*, but the *brāhmaṇa*s accept only the authority of the deity Soma.[184] Yet the actual relationship between sacred and temporal authority was one of interdependence. Various categories of *rājya* are listed of which the most eminent is 'the chief of the gathering' or the *sāmrājya*.[185] This is often translated as 'empire', but a more realistic rendering would be to regard it as a high status among *rājā*s (chiefs) and with the increasing tendency for clans to confederate, the status of *samrāj* would become inevitable. As a corrective to the assumption that the *rājā* held excessive power it is well to keep in mind that the same chiefs who are associated with the performance of the consecration rituals as part of their claim to *sāmrājya* were also the ones who carried out their raids in the dewy season and received a share of the booty.

Exalted titles such as *samrāj*, *vairāj*, *parameṣṭha*, *ādipati*, and so on are scattered throughout the texts and should not perhaps be taken too literally. The various ceremonies performed by the *rājā*s were in the nature of *saṃskāra*s, purification rituals and ceremonies for imbuing the *yajamāna* with power. These rituals were said to place the *rājā* in the proximity of the gods and gradually the *rājā* came to be accepted as divinely appointed. The gods were eligible to titles incorporating sovereignty, paramountcy, and overlordship, and as a consequence of these ceremonies the *rājā* also felt himself eligible for such titles. Thus the attributes of Indra and of the chief of the clan tended to merge and the one was seen in light of the other. Divine appointment drew the chief towards kingship but this was still short of claims to divinity. The latter became more common in the period after the rise of the monarchical state. The analogy with the gods also underlined the role of the *rājā* as the nourisher and the protector and protection was so important that it was equated with discipline and the avoidance of chaos.

It is stated that a people without a *rājā*, was a condition of anarchy.[186] The fear of anarchy is frequently alluded to which is not surprising in a society moving towards complex stratification. The *rājā* was in many ways the economic and political pivot of the lineage system. He integrated the control over territory with access to available resources as also production where productivity was a measure of the chief's efficiency. His position is symbolized in the linkage between the well-being of the clan and the physical well-being of the chief. This focus on the chief led to additional attributes associated with him. Not least among these was a connection with the gods and even if he was not himself regarded as divine, the insistence that the gods had intervened in his selection marked him out as a special person. This was not occasioned by a mere fancy for proximity to the gods, but the exigencies of an increasingly heterogeneous society demanded a category of persons who could be invested with authority. To concentrate power in one family could also have been the solution to tensions and hostility among the clans. In situations of migration to new areas, leadership plays an important part. Migration itself would help to stabilize political power by channelizing the potential for conflict into fission, provided settlements in new areas were attractive and did not involve constant battling against powerful previous inhabitants. A mechanism for assimilating such populations would allow migration to act as a safety-valve which prevented a major change towards state formation. The continual proliferation of such a system could have been checked by an obstruction to fission which would possibly have forced the change.

With the gradual concentration of power in the families of chiefs, there followed other changes which were eventually to move in the direction of encouraging the emergence of kingship. It is not easy to locate the point of change but the tendencies were clear. Election and selection was superseded by attempts at hereditary claims[187] as is evident from the genealogies, admittedly shallow in the early stages, as for example that of Sudās.[188] Genealogies of greater depth occur in the *Mahābhārata*, *Rāmāyaṇa*, and *Purāṇas*, and were compiled in a later period. The gradual emphasis on primogeniture safeguarded succession within the lineage. The link between the *brāhmaṇa* and the *kṣatriya* became stronger with the latter exchanging legitimation for gifts, *dāna*.[189] Implicit in this relationship was the idea that those who invest the *rājā* with divinity or legitimize him are alone permitted to remove him.[190] This was a far cry from the elected chief or legitimacy being based on kinship rights. The latter were still important but subject to Brahmanical approval as is evident from the story of the wicked *rājā* Veṇa whom the *brāhmaṇa*s had finally to strike down with stalks of the sacred *kuśa* grass.[191] Another important concession was the investment of the *rājā* with the right to punish (*daṇḍa*) and to make him exempt from punishment.[192] This was the necessary concomitant to his being made responsible for maintainance of law and order. However these aspects are not especially highlighted until the subsequent period.

Notions of divinity associated with the office of the *rājā* guaranteed the eventual transition to kingship. This restricted eligibility for the status of *rājā* to families already associated with the office. Earlier ideas of the well-being of the community being directly related to the health and well-being of the chief were reinforced at the rituals, particularly those focusing on rejuvenation, such as the *vājapeya*. Physical deformities of any kind invalidated claims to rulership and could create a crisis over succession. The blindness of Dhṛtarāṣṭra and the skin ailment of Pāṇḍu precluded both from uncontested succession and introduced the complication over the inheritance of the realm of the Kurus which had finally to be sorted out through a war. The sacerdotal status of the *rājā* also bestowed on him certain essential powers, necessary for the prosperity and fecundity of the kingdom, as for example, that of bringing rain. The king as 'rainmaker' is a widespread idea in many societies and its prevalence in the Indian tradition is recorded in a number of instances when drought accompanies the rule of an unrighteous *rājā* who has to be removed or goes voluntarily into exile before the rain falls again.[193]

The major sacrificial rituals such as the *rājasūya*, *aśvamedha*, *vājapeya*, became occasions for the consumption of wealth in lengthy ceremonies, some extending over many months. These were accompanied by lavish libations of milk and *ghī*, offerings of grain in various forms and the sacrifice of the choicest animals of the herd. The *yajña* took on some of the characteristics of the potlatch in literally burning up all this wealth. The redistribution of wealth through gift-giving on such occasions was primarily from the *kṣatriya yajamāna* to the *brāhmaṇa* priests. The change from animal herding to agriculture is reflected in the objects included as *dāna* and *dakṣinā* where heads of animals gradually gave way to preparations of grain and eventually to land. Only gold remains constant. The need for extensive consecration rituals would suggest that initially the position of the *rājā* as a superior among other *rājā*s was not so secure and required validation. If the *rājā* was selected to be the chief then he would not only have to prove himself but would also have to be invested with the requisite powers which would demarcate him from other *rājanya*s. This was prior to the assumption of such a status through the system of hereditary kingship. It is interesting that of the two families, it is the Pāṇḍavas establishing themselves at the new centre at Indraprastha who perform the *rājasūya* and not the well-entrenched Kauravas at Hastināpura.

Gift-giving served to reinforce social status and reciprocity between the dominant groups. The notion of obligation was seen as the priest performing services for the *rājā* and in return receiving gifts. Since in every case the gift was an object of considerable material value and therefore crucial to the livelihood of priests who had no other means of material support, it is ostensibly symbolic but in effect a fee.[194] Gift-giving was not restricted to an exchange between *kṣatriya*s and *brāhmaṇa*s. At the *rājasūya* sacrifice for example, initially gifts are brought by other chiefs as prestations to the *yajamāna*, the *rājasūya* of Yudhiṣṭhira being such an occasion.[195] The chiefs vye with each other in making valuable gifts, partly because the value of the gift reinforces their status and partly because it is expected that when they in turn perform the *rājasūya* a still more valuable gift will be returned.

Spectacular sacrifices involving the resources of the *rājā* were not the only occasions for gifting or redistributing wealth. Periodic sacrifices relating to changing seasons or to phases of the moon were part of the regular calender of observances among those of high status.[196] Social obligations were also sources of economic distribution. The *saṃskāra* rituals of the *Gṛhya-sūtra*s, and the domestic rituals enjoined upon every *gṛhapati,* were to be counted among such occasions both in expending wealth as part of the ritual and in prestations to the *brāhmaṇa*s. In addition, expiatory *prāyaścitta*[197] ceremonies became a regular requirement, particularly for those who travelled to areas beyond the pale, such as the *mleccha-deśa* of the Punjab and of the middle Ganga valley—areas which were looked upon as polluting, where the *yajña* rituals were not meticulously observed.

Food and feeding both for the living and the dead in the form of feasts and *śrāddha*s came to acquire central importance in the definition of prosperity. Hospitality and generosity even at the level of the *gṛhapati* were taken for granted. There are elaborate rules for the treatment of guests and the food fit to be served to guests.[198] These domestic rituals drew on the resources of the *gṛhapati*'s household and the wealth consumed was not booty from raids but the produce from cattle-rearing and cultivation carried out by the household. If a *gṛhapati* had obeyed the injunctions and observed each ritual as required by the *Gṛhya-sūtra*s it is likely that he would have been left with little to invest in other activities.

The *yajña* was a ritual occasion and one of major religious significance. But embedded in this and equally important was that a precondition to these rituals was the availability of an economic surplus which was consumed in the ceremony and in gift-giving. Wealth was destroyed rather than put to alternative use or invested.

Even the gifts to the *brāhmaṇas* had limited potential for creating a changed situation. The wealth was primarily provided by the *gṛhapati* in the form of tribute to the *rājā* and this was doubtless the reason for the statement that the *kṣatra* eats the *viś*. A successful raid or a victory in battle would also bring in booty which would contribute to the conspicuous consumption required in the *yajña*. Hence the heroic potentiality of the *rājā* was still of some consequence. The *dig-vijaya* or conquest of the four directions carried out by the Pāṇḍava brothers was an integral part of the *rājasūya* not only in terms of status and a declaration of political domination, but also to provide some of the necessities for the ritual. Tribute was the substitute for booty.

The burning of wealth through rituals was not just an irrational action, since the notion of long-term accumulation of wealth was absent at this time. The burning of wealth was part of what might be called a prestige economy. Some degree of economic redistribution took place in an indirect, restricted and ritualistic manner but was nevertheless noticeable since we are told that the *rājā* consumes the wealthy in the same way as fire consumes the forest.[199] The consumption of wealth on ritual occasions was a statement of status and political power. There was a sense of reciprocity with the gods who were the ultimate recipients of the wealth and were believed to bestow wealth on those who offered lavish sacrifices. The change in the political meaning of the ritual is evident in the changing form of the *aśvamedha* sacrifice. Whereas in the *Ṛg Veda* it is a relatively small affair aimed at conquering foes and acquiring prosperity, in the later Vedic texts it becomes an activity of political supremacy where the claim to the subjugation of others is a sequence to the initial ritual and is also a means of legitimizing control over new territories.[200] Echoes of the earlier society are maintained in the *yajña*s in the simulated chariot-races, cattle raids and games of dice, all of which are an essential part of the ritual. The sacrificial ritual enhanced the status of the *yajamāna* and the priest who performed it. The benefits of the latter were doubtless part of the reason why some *brāhmaṇas* came to be called very wealthy (*mahāśāla*). Temporal and sacral power is also symbolized in the relationship between the *rājā* and the *purohita*. The latter, at most merely the domestic priest of the chief's family, eventually becomes a formal office with the advent of kingship.

The destruction of wealth in the ritual placed severe limitations on these chiefdoms, limitations which acted as an obstacle to the easy transition to a state system. The establishment of a state system would require among other things either the weakening of such ritual prestations and channelling wealth in other directions or the generation of additional wealth to finance alternative activities. The *yajña* rituals were questioned but only by those who were searching for a path to salvation. The discourses in the *Upaniśad*s and *Āranyaka*s questioned the efficacy of *yajña*s but posited an opting out of society through renunciation rather than an alternative channelling of wealth. Renunciation in itself was of some, though limited, consequence to the stimulation of social change through possible changes in the *yajña* ritual. When renunciation was tied to a monastic community and this in turn was linked to lay support, then its role as a social catalyst began to take on serious dimensions.

The lineage system as it developed in the western Ganga valley resulted in a condition which might be called an arrested development of the state. The state was not bypassed but the lineage system did not develop into a state in this area during this period. Certain trends inclined towards the emergence of a state but others remained impediments. There was a consciousness of territory and an identity with territory. The chief was required to integrate territory with resources and with economic production and distribution, a role which concentrated attention on him. Access to larger resources came about with intensified agriculture and a demographic rise leading to the extension of agriculture. But the increase in resources was not sufficient to finance a state system. The concentration of powers in the hands of the *rājā* raised his status and effective control, but at the same time, lesser chiefs were not his appointees and were chiefs in their own right. There was minimal delegation of authority.

The unity of society and internal harmony was sought through the *varṇa* structure. There were no formal procedures for legal action and redress of wrong was linked to social pressures and expiatory rituals. External protection was highlighted in the office of the *rājā* with some indirect attempt to sanction his control over physical force in the close association of the *senānī* with his immediate retinue, as well as the tradition of leadership in battle being a prerequisite for the office. There were multiple prestations to support elaborate rituals maintaining the status of both the *rājā* and sacred authority but there was no systematic method of collecting an income to finance the institutions of a state, much of the wealth being consumed in the prestigious rituals.

The continuity of some elements of the lineage system was possible for various reasons. It was a successful mechanism for incorporating a diversity of ethnic and cultural groups where each group maintained its identity in a relationship of juxtaposition to each other. This probably accounts for the extensive segmenting off in the genealogy of the Candravaṃśi *kṣatriya*s the geographical reach of which included northern, western, and central India. The working out of the *varṇa* structure at this stage was not the codification of a new social formation but an elaboration of the lineage system in a way enabling its use as a framework within which social change could be registered and up to a point confined. Where land was easily available the system could reproduce itself through fission rather than have to undergo a change of form to accommodate the need for further resources or meet the pressure of numbers. Again, where land was easily cultivable without major cooperative organization and agriculture was reinforced by a strong pastoral base, the lineage system would serve the function of cohering groups without their having to subordinate themselves to a state. The western Ganga valley being favourable to such conditions did not require the major changes which were necessary in the middle Ganga valley. If the suggestion that agricultural niches were left relatively undisturbed in the Ṛg Vedic period and that there were no major agrarian innovations from the second to the early first millennium BC is acceptable, then there would have been no substantial technological change in the agrarian system requiring new mechanisms of control. The use of iron does not seem to have influenced agricultural technology until the middle of the first millennium BC. Its major impact in the earlier phase was to facilitate the clearing of land to a marginal extent, but much more significantly in its use in weaponry.[201] If the *kṛṣṇa ayas* of the Vedic texts is taken as iron, which is very possible, the use of iron would have been mainly in the making of arrow-heads, spearheads, knives, etc. This would undoubtedly have been the monopoly of the *rājā*s in their role as protectors. Clearing by burning was evidently possible in the Doāb as is described in the burning of the Khāṇḍava-Vana in order to establish the settlement at Indraprastha.[202] Iron technology was to become more necessary in the clearing of the marshlands and monsoon forests of the middle Ganga valley.

In the western Ganga valley the resources were neither sufficient to finance the institutions required for the establishment of a state nor were they directed towards the creation of such institutions. Archaeological evidence from the Painted Grey Ware culture points to the size of these communities (although larger and more numerous than previous settlements), being smaller than those of the subsequent period, that of the Northern Black Polished Ware. Territory was not seen merely as an area over which a *jana* had political control, for the territorial dimensions of marriage alliances were far wider, particularly for the *kṣatriya* caste. Like lineage, *varṇa* was a mechanism for assimilation but reflected a stratified society. The experience in the Kuru-Pañcāla area, as evident from Vedic literature and archaeology, appears to have been one of developing methods of accommodating diverse groups into a workable system based on control by lineage. The importance of the lineage base is reflected in the description of the Kuru-Pañcāla as among the *rājaśabdopajīvinaḥ* ('taking the title of *rājā*s', a term generally applied to chiefdoms), a statement which occurs in a text as late as the *Arthaśāstra*.[203] What is even more interesting is that the reference to the Kuru-Pañcāla comes in the section of the text which deals with the policy of a monarchy towards the *gaṇa-saṅgha*s or chiefdoms. The Kuru and the Pañcālas are listed among the pre-eminent of the *gaṇa-saṅgha*s, those of the Licchavis and Vṛjjis, as one category of the variants within that system. This would tend to question the description of the Kuru and Pañcāla *janapada*s being full-fledged monarchies in the Vedic period.

The relatively shallow descent groups of Vedic literature and the continual segmenting off of the Candravaṃśa lineages would point to the feasibility of migration as a method of easing tension rather than the necessity of evolving a system of control through the state. The migration eastwards to the middle Ganga valley presented a different ecological scene and one in which the lineage system and the role of the *gṛhapati* both underwent a change, and particularly so with trade impinging as a new factor. In this new situation the *kṣatriya* claimed greater power and prestations were incarnated as taxes. The prising out of the state, therefore, took place in the region adjoining the western Ganga valley and under changed circumstances.

Notes and References

1. V. Tripathi, *The Painted Grey Ware,* Delhi, 1976.

2. J.P. Joshi, 'Interlocking of Late Harappan Culture and Painted Grey Ware Culture in the Light of Recent Excavations', *Man and Environment,* 1978, vol. I, pp. 100–3.

3. R.C. Raikes, 'Kalibangan: Death from Natural Causes', in *Antiquity,* 1968, 42, pp. 286–91; Suraj Bhan, 'The Sequence and Spread of Pre-historic Cultures in the Upper Sarasvatī Basin', in A. Ghosh and D.P. Agrawal, *Radio-Carbon and Indian Archaeology,* Bombay, 1972, p. 252ff.; Suraj Bhan, 'Excavation at Mitathal 1968 (Hissar)', *Journal of Haryana Studies,* 1969, I, January, no. l, pp. 1–15; H.T. Lambrick, *Sind: A General Introduction,* Hyderabad, 1964; Gurdip Singh, *et al.,* 'Late Quaternary History of Vegetation and Climate of the Rajasthan Desert, India', *Philosphical Transactions of the Royal Society of London,* 1974, 267, no. 889, pp. 467–501; B. Ghose, Amal Kar and Z. Husain, 'The Lost Courses of Sarasvatī River in the Great Indian Desert: New Evidence from Landstat Imagery', *The Geographical Journal,* 1979, 145, pt 3, pp. 446–51; *idem.* 'Comparative Role of the Aravalli and Himalayan River Systems in the Fluvial Sedimentation of the Rajasthan Desert', *Man and Environment,* 1980, IV, pp. 8–12; Suraj Bhan, *Excavation at Mithathal (1980) and Other Explorations in the Sutlej–Yamuna Divide*, Kurukshetra, 1975; Suraj Bhan and J.G. Shaffer, 'New Discoveries in Northern Haryana', *Man and Environment,* 1978. II, pp. 59–68; K.N. Dikshit, 'Exploration along the Right Bank of River Sutlej in Punjab', *Journal of History,* 1967, 45, pt II, pp. 561–68; C. Ramaswamy, 'Monsoon over the Indus Valley during the Harappan Period', *Nature,* 1968, 217, pp. 628–9.

4. Gurdip Singh, 'The Indus Valley Culture', *Archaeology and Physical Anthropology in Oceania,* 1971, vol. 6, no. 2, pp. 177–89.

5. viii. 24.27; viii. 96; iv. 28.1; See also iii. 23.4.; x. 75; vii. 95; ii. 41. 16; vi. 61.

6. *Vedic Index,* (subsequently *V.I.*) ii. p. 434. This is Roth's reading. The verses cited carry no reference to its going to the ocean.

7. B. and R. Allchin, *The Birth of Indian Civilisation,* Harmondsworth, 1966, p. 200ff. The Copper Hoard culture which seems to have had its provenance in the middle Ganga valley but the artefacts of which are found in large numbers in the Doāb, remains controversial since some archaeologists associate it with the Ochre Colour Pottery culture on the basis of its having been found with this pottery at a few sites, but others regard it as a distinct culture which cannot be precisely dated because the copper objects are found in caches and rarely in excavations.

8. *Śat. Brāh.* xiii. 5.4.7; *-āla* as a termination is difficult to explain as an Indo-Aryan root. But it is worth noting that in Proto-Dravidian *āḷ* has a distinct meaning which would suit the present context. *DED* 341 *āḷ* refers to one who rules or controls. *DED* 342 gives *āḷ* the connotation of a man or hero. Pañcāla could therefore mean the five chiefs, as a confederacy, provided one can accept a bilingual and therefore a mixed form of Indo-Aryan and Proto-Dravidian.

9. F.E. Pargiter, *Ancient Indian Historical Tradition,* London, 1922.

10. *Ait. Brāh.* viii. 14; *Kausitiki Up.* iv. 1.; *Manu* ii. 17–74.

11. i. 42.8.

12. *Ṛg V.* viii. 86.2; iii. 47.4; v. 63.5; vi. 31.3.

13. *Ṛg V.* 3.47. 4; 5.63.5: 6.31.3.

14. *Tait Brāh.* i. 8.4.1.

15. *Ṛg. V.* ii. 24.6-7; *Vedic Index,* i. 471.

16. *Ṛg. V.* iii 43.5; ix. 35.5; 97.34; x. 67.8; *Ait. Brāh.* viii. 12.17; *Śat. Brāh.* ii. 6.4.2. ff. R.S. Sharma, 'Forms of Property in the Early Portions of the *Ṛg Veda*', P of I.H.C., 1973, pp. 94–101; 'From Gopati to Bhupati', in *Studies in History,* Jul–Dec. 1980, ii, no. 2, pp. 1–11.

17. *Ṛg. V.* ii. 1.1; iv. 20.1; vii. 69.1; x. 44.2-3; *Atharvaveda,* v. 18.1.

18. *Ṛg V.* vii. 96.2.; iv. 38.

19. *Ṛg V.* ix. 107.9.

20. *Ṛg V.* ii. 7.5; vi. 16.47; x. 91.14; x, 169.3; *Atharvaveda,* x. 10.

21. *Vedic Index,* i. p. 10; *Ait. Brāh.* i. 15; *Tait. Brāh.* ii. 17.11.1; *Śat. Brāh.* iii.4.1.2; *Apa. G.S.* viii. 22.3–11

22. *Atharvaveda,* xii. 4.38,53; 5. 36–9.

23. *Ṛg. V.* i. 83.1; iv. 32.17; v. 4.11.

24. *Ṛg. V.* i. 116.21; vi. 32.3.

25. *Vedic Index,* i. p. 336; ii. p. 82.

26. Romila Thapar, '*Dāna* and *Dakṣinā* as Forms of Exchange', in *Ancient Indian Social History: Some Interpretations,* New Delhi, 1978, p. 105ff.

27. Ibid.

28. I. 23.15; X. 34.13; X. 117.; X. 101.3; a hymn addressed to the *kṣetrapati* in IV. 57 is believed to be late although included in the early section of the text. E.W. Hopkins, 'Pragathikani', *JAOS,* 1896, 17, p. 84.

29. Romila Thapar, 'The Study of Society in Ancient India', in *AISH,* p. 211.

30. *Śat. Brāh.* I. 6.1.2–4.

31. R.L. Carneiro, 'A Theory of the Origin of the State', in *Science,* 1970, 169, pp. 733–8.

32. M.M. Deshpande and P.E. Hook, *Aryan and Non-Aryan in India,* Michigan Papers on South and South-east Asia, no. 14, 1978, Ann Arbor, 1979.

33. *Ṛg V.* VII. 83; VII. 18.

34. *Ṛg V.* I. 51.6; II. 19.6; VII. 8.4.

35. *Ṛg V.* VII. 18.

36. *Ṛg V.* VI. 27.7.

37. *Śat. Brāh.* XIII. 5.4 11; *Ait. Brāh.* II. 25; *Vedic Index,* I., p. 64ff. R.S. Sharma, *Śūdras in Ancient India,* 2nd ed., Delhi, 1980, p. 17.

38. Romila Thapar, *Exile and the Kingdom: some thoughts on the Rāmāyaṇa,* Bangalore, 1978. See also *Ṛg V.* X. 146. 1–3.

39. *Atharvaveda,* VII. 10.24; *Viṣṇu Purāṇa* I. 13. Romila Thapar, Origin Myths and the Early Indian Historical Tradition', in *AISH,* p. 294ff.

40. *Ait. Brāh.* VIII. 21.8; *Śat. Brāh.* XIII. 7.1.15.

41. *Ṛg V.* I. 161.10; IV. 57.4–8; X. 102.8.

42. *Strabo* XV. 1.13 and 20, quoting Megasthenes of the late fourth century BC.

43. K.A. Chaudhuri, *Ancient Agriculture and Forestry in Northern India,* Bombay, 1977.

44. *Vedic Index,* II., p. 187

45. *Vājasaneyi Saṃhita* XVIII. 12.

46. *Atharvaveda* VI. 91.1; *Śat. Brāh.* VII. 2.2.6; *Kaṭhaka Saṃhita* XV. 2.

47. X. 101. 5–7; I. 105.17.

48. *Śat. Brāh.* XIII. 4.2.17.

49. For example, R.S. Sharma, 'Class Formation and its Material Basis in the Upper Gangetic Basin, *c.* 1000–500 BC.', *IHR,* July 1975, II, no. 1., p. 1ff.

50. *Atharvaveda;* IV. 5.6; IV. 22.3; *Tait. Sam.* II. 3.1.3.; *Ṛg V.* VII. 55.5

51. I. 110.5.

52. *Śat. Brāh.* IV. 3.3.15

53. *Śat. Brāh.* xii. 7.3.8.

54. Ibid., iii. 3.2.8.; ii. 5.2.27.; vii. 1.1.4.

55. Ibid., xiii. 2.2.15, 2.9.6.

56. Ibid. v. 1.3.3.; xii. 7.3.15; v. 3.4.11.

57. *Ṛg V.* x. 173.6.

58. *Śat. Brāh.* i. 3.3. 15.

59. *Tait. Sam.* v. 4.6-7.: i. 8.11-12: *Śat. Brāh.* viii. 7.1.12; x.4.3.22: xii.7.3.15.

60. *Ait. Brāh.* viii. 12.17; *Śat. Brāh.* viii. 7.1.2.; viii. 7.2.2.; ix. 4.3.5.

61. *Ait. Brāh.* viii. 17.; *Śat. Brāh.* iii. 3.2.8.

62. *Śat. Brāh.* ix. 1.1.25.; ix. 1.1.18.

63. *Śat. Brāh.* iii. 1.1.9.

64. *Ṛg V.* i. 96.7.; *Nirukta* iv. 17.; S. Varma, *The Etymologies of Yaska,* Hoshiarpur, 1953, p. 51.

65. *Śat. Brāh.* iii. 9.3.7.

66. Ibid., ii. 5.2.24.

67. *Ṛg V.* x. 173

68. *Śat. Brāh.* ix. 4.1.1. 13.

69. *Ṛg V.* x. 173.1.

70. *Śat. Brāh.* ix. 3.1.13–14.; ix. 4.3.10.

71. *Ṛg V.* x. 124.8.

72. Ibid, x. 97.

73. *Atharvaveda* ii. 6.4.; *Tait. Sam.* v. 7.4.3.; *Vāj. Sam.* 18.48.

74. *Śat. Brāh.* iv. 1.4.1ff.

75. *Ṛg V.* x. 85.; *Atharvaveda,* xiv. 1 and 2.

76. *Ṛg V.* i. 12.6.; i. 36.5.; i. 60.4.; vi. 48.8.

77. Ibid., vi. 53.2.

78. *Tait. Sam.* ii. 5.4.4.

79. *Śat. Brāh.* v. 3.1.6.

80. *Ṛg. V.* x. 97.6.; x. 191.; *Atharvaveda* iii. 29.1.

81. *Ait. Brāh.* vii. 29.4.

82. iv. 57.8. *Kīnāśa* in later texts has an ambiguous meaning. The general sense is that of a cultivator who may not own the land he cultivates and is therefore better translated as a ploughman working for a wage and dependent on the owner. B.N.S. Yadav, 'The Kali Age and the Social Transition', *IHR,* 1978–9, v., nos. 1 and 2, pp. 37–8. Ṛg Vedic references to *kṣetra* suggest cultivated land or just land rather than individual holdings (i. 100.18.; i. 33.15.; iii. 31.15; v. 45.9; x. 85.4; x. 91.6).

83. K. Polanyi, *Dahomey and the Slave Trade,* 1966, p. 70ff.

84. *Ṛg V.* vii. 6.5.

85. For example, *Ṛg V.* i. 70.5.; v. 1.10. See also J. Gonda, *Ancient Indian Kingship . . .,* Leiden, 1969, pp. 12–13.

86. *Ṛg V.* VII. 6.5.; X. 173.6.; *Ait. Brāh.* VII. 29.
87. *Atharvaveda,* III. 4.2–3.
88. Goldman, *Ancient Polynesian Society,* p. 509; cf. *Śat. Brāh.* V. 2.3 9.
89. *Tait. Sam.* I. 8.9.2; *Kāṭhaka Sam.* XV. 4; *Tait. Brāh.* I. 7.3.5; III. 4.8.1. *Śat. Brāh.* I. 1.2.17; V. 3.1.9.
90. *Baudhāyana* D.S. I. 10.18.1.
91. *Arthaśāstra* II. 15;. *Viṣṇu D.Śā.* III. 22.
92. *Ṛg V.* VII. 82.6; VIII. 1.5; *Atharvaveda,* III. 29.3; III. 4.3; *Śat. Brāh.* XI. 2.6.14 qv.; *Vedic Index,* II, p. 387.
93. Pāṇini, IV. 3.75.
94. Goldman, *Ancient Polynesian Society,* p. 509.
95. *Śat. Brāh.* IV. 4.2.15; IV. 6.9.3-5; IV. 6.9.25; XI. 8.4.1ff; XII. 1.1.1ff.
96. *Ait. Brāh.* VII. 29.4.
97 . *Baudhāyana D.S.* II. 2.3.2ff.
98. *Aśvalāyana G.S.* II. 10.3.
99. Sabhā Parvan, 46ff
100. *Ṛg V.* I. 104.2; III. 34.9: II. 12.4.
101. H.W. Bailey, 'Iranian *Arya* and *Dāha*', *Transactions of the Philological Society,* 1959, p. 71ff.
102. *Naighantaka* 2.6.
103. III. 1.103.
104. Curiously the area inhabited by the *daha/dāsa* being the Indus valley would suggest an earlier nomenclature which I have argued elsewhere applied to this region and that is Makan. This in Proto-Dravidian would convey the same meaning of a man, or hero, or male. The name Suvīra is also indicative of the same meaning, being used for this region in a still later period and occurs frequently as Sindhu-Suvīra. Romila Thapar, 'A Possible Identification of Meluhha, Dilmun and Makan', *JESHO,* 1975, xviii, pt 1, p. 30ff.
105. *Annales* 10–11.
106. *Maj. Nik.* II. 144–50; *Samantapāsādikā* II., p. 238.
107. II. 12.4; 20.8; III. 12.6; IV., 16.13. 30.13; VIII. 40.6; X. 69.5-6; *Atharvaveda,* VII, 90.1–2. Blackness is also associated with the *asuras* and the *rākṣasas* and was probably symbolic of all those who were not speakers of Indo-Aryan.
108. *Ṛg V.* VI. 31.4; VII 99.5; *Ṛg V.* VIII. 32, 40, and 46; *Chand. Up.* IV. 2.1–5; *Vedic Index,* II. p. 355.
109. *Ṛg V.* I. 51.5–6, 103.8, 104.2; V. 30; VI. 20.7.
110. II, 11.4; IV. 28.4; VI. 25.2.
111. *Vedic Index,* I. p. 347; *Ṛg V.* I. 33.4; I. 51.8; VII. 6.3.
112. Pāṇini IV. 1.30; *Arthaśāstra* III. 13. In the *Ṛg V.* VI. 22.10 the *dāsas* and *āryas* are jointly invoked.

113. *Aśvalāyana G.S.* II. 8.6–8: cf. *Ṛg. V.* x. 20.9. The Licchavi clans are distinguished by a difference in colour but not skin pigmentation. *Mahāvagga* VI. 30.3–4.

114. *Śat. Brāh.* I. 5.3.2; I.7.2.22; II. 2.2.8; VI. 6.2.11.

115. Ibid. VI. 8.1. 1–2.

116. Ibid. I.6.1.2–4

117. *Tait. Brāh.* II. 2.9.5: *Maitrāyani Saṃhitā* I. 8.3.

118. *Yajñavalkya Smṛti* III. 61; Manu III. 31.

119. *Śat. Brāh.* XIII. 8.1.1. *Chāndogya Upaniśad* 8.8.5.

120. V. 63.3.

121. A curious reference to the bull *asura,* Vṛṣna, in the *Ṛg Veda,* III. 38.4 calls to mind the bull as a clan name which occurs so frequently in early Indian tradition in the form of Vṛṣṇi, Vṛṣabha, Ṛṣabha, not to mention the frequency of the bull on the Harappan seals.

122. *Śat. Brāh.* III. 2.1.23. Romila Thapar, 'The Image of the Barbarian in Early India', in *AISH,* p. 152ff.

123. E. Senart, *Le Mahavastu,* I, pp. 283–361, *Pāṇini* I. 2.65 ff.

124. *Baudhāyana* D.S., I. 1.2.1ff.

125. *Mahābhārata,* Ādi Parvan, 71ff: cf. Udyoga Parvan 104.121 and 147.3–13.

126. *V.I.,* I. p. 245ff.

127. Minoro Hara. 'A Note on the Sanskrit Word Jana', *Pratidānam,* The Hague, 1968, p. 256ff.

128. *Vedic Index,* I, p. 269; II., pp. 466–7. D.D. Kosambi, 'The Vedic "Five Tribes"', *JAOS,* 1967, 87, pp. 33–9. Yāska's *Nirukta* III. 8.8.; IV. 23.1, explains it as the five categories of *pitṛ, gāndharva, deva, asura,* and *rākṣasa.*

129. *Ṛg V.* I. 108.8; W.P. Lehman, 'Linguistic Structure as Diacritic Evidence on Proto-Culture', in G. Cardona *et al., Indo-European and Indo-Europeans,* Pennsylvania, 1970.

130. *Viṣṇu Purāṇa* IV. 10ff.

131. *Mahābhārata,* Ādi Parvan 57.

132. *Viṣṇu Purāṇa* IV. 18.

133. Echoes of the idea seem to continue in the later concept of the *pañca-vīra* or five heroes of the Vṛṣṇis, a segment of the Yādavas. The five heroes were eventually worshipped as part of a cult in Saurashtra, southern Rajasthan, and Mathura. The Tamil tradition of the Aimperumvelir, the five great *vel* chiefs is also curious, particularly as the Velir claim to be of Yādava descent. The notion of five constituting a unit is often found in the Indian subcontinent. The sacrificial ritual in the *Śat. Brāh.* involves five animals, listed as man, horse, bull, ram, and he-goat, and the *gṛhastha* is required to perform five *yajña*s during the day, etc.

134. This is evident from even later references to the *gaṇa-saṅgha* system as in Pāṇini VI. 2.34.

135. Yāska, *Nirukta,* II. 3. This presents a parallel with the Proto-Dravidian *vel.* DED 4562 and 4524 would suggest a homophone meaning the chief and the resplendent one.

136. E. Benveniste, *Indo-European Language and Society,* London, 1973, pp. 311–12.

137. G. Dumezil, *Mythe et Epopee,* I and II, Paris, 1968, 1971; *Flamen-Brahman,* Paris, 1935.

138. Later sources mention *kṣatriyas* moving to brahmanhood such as the Kāṇvas who were of the Ajamīḍha lineage. *Viṣṇu Purāṇa* IV. 19; Garga who was a Bharata, ibid.; Mudgala of the Candravaṃśa lineage, *Bhāgavata Purāṇa* IX. 21; and Harita of the Sūryavaṃśa, *Viṣṇu Purāṇa* IV. 3.

139. *Śat. Brāh.* VI, 4.4.13.

140. Manu, x. 1–73 discusses the origins of various *samkīrna jātis* of *sūdras.*

141. *Curtius Rufus* IX. 4; cf. *Mahābhārata,* Sabhā Parvan 48.14.

142. *Mahābhārata,* Sabhā Parvan 29.9.

143. A. Sharma, 'An Analysis of the Epithets applied to the Sūdras in Aitarey Brāhmaṇa VII. 29.4', *JESHO,* Oct. 1975, XVIII, pt 3, pp. 300–18.

144. Goldman, *Ançient Polynesian Society,* p. 418ff

145. *Ṛg V.* I. 105.7ff.

146. *Śat. Brāh.* V. 3.2.2; *Pañcaviṃśa Brāh.* VI. 1.11.

147. *Ṛg V.* VII. 33.10–13.

148. *Vedic Index,* I. p. 143, 366, II. 259.

149. Pargiter, *Ancient Indian Historical Tradition,* pp. 197, 307.

150. Ibid. p. 241.

151. Medatithi commenting on Manu III. 3 maintains that the *gotra and pravara* system was prevalent among the *brāhmaṇas* alone and quotes the *Aśvalāyana Srauta Sutra* I. 3 in support (P.V. Kane, *History of Dharmasastra,* II. 1, p. 493).

152. *Apastamba Śrauta Sūtra* 24.10.11–12

153. Romila Thapar, 'Social Mobility in Ancient India with Special Reference to Elite Groups', in *AISH,* p. 122ff.

154. *Vedic Index,* II. p. 83; *Ait. Brāh.* VII. 26; *Śat. Brāh.* III. 4.1.2; VII. 5.2.37–42.

155. Romila Thapar, 'The Archaeological Background to the Agnicayana Ritual', in F. Staal (ed.), *Agni,* Vol. I., Berkeley, 1982.

156. *Ṛg V.* x. 97.

157. *Atharvaveda* V. 22.14; *Baudhāyana* D.S., I. 1.2.13ff.

158. *Ṛg V.* II. 23.1; *Ait. Brāh.* I. 21.

159. *Vāyu Purāṇa* 88.4–5; 86.3; 94.51–2.

160. *Ṛg V.* vi. 59.7; ix. 76.2.; iii. 47.4.

161. *Ṛg V.* ii. 1.4; iii. 38.5–6; vii. 40.1; *Atharvaveda* i. 13.4.; *Vedic Index,* ii, p. 296. cf., RV. x. 11.8.

162. *Ṛg V.* ii. 1.16; i. 56.2.

163. *Ṛg V.* x. 91.2–9

164. R.S. Sharma, *Aspects of Political Ideas and Institutions in Ancient India,* p. 85ff.

165. J.P. Sharma, *Republics in Ancient India,* London, 1968, p. 72.

166. R.S. Sharma, 'Vidatha: The Earliest Folk Assembly of the Indo-Aryans', *JBRS* 1952, xxxvii, pts 3–4, pp. 429–48; J.P. Sharma, *Republics in Ancient India,* Leiden, 1968, p. 62ff.

167. cf. *RV* ii. 24.13; vii. 1.4; *Atharvaveda,* xix. 55.6; xii. 1.56; viii. 10.5; xx. 128.1.

168. *Ṛg. V.* x. 71.10; *Atharvaveda* vii. 12.3.

169. *Vedic Index,* ii., p. 426.

170. *Vedic Index,* i., p. 2; G. Held, *The Mahābhārata: an ethnological study,* London, 1935.

171. *Vedic Index,* i., p. 388

172. Ibid. p. 2ff.

173. *Atharvaveda* vii. 12.1; viii. 10.5–11; xii. 1.56. cf. *RV.* ix. 92.6; x. 97.6.

174. *Ṛg V.* x. 124.8. 166.4,173.1; *Atharvaveda* i. 9.3; iii. 4; iv. 22

175. *Ṛg V.* iii. 33. 7.

176. J.P. Sharma, *Republics in Ancient India,* p. 15.ff.

177. *Śat. Brāh.* v. 3.3.12; *Ait. Brāh.* viii. 5 ff; *Tait. Brāh.* i. 7.51 ff; *Pañcaviṃśa Brāh.* xviii, 8ff.

178. *Vedic Index,* ii, pp. 199–201

179. Gonda, *Ancient Indian Kingship . . .,* London, 1969, p. 65 ff.

180. *Maitrāyanī Sam.* ii. 6.5; iv. 3.8; *Śat. Brāh.* v. 3.1.1 ff; v. 4.4.7; *Tait. Brāh.* i. 7.3.1 ff; *Tait. Sam.* i. 8.9.1ff.

181. *Śat. Brāh.* v. 4.3.8.

182. *Śat. Brāh.* viii. 7.1.2, 7.2.2.

183. *Śat. Brāh.* i. 1.2.17, v. 3.1.9; *Tait Brāh.* i. 7.3.5; *Tait. Sam.* i. 8.9.2.

184. *Śat. Brāh.* v. 3.3.12.

185. *Ṛg V.* iii. 55.7, 56.5; iv. 7.1; v. 63.5; vi. 7.1; vi. 27.8; viii. 19.32; viii. 42.1.

186. *Ait. Brāh.* i. 14.6; *Tait. Brāh.* i. 5.9.1ff.

187. *Ṛg V.* x. 33.4.

188. *Vedic Index,* ii, p. 454

189. Romila Thapar, '*Dāna* and *Dakṣinā* as forms of Exchange', in *AISH,* p. 105ff.

190. *Śat., Brāh.* v.3.3.12.

191. *Mahābhārata,* Śānti Parvan, 59.115; *Viṣṇu Purāṇa* I. 13.

192. *Śat. Brāh.* v. 4.4.7.

193. The story of Devāpi in some versions combines the disqualification of a physical ailment with legitimacy associated with drought and rain. *Ṛg V.* x. 98; *Nirukta* II. 10; *Bṛhaddevatā* VII. 148ff; *Viṣṇu Purāṇa* IV, 20.

194. Romila Thapar, '*Dāna* and *Dakṣinā*'.

195. *Mahābhārata,* Sabhā Parvan, 30ff.

196. *Śat. Brāh.* I. 6.3.36; II. 5.2.48.; *Tait. Sam.* I. 6.10.33.

197. *Śat. Brāh.* I. 1.4.9; XII. 4.1.6; *Atharvaveda.* v. 22.

198. *Atharvaveda* IX. 6.3; *Śat. Brāh.* VII. 3.2.1; *Tait. Upaniśad* I. 11.2.

199. *Ṛg V.* I. 65.4.

200. *Ṛg V.* III. 53.11; *Śat. Brāh.* XIIIth *kānda; Tait. Sam.* VII. 4.16; *Taittiriya Brāh.* VIII. 1.1.1ff.

201. R. Pleiner, 'The Problem of the Beginning Iron Age in India', *Acta Praehistorica et Archaeologica,* 1971, 2, pp. 5–36.

202. *Mahābhārata,* Ādi Parvan, 199. 25 ff; 214–19.

203. XI. 1.5.

CHAPTER 6

The Evolution of the State in the Ganga Valley in the Mid-first Millennium BC*

The Ganga valley in the mid-first millennium BC provides a useful case for the study of state formation in early India. There are data from archaeology, especially in relation to the western Ganga valley, and from literary sources for both the western and the middle Ganga valley. It is possible to compare the conditions in the western region with those of the contiguous area in the central region and see the gradual change towards the coming of the state. In the absence of a firm chronology for the literary sources, it is not possible to date the changes in a precise manner, but the trends towards change can at least be recognized and discussed. The mid-millennium may be taken as an approximate dividing line between non-state and state systems and it is argued here that the evidence of the western Ganga valley indicates the continuity of a non-state system whereas that of the middle Ganga valley suggests the start of the process towards state formation. Added to this is the very considerable literature which now exists on the theoretical discussion on state formation.[1]

The significance of this process in the Indian subcontinent is that it was a continuing one in different regions until recent centuries. The emphasis in the sources on the need for a state in the absence of which there would be chaos arose from the constant need to justify new states. Erstwhile frontier zones of uncertain control would gradually evolve into states. The emergence of the state was

* This chapter was previously published in *Studies in History*, 1982, vol. 4, no. 2, pp. 181–96.

not a terminal point since pre-existing states would tend to change their character with the juxtaposition of new states. This requires a typology of state systems which has yet to be worked out.

This essay is concerned with the change from what has been called a lineage system to a state system. The lineage system is characterized by a distinctive social structure.[2] With marginal variations, it may broadly be said to consist of a corporate group of unilineal kin held together by bonds of genealogy, which is generally regarded as authentic but may be fictive. Stratification is essentially among lineages and there can be in some cases a separation between the senior lineage which holds power and the lesser or junior or cadet lines who are the providers of tribute and prestations to the former, which is then redistributed by the senior lineages through rituals and gifts. The family and its household is the unit of production. Ownership is a limited concept and applies at most to animal herds. Lineage rights of usage extend to pastures and to arable land. Ritual occasions are mainly sacrificial ceremonies when the lineage is present. External to the lineage are non-lineage groups which are generally small in number to begin with but depending on their function can become very powerful. Thus the shamans and priests tend to be powerful. Those captured in inter-tribal raids would have to work as slaves and labourers and would be deprived of power.

The state[3] is characterized by a concentration of political authority generally in the hands of an erstwhile senior lineage of which one family claims complete power, a claim which is legitimized by the priests as being based, among other things, on agencies other than human, such as an association with the gods. This authority is delegated to functionaries who constitute the administration. Legitimacy is also claimed on the basis of myths of origin. These, at a later stage, allow powerful families from groups not recognized as the earlier lineages, to assert authority. The state claims control over a well-defined territory which is defended by a standing army. The revenues for the state are collected through a system of taxes and consist of a contracted amount collected regularly by the officers of the administrative system. The revenue is directed towards a treasury which is the basis for the redistributive system organized by the ruler. The office of the latter is defined as that of protection both against external enemies and against internal disorder. The state also recognizes the importance of external relations, that is, relations with other states and these may be hostile or friendly. The lineage system and the state in the Indian context should not be seen as two sharply demarcated dichotomies. Although clear examples of both are evident in the sources, nevertheless the process of state formation is a gradual one and there are many overlaps from one system to another. It is part of the intention of this essay to suggest that the overlaps are as significant as the changes.

The *Ṛg Veda* and the later Vedic literature provide evidence of the lineage system. The *jana* constitutes the tribe which is made up of a number of clans, the *viś*. There is a demarcation between the senior lineages, *rājanya* and the lesser lineages which continue to be called the *viś*. *Rājanya* derives from *rājā/rājan*, which refers to the chief. Although some texts explain its etymology as the one who pleases,[4] this etymology is unacceptable and the derivation is more likely to have been from the root *raj*, to shine or to lead and direct.[5] There is some controversy as to whether the chief was elected by the *viś* or was selected by his peers in assembly.[6] Possibly, the idea of election was an earlier process and may well be reflected in the traditional meaning for the term. The word *viś* refers to a settlement and would therefore point to the lineages which settled on the land and were responsible for cattle-raising and agriculture. There are references to the *viś* of the *āryas* as well as the *dāsas* and some of the chiefs among the latter are said to be wealthy.[7] Land was held by the clan and could not be bestowed on anyone without the permission of the *viś*.[8] Pastures and grazing lands were plentiful but seem to have required some transhumance or migration, judging by the distances travelled by some of the *janas* such as the Pūrus. Wealth was computed in the form of cattle, horses, chariots, gold, and slaves, the latter being primarily female slaves doubtless captured in raids.[9] The importance of cattle wealth is suggested in cattle being listed as wealth and in the use of terms such as *gaviṣṭhi*, the search for cattle, which becomes synonymous with the term for a cattle-raid. The Paṇis who are described as cattle-lifters are also the most feared enemies. The evidence on what constitutes wealth is indicated in the famous *dāna-stuti* hymns of the *Ṛg Veda,* the eulogies by bards and priests on the magnanimous gifts bestowed on them by the *rājanya*s after successful cattle-raids and skirmishes.[10] In the division of wealth a major share would go to the *rājanya* and to the *brāhmaṇa.* The *rājanya* claimed it on the basis of being the protector of the settlement and the *brāhmaṇa* on the basis of his *mantra*s and rituals ensuring a successful raid as well as his eulogies ensuring immortality in the land of the living. The *rājanya* became the symbol of the clan's prosperity. The *brāhmaṇa* claimed to be the intermediary between men and gods. The redistribution of wealth between these two categories led to a re-inforcing of the status of each. The gift-giving and the redistribution took place at the time of the major *yajña* sacrificial rituals and these were not only the occasions for offering oblations to the gods but also the occasions for establishing the superior status of the *rājanya* and the *brāhmaṇa.* The Ṛgvedic chiefs based their power and wealth primarily on pastoralism although agriculture was known to the *Ṛg Veda*, and from archaeological evidence which goes back to pre-Harappan times. It is possible that the agricultural niches were cultivated by the non-lineage groups who were also the earlier settlers and who perhaps remained in these areas and did not migrate when the pastoralists arrived.[11] They would then have subordinated themselves to the pastoral chiefs, in a situation of what has been called environmental circumscription,[12] since the niches provided good agricultural land and migration away would have required an effort in clearing the waste land and forests before cultivation could be started. This would have led to a symbiotic relationship between the pastoralists and the cultivators and a situation of bilingualism, should the two have been speaking different languages, as is suggested in the fact of Vedic Sanskrit incorporating non-Aryan linguistic elements.[13] With the gradual but increasing emphasis on agriculture, the society of the cultivators although subordinate would have come to play an important role in Vedic society.

The later Vedic literature sees the gradual transition from an essentially pastoral economy to one where pastoralism continues but agriculture begins to supersede it. This is in part reflected in the offerings at the *yajña*s which still include the best livestock but also a variety of items made from grain. The geographical focus of this literature moves from the *sapta sindhu* (the seven rivers of the Indus) of the *Ṛg Veda* to the western Ganga valley and its eastern fringes. The archaeological culture of the Painted Grey Ware appears to coincide in terms of chronology and geographical distribution with the later Vedic literature. This is a culture with a mixed pastoral and agrarian economy with evidence of the cultivation of wheat and barley and probably of rice.[14] The latter has been found at a few sites and may have been locally grown or else imported from the area to the east of the Ganga–Yamuna *doāb*. Its increasing use in rituals suggests a gradual familiarity. There is evidence of the horse which is also attested to in the literature. Iron technology at this early stage seems to have been restricted to arrow-heads, spear-heads, blades, and knives.[15] It may well have been used in clearing waste land although literary sources refer more frequently to clearing by burning.[16] In any case the clearing of land points to an increase in agricultural activities. There is a scatter of fairly closely placed small settlements in the upper *doāb* mainly following the river courses. The confederacy of clans known as the Kurus and the Pañcālas emerges as the dominant group in the western Ganga valley. The territories where such clans settle are referred to as the *janapada*, literally where the tribe places its feet. Each *janapada* is identified by the ruling lineage whose name is given to the territory. This is indicative of greater authority invested in the ruling lineage and such lineages gradually drop the term *rājanya* and take on the designation of *kṣatriya,* from the root **kṣatra* meaning power. The *Śatapatha Brāhmaṇa* provides a wealth of evidence on this process.[17] We are told that the *kṣatriya* and the *viś* were originally close as reflected in the statement that the *kṣatriya* and *viś* once ate from the same vessel, which for a society concerned with the rules of commensality was a substantial indication of social proximity. In describing the relationship between the two, the analogy is often to superior and inferior categories within the same species, thus, the *kṣatriya* is the *soma* and the *viś* the *surā*, the *kṣatriya* is Varuna or Indra and the *viś* are the Maruts, and so on. But in addition to this it is also stated that the *kṣatriya* eats the *viś* as the deer eats grain. The superiority of the *kṣatriya* is always stressed. Furthermore, it is said that whatever the *viś* produces in that the *kṣatriya* has a share. The differentiation of status between the two is much sharper now although the common origins would still seem to be recognized. The fact of the *viś* providing prestations for the *kṣatriya* is made very evident. The prestations are referred to as *bali*[18] a voluntary tribute which in the Ṛg Vedic context referred to tribute from defeated foes as well as prestations from the *viś*; *bhāga*, which was a share of the produce or a share of the booty from raids;[19] and *śulka* which has the meaning of value or price and is used in the sense of a dower or a tribute.[20] It has been argued that these might have been taxes, as they were in later periods. It is however difficult to accept this argument since there is at this time no reference to *bali*, *bhāga* and *śulka* being of a specific amount, or paid regularly, or to there being special officers to collect these amounts; all of which are characteristic of a revenue system. The content suggests that they were still prestations and not taxes.

In addition to the *kṣatriya* and the *viś* there are two other groups which emerge as professional groups in this period. The *brāhmaṇa*s in addition to being controllers of ritual and magic and legitimizers of those in power also register a range of categories as priests. This was required by the change in the *yajña* rituals which had now become elaborate ceremonies sometimes extending over more than a year. Apart from the consecration and rejuvenation ceremonies for the *rājā*, the *yajña*s included fertility and prosperity rituals for the *jana* or for the family (*kula*) and these were held frequently in accordance with seasonal and calendric requirements. The *yajña* gradually became the central activity of Vedic society deriving its sanction from religious functions. But it was also the occasion for reiterating the status of the more powerful groups through gift-giving to the priests as well as establishing by the same process the status of those new to the higher reaches of society. Since the success of the *yajña* requires a large investment of animal and agricultural wealth, the ritual can also be said to have had embedded in it an economic role.

The other professional group was that of the *śūdra*s. The word itself is of uncertain origin and may be derived from **kṣudra* meaning small or low. It has been linked to the Sodroi tribes mentioned in classical sources,[21] but references to *śūdras* in Vedic literature do not suggest any particular tribe. The *śūdras* are mentioned only in the later Vedic literature (except for the single reference in the late hymn of the tenth *maṇḍala* of the *Ṛg Veda*) and clearly emerge as a separate group in this period. They are associated with agricultural labour and with craft and artisanal activities.

The recognition of increasing stratification is reflected in the change from the dual *varṇa* system (*ārya* and *dāsa varṇas*) to the four-*varṇa* system (*brāhmaṇa*, *kṣatriya*, *vaiśya*, and *śūdra*) which is the accepted system in the later Vedic literature. This was not just a division of two into four, but in fact the recognition of the further stratification in the *ārya varṇa* and a more specific connotation for the *dāsa varṇa*. The *brāhmaṇa*, *kṣatriya*, and *vaiśya* were regarded as *ārya*s or *dvija*s and the *śūdra*s were separate. The *ārya*s traced descent and were organized on a lineage system with exogamous *gotra*s characterizing the *brāhmaṇa* descent groups and the endogamous *vaṃśa* being frequently a feature of the *kṣatriyas*. The *śūdra*s on the other hand are specifically said to have no lineage ancestry, only the *varṇa* of their individual parents determining their status. Thus the *śūdra*s by being described as such were excluded from those who claimed lineage origin. The concept of *varṇa* was therefore a system for interlocking various types of stratification and its use was more theoretical rather than a description of ethnic or class groups. As a theory it is rooted in lineage-based society and acts as a carry-over from this in later times as well.

Embedded in this stratification are two groups which were later to take the form of what might be called class functions or of incipient classes. One of these was known to the *varṇa* system in the category of *śūdra*s, where the negation of a distinct lineage and the nature of occupation were the qualifying factors. In the post-Vedic period the *śūdra*s were increasingly cultivators and artisans. As a counterpoise to this group was the category referred to as the *gṛhapatis*. These were the heads of households and could belong to any of the *dvija varṇas*. Initially they seem to have been mainly of the *kṣatriya varṇa* but gradually *vaiśya gṛhapati*s are mentioned. It is possible that the basic unit of Vedic society was a householding economy in which a household, consisting of three or four generations of the family together with some labourers and slaves, constituted the producing unit, particularly when agriculture became the dominant economic activity. The *gṛhapati*s may well have been the entrepreneurs in the new settlement and those belonging to the lineages of the *viś* would have moved into *vaiśya* status. From cultivating allotted lands the family units would gradually have begun to claim permanent usage on the lands which they cultivated, usage rights which in the post-Vedic period could have constituted the basis to claims of family ownership over such lands. The increasing demarcation of function between the *kṣatriya* and *viś*, led to the emergence of the *vaiśya gṛhapati* in the post-Vedic period as the main landowning group but not excluding *gṛhapati*s of the other two *dvija varṇas*.[22] The wealth of the *gṛhapati*s supported the *kṣatriya* bid for greater power for the latter would take on the functions of protection at all levels and the former would remain the providers of prestations.

It is a debatable point whether the *rājā* of the later Vedic period remained a chief or became a king. In any case the transition was very gradual and even if kingship had evolved by this time it incorporated much of the tradition of chiefship. Two developments which assisted this process of change were the association of the office of the *rājā* with divinity[23] and the occasional reference to hereditary succession.[24] It is significant that the *rājā*'s association with divinity came about not through any claim to divine origins but through the rituals performed after he had been declared a *rājā*. A distinction has also to be maintained between the office of the *rājā* in the Vedic period and the emergence of the state. Very few of the characteristics of the state were apparent at this time. Strikingly absent is the mention of a standing army for protection against external aggression. Battles and campaigns are few and far between, the more frequent conflicts taking the forms of raids and skirmishes in which the *rājanya* would mobilize the clan. Similarly there is no mention of a legal sanction invested in the *rājā*. The symbolic *daṇḍa* is handed to him but without the backing of a *dharma-śāstra.* Social pressure remains the most effective means of redressing wrongs and expiation is often resorted to. Even more fundamental is the lack of a systematized revenue collecting administration. It could be argued that rather than encouraging state formation there was a series of factors which militated against the emergence of the state.

A state requires a considerable outlay of wealth to finance the institutions which are a part of its infrastructure. The wealth which was circulating in Vedic society was distributed and consumed in a manner which was not conducive to encourage the formation of a state system. There were two sources of wealth, one being the booty from raids and the other being the prestations deriving from cattle-rearing and agriculture made by the *viś* and the *gṛhapati*s to the *rājā.* The wealth was redistributed at the gatherings of the *rājanya*s or of the entire clan.[25] Gatherings such as the *sabhā, samiti,* and *vidatha* take on a further meaning if they are seen as the occasions when redistribution of wealth was also carried out. Such occasions were given a certain ritual form and this in turn bestowed sanctity and legitimacy on the distribution. The redistribution was confined to prestations moving from the *viś* and the *gṛhapati*s to the *rājanya*s and *kṣatriya*s and then circulating among the *kṣatriya*s and the *brāhmaṇa*s. Therefore power remained concentrated in the hands of the *kṣatriya*s and was legitimized by the *brāhmaṇa*s through rituals such as the *rājasūya*, *aśvamedha*, *vājapeya* and so on. These extended sacrificial rituals were the other occasion on which wealth was distributed in the form of *dāna* and *dakṣiṇā* by the *kṣatriya*s to the *brāhmaṇa*s reinforcing the status of each. The *yajña* was also the occasion when a substantial amount of wealth was consumed literally in the sacrificing of the choicest animals of the herd and in the burning up of the produce from dairying and agriculture. To that extent the *yajña* takes on some aspects of the potlatch. This destruction of surplus wealth is related to an absence of a sense of accumulating wealth, and accumulation, so necessary for state formation, is hardly evident. The archaeological evidence of the Painted Grey Ware does not indicate the kind of material evidence associated with societies accumulating wealth. In this the contrast with Northern Black Polished Ware levels of the subsequent period is noticeable. The later Vedic texts do not refer to monumental structures and even references to treasuries or store-houses of the *kṣatriyas* are infrequent. The power of the *kṣatriya* as the recipient of prestations and the distributor of wealth was not questioned and a change of political form was not required. Those who did question the sacrificial ritual opted out of society in the form of renouncers and forest hermits and did not encourage the challenging of the existing system at this stage. Their questioning related more to metaphysical concerns although their disenchantment with the existing system cannot be ignored.

A further mechanism for avoiding too great a tension from developing within the settlement, such as would require changing the system, was that clans in confrontation often migrated to new areas where the same structure was repeated and internal conflict was avoided. Such a 'fissioning off' of clans is clearly stated in the origin myths of many descent groups referred to in the Buddhist tradition.[26] Earlier, the archaeological evidence from the late second to the mid-first millennium BC relating to the Indo-Gangetic watershed and the western Ganga valley also reveals a very intensive pattern of migration. The spread of the Painted Grey Ware sites from a heavy concentration in the upper Ganga-Yamuna *doāb* to lesser concentrations in the central and southern *doāb* and the area east of the *doāb,* would point to migratory patterns. The symbolic meaning of the theme of exile so frequently occurring in epic literature and often associated with a crisis in political succession, would corroborate this trend. The avoidance of internal conflict in turn suppressed the tendencies which might otherwise have forced an authority system conducive to the emergence of a state.

The theme of migration introduces the new geographical location of the middle Ganga valley. This is made explicit in the description of Videgha Māthava migrating to the area east of the Sādanīra (Gandak)[27] river which is referred to as marshland; migration is also implied in the scatter of Painted Grey Ware sites along the northern fringe of eastern Uttar Pradesh as well at the confluence of the Ganga and Yamuna in Allahabad district. Black-and-red wares sites occur more frequently along the southern fringes of the Ganga valley and up along the Gandak suggesting a migration from central India, although the earlier provenance of the black-and-red wares is western India.[28] The routes of migration therefore from the western Ganga valley were along the Himalayan foothills of the *terai* region or skirting the Vindhyan outcrops towards south Bihar and then north along the rivers.

The middle Ganga valley was substantially marshy land and monsoon forest which would have been difficult to clear by burning except along the fringes. Clearing of the interior areas would have required better tools and considerable labour. Possibly it was in this area that iron technology for clearing land was more effective than in the western Ganga valley. Apart from Kosala, the ecological conditions were not very conducive to the breeding of cattle or the cultivating of wheat. Although cattle herds were still maintained the ideal pasture lands remained those of the western Ganga valley. Wheat cultivation appears fairly soon to have given way to rice which was the natural crop in this area. Thus Kośala was suited for the cultivation of rice and wheat whereas Magadha was especially suitable for the cultivation of rice.

The cultivation of rice (wet rice cultivation which was the more feasible form in this area) was the most productive but it required certain changes in the relationship towards land and agricultural technology[29] as compared to the western Ganga valley. With pastoralism becoming a subordinate economy settlements become more permanent. This was also a precondition to the increase in labour to clear marsh land and to manage rice cultivation. In normal circumstances rice was dependent on rainfall and therefore in an area of just the summer monsoon it would become a single crop cultivation. Rotation is only with leguminous plants. To obtain more than a single crop, irrigation would be necessary and this took the form of tanks, embankments, and channels taken off streams.[30] Alternatively a larger area of land would have to be brought under cultivation. Both of these meant an intensification in the employment of labour even though the area of land under rice produces a larger yield than the same area under wheat. The cultivation of rice together with irrigation and the extension of the cultivated area doubtless provided a surplus in excess of what was available in similar acreages in the western Ganga valley. However, this in itself was not a sufficient cause for major social changes and there were other factors influencing change.

The lineage system was continued in the middle Ganga valley in the *gaṇa-saṅgha*s or chiefdoms but it developed rather differently from its form in the western Ganga valley. The controlling lineage claimed *kṣatriya* status with the head of each family constituting the *rājā* who together sat in an assembly and claimed ownership of land as well as political control.[31] The land was not worked by the members of the *rājā-kula* but by the *dāsa-bhṛtaka* (slaves and labourers) and the distinction between the two categories was sharp.[32] Participation in ownership was by birth and therefore lineage connections were crucial. The worship of ancestral tumuli and memorials in the form of *stūpa*s and *caitya*s was part of the ritual to establish connections. The Vedic sacrificial ritual was not encouraged. There was therefore no private ownership of land by individuals in these societies and the power of the *gṛhapati* as a separate entity was reduced not only because of the insistence on the common ownership of land but also because of its being worked directly by labour. References to land revenue are absent although some taxes are said to have been collected from traders coming to the cities[33] associated with the *gaṇa-saṅgha*s. The residences of the *rājā-kula* were nucleated settlements which often evolved into towns. Sources of a later period refer to officers of an administrative category[34] but these were either anachronistic references or else the officials were part of a rudimentary administration which had not as yet taken on the characteristics of a full-fledged state system. The *gaṇa-saṅgha*s consisted either of a single clan such as those of the Śākyas, Koliyas and Mallas or else could be a confederation of clans as in the case of the Vṛjjis who incorporated the Licchavis and various others and had their settlement at the town of Vaiśāli. The distribution of the *gaṇa-saṅgha*s in the middle Ganga valley was largely in the area of present-day north Bihar and the adjoining areas of eastern Uttar Pradesh.

The highest status in these societies was given to the *kṣatriya*.[35] In the absence of large-scale *yajña*s the function of the *brāhmaṇa* would be limited. The *varṇa* system is referred to although more often in a theoretical sense as when the Buddha is describing the stages by which government was instituted together with social stratification.[36] Actual social distinctions relate more closely to the *jāti*s which are generally divided into two categories, the high and the low.[37] The emphasis on birth continues in the *jāti* system and becomes even more specific in the reference to the *ñāti* which has been rendered as, the extended kin-group.[38] References to *gṛhapatis/gahapatis* occur more often in the context of Kosala, Kāśī and Magadha, recognized as kingdoms.

The *gaṇa-saṅgha* system cannot be referred to as a non-state system since it has some of the germinal forms which were a precondition to the state, nor can it be called a state since the institutions associated with the infrastructure of a state are not present. It can perhaps best be described as representing a point along a continuum towards state formation, what Morton Fried,[39] has called stratified societies prior to the emergence of states.

The state emerges together with a monarchical system in Kosala and Magadha and the factors which led to this change relate to the lineage system and its transmutation into a state system. The continuation of the lineage system is perhaps most evident in the establishing of the *varṇa* status as a complementary system to whatever other changes took place. The essentials of a lineage society such as control over marriage alliances within a careful grid of hierarchy and social distance, the maintenance of lineage connections, commensality, and occupational activities adhered in form at least to the *varṇa* system. Parallel to this there emerged another stratification where the dual division into the *gṛhapati*s and the *dāsa-bhṛtaka*s was the main feature. The *gṛhapati*s could be of any of the three *dvija varṇa*s and the *dāsa-bhṛtaka*s were of the *śūdra varṇa* which by now had multiple sub-sections relating to cultivators, artisans, and subordinated tribal groups. The role of the *gṛhapati* as reflected in the *sūtra* literature of the post-Vedic period was of central importance and related both to the changes in agriculture and the beginnings of trade. The intensification of agriculture meant the production of a larger surplus. Not all of this was given in prestation or consumed in the sacrificial ritual. What remained in the hands of the *gṛhapati* became his personal wealth and this was particularly the case with the *brāhmaṇa gṛhapatis* who are described as *mahāśāla* or very wealthy.[40] With the claim to family ownership over the land cultivated the notion of private ownership became current. The rise of ideologies questioning the sacrificial ritual such as the discourses of the *Upaniṣads* and *Āraṇyakas* to begin with and subsequently the teachings of Mahāvīra and the Buddha loosened the ties of the *gṛhapati* to the prestation economy. This enabled him to use his wealth not only to enhance his status but also to invest in trade when the commercial economy became viable. In the latter situation it was the wealthy *gṛhapati* who became the *śreṣṭhin*[41] (he who has the best).

The roots of trade doubtless go back to the local circuits of exchange. These would arise from villages specializing in particular professions and products[42] such as the salt-makers' village and the potters' village and the carpenters' village. Such villages would have supplied the local markets or *nigama* of the Buddhist texts.[43] (The *nigama* seems to have been a market centre rather than a town since the commercial areas of towns are sometimes called *nigamas*.) Added to this were the itinerant herders and professionals who worked a regular circuit and complemented their basic activities with itinerant trade. Ironsmiths would have played a major role in fostering links along local circuits as they do to this day. The major iron deposits being limited to south Bihar, the peripatetic smith became a necessity. The routes of migration into the Ganga valley were to develop into regular trade routes. Thus the northern route along the Himalayan foothills, the Uttarapatha, linked the upper Ganga–Yamuna *doāb* via Kosala and Vaiśāli with Magadha. The southern route followed the right bank of the Yamuna and the Ganga past Magadha and into the adjoining region of Aṅga (Bhagalpur). This route was also linked through the Chambal river and the Malwa corridor to Ujjain and continued across the Narmada to the upper Godavari valley and came to be known as the famous Dakṣiṇāpatha (the southern route). The river system of the Ganga in itself provided a circuit of communication with major settlements at nodal points along the rivers which were to grow into the *mahānagaras* or the great cities of the later period.

Kosala controlled a vital segment of the Uttarapatha and this may explain why the capital was shifted to Śrāvastī in the north. Its earlier capital at Ayodhyā remained important, however, as it lay on the route to Kauśāmbi whose importance was based on its control of the southern route along the Ganga valley and its access to the main Dakṣiṇāpatha. Magadha lay as it were, at the confluence of the two routes and its extension eastwards to Aṅga and the Ganga delta. Magadhan antagonism towards Vaiśāli was almost inevitable since Vaiśāli was crucial to the control of the Uttarapatha as also was Kosala which Magadha eventually annexed. Magadha also controlled the Vindhyan route to central India via the Son valley. The eventual shift of the Magadhan capital from Rājagṛha to Pāṭaligāma on the Ganga river was again to enable it to control the terminal point of these routes.

Routes and itinerant traders do not in themselves lead to the development of commerce. The larger circuit of trade was developed on the basis of exchange between areas more distant. Such exchanges may have been initiated by marriage alliances among the *kṣatriya* families and exchanges of prestigious goods. Such alliances were frequent in the middle Ganga valley but were also known to extend further in contacts between the *kṣatriya* families of Kosala and Kekeya for instance. These alliances would have fostered an elite trade in luxury goods acting as a counterpart to the more mundane but necessary exchanges involved in the circuits of iron-smiths and salt traders. Salt, metals, textiles, and pottery were the standard items of trade at this time.[44] The distribution of the Northern Black Polished Ware with its provenance in the area between Varanasi and Patna is an indicator of the gradual rippling out of trading circuits. That there may have been some demands on Indian goods from areas within the Indian subcontinent but included in non-Indian states, such as Gandhāra would have to be examined. Gandhāra was a part of the Achaemenid empire and items of Indian manufacture are said to have been used in west Asia.[45] Similarly, the possibility of a sea trade between Mesopotamia and the west coast of India to which there are tantalizingly ambiguous[46] references may have provided a further incentive to trade within the northern part of the subcontinent.

That the trade was based on a recognized medium of exchange would seem clear from the discovery of punch-marked coins in silver and copper from various urban sites going back to levels of the mid-first millennium BC. This evidence is corroborated by the descriptions of coins in the grammar of Pāṇini.[47] Although there is some controversy[48] as to who issued the coins it would seem that they are in the main local issues since the combination of designs punched on the coins tend to relate to particular areas. This would suggest that the mechanism of trade was relatively decentralized although the state derived a revenue from it.

The trading community of *vaṇijas* and *seṭṭhis* (traders and merchants) came from the ranks of the *gṛhapatis* and by now the activities of the *vaiśya* are also described as cattle-rearing, agriculture, and trade. The *gṛhapatis* as landowners experienced further changes. The private ownership of land resulted in some very rich households of landowners. But it also led to the subdivision of landholdings and the cultivation of land by tenants some of whom as cultivators had *śūdra* status. Mention is also made of revenue collected from those who cultivated land. Assessment officers measured the land and its produce and calculated the taxes.[49] The king's share was later said to have been one-sixth *ṣad-bhāga* of the produce and this was collected at regular intervals.[50] That these were not prestations but a range of taxes is clear from the fact that in each case it was a contracted amount, stipulated in advance, regularly collected and channelled through an administrative hierarchy of officers. The justification for tax collection is explained in the theory that when stratification became intense and disorder prevailed in society, it was decided that one person should be selected or nominated to maintain law and order and to protect society; and the wages for both these functions were to be gathered as taxes by the ruler.[51] With the establishment of a revenue collecting system political authority began to see the additional advantage of opening waste land to settlers.[52]

These changes brought about the presence of two new groups, the traders and the peasants. Since there was no separate identity for them in the *varṇa* system they were included, together with other groups in the *vaiśya* and the *śūdra varṇa* respectively.

Furthermore, both indicated the weakening if not the breaking in some areas, of the prestation economy as the main economic force. In this they were assisted by the new ideologies of Buddhism and Jainism which, even though they arose among the *kṣatriyas* of the *gaṇa-saṅghas*, were more vigorously preached in the cities of the kingdoms of Kosala, Kāśī, and Magadha. The new ideologies were not in favour of burning wealth in the *yajñas* but rather in accumulating and investing it.[53] That accumulation required austerities is fully supported in the exhortation to the lay-followers to refrain from indulgences of various kinds and lead a balanced and generally puritanical life. Brahmanical sources were suspicious of those who lived in cities and objected on principle to the investment of wealth and the earning of interest on investment.[54] Buddhist sources on the other hand, eulogize the *seṭṭhi,* encourage usury, and are generally sympathetic to the urban dwellers. With the weakening of clan ties the monastic institutions provided new networks of relations and this was strengthened in the idea of the lay-follower and the monk being interdependent. Many of these new ideologies harked back to the values of the lineage society in as much as social groups were more egalitarian and the individual had a predetermined niche. These values were sought to be resurrected or continued in the monastic institutions. But the contradiction in the situation was that in order to maintain the monasteries the new religions required, in the initial stages, both the direct patronage of the state as well as a society rich enough to support the monks through alms. Such a society would presuppose at least the rudiments of a state, and to that extent a decline in lineage society.

Theories of the origin of the state shift the focus from the *rājanya* who protects the *jana* to the *kṣatriya* who both protects as well as maintains law and order and whose control grows out of a notion of sovereignty. Ultimately even the *kṣatriya* is not sufficient and the state is visualized as the intermeshing of seven elements or limbs (*prakṛtis* or *aṅgas*) among which the king is one of the elements.[55] The others are *amātya* (ministers and administration in general), *janapada/rāṣṭra* (territory), *durga* (fortified settlement or royal capital), *kośa* (treasury), *daṇḍa* (force, army or the right to coercion), and *mitra* (external ally). With the discussion of the *saptāṅga* theory in the Kauṭilya *Arthaśāstra* the concept of the state can be said to have arrived. The prestation economy of the lineage society was now, in the middle Ganga valley, largely a formal ritual of legitimation which was performed by some kings. Thus Pasenadi of Kosala had all the required *yajñas* performed when he became king.[56] But the *yajña* consumed only a part of the wealth. On a lesser scale this was also true of the *gṛhya* sacrifices which in terms of economic outlay did not consume the substantial part of the household's wealth. It is significant that the most powerful monarchies of the middle Ganga valley, namely, those of the Nandas and Mauryas, ignored Vedic rituals, supported the 'heterodox' sects and not surprisingly are described in brahmanical sources as *śūdra* and *adharmaḥ*.[57]

This attempt at examining the process of state formation in the middle Ganga valley suggests a complex process involving a series of inter-related changes. It is also a gradual process and even when the state is established it is not a unitary, monolithic, centralized state to begin with nor do the earlier forms totally disappear: in fact there is an overlap which continues for sometime. This overlapping situation accounts in part for the complicated stratification registering caste groups and also the movement towards incipient classes, the two systems sometimes converging. The mobility of the group and its ability to migrate in a condition of tension reduces the trend towards state formation since migration enables groups to readjust without changing their social forms. The amount of wealth produced and the direction given to the use of wealth is also crucial as a factor inhibiting or encouraging the formation of a state. Ideologies have also to be considered central to frustrating or developing the notion of the state. As a continuing historical process, state formation requires an analysis not merely of the transition from non-state to state but also the typologies of states as they take form under varying circumstances.

Notes and References

1. R. Cohen and E. Service (eds), *Origins of the State,* Philadelphia, 1978; H.J.M. Claessen and P. Skalnik (eds), *The Early State,* The Hague,

1978; L. Krader, *Formation of the State,* New Jersey, 1968; M. Fried, *The Evolution of Political Society,* New York, 1967.

2. I. Goldman, *Ancient Polynesian Society,* Chicago, 1970; J. Middleton and D. Tait, *Tribes Without Rulers,* London, 1964; *Political Systems and the Distribution of Power,* ASA Monographs 2, London, 1965.

3. L. Krader, *Formation of the State; Arthaśāstra,* I.8.

4. *ranjitaśca prajāh sarvastena rājeti śabdyate . . . Mahābhārata,* Śānti Parvan, 59, 127ff.

5. Cf. Proto-Dravidian *vel.* DED 4562 and 4524. For a discussion on the etymology of *rex* and *rājā* see E. Benveniste, *Indo-European Language and Society,* London, 1975, pp. 311–12.

6. *Ṛg Veda,* X.173.1; X.124.8; J.P. Sharma, *Republics in Ancient India,* Leiden, 1968.

7. *Vedic Index,* II, p. 305; I. p. 356.

8. *Śatapatha Brāhmaṇa,* VII.1.1.4–8; *Aitareya Brāhmaṇa,* VIII.21.8.

9. Romila Thapar, '*Dāna* and *Dakṣiṇā* as Forms of Exchange', in *Ancient Indian Social History: Some Interpretations,* New Delhi, 1978, pp. 105ff.

10. Ibid.

11. Suraj Bhan, *Excavation at Mitathal (1980) and other Explorations in the Sutlej-Yamuna Divide,* Kurukshetra, 1975; Suraj Bhan and J.G. Shaffer, 'New Discoveries in Northern Haryana', *Man and Environment,* 1978, II, pp. 59–68; K.N. Dikshit, 'Exploration along the Right Bank of River Sutlej in Punjab', *Journal of History,* 1967, 45, part II, pp. 561–8; J.P. Joshi, 'Interlocking of Late Harappan Culture and Painted Grey Ware Culture in the Light of Recent Excavations', *Man and Environment,* 1978, II, pp. 100–3.

12. R.L. Carneiro, 'A Theory of the Origin of the State', *Science,* 1970, 169, pp. 733–8.

13. M.M. Deshpande and P.E. Hook, *Aryan and Non-Aryan in India,* Ann Arbor, 1978.

14. K.A. Chaudhuri, *Ancient Agriculture and Forestry in Northern India,* Bombay, 1977; V. Tripathi, *The Painted Grey Ware, an Iron Age Culture of Northern India,* Delhi, 1979.

15. R. Pleiner, 'The Problems of the Beginning Iron Age in India', *Acta Praehistorica et Archaeologica,* 1971, 2, pp. 5–36.

16. For example, the Khāṇḍava-vana which was cleared to establish the settlement of Indraprastha, *Mahābhārata,* Ādi Parvan, 199.25ff, 214–19.

17. IV.3.3.15; XII.7.3.8; III.3.2.8; II.5.2.6; II.5.2.27; VII.1.1.4; III.l

18. *Ṛg Veda,* VII.6.5; X.173.6; *Atharvaveda,* III.4.2.3.

19. *Taittirīya Samhitā,* I.8.9.2; *Taittirīya Brāhmaṇa,* I.7.5.

20. *Ṛg Veda,* VII.82.6; VIII.1.5; *Atharvaveda,* III.29.3.

21. *Curtius Rufus,* IX.4; cf. *Mahābhārata,* Sabhā Parvan, 48.14; *Pāṇini,* II.4.10.

22. As is clarified in the *Gṛhyasūtras* which provide for a variation in the domestic ritual depending on the *varṇa* of the person, e.g., *Āśvalāyana Gṛhyasūtra,* I.19.

23. J. Gonda, *Ancient Indian Kingship from the Religious Point of View,* Leiden, 1969.

24. Hereditary succession is emphasized in the two epics but is infrequently referred to in Vedic literature.

25. The function of these assemblies have been discussed at length by various scholars whose views have been summarized and added to in R.S. Sharma, *Aspects of Political Ideas and Institutions in Ancient India,* Delhi, 1968 and J.P. Sharma, *Republics in Ancient India,* Leiden, 1968.

26. Romila Thapar, 'Origin Myths and the Early Indian Historical Tradition', in *Ancient Indian Social History: Some Interpretations,* pp. 294ff.

27. *Śatapatha Brāhmaṇa,* I.4.1.14–17.

28. D.P. Agrawal and S. Kusumgar, *Prehistoric Chronology and Radio-Carbon Dating in India,* New Delhi, 1974, pp. 138ff.

29. E. Boserup, *The Conditions of Agricultural Growth,* London, 1965; M.R. Haswell, *The Economics of Subsistence Agriculture,* London, 1967.

30. W.B. Bollee, *Kunāla Jātaka,* London, 1970, pp. 1ff.

31. *Dīgha Nikāya,* II.73ff.

32. N. Wagle, *Society at the Time of the Buddha,* Bombay, 1966, pp. 134ff.

33. This reference is from a much later text the *Sumaṅgalavilāsinī,* I.338.

34. Ibid., II.59; II.673.

35. *Dīgha Nikāya,* I.97–107.

36. Ibid., III, 80–98.

37. *Aṅguttara Nikāya,* I.162.

38. Wagle, *Society at the Time of the Buddha,* pp. 122ff. V.S. Agrawala, *India as Known to Pāṇini,* Varanasi, 1963, p. 93.

39. M. Fried, *The Evolution of Political Society,* 1967, pp. 185ff.

40. *Saṃyutta Nikāya,* I.74.

41. *Aṅguttara Nikāya,* IV.282; *Mahāvagga,* I.7.4; *Cullavagga,* VI.4.1.

42. *Vinaya Piṭaka,* I.207; *Aṅguttara Nikāya,* II.182.

43. *Dīgha Nikāya,* I.7; *Majjhima Nikāya,* I.429; I.488.

44. Agrawala, *India as Known to Pāṇini,* pp. 240ff.

45. E.J. Rapson, *The Cambridge History of India,* Cambridge, 1922, vol. I, 1935, pp: 391ff.

46. Ibid.

47. *Pāṇini,* V.I.19–37.

48. D.D. Kosambi, *Indian Numismatics,* New Delhi, 1981.

49. *Jātaka,* III, 376.

50. Manu, 7.131; 8.305–8. *Arthaśāstra,* II, 15; *Baudhāyana DS,* I.10.6.

51. Ibid.

52. *Dīgha Nikāya,* III.80–98.

53. Ibid., III.188.

54. *Baudhāyana Dharmasūtra,* I.5.10.23–25; *Vasiṣṭha Dharmasūtra,* II.40–42.

55. *Arthaśāstra,* VI.l.

56. *Saṁyutta Nikāya,* III. 1.9.

57. F.E. Pargiter, *The Purana Texts of the Dynasties of the Kali Age,* Oxford, 1913, pp. 25ff.

CHAPTER 7

Black Gold

*South Asia and the Roman Maritime Trade**

The writing of the early history of South Asia has been largely land-locked. Major studies of the Indian Ocean or the lesser seas generally begin with the rise of Islam. In choosing to speak on an earlier period my intention is not only to underline the continuity of maritime contacts, but also to go behind the artefacts, as it were. The significance of trade lies not only in the items exchanged but also in the nature of the exchange and the mutation of the cultures communicating through the trade. Trading diasporas, where traders as a distinct quasi-cultural group provide channels for the movement of goods between disparate societies, is one aspect of trans-cultural trade,[1] but interventions in the evolution of societies are equally significant. A diversity of items changed hands; some as objects of simple exchange or of purchase, others perhaps as fetishized commodities. The same cargo may play multiple roles. My endeavour in trying to shift the focus in these directions is necessarily hedged in by the limitations of the current evidence which may involve asking more questions than providing answers.

Roman maritime trade was the first extensive contact between Europe and Asia. The geographical pattern of the contact—the foci of maritime trade, the locations of harbours, the routes using monsoon winds and ocean currents—recurred in later centuries

* This is an expanded version of the South Asia Lecture given at the South Asian Studies Association Conference at Armidale in July 1992. It was originally published in *South Asia,* n.s., vol. 15, no. 2, 1992 pp. 1–28.

with similar overlaps of traders, commercial interests, and cargoes. But those who provided its investment changed over time as also did the economic relations between traders and host countries. Trade with Asia remained, as an activity, somewhat distant to the Romans themselves, except that with the exotica which the trade brought to them they fantasized about the east, a fantasy which is encapsulated in the phrase, *ex oriente lux.* The actual merchants were mainly Greek or Jewish from Egypt and the eastern Mediterranean as well as Palmyrene and Levantine from the Hellenized world. The financial outlay appears to have been largely from this area although it has been argued that wealthy Romans invested in this trade.[2] But increasingly these traders had the backing of local Roman administration and among others, catered to the expensive tastes of Roman patricians. Although the eventual market was Rome, the actual functioning of the maritime trade focused on Egypt and to a lesser extent on the eastern Mediterranean. From the South Asian perspective one could as well use the nomenclature familiar from those times and refer to it as the Yavana maritime trade.[3]

The commonly used phrase, 'Roman maritime trade with India' refers to the categories of trade and exchange through maritime channels between the eastern Mediterranean as a part of the Roman empire and various regions of the Indian subcontinent. The term 'Roman' is not intended to suggest that Rome itself conducted the trade but refers rather to the fact that the administration of the trade and the profits thereof in the eastern Mediterranean were within the control and jurisdiction of the Roman imperial system. The volume of trade and its impact on Indian centres varied; but where it was substantial, there the Roman maritime trade can be viewed as a significant factor of economic and social concern. It speaks for the profits of the trade that in spite of difficulties it was pursued for so long. The Indian markets supplied exotic and aromatic plants and spices—nard, bdellium, costus, aloes, and pepper; semi-precious stones—chalcedonies, beryls, and pearls; a variety of textiles—silk, fine linens and cotton; timbers such as teak and ebony and fragrant sandalwood; all from different parts of the subcontinent, and even tortoise shell and perhaps cinnamon from Sri Lanka and Southeast Asia. The traders from Egypt brought to South Asia a range of goods but most frequently lead, tin, coral, glass, wine and above all in the largest number, Roman coins in gold and silver, used in varying ways in different parts of the subcontinent. Judging by the presence of coins in South Asia, the trade commenced on the cusp of the Christian era, with the earliest major collections of coins being those of imperial Rome, reaching its peak in the first century AD. Recent finds of coins of the Roman Republic in south India, antedating the imperial issues, may point to a possibly earlier start to contacts, and this has also been argued from archaeological and palaeographical data.[4] It has, however, also been argued that the coins of the Republic could have been circulating together with early Imperial coins and do not, therefore, indicate an earlier start to the trade. The Ptolemies had some idea about the potentials of such a trade even if they did not fully explore it.

Roman maritime trade in the Indian Ocean makes a neat arc from Alexandria to Malacca and if I may borrow a phrase, it was held together by the 'urban gravitation'[5] of Coptos on the Nile, Barygaza in western India, Sopara in the western Deccan, Muziris on the Malabar coast and Kāveripaṭṭinam in the Kaveri delta, and their expansive hinterlands. As it inched its way eastwards it threaded through these distinct segments often underlining diverse socioeconomic patterns. The sea creates its own frontiers and zones of activity and these, do not invariably coincide with the boundaries of land-based territories. Just prior to the Roman trade the Hellenistic kingdoms, motivated by politics and commercial interests, began to re-explore earlier links. By the third century BC, Mauryan contact with the Hellenistic kingdoms of the Seleucids, Ptolemies, and their neighbours are well-established.[6] The Roman maritime trade extended the geographical area of these contacts and realized the potential of economic activities.

Localized circuits of exchange and trade, linking ports and extending into hinterlands sometimes quite far into the interior, existed prior to the Roman trade. Among these were those from the Mediterranean towards the Red Sea pursued by the Phoenicians; the two coasts of the Red Sea involving local seafarers as well as the Ptolemaic search for elephants, which extended this circuit to east Africa and more hesitantly perhaps to South Asia; the caravan trade of southern Arabia with the eastern Mediterranean; the commerce between Syria and the Arab Persian Gulf with the Seleucids encouraging Indian commercial links;[7] the ports in western India drawing on the prosperous commercial centres in the hinterland of northern India and maintaining contact, probably through a looping trade, with ports along the coast of the Arabian peninsula, many of which were dependent on this trade for import of food, especially rice, sugar, sesame oil, and *ghī,* as well as cotton cloth; the circuits of the Megalithic people of the Indian peninsula and of Sri Lanka further underscored by Mauryan intervention; possible east coast connections with areas across the Bay of Bengal; and the exchange networks within the islands of Southeast Asia extending to southern China.

Trade in consumables and food items could well remain a down-the-line coastal trade. But the trade in luxury items, as well as the availability of a large fleet of ships financed by commerce from Egypt and the eastern Mediterranean, encouraged greater risks. A faster mid-ocean route, regularly using monsoon winds, becomes more attractive for such trade. Ideally it was limited to a brief period of the year when the harbours of the west coast of India are serviceable in September and which enables a return to the Red Sea later with the start of the northeast monsoon. The return journey had to be undertaken by December or at the latest, January. Setting out too early, even with using the southwest monsoon, was not only hazardous but entailed a longer wait in an Indian harbour before returning.[8] The gradual emergence of the Red Sea as the main artery of Roman maritime trade to the east dislodged the pre-eminence of the Arab Persian Gulf. The Red Sea route avoided the hostile Parthians closer to the Persian Gulf, required negotiation with the more malleable Arab traders and brought the west coast of India into quicker contact. The Red Sea route did, however, require the taking on board of archers as a protection against piracy.[9] Cargo arriving at the ports of the Red Sea was transported overland to Coptos and from there taken down the Nile to Alexandria. Such transportation was familiar to the Egyptian administration and economy since grain had been regularly transported down the Nile from Upper Egypt to Alexandria under the Ptolemies. The small-scale canal transportation was in Egyptian hands but the large-scale grain business on the Nile was controlled by the Greeks from Alexandria. The Levantines also participated in this trade.[10] The earlier transportation formed an important circuit and was doubtless easily adapted to include the cargoes from the east. Roman trade over-arched some of the existing circuits but this did not result in their termination, in fact to the contrary, it could act as an incentive to increasing their activity. A fuller assessment of this trade would require a view beyond the circuits to their hinterlands and these differ widely, but in attempting to analyse the trade these differences have to be considered.

Discussions on the Roman economy have generally projected a predominantly agricultural economy with trade playing a marginal role in what has been referred to as the presumed cellular self-sufficiency of the ancient economy. This view is now changing as it is taking cognizance of the nature of the role of trade.[11] Whereas in its social attitudes Roman patrician society was prejudiced against trade and traders, as an economic activity it was significant not only to the Roman economy but also to the patrician lifestyle.[12] The question has been posed as to whether the Roman empire constituted a world-system in terms of the World Systems Analysis[13] where Roman trade would be an important manifestation. As an area of investigation within this theory, the Roman trade with Asia would be additionally significant if in fact there was an imperial policy towards it as well as imperial investment, as has been suggested.[14] The theory assumes a differentiation between two social systems: one was the small, subsistence economy, largely autonomous and not part of a tribute demanding system; the other was the large state containing a multiplicity of cultures and a division of labour related to the most efficient form of production. Of the latter kind there are two categories: the world empire and the world economy. The world empire is linked by a uniform political system which dominates the various interrelated societies within its boundaries and with enough agricultural surplus to maintain artisans and the administrative stratum. The world economy is fundamentally different with no political unity and with the redistribution of the surplus via the market. It is divided into core states and peripheral states where the former extracts the surplus from the latter in the form of resources. The frontier between the two is the semi-periphery which can also act as a link. The operation of the system revolved around two dichotomies based on unequal exchange: control over production and the appropriation by the centre of the produce of the periphery.[15] The theory concedes that some pre-capitalist world economies may be postulated, such as in China, Persia, and Rome, but these changed into world empires.

Relating primarily to capitalism and excluding the pre-capitalist world, the theory appears nonetheless to have caught the fancy of archaeologists and has been used to investigate centre–periphery relations in various sectors of the Roman empire and in other areas of the ancient world.[16] Whereas the Roman empire may or may not confirm to the world empire model, the world economy model seems inapplicable to Roman trade with Asia. Trade alone does not necessarily define centre and periphery nor result in a hegemony of the centre over the periphery even if the trade in pre-capitalist societies was more extensive than is envisaged in the theory. However, trade can act in some places as a catalyst whereas in others it is subordinated to local economic patterns. Some of the questions which the World Systems Analysis and its critique have raised, such as the nature of centre–periphery relations, could be pertinent to the changes which occurred in the areas involved in the trade. Perhaps the nature of a centre–periphery relationship can be sought in the smaller circuits where new forms of economic and political power emerged in association with the changes brought about by the trade, but these would not necessarily conform to the model. Thus in the context of the Roman trade, the dominance of the Cambay region in western India suggests a pattern almost of a centre–centre trade. As a contrast, the Malabar coast remains ambiguous and does not conform to an easily recognizable pattern.

What is of greater significance is an assessment of conditions in areas to which the trade reaches out, the differences from region to region and the perception, both cultural and economic, of the foreign traders among those with whom they trade. Mechanisms of exchange were neither uniform nor universal. They included barter, gift-exchange, formalized trade, and monetized commodity exchange involving markets. Some of these categories co-existed in the same region but there was usually a priority among them which differed among different cultures. Each had its own complexities, even barter, which is generally dismissed as simple.[17] Barter could occur in the absence of money or in a condition of paucity of coins or even as a form of social distancing from commercial activities. The social back-up of barter was frequently the larger group of the family or the clan. A backing for the exchange of commodities came from more impersonal organizations such as guilds or corporations of traders. Gift-exchange underwrites social relations but also requires strategy and calculation.[18] Where a trade item is converted into a gift, even money can be absorbed as a valuable rather than a currency. Cargo can also consist of fetishized objects. It is thus as well to remind ourselves that, 'A commodity appears at first sight an extremely obvious, trivial thing. But its analysis brings out that it is a very strange thing, abounding in metaphysical subtleties and theological niceties.'[19] To assess the value of an item, therefore, involves looking at many dimensions of a society.

This in turn relates to the items exchanged and the mechanism of obtaining these. Raw materials are extracted from some areas, while in others trade demands sophisticated production. Exchange involved a series of transactions, some between the foreign trader and the local middleman or the merchant and some between the latter and the supplier of cargoes. Such transactions would register a regional divergence. Hinterlands are governed by varying characteristics and changed over space and time. Existing economies influenced the nature of the trade, and changes in the pattern of trade are pointers to social change. Activities under the rubric of trade are of many kinds and these are linked to itinerant pastoralism, travelling pedlars, clan chiefs, middlemen, traders. These may exist separately or be knitted together in an overarching trade. Thus whereas peddling is an occupation, trade requires an investment.[20]

Traders and ships crews are carriers of a particular culture. Their initial incursions have to be backed by a political interest if a literate high culture is to be introduced. From the western perspective the trade acted as a link between exchange nodes, ports of call, and perhaps the mobile settlements of the traders from the west. From the perspective of those on whom the Roman traders called, the view is different. Within the boundaries of the Roman maritime trade in Asia there is the striking difference between the rather limited Mediterranean cultural imprint on India, and on the other hand, what has been called the 'indigenization' of Indian culture in Southeast Asia. Yet both were not unrelated to the initial demands of the Roman trade.

The interpretation of Roman maritime trade with South Asia has moved from listing items and claiming cultural influences to assessing social and economic patterns.[21] At first studies remained close to the texts, usefully identifying ports and items. The focus shifted with the introduction of archaeological and numismatic data. The argument was frequently posed in terms of Roman influence on India. Viewed from the Indian perspective, the widespread distribution of Roman gold and silver coins in peninsula India would superficially suggest that the trade had overwhelmed Indian networks of exchange. However, the complaint of Pliny that the oriental trade was draining the finances of Rome[22] was read as a statement of the economically superior position of India. But the impact of the trade and the imprint of wealth varied in different parts of India largely because of the dissimilar conditions in the subcontinent, which makes generalizations about India as a whole in relation to this trade, questionable. The evidence of coins alone suggests a pattern which points to divergences in different areas. Backed by other evidence the variation stands out even more strongly. Given this, neither barter nor market exchange appears to have been universal.

Western India, including the ports of Barbaricon and Barygaza (Bhṛgukaccha, Bhārukaccha/Bharuch) was known not only to the maritime traders of West Asia but also as an extension of the overland trade from West Asia to India. Barygaza is mentioned more frequently than any other emporium and inevitably had an important role in the Roman trade. Barbaricon was the port to the capital further up the river. The silting up of Barbaricon, known to happen in the Indus delta, may have ended its existence as a port and led to a convergence on Barygaza coinciding with the inclusion of central India as an area of production and internal trade. At the other end of this circuit there is little evidence of Indian ships docking in the northern ports of the Red Sea and this may have been partly because Indian ships were not permitted beyond Ocelis.[23] The Sabaeans in southwest Arabia are said to have acted as middle-men between India and the Mediterranean world, prior to the development of the Roman trade.[24] Perhaps the coral reefs made it dangerous and only the local seamen could handle these conditions. [25] The *Periplus,* a traders' manual probably dating to the mid-first century AD, states that Aden declined as a port after Ptolemaic times and this doubtless coincided with the growth of the Red Sea ports such as Berenice, Myos Hormus, and Leucos Limen (Quseir-al-Qadim).[26] Strabo refers to a fleet of 120 ships sailing from Myos Hormus to India.[27] This was a radically different situation from the coastal voyages of the earlier trade. It suggests considerable control over shipping in the Red Sea and raises the question of who administered the control—local Arab interests or the Roman administration. The appointment of an official, the *epistrategos,* in charge of the Red Sea and the eastern desert of Egypt, which was a Roman continuation of a Ptolemaic practice, would suggest that the local Arabs were edged out of the major trade. The inability or the prevention of Indian ships moving freely in the Red Sea might have been one of the reasons for the initiative of the Indian trade going into Egyptian hands. Indians as individual merchants are however listed as among those who trade in Egypt and are known at Alexandria.[28] Ostracon inscriptions in Prākrit at Quseir have been read as referring to merchants[29] and graffiti in Tamil Brāhmi on potsherds from the same area could be Tamil names.[30] The connections appear to have been with south India.[31] A much-discussed Greek inscription found closer to the Nile refers to an Indian, Sophon (probably Subhānu) who addresses a prayer to the god Pan and was evidently a Hellenized Indian.[32]

Western India shows a familiarity with more than one pattern of exchange. The Ābhīras, who were initially itinerant pastoralists but later took to other occupations, give their name to the coastal area which was now associated with a sophisticated commerce. Barygaza was also a manufacturing centre and therefore imported some raw materials as well as commodities such as silverware, wine, and perfume not to mention slave girls and musicians.[33] The hinterland of Barygaza from Saurashtra to central India included more distant areas from where silk and Kashmir nard was brought to be exported to the west. The rich trading centres of this hinterland such as Mathura and Ujjain, were familiar with monetary media and had used local high-value coins contemporary with the arrival of the traders from the eastern Mediterranean. The paucity of Roman gold coins in northern India may not have been because the Kuṣāṇas melted the metal to mint their own coins, but because there was little need for yet another monetary medium in the area, although there may be more grounds for suggesting that the Kṣatrapa silver currency of western India re-used Roman originals.[34] Many parts of the Indian subcontinent, including western India, had known the circulation of punch-marked coins. Although this coinage is distinct from that associated with the Roman trade, nevertheless some familiarity with monetary exchange has to be assumed for the areas where the punch-marked coins circulated. In the first century AD there is an import of Roman *denarii* into western India which, it is said, can be exchanged with much profit for the local currency,[35] but this declines. The Roman trade at Barygaza appears to have been handled by local merchants. Given the variance in forms of trade and the circulation of coins in the area, it is unlikely that the nature of this exchange was limited to barter rather than commerce as has been suggested by way of an explanation for the lack of Roman coins. The nature of the commercial exchange in itself may have precluded the presence of Roman coins although indigenous coins are available.

Further down along the west coast were the port of Suppāra (Suppāraka/Sopara) and the city of Kalliena (Kalyāna). The importance of the former dates to the Mauryan period. In a Buddhist *Jātaka* story it is linked to Bhārukaccha and associated with mariners and seamanship.[36] The hinterland of the two ports fanned out to central India and the Deccan, the network of which can be mapped by epigraphic references at Buddhist sites to donors from various places.[37] The resources of this hinterland had been earlier tapped by the local Chalcolithic and Megalithic people. The Mauryas in turn had sought access to timber, a large range of semi-precious stones such as carnelian, quartz, and agate used for making beads and other forest produce. Processes of exchange were therefore a familiar activity moving towards more complex forms of exchange, but there was a continuity in the items sought by the western trade. The tapping of resources was juxtaposed with centres of production and with towns controlling a sophisticated trade along the routes to the ports. Paithan and Ter in the western Deccan are said to send textiles along almost impassable routes to Barygaza. Bhokardan in the same area was a bead-making centre.[38] The nexus between elite politics and mercantile communities is evident from royalty investing sums of money in craftsmen's guilds by way of a donation, with the interest on the investment going to the Buddhist monasteries.[39] Cash donations involving large sums of money are again indicative of the widespread use of monetary exchange in western India and the western Deccan. The distribution of Sātavāhana coinage in the Deccan confirms the same. Although some rulers built rest-houses along the longer routes, nevertheless the monasteries must have acted as staging points as they do elsewhere. At those where the halt was necessary prior to facing the difficult terrain of the *ghat*s such as at Nasik, Junnar, Karle, Bedsa, and Kolhapur, or at terminal points such as Barygaza or Sopara, the endowments in the vicinity were impressive.[40] Even the monastic complex at Kanheri near Sopara was associated with what has been called a 'sub-urban complex'.[41] Frequent and sizeable donations by traders and artisans point to a growth in the commercial economy as compared to the earlier period and in the general expansion of subcontinental and trans-Asian trade, the maritime trade with Egypt played no small role in these parts. A significant body of donors were women—wives of traders, artisans, and small-scale landowners as well as nuns.

Inscriptions refer to a large range of professions involved in the production of a variety of commodities. Among these, goldsmiths and workers in semi-precious stones are prominent and this is backed by archaeological evidence of bead-working in the western Deccan.[42] Donors at Buddhist sacred sites, identify themselves with towns in the area. Guilds of ivory-carvers, weavers, potters, oil-pressers, bamboo-workers, and corn dealers are also mentioned.[43] Categories of persons involved in trade include the *seṭṭhi* or financier, the *vanij* or merchant, the *sārthavāha* or transporter and the *negama* who is associated with the market. Other sources describe ships arriving in port with merchants bidding for cargo, of merchants at border towns or in dialogue with producers.[44]

Not surprisingly a large range of items associated with the eastern Mediterranean surfaces at sites in the western Deccan.[45] Some were imported and others were local imitations. Smaller objects, such as bronze figures and Roman lamps, had their local imitations. Clay bullae suggest the same. Roman amphorae, generally containing wine or oil, were bulk items and may well have doubled as ballast. Judging by the distribution of the sherds there appears to have been a brisk market for wine. It has been argued that luxury trade required bulk goods as an economic balance since bulk goods with a saleable value maximize cargo space and freight revenue.[46] The large number of items from the Mediterranean which turn up in western India may also have come through the overland trade although coastal sites appear to have been quite active. More specific to the western Deccan are items such as clay seals of Roman design, double-moulded terracotta figurines, bronze statuettes—appropriately of Poseidon, Eros, and Atlas, household objects such as metal cups, mirrors, a wine jug, a candlestick stand, and a variety of Roman glass.[47] Were these the belongings of visiting Yavana merchants or, of Indian merchants who had brought them back as souvenirs from their travels west? These were not invariably bulk items but markers of gracious living. Given the frequency of local imitations, Roman objects were prized and may have even been purchased for money. Thus coral brought from the west was valued for the same reason as in the Mediterranean lands: it was a talisman against illness and evil. Imported coral was doubtless thought to be more effective than that available close by.

Roman trade with Barygaza and the western Deccan was therefore conditioned by a locally well-established economic exchange. The commercial advantages outweighed the navigational difficulties of a bad anchorage at Barygaza and the former assumed a familiarity both with local commerce as well as its extensive hinterland. In political terms this implied reasonably powerful states with some concern for the furtherance of the trade. A recognition of the economic importance of the Roman trade world explain why ships arriving at Kalyāna were escorted under guard to Barygaza, given the hostilities between the Śakas and the Sātavāhanas.[48] Clearly the profits from the Roman trade were highly attractive, hence the competition between local powers to capture the trade. This was not a profitable barter or a localized exchange but included a transit trade as well since the destinations of the items were often quite distant, as is frequently so with luxury goods.

Further south the picture changes. In most parts of south India, barring the major settlements registering the presence of the Yavanas, there are fewer Roman artefacts but a strikingly larger number of coins, particularly in hoards. This is suggestive of a different dialogue underlying trade. Roman trade with the Malabar coast, focuses on a new item much in demand namely, black pepper. So profitable was this trade to the suppliers of pepper that this item could indeed be called 'black gold', the pepper being exchanged for gold.[49] The volume of black pepper exported must have been enormous because it was the cheapest of the peppers according to Pliny[50] and was paid for in coin. Possibly the pepper was also used as ballast on the journey back.[51] Pliny mentions a price for the pepper, early Tamil sources refer only to exchanging it for gold. Pliny adds that the pepper grew extensively in the area to the east, Cottonara, and was collected and sent in canoes made of hollowed out tree-trunks, to the emporium at Muziris.[52] That it was extremely valuable is also clear from Pliny who states that it was easy to adulterate it with locally available mustard seeds at Alexandria.[53] The demand for other items included semi-precious stones and the popularity of beryl is indicated by Roman coins which tend to cluster around the beryl mines near Coimbatore, a location which was also on the overland route to the east coast.

Those who grew the pepper were likely not to have been the same as those who mined the beryl.

The presence of semi-precious stones and their distribution again goes back to Chalcolithic and Megalithic sites in the peninsula prior to the Roman trade. Megalithic exchange networks also carried a range of metal artefacts which have been found in burials. These were mainly weapons, agricultural implements such as hoes, and horse-bits, generally of iron. Also included as grave furnishings were carnelian and gold beads and jewellery. The exchange could have been an itinerant pedlar's exchange but more likely it was an exchange among the elite of goods which conferred status. The proximity of the Kolar gold-fields and auriferous veins in Karnataka, where numerous Aśokan inscriptions were located, also provides evidence of the Megalithic people and the Mauryan administration working these sites.[54] Spectacular remains of gold objects in Megalithic burials are few and possibly the gold was sent back to the Mauryan capital. The working of gold mines and veins would have added to the importance of gold in the local system of exchange and perhaps encouraged its hoarding when available.

The discovery of a sizeable amount of high-value silver and gold Roman coins, occurring as stray finds and in hoards, in the peninsula, raises many questions relating to the Yavanas and to the local persons involved in the exchange. It has been argued that the silver *denarii* found in larger numbers were widely used in the transactions of the earlier period of the trade and the introduction of gold coins came later and that the silver coins were tied to the trade in beryl and semi-precious stones.[55] Interestingly, Tamil sources associate pepper with gold. However, the basic question remains that of explaining why the coins were found mainly in hoards. The explanation may cover more than a single function for the coins, and the need to hoard them may have been due to a coinciding of various factors.

Were the coins hoarded against brigandage or alternatively paid as protection money to ensure the safe passage of goods from one coast to the other? Could it be that the hoards were intended as investments in further trade on the part of visiting traders? Were the coins in southern India and the western Deccan indicators that larger quantities of merchandise were bought for the Roman markets?[56] Roman coin hoards in India tend to be of specially selected coins with a high degree of metal purity.[57] Minted in the context of market exchange, they could become a measure for the commoditization of other items. It has been suggested that Roman coins were used as bullion. This is more likely to apply to silver coins for if the high point of gold mining in Karnataka was during the period from 200 BC to AD 200,[58] there may not have been a need to use gold coins as bullion.

Gold and silver coins as items of consumption outside the context of market exchange could be linked to status hierarchies in which those who had access to these coins were in positions of dominance. Although some items are both necessities and luxuries, their particular role can be differentiated according to the circumstance in which they occur. Luxuries have been described as goods whose principal use is rhetorical and social, they are incarnated signs and respond to political necessity.[59] Commodities subsume value and labour value and value arises from the social context of the object. The intention of exchange can be the enhancement of status or of economic profit and this would be decided by the category of exchange—barter, gift exchange, or commodity trade.

Could the hoards be evidence of a system of gift exchange among indigenous chiefs and ruling families which might have continued from the chiefships of the earlier period? Gift exchange does encourage the accumulation of wealth up to a point. If so then coins would not be used as high-value currency but would be regarded as symbols of status. The political hegemony of the Cēras, Cōḷas and Pāṇḍyas in south India, in competition with the chieftains—the Velir, is evident by the turn of the Christian era from Tamil sources. Even Pliny makes a distinction between the king of Muziris, Caelobothra (the Latin for Ceraputra? echoing an earlier clan identity), and the tribe/*gentis* Neacyndi controlling the port at Porakud, a port also used by the Pāṇḍya king whose capital was further inland.[60] Chiefships and kingships co-existed. Pliny also states that local conditions were changing as reflected in the changing names of tribes, ports, and towns. Power was garnered in the traditional manner through marriage alliances and conquests, hence the poems of love and war in the Śaṅgam anthologies.[61] Wealth had earlier been collected but periodically distributed in the holding of great feasts which took on the character of a potlatch. The politics of monarchies was relatively recent in these kingdoms. As they moved towards consolidating kingdoms, the expenses of maintaining both kingship and the state increased. The availability of wealth became imperative. Prestige goods in order to be effective have to be circulated and the hoarding of these would have another meaning. If the coins did not circulate as wealth, their possession may have been of symbolic importance. Control over prestige goods is an enabling factor providing social and economic power useful to negotiating alliances. It is assumed that it was the families of the chiefs and the emergent royal families who, constituting the elite, controlled the goods. They not only had the will and the ability to accumulate wealth but could do so cutting across the identity of the clan. The ready availability of high-value coins as prestige goods may have encouraged this process. The intrinsic value of the early imperial Roman coin was obviously recognized. Does the presence of Roman coin hoards suggest that in addition to an established commercial system in the coastal areas of south India, there was also in the hinterland, the prevalence of forms of barter? The coin therefore did not have the single function for which it was minted but could be used variously in accordance with the activities of the recipient and the nature of exchange.

What then was the impact of the Roman trade on such a society? Were the coin hoards seen as status symbols representing an accumulation that was not put to an economically productive use? Or did they contribute to the accumulating activities of the elite groups through whom the local resources were gathered and exchanged and which accelerated and intensified hierarchies? Such groups may eventually have indulged in some entrepreneurship themselves. The exports local to the region were mainly natural resources and not crafted products. The *Periplus* refers to villages and marts along the Malabar coast rather than urban commercial centres with the exception of Muziris and Nelkynda.[62] It records the import of wheat into Muziris presumably to feed the Yavana merchants negotiating with local middlemen or the crews of the ships waiting for the northeast monsoon in order to sail back to the Red Sea. Muziris as an emporium draws for export, cargoes from the east coast, including Chinese silk, Gangetic nard and tortoise shell from Southeast Asia. Its imports are a great amount of money and other items not too different from elsewhere. But its hinterland is different from that of Barygaza. The activities at Muziris may not initially have been all that integrated with the hinterland and this may have changed gradually. The change is reflected in Tamil sources. The earlier Tamil source, the *Śaṅgam* literature has a larger space for chiefdoms and the Yavanas are alien, whereas the somewhat later Tamil epics, the *Śilappadi-kāram* and the *Maṇimēkalai,* assume monarchy to be the more familiar system with cities as centres of commerce in some of which the Yavanas have settled. Transactions within the trade would have moved from the one to the other.

Roman trading contacts on the eastern coast of south India were with a society familiar with commercial exchange although perhaps not as sophisticated as the markets of Barygaza and the western Deccan. Punch-marked coins circulated in Tamil Nadu[63] and may have come as a result of increased trade in the post-Mauryan period. Tamil Brāhmī votive inscriptions found in greater profusion to the east of Coimbatore, suggest the presence of professionals and craftsmen but even in their Buddhist and Jaina identity they do not carry the power and the patronage of the community associated with the monastic centres of the western Deccan. The wharf at Kāveripaṭṭinam and the presence of Yavanas at the port in later times points to the continuing importance of the area. Roman traders located their bases at Arikamedu and Kāveripaṭṭinam, both of which, prior to this, may have been collection points for goods.[64] The location of Arikamedu has been associated with one of the strongholds of the Velir chieftains.[65] As bases, these would have been linked to resources both from Sri Lanka to the south and from the east coast of India along the major river deltas to the Ganga and possibly Southeast Asia.[66]

Earlier excavations at Arikamedu yielded Roman artefacts and what was interpreted as evidence for the manufacture of textiles.[67] A more recent excavation suggests that the settlement in the previous period had links with local exchange networks.[68] What is also of interest is that the amphorae sherds indicate that they were containers of wine, oil, and garum, the latter two suggesting the presence of foreign consumers.[69] The presence of foreign merchants who brought their goods to Kāveripaṭṭinam and who had left their homes and settled there and who spoke a variety of languages is mentioned in the *Śilappadikāram*[70] although the text is later than the first century AD. Recent excavations as Alagankulam suggest a possible trading-station in the Vaigai delta servicing the Pāṇḍyan territory.[71] It has been plausibly argued that Roman ships did not initially round the Cape because of navigational problems and thus the overland route from near Coimbatore—the Palghat gap—to the east coast became the regular route. Furthermore Indian seamen, using indigenous boats, fetched and carried cargo between the two coasts.[72] Payment for this trade may have required a large monetary outlay which could have been delivered to merchants and middlemen along the safer land route. Hence the location of major coin hoards along this route.

Settlements of Yavana traders were not colonies since that would imply that there was an appropriation of resources, land and labour, and some degree of permanency which was not the case. The nature of the settlements were by no means identical. Some might have been trading stations with a quick change of visiting traders using local agents as mediators in the trade. The emporium at Muziris may have been one of these. The manufacturing of items locally which were specific to this trade, such as textiles, may have encouraged merchants to live more permanently in the settlements as at Arikamedu and Kāveripaṭṭinam. It is possible that Paithan and Ter in the western Deccan which are also associated with the production of textiles for this trade may have played a similar role given the Yavana settlement at Dhenukākata. This would point to a more-than-casual lateral intervention in the production of items.

In the eastern Deccan, at one site Roman pottery and other artefacts have been found together with Megalithic pottery pointing to an interaction between the two.[73] The area had been under Mauryan administration, had coastal links with ports along the deltas as far north as the Ganga and was also linked to the routes going inland to central India and to the western Deccan. Khāravela in Kalinga, generally dated to about the first century BC, boasts of conquering a confederacy of the Tamils which may be just a boast but could reflect an east coast network.[74] He also refers to defeating the Sātavāhana king at the Krishna river and to receiving pearls from the Pāṇḍyan king. Important Buddhist centres with votive inscriptions, such as at Bhaṭṭiprolu and Amarāvatī, indicate organized mercantile activities involving market centres and towns as well as agrarian prosperity and some date to the period just prior to the Roman trade.[75] Substantial Roman coin finds occur in Andhra Pradesh, particularly in and around the Krishna valley.[76] The *Periplus* has a sparse reference to ports in this area—the region of Masalia—but gradually, judging by coin finds and the more detailed references in Ptolemy to Maisolia (Masulipattam),[77] Roman trading interests appear to have increased. Ptolemy provides details of urban activity and the sources agree that it was a production centre for cotton fabric. The wharf at Dharanikota (ancient Dhānyakakata), the port of the settlement at Amarāvatī, continued to be used until it was silted up in the third century AD[78] by which time Roman coins became scarce.

Coin hoards from the region around the Krishna valley contain high-value coins. As is also the case in some south Indian hoards, a few are defaced either by a bar or slashed and others carry small punch marks.[79] There appears to be a greater frequency in slashing gold coins than defacing silver coins and the latter seem to be restricted to the Krishna valley. The defacing of these coins is unlikely to have been because of Hinayana Buddhist iconoclasm as has been suggested, since Buddhism by now had its own icons and had not objected to royal portraits elsewhere in India. It was more likely to do with differentiating between those coins minted prior to Nero's debasement of coins or with an attempt to prevent these coins from being sent back to Egypt.[80] The defacement ensured that their currency was restricted to the Indian circuits of the trade and particularly along the east coast. This might further relate to Yavana interest in resources from Southeast Asia and the need for readily available specie in areas which had links with these resources. (Ptolemy mentions in his discussion of Maisolia that the point of departure for ships going to the Khryse or Southeast Asia was on this coast.) Yet it is curious that only a small percentage of the coins are defaced. High-value coins in the Krishna valley are unlikely to have been used only as symbols of status, as might have been the case in some parts of south India, since there was a familiarity with monetary exchange based on a system of indigenous coins. The use of punch marks may even suggest an attempted continuity from earlier practice.

The lure of trade further east was possibly because of the fabled lands of gold, the *suvarṇa* prefixes in the Sanskrit place names and the possibility of an alternate route to Chinese silk and other items not easily available in India. The *Periplus* gives few details of ports and harbours along the northern half of the east coast. A major commercial port called Ganga, on the delta, was evidently the point at which the trade along the Ganga valley came to settle. Its identity remains uncertain although it has been linked to Tāmralipti (Tamluk),[81] the most active port in the delta going back to the Mauryan period with an extensive hinterland of the Ganga plain. Eastwards the picture is vague for the *Periplus* refers only to Thina as the silk producing land. However, the geographer Ptolemy, writing at a later date in the second century AD (and with possible interpolations), provides more details of the ports and produce from the Ganga delta to the Gulf of Siam, a circuit which gradually comes into greater use. This circuit continues to be referred to as 'India', suggesting the strong imprint of Indian trade at these ports.

There has been much discussion on the mutation in some parts of Southeast Asia initiated by incidental and later more organized exchange with Indian traders.[82] The process remains, elusive but hypotheses can be suggested. In clan-based societies reciprocal relations are achieved through maintaining the status quo or allowing only a limited deviation. Exchange activities with those outside the clan would introduce social imbalances and alter the existing economic forms. Such changes would encourage the accentuation of political control by those already in some positions of authority. A link between alien traders and emergent chiefs would have enhanced the power of the latter and might possibly have impeded the growth of indigenous traders. Initially at least the items traded would tend to be redistributed except where they were regarded as prestige goods. With the emergence of states, however, relations between Indian traders and local royalty in the kingdoms drew on a variety of cultural elements as well. Among the cultural imports into Southeast Asia were the coming of Buddhism and Brahmanism, where both were to provide ideologies of political control to the local elite. Buddhism tends to be less acceptable to clan-based societies for whom Brahmanical sacrificial rituals were easier entry points into an imported ideology and could, be more comfortably adjusted to local mores and beliefs. When exchange turned into trade, however, Buddhism perhaps became more attractive because of its social ethic which included a partiality for the accumulation of wealth and investment in commerce. But there was an increasing tendency for the two to fade into each other.

Unlike the Indian Ocean trade of later times when Islam and Christianity provided a religious backing to the trading networks, the Roman trade did not carry a religion. Those that came from the Mediterranean were largely worshippers of Greco-Roman and Egyptian deities, with possibly some early Christians. There is an absence of recognizable representations of such deities in India.[83] Nor is there a presence of Christianity at this time although the picture changes by the middle of the millennium.[84] Christian texts written in the eastern Mediterranean begin to mention Christian missions from the second century AD and the establishment of the Church in south India and Sri Lanka by about the sixth century AD.[85] The council of Nicea in AD 325 lists an Indian connection and there is later evidence of a Nestorian mission. Still later, Syrian Christians are said to have settled in Kerala.[86] If at all a wide-ranging religious ideology is to be associated with this trade, then it seems to have been Buddhism which spread along the trade routes and where possible, provided an ideological infrastructure which helped to integrate a diversity of mercantile and political interests with religious concerns. These were possibly germane to the almost contradictory tradition of the Christian hermits in Syria and Egypt[87] and the royal cults of Cambodia and Indonesia.

Indian perceptions of those that came from the west, the Yavanas, varied.[88] The north Indian experience of the Yavanas was initially in the context of aggression and military hostility: the campaigns of Alexander and later of the Indo-Greeks. Consequently in some Brahmanical texts, the Yavanas are reviled and regarded as oppressors.[89] When the Indo-Greeks ruled in northern India there was a problem about giving them a rank in the hierarchy of caste and they were slotted as *vrātya-kṣatriya*s or literally, the degenerate *kṣatriya*s. Yavanas arriving as peaceful traders do not find an entry in Brahmanical texts. This was in part because the good *brāhmaṇa* was told to avoid the cities, the traders and their means of livelihood such as usury, and to refrain from crossing the seas. Needless to say few *brāhmaṇa*s paid attention to these injunctions. *Brāhmaṇa* hostility to the Yavanas also derived from the fact that the latter, both as royalty and as traders, were substantial patrons of the various Buddhist sects who by now were regarded as heretics by the *brāhmaṇa*s. This did not, however, preclude more than just a passing interest in some categories of technical knowledge. Familiarity with Hellenistic ideas on medicine and horoscopy is evident from various texts. The *Yavana-jātaka,* a text on horoscopy is believed to be based on a Greek text from Alexandria and dates to the early Christian era and was probably written in western India.[90] It would seem that a few Greek-speaking persons may have been settled in western India and had a high status since they use the title of *rājā.* The text has a Brahmanical idiom and perspective and is contemptuous of other religious sects which it describes as *pāṣaṇḍa*s or heretics.[91] The use of such a text may not however have been limited to the *brāhmaṇa* elite.

The Buddhist view of the Yavanas was different. There was a curiosity about Yavana society and there is a tradition of Buddhist missions having been sent to Yavana lands to proselytize. Buddhist texts respect traders and merchants, and Buddhism derived a considerable patronage from the support of mercantile groups in Indian society. Consequently traders and commercial centres were not treated as marginal. Wealthy Buddhist Yavanas are mentioned in the votive inscriptions at Buddhist sacred sites in the Deccan.[92] Some have Prākritized Indian names but were not Indians else they would not have claimed to be Yavanas.[93] In one case the donor describes himself as a northerner but in most instances the term Yavana alone is used. As worshippers of Isis or Poseidon, their 'pagan' beliefs would not have stood in the way of an acceptance of Buddhism. If anything, it would have admitted them to the dominant religious idiom of the traders of western India. If an early reading of these inscriptions is correct that some among the Yavanas came from Gata, then it may be suggested that this should not be identified with Trigarta or Jallandhar in northern India, but could be the Prākrit form of Coptos (Coptos>Gapta>Gata). However, recent readings have related the suffix *gata* to *saṇgata* as in a corporation[94] or else interpret *gata* as part of the Yavana name and not a place.[95] But it is unlikely that the suffix *gata* was a recognized Yavana name-ending. There are references in Greek and Latin sources to persons from Egypt being in India and Coptos was the emporium which handled the trade from India.[96] That a merchant from Coptos could declare himself a Buddhist and be involved in the maritime trade with the western Deccan, also provides a logical context. The inscriptions mention that some of these Yavanas were associated with Dhenukākata which has been variously identified but was probably close to Karle in the western Deccan.[97] That Dhenukākata was a commercial centre is suggested by its description as a *vaniya-gāma*.[98] It is not surprising that the maximum integration between Yavanas and Indians was in an area where commerce was developed. One expression of this integration appears to have been a bi-lingualism in Hellenistic Greek and Prākrit although there must have been a bi-lingualism in Greek and Tamil as well.

Tamil Śangam literature provides yet another facet of Indian views of the Yavanas. There are descriptions of the beautiful ships of the Yavanas, laden with gold which they exchanged for pepper.[99] Mention is also made of the cool fragrant wine brought by them in elegant jars.[100] Sometimes the tone is hostile as when a Cēra chief is said to have captured the barbarous Yavanas and divested them of their wine and their wealth.[101] Cēra hostility towards the Yavanas is repeated in the epics of the subsequent period.[102] To the Tamil speakers of the south, Yavana speech was a harsh and barbarous language. In the Tamil epics the relationship seems to have changed as they describe the Yavanas in the port of Kāveripaṭṭinam not as passing visitors but as resident craftsmen or even employed as city guardsmen.[103] They are said to live in a separate section of the city and are distinguished by their wealth. This remains a more distanced view of the Yavanas than in the western Deccan. In spite of the presence of Buddhists in the area there are no Yavana Buddhists. Thus the difference in the nature of the trade and exchange is also reflected in these facets of the Yavana relationship with the people of the subcontinent.

The Roman trade may not have bestowed a common belief system on the lands which it touched, but Roman coins became legal tender in large parts of the Indian Ocean. The role of the trade in the Roman economy is significant and has been commented upon both by contemporaries and by modern historians. The starting point of what has become a debate are the statements by both Pliny and Tiberius that the wealth of Rome was being drained by the purchase of articles of feminine vanity and of luxury from the east.[104] Tiberius, in a letter to the Roman senate, objected to the conspicuous consumption of Roman patricians in the grandeur of their villas, their numerous slaves, their silver, gold and objects d'art, their fine clothes and the jewels of the women, many of these items coming from distant lands. Pliny at one point mentions a drain of fifty-five million sesterces; and elsewhere he assessed the drain of wealth to India, Arabia, and China as one hundred million sesterces.[105] Such statement were taken literally and it was argued that this trade contributed to the economic pressures on the Roman empire which facilitated its decline.

An early attempt at refuting this view[106] pointed out that there was a rigorous control over *ad valorem* customs duties of up to twenty-five per cent on imports from the east into Egypt and the re-exporting of such goods from Alexandria. The actual loss of gold was not high because of the supply from the gold mines of Spain and treasure captured in campaigns. In fact, the price of gold on the Roman market dropped somewhat at the end of the first century AD just after the period of the maximum despatch of gold coins to the Indian trade. Another argument rejecting the fleeing of gold from Rome in the eastern trade maintains that the Romans exported wines, tin, and lead and that the Indians exchanged goods for goods, not having a sufficient monetary outlay.[107] The latter statement is open to question since, as we have seen, a uniform pattern of exchange did not prevail in every part of India. The monetary outlay in northern and western India appears to have been sufficient for the trade. Coin hoards in themselves are not the sole evidence of a financial drain, for the nature of the exchange would have to be examined. The total number of Roman coins in India is small as compared to those found in hoards on the northern frontier of the Roman empire[108] where money was used to buy off the barbarians and therefore played a different role from that of the hoards in the Indian peninsula. A further perspective on this question argues for looking at other features unconnected with maritime trade which contributed to a decline in the Roman economy. These include the over-expansion of global consumption in the Antonine age, the economic pressure on the state arising out of the system of doles, the fiscal pressures on medium and small scale landowners and the evasion of taxes by large property owners as well as the increased expenditure on the army and the bureaucracy and on keeping the barbarians at bay.[109] A more recent debate focuses on doubts regarding an economic decline.[110]

Egypt was the focal point of the eastern maritime trade in the Roman empire.[111] It attracted a larger volume of trade from the east than from the cargoes of the Mediterranean.[112] The initial thrust of the Ptolemies in the eastern direction was extended when Egypt became a province of the Roman empire.[113] Shipping was largely controlled by wealthy Alexandrian merchants who had a monopoly over the Red Sea trade. The Roman administration continued the Ptolemaic office of the *espistrategos* of Thebaid, the prefect of the Red Sea, who had command over the eastern desert and controlled the caravan routes and customs dues levied at Coptos.[114] He also kept a check on the tariffs collected on this route and the tariff rates suggest that small-scale transportation was as frequent as the larger caravans. Heavy fees were charged for the use of these routes which had to be kept well-guarded to ensure a safe passage for the trans-shipment of cargo.[115] The maintenance of a garrison at Coptos may have been required for this purpose as well.[116] The caravan routes from the Red Sea ports to inland centres in Egypt were run by private companies.[117]

A papyrus document containing a contract between a merchant and a ship's captain refers to shipments of goods from India and dates to the second century AD.[118] Views differ as to where exactly the contract was drawn up, either in Muziris or Alexandria or at a port of the Red Sea where the cargo was off-loaded. The contract relates to cargo from Muziris and its transport from the port to the Nile and its safe arrival in the warehouse of the merchant in Alexandria. The cargo which is the subject of this contract consisted of 700 to 1,700 pounds of Gangetic nard, about 4,700 pounds of ivory and a variety of textiles totalling about 790 pounds—all luxury goods and subject to a twenty-five per cent customs duty on import. Curiously pepper is not included in the list. The contract points to a very large capital investment and this had to cover not only the cost of the cargo but also the maintenance of a crew and its stay in India while waiting for the return monsoon, and protection of the cargo from brigandage en route. Possibly Pliny was troubled by such large investments of capital. Yet if one voyage was so costly, the drain of fifty-five million sesterces does not seem totally out of proportion. What the Muziris contract does underline is that the trade with south India was substantial in the second century AD with Muziris continuing to be the emporium for goods even from the east coast. The enormous financial outlay required in this trade as is evident from the contract, does rather diminish the importance of the quantitative aspect of the Roman coin hoards in peninsular India.

Bullion was sold in the open market at Coptos and Alexandria where the former is particularly associated with silver bullion.[119] That Coptos was extremely important to this trade is evident from the large numbers of Greek *ostraca* recording accounts and receipts.[120] These receipts and the evidence of the Muziris contracts point not only to the outlay on this trade but also to complex banking systems in Egypt. High taxes were levied on the various processes of textile production,[121] presumably to encourage the import of textiles rather than raw material. Perhaps this accounted for the vats at Ter and Arikamedu.

Coptos was the bustling business centre and was sufficiently cosmopolitan for Greek families and others such as Hellenized Egyptians, Levantines, traders from Palmyra to be the main actors in the Indian trade.[122] That women were also representatives of trading houses and were ship-owners and merchants goes back to Ptolemaic times.[123] Coptos was the centre for collecting and handling cargo to be forwarded either eastwards or to Alexandria. The ultimate control lay in the hands of the merchants from Alexandria whose representatives were resident at points along which the cargo moved. Alexandria was the centre financing the trade, organizing the sale and purchase of cargoes and arranging the trans-shipment of large quantities to Rome. It would seem that although the tastes of the Roman patricians were met by this trade, its commercial base remained in the Roman province of Egypt. Egypt, therefore, can be viewed as the periphery to the centre at Rome, or else as the centre to the periphery in the eastern Mediterranean.

The spectacular profits of the trade for Mediterranean traders encouraged the fabulous in descriptions of Asia. What is perhaps curious is that despite the close contacts resulting from the trade with the Yavanas and the visibility of the transactions, the Indian world has left us no descriptions of places and peoples visited in the course of this trade.

And what of Rome and its citizens whose demands sustained this trade? Rome, it has been said, was a consumer city par excellence, and the eastern luxury trade was crucial to its lifestyle. This was recognized in more than just the complaints of Tiberius and Pliny. In what has been referred to as the apocalyptic cartoon language of one book of the Bible—*The Revelations of St John*—Rome is projected as the 'scarlet harlot' and its opulence and evil ways are denounced.[124] The denunciation coincided with the peak period of the eastern trade. St John prophesies doom on the death of Rome and adds that, ' . . . merchants the world over have grown rich on her bloated wealth, but when she dies they will mourn, as no one will buy their cargoes of . . . jewels, pearls, silks and fine linen, of scented woods, ivories . . . cinnamon and spice . . . ' But trade falsified the dire prophecies of St John. The regular visits of merchant ships to India continued into Late Roman times.[125] Given the author of the prophecy, it was all the more ironic that in the fourth century AD Constantine donated to the eastern churches vast quantities of incense, perfume, nard, balsam, and pepper.[126] It is not clear as to what the churches would have done with these donations. They may have used a small amount in church rituals but probably sold the bulk on the market, deriving a substantial revenue from the sale. The cargo listed by St John had a constant market in the Mediterranean, providing a continuity to the trade with South Asia well after Roman times. And in later centuries there were to be, many more cities in Europe emulating the 'scarlet harlot'.

Notes and References

1. P. Curtin, *Cross-cultural Trade in World History,* Cambridge, 1984.
2. M.G. Raschke, 'New Studies in Roman Commerce with the East', *Aufsteig and Niedergang der Romischer Welt,* Berlin, 1978, p. 646.
3. *Yavana* from the Prākṛit *yona,* was initially the term used for Greeks but soon came to be applied to all those who came from West Asia and even further west.
4. P. Turner, *Roman Coins in India,* London, 1989, pp. 6–7, 42–3, 90. V. Begley, 'Arikamedu Reconsidered', *American Journal of Archaeology,* 87, 1983, pp. 261–482. See also, R. Nagaswamy, 'Alagankulam: An Indo-Roman Trading Station', in C. Margabandhu et al. (eds), *Indian Archaeological Heritage,* Delhi, 1991, pp. 247–54.
5. K.N. Chaudhuri, *Trade and Civilisation in the Indian Ocean,* Cambridge, 1985, p. 165.
6. Romila Thapar, 'Epigraphic Evidence and some Indo-Hellenistic Contacts During the Mauryan Period', in S.K. Maity and U. Thakur (eds), *Indological Studies, Prof. D.C. Sircar Commemoration Volume,* New Delhi, 1988, pp. 15–19.

7. J.F. Salles, 'The Arab Persian Gulf under the Seleucids', in A. Kuhrt and S. Sherwin-White, *Hellenism in the East,* London, 1987, pp. 75–109. F. Millar, 'The Problem of Hellenistic Syria', ibid., pp. 110–33. D.T. Potts, *The Arabian Gulf in Antiquity,* vol. II, Oxford, 1990.

8. L. Casson, 'Rome's Trade with the East: The Sea Voyage to Africa and India', *Transactions and Proceedings of the American Philological Association,* 110 (1980), pp. 21–36. Pliny, *Natural History,* 6.26.106.

9. Pliny, *Natural History*, 6.26.101.

10. D.J. Thompson, 'Nile Grain Transport under the Ptolemies', in P. Garnsey, K. Hopkins, C.R. Wittaker (eds), *Trade in the Ancient Economy,* London, 1983, pp. 64–76.

11. K. Hopkins, 'Introduction', in P. Garnsey et al., *Trade in the Ancient Economy*, London, 1983, pp. ix–xxv.

12. R. Duncan–Jones, *Structure and Scale in the Roman Economy,* Cambridge, 1990, pp. 29, 46ff. H.W. Pleket, 'Urban Elites and Business in the Greek Part of the Roman Empire', in P. Garnsey et al., *Trade in the Ancient Economy*, pp. 131–44. J.H. D'Arms, *Commerce and Social Standing in Ancient Rome,* Cambridge, Mass., 1981.

13. G. Wolf, 'World Systems Analysis and the Roman Empire', *Journal of Roman Archaeology,* 3, 1990, pp. 44–56.

14. S. Sidebotham, *Roman Economic Policy in the Erythra Thalassa, 30 BC to AD 217,* Leiden, 1986. But see also L. Casson, *Periplus Maris Erythraei* (hereafter *PME*), New Jersey, 1989, pp. 32–3, for the more generally accepted view that the trade was in private hands.

15. E. Wallerstein, 'A World-System Perspective on the Social Sciences', in *The Capitalist World Economy,* Cambridge, 1979, pp. 152–64.

16. M. Rowlands, M. Larsen, and K. Kristiansen (eds), *Centre and Periphery in the Ancient World,* Cambridge, 1985. P. Kohl, 'The Use and Abuse of World Systems Theory', *Advances in Archaeological Method and Theory,* 11, 1987, pp. 1–35. C. Edens, 'Dynamics of Trade in the Ancient Mesopotamian World System', *American Anthropologist,* 94, 1 (1922), pp. 118–39. T. Champion (ed.), *Centre and Periphery, Comparative Studies in Archaeology,* London, 1989. J. Schneider, 'Was there a Pre-capitalist World System?', *Peasant Studies,* 6, 1, 1977, pp. 20–9.

17. C. Humphrey and S. Hugh–Jones, *Barter, Exchange and Value,* Cambridge, 1992, Introduction.

18. C.A. Gregory, 'Gifts to Men and Gifts to God: Gift Exchange and Capital Accumulation in Contemporary Melanesia', *Man,* n.s., 15, 4, 1980, pp. 625–52. *Gifts and Commodities,* London, 1982.

19. K. Marx, *Capital,* I, Harmondsworth, 1976, p. 163.

20. J.C. Van Leur, *Indonesian Trade and Society,* The Hague, 1967.

21. H.G. Rawlinson, *Intercourse between India and the Western World, from the Earliest Times to the Fall of Rome,* Cambridge, 1916. E.H. Warmington, *The Commerce between the Roman Empire and India,* London, 1928, 1974 revised. J.I. Miller, *The Spice Trade of the Roman Empire,* Oxford, 1969. R.E.M. Wheeler, A. Ghosh and Krishna Deva, 'Arikamedu: An Indo-Roman Trading Station on the East Coast of India, *Ancient India,* 2, 1946, pp. 17–125. R.E.M. Wheeler, *Rome Beyond the Imperial Frontier,* London, 1955. 'Roman Contact with India, Pakistan and Afghanistan', in W.F. Grimes (ed.), *Aspects of Archaeology in Britain and Beyond: Essays Presented to O.G.S. Crawford,* London, 1951, pp. 345–81.

22. Pliny, *Natural History*, 6.26.101.

23. *Periplus,* pp. 25–6. Motichandra, *Sārthavāha,* Patna, 1953, pp. 119ff.

24. P.M. Eraser, *Ptolemaic Alexandria,* 1, Oxford, 1972, p. 543.

25. K.N. Chaudhuri, *Trade and Civilisation*, p. 130.

26. *Periplus,* pp. 18–19, 26. Strabo, 16.4.22–4.

27. Strabo, 2.5.12; 2.118.

28. W. Scmitthammer, 'Rome and India: Aspects of Universal History During the Principate', *Journal of Roman Studies,* 69, 1979, pp. 90–106.

29. R. Salomon, 'Epigraphic Remains of Indian Traders in Egypt', *Journal of the American Oriental Society,* 3, 4 (1991), pp. 731–6.

30. Two pot-sherds with Tamil Brāhmī inscriptions—*catan* and *kapan*—were found at Quseir-al-Qadim, a port on the Egyptian side of the Red Sea, D.S. Whitecomb and J.H. Johnson, *Quseir-al-Qadim 1978: Preliminary Report,* Cairo, 1979; *Quseir-al-Qadim 1980: Preliminary Report,* Malibu, 1982.

31. Tamil Brāhmī graffiti on pot-sherds also occurs at Arikamedu. R.E.M. Wheeler, A. Ghosh, and Krishna Deva, 'Arikamedu: An Indo-Roman Trading Station on the East Coast of India', *Ancient India,* 2, 1946, 109ff.

32. Salomon, 'Epigraphic Remains . . .'

33. Casson, *PME,* pp. 22ff.

34. P. Turner, *Roman Coins from India,* London, 1989.

35. *Periplus,* p. 49.

36. *Suppāraka Jātaka,* 11.463.

37. Romila Thapar, 'Patronage and Community', in B. Stoler Miller (ed.), *The Powers of Art,* Delhi, 1992, pp. 1–34. Vidya Dehejia, 'Collective and Popular Bases of Early Buddhist Patronage: Sacred Monuments, 100 BC–AD 250', ibid., pp. 35–45.

38. S.B. Deo and R. Gupte, *Excavation at Bhokardan,* Nagpur, 1974.

39. *Epigraphia Indica,* 8, 1905–6, pp. 82ff, 89ff.

40. *Epigraphia Indica,* 5, Lüders List nos 1131, 1133, 1099. K.L. Mahalay, 'Rise and Fall in the Commercial Significance of the Deccan

Caves', *Deccan Geographer,* 11, 1973, pp. 1–17. C. Margabandhu, 'Trade Contacts Between Western India and the Greco-Roman World', *Journal of the Economic and Social History of the Orient,* 8, 1965, pp. 316–22. H.P. Ray, *Monastery and Guild,* Delhi, 1986.

41. M. Meister, 'Sub-Urban Planning and Rock-cut Architecture', in *Madhu: Recent Researches in Indian Archaeology and Art History,* Delhi, 1981, pp. 157–64.

42. H.D. Sankalia, S.B. Deo, and B. Subbarao, *Excavations at Maheswar and Navdatoli, 1952–3,* Poona, 1958; B.K. Thapar, 'Prakash 1955: A Chalcolithic Site in the Tapti Valley', *Ancient India,* 20, 21, 1964–5, pp. 5–167. S.B. Deo and R.S. Gupte, *Excavations at Bhokardan, 1973,* Nagpur, 1974; B.N. Chapekar, *Report on the Excavation at Ter,* Poona, 1969.

43. J. Burgess and B. Indraji, *Inscriptions from the Cave Temples of Western India,* Delhi, 1976 (reprint), pp. 47, 54.

44. *Cullaka-seṭṭhi Jātaka,* 1.4; *Akatannu Jātaka,* 1.90; *Makasa Jātaka,* 1.44; *Sussondi Jātaka,* 5.360.

45. C. Margabandhu, 'Two Clay Bullae (medallions) from Junagarh', *Visvesvaranand Indological Journal,* 8, 2 (1975), pp. 1–7. *Archaeology of the Sātavāhana Kṣatrapa Times,* Delhi, 1985.

46. K.N. Chaudhuri, *Trade and Civilisation,* pp. 184ff.

47. H.D. Sankalia and S.B. Deo, *Report on the Excavations at Nasik and Jorwe, 1950–51,* Poona, 1955. H.D. Sankalia et al., *From History to PreHistory at Nevasa, 1954–56,* Poona, 1960. B. Subbarao, *Baroda Through the Ages,* Baroda, 1953. R.N. Mehta and S.N. Chowdhury, *Excavations at Devnimori,* Baroda, 1966. R.N. Mehta and D.R. Shah, *Excavations at Nagara,* Baroda, 1968. S.B. Deo and R.S. Gupte, *Excavation at Bhokardan,* Nagpur, 1974. Relevant reports in *Indian Archaeology—A Review.* M. Dikshit, *History of Indian Glass,* Bombay, 1969.

48. J.A.B. Palmer, 'Periplus Mari Erythrae, the Indian Evidence as to the Date', *The Classical Quarterly,* 41, 1947, pp. 136–40. D.W. Macdowall, 'The Early Western Satraps and the Date of the Periplus', *The Numismatic Chronicle,* 4, 1964, pp. 271–80. G. Mathew, 'The Dating and Significance of the Periplus of the Erythreaen Sea', in N. Chittick and R.I. Rotberg (eds), *East Africa and the Orient,* London, 1975, pp. 147–63. See also L. Casson, 'Śakas versus Andras in the Periplus Mari Erythrae', *Journal of the Economic and Social History of the Orient,* 26, 2, 1983, pp. 164–77, for a different reading of the text.

49. *Akam,* 149.7–11.

50. Pliny, *Natural History,* 12.14.28. Four *denarii* per pound for black pepper and seven and fifteen respectively for white and long pepper.

51. K.N. Chaudhuri, *Trade and Civilisation,* p. 191.

52. Pliny, *Natural History,* 6.26.105. L. Casson, *PME,* p. 221. *Periplus,* p. 56.

53. Pliny, 12.14.28.

54. F.R. Allchin, 'Upon the Antiquity and Methods of Gold Mining in Ancient India', *Journal of the Economic and Social History of the Orient*, 5, 2, 1962, pp. 195–211. 'Antiquity of Gold-mining in the Gadag Region—Karnataka', *Madhu*, Delhi, 1981.

55. Turner, *Roman Coins from India*, p. 16.

56. Warmington, *Commerce* . . . , Delhi, 1974, pp. 277, 292.

57. D.W. Macdowell, 'Indian Imports of Roman Silver Coins', paper read at the Third International Colloquium, Nasik, 1990.

58. Allchin, 'Upon the Antiquity . . .'.

59. A. Appadurai (ed.), *The Social Life of Things: Commodities in the Cultural Perspective*, Cambridge, 1988, Introduction.

60. Pliny, *Natural History*, 6.26.105.

61. K. Kailasapathy, Tamil *Heroic Poetry*, Oxford, 1968. A.K. Ramanujam, *Poems of Love and War*, New York, 1985. K.V. Zvelebil, *Tamil Literature*, Wiesbaden, 1974. *The Smile of Murugan*, London, 1973.

62. *Periplus*, pp. 53–6.

63. K.V. Raman, Presidential Address, Numismatic Society of India, Visva Bharati, 1990. A recent report of finds said to be of indigenous coins of the Cēras, Cōḷas and Pāṇḍyas of this period, with one coin at least showing a trace of Roman numismatic influence, suggests fresh dimensions to the numismatic evidence and the exchange systems should these be found to be authentic. R. Krishnamurthy, 'Śangam Period Chera Silver Coin with a Portrait and a Legend', paper read at the First Oriental Numismatic Congress, Nagpur, 1990. See also the publications in Tamil by the same author on Cōḷas and Pāṇḍyas and Malaiyamān coins, 1986–90. R. Champakalakshmi, pers. com.

64. R.E.M. Wheeler, *Ancient India*, 2, 1946, pp. 17–24. Begley, 'Arikamedu Reconsidered'.

65. The identification is with Virai and has been discussed in R. Champakalakshmi, 'Archaeology and Tamil Literary Tradition', *Puratattva*, 8 (1975–6), pp. 117ff. I. Mahadevan, 'The Ancient Name of Arikamedu', in N. Subrahmaniam (ed.), *Surya Narayana Sastri Centenary Volume*, Madras, 1970, pp. 204ff.

66. The *Śilappadikāram*, 14.116. Refers to aromatic wood and camphor being brought to the port of Kāveripaṭṭinam and this, it has been suggested, may have been cargo from Southeast Asia. V.R.R. Dikshitar, The *Śilappadikāram*, Madras, 1939, 14.116n. I. Mahadevan has read the graffiti on one potsherd as a name in Old Sinhalese.

67. R.E.M. Wheeler, A. Ghosh, and Krishna Deva, 'Arikamedu: An Indo-Roman Trading-station on the East Coast of India', *Ancient India*, 2, 1946, pp. 17ff.

68. Begley, 'Arikamedu Reconsidered.'

69. Casson, *PME,* pp. 228–9.

70. *Śilappadikāram,* 6.128–44; 5.7ff.

71. Nagaswamy, 'Alangankulam . . .'

72. L. Casson, 'Rome's Trade with the Eastern Coast of India', *Cahiers d'Histoire,* 1988, pp. 3–4, pp. 303–8.

73. H. Sarkar, 'Kesarpalle 1962', 22, *Ancient India,* 22, 1966, pp. 37–74.

74. Hathigumpha inscription. D.C. Sircar, *Select Inscriptions . . . ,* I, Calcutta, 1965, pp. 213–20. An early second-century inscription at Guntur could be that of an Aira Mahāmeghavāhana ruler, thus lending some credence to Khāravela's claim. Velpuru inscription, *Epigraphia Indica,* 32, pp. 82–7.

75. *Epigraphia Indica, 2,* pp. 323–9; 15, pp. 258–75.

76. P.L. Gupta, *Roman Coins from Andhra Pradesh,* APGMS, No. 10, Hyderabad, 1965. Turner, *Roman Coins . . . ,* pp. 29ff.

77. *Periplus,* p. 62. Ptolemy, 7.1.15–93.

78. K. Raghavachari, 'Dharanikota', in A. Ghosh (ed.), *An Encyclopaedia of Indian Archaeology,* II, Delhi, 1989, p. 126.

79. Turner, *Roman Coins . . . ,* pp. 32–6.

80. Ibid., p. 41.

81. Casson, *PME,* p. 236.

82. I.W. Mabbett, 'The "Indianisation" of Southeast Asia: Reflections of the Prehistoric Sources', *Journal of South East Asian Studies,* 8, 1, 1977, pp. 1–14; H. Kulke, *The Devaraja Cult,* Cornell, 1978; H. Kulke, 'The Early and the Imperial Kingdom in Southeast Asian History', in D.G. Marr and A.C. Milner (eds), *Southeast Asia in the 9th–14th Centuries,* Singapore, 1986.

83. R. Fynes in his unpublished D.Phil, thesis, 'Cultural Transmission between Roman Egypt and Western India', Oxford, 1991, argues that the evolution of the goddess Pattini in south India was deeply influenced by the cult of Isis. This is a plausible idea but the evidence is not wholly convincing. Isis was of course the major deity at Coptos. W.M.F. Petrie, *Koptos,* London, 1986, pp. 17ff.

84. A.E. Medlycott, *India and the Apostle Thomas,* London, 1905. E.O. Winstedt, *The Christian Topography of Cosmas Indicopleustes,* Cambridge, 1909. S. Neal, *A History of Christianity in India: the Beginnings to AD 1707,* Cambridge, 1984.

85. Winstedt, *Christian Topography . . . .*

86. S.G. Pothan, *The Syrian Christians of Kerala,* Bombay, 1963, pp. 101ff. In the second millennium AD there is a Christian diaspora which links the Christians of south India to those in the eastern Mediterranean trade, a reversal of the situation of the Yavanas who became Buddhists.

87. P. Rousseau, *Ascetics, Authority and the Church*, Oxford, 1978.

88. Romila Thapar, 'Indian Views of Europe: Representations of the "Other" in History?'

89. J.E. Mitchner, *The Yuga Purāṇa*, Calcutta, 1986; D.C. Sircar, *Studies in Yugapurāṇa and Other Texts*, Delhi, 1974.

90. D. Pingree, *The Yavanajātaka of Sphujidhvaja*, I, Camb. Mass., 1978, Introduction and Text.

91. Chapters 21 and 22.

92. G. Buhler and J. Burgess, 'Report on the Buddhist Cave Temples and their Inscriptions', *Archaeological Survey of Western India*, 4 (reprint), Varanasi, 1964, pp. 82–140. *Epigraphia Indica*, 7 (1902–3), pp. 47–74; 8 (1905–6), pp. 59–96; 18 (1925–6), pp. 325–9.

93. J. Burgess and B. Indraji, *Inscriptions from the Cave Temples of Western India*, nos 7, 10 (reprint), Varanasi, 1976, pp. 31–2; *Epigraphia Indica*, 7, pp. 53–5. See also the discussion on a possible rock-cut Buddhist temple at Petra, H. Goetz, 'An Unfinished Early Indian Temple at Petra, Transjordania', SD aus, *East and West*, n.s., 24 (1974), pp. 245–8.

94. Pingree, *The Yavanajātaka*.

95. S.C. Laeuchli, 'Yavana Inscriptions of Western India', *Journal of the Asiatic Society of Bombay* 1981–4, pp. 56–9, 207–21.

96. Strabo, 2.3.4; 17.1.45. Pliny, *Natural History*, 6.26.101. Raschke, 'New Studies in Roman Commerce', p. 241. Scmitthammer, 'Rome and India . . .'

97. D.D. Kosambi, 'Dhenukākata', *Journal of the Asiatic Society of Bombay*, n.s., 30, 2, 1955, pp. 50–71.

98. *Epigraphia Indica*, 18, 1925–6, p. 326.

99. *Akam*, 149.7–11.

100. *Puram*, 56.16–21; *Puram*, 343.1–10.

101. *Patirrupattu* II, patikam, pp. 4–10.

102. *Śilappadikāram*, 28,142; 29. Usal's song.

103. *Maṇimēkalai*, 19, 108. *Śilappadikāram*, 5.7ff; 14.62.

104. Tactius, *The Annals*, 3.52–4. Pliny, *Natural History*, 6.26.101; 12.41.84.

105. Pliny, *Natural History*, 6.101; 12.84.

106. Miller, *Spice Trade of the Roman Empire*, pp. 222ff.

107. P. Veyne, 'Rome devant la pretendue fuite de l'or . . .', *Annales*, 34, 2, 1979, pp. 21 Iff. A detailed picture of the items which travelled within Egypt as part of this trade is provided by A.C. Johnson, *Roman Egypt to the Reign of Diocletian*, Baltimore, 1936.

108. Raschke, 'New Studies in Roman Commerce', p. 673.

109. A. Bernardi, 'The Economic Problems of the Roman Empire at the Time of its Decline', in C.M. Cipolla, *The Economic Decline of*

Empires, London, 1970, pp. 16–83. R. Duncan-Jones, *Structure and Scale*, pp. 172–3.

110. G. Gunderson, 'Economic Change and the Demise of the Roman Empire', *Explorations in Economic History*, 13, 1, 1976, pp. 43–68. J.L. Anderson and T. Lewit, 'Contact with the Barbarians? Economics and the Fall of Rome', ibid., 29, 1, 1992, pp. 99–115.

111. In AD 297 Coptos was destroyed by Diocletian and in AD 273 Palmyra was sacked by Aurelian.

112. J. Paterson, 'Salvation from the Sea . . . ', *Journal of Roman Studies*, 2, 1982, pp. 146–57. That there was a trade with the western Mediterranean is indicated by the stamps on the amphorae. Other items traded in the Mediterranean such as timber and marble are not part of the Egyptian economy.

113. R.P. Duncan Jones, *The Economy of the Roman Empire*, Oxford, 1974. P.A. Brunt, *Journal of Roman Studies*, 71, 1981, pp. 162ff.

114. Petrie, *Koptos*, pp. 26–7.

115. S.L. Wallace, *Taxation in Egypt*, Princeton, 1933, p. 253.

116. Petrie, *Koptos*, pp. 32–3.

117. Johnson, op. cit., pp. 400ff.

118. L. Casson, 'P. Vindob. G. 40822 and the Shipping of Goods from India', *Bulletin of the American Society of Papyrologists*, 23, 1986, pp. 73–9. L. Casson, 'New Light on Maritime Laws: P. Vindob, G. 40822', *Zeirschrift fur Papyrologie und Epigraphik*, 84 (1990), pp. 195–206. The document was earlier published by H. Harrauer and P. Sijpesteijin, 'Ein neues Dokument zu Roms Indienhandel, P. Vindob. G. 40822', *Anzeiger der Osterreichischen Akademie der Wissenschaften*, 122, 1985, pp. 124–55.

119. L.C. West and A.C. Johnson, *Currency in Roman and Byzantine Egypt*, New Jersey, 1944, pp. 180ff.

120. J.G. Tait, *Greek Ostraca in the Bodleian Library at Oxford, and Various Other Centres*, I, London, 1930.

121. S.L. Wallace, *Taxation in Egypt*, Princeton, 1938, pp. 181ff.

122. Tait, *Greek Ostraca* . . . .

123. D.J. Thompson, 'Nile Grain Transport under the Ptolemies', in P. Garnsey et al., *Trade in the Ancient Economy*, pp. 64–76. D. Meredith, 'The Roman Remains in the Eastern Desert of Egypt', *Journal of Egyptian Archaeology*, 38, 1952, pp. 94–111; 39, 1953, pp. 95–106. This point has been discussed in some detail by Richard Fynes in his unpublished Oxford D.Phil, thesis, 'Cultural Transmission . . .'

124. T.F. Glasson, *The Revelation of John*, Cambridge, 1965, chapter 18. Babylon in *The Relevations* was the code name of Rome. The phrase 'scarlet harlot' was used by Keith Hopkins who drew my attention to this passage.

125. C.R. Whittaker, 'Late Roman Trade and Traders', in P. Garnsey et al., *Trade in the Ancient Economy*, p. 167.

126. L. Duchesne, *Le Liber Pontificalis: Texte, Introduction et Commentate*, 1, Paris, 1955–7, p. 174: III, p. 177 and p. 194. The amounts referred to were aromate 200 pounds, nardinum 200 pounds and balsam 35 pounds. I am grateful to Simon Price for help in locating the references and to Keith Hopkins for referring me to the text.

Section III

Changing Political Formations

CHAPTER 8

The Mauryan Empire in Early India*

The idea of empire in India became part of historical discussion in the nineteenth century. The notion of a British empire led to a search for earlier empires in Indian history and mention was made of the Mauryan, the Gupta and, pre-eminently, the Mughal empires. The British empire was projected as a successor to the earlier ones, enhancing the prestige attached to the British conquest of India. In the context of European history, the British empire was viewed as modelled on the Roman.

The distinctive difference between old and new was said to be that India's pre-British empires had conformed to the model of Oriental despotism, a concept rooted in descriptions of the Persian empire in Greek sources, endorsed by the grandeur of medieval Islamic courts.[1] Even the dialectical analyses of Karl Marx failed him when it came to Asia; his Asiatic Mode of Production drew heavily on the concept of Oriental despotism.[2] These layers of history moulded the idea of India having had a series of empires exhibiting extraordinary wealth derived from despotic oppression. In the indiscriminate use of the term 'empire' by subsequent historians of India, many Indian kingdoms have been given this label without an attempt at defining empire.

The stereotype of empire culled from these models in the late nineteenth century hinged on territory, revenue, and ideology. The territory, acquired through conquest, had to be extensive;

* This article is a revised version of a plenary lecture delivered at the 74th Anglo-American Conference of Historians, 'States and Empires', in the Beveridge Hall, Senate House, University of London, 7 July 2005.

the administration had to be centralized, with power focused on the king as emperor, although authority also lay with the officers maintaining the laws; and the ideology had to support attempts at cultural uniformity. When applied to Asian empires, conquest meant large armies both to acquire and control far-reaching territories and to generate a prosperous economy through booty and prisoners-of-war. The provinces, uniformly administered, channelled the revenue to the centre. It was said that the king claimed ownership of the land, a statement based on Hellenistic sources about Asia and doubtless quoted in the nineteenth century to justify similar modern colonial claims. The revenue came through peasant agriculture, described as slave labour, although Indian sources differentiate between lower caste labour and slaves and do not associate slaves with agricultural production on a substantial scale. Commerce was thought to have been of marginal importance. The administration concentrated on revenue from agrarian sources, intended largely for the enrichment of the ruling class. The ideological confrontation was between the civilized and the barbarian, and religion became an agency of civilizing the barbarian.

Past 'glory' was measured by monumental architecture, imperial edicts, and grand public works. Significantly, the crucial factor of economic appropriation, although admitted as part of the scheme, was dismissed at a simplistic level. There was little analysis of the relationship between empire and its constituent parts. This would have required a typology of states, of the economies that went into the making of states, and of their relation to the empire. Pre-modern Indian empires are named after dynasties and this gives little clue to the differentiation between kingdoms and empires.

The characteristics of empire have been widely discussed in the context of colonial empires and some of these are relevant to earlier empires as well. Thus, empire assumes absolute sovereignty on the part of those ruling and sovereignty is exercised through the right to wage war and to make laws.[3] Size was measured in terms of extensive territories beyond the homeland. This allowed for a differentiation between core and periphery, with the assumption that, the core being dominant, its culture was superior to that of the periphery. In a sense this also encouraged an attitude of internal colonialism. Although diversity was recognized, it did not imply equality between diverse communities. Different cultural levels are registered within elite and non-elite groups, but these are not necessarily sharp demarcations. Empires grew out of states and communities that were previously independent. The aspiration of empire-builders was to achieve universality, perhaps through an over-arching ideology. The fear of cultural divisiveness leading to political dismemberment was always present.

The tension and play between the core and the periphery was a significant aspect of imperial policy. Culturally distant communities could be viewed as barbarians or as outside the social pale, requiring efforts, where possible, to incorporate them by converting them to the culture of the core region. This inevitably meant that the latter had also to undergo some change. Often this incorporation required enlisting the local elite who, in return for allowing them their existing wealth, status, and power, ensured the obedience of the local people, as well as their willingness to provide a militia and to be taxed for revenue. Such arrangements often involved some degree of violence. Symbols of conquest were made visible through monuments and inscriptions glorifying imperial power.[4] The ideology of power legitimized economic demands and these were facilitated through the conquest of territories that had economic potential. Since the system rested on exploitation, tribute of every variety—in cash, in kind, or in human labour—became essential. This was also the basis for the provisioning of armies which both conquered territory and policed it.

Some of these features can be observed in the Mauryan empire. The more significant question, however, is the manner in which they are interrelated. This not only differs from empire to empire but also from the model accepted by earlier historians. Rather than seeing empire as a radical change or a static pattern, it might be helpful to the investigation of pre-colonial empires if they are viewed as a further and more evolved form of the state. Therefore, the formation of states becomes a precursor to empire and in the typology of states empire becomes a distinctive form.

The emergence of empire in India was gradual. In about the sixth century BC there are references to well-established kingdoms, the *rajyas*, and also to the *gaṇa-saṅghas*, the chiefdoms of clan-based societies. These polities are each identified as a community of common ancestry, custom, language, and religion,[5] but they had divergent views about the origins of the state. Brahmanical sources of that time approved of the kingdoms and held that, although the state emerged from a contractual relationship among people, the contract had to be validated through the intervention of deity. At the practical level the requirements of the state were said to be its seven limbs, the *saptāṅga*: these were the king, the territory, the ministers and officers, the fortified capital city, the treasury, the resort to coercion, both militarily and through punishments, and the ally.[6] The king's duty was to protect his subjects, referred to as *prajā*—literally, children—and to enforce the *dharma*—the social obligations and sacred duties of members of society—and, if necessary, to resort to *daṇḍa*, or coercion, in order to do so.

Brahmanical sources ignored the chiefdoms but the latter drew their legitimacy from contemporary Buddhist, Jaina, Ajivika, and other heterodox thinkers, referred to jointly as the Shramanas. Buddhist theory argued for a social contract, but one devoid of divine intervention since at this time gods were largely extraneous to the Buddhist scheme of things.[7] The confrontation between kingdoms and chiefdoms, therefore, was not restricted to the eventual conquest of the latter by the former, but also included the continuing and opposed theoretical explanations of how the polities evolved. This duality of thought moved along parallel paths and is especially evident in discussions on social ethics, notably in the context of the debate on *ahiṃsā*/non-violence. Whereas Brahmanical views held that violence was justified if social obligation required it, the Buddhist view was firm that conforming to the Middle Way of avoiding extremes should be the more persuasive ethic.

By about the fifth century local cultural variations had surfaced, orthodox ritual practices were being questioned, and there were arguments over the diverse theories, many denying divine revelation and claiming derivation from attempts at logical analysis. The comfortable earlier orthodox system was beginning to come apart. This was the point of change. The large kingdom of the Nandas annexed the earlier small polities and was itself a departure from what characterized these polities. In contrast to the rulers of the earlier states those of the Nanda dynasty were said to be of low social status. Politics was becoming a relatively open field and kingship was not restricted to the upper-caste aristocracy as the Brahmanical normative texts advised.

The kingdom of the Nandas extended across almost the entire Ganges plain and had its nucleus in the middle region of the plain in the territory of Magadha (present-day south Bihar), which had been among the earliest kingdoms dating to the sixth century BCE. Magadha was an important political and economic heartland, apart from being the focus of contending philosophical sects. It was the spine of the Ganges plain, through its control of traffic on the river and its tributaries, and it was further strengthened by its extensive rice-land, forest wealth, and copper and iron deposits. Expanding these resources required the availability of labour, obtained possibly from prisoners-of-war and by relegating the lowest castes to this manual work. The kingdom was also associated with considerable wealth derived from the systematic collection of revenue. This allowed the maintenance of an army so large that it is thought to have discouraged the soldiers of Alexander the Great from continuing the Greek campaign eastwards. The Nanda king was soon overthrown by the young Candragupta, the first Mauryan ruler, acting on the advice of Kauṭilya, the author of the well-known treatise on political economy, the *Arthaśāstra*. Magadha became the hub of the Mauryan empire—this was the inheritance of the first Mauryan ruler.

This article primarily draws on three historical sources. The first and most important of these consists of the edicts of the emperor Aśoka, which were inscribed on rock surfaces and specially erected pillars in various parts of his empire. Some of these edicts, or statements, are personal in nature and some reflect his concerns as a statesman and ruler; they can be precisely dated and refer to events and personalities of that period. The second source is the account of Mauryan India written by Megasthenes, a friend of Seleucus Nicator, who ruled the territories in West Asia on the death of Alexander. It is said that Megasthenes came as ambassador to the Mauryan court. Unfortunately his original account does not survive and all we have are lengthy paraphrases from the original incorporated into geographical works and biographies of Alexander written in subsequent centuries by Strabo, Diodorus, and Arrian.[8] The third source—the *Arthaśāstra* of Kauṭilya—is more controversial as its date is uncertain. Most historians take it to have been written in an early form in the reign of the first Mauryan ruler, as Kauṭilya was his minister, but this form was revised and possibly rewritten in the third century AD. A linguistic study of the text suggests different periods of composition for different parts.[9] The section that parallels aspects of Mauryan administration is the one that seems to be the earliest in date, and it is this section that is most frequently quoted as relevant to the concepts of Mauryan economic polity.

The dates of the Mauryan empire are roughly from 321 to 185 BC. It was founded just after the campaign of Alexander of Macedon, who marched through northwestern India from 327 to 325 BC and then returned to Babylon. It was a close successor to the Achaemenid Persian empire to the west of it. Territories at the eastern frontier of the Persian empire in the Indus plain were the western frontier lands of the Mauryan. The closeness is also evident from a few stylistic similarities associated with the Mauryan empire: Mauryan royal patronage, it has been argued, may have borrowed some Persian forms, although the Mauryan style is quite distinctive. The chronological hyphen between the two empires was Alexander.

Interestingly, there is no mention of Alexander in Indian sources. But in subsequent generations there were close links between the Mauryas and the Hellenistic kings who succeeded to the territories that he annexed. Spatially the Mauryan empire controlled virtually the entire subcontinent, and in addition included eastern Afghanistan. The latter was an asset; at the crossroads of an embryonic pan-Asian trade, it was ideally placed to serve as a source of revenue and a forum for more stimulating cultural exchange between multiple communities of Greek, Aramaic, and

Prākṛit speakers.[10] The chiefdoms of the far south of India were not included, probably because they were of marginal importance. Their potential became visible in the post-Mauryan period with the extensive commercial exchange between the merchants of Alexandria and those of the Indian peninsula. The territories of the Mauryan empire were contiguous, which made administration less complicated. To date, estimates of population—a figure of 181 million has been suggested—have been vastly exaggerated; more reliable demographic studies are awaited.

Apart from textual sources, the Mauryan presence is visible from artifacts, but these are of a limited kind. The more significant were the imperial edicts inscribed in various parts of the empire, indicating a Mauryan presence. A particular luxury-ware pottery—the Northern Black Polished Ware—and silver and copper punch-marked coins are associated with the period immediately before and increase in the Mauryan period. Their distribution is taken as an indicator of the locations touched by imperial administration and commerce. Terracotta figurines were noticeably common and many suggest popular fertility icons. Some sealings have been found with Prākṛit names, inscribed in the Brāhmī script used in the edicts, but the style used is less refined. Iron objects associated with city life occur with other finds; urban sites have brick-built structures, and houses have terracotta ring wells and soakage jars.[11] The empire was an area of multiple and diverse cultures, speaking a variety of languages, reading a variety of scripts, and varying immensely in forms of worship, in economic patterns, and in social organizations. Some of the conquered territories had earlier been kingdoms and some chiefdoms. As such, the kingdoms at least were forerunners of a system that mutated into empire. How was this territory and its varied patterns of living to be welded together into an empire?

The Mauryas were an obscure family referred to contemptuously in Brahmanical sources as being of the lowest caste and heretics because they patronized the heterodox sects of Jainas, Ājīvikas, and Buddhists, all three of which accorded them the high *kṣatriya* status of the aristocracy in their narratives. Candragupta campaigned in central and western India, which secured the routes to the peninsula as well as to the ports of the west coast which had maritime contacts with West Asia. A campaign in the northwest against Seleucus Nicator was terminated in a treaty which brought territories in eastern Afghanistan into the Mauryan sphere. Seleucus sent an ambassador, Megasthenes, to the Mauryan capital at Pāṭaliputra (modern Patna), and his observations on India, the *Indica*, have survived paraphrased in later Greek texts.[12] Some Greek commentators have doubted that Megasthenes spent time at the Mauryan court and suspect that he picked up his information from Indian visitors to eastern Afghanistan. It is certainly surprising that he makes no specific mention of the Mauryan emperor. Greek accounts of India began largely as fantasy, such as that of Ktesias, and then gradually became more reliable in their descriptions. The overlap between the two is apparent in some parts of the narrative by Megasthenes. The major problem is that the original text has not survived and, as mentioned above, what we have are paraphrases in later writings, which do not necessarily always tally.

Candragupta was succeeded by his son, Bindusāra, who appears in a number of sources. He is said, for example, to have asked Antiochus I to send him a gift of sweet wine, figs, and a sophist.[13] A much later Buddhist text mentions his having conquered the land between the two seas—a reference it would seem to the conquest of the peninsula.[14] Tamil poems refer to the chariots of the Mauryas racing through the landscape, although they never in fact conquered so far south.

Bindusara's son Aśoka was the most remarkable of the Mauryan kings. Although virtually forgotten in the subsequent hegemonic Brahmanical tradition, he was much lauded in Buddhist texts, having been a Buddhist himself.[15] Information on his reign comes primarily from his many edicts, which provide an unusual glimpse of imperial rule.[16] The elaborate discussions on social ethics and kingship in post-Mauryan texts authored by *brāhmaṇa*s were probably provoked by the projection of Aśoka as a role model in Buddhist literature.[17] The concept of the *cakravartin* (the universal monarch), mentioned in the post-Aśokan period, again registers a difference between Brahmanical and Buddhist views.

The first gives primacy to conquest and the protection of caste society, with a social ethic differentiated according to caste; in the Buddhist concept, primacy is given to the universally applicable social ethic, projected as the law that protects society, and not to conquest.

The territories of the Mauryan empire were at their most extensive during Aśoka's reign. This is gauged by the location of his edicts in various parts of the subcontinent and by the languages and scripts in which they were written, differing according to location. Aśoka refers to the territory that he ruled by the commonly used name, Jambudvīpa—the land of the rose-apple tree. This is difficult to define as a geographical area (in cosmology it was the central place in the inhabited world), but the sense of extensive territory is indicated in his reference to the state that he ruled as *vijita*, literally, that over which he has victory, probably better understood as sovereignty. He suggests the range of his empire not in geographical terms but by mentioning the more important peoples over whom he rules, settled in various parts of the subcontinent. He also defines his territory by reference to his neighbours, the Hellenistic kings to the west and the chiefdoms of south India. Despite the size of the territory over which they held sway, Mauryan ambition was not one of unlimited expansion or there would have been campaigns against both these neighbours.

The Mauryas did not take what could be called imperial tides. Aśoka uses *devānaṃpiya* (the beloved of the gods), in his inscriptions. It neither connoted power derived from the gods nor was used by the kings who followed the Mauryas. In one edict he calls himself by the seemingly simple title of 'the *rājā* of Magadha'. This is in striking contrast to even quite minor rulers who soon afterwards regularly refer to themselves as *mahārājādhirāja*—the great king, the king of kings. Calling himself the *rājā* of Magadha, in effect, implied much more than the title suggests since Magadha was the heartland of the empire. Clues to empire need not lie in royal titles.

The first major event of Aśoka's reign, eight years after his succession, was his campaign in Kalinga, in eastern India.[18] He confesses his remorse at the suffering and death caused by this action, and mentions the resulting deportation of 150,000 people, the death of 100,000, and many more who perished unknown. This seems to have inspired his commitment to forsake violence and war, a policy that he hoped would also be followed by his descendants. The empire was large enough for there to be no need for fresh conquests, yet in terms of imperial ambitions this was a significant self-imposition. It could be argued that perhaps a fiscal crisis also encouraged the forsaking of war, but there is no mention of a reduction of the army. Aśoka's attempt to discourage warfare contradicts a conventionally accepted characteristic of empire, namely, the glorification of continuous conquest. There was no major campaign by Aśoka's successors and, assuming that the size of the army had been stabilized, the peasantry would have remained on the land. Megasthenes states that the cultivators were the largest section of Indian society, and adds that they continued to till their fields even when there was a battle being waged near by, and were unarmed.[19]

The Mauryan empire was described above as a highly centralized bureaucracy controlled by an efficient hierarchy of officers. But there are problems with this pattern. It assumes a pyramidal form of administration with the ruler and his court at the peak. Below this is a neat division of the empire into provinces, further subdivided into smaller, similar units and with parallel hierarchies of administrators. The edicts do refer to smaller administrative units but these were not identical in every part of the empire. With regard to the hierarchy of officers, the edicts refer to far fewer of them than the texts. It would also seem that officers were appointed from the ranks of local people and this again would tend to have decentralized the administration. A centralized pattern relies on rapid communication between the different sections of the administration, but distances within the Mauryan empire were extensive. It has been calculated that it would have taken routine messengers from provincial centres at least two months to reach Magadha and return home.[20] Given this, it is likely that many decisions were taken locally.

The administrative and economic patterns of the empire might be better seen as more decentralized and less uniform. This would also point to unequal power relationships between various parts of the empire, both among themselves and with the centre. Three administrative patterns can be suggested, applicable to different locations and with a gradation of control from the centralized to the local: first, there is the single metropolitan state, second the core areas, and third the peripheral areas.[21] The metropolitan state had its nucleus in Magadha and included the imperial capital at Pāṭaliputra but extended across the entire Ganges plain. The area is in a sense demarcated by the location of specially erected pillars on which a later set of edicts was inscribed in the twenty-sixth and twenty-seventh years of Aśoka's reign. In these the emperor reviews his activities and achievements—a kind of retrospective of his reign, among other things. The pillars are substantial monolithic columns, located only in the Ganges plain and characterized by a superb polish and impressively sculpted elaborate capitals. There is no mistaking that they are imperial markers. They are a striking contrast in style to the heavily ornamented terracotta figurines found in the region and elsewhere. Pāṭaliputra, as the capital, monopolized monumental architecture incorporating halls and palaces. The city was enclosed within a vast palisade with regularly placed towers, described with some degree of awe by Megasthenes, whose words are endorsed in part by excavations.

The metropolitan state would have been administered directly and centrally. It had a history in the rise to importance of Magadha over the two previous centuries. It could well have been administered according to the centralized norms suggested in the *Arthaśāstra*, with a focus on revenue. The revenue intended for the imperial treasury would be brought to Pāṭaliputra to be redistributed in a manner conducive to the imperial economy and administration. The pattern of redistribution suggests that much less was spent on secular monumental architecture than was the case under imperial systems in other parts of the ancient world. Nevertheless, some royal patronage was expended on Buddhist monuments at the three sites where Aśoka addressed the *saṅgha* (the Buddhist order). We also know that the officers were instructed to record the donations of the queen.[22] Whereas the post-cremation relics of the Buddha and of important Buddhist monks were buried within huge *stūpas*—tumuli decorated with stone sculpture—the relics of kings were not preserved. Cremation did not encourage the construction of graves and tombs and thereby denied to the historian of India a valuable collection of objects from the past.

A major drain on the economy appears to have been the payment of salaries to the upper levels of the bureaucracy, quite apart from the cost of maintaining an army. The relative cost of a domestic slave—and slaves were largely domestic—was approximately the same as the salary of an artisan working for the state, low compared to that of a public official. The *Arthaśāstra* recommends that senior officers receive forty-eight times the salary of a clerk, and ministers double that.[23] Unfortunately we do not have evidence of actual salaries paid but even notionally this would have been a huge burden on the treasury. That the upper classes lived well is evident from the representation of rich donors at Buddhist sites of the second century BC. Salaries were computed in coins, and where revenue was collected in kind were more likely to have been paid locally. Since all manner of human activities were taxed, including magicians and prostitutes, tax collection required not only control by the administration but co-ordination as well.

The building of roads and rest houses was part of public expenditure and served many purposes: moving the army, facilitating administration, and opening up trade through linking towns. One set of edicts is located on the route from Magadha to the peninsula. Pliny mentions an impressive royal highway from Taxila in the northwest to Pāṭaliputra, a road which was to be rebuilt more than once in later times.[24] The centrality of trade to the income of the state is underlined in lists of committees and supervisory officers inspecting and valuing items and organizing their sale, mentioned by both Megasthenes and Kauṭilya.[25]

The second of the three administrative categories is that of the core areas. They were not colonies but were often the nuclei of provincial administration. These lay beyond the Ganges plain and were located in parts of the northwest, western India, the southern part of the peninsula and the east. They are generally indicated by clusters of Aśokan edicts engraved on rock surfaces. The area extending from the northwest to eastern Afghanistan, for example, had a population of Prākṛit, Greek, and Aramaic speakers and the edicts are inscribed in all these languages. Western India was Prākṛit-speaking, as was Kalinga in the east, but differences of dialect are registered in the edicts. The cluster of edicts in Karnataka in the south are also in Prākṛit, although the local language in the southern regions was of Dravidian origin. Some of these edicts are addressed to local officers in charge of the area and posted to its central city. The officers were required to read the edicts to the populace, or to any interested parties, and presumably to translate them where the language was not understood. Each core area was the nucleus of a larger unit, frequently governed by members of the royal family, being groomed for more responsible functions at the centre.

The core areas were economically active but differentiated. Their economic potential was exploited and restructured to support the empire. In the northwest the nodal points in the overland exchange between northern India and West and Central Asia were the cosmopolitan centres where the edicts were located. In Afghanistan the major centres were Kandahar and locations in the northeast of the country. Edicts inscribed at Shahbazgarhi and Mansehera seem literally to point towards the routes to Central Asia. There is a tradition that associates Aśoka with having travelled to Khotan, and although this was said to be fantasy a century ago, more recent discoveries of routes from the northern parts of the subcontinent to Central Asia suggest that a revision of these ideas may be necessary. Commercial wealth and the status that it brought gave a degree of autonomy to the elite of the area in the pre-eminent cities such as Kandahar and Taxila. References to the citizens objecting to the repressive policies of the Mauryan officials are associated with Taxila.[26] In the first example the young prince Aśoka was sent to quell the revolt and his arrival was welcomed by the citizens. A couple of generations later the same story is narrated and this time it is Aśoka's son Kunāla who is sent. There is recognition of official high-handedness which was curbed immediately and effectively through imperial intervention.

By way of contrast, western India—Gujarat and Malwa—was a rich agricultural region, with an Iranian local governor named

Tushaspa. Among the Mauryan investments in this area was the construction of a dam. That it was crucial to the agriculture of this region is evident from a series of later inscriptions at the site that refer to the renovation of the dam each time it was breached subsequently, over a period of about 700 years.[27] Irrigation systems, provided and controlled by the state—referred to by some modern historians as hydraulic machinery—were cited as characteristic of oriental empires and a major source of expenditure. There is a contradiction here between Megasthenes, who refers to officers supervising the release of water for irrigation, as in Egypt, and the *Arthaśāstra,* which reveals a preference for irrigation managed privately by cultivators and landowners, even to the extent of their being given some tax exemptions for doing so. This dam in western India was the single irrigation system built by the Mauryan state.

The edicts in the south point to yet another economic activity, since they frequently occur in the proximity of the region's heavily worked gold mines. The *Arthaśāstra* refers to the transport of this gold and semi-precious stones from the south to the treasury at the centre. Kaliṅga, on the coast of eastern India, was in some ways a counterpart to the northwest, as the maritime trade going southwards along the eastern coast of India would have to pass through it. Before the Mauryas, archaeology provides evidence of Chalcolithic and Megalithic societies. The Mauryan period shows urban sites in these areas: Sopara in western India; Shishupalgarh in eastern India; and a number of coastal towns, together with a cluster in the Krishna and Tungabhadra plains of the south. Sannathi lies in the heart of the peninsula and was evidently linked both to the Vindhyan sites and those of the south. New settlements of an urban nature meant some increase in settlement densities.

Although some of the produce and revenue from the core areas was sent to the capital, some would have been used locally. The proportion for each cannot be assessed on the available evidence. Given the distance from the capital, control was doubtless flexible, with many decisions being taken locally. The core areas had either earlier been independent states, as in the northwest, or were in the process of developing that potential, which they did in the post-Mauryan period. Responding to the needs of imperial revenue, their economies were restructured, and this might have encouraged them to become rival centres of power, grouped around political factions and different religious ideologies, enabling them to emerge as independent kingdoms on the decline of the empire.

The third administrative category consisted of the peripheral areas—the waste land, the pastoral tracts, and the forests—all of which were considerable in the period under consideration. They were peripheral in terms of their economic potential, but geographically they were scattered. They lay in the interstices of core areas and not necessarily only at the frontiers of the empire. Much of the peninsula, apart from the river valleys, was forested, as was the Vindhyan region extending through central India. A large stretch of Sind and Punjab and western Rajasthan was not closely settled. These were areas where the edicts have not so far been found but some of their inhabitants are mentioned therein. It was difficult to conquer such regions and bring them under direct control; administration would have tended to skirt round them. Imperial officers probably had closer links with the local chiefs from whom they collected whatever revenue was available, generally in the form of animals and forest produce, such as elephants, timber, and semi-precious stones.

Curiously, the only group of people whom Aśoka threatens in no uncertain terms is the *aṭavikas*, or forest-dwellers, who were in the main hunter-gatherers.[28] His reasons are unclear, but the *Arthaśāstra* states that they sometimes burned the crops of the cultivators, presumably where forests had been cleared and the land of the forest-dwellers encroached upon by cultivators. Burning the crops would be the most effective method of retaliation (Aśoka does specifically ban the indiscriminate burning of forests). It is also said that forest chiefs made unreliable allies,[29] again presumably when armies were traversing their lands. Since the forest-dwellers were primarily hunter-gatherers, they may have found Aśoka's ethic of non-violence unacceptable. In later times, however, converting forest-dwellers into peasants became a more regular activity.

The intervention of the state would have occurred and been perceived very differently in each of these three categories. The

Ganges plain was by now familiar with a system of maximum intervention. The clearing of marshland and forest required a heavy investment of labour before it could be settled. Since slave labour was not used extensively for agriculture or commercial production the availability of labour was ensured through identifying certain castes as those who provided labour—their subordination was further guaranteed by ranking them as low. The availability of labour would also have helped to promote wet-rice cultivation. This gradually became central to agrarian activity wherever it was feasible, since the yield per acre was higher than other crops with more than a single harvest in the year. Consequently, there was the potential both for a food surplus and for increased revenue, provided that the agrarian resource was properly organized.

The *Arthaśāstra* advises that land referred to as *sīta,* or royal, should be cultivated by tenant farmers.[30] It is unclear whether these were small-scale farmers or agricultural labourers, cultivating for the state and retaining a small part of the produce for themselves but giving up the bulk of their crops as revenue. Megasthenes refers to *georgoi* but there is confusion in his account as to whether they paid a tax or a rent. The *Arthaśāstra* suggests that the state should also bring and settle *śūdra* cultivators on waste land and establish a variety of tenancies. These cultivators were, however, distinct from private landowners, who also paid taxes directly to the state. Although private ownership of land is referred to often enough in Buddhist sources, the purchase of land with money is rarely mentioned. Most landownership came from hereditary rights, particularly after the breakdown of clan ownership into family holdings, or through grants from royalty. The latter, however, was not as common at this point as it was to become later. Private estates are not mentioned with any frequency and come into prominence only some centuries later when royal grants, especially to religious beneficiaries and institutions, became an extremely lucrative source of revenue for the grantee.

Empire changed rural land-holding patterns, with more land being cultivated as state land, but by cultivators settled on it by the state and assessed for revenue. At least two types of taxes on agriculture are well established: *bali* was the tax on the amount of land cultivated; and *bhaga* the tax that was a share of the produce, generally a sixth or an eighth, but it could be higher in an emergency.[31] It is likely that the 150,000 people deported after Aśoka's Kaliṅga campaign were settled on uncultivated land and converted into peasants.[32] The degree and distance to which populations can be moved and resettled might, in the context of early India, be another distinction between kingdoms and what I am referring to as empire.

Merchants and financiers investing in trade often came from the families of tax-paying landowners. Commercial activities were tightly controlled, with the required registration of merchants and artisans and with merchandise being processed through a series of tolls and taxes. The coins used extensively in the Mauryan empire are of silver and copper and are stamped with a variety of symbols.[33] The prototype for these coins is traced by some numismatists to Lydian bar coins of the sixth century BC. Some issues carry a legend mentioning organizations linked to towns, suggesting the parallel presence of a more localized system. The Mauryan economy extended the use of money, beyond the obvious trade routes, judging by the widespread finds of punch-marked coins in the subcontinent.

It has been argued in one study that, on the basis of the identification of particular symbols with particular rulers, there was a debasement of silver coins in the later period of the empire, indicating a fiscal crisis. Further evidence for the latter is also thought to come from references to double-cropping. It could be asked if this was debasement or the use of two metals, suggesting a sensitivity to the value of silver and especially so given that silver was not widely available at this time in India. Was there an increased demand for silver coins? Would the debasement of silver alone have had a major impact on the economy or was it a manifestation of other factors causing a fiscal crisis?

The core areas, having been kingdoms or having the capacity to be so, tended to be more uniformly developed and more purposefully administered, generating revenue from agriculture and/or trade. This made them potentially important and more liable to be conquered. They were likely to have been incorporated into the administrative structure fairly easily since they were already familiar with its rudiments. These were the areas of resistance when the empire weakened and they emerged as independent kingdoms in post-Mauryan times.

The relationship of the metropolitan state to the peripheral areas was different since the former did not develop these areas as economic assets but creamed off what was needed from existing agencies; nor did it introduce new forms of administration. Peripheral areas were probably acquired more through a process of osmosis than conquest and were controlled more by fiat than by an extensive network of administration. These were the areas where, after the empire declined, either clan-based societies resurfaced, as in Rajasthan and Punjab, or small kingdoms evolved, as in the peninsula. The interdependence of Mauryan administrators and the chiefs of clans in such areas would have encouraged the latter to recognize the potentialities of state systems. That there was an imperial influence is suggested by post-Aśokan inscriptions in Tamil in the south adapting the Brāhmī script of Mauryan inscriptions to Tamil and largely recording the activity of chiefs of clans mutating from chiefship to kingship, and merchant patronage to Buddhist and Jaina monks.[34]

Cultural assimilation would have been facilitated where there were settlements of the hegemonic culture among those it was seeking to absorb. Given the variation in patterns of control there was also the problem of supervising a large bureaucracy. This was done by the emperor travelling through his dominions; by his senior officers—the *pradeśika* and the *rajjuka*—making quinquennial tours; and by using junior officers and others as informers and spies.[35] There were other ways of attempting to introduce conformity. A statement in one of the edicts suggests a possible uniformity of laws in the empire, but this must have been limited as it is not apparent in the successor states. Customary laws, with their diversities and variant forms, were more prevalent, as among the castes that constituted Indian society. Brahmanical sources speak of four ritual statuses and of multiple groups identified by occupation, ethnicity, and custom. Megasthenes speaks of seven divisions and gives them caste-like features, stating, for example, that marriage circles and occupation were specified and that transactions cutting across these divisions were not permitted.[36] But surprisingly, Aśoka does not mention any form of caste. This would suggest that it was more important to theories of social organization and less formalized in practice at this time. Converting non-caste groups to castes as a method of assimilation became a significant process in later periods, but the practice is not referred to in Mauryan sources.

Given the absence of a dominant code and the presence of a multiplicity of others, an attempt was made by Aśoka to introduce a single code of social ethics. His intention was to persuade the people of the empire to adopt his understanding of social ethics, which he referred to as *dhamma.* This was not just a pious wish. He re-iterated the *dhamma* repeatedly and appointed special officers to encourage its adoption. They were also directly involved in various policies and practices relating to the welfare of his subjects. *Dhamma* was the term commonly used by the Buddha for what he taught. It referred to the universally applicable ethics required of the individual in social behaviour and norms. At one level, an individual's endorsement of this ethic would ensure that he or she acquired merit and consequent liberation from rebirth; at another, it was directed towards creating a tolerant society and avoiding discord. The Sanskrit form, *dharma*, used in Brahmanical texts, referred to the differentiated social obligations and sacred duties required of each caste separately in accordance with Brahmanical norms. There was, therefore, a tension in the application of the two terms as the implications were not identical. This was an important duality of the times. The Mauryan rulers were open to non-Brahmanical ideas and were claimed as patrons of the heterodox sects. In using the term *dhamma*, Aśoka was closer to the Buddhist connotation than to the Brahmanical, but he gave it a uniquely nuanced interpretation.[37] This is especially clear from the Greek rendering of his edicts, in which *dhamma* is not explained as the teaching of the Buddha, but is translated as *eusebeia* (virtue, reverence). Aśoka was not confining himself merely to spreading the message of the Buddha; he was reflecting his understanding of the centrality of social ethics to kingship and to a king's relationship with his subjects. Power and governance are not unconnected; power takes many forms, such as the networks that link individuals to each other, or to society or to governance. The ethic was intended for the individual but was seen as part of a complex social organization. Power can be coercive but such power is distinctly different from the attempt to persuade. Aśoka's edicts are concerned with his definition of social ethics, his attempts to persuade his subjects to conform to these ethics, and his assessment of his own attempts to infuse a new ethic. The *dhamma* did not recognize ethnic and cultural boundaries, and this in turn facilitated the development of local cultures in a less uniform fashion than is assumed for empires.

That there were tensions in the societies of the empire comes through in the edicts. To take one example, Aśoka's *dhamma* maintains that people should respect *brāhmaṇa*s and *śramaṇa*s, and sects with diverse philosophies should respect each other's views. Equal respect for all sects was, however, unacceptable to the *brāhmaṇa*s, who claimed the superiority of divine revelation. The orthodox would have resisted the efforts of the emperor to insist that all sects be respected—the patronage by wealthy financiers and merchants of the heterodox sects was irksome to them. Similarly, the movement and settlement of populations by the state could cause conflict. It led to an increase in the number of peasants, but not necessarily to their becoming better off economically. The resistance of the forest-dwellers was an opposition to the Mauryan state encroaching on their forests and hunting grounds, an opposition that was to be a continuing feature of Indian history.

The Mauryan empire was host to a variety of distinctive cultures. Perhaps the most cosmopolitan gatherings were in the cities of the northwest inhabited by Iranians, most of whom were Zoroastrians, and by Greeks and others imprinted with Hellenistic culture, as well as by Buddhists who were doubtless at this stage largely Indian. In the peninsula, settlements before the Mauryan empire were frequently megalithic sacred sites, some connected to later Buddhist structures. Tamil was the spoken language in the south but the earliest script it used was adapted from the Brāhmī script used in the inscriptions of Aśoka.

Diverse cultures and diverse languages sometimes encouraged interconnections, but at other times they seeded confrontation. A broad-based social ethic could have welded together the various groups. The *dhamma* generally pointed to universally acceptable norms in its emphasis on tolerance and non-violence as prime values. Its social ethic concerned families and communities and the relations between them, and relations between parents and children, masters and servants, friends and acquaintances, the young and the aged. This was not a radical programme but, because of its simplicity, it had to be constantly re-iterated. Its effectiveness lay in its being the attempt by the ruler to reach out to his subjects, and the tone, therefore, is conversational and informal. Some degree of paternalism enters the mood when Aśoka speaks of all men being his children. This universal monarch was less given to conquest and more to ensuring that social ethics took root. It is impressive that the attempt to seek validation from divine sources was minimal and marginal. But states are not moral agents—they are power systems. The endorsement of the *dhamma* by the state faded with the Mauryas. Nevertheless, its essential features continued and have often been central to debates on social philosophy in later times. It could be argued that it has been a visible strand in many movements that distanced themselves from orthodoxies—whether political, social, or religious—and, ironically, from the authority of the state.

Empire, as understood here, was a specific polity, controlling a demarcated territory, with sovereign authority over its subjects exercised through administrative supervision and a philosophy of persuasive association. The territory was more extensive than that of kingdoms, but not uniformly administered. Power, in this system, was expressed in a variety of ways—economic restructuring, cultural hegemony, and persuasion towards ethical norms. This kind of empire is a more complex and evolved form of the state, as it incorporates a variety of existing states or potential states of different kinds. Before being included in empires kingdoms have a nucleus of a presumed community claiming common descent, social sanctions, language, and patterns of living. The incorporation of such kingdoms into an empire does not imply their integration within an overarching uniform pattern to the point where their identities are erased; it implies a flexibility in which some earlier identities are retained and some changed. These are perhaps best seen in the diversities that emerge on the break-up of the empire.

Such a flexibility can be observed through various imperial functions. Divergent economies were recognized and treated as distinct—this placed a premium on the empire restructuring some of these economies because of financial or administrative needs. Such activity differentiated empire qualitatively from kingdom. Kingdoms had relatively less scope for adjusting diverse economies or changing them effectively within their own territories. Imperial policy brought more land under cultivation, creating a larger peasantry. Protected routes and roads opened up distant areas to exchange, and this introduced migrations of new peoples whose settlements became part of a new landscape.

Attempts were made at establishing a tolerant social interface through notions of culture and ethics. The upper levels of imperial society flaunted status, but urban centres were cosmopolitan and supported ideologies that allowed of catholic ideas, such as those of the heterodox religions. These were to spread rapidly, travelling with the traders. Belief systems underwent mutation, with a sharper divide between the orthodox and heterodox. Imperial power had to assess the advantages of where to place its patronage.

The imprint of such an empire on successor states was subtle and became visible in unexpected ways. Erstwhile core areas mutated into kingdoms with more than a hint of Mauryan administrative and economic patterns. An Aśokan pillar was repeatedly used to carry statements by later kings, invoking legitimacy, even by those who were not only unable to read the edicts but who acted in a manner contrary to the *dhamma* of Aśoka. Above all, there was a continuing debate on what constituted social ethics in relation to power. Perhaps, therefore, it is not too great an exaggeration to say that the first Indian empire, in many ways, gave a direction to Indian history.

Notes and References

1. R. Thapar, 'Ideology and the Interpretation of Early Indian History', in R. Thapar, *Cultural Pasts: Essays in Early Indian History*, Delhi, 2000, pp. 3–20.

2. D. Thorner, 'Marx on India and the Asiatic Mode of Production', *Contributions to Indian Sociology*, ix, 1966, pp. 33–66, at pp. 33ff.

3. S. Howe, *Empire: A Very Short Introduction*, Oxford, 2002, pp. 13ff.

4. Ibid., pp. 36ff.

5. R. Thapar, *Early India: From the Origins to AD 1300,* Delhi, 2003, pp. 137–73.

6. *The Kautiliya Arthaśāstra*, R.P. Kangle (ed.), 3 vols, I, 6.1. Bombay, 1965–72.

7. *Digha Nikāya*, T.W. Rhys Davids and E. Carpenter (eds), 3 vols, 1890–1911, II. 253.

8. R. Thapar, 'The Mauryas Revisited', in Thapar, *Cultural Pasts*, pp. 488–519.

9. T.R. Trautmann, *Kautilya and the Arthaśāstra*, Leiden, 1971.

10. Prākṛit was the language used by the majority of the subjects of the empire and was of the Indo-Aryan group.

11. F.R. Allchin, *The Archaeology of Early Historic South Asia*, Cambridge, 1995, pp. 185–274.

12. J.W. McCrindle, *Ancient India as Described by Megasthenes and Arrian*, Calcutta, 1877.

13. Atheneus, ch. iii, sect. 444, ch. xiv, sects., 652–3.

14. Taranatha, *Geschichte des Buddhismus in Indien*, St. Petersburg, 1869, pp. 80–9.

15. R. Thapar, *Aśoka and the Decline of the Mauryas*, 2nd edn., Delhi, 1997.

16. E. Hultzsch, 'The Inscriptions of Asoka', *Corpus Inscriptionum Indicarum*, I (new edn., 1925); J. Bloch, *Les Inscriptions d'Asoka*, Paris, 1955.

17. *The Mahabharata*, (tr.) J.L. Fitzgerald, vol. 7, Chicago, 2004, 12. 114ff.

18. Major Rock Edict XIII (Bloch, pp. 125ff).

19. Strabo, *Geography*, xv, 1.40.

20. G. Fussman, 'Central and Provincial Administration in Ancient India: The Problem of the Mauryan Empire', *Indian Hist. Rev.*, xiv, 1987–8, pp. 43–72.

21. Thapar, 'Mauryas Revisited', pp. 462–519.

22. Thapar, *Aśoka and the Decline of the Mauryas*, pp. I78ff.; The Queen's Edict, 'La Reine' (Bloch, p. 159).

23. *Arthaśāstra*, 5.3.

24. Pliny, *Historia Naturalis*, vi. 21; Bloch, p. 170.

25. Strabo, xv, 1.50 (*Arthaśāstra*, 2.16).

26. *Divyāvadāna,* E.B. Cowell and R.A. Neil (eds), Cambridge, 1886; J.T. Przyluski, *La legende de l'empereur Asoka*, Paris, 1923, pp. 232ff.;

Mahāvaṃsa, 5.150; *The Aśokāvadāna*, S. Mukhopadhyaya (ed.), New Delhi, 1963; J. Strong, *The Legend of King Asoka*, Princeton, N.J., 1983.

27. Thapar, *Aśoka and the Decline of the Mauryas*, p. 118.

28. Major Rock Edict XIII and Pillar Edict V (Bloch, pp. 125ff. 165ff.).

29. *Arthaśāstra*, 2.1.36.

30. *Arthaśāstra*, 2.1.24.

31. The Rummindei Inscription (Bloch, p. 157).

32. Inscription and text use the same term for deportation, *apavuḍhe* (D.D. Kosambi, *Introduction to the Study of Indian History*, Bombay, 1956, p. 196; *Arthaśāstra*, 2.1.1; Major Rock Edict XIV (Bloch, p. 126)).

33. The correspondence of these symbols with particular Mauryan rulers is the subject of debate (Thapar, *Aśoka and the Decline of the Mauryas*, pp. 241ff; J. Allan, *Catalogue of the Coins of Ancient India*, 1936; D.D. Kosambi, *Indian Numismatics*, New Delhi, 1981; E. Errington, 'A Survey of Late Hoards of Indian Punch-marked Coins', *Numismatic Chronicle*, clxiii, 2003, pp. 69–121.

34. I. Mahadevan, *Early Tamil Epigraphy: From the Earliest Times to the 6th Century* AD, Cambridge, Mass., 2003.

35. Thapar, *Aśoka and the Decline of the Mauryas*, pp. 103ff.

36. Strabo, xv, 1. 39–49.

37. Thapar, *Aśoka and the Decline of the Mauryas*, pp. 137ff.

CHAPTER 9

Society and Economic Activity in the Late First Millennium BC*

A study of the social and economic conditions of Mauryan India is essential to a proper understanding of the policy of Aśoka. Furthermore, the particular type of administration started and developed by the Mauryas, that of a centralized bureaucracy, was possible because of these conditions which helped to fashion this administrative system. The influence of social and economic factors upon each other is equally important. No single force is entirely responsible for the development of a society, be it a religious force, an economic system, or a philosophical movement. Each of these forces is interrelated and plays a significant part in the general development. Nevertheless the economic factor, because it is so closely associated at a primary level with the sheer physical fact of livelihood, can modify the form of a society. If the study of the history of a period aims at authenticity, it must of necessity take into consideration the role of various forces.

An analysis of the social factors moulding a society, and an examination of the economic forces, may often merge one into the other, since the two are closely related. That these two features of Mauryan life are of particular significance during this period is clear from the fact that the organization of the empire meant the acceptance of a new type of economy, which in turn affected the social order. In the pre-Mauryan period, the early pastoral economy had changed to a village economy based on agriculture. This was

* This chapter was originally published as 'State and Economic Activity' in *Aśoka and the Decline of the Mauryas*, London, Oxford University Press, 1961.

a natural step after the forests had been cleared, and agrarian village communities became the general pattern in the Ganges valley. Comparative permanence of settlement brought with it the organization of other facilities such as trade, to which again the Ganges was well suited since it provided river transport. The development of trade led to the establishment of the mercantile community through a system of guilds. These were a predominant factor in urban life, and consequently introduced a new force into existing society. Gradually, as this change in the economy spread from the Ganges valley to other areas, it became possible to regard these areas as one unit. This in turn, once it was brought under a single political control, considerably facilitated the administrative system. Administrative ideas could be developed more easily since the same general pattern existed in most areas.

This is not to suggest that no other type of economy was possible once the agrarian economy became permanent. Variations on the economic structure continued to exist, but generally tended to be concentrated in areas where they were more advantageous. The expansion of the agrarian economy accelerated the realization that a single predominant economy facilitated the evaluation of taxes. For instance, coastal areas dependent on maritime trade would continue the trade or increase it as the case may be, but nevertheless would be regarded as areas specifically devoted to one main economic pursuit and would be taxed accordingly. There was much to be gained by those governing a settled economy, which would permit a near-permanent establishment of taxation systems and tax-rates. It is not surprising, therefore, that Kauṭilya, the theorist of the politico-economic basis of the Mauryan state, devotes an important part of the *Arthaśāstra* to the application of taxation.[1] The predictability of revenue in the form of taxes created a feeling of economic and social security. It also simplified the working of the administrative system, in so far as in its embryonic stages administration was largely a matter of collecting taxes. Social security led to the utopian desire to organize society, in such a way that it would function consistently and with advantage to its constituents.

Social organization had already begun in the Vedic period. Based on the organization of social labour, the system of dividing society into four castes had emerged. Until the Mauryan period the system tended to be fairly fluid and examples can be quoted of considerable social mobility.[2] The position of the first two castes for instance, the *brāhmaṇa*s and the *kṣatriya*s, was interchangeable. The prince often appeared to be socially superior to the *brāhmaṇa* who was regarded very much as a mere priest and was on occasion ridiculed. Buddhist literature frequently gives the list of the four castes as Khattiyas, Brahmanas, Vessas, and Suddas, suggesting thereby that in the time of the Buddha the *brāhmaṇa*s had a position socially inferior to that of the *kṣatriya*s.[3] By the Mauryan period, it would appear that the *brāhmaṇa*s had gained the upper hand. Although the later rigidity of the caste system was not prevalent in all its forms in Mauryan times, the process of crystallization had begun. Certain priorities and privileges for the *brāhmaṇa*s were accepted as a matter of course.[4] The earlier indication in the *Brāhmaṇa*s of the leading role of the *purohita* in matters relating to the state, is emphasized in the *Arthaśāstra*.[5] The theoretical aspect of the caste system had been fully accepted, as is evident from Megasthenes' account of Indian society. Buddhism could have been a check on increasing *brāhmaṇa* power, but it was never effectively used as an anti-Brahmanical weapon. Once triumphant, Brahmanical forces held fast to their position by all and every means, as is amply demonstrated by Manu, and the rigidity of the caste system became a permanent feature.

In considering social organization in ancient India, a useful approach is that of examining the reports made by contemporary visitors and foreign sources on the same subject. Greek and Latin sources for instance refer to the caste system in India, and the majority of these references may be traced largely to the account of Megasthenes. We intend to use the comments of Megasthenes as a basis for our discussion, not because we believe them to be more reliable than any other source, Indian or foreign, but because they take into consideration the more predominant features of Mauryan social life without any marked bias; they are meant largely to record and not to maintain a particular point of view.

Megasthenes states that Indian society was divided into seven classes. These he lists as philosophers, farmers, soldiers, herdsmen, artisans, magistrates, and councillors.[6] Arrian states that there are about seven but does not speak with certainty.[7] This observation of Megasthenes is only partially based on fact. The idea of society being divided into groups was no doubt a prevalent one, and the system must have been explained to him by local *brāhmaṇas*. But the number of classes and the categories must have become confused in his mind. His divisions appear to have been rather economic divisions than social. This is understandable because the system of the four *varṇas* or castes originated in an economic division, and it is possible that vestiges of this origin remained in Mauryan times. It is obvious that the divisions of Megasthenes could not follow rules of endogamy and restrict themselves to their own trade.[8] He appears to have confused his own observations with Brahmanical theory. The numerical confusion may be due to the fact that in writing his account, possibly some years after his visit to India, he may have accidentally arrived at the number seven, forgetting the facts as given to him. We must also keep in mind that the fragments remaining to us are not the original accounts but are quotations from the original. Some of the inconsistencies may be explained by erroneous quoting on the part of later authors. Megasthenes may also have had in mind the description of Egyptian society as given by Herodotus, who enumerates seven social classes in Egypt.

Amongst the general remarks Megasthenes makes about the various castes, he states, 'No one is allowed to marry outside of his own caste or to exercise any calling or art except his own.'[10] But he adds elsewhere, 'and exception is made in favour of the philosopher who for his virtue is allowed this privilege'.[11] This passage is reminiscent of a later text, the *Dharmaśāstra* of Manu, where *brāhmaṇas* are permitted marriage with a lower caste.[12]

The first caste mentioned by Megasthenes is that of the philosophers. This group is generally believed to represent the *brāhmaṇas*. Before examining Megasthenes' comments on this group, its position in traditional literature may be considered. Richard Fick is of the opinion that the *brāhmaṇas* are divided into two groups, and his suggestions based on near-contemporary literature are convincing.[13] The two categories consist of the *udicca brāhmaṇas*, the more orthodox ones who were the teachers and the priests, and the *satakalakkhana brāhmaṇas* who were the worldly ones, superstitious and ignorant. The latter practised fortune-telling and magic. Sacrifice was the stock remedy for all ills, and wealth came to the *brāhmaṇa* each time he conducted a sacrifice. Thus the ban on the killing of animals by Buddhists may have been resented by these *brāhmaṇas*, as also Aśoka's disapproval of *maṅgalas* and other ceremonies which he regarded as being valueless. The second group of *brāhmaṇas* was sometimes driven to non-brahmanic activity through economic necessity. For example a *brāhmaṇa* living on the edge of a forest might take to carpentry if there was a surplus of priests in the area.[14] Thus it would seem that some degree of mobility within the caste was allowed provided it was the direct result of economic pressure. However, on the whole the laws of endogamy were strictly observed, and marriage within the *brāhmaṇa* caste preserved the Brahmanical birth; this prevented the *brāhmaṇas* from merging with the rest of the population.[15]

Fick makes particular mention of the *purohitas* who, it would seem, were not content with the occasional care of political affairs but were greedy for more permanent power.[16] This policy naturally had a disastrous effect on a weak or superstitious king who would find himself a pawn in the hands of the *purohita*. Although the *Jātakas* are certainly prejudiced against the *brāhmaṇas*, they nevertheless do present the other side of the story, a view of the *brāhmaṇa* as he appeared to members of the lower order. Megasthenes' description of the *brāhmaṇa* is certainly more sympathetic than the one we find in the *Jātakas*.[17] His remarks on the philosophy of the *brāhmaṇas* suggest that in this instance he made some reliable observations. He mentions briefly at one point that the *brāhmaṇas* offer sacrifices and perform ceremonies for the dead and foretell the future. He adds that they are small in numbers but very powerful.

In another longer fragment he classifies the philosophers into two groups, the *Brachmanes* and the *Sarmanes*.[18] The *Brachmanes* undergo a severe training in a retreat and study there for thirty-seven years. This number is strikingly close to that given by Manu, who states that the maximum length of time that a man can spend as a *brahmacārin* is thirty-six years.[19] The *Brachmanes* then return to a family life. They eat meat but not the flesh of animals employed in labour, therefore they refrain from eating the flesh of cows, oxen, horses, and elephants. They are permitted many wives and consequently have many children. The children do most of the work since there are no slaves in Indian society. The women are kept in ignorance of philosophy. Megasthenes appears to have taken an interest in the philosophy of the *Brachmanes* since he adds that they believed that life was a dream-like illusion. This appears to be a reference to the doctrine of *Māyā* current in Indian thought. Death was not associated with fear and terror but was accepted with a certain anticipation, since they believed that dying was the real birth. He states that their ideas about physical phenomena were crude, but that they did hold some beliefs similar to the Greeks, for example, some of their cosmological theories.

The *Sarmanes* he divides further into various smaller groups.[20] The *hylobioi* are the most respected of these, and they live as ascetics. The second group are the physicians and finally, the diviners and sorcerers. This appears to be a confused description since it suggests the two categories of *brāhmaṇa*s mentioned earlier, the ascetics and the more worldly *brāhmaṇa*s, but it hardly agrees with the usual description of Buddhist and Jaina *śramaṇa*s. Megasthenes must surely have known about Buddhists if he took an interest in religious ideas. It is possible that in later years he confused the two groups of *brāhmaṇa*s, the *udicca* and the *satakalakkhana* and referred to the latter as the *Sarmanes*. Timmer believes that Megasthenes confused the *Sarmanes* with the *vānaprastha* stage of the four *āśrama*s of orthodox Hinduism.[21] In Hindu religious works they would not be regarded as true ascetics. The reference to their leaving their retreats after thirty-seven years and becoming householders would suggest that they were *brahmacārin*s. The four stages were a theoretical subdivision and it is unlikely that they were rigidly adhered to by even the majority of the 'twice-born' Hindus. For all its physical deprivations the life of the ascetic was free from personal and social responsibility. It would not be incorrect, therefore, to suggest that for the majority of ascetics, their vocation may well have been an escape from the drudgery of daily life in organized society.

In another fragment there is an even more confused account of a group of philosophers, again called *Brachmanes*.[22] The confusion is not surprising since the passage is quoted in an early Christian text, the Pseudo-Origen *Philosophia*, which has been dated to the third or fourth century AD. This group of *brāhmaṇa*s is said to subsist on gathered and fallen fruit. They live in the region of the Tungabhadra river in southern India, but they wander about completely naked, as they believe that the body is merely a covering for the soul. Not surprisingly they are also said to be celibate. There follows a passage containing a very muddled account of the mysticism of the words used by this sect. References to God being very frequent amongst them it is possible that this may have been a colony of *brāhmaṇa* ascetics. The description, however, tallies far more closely with that of Jainas living in southern India. The ban on eating food cooked by fire and living instead on fruit is quite in keeping with certain orthodox Jaina practices.[23] The location of the group at Tungabhadra again suggests the Jainas. Jaina sources state that Chandragupta Maurya went to south India with Bhadrabāhu and he may well have spent his last days in this region. Unfortunately Megasthenes does not state clearly whether he actually went as far as the Tungabhadra to see these ascetics, or whether this was a part of the Mauryan empire, and the life of these ascetics was reported to him. The fact of their nakedness agrees with the beliefs of the *digambara* sect of Jainas.

Megasthenes' comments on the privileges of the philosophers are interesting. Amongst them he mentions the exemption from taxation. Diodorus states that they were free from any kind of service,[24] but Arrian writes that they were free of all duties to the state except that of state sacrifices.[25] This freedom is granted to them on condition that their predictions to the state synod are correct. It is not clear whether those who did not accurately forecast the future were made to pay. It is possible that the reference to duties and services to the state may have been forced labour or *viṣṭi* which was current in Mauryan times and which we shall discuss in detail later. Megasthenes also reports that philosophers who make incorrect predictions have to remain silent all their lives. Again it is not explicit whether this meant complete silence or only a prohibition on forecasting events. The fragment quoted by Diodorus states that philosophers are hereditary, but this disagrees with the fragment quoted by Arrian, according to which anyone can be a philosopher, the only deterrent being that it is a hard life.

Timmer is of the opinion that it appears from these fragments that Megasthenes based his caste divisions on observation and not on information.[26] We feel, however, that he must have had some knowledge, although confused, of the Indian caste system. His observations do present certain generally acceptable points. It is clear that the *brāhmaṇa*s were a privileged section of society, despite the fact that they were numerically small. They were not expected to contribute their share in forced labour, and it would seem, were on the whole exempted from taxation. This in itself was a valuable right, singling them out immediately as a special body. Nor does this position change too radically judging from the information of Indian sources. It is clear from the frequent references to the *brāhmaṇa*s and *śramaṇa*s together in the Aśokan edicts and his constant exhortation to his subjects that they should be respected, that they were granted special treatment and were almost a pampered section of society, their religious merit being taken into account in place of productive labour.

With the growth of the agrarian economy the cultivator began to assume an increasingly important economic role. His social position was inferior but his economic position could not be ignored. According to Megasthenes, the second class among the seven Indian castes was that of the farmer.[27] This class was numerically large and was devoted to the land. It was generally left unmolested by armies fighting in the neighbourhood.[28] He states further that all the land belonged to the king and was cultivated by the farmers for the king. The cultivators paid one-quarter of the produce in tax. In addition to the tax they paid a land tribute to the king. Strabo's quotation from Megasthenes is in agreement with the above except on the matter of taxation. Strabo maintains that the cultivators received one-quarter of the produce from the king as payment.[29] The fragment in the writings of Arrian does not specify the amount when referring to taxation. He merely states that the husbandmen cultivate the soil and pay tribute to the kings and the independent cities.[30]

It would seem that the cultivators formed the majority of the Indian population, a situation which has not changed to this day. They were kept disarmed according to all accounts, and their sole task was the cultivation of the land. Some villages were exempt from taxation but this was only in lieu of providing soldiers.[31] Megasthenes maintains that the peasants were left untouched during a war. This no doubt was the theoretical ideal, but it is hardly likely that when hard-pressed in battle the king did not employ whatever manpower was available in the form of local peasants, or attack the villages in enemy territory. The figures quoted by Aśoka of the dead and wounded in the Kalinga war, even if they were exaggerated, could hardly refer only to army casualties.[32] Of the one hundred and fifty thousand people deported from Kalinga, a fair percentage must have been peasants who were probably made to clear forested regions and to cultivate virgin lands. The organization of the commissariat department of the army must have depended quite considerably on local supplies, and this must surely have led officially or unofficially to peasants being forced to surrender their own supplies.

In an effort to relate the castes as listed by Megasthenes and the traditional Indian division, it has been suggested that the cultivators were the *śūdra*s,[33] and that new villages were built in the waste land by deported *śūdra*s from over-populated cities and from conquered areas. They were kept unarmed and under state control and the state took their surplus wealth. The *śūdra* helot had come into his own under state control to make large-scale slavery unnecessary for food production. The *Arthaśāstra* suggests the formation of villages either by inducing foreigners to immigrate, or by causing the excessive population of the heavily populated centres to emigrate to the newly settled areas (*paradeśāpavāhanena svadeśābhisyandavamanenavā*).[34] The foreigners referred to in this context were most probably people from conquered areas; *śūdra*s may well have been deported from over-populated areas. Naturally the *śūdra* peasants would not be the only settlers to move to virgin lands. Members of other professions necessary for the establishment of a village would also be included, as for example, carpenters and merchants. The distinction rested no doubt on *śūdras* being ordered to move and the others going voluntarily for improved economic prospects. Village economy under the Mauryas emphasized the collective efforts of each village.[35] The village tended to develop into a self-sufficient unit in so far as the everyday needs of the villagers were concerned. The overall authority was with the state and the economic integration of the village into a larger unit, the district, was supervised by the administrative officials of the state.

Megasthenes' statement that the land was owned by the king is open to debate and some historians are of the opinion that this was incorrect. In defence of the latter it has been stated that the various texts quoted on this matter should be interpreted as referring to the king as the protector of the land, and not as the owner.[36] The area of the Mauryan empire was so vast and at such dissimilar stages of development, that it is in fact impossible to maintain that one particular type of landownership existed. In our discussion of the subject we shall restrict ourselves to the region of the Ganges plain, and more particularly Magadha, with which area both Megasthenes and the Indian texts were most familiar. The possibilities of landownership in Mauryan society are five, the king: the state, large-scale land owners, communal ownership, and the cultivators. Nowhere in any of the sources is there even a hint of land being owned by the cultivators, and this is not surprising since most of them were *śūdras*. Communal ownership was a much later conception and did not become current until quite a few centuries after the Mauryan period.[37]

Fick draws attention to the frequent references to *gahapatis* and *gāmabhojakas* in the *Jātakas*, both of whom appear to control large areas of land.[38] They are said to have employed hired labourers on the land, whose living conditions were poor but not nearly as bad as those of the *dāsa* (slave). The precise function of the *gahapati* during this period remains uncertain. Fick suggests two possibilities, that the term referred either to the landowning gentry, or to the rich urban families. If the term referred to the former then it is strange that an extensive landowning gentry did not produce a political system to incorporate its position, as was the case in later centuries in Mughal India, or in the feudalism of

Europe. No known social category of Indian society of the period coincided with such a landowning gentry. It is possible that the *gahapatis* were a class of entrepreneurs who were responsible for the development of villages in the new areas, and acted as financiers both to the cultivators and the tradesmen. Thus while they were strictly neither landowners nor tax-collectors, they did have a semi-official status. As wealthy merchants many may have acquired land of their own, apart from the state lands, and not sufficiently large as to form an independent source of income. The term *gāmabhojaka* also occurs widely in Pāli literature. Bose interprets it as a landlord, either in the sense of a man who has acquired territory and has had it confirmed by the king, or as a man who has been given a village as reward for services.[39] Here again, the implication was probably an emphasis on the revenue derived from the land rather than on the ownership of the land.

The question may be clarified further by examining a few of the terms and ideas prevalent in the Indian texts. Originally the king was not the owner of the land, which is apparent from the story of the king Viśvakarman Bhauvana who was rebuked by the earth when he treated the land as his private property.[40] But gradually the position changed. Later law books refer distinctly to the ownership of the land by the king. Kātyāyana, for instance, states that the king is the lord of the earth but not of any other wealth, and that he may take one-sixth of its fruit.[41] As one authority points out, there is a distinction in Brahmanical law between the ownership of land and the enjoyment of land.[42] For the former the word *svam* (and its derivatives, *svatra*, *svāmya*, *svāmitra*) are used. For the latter the word *bhoga* is used. Thus there would be a difference between the land personally owned by the king, which he could dispose of as he wished, and the state lands, whose tax he received as the head of the state, and which he did not therefore own, but merely enjoyed their produce. Private donations of land to religious sects or to anyone to whom the king wished to make a private gift, would be made from the lands he owned in his personal capacity and not from the state lands.

Thus we have a reference in the *Arthaśāstra* to the crown lands.[43] These are the lands owned personally by the king, the income of which formed part of what would be termed in modern times the privy purse. The rest of the land theoretically would belong to the state. Here, however, usage complicates theory. Since the king is in fact by this time regarded as the state, it is extremely difficult to distinguish between the king in his personal capacity and the king as the head of the state. The same chapter of the *Arthaśāstra* dealing with the work of the superintendent of agriculture, treats of the administration of the land as if it was owned by the king, which it was, in his capacity as the head of the state. Since the conception of the state in Indian political thought was not developed at this stage, this distinction in the power and position of the king was not made. The subtle and gradual change from the king not owning the land to the king as the sole land owner is apparent from the work of later theorists.[44] Arrian, maintaining that he is quoting from Megasthenes, states that the same payment was made by the cultivators in the monarchies as in the republics. This would stress the point that in the monarchical lands the king, being the representative of the state, was regarded as the owner of the land.

A small section in the *Arthaśāstra* deals with the sale of land and buildings.[45] It appears that this category of land might be bought by those who were willing to bid for it. Timmer explains this passage by the fact that land was not completely and absolutely the property of the individual; the Indian idea of property being based on the just and fair use of a thing, as opposed to the Western idea which implies more absolute ownership.[46] The passage seems to treat this land as subsidiary to the buildings upon it. State ownership of land did not exclude individuals from owning small areas of cultivable land, which they could cultivate themselves with a little assistance. It merely means that small-scale ownership of land was not the dominant feature.

The distinction made by Diodorus between land tribute and the tax paid to the treasury, may be explained as implying a rent for the land distinct from the tax on its produce.[47] This appears to indicate a heavy total taxation. Since Diodorus alone refers to it, it is possible that there may have been some confusion regarding the interpretation of the source from which he obtained this evidence. Alternatively it is possible that in some areas, the tax of one-quarter of the produce applied only to certain crops, the land tribute being the basic revenue. Ghoshal has pointed out that later two types of revenue was obtained from the land. One was known as *bhāga*, based on the idea of the early Vedic tribute or *bali*, and the other was *hiraṇya*, that is, the cash tax on special classes of crops.[48] Thus it may have been possible under very special conditions to apply both types of revenue in one area.

Although Arrian does not mention the amount that was paid in tax, other writers quoting Megasthenes give the figure as one-quarter of the produce of the soil.[49] Strabo states that the cultivators received one-quarter of the produce as their payment, the rest of the produce presumably going to the king. This discrepancy may have been due to an error on the part of Strabo or the source from which he took his information, and, instead of stating that the cultivators paid one-quarter of the produce to the king, he states that they received the same amount. The other possibility is that he is here referring to those cultivators who are working as labourers on the crown lands although he does not make this clear. They would receive one-quarter of the produce as their wages. The remaining three-quarters would go to the king, providing a substantial income for him. Such revenue is referred to in the *Arthaśāstra*.[50] The revenue being assessed at one-quarter was perhaps a general estimate or was applicable only in very fertile areas such as the region around Pāṭaliputra with which Megasthenes was most familiar. The precise amount must have varied according to local conditions. An example of such a variation in tax occurs in the *Arthaśāstra*, where the type of irrigation provided, changes the amount of tax on the water, this ranging from one-fifth to one-third.[51] The same must undoubtedly have been the case with land tax, but with possibly a smaller degree of variation. One-quarter of the produce is more than the normal amount suggested by most Indian texts, which is one-sixth.[52] Variations occur of one-eighth, one-tenth or even one-twelfth. The *Arthaśāstra* advises that in a period of emergency, the tax may be raised to one-third or one-quarter, or a system of double cropping may be adopted, but only in fertile areas irrigated by rain water.[53] Some historians have maintained that one-quarter was a high tax and consequently a heavy burden on the people, which could easily have led to a justified rebellion against the government.[54] Admittedly one-quarter as a regular tax was high, but later centuries saw worse, when during the reign of Akbar for example, one-third was the regular amount in tax.[55]

The Rummindei inscription is the only Aśokan inscription which makes a precise reference to taxation.[56] We are told that because the village of Lumbini was the birthplace of the Buddha, the king exempted it from taxes, and it was paying only an eighth share of the produce. The word used for the first item is *udbalike*, which generally conveys the meaning of freeing from *bali* or tribute. This probably refers to the land tribute which every village had to pay. The *aṭṭhabhāgiye* or eighth share, no doubt refers to the produce of the soil.[57] It is uncertain whether this was a reduction from the normal amount paid, which may have been a quarter or one-sixth, or whether it referred to the continuance of the usual amount of one-eighth. Had it been the latter there would have been no necessity for the king to have mentioned the tax. Since the village was now exempted from land tribute, it is more likely that the tax would be reduced by only a small amount and not by half. Thus the usual tax in this area must have been one-sixth. This would suggest that the assessment was lower in the area of Rummindei as compared to the tax of one-quarter in the region of Pāṭaliputra. This was probably due to the fact that the land as far north as Rummindei, was not as fertile as that nearer the Ganges. Variations in taxation must have been introduced as the settlements spread farther away from the fertile region of the Ganges basin. It is therefore possible that Megasthenes' statement of the assessment of revenue being one-quarter was based on the amount collected in the vicinity of the capital, which he assumed applied to the entire country.

Another interesting fact which emerges from the Rummindei inscription is that the king deals directly with the question of exemption from land tribute. If there had been any intermediary in the form of a landowner, the king would have had some difficulty in granting the exemption, since it would have affected the landowners' economic position. One of the possible ways of building up a system of landlords appears not to have been in use.

Megasthenes mentions that military officers were paid in cash.[58] This eliminated the necessity of granting them land revenue by way of payment as was done by most later Indian governments, both Hindu and Muslim. Land revenue given to religious sects did not imply a transfer of ownership but literally only the gift of the revenue, so that the members of the sect in question did not have to work for a living. Where the transfer of landownership was involved, it was known as a *brahmadeya* gift.[59] Certain rights of the king listed in the *Arthaśāstra* imply that his ownership of the land was tacitly accepted even though it was not theoretically stated.[60] The fact that the king could demand a compulsory second crop in time of need is such a right.

It is clear that in the Mauryan period the state officials such as the revenue collectors made a direct assessment of the land under cultivation.[61] The assessment was based not on the combined lands of the village as a whole, but considered the details regarding each cultivator and member of the village. The first step in the process of assessment was the subdivision of the lands of the village into categories of high, middle, and low quality. The village was then listed under one of the following heads: villages that were exempted from taxation (*parihāraka*), those that supplied soldiers (*āyūdhiya*), those that paid their taxes in the form of grain, cattle, gold (*hiraṇya*) or raw material (*kupya*), and those that supplied free labour (*viṣṭi*) and dairy produce in lieu of taxes. It is thus amply clear that the administration took into consideration all local features before any assessment was made.

Megasthenes states that there were no famines in India,[62] which is something of an exaggeration, since Indian sources do mention their occurrence. Jaina tradition has it that there was a famine in the reign of Chandragupta Maurya.[63] Evidence of such conditions may also be gathered from the two Mauryan inscriptions at Sohgaurā and Mahāsthān, which are concerned specifically with measures to ameliorate famine conditions in the Ganges valley.[64] Either Megasthenes was attempting to describe India in such glowing terms that he wished his readers to believe that it was a land of plenty which never suffered from famines, or, as is more likely, he left India just before any famine occurred.

Increased centralization under the Mauryas, more particularly during the reign of Aśoka, meant an increased control of the state over the economy. The administrative system was improved and developed and was made capable of examining and controlling even the minutiae of the economic structure. The king in turn, both controlling and co-ordinating this system, assumed a corresponding increase in power. The cultivator came into direct contact with the administration, which to him signified the state. The king became an even more remote symbol than before, and the immediate world of the cultivator was concerned with officials, a condition which was to remain current for many centuries.

The third caste listed by Megasthenes is described as that of shepherds and herdsmen.[65] They are said to be nomads and are the only group of people who are permitted to hunt animals. They were probably called in when an area had been cleared and they were needed to rid it of whatever wild animals remained. There is no confirmation in Indian sources of their existing as a major class, but the mention of the Ābhira or Ahīr caste in later texts would suggest that they existed in smaller groups, probably as a subcaste. Megasthenes adds that they paid tribute in cattle. It may be suggested that these were the remnants of the pastoral Aryans, who were still nomads living on the waste lands and had not yet settled down in an agricultural occupation.

The *Arthaśāstra* does not pay much attention to herdsmen or shepherds. Its remarks on this subject are largely general, as for instance the statement that, 'the king shall make provision for pasture grounds on uncultivable tracts'.[66] That there was no particular caste whose work was the care of animals is confirmed by a lack of evidence to the contrary. Megasthenes looked on them as a caste because he was thinking in terms of economic divisions. In the hierarchy of the social order the shepherds may have been included among the *śūdra*s. Although, as we have suggested above, they may have been of Aryan origin, nevertheless the nature of their occupation would relegate them to the lowest order. If they tended domestic animals then they were probably included with the cultivators. If they were huntsmen leading a nomadic life they would still be regarded as degenerate Aryans by those that were now living in settled communities.

Of the domestic animals reared and maintained by herdsmen cows, buffaloes, goats, sheep, asses, and camels are mentioned.[67] Horses and elephants were also maintained but they came under a different category and had their own superintendents, presumably because they were important for military purposes.[68] Draught oxen are also referred to,[69] so the wooden plough drawn by an ox must have been known to the cultivator. The cow is certainly the most important of these domestic animals. There is no reference to its being a sacred animal, but the value of the cow is appreciated. Dairy products and hide were regarded as the chief commodities for which the cow was bred. This is borne out by the statement in the *Arthaśāstra* that when a man rears a herd of cows he has to pay the owner a certain quantity of clarified butter per year, together with the branded hide of the cows that may have died during that year.[70] Although the cow was not killed for its meat, cow's flesh was eaten. We are told that the cowherd may sell either the flesh or the dried flesh of the cow when it has died.[71] Another passage states, 'Cattle such as a calf, a bull or a milch cow shall not be slaughtered'.[72] The reason for this is obvious since they were animals of labour and provided dairy produce, and were consequently of considerable value. Presumably if cattle died a natural death then the flesh could be sold. With regard to Megasthenes' remark that the herdsmen paid tribute in cattle, it appears from the *Arthaśāstra* that the tribute was paid not in cattle but in dairy produce. A certain percentage or share of the produce is given either to the owner of the herd, or to the superintendent of cows.[73] The reference to the owner of the herd points to the fact of private ownership of cattle. Herds were not maintained only by the state but also by wealthy individuals. The work of the superintendent included the collecting of taxes, inquiring into the condition of the animals, and the work of the herdsmen.

Aśoka made repeated requests in his edicts that animals should be treated with kindness and care. At one point he mentions that arrangements have been made for the medical treatment of animals in his kingdom and also in neighbouring areas and countries.[74] Furthermore, trees have been planted along the main highways, and wells have been dug, so that men and cattle may have access to water and may rest in the shade of the trees. In a further edict he calls upon his subjects to abstain from killing animals. He himself had reduced the number of animals killed daily in the royal kitchen to two peacocks and a deer and even the killing of these would not continue for long. With the same idea in mind, he discontinued the favourite pastime of earlier monarchs, the royal hunts.[75] This policy was no doubt prompted both by a genuine regard for animals and by the fear that indiscriminate killing would harm the country's livestock. The sacrificing of animals was a particularly harmful custom, since, to propitiate the god fully, the best animal of the herd was selected as the victim. Had non-violence been Aśoka's only purpose in instituting this ban on the killing of animals, then surely by way of an example the royal kitchen would immediately have ceased to cook meat.

The 5th Pillar Edict contains a detailed list of animals that are not to be killed under any circumstances, and a further list of animals and creatures which are declared inviolable on certain days.[76] The superficially arbitrary nature of the first list has long been a great puzzle. Why geese, queen-ants, and iguanas should be declared inviolable seems hard to explain. The king concludes the list by stating that all quadrupeds which are neither useful nor edible should not be killed. This is a justifiable ban on unnecessarily killing animals. If this list of animals is compared with the names of animals mentioned in Book XIV of the *Arthaśāstra*, some connection can be traced. This section is devoted to the making of spells and poisons incorporating various parts of the bodies of a wide range of creatures. The lizard family occurs with great frequency, and as the iguana is also a member of the lizard family, we may postulate that some of these animals were declared inviolable because they were used in the making of poisons and magic potions. Aśoka's disapproval of sacrifices and what he calls useless ceremonies and rituals is apparent from a number of edicts.[77] His objection to the use of certain animals in magical rites, may have resulted in this edict; this may have been a subtle attempt on his part to undermine the influence of sorcerers and magicians on the more gullible section of the population.

In the chapter dealing with the superintendent of the slaughter-house, there is a list of animals and birds that are to be protected from molestation.[78] Animals with a human form are included. This probably refers to monkeys. Fish of all kinds are mentioned in the list, and also the following birds: swans, geese, parrots, and *mainās*, which are included in the edict. Animals coming under the general description of 'other auspicious animals' are included in the edict. Unfortunately there is no explanation in the *Arthaśāstra* as to why these animals should be protected. The ban on catching certain fish can be explained on the basis of their being inedible.[79] The edict continues with the statements that she-goats, ewes, and sows which are with young or in milk, and young ones under six months are also inviolable. This statement hardly needs any explanation. Aśoka obviously considered it a heartless act to kill animals in such conditions, and furthermore, they were all domesticated animals, bred for meat and subsidiary products.

Fish generally are prohibited from being caught and on certain days even the sale of fish is prohibited. The latter has been explained on the basis that the indiscriminate catching of fish interferes with their natural breeding habits.[80] Thus the ban on the sale of fish on certain days, mentioned in the edict, was a means of regulating the sale of fish evenly throughout the year. Fish were regarded as an important commodity in Mauryan times. A toll had to be paid on the capture of fish and birds which amounted to one-tenth of the catch.[81] Although in the *Arthaśāstra* fish is classed as edible food and the organization of fisheries was given much thought, it was also used for various other purposes. The value of fish manure for instance was known. The poisoning of fish in streams running into enemy territory was one of the many means of undermining enemy strength, and it would seem, therefore, that fish was commonly eaten.

There is a curious reference in the Kandahār inscription to the hunters and fishermen of the king. It occurs in a sentence which reads as follows,

> . . . And the king refrains from [eating] living beings, and indeed other men and whosoever [were] the king's huntsmen and fishermen have ceased from hunting . . .[82]

It may be suggested that this refers to the hunters and fishermen employed by the king on his estates or for his private purpose. We know for instance that Aśoka stopped the royal hunts. But if fish was an important article of diet in Mauryan times it would have been impossible for the king to have banned the catching of fish. The wild forest areas must have needed the hunters to make the regions comparatively safe for travellers. It is hardly possible that all the hunters and fishermen throughout the empire had ceased to hunt and to fish.

One of the more important results of the political unification of India under the Mauryas, and the control of a strong centralized government, was the impetus given to the various crafts. With the improvement of administration, the organization of trade became easier and the crafts gradually assumed the shape of small-scale industries. Megasthenes refers to the artisans and craftsmen as the fourth class in his seven-fold division of Indian society. He writes of them that some pay tribute and render to the state certain prescribed services. Diodorus maintains that they were the armourers and implement-makers. They were exempted from paying tax and instead were paid wages by the royal exchequer.[83] Arrian explains that most of the artisans and handicraftsmen paid a tax to the state. The exception were armourers and ship-builders who received wages from the state.[84] It would appear that certain members of the artisan class were exempted from tax, since they were employed directly by the state. In the case of armourers it is not surprising that they were state employees. Those that rendered the state certain services probably worked for the state for a fixed number of days per year. This would be regarded as service tax in addition to the regular tax.

It is apparent from remarks both in European and Indian sources that the artisans were systematically organized. For instance, there is general agreement that finished products were not only taxed immediately, but were also stamped by a special officer with a particular stamp, in order to distinguish the new goods from the old unsold goods.[85] Such a high degree of organization on the administrative side meant that the producers of the commodity must have been organized into a working system as well. The sources frequently refer to the system of guilds which began in the early Buddhist period and continued through the Mauryan period. Fick, in tracing the history of the guilds suggests that topography aided their development, in as much as particular areas of a city were generally inhabited by all tradesmen of a certain craft.[86] Tradesmen's villages were also known, where one particular craft was centred, largely due to the easy availability of raw material.[87] The three chief requisites necessary for the rise of a guild system were in existence. Firstly, the localization of occupation was possible, secondly the hereditary character of professions was recognized, and lastly, the idea of a guild leader or *jeṭṭhaka* was a widely accepted one.[88] The extension of trade in the Mauryan period must have helped considerably in developing and stabilizing the guilds, which at first were an intermediate step between a tribe and a caste. In later years they were dominated by strict rules, which resulted in some of them gradually becoming castes. Another early incentive to forming guilds must have been competition. Economically, it was better to work in a body than to work individually, as a corporation would provide added social status, and when necessary, assistance could be sought from other members. By gradual stages guilds developed into the most important industrial bodies in their areas.

Having arrived at a point when the guilds controlled almost the entire manufactured output, they found that they had to meet greater demands than they could cater for by their own labour and that of their families; consequently they had to employ hired labour. This consisted of two categories, the *karmakaras* and the *bhṛtakas* who were regarded as free labourers working for a regular wage, and the *dāsas* who were slaves.[89] Aśoka refers to both categories in his edicts when he speaks of the *bhatakas* and the *dāsas*.[90] Thus by the Mauryan period the guilds had developed into fairly large-scale organizations, recognized at least in the northern half of the subcontinent if not throughout the country. It would seem that they were registered by local officials and had a recognized status, as there was a prohibition against any guilds other than the local co-operative ones entering the villages.[91] This suggests that a guild could not move from one area to another without official permission. Furthermore, they must by now have developed a social hierarchy within their class of artisans, based on their occupations. A chapter in the *Arthaśāstra* describing the buildings within the city throws some light on the social status of various professions; this varies according to their location and in relation to the parts of the city inhabited by their social superiors.[92]

Because of the guild organization individual members possessed certain rights. For example, they were protected against injury and theft. If a craftsman was hurt, the person responsible was put to death.[93] Presumably this law only applied during the time he was actually working. A person accused of stealing articles belonging to an artisan had to pay a very heavy fine of 100 *paṇas*.[94] There were equally strict rules against deception by artisans. People were told to be cautious when trusting money to artisans, even when they belonged to guilds.[95] The fact of belonging to a guild must have acted as a check on fraudulent practices. If a particular artisan was caught in such an act it is unlikely that he would be permitted to continue as a member of the guild, and for an artisan to work independently appears to have been extremely difficult.

Wages were determined according to the quality of the work and the quantity produced. The wages of the weaver, for instance, depended on whether the threads were spun fine, coarse, or of middle quality, and in proportion to the quantity woven.[96] The system of fixed wages for a given amount was also known. Further payment or reward was made for work done during holidays. Strict supervision and examination of the product was enforced. Fines and penalties for inferior or fraudulent work were very severe. Kauṭilya was of the opinion that wages were to be paid according to the amount of the work completed.[97] Thus if a commission was half-finished the artisan was to be paid only for the completed part. The whole payment would be made after the work was completed either by the artisan or a substitute, or else the artisan would have to compensate the man who commissioned it. This system was applicable both in the case of individual artisans and the guild as a unit.

It would seem that artisans' guilds were not the only ones in existence. The corporation of soldiers played an important part in the recruiting of an army.[98] It is clear that these were not regular soldiers who had formed themselves into guilds (*śreṇī*), but were more akin to the modern reserve force. The army, we are told, consisted of hereditary troops, hired troops, corporations of soldiers, troops belonging to an ally, and wild tribes. The term hereditary troops undoubtedly refers to the standing army, which was directly employed by the state on a permanent basis. Hired troops were temporarily employed as and when they were needed. The remaining categories of soldiers, other than the corporation soldiers, were probably also employed only in time of need. Unlike the cultivators, the artisans were probably allowed to carry arms, and therefore could be called upon to serve in the army during a war. Those that were fit to be thus called up were perhaps listed and, in addition to their guild, belonged to a military corporation.[99] That they were not as efficient as the trained soldiers is clear from a further paragraph in the same chapter. Here it is explained that the soldiers belonging to a corporation and not to the regular army, can be put into action when the enemy's army consists of similar troops, suggesting thereby guerilla, warfare rather than pitched battles.

The *Arthaśāstra* in discussing the work of administrative superintendents, relates it to the working of a number of guilds. Evidence of the products manufactured by these guilds is corroborated by European classical sources and by archaeological remains. Weapons manufactured by the armoury are listed in great detail.[100] Arrian mentions that Indian infantrymen carried bows, javelins, and swords, and each cavalryman was armed with two lances.[101] Excavations at Hastināpur have revealed the regular use of metal for domestic and military purposes showing a technological advance over the earlier period.[102] Barbed and socketed arrowheads of iron were found amongst the weapons.

A wide range of metals was known and special characteristics as regards the mining and manufacture of these are noted. This knowledge extends both to utilitarian metals such as iron, copper, and lead, and to precious metals such as gold and silver. There are remains of copper antimony rods and nail-parers from Hastināpur and other copper and bronze objects from the Mauryan strata at Bhir Mound in Taxila.[103] The copper bolt found on the Aśokan pillar at Rāmpūrvā and the copper cast coins dated to the Mauryan period are further evidence of the use of this metal.[104] The demand for iron appears to have increased during the Mauryan period. Iron objects at the earlier levels at Bhir Mound consisted of adzes, knives, and scrapers. The later level shows a wider use of iron, including weapons, tools, agricultural implements, and household vessels.[105]

Precious metals such as gold and silver and precious stones of many kinds were much in evidence during this period. Kauṭilya has a fair amount to say on the work of the superintendent of gold and the duties of the state goldsmith.[106] A further chapter is concerned entirely with the examining of gems that are brought to the royal treasury.[107] Strabo describes an Indian festive procession where royal attendants carry an abundance of objects made of gold or inlaid with precious stones.[108] Evidence of jewellery of various kinds was found at Hastināpur and at the site of Bhir Mound. It seems that the goldsmiths' and jewellers' guilds were kept busy with royal orders and commissions from the wealthy citizens.

The craft of stone-cutting and working in stone needs no literary evidence to confirm the excellence of its quality. The Aśokan pillars with their capitals are sufficient evidence. How this degree of excellence was reached is still something of a puzzle, since no example of stone sculpture which can be dated with certainty to a pre-Mauryan period is extant. The extensive use of wood in pre-Mauryan times and the equally extensive use of stone in the post-Mauryan period, suggests that the Mauryan period itself was a period of transition in this matter.[109] It is fairly evident that most of the craftsmen responsible for the stone work of the Aśokan period which has survived were trained in the northwestern part of the empire, probably at Taxila. The uniformity of workmanship certainly suggests a common centre. In a place like Taxila the Indian craftsmen would also be in contact with Iranian craftsmen who were already familiar with the medium of stone. Remains of Mathura and Chunar sandstone at Bhir Mound suggest a confirmation of this hypothesis.[110]

The guild of wood-workers must also have been amongst the more active guilds. The *Arthaśāstra* suggests that cities were built largely of wood since the city superintendents had to pay special attention to precautions against fire.[111] Fire is listed as the first of the national calamities.[112] Although there are indications of brickwork and in fact, archaeologists recognize a particular sized brick as Mauryan, wood must have been used fairly extensively.[113] It was probably a cheaper building material than stone since the clearing of the forests covering the waste lands must have provided ample supplies of timber. Pāṭaliputra had a wooden palisade surrounding it.[114] Associated with woodwork are craftsmen working in ivory and bone. Remains of ornamental objects in these two materials were found at Bhir Mound.[115] Art historians have maintained that much of the low-relief carving on the gateways at Sanchi was based on wood and ivory prototypes.[116]

Guilds of textile-workers must also have been prominent during the Mauryan period. The *Arthaśāstra* mentions places specializing in certain textiles.[117] Cotton fabrics were made at Madhurā, Aparānta, Kaliṅga, Kāśī, Vaṇga, Vatsa, and Mahiṣa. Cotton manufactured at Aparānta may well have been exported from Broach to the west. Other varieties of fabrics are also mentioned. Among them are the *dukūla*, a white, soft textile, and the *kṣauma*, a type of linen. The manufacture of woollen blankets and other woollen fabrics was also known. Greek sources mention processions in which important persons appeared dressed in garments made of cloth embroidered and interwoven with gold.[118]

Surprisingly enough, Kauṭilya does not mention the potter's craft, beyond a brief mention of trade in earthenware pots. Considering the frequency with which pots and potsherds are found in Mauryan sites, the potters' guilds must have been flourishing ones. Earthenware pottery was common enough not to warrant special mention. But since the black polished ware was extensively used by the upper classes of Mauryan society, and was evidently a more exclusive type of pottery one would expect Kauṭilya to have given some description of it.[119] However, since he does not claim to mention every craft, but only those that are necessary to his general exposition, it is possible that the pottery-makers were thus left out.

Trade regulations are carefully planned and suited to a well-organized system. The sale of merchandise is strictly supervised by the state. The superintendent of commerce, when valuing an article, takes into consideration the rise and fall of prices and the means of transportation.[120] The latter causes a difference in the price of the article, since transportation by water is cheaper than transportation by land. Merchants importing foreign goods can claim a remission of trade tax, so that they can derive a profit from the sale of goods from a foreign country. The trade tax was probably the same as the state dues. This consisted of one-fifth of the toll dues, and the toll tax was one-fifth of the value of the commodity. There was a control on prices as well, since it was the responsibility of the superintendent of commerce to prevent the merchant from making too great a profit such as would harm the people. The percentage of profit to the merchant was fixed and excess profits went to the treasury.[121] The amount consisted of 5 per cent on local commodities and 10 per cent on foreign produce.[122] This beneficial control on prices was a boon during normal periods. However, in times of need, when the treasury required replenishing, the merchant was no doubt encouraged to ask for a high price, since that would result in a larger amount for the treasury as well. The general control over prices and profits extended even to regulating the earnings of the middleman.[123] It would seem that supply and demand were also regulated, both within a certain area and with regard to a particular commodity. But as it was not possible to calculate overall production and consumption, this measure could take effect only in a very superficial way. Since the process of controlling and diverting production was an extremely slow one in those times, crises in over-production of a particular commodity must surely have occurred. The sale or mortgage of old goods could only take place in the presence of the superintendent.[124] This rule was enforced largely to avoid deception, to prevent old ware being passed off for new.

The general tax levied on merchandise appears to have been one-tenth, although it probably varied with each commodity.[125] It ranged from one-twenty-fifth, the tax on certain qualities of textiles, to one-sixth, the tax on flowers, vegetables, and so forth. Since all merchandise was taxed, it was a punishable offence to buy anything in the place where it was manufactured, that is, before it had been taxed and priced. Commodities manufactured in the country were stamped in the place of manufacture, those that came from foreign parts were stamped at the toll-gates. Since the toll was based on the value of the commodity it was probably paid in money and not in kind. Although the tax on foreign goods might be remitted so as to encourage foreign trade, foreign traders were not particularly welcome. The artisan or the merchant was made responsible for the good behaviour of another member of his profession who came and resided in his home.[126] Thus a person known to the former would be vouched for, but a stranger would have no one to act as a referee for him. Any fraudulency with regard to weighing and measuring a commodity in order to fix the price was severely punished.[127] The degree of punishment for the degree of crime in this matter is stated in detail. Similarly, the gaining of more than the specified profit is considered a punishable offence.

About the practice of usury, Megasthenes states that Indians neither put out money at usury, nor know how to borrow.[128] In view of the economic activity we have described above this seems hardly possible. From Buddhist literature it would appear that the commercial community of the time had a highly developed sense of business administration, judging by the way in which resources and fortunes were consolidated. An appropriate passage runs thus,

> The wise and moral man shines like a fire on a hilltop, making money like the bee which does not hurt the flower. Such a man makes his pile as an anthill, gradually. The man grown wealthy thus can help his family and firmly bind his friends to himself. He should divide his money in four parts: on one part he should live, with two expand his trade, and the fourth he should save against a rainy day.[129]

It is unlikely that there was no system of private banking to assist a business man in his transactions. Kauṭilya deals with organized moneylending in the *Arthaśāstra*. It would seem that there was no ban on such activity, since money could even be lent from the treasury on interest paid at fixed periods.[130] Details are given of the amount of interest that can be legitimately charged in certain situations.[131] Fifteen per cent per annum appears to have been the average rate of interest on borrowed money. A special commercial interest is mentioned (*vyāvahārikī*), and this works out at 60 per cent per annum. This high rate of interest was probably charged for commercial activities involving sea voyages or lengthy travels. It is possible that the rate of interest was controlled by the state and this may have given the impression of there being no usury.

Greek sources speak of tax evaders being sentenced to capital punishment (*kleptim totelos*).[132] It has been argued that this may not mean evading the tax, but stealing it from the collector.[133] In the *Arthaśāstra* there is no mention of capital punishment for such a crime.[134] The punishment is merely the confiscation of goods or the payment of a fine. As the latter source places considerable emphasis on the crime of stealing from the collector, it would seem that it was known and practised. It is probably more correct to treat the Greek phrase as a reference to this crime. In consulting the *Arthaśāstra* for evidence of economic organization during the Mauryan period, and the administration of trade and commerce, it must be remembered that the picture presented by Kauṭilya is that of the ideal state. We cannot accept the belief that the Mauryan state was run along these lines in every detail. The *Arthaśāstra* suggested general policies and described various ways in which these policies could be implemented. Undoubtedly the general policy of the *Arthaśāstra* and that of the Mauryan state were very similar and the administrative system of the Mauryas was largely inspired by the ideas in the *Arthaśāstra.* It is, however, reasonable to expect that there were discrepancies. Economic organization on such a detailed scale was a new feature in the politico-economic system of the country. The practical application of these ideas must certainly have resulted in a few lapses. It is difficult to believe, for instance, that merchants importing goods from a foreign country or a distant area, with all its attendant risks, would be willing to accept so low a profit as the official rate of one-tenth which we have already discussed. It is more probable that the officers may have been bribed and the matter of profits privately settled between the superintendents and the merchant.

Trade routes during this period tended to follow the main highways and the navigable rivers. Sea trade was conducted both with the West and with the upper coast of Burma. There is an interesting discussion in the *Arthaśāstra* on the efficiency of land and water routes.[135] The water route is certainly cheaper but it is not a permanent route nor can it be defended in the same way as can a land route. A route that follows the coastline is preferred to a mid-ocean route, because the former may touch the various ports along the coast and thus perhaps enhance commerce. A navigable river is thought to be a fairly safe route. Of the land routes, those going northwards towards the Himalayas are said to be better than those going south. This was presumably because the northern region was better known and was better served with well-known roads than the southern region. The opening up of the south by northern traders was at that period a comparatively recent venture.

Kauṭilya, however, contradicts the above suggestion that the northern routes are better, because he evaluates the routes on the basis of the trade connections they provide. He decides that trade prospects in the south are more numerous and the commodities available are of greater value than in the north. It is suggested that of the routes leading to the south it is wiser to follow those traversing the mining areas as these are frequented by people. This would avoid the necessity of long distances of solitary travel and it would again allow an opportunity of trading en route with the people and habitations. A cart-track is preferred to a footpath and a route which can be traversed by pack animals is naturally all to the good.

A list of the various routes in use in pre-Mauryan India has been compiled largely from Buddhist sources.[136] These routes must have continued in use during the Mauryan period. The more important of these routes were the north to southwest route (from Śrāvastī to Pratiṣṭhāna), the north to southeast route (from Śrāvastī to Rājagṛha), and the east–west route which followed the river courses of the Ganges and the Yamuna. The desert of Rājasthāna was known. The port of Bhārukaccha (Broach) on the west coast was frequently mentioned, and Baveru (Babylon) was known as a trading centre in the west. These routes we may assume were frequently used by the Buddhists in the fifth and fourth centuries BC. These were the nucleus of the communications which were later to spread across the extent of the Mauryan empire. The Buddhist emphasis on pilgrimage no doubt assisted in the care and maintenance of these routes. At the same time the development of commerce both along the Ganges and in the western part of the country made it imperative that good communications be maintained.

With the spread of the Mauryan empire from Pāṭaliputra outwards, communications had naturally to be extended as far as the frontier or even farther. The development of bureaucratic administration contributed to the necessity for such communications, since the officials had constantly to be in touch with the capital cities. Thus, there were not only the main routes traversing the empire or radiating from Pāṭaliputra, but the provinces had also to be served with their own smaller network of routes. Mauryan administration seems to have employed a special group of officials whose concern was with the building and maintenance of roads. These are referred to by Megasthenes as *agoranomoi*, the literal meaning of the term being 'market commissioners'.[137] But their work was related to communications. They were responsible for the construction of roads. At every ten stadia signposts were erected recording distances, by-roads, and other such information. This remark is reminiscent of the 7th Pillar Edict where Aśoka states that he has had wells dug at every eight *kos* which is a distance of about nine miles.[138]

The Royal Highway from the northwest (in the region of Taxila) to Pāṭaliputra was considered the most important route; it has continued to be so through the centuries, being familiar today to modern Indians as the Grand Trunk Road. It has been described in some detail in a Latin source.[139] There was an extension eastwards which was said to have reached as far as Tāmluk or even farther to the mouth of the Ganges. It was equally important from both the commercial and the strategic point of view. Before the development of sea-trade it was the chief trade route with the west, Taxila being the point of exchange. Even for inland trade it was frequently used since there was considerable exchange of goods between the Ganges region and the northwest.[140]

Evidence of routes to south India is scanty. Journeys as far as the Vindhyas were probably not extraordinary events, but travelling farther south may have been something of an adventure. The sea route along the western coast from Broach and Kathiawar to ports on the southwestern coastline and Ceylon, appears to have been in use. We are told for instance that Vijaya, the first king of Ceylon, travelled from Sopārā on the west coast to Ceylon.[141] The east coast sea route appears to have had heavier traffic. Ships sailed from Tāmluk to various ports along the east coast, some going farther south to Ceylon.[142] The importance of Kaliṅga to the Mauryan empire was due largely to its strategic position. Lying between the Mahānadī and Godāvarī rivers it could control the sea traffic between Vaṅga and the south. Kaliṅga in hostile hands would thus be a perpetual danger to this route. Furthermore, it obstructed the land routes to the south, since the easier routes following the river valleys were in the Kaliṅgan territory.

Land routes across the Deccan plateau would naturally tend to follow the river valleys as far as possible. One of the obvious routes to south India would be along the Son valley as far as Sahasrām, then over the plateau descending later to Tosalī in Kaliṅga, and along the coast to the Krishna delta. The road farther along the Krishna valley would lead to the Raichur area. The Tungabhadra valley leading off the Krishna would give access to northern Mysore. Another route from Pāṭaliputra following a more inland course would branch off at Rūpanāth and would meet a northern tributary of the Godāvarī in the Wainganga valley. At the mouth of the Godāvarī it would go south to the Krishna river and then follow the Krishna valley. Another route may have followed the west coast, from Pratiṣṭhāna to Sopārā and farther south.

The reasons for suggesting that the routes followed the river valleys are largely geographical. The height of the Deccan plateau is on an average 1,200 to 3,000 feet, which is certainly not too great a height over which to travel. The problem of crossing this plateau is that it rises sharply from low-lying areas, which would necessitate steep ascents and descents in the roads. But where there are rivers the change from plain to plateau is broken by large valleys which render the rise considerably more gradual, thus making the area far more accessible by road. Furthermore river transport, which must have been used as it is to this day, made it more economical to travel along river valleys. The plateau being a dry area and thickly wooded in those days, not much of it having been cleared, was not particularly safe for a single traveller. Travelling along river valleys, more thickly inhabited than the plateau, was a much safer proposition.

Routes leading from the empire to countries outside the border were concentrated mainly on the western and northwestern frontier. There appears to have been contact between the eastern province and the upper Burma coast,[143] but contacts farther east during this period are not recorded. Relations with the Hellenic world were fairly close. The routes from India westwards have been discussed in some detail by a modern historian of Indo-Greek history, Tarn. He classifies them into three main groups.[144] The first was the northern route and of comparatively minor importance. It ran from Taxila to Kabul, thence to Bactria, the region of the Oxus, the area south of the Caspian Sea, Phasis (in the Caucasus) and terminated at the Black Sea. The second group consisted of three routes which were used extensively in the third century BC. One was from India to Ecbatana via Kandahar and Herat, and was the most important. The recently discovered Aśokan inscription at Kandahar confirms this view. The Greek and Aramaic texts would point to a large Greek and Iranian population at Kandahar, whose livelihood may have depended largely on the prosperity of this trade route. Another less important route branched off at Kandahar and followed the direction of Persepolis and Susa. A further and more southerly route in the second group ran from India to Seleucia via the Persian Gulf and the Tigris river. From Seleucia roads branched off in various directions to Ephesus, Antioch, and Phrygia, and to Edessa, Damascus, and Tyre. This southern route was probably started after Alexander's army had marched in that direction on its return from the Indian campaign. But it never developed into an important route, probably owing to climatic difficulties, and the barrenness of the areas through which it passed in the first half of its length. The third route discussed by Tarn was the sea-route from the west coast of India to ports along

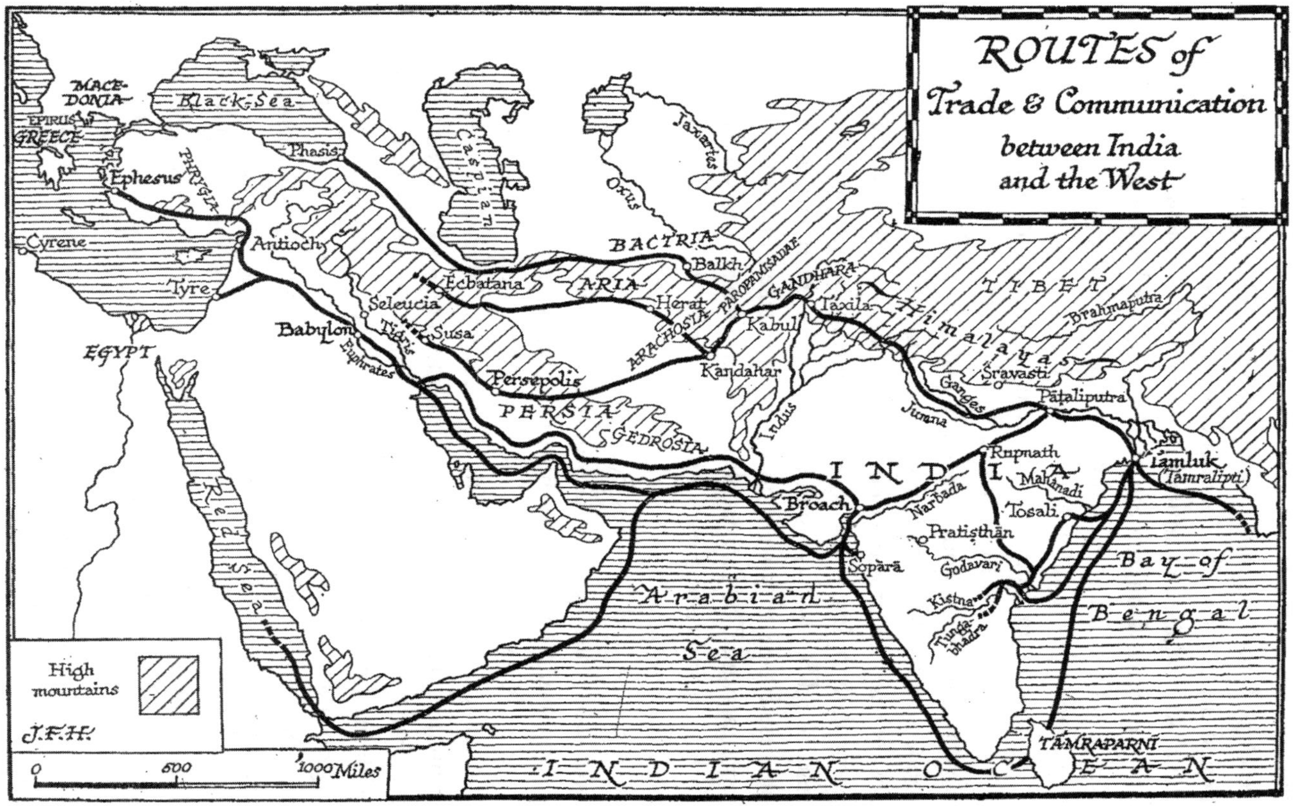
ROUTES of Trade & Communication between India and the West
MACEDONIA
EPIRUS
GREECE
Black Sea
Ephesus
PHRYGIA
Phasis
Caspian
Jaxartes
Oxus
Cyrene
Antioch
Tyre
EGYPT
BACTRIA
Balkh
Ecbatana
ARIA
Herat
Seleucia
Susa
Tigris
Babylon
Euphrates
Persepolis
PERSIA
GEDROSIA
ARACHOSIA
PAROPANISADAE
GANDHARA
Kabul
Kandahar
Taxila
TIBET
Himalayas
Brahmaputra
Sravasti
Ganges
Jumna
Pātaliputra
Indus
INDIA
Rupnath
Mahanadi
Tamluk
(Tāmralipti)
Broach
Narbada
Tosali
Pratisthān
Sopārā
Godavari
Kistna
Tungabhadra
Bay of Bengal
Arabian Sea
Red Sea
TĀMRAPARNI
INDIAN OCEAN
High mountains
J.F.H.
0
500
1000 Miles
Map 9.1

the southeastern coast of Arabia, particularly to a point which later developed into the modern port of Aden. During the Mauryan period the ports on the Arabian coasts must already have become the centres where Indian traders exchanged their goods for those of the eastern Mediterranean, the latter having been sent down the Red Sea, though undoubtedly the trade had not developed to the degree to which it did in later centuries.

References in Buddhist literature to merchants undertaking long journeys are very frequent.[145] These cross-country journeys were full of terror both imaginary and otherwise. If the fear of robbers and wild animals was not enough, the imagination was always ready to provide a host of demons. Desert journeys were particularly trying. These were conducted only at night, when the stars could be used as a guide.[146] Owing to the hazardous nature of these travels they were normally undertaken in the form of a large caravan. The *Jātaka*s also contain references to sea voyages with some interesting remarks on navigation. For instance, crows were used for piloting a vessel since they were known to fly in the direction of land.[147] It has been suggested that this practice was borrowed from the early Babylonians and Phoenicians.[148]

Ship-building was known to the Indians in the pre-Mauryan period. Arrian states that during Alexander's campaign, the Kathyioi, a tribe living in the Punjab, had large dockyards and supplied galleys and transport vessels to the Greeks.[149] The tribes living along the banks of the Indus must have been acquainted with maritime traffic because there had been trade between this region and that of the Sabaeans at an earlier period.[150] Strabo writes that the Mauryas maintained ship-building as a state monopoly.[151] Ship-builders hired ships to merchants for use on rivers as well as on the seas. The state appears to have had a considerable control over the ship-building industry judging by the remarks of the *Arthaśāstra.*[152] Sea-going vessels and ships on rivers and lakes were in the charge of a special officer, the superintendent of ships. Pirates' ships or those bound for enemy country, or any ships disobeying the regulations were to be destroyed. Presumably this law was not taken too literally. Capturing such a ship would suffice. Merchandise coming by ship and damaged owing to sea conditions, could either be exempted from toll, or the toll in this case might be reduced.[153] This was a particularly helpful provision for maritime trade. The sailing ships of those days being what they were, it was hardly possible to take sufficient precautions against damage, as for example, from sea spray.

Much of the small-scale trade must have consisted of the exchange of local products between neighbouring areas. Of the more expensive and adventurous trade we have some mention in the *Arthaśāstra*.[154] The northern areas exported blankets, skins, and horses, while from the south came conch shells, diamonds, and precious stones, pearls and gold. There is, unfortunately, no indication of the objects that were traded with the West during this period. This trade developed enormously in the next two centuries, when we do have information of the commodities that were traded. At this later period various sources mention that India sent to the West, pepper, cinnamon, and other spices, pearls, diamonds, carnelian, sard, agate, Indian cotton cloth, peacocks, parrots, and ivory work.[155] Among the merchandise imported from the West were horses, red coral, linen, and glass.[156] We may assume that much the same type of merchandise was traded in the earlier period under the Mauryas, but probably in smaller quantities. Even more important than the actual exchange of goods is the fact that this trade carried with it a transmission of ideas and practices. As the volume of trade increased, the areas within which the trade was conducted became more familiar, resulting in greater knowledge and understanding.

The last three classes listed by Megasthenes, that of the soldiers, the administrative officials, and the councillors, are dealt with in the chapter on the administration of the country.

The role of women in Mauryan society is of some significance. It was taken for granted that their position was subordinate to that of the men. This is particularly the case in the type of society envisaged by the *Arthaśāstra*. Brahmanical treatises were usually severe with women, who, in later works are regarded without equivocation as an inferior species. The Buddhists were much more humane in their attitude. The decision to allow nuns in the Buddhist Order was one of tremendous importance, whereas their

Brahmanical counterparts would not even admit of education for women. It has been suggested and with some justification, that for a woman life in Buddhist society was not so trying as life in Brahmanical society, since she was not regarded primarily as a child-bearer.[157] The birth of a son was not necessary to Buddhist ritual as it was to Hindu ritual. Since Buddhist society accepted unmarried women, the women tended to be less concerned with finding husbands and consequently less subservient. All the same, marriage was still regarded as the most suitable occupation for a woman. Working women were restricted in their work. The only possibilities seem to have been those of performing in circuses and plays, working as domestic slaves, either in private homes or in royal palaces, and as a last resort, setting themselves up as prostitutes and courtesans. At a later stage, when Hindu ideas on this matter began to infiltrate into Buddhism the woman's importance, even within the home, declined and the older Brahmanical attitudes were revived.

Megasthenes and Arrian in speaking of the manners of the Indians, mention the prevailing attitudes towards women and their place in Indian society. Megasthenes writes that Indians marry many wives.[158] There appears to have been a fixed bride-price consisting of a yoke of oxen to be exchanged for the bride. Probably most people who could afford it had a yoke of oxen for pulling carts and carriages. Those who did not possess the oxen must have paid the equivalent in value. The *Arthaśāstra* refers to the giving in marriage of a maiden for a couple of cows.[159] This practice is called *ārṣa-vivāha* and is described as an ancestral custom. It is also included as one of the eight types of possible marriages. It would seem that the two cows were symbolic and the equivalent in value would be equally acceptable. Megasthenes seems to suggest that some of the wives were solely concerned with bearing children whilst the others assisted their husbands in their work. The latter category would apply more to the cultivators than to any other class, since it is possible that women worked in the fields, but it is highly unlikely that they would be permitted to assist in any other kind of work, particularly in the towns. It is possible that Megasthenes was referring only to the domestic sphere, where, in well-to-do families, some of the wives would maintain and supervise the household, while others would look after the children.

The unchastity of Indian women is commented upon. Wives prostitute themselves unless they are compelled to be chaste. Arrian writes that for the gift of an elephant even the most chaste of Indian women would be willing to stray from virtue.[160] Apparently it was regarded as a great compliment since it meant that she was worth an elephant. Judging from the frequently repeated stories in Indian sources of the adventures of various Hindu gods with the daughters of high caste Hindus, there appears to have been considerable laxity in these matters. This is not surprising. With regard to sexual matters the Hindu moral code was, during this period, free from the guilt complexes which other religions have associated with sex, and consequently a far healthier attitude of mind was exhibited. However, even the Hindu attitude was not without blemish. Owing to the subordination of women in society, it resulted in curious situations. For instance, the state did not ban prostitution but in fact derived a tax from it.[161] Prostitutes were protected against being maltreated. They could also if necessary be called upon to act as spies for the state.

The women employed in the royal palace either worked in the harem,[162] or were responsible for looking after the king.[163] Those in the latter category were bought from their parents. Evidence of the king's personal attendants being women is confirmed by the *Arthaśāstra*, where the king is advised to maintain an armed bodyguard of women.[164] The king's hunting expeditions seem to have been very elaborate. Even on this occasion the king was encircled by armed women. These precautions may have originated in the idea that men, since they were not as subservient as women, would be more liable to corruption and might turn against the king; whereas women, knowing their weak and inferior position in society, would be only too glad of the prestige of serving the king and would therefore be meticulous in their care of him.

One occupation from which women are not debarred is that of weaving.[165] In fact the *Arthaśāstra* suggests that women of all ages can be gainfully employed by the superintendent of weaving.

But this occupation is suggested largely for deformed women, widows, ageing prostitutes, or women compelled to work in default of paying fines. A married woman or an unmarried woman not belonging to any of these categories, if she had to seek such employment, would work at home. This chapter indirectly reveals social conventions with regard to women. For instance, there are three main degrees in the segregation of women; the women who do not leave their houses (*aniṣkāsinyah*), those whose husbands have gone abroad, and those who are crippled and have to work in order to maintain themselves. It is suggested that where possible a maidservant should act as the go-between when the woman has to send for yarn or return the woven material. Where this is not possible then the superintendent is permitted to deal directly with the woman, but she must visit the office only when the light is dim, so that he cannot see her clearly, and that he must restrict his conversation strictly to the work in question.

The *Arthaśāstra* further discusses the position of women in the chapters concerning marriage, and the relationship between husband and wife.[166] The social role of married women is still more flexible than in later centuries. The marriage of a widow outside the family of her in-laws is not unheard of; she must obtain the consent of her father-in-law. Divorce was permitted if both husband and wife wished it under certain circumstances, but this only applied to those marriages which were either voluntary unions or abductions, or contracted with a high bride-price. The types of marriage which were considered more respectable, were those held completely in accordance with social custom and these could not be dissolved. Here again we must remember that this section of the work was a theoretical discussion of possible situations. Whether in practice, social convention permitted the above-mentioned usages cannot be stated for certain. No doubt public opinion, then as now, must have influenced the day to day working of these laws.

Megasthenes has stated in his account that there were no slaves in India.[167] This remark has led to much debate, since the existence of slaves is mentioned in Indian sources, and in fact, most of the labour power was supplied by slaves and hired labourers. It is possible that Megasthenes, having the Greek conception of slavery in mind, did not recognize the Indian system which was different from that of the Greeks. If, for instance, Mauryan slavery was organized according to the system described in the *Arthaśāstra*, then Megasthenes was right. The Indian *dāsa* was not identical with the Greek *doulos*, since the former could own property and earn for himself.

Of the slaves and hired labourers employed to provide labour power, the latter were in a more elevated position than the slaves. They were paid wages in accordance with the amount of work they completed and were not owned by the employer. As we have noticed earlier, much hired labour was employed by the artisans. They were also used as agricultural and domestic labourers and are known to have worked on ships as well.[168] The social position of these labourers was extremely low and was almost on a par with the outcastes. The *Arthaśāstra* concerns itself with details about their wages, but does not suggest any action for the improvement of their condition. Wages were either fixed according to their work or there was a standard wage of one-tenth of their produce.[169] The system of hired labour is to be distinguished from forced labour or *viṣṭi*, which was in practice in Mauryan times. Megasthenes mentions that artisans worked for the state for a certain number of days in lieu of paying tax.[170] A similar system existed for land cultivators. The *Arthaśāstra* refers to it and warns against the tyrannical use of *viṣṭi*. The king is supposed to protect the cultivator from the oppressive infliction of forced labour by his subordinates.[171]

Arrian writes that, 'all Indians are free and not one of them is a slave. The Lacedaemonians and the Indians here so far agree. The Lacedaemonians however hold the helots as slaves and these helots do servile labour; but the Indians do not even use aliens as slaves, and much less a countryman of their own.[172] Strabo affirms that in India no man is a slave.[173] Diodorus quotes Megasthenes as saying that, 'the law ordains that no one among them shall under any circumstances be a slave, but that enjoying freedom they shall respect the equal right to it which all possess'.[174] The passage following this speaks of an equality of laws not excluding an inequality of possessions. This passage provides the clue to the above ideas. Following the textual emendation made by Timmer, the passage runs, 'for they who have learnt neither to stand over or under others, must have the best life in all conditions. It is foolish to make the laws the same for everybody and yet keep the status unequal.[175] Timmer rightly sees in this passage an attempted criticism of the Greek system. Megasthenes is suggesting that the Greeks cannot see that an equality of laws and slavery are incompatible. The reference to slavery need not have been a description of Indian conditions. It may well have been an attempt at propaganda against slavery in Greece.[176] Agitation against slavery had begun with the attacks on the system made by Diogenes and the Cynics. Megasthenes either did not recognize the existence of slavery in India, or else used his account as a polemic on the debate regarding slavery in Greece. It is also possible that Arrian inserted the comparison with Sparta to the original statement of Megasthenes to give more point to the statement in the minds of his Greek readers.

It is possible that Megasthenes may have referred to it in his original text, but later editors may have deleted it and added their own comment believing the latter to be more correct. From Buddhist literature it appears that slaves were of three types: those that were inherited from one's father, those that were bought or were given as a gift, and those that were born in the house.[177] It must also have been the practice to make prisoners-of-war work as slaves. Aśoka's 13th Rock Edict mentions the deportation of 150,000 people from Kaliṅga.[178] It is unlikely that the entire number were enslaved, but a certain percentage of them must have been employed as slaves. The majority were probably sent as settlers to newly cleared areas as the *Arthaśāstra* suggests.[179] By the time of Manu in the early centuries AD, this practice had become a regular one.[180] Slavery as a result of punishment (*daṇḍadāsa*) is also known in the *Jātaka*s and is referred to in the *Arthaśāstra*.[181] Domestic service in households was probably the most common work for slaves. They were used as personal attendants by their owners. Some may have worked as agricultural labourers, others among artisans. It is possible that a man owning many slaves may have on occasion, hired them out for general purposes.[182]

The *Arthaśāstra* describes another group of slaves which affirms the fact that slavery in India was not so severe as in Greece. It is said that in normal circumstances, an *ārya* should not be subjugated to slavery, but it is possible that due to some misfortune, family troubles, or the necessity for earning more money than usual, an *ārya* may temporarily work as a slave.[183] He can buy back his freedom when his term of agreement is over, and resume his normal life. This reference is of importance since it establishes the fact that even though a slave had no freedom, nevertheless he had a social position and was regarded as another category of labour force. The lowest order in the social scale of Mauryan society was not the slave but the outcaste, the person belonging to the despised classes. Thus the social degradation of being a slave was not as great in India as in Greece. To a casual Greek visitor of the period, slavery in India was of a better nature than it was in Greece, but he would at the same time fail to understand or recognize the condemnation of the outcastes by the rest of Indian society.

Both the *Jātaka*s and the *Arthaśāstra* suggest a generally humane attitude towards the slaves.[184] The latter mentions various regulations for the protection of slaves. The children of a man who has sold himself as a slave shall not be slaves. A slave is permitted to own what he has earned and to inherit from his father and bequeath to his kinsmen. Proper treatment of female slaves is insisted upon. If a female slave has a child by her owner, both mother and child are immediately recognized as free. The king is expected to chastise those who do not give heed to the claims of their slaves.[185] Such were the prescribed regulations which no doubt were followed on the whole. But there must also have been lapses. Some *Jātaka* stories refer to the misery of slaves, who had to suffer beatings, imprisonment, and malnutrition at times.[186] In his edicts, Aśoka frequently appealed to his subjects to treat their slaves and labourers with kindness.[187]

The main distinction between the slaves and the outcastes was, that the former could not be considered impure since they were in constant and close attendance on their masters.[188] They lived with the family and not in segregated parts of the town as did the outcastes. The despised classes or *hīnajāti* consisted of people in an assortment of occupations largely concerned with things that were considered unclean. There was complete social segregation between them and the rest of society, and they had no hope of being accepted in the main body of society.[189] The *caṇḍāla*s are an example of such outcastes. They were supposed to have originated as the result of a *brāhmaṇa-śūdra* union and were therefore of very low caste.[190] The reference to *Caṇḍāla-bhāṣā* which occurs in a *Jātaka* story suggests an aboriginal speech.[191] They were restricted in their occupations to being public executioners, cleaning the cremation grounds, hunting and performing as acrobats and jugglers.[192] Leather-workers were despised and because of this the *rathakāra*s were also considered degraded, since their work involved handling leather. The *veṇa* caste were basket-makers and flute-makers and were probably also of aboriginal origin. The *nesāda* caste lived by hunting and fishing, and probably came from areas lying on the edge of the cultivated land.[193] To the settled cultivators the occupation of the *nesāda* was inferior. Potters, weavers, barbers, dancers, snake-charmers, and beggars were all grouped together as despised castes.[194] It is of some interest to notice that their caste names refer directly to their profession or work.

The outcastes accepted this position of social ostracism because they were numerically not strong enough in each area to take objection to it. They lived together with their families outside the towns or concentrated in a small area within, and were thus at a disadvantageous position in relation to the rest of the town. They were not banded into guilds which could act as organizing bodies. The fact that they were deliberately kept uneducated made their position even weaker.[195] The description of the despised classes in the *Jātaka*s is borne out by the *Arthaśāstra*, particularly in connection with the *caṇḍāla*s. It is stated in no uncertain terms that 'heretics and *caṇḍāla*s shall live beyond the burial grounds', that is, well outside the boundary of the city.[196]

Archaeological evidence reveals that towns were built according to a plan and that houses were well constructed.[197] The house plan was generally a simple one, a central courtyard with rooms surrounding it. The rooms on the ground floor were often smaller than those above, and this, it has been suggested, was because in wealthy households the slaves and servants would live on the ground floor and the family upstairs. The lay-out of Mauryan cities improved considerably in the later Mauryan period and the Śuṅga period, when they were planned in a more regular and controlled pattern.[198] Municipal responsibilities such as the drainage system were evidently well organized even at the earliest period.

It would appear from literary and archaeological evidence that the Mauryan period was one of an expanding economy. New possibilities of the development of various crafts on a large scale were being realized, particularly in the context of increasing trade and all its attendant commercial advantages. The benefits of an agrarian economy were also revealed for the first time on an extensive scale and this type of economy assumed a degree of permanency. Together with this economic change, social organization developed along a pattern which was to remain comparatively unchanged for the next couple of centuries.

Notes and References

1. *Arthaśāstra*, Book II. R.P. Kangle (ed.), *The Kauṭilya Arthasastra*, Bombay, 1965.
2. Rhys Davids, *Buddhist India*, New York, 1903, p. 56.
3. *Aṅguttara Nikāya*, III, pp. 362ff.; *Jātakas*, III, 19; IV, 205.
4. *Arthaśāstra*, II, 28.
5. Ibid., I. 10.
6. Diodorus, II, 40–41.
7. *Indica*, XI.
8. J. Timmer, *Megasthenes en de Indische Maatschappij*, Amsterdam, 1930, p. 66.
9. *Histories*, II, 164.
10. Diodorus, II, 40.
11. Strabo, XV, 1, 48.
12. III, 13.
13. Richard Fick, *Social Organization in North-East India in Buddha's Time*, Calcutta, 1920, p. 212.
14. *Jātaka*, IV, pp. 207ff.
15. Fick, *Social Organization in North-East India in Buddha's Time*, p. 212.
16. Ibid., pp. 174, 187.

17. Diodorus, II, 40.

18. Strabo, XV, 1, 59.

19. III, 1. *Brahmacārya*, was the first *āśrama* or stage of the four stages in the life of a Hindu. The first was the period of religious study and celibacy. This was followed by periods of being a householder, then learning to renounce the world, and becoming a hermit, and finally renunciation.

20. Strabo, XV, 1, 59.

21. Timmer, *Megasthenes en de Indische Maatschappij*, p. 105. The *vānaprastha* stage is the third stage, that of being a forest hermit.

22. Pseudo-Origen, *Philosophia*, 24.

23. Jean Filliozat, *L'Inde Classique*, Paris, 1995, pp. 2447–54.

24. Diodorus, II, 40.

25. *Indica*, XI.

26. Timmer, *Megasthenes en de Indische Maatschappij*, pp. 66–9.

27. Diodorus, II, 40.

28. Cf. Breloer in *Grundeig*, p. 119. A Buddhist work, the *Abhidharmakośavākhya* (*IHQ*, II, No. 3, 1926, p. 656), states, 'Philosophers should follow logic in debate, even as kings allow peasants to go on working, even when enemy country is over-run'.

29. XV, I, 40.

30. *Indica*, XI.

31. *Arthaśāstra*, II, 35.

32. R.E. XIII, Kalsi. Juler Bloch, *Les Inscriptions d'Aśoka*, Paris, 1950, p. 125.

33. D.D. Kosambi, *Introduction to the Study of Indian History*, Bombay, 1956, pp. 185, 218.

34. II, 1.

35. Rhys Davids, *Buddhist India*, p. 49.

36. K.P. Jayaswal, *Hindu Polity*, vol. ii, Bangalore, 1943, pp. 173–88.

37. It is referred to in a medieval work, *Jaiminī nyāyāmālavistāra*, p. 358.

38. Fick, *Social Organization in North-East India in Buddha's Time*, pp. 253, 305.

39. Richard Fick, *Social and Rural Economy of Northern India*, Calcutta, 1920, p. 38.

40. *Śatapatha Brāhmaṇa*, XIII, 7, I, 15.

41. P.V. Kane, *Kātyāyanasmṛtisaroddhara*, Bombay, 1933, pp. 16–17.

42. U.N. Ghoshal, *The Agrarian System in Ancient India*, Calcutta, 1930, p. 84.

43. II, 24.

44. Manu, *Dharmaśāstra*, VIII, 39.

45. III, 9.

46. Timmer, *Megasthenes en de Indische Maatschappij*, p. 123.

47. Diodorus, II, 40.
48. U.N. Ghoshal, *Agrarian System in Ancient India*, Calcutta, 1930, p. 6.
49. *Indica*, XI; Diodorus, II, 40; Strabo, XV, 1, 40.
50. I, 6.
51. II, 24.
52. U.N. Ghoshal, *Contributions to the History of the Hindu Revenue System*, Calcutta, p. 58; Manu, *Dharmaśāstra*, VII, 130.
53. V, 2.
54. H.C. Raychaudhuri, *Political History of Ancient India*, Calcutta, 1923, pp. 363ff.
55. W.H. Moreland, *The Agrarian System of Moslem India*, Calcutta, 1929, p. 91.
56. Bloch, *Les Inscriptions d'Asoka*, p. 157.
57. Fleet, *JRAS*, 1908, p. 479.
58. Diodorus, II, 41.
59. A. Bose, *Social and Rural Economy of Northern India*, Calcutta, 1961, p. 18.
60. V, 2.
61. *Arthaśāstra*, II, 35.
62. Diodorus, II, 36.
63. *Pariśiṣṭaparvan*, p. lxxi, VIII, pp. 415ff.
64. D.C. Sircar, *Select Inscriptions Bearing on Indian History and Civilization*, 1965, pp. 82, 85.
65. Diodorus, II, 40.
66. II, 2.
67. *Arthaśāstra*, II, 29.
68. Ibid., II, 30, 31.
69. Ibid., 29.
70. II, 29.
71. Ibid.
72. II, 26.
73. II, 29.
74. II R.E. Girnar. Bloch, *Les Inscriptions d'Asoka*, p. 94.
75. I, IV, VIII R.E. Girnar. Ibid., pp. 91, 98, III.
76. Ibid., p. 165.
77. IX R.E. Girnar. Bloch, Ibid., p. 113.
78. *Arthaśāstra*, II, 26.
79. Hora, *Archives Internationales d'histoire des Sciences*, no. 15, 1951, pp. 405–12. The author states that the fish named in the edict are common to Gangetic waters, and are regarded as inedible even to this day. They were probably known to be inedible even in the third century BC.
80. Ibid.

81. *Arthaśāstra*, II, 1; II, 2; II, 24; XIV, 1.
82. *JA*, vol. ccxlvi, pp. 2–3.
83. Diodorus, II, 41; Strabo, XV, 1, 46.
84. *Indica*, XII.
85. Strabo, XV, 1, 50; *Arthaśāstra*, II, 21.
86. Fick, *Social Organization in North-East India in Buddha's Time*, pp. 279, 280.
87. For example, the carpenters' village outside Banaras, which developed because of the forest nearby. *Alīnacitta Jātaka*, II, 18.
88. There are references in the *Jātaka*s to the *jeṭṭhaka* or president of a particular craft. *Jarudpana Jātaka*, II, p. 295.
89. *Arthaśāstra*, III, 13, 14.
90. IX R.E. Girnar. Bloch, *Les Inscriptions d'Asoka*, p. 115.
91. *Arthaśāstra*, II, 1.
92. *Arthaśāstra*, II, 4.
93. Ibid., III, 19; Strabo, XV, 1, 54.
94. *Arthaśāstra*, II, 13.
95. Ibid., IV, 1.
96. Ibid., II, 13.
97. Ibid., III, 14.
98. Ibid., IX, 2.
99. A similar system prevailed in England during the Tudor and Stuart periods.
100. *Arthaśāstra*, II, 18.
101. *Indica*, XVI.
102. B.B. Lal, *Ancient India*, 1954, vol. x, p. 16.
103. Ibid.; Marshall, *Taxila*, vol. i, Calcutta, 1951, p. 103.
104. Panchanan Neogi, *Copper in Ancient India*, Calcutta, 1918, pp. 18–20.
105. Marshall, *Taxila*, vol. i, Cambridge, 1951, pp. 104, 107.
106. II, 13, 14.
107. II, 11.
108. Strabo, XV, 1, 69.
109. Cf. *Jātaka*s, I, p. 470.
110. Marshall, *Taxila*, vol. i, Cambridge, 1951, p. 103.
111. II, 36.
112. IV, 3.
113. Lal, *Ancient India*, 1954, vol. x, p. 159
114. *ARASI*, 1912–13. pp. 53 ff.
115. Marshall, *Taxila*, vol. i, p. 103.
116. *History and Culture of the Indian People*, vol. ii, p. 541.
117. II, 11.

118. Strabo, XV, 1, 69.
119. See Appendix IV.
120. *Arthaśāstra*, II, 16.
121. Ibid., II, 22.
122. *Arthaśāstra*, II, 21.
123. Ibid., IV, 2.
124. IV, 2.
125. I, 13; II, 22.
126. II, 36.
127. IV, 2.
128. Aelian, V, L, iv, 1.
129. *Digha Nikāya*, iii, p. 188 (trans. A.L. Basham).
130. II, 8.
131. III, 11.
132. Strabo, XV, 1, 50.
133. Timmer, *Megasthenes en de Indische Maatschappij*, p. 217.
134. II, 8.
135. VII, 12.
136. Rhys Davids, *Buddhist India*, pp. 103 ff.
137. Strabo, XV, 1, 50.
138. Bloch, *Les Inscriptions d'Asoka*, p. 170. Bloch has translated the term *aḍḍhakosikya* as half a *kos*, but we prefer Hultzsch's reading based on Fleet's argument that the *aḍḍha* is derived from the Sanskrit *aṣṭam* (Hultzsch, *Corpus Inscriptionum Indicarum*, vol. i, p. 135 n. 1; *JRAS*, 1906, pp. 401ff.). The precise length of a *kos* is difficult to ascertain, since the length of the *yojana* (4 *kos*) varied from five to nine miles. The digging of wells and the construction of rest houses at every half a mile would not have been necessary. The same every nine miles would be the right distance in view of the fact that travellers who walked for most of their journey would need to rest after a nine-mile walk.
139. Pliny, *Historia Naturalis*, VI, 21.
140. *Arthaśāstra*, II, 11.
141. *Mahāvaṃsa*, VI, 46, 47.
142. Ibid., XI, 38.
143. See Ch. II.
144. W.W. Tarn *Hellenistic Civilization*, London, 1927, pp. 211 ff.
145. *Jātakas*, vol. ii, p. 248; vol. iii, p. 365.
146. Ibid., vol. i, p. 107.
147. Ibid., vol. iii, pp. 126–7, 267.
148. Fick, *Social Organization in North-East India in Buddha's Time*, p. 269.
149. *Anabasis*, VI, 15.

150. E.H. Warmington, *Commerce between the Roman Empire and India*, Cambridge, 1928, p. 64.

151. Strabo, XV, 1, 46.

152. II, 28.

153. Ibid.

154. VII, 12.

155. Warmington, Commerce between the Roman Empire and India. pp. 162, 167, 180, 210.

156. Ibid., pp. 150, 263, 264.

157. I.B. Horner, *Women under Primitive Buddhism*, London, 1930, pp. 22 ff.

158. Strabo, XV, 1, 53–56.

159. III, 2.

160. *Indica*, XVII.

161. *Arthaśāstra*, II, 27.

162. Ibid., I, 20.

163. Strabo, XV, 1, 53–5.

164. I, 21.

165. *Arthaśāstra*, II, 23.

166. III, 2; III, 3.

167. Diodorus, II, 39.

168. A. Bose, *Social and Rural Economy of Northern India*, Calcutta, 1961, p. 424.

169. III, 13.

170. Strabo, XV, 1, 46.

171. II, 1.

172. *Indica*, X.

173. XV, 1, 54.

174. Diodorus, II, 39.

175. Timmer, *Megasthenes en de Indische Maatschappij*, p. 274.

176. Ibid., pp. 274–6.

177. *Vinaya Piṭaka: Bhikkhunīvibhaṅga Saṅghādisesa*, I, 2, 1.

178. Bloch, *Les Inscriptions d'Asoka*, p. 125.

179. II, 1.

180. Manu, *Dharmaśāstra*, VIII, 415.

181. *Kulavāka Jātaka: Jātaka*s, vol. i, p. 200; III, 13.

182. Bose, *Social and Rural Economy of Northern India*, p. 413.

183. III, 13.

184. For example, *Nānacchanda' Jātaka: Jātaka*s, vol. ii, p. 428; III, 13.

185. II, 1.

186. *Jātaka*s, vol. i, pp. 402, 451.

187. IX, XI, XIII R.E.; VII P.E.

188. Fick, *Social Organization in North-East India in Buddha's Time*, p. 312.

189. Bose, *Social and Rural Economy of Northern India*, p. 435.

190. Manu, *Dharmaśāstra*, X, 12.

191. *Citta-sambhūta Jātaka: Jātakas*, vol. iv, p. 391.

192. Bose, *Social and Rural Economy of Northern India*, p. 435.

193. Ibid., pp. 447–55.

194. Ibid., p. 483.

195. *Citta-sambhūta Jātaka: Jātakas*, vol. iv, pp. 390 ff.

196. II, 4.

197. Marshall, *Taxila*, vol. i, pp. 91–101.

198. R.S. Sharma, *Ancient India*, 1953, vol. ix, p. 168; Lal, *Ancient India*, 1954, vols x–xi, pp. 5 ff.

CHAPTER 10

Text and Context

*Megasthenes and the Seven Castes**

Despite the proximity of the Hellenistic Greeks there is little that Indian sources have to say about them. If the Mauryas sent ambassadors to the courts of the Seleucids, Ptolemies, and Macedonians there are no ambassadors' journals; nor are there any records of enterprising merchants who may have travelled to and traded at the markets of Antioch and Alexandria. There is a curious lack of interest in exterior landscapes of other regions which pervades the Indian ethos of earlier times. This is in strong contrast to the Greeks who were not only anxious to explore but also to describe what they had seen, even to the point of being accused of having invented the marvels which they associated with India. Admirals, navigators, and ambassadors from West Asia have left narratives of their travels and observations.

Among the latter was Megasthenes, who came from the Seleucid court and is believed to have visited the Mauryan capital and other parts of the state and has recorded his impressions in an account entitled *Indica.* This work, unfortunately, has been lost and what survives of it is in the form of what are generally referred to as 'quotations' from later writers concerned with the Hellenistic

* I am grateful to the late Lillian Jeffry for reading the Greek texts with me and to Peter Fraser, Sally Humphreys, and the late Simon Price whose comments on an earlier draft led to useful revisions. I am also grateful to Anthony Michaelis for help with the German texts.

This was one of the two Deuskar lectures I gave in Calcutta and these were published as *The Mauryas Revisited*, published for Centre for Studies in Social Sciences, Calcutta, by K.P. Bagchi & Co., Calcutta, 1987.

world. Since the quotations are not invariably in agreement their reliability becomes uncertain. Further those who quote these passages with reference to India are authors whose interest in India is relatively marginal and is an appendix to a broader and more central concern with West Asia and the eastern Mediterranean. Nevertheless, the quotations from Diodorus, Strabo, and Arrian have been used extensively by scholars in studying the Mauryan period and have raised a large number of controversies. I would like in this essay to consider a small segment from these quotations, the passages referring to the so-called seven 'castes' of Indian society and re-examine these passages. Such a re-examination raises a number of questions. Were the passages in the later authors' quotations from the original or were they a paraphrased version? Was Megasthenes referring to caste when describing Indian society? How reliable are his descriptions of the royal ownership of land? Were the accounts of India influenced by the historiography and the perceptions of Hellenistic culture which formed the intellectual background of these authors? Equally pertinent is the question of the modern interpretation of these texts. There has been a tendency to regard classical authors writing on India as largely reliable perhaps because of the sparseness of Indian descriptive sources. Such questions require attention even if they cannot be conclusively answered.

Megasthenes is quoted as having listed the following seven divisions of Indian society: philosophers, cultivators, herdsmen, artisans and traders, soldiers, overseers, and councillors. The divisions are referred to in the Greek texts either as *merē* or *genē* and these terms have been variously translated as 'division', 'class', or 'caste'. Altheim uses 'class' for both *meros* and *genos* (the terms used in the original Greek).[1] Oldfather translating Diodorus renders *merē* as 'castes'[2] as also does Jones translating Strabo,[3] whereas Brunt uses 'classes' for *genea* in Arrian.[4] McCrindle translating Strabo refers to *merē* as 'parts' and *genē* as 'castes' both in the case of Strabo and Arrian. Because of its being a description of Indian society perhaps the term 'caste' has been commonly and arbitrarily used and there is now an established reference to the seven 'castes' of Megasthenes.[5]

According to R.C. Majumdar, 'His (Megasthenes) description of the seven castes which are unknown to Indian literature or tradition may be cited as an example where, on a few basic facts he has reared up a structure which is mostly inaccurate and misleading'.[6] This statement results from a lack of careful reading and understanding of the text. If Majumdar had been sufficiently meticulous he would have realized that not every translation of the original texts uses the word 'caste'. As has been pointed out in a rejoinder to him[8] it is not justified to berate Schwanbeck, who put together the fragments relating to India, because even he cautions against an indiscriminate use of the text. In the introduction to Oldfather's translation of Diodorus, the translator makes it clear that he is uncertain whether Diodorus is paraphrasing directly or indirectly. The more significant question it would seem is, why was there this confusion?

The question of how Megasthenes arrived at these seven 'castes' has now become a hardy perennial among the controversies relating to early Indian history. Many suggestions have been made on the interpretation of the seven but there is no general agreement. If Megasthenes was referring to the *varṇa* organization of Indian society then he should have listed only the four castes of *brāhmaṇa*s, (priests), *kṣatriya*s (warriors and landowners), *vaiśya*s (traders and artisans), and *śūdra*s (artisans and cultivators) and possibly should also have mentioned the fifth group, that of the untouchables, or at least the *caṇḍāla*s. If however he was referring to the *jāti* organization then the number of castes would be innumerable and would certainly exceed seven. They might even have had to be divided into the high and the low as is common in Buddhist texts. Why then did Megasthenes give a precise list of seven? Was he merely repeating what Herodotus earlier had said about there being seven major divisions of Egyptian society as some scholars have argued?

Among those who have written at length on this theme are Otto Stein,[8] B.C.J. Timmer,[9] and B. Breloer.[10] Stein doubts that Megasthenes had discussions with Indians on caste since his information does not conform to what we know about caste in the Mauryan period or to the statements in the *Arthaśāstra* of Kauṭilya, some sections of which are of the Mauryan period. Timmer was of a different opinion and felt that Megasthenes did have some familiarity with Indian theories about caste to which he probably added some oral information. Breloer makes the interesting observation that the list given by Megasthenes differs from those of Pliny and Solinus both in sequence and in number since the latter two do not refer to overseers/spies as a separate group. Breloer makes a worthwhile distinction between the division according to *merē* which he argues related to fiscal units and the reference to *genē* which were concerned with the social ordering of the community. He argues that it was Arrian's confusion between the two which resulted in fiscal divisions being seen as castes by modern scholars. This suggestion requires that there be some analysis of the concepts of *merē* and *genē.* Van Buitenen has argued that the seven divisions should be seen as forming three groups, each determined by services to the state and fiscal requirements, what he calls, tax categories.[11] Thus the philosophers do not serve the state nor do they pay taxes. The soldiers, overseers, and councillors are paid by the state and therefore do not pay taxes. The cultivators, herdsmen, artisans, and traders do not perform services for the state but pay taxes. The seven divisions therefore were essentially fiscal and were listed so by Megasthenes from observation and from information relating to the treasury. The argument is plausible to some extent but one wonders why then did Megasthenes not list them as three distinct groups rather than seven. The distinctions also do not always hold since in some cases the philosophers do serve the state in that they are supposed to foretell weather conditions and events and some among the artisans also served the state and paid no tax.

In taking up this question again I am proposing a change of focus rather than an attempt to solve the problem and the change of focus may help eventually in arriving at a solution. The question is generally analysed by comparing the text of Megasthenes, or rather the variant texts purporting to be quotations from Megasthenes, with contemporary Indian sources, especially the *Arthaśāstra* of Kauṭilya. I would like to argue that there is also a need to look more analytically at the Greek texts and at Hellenistic historiography which forms their ideological context.

The earliest quotation comes in the writings of Diodorus Siculus who, as his name indicates, was a resident of Sicily but visited Egypt in the mid-first century BC. His description of India is part of a larger work, *Library of History*, which was substantially concerned with the eastern Mediterranean and whatever was known of neighbouring north Africa and Asia and which he based on earlier Greek accounts such as that of Megasthenes. This is not regarded as a highly scholarly work but more as a summary of contemporary knowledge about these regions.

Diodorus, quoting Megasthenes, writes that the Indian people (*plethos*) are divided into seven *merē*.[12] The word *meros* (in the singular) refers to a share or a portion, a heritage, a part, a lot. The sense of a part is in contrast to the whole and also carries the meaning of a branch. Diodorus then goes on to state that no one is allowed to marry a person of another *genos* or follow another calling or trade. Interestingly, the word used in this section of the passage is not *meros* but *genos* which has a different meaning.[13] *Genos* means kind or variety and is largely used of divisions relating to race, stock, family, direct descent, and birth and has a common usage in Greek as 'clan'. Where Herodotus in his *History* refers to the seven *genē*[14] in Egypt the word has been variously translated into English as nation, tribe, class, and clan: a sad reflection on the vagaries of translation. Herodotus lists the seven *genē* as priests, warriors, cowherds, swineherds, tradesmen, interpreters, and boatmen. Curiously, cultivators are absent which is particularly strange for Egypt. Diodorus therefore uses one word for the general divisions of society which he refers to as the *merē* and another for the rules of marriage and hereditary occupation which derive from *genos*, although he illustrates it by reference to the *merē*, giving the example of a soldier not becoming an artisan or an artisan a philosopher.

As regards the seven divisions, the first is described as the order of the *philosophoi*, a general term translated as philosophers and the description seems to refer to *brāhmaṇa*s (and that too the more learned or *śrotriya brāhmaṇa*s). They are small in number but have a high status. They are exempt from all public duties and are neither the masters nor the servants of others. They perform sacrificial rituals and live off gifts and honours, suggestive of the *dāna* and *dakṣiṇā* given to *brāhmaṇas*. They make predictions about climate and weather for the state and those who err in their predictions are thereafter silent. This was an important public duty in an economy dependent on agriculture. It is curious that there should have been no reference to the *śramaṇa* sects associated with Buddhism, Jainism, the Ājīvikas and other such religious and philosophical movements of the period, as there is in other works quoting from Megasthenes. Perhaps this section was deleted by Diodorus; for it is hard to explain why the term *philosophoi* was used when the functions described relate more closely to those of the priests, *hiereis*.

The second division is that of the *georgoi*, the cultivators who are exempt from public service and from war. They stay on the *chora*, the rural area and do not go to the *polis* or city. For cultivating the land they pay a *misthos* to the king since all of India is royal land and no private person can possess land. Apart from the *misthos* they pay one-fourth (of the produce) to the treasury. *Misthos* is generally regarded as a wage or payment for work done or hired service, or allowance for public service but can also be translated as rent. There are therefore two payments made by the cultivators, one on the land cultivated and the other a share of the produce. This would appear to agree with the two taxes mentioned in Indian sources, the *bali* and the *bhāga*. The Rummindei inscription of Aśoka mentions both.[15] *Bhāga* is clearly a share of the produce and is normally stated to be one-sixth in Indian sources. Thus one-fourth would be higher. *Bali* may have been a tax on the area of land cultivated although it does not indicate a connection with a wage nor does it necessarily imply royal ownership of land. That all land is royal, that is, owned by the king is contradicted by Indian sources.[16] Possibly the statement was derived from the notion of the *sītā* or royal lands also referred to in the *Arthaśāstra*.[17] The *sītā* lands would be similar to the *chora basilīke* of the Seleucids and the Ptolemies. The word *misthos*, however, seems ambiguous when referring to what the tenants pay to the state. If the cultivators were working the land owned by the state as labour then the state would have been paying the cultivators a wage or *misthos*. The closest equivalent in Sanskrit would be *bhaṭa* or *vetana*.[18] *Misthosis*, however, can mean letting for hire or lease and may refer to the state leasing land. The cultivators in this case would be tenants of the state and paying a rent.

The category of *boukoloi* and *poimenes*, herdsmen and shepherds, appear to be a nomadic group as they live in tents and include hunters. These are suggestive of pastoralists not quite settled and of their closeness to forests which often formed the major grazing grounds as Kauṭilya suggests.[19] Interestingly, Diodorus does not use the word *meros* for these nomadic groups but refers to the *phylon* of shepherds and herdsmen, a word generally used for tribe. Grazing in forests would require pastoralists to be hunters as well in order to clear the area of predators before their animals could safely graze. Forests located on the borders between kingdoms acted as frontier zones and their inhabitants would tend to be left alone. If they were not incorporated into caste society, they would generally be regarded as different. The term *phylon* does suggest this. The nomadic nature of such groups may have been due to their practice of transhumance in many areas or to the circuits of grazing which required seasonal shifts.

The category of artisans, the *technitai*, are described as implement-makers who are exempt from taxes and receive maintenance from the royal treasury. Presumably they work for the state but this is not the same as required service or labour in lieu of tax as is suggested by the Sanskrit *viṣṭi*.[20] The *Arthaśāstra* refers to certain categories of artisans such as armour-makers being employed by the state[21] but the major part of the artisans work independently.

The soldiers, *polemistai*, refer to the standing army. If the figures given for the Mauryan army in other Greek and Latin sources are to be believed then the soldiers would have constituted a substantial number.[22] The *ephoroi* were the overseers and the term since it implies secrecy, is also translated as spies whose function was to enquire into and inspect all sections of government work and report back to the king, or in the case of kingless states, to the archons or senior administrators. *Ephoroi* was the standard Spartan term for officials and they were required to make reports to the king. This group is familiar from Indian sources where the *Arthaśāstra* refers to the *adhyakṣa*s or superintendents of various departments[23] and Aśoka refers to the *pulisā* in his inscriptions.[24] Their presence in the kingless states, presumably the *gaṇa-saṅgha*s or the *gaṇa-rājyas* points to a more sophisticated concept of administration which is corroborated by the association of a hierarchy of officials in the state of the Vṛjjis but mentioned in Buddhists texts of a later period.[25]

The reference to the seventh category as the *bouleuon* and *sumedreuon* underlines Diodorus' statement that they were not ordinary advisors but were members of recognized administrative bodies of high status. The Boule was a formally constituted body of advisors or any council of a Greek city as also was the Synod. Both the Boule and the Synod were well-established institutions in the Greek states of Asia Minor as well. The nearest equivalent would be the *sabhā* or *pariṣad* of Mauryan times and this category probably referred to the *amātya*s and *mahāmātra*s of the Mauryan administration.

Our second author Strabo, also quotes from Megasthenes in his famous work, *The Geography.*[26] Strabo was born in Pontos in Asia Minor and was therefore even closer to the Hellenistic world and was a slightly later contemporary of Diodorus, having written his book at the turn of the Christian era. His father and grandfather were involved in the politics of Roman generals and he himself was not only familiar with Rome but had also worked at Alexandria in Egypt. His book is knowledgeable on the eastern Mediterranean though doubtless the interest in Asia increased with the spurt in the Roman trade with the east. Strabo was writing at the peak period of the trade with India and one would therefore expect fuller information as compared to earlier texts.

Strabo refers to the people (*plethos*) of India being divided into seven *merē* and lists these in much the same way as Diodorus although with some variants. However, when speaking of marriage and occupation he refers to the groups as *genē* and repeats the information regarding the restrictions of marrying within the *genos* and keeping to the same occupation. However, he adds that only the philosophers can marry outside their *genos.*

Strabo's description of the *philosophoi* refers to the *brachmanes* but also includes another quotation from Megasthenes which

Strabo reads as *garmanes.*[27] This seems to be a mistaken reading for *śramaṇas*. The dual division of the *brāhmaṇas* and the *śramaṇas* is corroborated in the inscriptions of Aśoka.[28] Strabo's description of the *brachmanes* carries hints of the system of the four *āśramas* which was considered as the ideal curriculum for a *brāhmaṇa;* that of the *garmanes* ranges over what would be identified as forest ascetics, *saṃnyāsins*, shamans and *bhikṣus*. Elsewhere in the text Strabo mentions the *brachmanes* and those opposed to them as the *pramnae*, 'a contentious and disputatious sect', of whom there are many varieties.[29] Possibly *pramnae* was a garbled version of *parivrājaka* which the various categories seem to resemble.

As regards the *georgoi* or cultivators, he repeats the statement that the *chora* or countryside is *basilīke* or royal and that the farmers cultivate it for a *misthos* and also pay one-fourth of the produce. The statement that the *chora* is royal implies ownership by the king but Strabo does not explicitly state the absence of private property in land as does Diodorus. H.L. Jones, translating this passage, has glossed it as, 'the farmers cultivate it for wages on condition of receiving a fourth part of the produce'. This reading makes it a very different statement from that of Diodorus and the gloss is not acceptable to many scholars. It would suggest exceptionally well-paid cultivators since they would keep one-fourth of the produce and be paid a wage for their labour on the land. This was unlikely at the time. One may well ask whether it was necessary to attract cultivators to the state lands in order to extend agriculture? This may be compared to Kauṭilya's advice to the king to bring families of *śūdra* cultivators to settle on waste land or deserted land.[30] The *Arthaśāstra* mentions share-croppers *ardha-sītaka*, in the cultivation of *sītā* lands. Reference is also made to those who give their labour to cultivate land for a share (*bhāga*) of a fourth or a fifth but they do not receive a wage as well.[31] Those that receive a wage do not have to pay a part of the produce. The problematic word in the Greek texts is *misthos* with its meaning of both wage and rent and either meaning would change the premises of taxation. Perhaps Megasthenes did not think it necessary to comment on privately owned land with its range of tenures and therefore confined himself to discussing only the royal land which as a legal form was in any case both familiar and of greater consequence from his Hellenistic experience. Possibly royal land or the *chora basilīke* had a different revenue demand in the Hellenistic states and therefore Megasthenes felt it necessary to comment on the Indian system.

Strabo then refers to the herdsmen (*poimenes*) and the hunters (*thereutai*) where only the first term is the same as that used by Diodorus. The description of this group is similar to that of Diodorus except that Strabo adds that no private person is permitted to keep a horse or an elephant. Both of these were rare commodities. Horses had to be imported into India and elephants could not be bred but had to be captured, the procedure having been described by Megasthenes.

In his fourth category Strabo includes those that sell their physical labour, that is, hired labourers and the retail traders or petty traders in the market place, the *kapelikoi*.[32] Some among them adds Strabo are employed by the state alone such as the armour-makers and ship-builders and they receive a *misthos*/wage and provisions from the king. Other artisans pay a tax, *phoros*, to the state and render prescribed services to the state *(leitourgiai)*. These services may be compared to the *viṣṭi* referred to in the *Arthaśāstra*.[33]

The soldiers (*polemistai*) are described as in Diodorus, so also are the overseers (*ephoroi*). The details of the work of the latter are, however, spelt out more fully and in this the text of Strabo differs from the others. We are told that they keep the rivers in proper condition, inspect the canals and sluices from which water is distributed, measure the land as in Egypt, collect the taxes, superintend the crafts, as well as the building of roads, and the work of the city commissioners and those in charge of armaments. Strabo's experience of administration in Egypt seems to have influenced this description and some scholars doubt that it was included in the original text of Megasthenes.[34] Its general tenor, however, is also suggestive of the work of the *adhyakṣa* in the *Arthaśāstra*. The rendering by some scholars of the *ephoroi* solely as spies would seem from this text to be exaggerated. Some overseers would certainly have used spies as part of their system of work but that docs not justify translating the term *ephoroi* as spies. The seventh category about which Strabo has little to say are listed as the *sumbouloi* and the *sunedroi*, both terms again connected with the Boule and the Synod and suggestive of advisors of high rank. He adds that their work covers the entire range of administration since they hold the chief offices of state.

The third text which drew on the original of Megasthenes was the *Indica* of Arrian.[35] The author was a native of Bithynia (Asia Minor) and wrote in the early second century AD about four hundred years after Megasthenes. He held high offices under the Romans largely because of the patronage of Hadrian but eventually retired to Athens. He wrote extensively on a variety of subjects but was more centrally a historian and deeply influenced by Xenophon. He was easily the most scholarly of the three authors under discussion. Arrian was also involved in the intellectual movement of the early centuries AD which has come to be called the Second Sophistic.[36] This expressed itself in a nostalgia for the classical period of Athens recalling the achievements of Athens in the fifth century BC by imitating Attic prose and literary forms and often writing in what was by now the archaic Ionian Greek. This movement was in part the result of the prosperity of the Hellenized cities of the eastern Mediterranean in the face of what was seen as subservience to Roman power. Arrian's major work was a history of Alexander of Macedon, the *Anabasis*, and this in a way led to a number of accounts of regions such as Parthia and India where Alexander had campaigned. Arrian used as sources for the *Anabasis*, Ptolemy as well as a large number of contemporary accounts of Alexander such as those of Nearchos, Onesicritus and Aristobulus. The *Indica* is, however, only a coda to the *Anabasis* since this was not the primary interest of Arrian. As has been rightly said, for Arrian, India had a marginal role between the Macedonians and the Persians who in his perception were the dominant powers at the time of Alexander.[37]

Quoting from Megasthenes he states that all the Indians are divided into seven *genea.*[38] This is different from the earlier two authors who refer to these divisions as *merē.* Was he quoting more precisely from Megasthenes or, was he merely copying Herodotus?

Was he substituting a term which he thought was closer in meaning to the concept of caste? Alternatively he may have argued that since the crucial unit involving marriage and occupation was termed the *genos*, it would be more logical to use the same word for the seven divisions as well.

The first category he labels as *sophistai* and therefore differs from the earlier authors. His description is close to that of the *philosophoi* and the *brachmanes* of the earlier authors yet the choice of the word *sophistai* is curious. It refers to philosophers and teachers, especially peripatetic, and those skilled in art. The religious connotation is less evident in this term. He may have had in mind also the renewal of interest in the sophists as the wise men of a society, during his lifetime. This would agree with his statement that anyone in India can become a sophist, but few do because they have to lead such a hard life. Yet in the *Anabasis* he refers to the *brachmanes* as Indian *sophistai* and at another point refers in a general way to Indian sophists.[39] But his description of the sophists has less of Brahmanical belief and practices and more of an extensive range of renunciatory sects: in fact more of the *śramaṇa*s than of the *brāhmaṇa*s.

The cultivators (*georgoi*), according to him, pay *phoros* to the kings and the cities which are self-governing. *Phoros* literally refers to payments of tribute. Arrian makes no reference to ownership of land or to royal ownership. Interestingly, in the case of the third category, that of the herdsmen and pastoralists (*boukoloi*, *poimenes* and *nomeis*) they are again described as nomadic but are said to pay a *phoros* from the produce of their animals. The same term *phoros* is used even though the animals are not state owned. This would suggest that in the context of land, *phoros* was a tax and not a rent and was probably a share of the produce. The statement is again repeated for the fourth category described by Arrian as the *demiourgikon* and the *kapelikon*, the artisans and traders. Interestingly *demiourgikon* was the term used for artisans and traders in classical Athens. This category are also said to have paid a *phoros* to the state. The only exceptions are the armourers, shipwrights, and sailors employed by the state who are paid a *misthos*. *Misthos* in this case was the wage paid by the state to those whom it employed.

The fifth category of soldiers of *polemistai* are paid so well by the state that they can afford to maintain others on their pay. Again the word *misthos* is used here. In place of the *ephoroi* Arrian uses the term *episkopoi* which has a stronger sense of inspecting and overseeing. The seventh category are the *bouleuomenoi* who deliberate on state matters with the king and with the archons in the autonomous cities. It is from this group that the officers of state are selected and the list of functions given by Arrian would again point to the *mahāmātras* of the Mauryan state, although such functions would be performed by senior officers in any well-developed administration.

Arrian concludes with the statement that to marry out of any *genos* is unlawful as also to change professions from one *genos* to another. This is permitted only to the *sophistai.* The consistency of the statement relating to marriage and occupation in all three texts makes it clear that this at least was common to all and undoubtedly went back to Megasthenes. The listing of seven divisions was also common although the element of variation in the terms used suggest that it was more an adaptation from Megasthenes than an actual quotation. Only the terms for cultivators (*georgoi*), herdsmen (*poimenes*), and soldiers (*polemistai*), are common to all three versions. The other terms generally occur in two out of three texts and not always consistently. There are, as we have seen, discrepancies on the question of agrarian revenue. Similarly the details regarding the first category differ. The crucial term used for the seven divisions varies and two authors use *merē* and *phylon* and the third uses *genē.* All three, however, use *genos* with reference to marriage relations. Thus the quotations from Megasthenes are only approximate quotations or paraphrased versions. Arrian's style is recognizably different from that of Diodorus and Strabo and his version attempts to give perhaps only the gist of what Megasthenes may have said. The difference may partially also be due to his writing in the Ionian dialect. Clearly the meaning of 'quotation' should not be taken in the more modern sense of stating the actual words of the source. Each author seems to have paraphrased Megasthenes in his own words.

On the question of editing and paraphrasing Megasthenes, Arrian would have had no qualms since he was convinced that most accounts of Alexander's activities and subsequently of his dominions were exaggerated in order to flatter the Macedonian.[40] Onesicritus was generally held in better esteem perhaps because he was a philosopher and a pupil of Diogenes and because he was a contemporary of Alexander. That he influenced Arrian is suggested for example by his consistent use of the term 'sophist' for what might be called Indian 'holy men' which usage was followed by Arrian.[41] Another source regarded as reliable by Arrian was the account of Nearchos who wrote not in Ionian Greek but in a *koiné* requiring Arrian to paraphrase his views.[42] Arrian in any case had his doubts about the reliability of the text of Megasthenes on areas of India beyond the northwest which Megasthenes may possibly not have visited.

Modern historians have debated the veracity of Megasthenes and it is as well to remember that he was regarded with suspicion even by his contemporaries. We are told that he was sent by Seleucus Nicator on an embassy to Sandrocottos (Chandragupta) who had his capital at Palibothra (Pāṭaliputra).[43] The book would then have been a description of his visit to India at the time of Chandragupta, the first Mauryan king. Strabo adds that Deimachus was sent on a similar mission to the son of Sandrocottos, Amitrachades (that is, the son of Chandragupta, Bindusara), and he too left an account and goes on to say that the accounts of Nearchos and Onesiciritus were however more truthful.[44] Dionysius is believed to have been sent by Ptolemy Philadelphus of Egypt to ascertain the truth of the account given by Megasthenes. Eratosthenes maintains that Megasthenes and Deimachus accused each other of falsehood.[45] Arrian states that Megasthenes lived with Sibyrtius, the satrap of Arachosia (in modern Afghanistan) and Gedrosia and often visited Sandrocottos.[46] He may thus have spent most of his time in Kandahar and his perspective on India may therefore have focused more on northwestern India than on the Ganga valley. That Kandahar was an important Greek city, possibly the Alexandria in Arachosia, is suggested by recent excavations and finds.[47] Megasthenes was familiar with the Seleucid satrapy and kingdom and if he resided in Arachosia then there would be some

Seleucid influence in his picture of India. Among later authors, Clement of Alexandria[48] refers to Megasthenes as an historian and Pliny disapproves of both Megasthenes and Dionysius.[49] Thus the veracity of Megasthenes' account may well have been tempered by his inability to obtain detailed information and therefore the Hellenistic and Seleucid imprint may have been greater than has been recognized so far. The quotations from Megasthenes, if seen in the light of this as well, may not have been taken too literally. They may have been introduced and amended by each author partially to give legitimacy to his own descriptions.

The historiographical ancestry of the *Indica* of Megasthenes is linked to similar writing in Egypt and Babylon as has been pointed out. In the Hellenistic world the account of Egypt written before the end of the fourth century BC by Hecataeus of Abdera, was widely read and respected and treated as a model.[50] The state of Egypt was idealized and projected as a new kind of society which had earlier even excited the interest of Plato. Hecataeus though apparently concerned with Pharaonic ideas and the antiquity of Egypt, was at the same time eulogizing the Ptolemies. Manethon, an Egyptian writing in Greek in the early third century BC, reiterated these ideas.[51] The challenge was taken up from another direction when Berossus the Chaldean wrote a history of Babylon which he dedicated to Antiochus I and which was partially a Seleucid reply as it were, to Hecataeus, suggesting that there were systems other than the Egyptian considered worthwhile as forms of government and society.

Megasthenes it has been argued, was doing the same in writing on India.[52] He was also seeking a Utopian society and was projecting India as such. The magic and the marvels were somewhat reduced especially when compared to the discredited earlier account of Ktesias. But the exotica remained. At another level it was a society which gave maximum honour to philosophers, which insisted on the hereditary nature of occupations and which did not require slaves; all these ideas evoked the interest of contemporary Greeks.[53] Nevertheless, in the actual structure of the *Indica*, the account of Hecataeus seems to have been the model in as much as it was divided into sections on cosmology, geography, king-lists (of a sort), the organization of society and social customs.[54] This format was to be frequently used by Hellenistic writers. Historiographically Arrian is the most important of the three authors quoting from Megasthenes and was influenced by the structure of the earlier *Indica*.[55] His account is also divided into similar sections and he is even more determined to leave out the marvels and the curiosities with which descriptions of India abounded, what he refers to as the gold-digging ants and the gold-guarding griffons.

Apart from the historiographical context, there is also the question of the influence of prevalent forms in the Seleucid and Ptolemaic systems which may have coloured the perception of India. The Hellenistic imprint can probably be seen more clearly in the statement on landownership and agrarian revenue. The economy of the Seleucids, the neighbours of the Mauryas, based largely on agrarian revenue listed as the most important categories of land, the *chora basilīke* or the private estates of the king, and the land owned by the independent Greek cities.[56] The king assigned land from the *chora basilīke*. But the existence of royal estates did not preclude ownership of land by the temples or tribes or even private ownership. The *chora basilīke* was cultivated under the supervision of officials by hereditary tenants who paid in cash or kind and the payment could also be in the form of a part of the harvest. The payment was for the use of the land which was said to belong to the king, and was based on earlier prevailing systems. Megasthenes would therefore have been familiar with the notion of the *chora basilīke* and the Mauryan *sītā* lands may have seemed to him to be the exact counterpart of the Seleucid system. The cultivation of land by the state even if not to the exclusion of private ownership of land, is referred to in the Kauṭilya *Arthaśāstra*, where the king is advised to settle new land or deserted land with *śūdra* cultivators.[57] This would have been a major change in the economic picture from earlier times and may have been much talked about; hence suggesting to Megasthenes that the *sītā* lands were far more important than any other system of tenure. The statement regarding cultivation and the payment of a *misthos* may well have been confined to such lands and was not meant to exclude private ownership.

The reference to self-governing cities is puzzling. Although a familiar feature of Hellenistic Asia Minor they are not referred to in Indian sources, unless Megasthenes had in mind a vague notion of the *gaṇa-saṅghas* each of which had an urban centre as its nucleus. The *polis* system of self-governing cities has been described as a pillar of Seleucid power. Lands were assigned to the cities from the estates of the king's land. The cities had considerable autonomy in issuing coins and collecting taxes. The advantage to the Seleucids was that such cities paid a *phoros* or tribute to the ruling family.

The reference to taxes paid to the king and to the self-governing cities in the same passage is so characteristic of the Seleucid system that one may be justified in arguing that this statement could have been taken from the Seleucid system and applied to the Mauryan. Interestingly, it is only Arrian, with his experience of Asia Minor who mentions the self-governing cities. Neither Diodorus nor Strabo refer to these, perhaps because they were more familiar with the Ptolemaic kingdom where such cities did not exist.

For both Diodorus and Strabo it was the Ptolemaic state that was possibly the model for systems relating to the Orient, particularly with the increasing communication between the Red Sea and the Indian subcontinent at the turn of the Christian era. The prevalent view in Egypt had been that the gods were the owners of the land and since the kings were their descendents this enabled them to claim ownership.[58] The *chora* was the estate of the king. Political philosophy was dominated by the idea that the king owns and manages the land and has the right to compulsory labour. Agriculture under the Ptolemies was carefully controlled by a large body of officers who assessed and measured the land and managed the distribution of water, all of which was geared to the goal of revenue collection. Land owned by the king, royal land, was cultivated by peasants under royal control, the *georgoi basilikoi*,[59] who were under contract to the king by which they paid a share of the produce to the king and cultivated according to instructions. This did not exclude other categories of ownership such as temple lands, service tenures, and privately owned land, although royal ownership was the predominant form. Could this have influenced the comprehension by Diodorus and Strabo of agriculture in India as described by Megasthenes and led to the confusion between the two senses of *misthos*?

In Hellenistic states taxes were paid to the king only from the *chora basilīke.* Other categories of landowners such as temples, autonomous cities and individuals, received the contracted amounts from the peasants and had their own arrangements with the king. Since the major land revenue was from the *chora basilīke* Megasthenes may have assumed that the same was applicable in India and that there was no need to mention other tenurial arrangements. By the time that Arrian was writing, the economy based on the *chora basilīke* had ceased to exist in both the erstwhile Ptolemaic and Seleucid areas. This might in part account for his not referring to the royal ownership of land but merely to the *phoros* paid by the cultivators.

The historiographical context is equally important on the question of social divisions. The term *meros/merē* is familiar to Greek thought particularly through the writings of Aristotle, who would also have had an intellectual influence on Megasthenes. Aristotle's ideas appear to have been known in the centres of Hellenistic activity. It has been suggested that one of his more celebrated disciples, Klearchus, was active at Ai-Khanum the Greek city on the Oxus.[60] Furthermore, that he drew attention to the religion and philosophy of the Persians and the Indians. The Hellenistic cities were doubtless the meeting point of a variety of ideas and theories. In his *Politics*, Aristotle refers to various concepts which seem also to be reflected in the views of Megasthenes. Thus he states that each citizen body was composed of a number of *merē* or parts having widely varying characteristics.[61] He then lists the parts of the citizen body as the *georgoi* or cultivators, the *banausoi* or artisans, the *agoraioi* or traders (including the *emporoi* or inter-state merchants and the *kapeloi* or petty traders) and finally the *thetikon* or labourers working for a wage. In some places soldiers are added as a fifth group.[62] All these are said to constitute the larger mass of people, the *plethos.* Interestingly, both Diodorus and Strabo refer to the *plethos* or people of India being divided into seven *merē.* Aristotle adds that in every city there are three *merē*—the rich, the poor and those of the middle group.[63] He emphasizes the difference between the rich and the poor and an important element in this difference is honour or *timē* which also bestows status on a person. He states that the rich are armed and the poor are unarmed.[64]

In the general discussion on the constitutions associated with oligarchies and democracies, numerous divisions of people are listed as the *merē*. Generally these include farmers, artisans, traders, seafarers, labourers, and servile groups. The classification of the *merē* was a matter of considerable debate at this time and presumably Megasthenes was aware of this debate and perhaps had it in mind when composing the *Indica*. In discussing the important officers of government, Aristotle heads the list with designations which are included in the list of *ephoroi* in Strabo.[65] Similarly, in passages referring to the requirements of a state the responsibilities of those concerned with food, handicrafts, arms, wealth, religion, and decision-making are again suggestive of the divisions listed by Megasthenes although such divisions are so general that they could apply to virtually any society.[66] According to Aristotle the divisions into *merē* are necessary in order to separate functions and that this was established long since in many areas such as Egypt and Crete.[67] It has recently been argued that the Aristotelian concept of *merē* virtually means class since property qualifications and the functions they perform in the productive process are an important aspect of a *meros*.[68] Aristotle ends up with a basic division between the propertied and the propertyless and takes a man's economic position as determining his behaviour. But the *merē* as listed by Aristotle or Megasthenes do not have distinct property qualifications. The *merē* of Megasthenes can perhaps be better explained, as being linked to production although even this is not an exhaustive criterion for each category. To use class in the modern sense for *meros* would also be misleading as the groups mentioned by Megasthenes do not constitute classes. Megasthenes also mentions that the category of philosophers and of councillors are regarded with respect and have high status or *timē*. The property qualifications or role in production of the former at least would be unimportant to their status. The *georgoi* or peasants, presumably making up the poorer sections of society were kept unarmed. Doubtless the importance of this statement also relates to the argument in Aristotle that arms should be restricted to the rich. That the peasants could continue working in their fields whilst a battle raged in the vicinity, seems to have impressed the Greeks, particularly as the latter had often to resort to conscription.

The seven *merē* of Megasthenes if seen from the perspective of the Aristotelian concept of *merē* make good sense. They are a list of the important divisions of the population involved in the functioning of society. They can be further divided into three broad groups: the first, the philosophers and sophists are those with the maximum honour or *timē* and prescribe on matters religious; the next three constitute a second group concerned with economic production since they consist, of cultivators, herdsmen, artisans and traders; and the last three constitute the third group that of persons responsible for administrative functions, namely, soldiers, officials, and councillors.

Why did Megasthenes choose the number seven for the *merē* of India? This may have been based on the seven divisions in Egypt as listed by Herodotus. But it is equally possible, as it has been argued, that a current Indian concept may explain this number. With the gradual evolution of the monarchical state in India, there emerged by the late fourth century BC the notion of the constituent elements of the state. This concept was referred to as the *sapta-prakṛti* or more commonly later as the *saptāṅga.*[69] These were the seven elements or the seven limbs of the body politic. The listing of the seven elements was of course different from the *merē* of Megasthenes. The *saptāṅga* consisted of the king, the ministers, the capital, the treasury, the army or a form of authority, territory, and allies. Possibly when enquiring about notions regarding the polity and the state, the seven elements were quoted to Megasthenes and he remembered the figure but reconstructed the elements on the principles of the *merē* which were more familiar to his own intellectual background.

It is possible, therefore, that the original text of Megasthenes may have used the word *merē* and have derived the number seven from the *saptāṅga* theory. Arrian perhaps then replaced *merē* by *genea* and retained the term *genos* when it came to marriage and occupation. He may also have seen in this description a similarity in the use of *genos* with the meaning given to it in the classical period of Athens.

The reference to *genos* states the two important characteristics of caste as marriage rules and restrictions and those relating to occupation. Here again Megasthenes picked up the salient points about caste organization but perhaps confused caste with *meros.* It is also important to consider whether he was referring to *varṇa* or *jāti.* It would seem that he was not referring to *varṇa* for a variety of reasons. *Varṇa*s were four in number, possibly five, but never seven. The seven categories are described by Megasthenes not by special names but in general descriptive terms. Where *brachmanes* may well refer to the first *varṇa*, *brāhmaṇa*, there is no further mention of the remaining three. Of the latter the *kṣatriya*s and the *śūdra*s as names of ethnic communities were familiar to the Greeks since they are mentioned in the accounts of the campaign of Alexander in the form of Xathroi and Sydracae.[70] There is curiously no mention of the untouchables or even the *caṇḍāla*s or the concept of pollution which should have been a strikingly new feature to an observer from another society. (This could be attributed not to a lack of observation but to the influence of a Greek model of social divisions.) The occupational groupings are also not suggestive of *varṇa* since it would not have been common to find hired labourers, artisans, and traders listed as belonging to one *varṇa*; the former were frequently of *śūdra* status and the latter *vaiśya.* Had Megasthenes been reflecting the dominant ideas of the middle Ganga valley it is possible that he would have listed the *kṣatriya*s as first which was the case in Buddhist and Jaina writings. High status being given to the *brāhmaṇa*s might suggest the influence of Brahmanical thinking, except that the compound of *brāhmaṇa* and *śramaṇa* occurs in the Aśokan inscriptions as a general category and included those in a religious vocation or renouncers and teachers and therefore of high status. The joint mention of *brāhmaṇa*s and *śramaṇa*s would again suggest a category other than that of the *varṇa* since the *brāhmaṇa*s and the *śramaṇa*s (in many cases) regarded each other with considerable hostility.[71]

Whereas, the *Dharmaśāstra* texts give priority to *varṇa* as the pattern of social organization, it has been argued that this was more in the nature of a theoretical model or norm or reflective of ritual status; and, that, as is evident from Buddhist sources, *jāti* organization was the more recognizable and effective social form, in which both kinship and marriage as well as occupation were important factors of identity. The term *genos* which implies a blood/kin connection would be more indicative of *jāti.* Interestingly *genos* is regarded as a cognate of the Sanskrit *jana* which shared the root *ja* with the word *jāti.*

Genos has its own history.[72] Fustel de Coulanges has argued, that *genos* was a corporate group with common 'property' and collective activities as well as symbols of unity. Later writers have argued that it was a form of grouping to which only some families belonged and it developed particularly in Athenian aristocracy. The rich encouraged a pride of lineage to symbolize superior status. Originally they were of the noble *eupatridai* order but gradually families began to claim rights to certain offices and this became parallel to property and each such group of families constituted a *genos.* One family reiterated this right by insisting on a rule of endogamy. The right also constituted its identity as a corporate group.

If we argue that Megasthenes was revised by Arrian as is suggested by Breloer then the explanation for Arrian having replaced *meros* by *genos* would require a finer linguistic analysis of the use of *genos* in the Greek context and its various meanings. Recent studies of *genos* do not help us in arriving at a more precise definition of its use either by Megasthenes or Arrian.

It could of course also be argued that *meros* and *genos* were used arbitrarily, if not interchangeably, in descriptions of alien societies; and that there was no technical meaning attached to either of them since both Herodotus and Arrian use *genos* for social divisions in societies as distinct as those of Egypt and India. One would then have to look for the specific description of Indian society which might suggest something distinctive, namely, caste. Megasthenes understood the essentials of a caste society when he emphasized the importance of endogamy in marriage, all except for the *brāhmaṇas*;

and of course, the principle of hereditary caste status as well as the association of caste with occupation and the restrictions on changing occupation. In this passage from Megasthenes as it has come to us in the three versions which have been discussed, there is a juxtaposition of two statements. First, that Indian society was divided into seven parts. Secondly, that Indian society had specific rules of marriage and occupation. These rules were then illustrated by reference to the seven parts resulting in perhaps an incorrect merging of the two ideas by Megasthenes. His confusion lay in identifying his divisions, the *merē*, with the notion of social divisions in India constituting an endogamous unit and governing hereditary occupations.

The utilization of texts from the ancient period remains a complicated process and requires the removing of many veils of obscurity. With greater research into the precise meaning of terms and inevitably, therefore, of historical interpretation, the translations made in the nineteenth century of such sources have often to be re-examined. There is also the need to be aware of the perceptions of the original authors and of those who in later periods paraphrased the original. This I have tried to demonstrate in arguing that references to the agrarian structure owe more perhaps to the imprint of the Seleucid and Ptolemaic systems than to an authentic description of the Mauryan. Whereas Diodorus and Strabo mention the *chora basilīke* and refer to the payment of a *misthos*, Arrian makes no mention of royal ownership of land and refers only to a *phoros* or tax. The *chora basilīke* was the most important agricultural land in the Seleucid and Ptolemaic states and it was the equivalent of this which Megasthenes was seeking and to which he refers. The phrase *chora basilīke* is so closely linked to those two states that its use for Mauryan India echoes the other two.

The importance of crown lands to the Mauryan economy has been argued on the strength of references to *sītā* lands in the *Arthaśāstra* and to Megasthenes' statements regarding the *chora basilīke.* I have tried to show that it is necessary to examine the context of such descriptions before taking them as factual. If the Kauṭilya *Arthaśāstra* was in fact a text concerned primarily with the revenue of the metropolitan state, the discussion on *sītā* lands would have to be central. The same would be true of Megasthenes if he was describing the *sītā* lands when referring to the *chora basilīke.* My problem is with the statement that there were only crown lands. This seems to be both partial and influenced by conditions prevalent elsewhere, as I have tried to argue. That there is disagreement in the three texts following Megasthenes on the ownership of land would point to Megasthenes not having made a clear statement. Was this because the incidence of crown lands was not as extensive as Diodorus and Strabo would have us believe? The confusion in these two authors over whether *misthos* refers to rent or tax or whether it was a wage would indicate that the text of Megasthenes was not categorical on this crucial matter. Or, that the confusion has arisen because there were other tenures which have not been listed by Megasthenes, but whose contractual conditions had entered the original discussion.

The seven subdivisions of Indian society as listed by Megasthenes which doubtless drew on some observation, present features of Indian society which require attention. Clearly the definition is in terms other than *varṇa* and is most likely *jāti.* The two characteristics on which there is complete agreement are those referring to endogamous marriage and hereditary occupation. (This is so firmly stated that one almost suspects Megasthenes of having read modern Indian ethnography!) It would seem that a certain parochialism in the functioning of caste is indicated and here I would like to repeat that there is a need to look at caste along its vertical axis first, when trying to assess its role in production.

The Greek in Megasthenes saw these subdivisions as universal categories, but he lists them in no known order. If he began with the *brāhmaṇas* and *śramaṇas* because they are the most highly respected, he should have proceeded to the next most highly respected group, that of councillors and advisors. But the latter come last and instead the second category are the cultivators because they are the largest in number. He nowhere mentions that they are regarded as of low status. That they are the largest in number would bear out the dependence at this time on agricultural revenue.

Herders and huntsmen which even in Buddhist sources are listed as low, are not referred to as such. But significantly they are identified by *phylon* or tribe, suggesting that they might have been regarded as somehow outside the usual framework of caste society. Were these the *aṭavika* or forest tribes mentioned by both Aśoka and Kauṭilya?

If they were outside the caste structure then they would have been more mobile. Why then were they not deported and used as labour? Was it because it was thought safer to leave them in their forests, so that resources from the forests could be more easily tapped through them? That they did provide revenue in kind is explicitly stated. This may have led to these areas being deliberately cordoned off, to prevent interference. Or was it because hired labour and the large number of cultivators sufficed for Mauryan economic ambitions?

The commercial economy is neatly tied up in one package which binds together hired labour, artisans, and traders, suggestive of the urban guild which in the post-Mauryan period was to integrate all three groups.

Megasthenes elsewhere, makes an important statement which has been dismissed by historians as it appears to conflict with Indian sources. He states that there were no slaves in India and in this respect draws on the similarity with Sparta.[73] Perhaps the clue to his meaning lies in the reference to Sparta. Spartan helotage was very much a Spartan phenomenon in the Greek world and there was some discussion as to whether helotage was the same as the more general form of slavery, that of the *doulos*. These were individual slaves and unlike the helots were not an enslaved community owned by the state. What Megasthenes was probably commenting on was the absence of a *doulos* type of slavery with slaves used on a large scale in both agricultural and artisanal production. Indian sources do provide evidence of slaves of the *doulos* variety, that is, men and women owned outright as property, with no legal rights or status and not receiving a wage. However, such slaves although used in production, appear in large numbers as domestic slaves. What is interesting is that Megasthenes although aware of the issue, does not notice the use of either slaves or hired labour in agricultural production. This may have been because if they were paid even a minimal wage as some slaves were, they would not strictly speaking qualify as *doulos*.

There was a time when it was argued that the most reliable source material on ancient India was the literature which emanated from Hellenic and Hellenistic authors. Modern scholars were imbued with the notion that somehow the Greek tradition because it had what Europe recognized more easily as, 'a sense of history' could therefore be depended upon by historians. The world of Vincent Smith may have ended but its resonances still reach out to us as do those of scholars who vehemently insist that such sources by virtue of being 'foreign' cannot be relied upon. Because of the paucity of descriptive narrative sources from the Indian tradition for the first millennium BC, the Greek texts also came to be regarded as more reliable than the Indian in depicting the actual conditions of society, rather than the theory behind the institutions. Hence the acute problem over the 'seven castes'. I have tried to argue that even these texts and their context require a more critical investigation before their statements can be taken as fact. This is not an attempt at Orientalism in reverse, for this exercise would be necessary in using any textual material, no matter what its authorship or content.

I have tried to show that the need to consider the ideological influences on the authors of texts becomes significant in that authors are given to ideological positions whether they are aware of these or not. It would be as well to keep in mind Arnaldo Momigliano's assessment of the ancient historians when he writes, 'Greek and Roman historians in fact, after Herodotus, did very little research into the past and relatively seldom undertook to collect first-hand evidence about foreign countries. They concentrated on contemporary history or summarized and reinterpreted the work of former historians'.[74] The use of such literary sources then becomes an enterprise in going beyond the obvious: a process which requires of historical study a proximity both to the comparative method and to historiography.

Notes and References

1. F. Altheim, *Weltgeschichte Asiens in Griechischen Zeitalter*, I, Halle, 1974, pp. 257–64.

2. C.H. Oldfather, *Diodorus of Sicily*, II, Cambridge, Mass., 1979.

3. H.L. Jones, *The Geography of Strabo*, Cambridge, Mass., 1966.

4. P.A. Brunt, *Arrian*, II, Cambridge, Mass., 1983.

5. J.W. McCrindle, *Ancient India as Described by Megasthenes and Arrian*, London, 1987, pp. 83ff.

6. R.C. Majumdar, 'The Indica of Megasthenes', *JAOS*, 1958, 78, pp. 273–6.

7. K.D. Sethna, 'Rejoinder to R.C. Majumdar', *JAOS*, 1960, 80, pp. 243–8. The question of the reliability of Megasthenes has been under discussion since Schwanbeck put together the fragments. For more recent views, see, T.S. Brown, 'The Merits and Weaknesses of Megasthenes', *Phoenix*, 1957, XI, pp. 12–24; 'The Reliability of Megasthenes', *American Journal of Philology*, 1955, 76, pp. 18–33; A. Zamarini, 'Cli *Indika* di Megasthenes', *Annali di lettere et Filosophia*, Series III, XII, I. Pisa, 1983, pp. 73–149. J.D.M. Derrett presents an interesting case of the transformation of a theme in, 'The History of "Palladius on the Races of India and the Brahmans"', *Cl. Med.* (1960), 21, pp. 64–135.

8. O. Stein, *Megasthenes und Kauṭilya*, Wien, 1921.

9. B.C.J. Timmer, *Megasthenes en de Indische Maatschappij*, Amsterdam, 1930.

10. B. Breloer, *Kauṭilya Studien*, Bonn, 1927–34.

11. J.A.B. van Buitenan, 'The Seven Castes of Megasthenes', *AOS*, Middle West Branch Semi-centential Volume, D. Sinor (ed.), Bloomington, pp. 228–32.

12. II.40. F. Jacoby, *Die Fragmente der Griechischen Historiker* (*FGrH*), Leiden, 1958, 715 F4 (35–42).

13. Liddell and Scott, *Greek-English Lexicon.*

14. *Histories*, I.56.101; II.164.

15. J. Bloch, *Les Inscriptions d'Asoka*, Paris, 1965, p. 157.

16. *Arthaśāstra*, III.9 and 10; *Uvāsagdāsao*, II.52–4; *Baudhayāna Dharma Sūtra*, I.5.11.11ff; II.2.3.3ff. *Vasiṣṭha Dharma Sūtra*, XVI.13.

17. *Arthaśāstra*, II.24.

18. Ibid., II.29.1–3 of wage to *dāsa-karmakara*, II.24.28.

19. Ibid., II.34.6.

20. Ibid., II.1.33–7; VIII.1.19–20; II 35–1–4; X.1.9; 17.

21. Ibid., II.18.1.

22. Romila Thapar, *Aśoka and the Decline of the Mauryas*, London, 1961, pp. 118–20.

23. *Arthaśāstra*, Book II.

24. Pillar Edict, IV, J. Bloch, *Les Inscriptions . . .*, p. 164.

25. *Sumaṅgalavilāsinī*, II.673.3; *Kunāla Jātaka*, 536.

26. XV.1.39–41, 46–9. *FGrH*, 715 F 19.

27. XV.1.59ff; *FGrH*, 715 F.33.

28. J. Bloch, *Les Inscriptions . . .* , pp. 97, 99, 115.

29. XV.1.70, *FGrH*, 721 F 15.

30. *Arthaśāstra*, II.1.

31. Ibid., 4.1.10ff, 2.29.2.

32. M.I. Finley, 'Aristotle and Economic Analysis', *Past and Present*, 1970, 47, p. 16.

33. See f.n.20.

34. F. Jacoby, *FGrH*, 715, suggests that 715 F 19, p. 624 is an addition from F 31 (52).

35. A.B. Bosworth, *A Historical Commentary of Arrian's History of Alexander*, I, Oxford, 1980.

36. E.L. Bowie, 'Greeks and their Past in the Second Sophistic', *Past and Present* (1970), 46, pp. 3–41; G.W. Bowersock (ed.), *Approaches to the Second Sophistic*, University Park, 1974.

37. P. Vidal–Naquet, *Flavius Arrian Entre Deux Mondes*, Paris, 1984, p. 383, in Arrian, *Historie d' Alexendre*, traduit par Pierre Savinal.

38. *Indica*, XI and XII.

39. *Anabasis*, VI, 16.5; VII. 1.5–6.

40. L. Pearson, *The Lost Histories of Alexander the Great*, Oxford, 1960, pp. 5ff. T.S. Brown, *Onesicritus, A Study in Hellenistic Historiography*, Berkeley, 1949.

41. Onesicritus in Strabo, XV.1.58–66; Plutarch, *Alex.*, 65; Arrian, *Anabasis*, 7.3.6; *Indica*, XI.7.

42. P.A. Stadter, *Arrian of Nicomedia*, Chappel Hill, 1980, pp. 112ff.

43. Strabo, XV.1.36.

44. Ibid.

45. *Exp. Alex.*, V.vi.2 (2).

46. *Anabasis*, V.6.2; *Indica*, V.3.

47. P.M. Fraser, 'The Son of Aristonax at Kandahar', *Afghan Studies* (p. 80), 1979, 2. pp. 9–21.

48. *Sylb.*, pp. 132–42.

49. *Hist. Nat.*, VI.21.

50. O. Murray, 'Hecataeus of Abdera and Pharaonic Kingship', *JEA*, 1970, LVI, pp. 141–71.

51. P.M. Fraser, *Ptolemaic Alexandria*, I, Oxford, 1972, pp. 505ff.

52. O. Murray, op. cit., 'Herodotus and Hellenistic Culture', *CQ*, 1972, XXII, pp. 200–13.

53. P.M. Fraser, *Ptolemaic Alexandria*.

54. Ibid.

55. P.A. Stadter, *Arrian of Nicomedia*.

56. M.I. Rostovtzeff, *The Social and Economic History of the Hellenistic World*, Oxford, 1967, pp. 464ff. E. Bikerman, *Institutions des Seleucids*, Paris, 1938, Domenico Musti, 'Syria and the East', in *The Cambridge*

Ancient History, VII, 1, pp. 175–220. S.M. Burstein, *The Hellenistic Age . . .* , Cambridge, 1985, No. 19, pp. 24–5. C. Brunner, 'Geographical and Administrative Divisions: Settlements and Economy', in E. Yarshater (ed.), *The Cambridge History of Iran*, 3 (2), Cambridge, 1983, p. 713.

57. *Arthaśāstra*, II.1. A similar description of the founding of a colony is referred to in a letter of Antiochus III dating to the late third century BC. S.M. Burstein, *The Hellenistic Age . . .* , No. 29, pp. 37–8.

58. M.I. Rostovtzeff, *The Social and Economic History of the Hellenistic World*, pp. 255ff. H. Kreissig, 'Landed Property in the Hellenistic Orient', *Eirene*, 1977, 15, pp. 5–26. Eric Turner, 'Ptolemaic Egypt', in *The Cambridge Ancient History*, VII, 1. pp. 118–74. M.I. Rostovtzeff, *A Large Estate in Egypt in the Third Century BC*, Madison, 1922.

59. Rostovtzeff, *SEHHW*, pp. 272ff.

60. L. Robert, 'De Delphos a l'Oxus . . . ', *Compte Rendus des Seances de l'Academie des Inscriptions et Belles-lettres*, Paris, 1968, pp. 416–57. S.M. Burstein (ed. and trans.), *The Hellenistic Age . . .* , Cambridge, 1985, p. 67.

61. *Politics*, IV.3.4.

62. Ibid., VI.7.

63. Ibid., IV.II.

64. Ibid., II.8.

65. Ibid., VI.8.

66. Ibid., VII.8, 9.

67. Ibid., VII.10.

68. G.E.M. de Ste Croix, *The Class Struggle in the Ancient World*, London, 1983, pp. 77ff; 'Karl Marx and Classical Antiquity', *Arethusa*, Spring, 1975, 8.1. pp. 7ff.

69. *Arthaśāstra*, VII. This idea is touched upon in a paper by H. Falk, 'Die Sieben "Kasten" des Megasthenes', *Acta Orientalia*, 1982, 43, pp. 61–8.

70. Arrian, XV.4; Quintus Curtius Rufus, 9.3; Strabo, XV.8; XV.1.33.

71. Patañjali, *Vyākaraṇa Mahābhāsyam*, ii.4.9 (I.476).

72. S.C. Humphreys, 'Fustel de Coulanges and the Greek *genos*', *Sociologia del Diritto*, 1982, 3, pp. 35–44; *Genos* has been interpreted in a multiplicity of ways from family and birth to clan, lineage .and caste. In each case a kin or blood tie is important and a distant ancestor, real or fictive, is involved. F. Burriot, *Recherches sur la nature de Genos*, Paris, 1976.

73. Diodorus, II.39.

74. A. Momigliano, 'Herodotus in the History of Historiography', in *Studies in Historiography*, New York, 1966, p. 130.

CHAPTER 11

Aśoka

*A Retrospective**

To speak of the king Aśoka of the Maurya dynasty in a retrospective vein is to trace virtually the entire span of Indian history. The question frequently asked is why this extraordinary ruler was seemingly ignored in the past and why he became so prominent in recent times. Subsequent to his reign, he is thought to have been gradually set aside. Only in recent times were his inscriptions deciphered providing evidence of his ideas and actions. Nevertheless, we have to ask whether the ideas he propagated, especially his concepts of kingship and of social ethics, were actually ignored through much of Indian history or whether they were appropriated or contested and if so, by whom, in what form; and are we still appropriating them, or contesting or ignoring them, in any essential way?

Many modern assessments have largely tended to view Aśoka only as a Buddhist. When placed in a historical context in more recent times, the man and his ideas come to be liberated from this single perspective. We need to see him both as a statesman in the context of inheriting and sustaining an empire in a particular historical period, and as a person with a strong commitment to changing society through what seems to have been a concern for social ethics.

* Based on the Keynote Address delivered at the Conference on 'Ashoka and the Making of Modern India' held in Delhi, 5–7 August 2009. Originally published as 'Aśoka: A Retrospective', in *Economic and Political Weekly*, vol. 44, no. 45, 7–13 November 2009, pp. 31–7.

Empires of the ancient world are often thought to have operated through the violence of conquest and the persuasion of ideology, the latter often intended to bring about a relative cultural uniformity. The method of conquest and the resistance to it varied, requiring subsequent adjustments in systems of governing and in cultural expression. Ancient empires incorporated contiguous territories, which allowed of some broad-based similarities that crossed their frontiers. Nevertheless, disparities persisted. This was unlike colonial empires conquered across the oceans. These required new cultural articulations but did not necessarily aim at cultural uniformity.

The variations within the Mauryan Empire were immense and continued into later times. Ecologies changed from region to region, as did social forms and economies. The area was a subcontinent of multiple and diverse patterns of living, of languages and of forms of worship. This is apparent not only from textual sources but even more so from the excavation of sites of this period. The Mauryan system attempted to incorporate the diversity, but the degrees of assimilation in the regions were not similar as is particularly evident from the diverse cultural patterns that emerged on the disintegration of the empire. How was this diversity to be welded into an empire?

The Aśokan edicts might be the best way of initiating a reassessment of the king and the nature of his policies. Most of the edicts are personal statements of how he saw himself as combining political sovereignty and governance with closeness to what have been regarded as heterodox views. They were heterodox *vis-à-vis* Brahmanical orthodoxy, but the larger number of his subjects would not have found them alien. His reading of political sovereignty, both the conquest of Jambudvīpa and the welfare of his *prajā,* subjects,[1] did not contradict his perspective on required policies. The edicts, moving between the two, often take shape as a discourse on governance and ethics.

Aśoka had to explain his understanding of *dhamma,* given the multiplicity of senses in which the term was being used. This ranged from the *dharma* of the *varṇāśrama-dharma* in which the obligations of caste were pre-eminent, to the questioning of this by various *śramaṇa* sects such as the Buddhists and Jainas. For Aśoka, *dhamma* was essentially a code of ethical behaviour and the benefits thereof. This had parallels with Buddhist teaching, but the two are not equated in the public domain. Thus, in the Greek and Aramaic renderings of his edicts, he uses terms that have a context in these languages and a meaning close to his definition of *dhamma*, as for example, *eusebeia* meaning virtue, in Greek.[2] He does not refer to it as the teachings of the Buddha. It would seem that he was attempting to universalize a code focussed on social ethics and on the accommodation of diverse views. His *dhamma* did not derive from divine inspiration, even if its observance promised heaven. It was more in keeping with the ethic conditioned by the logic of given social situations.

His formulations of *dhamma* were intended to influence the conduct of categories of people in relation to each other, especially where they involved unequal relationships. There was a repeated emphasis on harmonious social relations and often, though not always, of categories described almost as opposite pairs, as for example, parents and children, kinsmen and friends, teachers and pupils, employers and employees, *brāhmaṇas* and *śramaṇas*. The empire included a spectrum of societies where these categories were variously organized. The underlining of this social ethic was virtually the reversal of the other system, the *varṇāśrama-dharma*. Aśoka mentions neither *varṇa* nor *jāti*, nor does he refer to caste relations as important. More general values were also called up, such as not injuring animals and humans, being forgiving, observing piety, and adhering to the truth.

His advocating tolerance and non-violence as official policy made him an unusual ruler. However, there is a small but significant discrepancy in what he propagated and in a couple of policy actions. These suggest that *ahiṃsā* as his official policy had limits, determined by the circumstances.

Hostility between the *pāsaṃḍās*/sects—orthodox and heterodox—and dissident groups evolving into sects required that the social ethic had to highlight tolerance among these. Aśoka sought the advancement of the essentials of all sects, and this, according to him, was only possible if each treated the other with respect.[3] He states that in honouring the views of others' sects one is honouring one's own sect. Yet, this sits uncomfortably with his edict ordering the expulsion of dissident monks from Buddhist monasteries.[4] Possibly, for him there was a distinction between activities within the Buddhist *Saṅgha*, and the need to rule without ideological prejudices. Monastic disputes were to be expected, as the institution of monasteries had almost become polities in miniature. Contentions over rules and authority could disturb the general equilibrium sought by governance. Nevertheless, his statement that all sects should be treated with equal respect was an innovation both in politics and among religious groups. This strand of thought was not unfamiliar in later times among those sects that aspired to universalistic values. The popular but somewhat ineffective current definition of secularism in India—*sarva-dharma-samabhava*—suggests a distant parallel with the Aśokan idea and echoes some of its insufficiencies.

More striking in an imperial system was Aśoka's claim to forsaking war and violence. However, this had a caveat. If war was unavoidable, then he hoped that the victorious would be satisfied with light punishments.[5] Curiously, however, the *aṭavikas,* the forest-dwellers, were at the receiving end of a fierce threat by the king of being killed—without any ostensible reason. Did this result from the encroachment by the state into forests and the resistance to this by forest-dwellers? This, of course, has been a continuous activity in Indian history and still persists.

The choice of such an ethic privileging *ahiṃsā* and the idea of tolerance as mutual and equitable respect among competing groups may also have been influenced by the problems of governing a subcontinental territory. The inaudible dialogue between the edicts and the ideas that became the prescriptions of the *Arthaśāstra* suggests seeming similarities but significant differences. For Kauṭilya, political integration required conquest followed by a centralized administration. Proximity to this model was frequently resorted to in discussions on administration in Orientalist discourse, but the severity of the centralization would have been difficult in practice. Far more investigation is needed to try and approximate the reality of administration in those times, with its varying regional patterns.

This was what I had attempted a couple of decades ago in a reconsideration of the notion of empire and its administration for those times. The edicts seem more sensitive to a flexible administration. This is demonstrated in Aśoka's orders to his officers and in the functions of the *dhamma-mahāmattas,* specially appointed officers concerned centrally with the well-being of his subjects. Adjustments to local conditions in the patterns of governance were likely, and I have suggested that administration was diversified.[6] Whereas there was a relatively centralized administration in the Ganges plain with its epicentre in Magadha at that time, this was somewhat different from the less centralized administration in other areas—Gandhara, Saurashtra, Kalinga, and Karnataka. Diversity in administration would reflect diverse socio-economic conditions. The economy of the Gangetic Plain continued to be largely based on agriculture, and if the advice of Kauṭilya was followed there were increasing areas being brought under cultivation with state organized settlements of peasants. Together with this, the growth of towns reflected the on-going commercial activities, where river trade played a significant role. The revenue produced by both activities was substantial. This region seems to have been demarcated by the location of the pillar edicts, and this is what I have referred to as the metropolitan state. With its history of kingship and of caste society, it was distinct from other areas where both these were relatively less established.

The core areas in the fringes of the empire were less centrally administered owing largely to difficulties in rapid communication. Their economies drew on local production in which commerce often played an important role. For Gandhara, it was the commercial nexus with west Asia and its tentative beginnings with central Asia. The post-Mauryan period saw connections between the Northwest and the Ganges Delta. Nevertheless, the cultures that evolved were far from identical. There is no mistaking a Buddhist icon from Gandhara and those crafted at Mathura or at Amaravati. Quite how such differences were maintained despite their working within a similar discourse is a matter for historical investigation. For Karnataka, the local gold mines were an important resource. Communications along the east coast made the connections easier with the north but there must also have been links southwards.

The societies in these core areas were likely to have been fairly mixed as is attested by inscriptions. The presence of Greek and Aramaic speakers in the northwest is evident from the need to render Aśokan inscriptions into both these languages and the location of other Greek inscriptions in and around this area. Brāhmī inscriptions found further south than the Aśokan have been read as Tamil-brāhmī.[7] These have been dated from the second century BC. They have occasional references to the chiefs mentioned in the Śangam poems, and to local traders, and there are also votive inscriptions involving the presence of Jaina monks. Unlike in the northwest, Aśoka did not consider rendering his edicts into Tamil and having them engraved in these areas. Doubtless there was no political compulsion since chiefdoms were less important than kingdoms. The use of varying languages would reflect cultural differences among the populations of these regions.

The forested territories probably experienced a minimal control provided that the forest dwellers were forthcoming with their produce. Lack of cooperation may have been the reason for the dire threats from the king. These were the peripheral areas supplying timber, elephants, and mineral wealth. Those involved with the production of such resources were not settled populations and were generally regarded as outside the social pale of caste.

The differences did not constitute sharply defined boundaries. There were doubtless some internal zones in the subcontinent where economies partially overlapped. Such diversity could not be removed or ignored and the administration of Jambudvīpa had to be sensitive to differences. The range of economic resources that produced particular categories of revenue also required an adjustable administration. At one level, the *dhamma* may have been an attempt to provide a pivot in the form of a persuasive ethic. An imperial system need not have been uniformly centralized, nor was the centralization identical, since regional differences could not be dismissed. This is made apparent in the concession to regional elements in the languages of the Prākrit inscriptions. Not only do these differences relate to regional usage but some could have also been a continuation in the preference for using a more familiar local language. The Achaemenids showed some sensitivity to this practice. Issued by the king, inscriptions were symbols of power and authority. But their reading and implementation were through local administration. This reflects a local authority that might have been closer to the people despite the commanding status of the emperor.

The attempt to universalize, such as it was, lay perhaps in the propagation of the social ethic as a new form of governance moving beyond the identities of clan, caste, or sect. It was an attempt at propagating what was thought to be a common way of life, a believed past and a universal ethic. Significantly, there is an absence of reference to what might have been a folk repertoire deriving from the epics, which would suggest that this had not as yet travelled long distances.

The ideology of *dhamma* differs from what we associate with ancient empires where, for instance, the validation of imperial rule generally came from a deity or through claims to divinity. Aśoka's references to deities are more in passing. For example, the title of *devānaṃpiya*—the beloved of the gods—which he used together with *rājā,* had little resemblance to the more exaggerated titles of post-Mauryan times; or his claim that because of the wide-spread practice of *dhamma,* the *deva*s, referring either to gods or kings, were now mingling with the people, is a statement the meaning of which remains controversial.[8] He refers to the sound of the drum heralding *dhamma* and displays of heavenly chariots, of elephants, balls of fire, and celestial forms (*divyāni rūpāni*)[9] almost as an ancillary to spectacle and magic. In the Aśokan cosmos, the gods are rather shadowy figures with uncertain roles rather than being the omniscient ones who control the universe.

The distinction between his being persuaded of the Buddha's teaching with some attachment to the *Saṅgha*, and his perception of himself as a ruler with a distinct purpose, can be observed in references to him from later sources. These can perhaps be differentiated into three categories. The first is obviously Aśoka as the exemplary king of the Buddhist texts, as in the *Aśokāvadāna* of the northern Buddhist tradition or the *Dīpavaṃsa* and

Mahāvaṃsa of the Pāli Theravāda tradition. The second is the seeming disappearance of Aśoka in Brahmanical texts, something that has been questioned in recent times. The last would be the few but significant associations with him, directly or indirectly, by later rulers in their inscriptions.

The decipherment of the *brāhmī* script in the nineteenth century drawing on the Aśokan inscriptions required identifying the author of these. The *Mahāvaṃsa* of the mid-first millennium AD provided some initial clues to the identity, and this in turn tended to colour the image of Aśoka. In the Theravāda tradition, he was not only a royal patron donating largesse but also initiating the proselytizing of Buddhism. The later claim that the Mauryas were in origin a clan linked to the Śākyas was attractive to the authors of the Sri Lankan chronicles. The political advantage of linking the coming of Buddhism to Sri Lanka with Mahinda, said to have been the son of Aśoka, was that this claim associated him with a pre-eminent ruler and that too from the clan of the Buddha himself. Underlying the narratives of conversion and miraculous happenings, sovereign authority remained the issue.

Much has been said about the spread of Buddhism being ensured by the missions of Aśoka. He instituted a body of *dhamma-mahāmatta*s concerned with the general welfare of his subjects. They were sent as emissaries of the king even to the *Yona*s, the Hellenistic world. But were they preaching Buddhism? Hellenistic sources are silent about such supposed missions. The only part of the then Hellenistic world where Buddhism had a presence was Gandhara, and this was within the empire. The spread of a religion requires more than just missionaries backed by royalty.

The really impressive spread of Buddhism dates to the post-Mauryan period when both *stūpa*s and patrons multiplied. The patrons were occasionally royalty but more frequently the laity—householders, small-scale landowners, artisans and traders, and monks and nuns. They gave of their skills and made donations as reflected in their votive inscriptions at Buddhist monuments. The emergence of many kingdoms and the importance of urban and rural householders, *gahapati*s, diversified patronage.[10] Such a backing from society was required for supporting the renouncers.

Buddhist presence in new areas, which some Buddhist authors attribute to the missions of the king, finds little corroboration in other sources.

The appropriation of Aśoka by the northern Buddhist tradition in texts such as the *Aśokāvadāna* dates to the early centuries AD.[11] Less politically oriented than the Sri Lankan chronicles, these versions present the king as acting closely to the wishes of the elders of the *Saṅgha*. Dramatic stories and miracles, the common currency of both Buddhist traditions, begin to reach a new high: The wicked *caṇḍa-aśoka* is converted to the righteous *dharma-aśoka*; the miraculous overnight construction of 84,000 *stūpas* for placing the relics of the Buddha—the distribution of the relics underlining Aśoka's sovereignty; or, the king donating his kingdom to the *Saṅgha*, which had to be retrieved by the ministers at the order of his grandson. Was this indeed an attempt to reconcile the *cakkavatti* with the *bodhisatva*?

Aśoka's own declaration of his closeness to Buddhism points to a gradual process. He refers to himself as an *upāsaka*; as approaching the *Saṅgha* (*saṅghe upeti*); visiting the Bodhi-tree (*ayāya saṃbodhim*); and there is also a controversial reading of his travelling with the relics of the Buddha.[12] The *dhamma* is described as an ancient tradition (*porānā pakiti*). Whether or not the authors of the various Buddhist texts knew about the edicts, they preferred to selectively embroider on the narratives of their own making.

The contemporary function of narratives underlining the requirements of the ideal king may have been intended to instruct the new patrons—the royalty of the Indo-Greeks, Śākyas and Kuṣāṇas. In the *Milinda-pañho,* a discussion between a Buddhist monk and the Indo-Greek king Menander, Aśoka is said to have witnessed an act of truth performed by a prostitute, who was able to roll back the waters of the Ganges, thereby demonstrating the power of the teaching.[13]

That the Buddhist traditions had their own take on Aśoka is evident from the absence of any mention of the Kalinga campaign as significant to the formulation of his understanding of *dhamma*. The king describes his remorse and repentance at the suffering caused by him in an edict[14] located everywhere except, interestingly, in Kalinga. These two specific edicts are addressed to his officers in the region.[15] He orders them to ensure the welfare of the people, encouraging them to trust the king as a child would its father—a trust that surely was needed after the campaign. If the monks had read the inscriptions they might have described the conversion as taking place on the battlefield, as some historians have done in our time. But regret and repentance, recollected in tranquility, is too tame for the drama of conversion.

It might also be worth asking what such a 'conversion' could have entailed. Religious articulation was multiple, characterized by the presence of a variety of heterodox and orthodox sects, some strongly opposed, others less so. If the combination of the exercise of power and the practice of Buddhism was problematic, this seems not to have been the concern of Buddhist texts.

The transmission of information being largely oral, the stories from these texts would have entered the repertoire of folklore. Locations became associated in historical memory with Aśoka and drew their importance from this association. Travel accounts of the Chinese Buddhist pilgrims, who came in the fourth and seventh and later centuries AD, narrate the stories more likely from the northern tradition. Fa Hien attributes some of them to inscriptions from Magadha.[16] Xuanzang in the seventh century writes of vast numbers of *stūpas* built by Aśoka located all over the subcontinent.[17] Perhaps he was influenced by the story of the 84,000 *stūpas*. He also refers to at least half-a-dozen stone pillars largely in the Ganges heartland, each with different animal capitals. But he has less to say on the possible readings of inscriptions. Perhaps by now the script could not be read, because he mentions a *stūpa* built by Aśoka in Kalinga but does not refer to the campaign. Whether built by Aśoka or not, the *stūpas* are nevertheless attributed to him. Were they the symbols of a Buddhist king or had they become the historical legitimation of a site?

By this time the tradition with its many legends had accompanied the spread of Buddhism to various parts of Asia. Aśoka emerged as the *cakravarti* of the Buddhist world beyond the subcontinent. But in India he received little mention. Yet, even if he had been marginalized as a ruler, the question remains whether his ideas and attempts at a particular form of governance were part of discussions on kingship and ethics.

In the eyes of Vedic Brahmanism and later Purāṇic Hinduism, Śramaṇic sects were heterodox—the *pāṣaṇḍās*/sects of the *nāstikas*, those who did not believe in deities. The heretics were more successful in the competition for royal patronage in the immediate post-Mauryan times. This was doubtless resented by the orthodox. However, as was argued many decades ago, there was little in the way of Brahmanic revival as a result of Śuṅga rule. The post-Mauryan period witnessed an efflorescence of Buddhism through an expansion in patronage within the subcontinent and beyond. Texts of Brahmanical authorship did not name Aśoka as the object of their hostility but were opposed to the teaching of the Buddha, which gave shape to some of the principles of the *dhamma*. Aśoka is ignored or reduced to a mere name in the dynastic lists of the *Purāṇas*. 'Mahāmoha' is the name used for the Buddha and for Mahāvīra in the *Purāṇas*, because the authors projected them as deluded and maintained that they deliberately deluded others. The hostility seems to find expression in the changing meaning of the term *devānaṃpriya*.[18]

This was taken as a title by a few kings but is particularly associated with Aśoka. The Sri Lankan chronicles are familiar with it and maintain that it was adopted by their king Tissa. Its precise connotation remained controversial with some grammarians stating that it was a term of contempt and others that it was an honorific. The meaning of *deva* varied from gods to kings to fools depending on the context.

The *Mahābhārata* has an ironic statement about a king called Aśoka, presumably the Mauryan: that among those celestials who were born on earth was the *mahāsura* Asva who became the *rājā* Aśoka,[19] described as *mahāvīrya parākrama,* a great conqueror. Many of the *rājās* so created are those who were hostile to the heroes. Recent research on the Śāntiparvan and Udyogaparvan of the *Mahābhārata* suggests that the dilemmas faced by Arjuna and Yudhiṣṭhira reflect some element of Buddhist thought and an echo of what might have been the debates that grew out of Aśoka's *dhamma*. More specifically the questioning of the *kṣatriya* model might have been encouraged from the presence of some Aśokan ideas. Yudhiṣṭhira's initial rejection of rulership exposed the tension between renouncer and householder and his wish being to opt for the former. The process of his being persuaded to renounce renunciation was often through arguments opposed to heterodox thinking.[20]

The discussion of kingship in the *rājadharma* section tends to focus on the king rather than the institutions of the state. The earlier Buddhist experience seems to have toyed with appropriating the legitimacy of the ruler as a way of ensuring closeness to power. This may have been thought necessary if the institution of kingship was to be part of Brahmanical enterprise. With the emergence of state systems, the nature of kingship had changed. From another perspective, and assuming that the *rājadharma* section is post-Mauryan in date, as is now being suggested, it could be argued that although there was an awareness of Kauṭilya's notion of *saptāṅga* (the seven constituents of the state), the function of these in the Aśokan state were not the same as envisaged in the *Arthaśāstra.*

A central point of debate is likely to have been around the definitions of the social code. The *varṇāśrama-dharma* of the normative texts was not universally accepted. The values of the *kṣatriya dharma* highlighting war where necessary violated the ethic of *ahiṃsā.* But as a *kṣatriya* it was Arjuna's *svadharma* to go to war. Arjuna's dilemma also revolves around the legitimacy of violence against kinsmen, an appropriate concern for a clan society on the eve of fading out. The insertion of the *Bhagavad Gītā* would have been necessary to counter the questioning of the morality of violence and to argue that where it involved the destruction of evil there it was justified. To this was added the notion that death is not death since the soul is immortal. This was problematic for those who denied the soul.

The *Gītā* can perhaps be read at one level as a response to the polemic of interweaving *ahiṃsā* with politics. This would have to have been faced frontally if there continued to be a memory of Aśoka having explored the relationship between kingship and *dhamma.*

From later inscriptions we know that the Mauryas had not been forgotten. Probably some people may still have read the edicts.

Yudhiṣṭhira's pronouncements against violence speak of the evils of war, possibly reflecting a debate among post-Aśokan polities. His remorse and rejection of violence is reminiscent of Aśoka's Major Rock Edict XIII relating to the Kalinga campaign. Yudhiṣṭhira states that no *dharma* is as sinful as the *kṣatriya dharma* because a king during a campaign slaughters a multitude of people—*rājā hanti mahājanam.*[21] Others justify war by the more usual argument that it removes evil, without explaining how evil is to be differentiated from good, apart from referring to the normative code.

The *gaṇa-saṅgha*s, chiefdoms, of the middle Ganges plain appear to have been incorporated into the empire. This process would have meant that some coercion was inevitable, but Aśoka maintained that persuasion was the preferred way. Subsequently, when the Mauryan Empire disintegrated, new kingdoms emerged. The restitution of old polities, to whatever extent, and the creation of new ones inevitably involved violence. So although the players on the epic stage were heroes of past times, some of the quandaries they faced remained relevant to their contemporary times.

An example of the marginalization of the memory of Aśoka in a Brahmanical ambience subsequent to the seventh century AD is captured in the re-use of an Aśokan object. The stone *pīṭha* of the image in the Candralamba Temple at the site of Sannathi in Karnataka was identified as a slab with an engraving of Aśoka's edicts that included the Separate Edicts.[22] A section in the centre was cut out to hold the tenon at the base of the image. Did the *brāhmaṇa* literati not want to know what had been engraved so carefully on the slab? Or, were they unable to read the script by now and had no curiosity about knowing what it might have said? Did they assume it was a religious invocation but nevertheless cut into it? Or was it a deliberate act of contempt? Why the Separate Edicts were engraved at Sannathi remains an enigma, since there is no reference to a local campaign.

Another act of vandalism but of a lesser kind is also on record. A set of caves in the Barabar and Nagarjuna hills in south Bihar were donated by Aśoka and by his grandson Daśaratha to the Ājīvika sect. The donations are recorded in brief votive inscriptions.[23] These are so far the earliest attested donations of caves. The word *ājīvikehi* has been erased in some inscriptions. The caves were subsequently occupied by Buddhist monks and then by Hindu ascetics, as they still are. There is uncertainty as to the date of the erasure, but it would have to be of a date when the script could still be read. Was this a statement of hostility towards the donors who were viewed as patrons of the heterodox? Or was the hostility directed towards the Ājīvika sect from their rivals? It was probably the latter since it was an attempt to acquire property by fraud.

It has been suggested that the idea of the structure of these caves may have been Achaemenid in origin. However the Vindhyan ranges across central India provide evidence of cave sites, some pre-historic, and many with rock art. Megalithic sites of the first millennium BC sometimes take the form of caves cut into laterite rock. Possibly the use of caves by the heterodox sects was a continuation of an earlier practice as was the occasional association of Buddhist sites with tumuli and pillars. The architecture of these forms was given a greater aesthetic visibility in the post-Mauryan period.

A rather different mood emerges from Kalhaṇa, who, in his history of Kashmir, the *Rājataraṅgiṇī*, written in the twelfth century, refers to Aśoka's activities in Kashmir.[24] He is said to have ruled over the entire earth, been a follower of the Jinaśāsana, built *stūpa*s at specifically mentioned places, and established the wealthy town of Śrinagara. He restored a Śaiva temple and the deity granted him a son, Jalauka, who ousted the *mleccha* from the country. The author, although not a Buddhist, seems to have been familiar with the Buddhist accounts and approves of the king. It reflects an attempt to reconstruct the past from local records and traditions. Significantly, Aśoka is mentioned by name and represented as a monarch of considerable standing. Kalhaṇa was intellectually many cuts above the authors of the *Purāṇa*s, and his perspective is refreshingly different.

But this also raises the question of whether Aśoka, ignored in Gupta times and soon after, was restored to some respect by the time of Kalhana? Perhaps one may be permitted to speculate on this. The earlier period had seen confrontations between Purāṇic Hinduism and the Śramaṇic religions at various levels, from differences in philosophical explanations to competition for patronage. *Brāhmaṇa* authorship had by now acquired the mechanism of legitimizing royalty through reconstructing genealogies and validating the creation of new castes of *kṣatriya*s, as stated in the *Purāṇa*s,[25] and by claiming various other powers. Their authority was enhanced with grants of land from royalty. To this was added the incorporation of various forms of religious articulation. Sanskrit, the language of the elite and the learned, replaced Prākrit in the royal courts. With their success being confirmed, it would have been possible for this authorship to make concessions to those whom they had earlier opposed.

The third category of sources undermined the first two. This consisted of persons who either referred directly to Aśoka or who used Aśokan objects to derive historical legitimation. Aśoka was mentioned in inscriptions other than his own, and his pillars were re-used, perhaps for historical legitimacy.

An early inscriptional reference to him comes from a Buddhist *stūpa* at Kanaganahalli near Sannathi in Karnataka.[26] Two low-relief panels carry label inscriptions identifying the person represented as *raya asoko.* One shows a royal personage accompanied by some women, and the other depicts worship at a shrine. These seem not to be portraits with identical facial features but conventional representations. Aśoka is treated on par with contemporary Sātavāhana rulers, also called *raya*/*rayo.* He is not given the title that he took in his own inscriptions. The form *raya* occurs in his edicts but generally as part of the longer title. On one occasion he calls himself *lājā māgadhe* when addressing the *Saṅgha* (the replacement of 'r' by 'l' being a characteristic of Magadhan Prākrit).[27] Aśoka having ruled a century or two prior to this, the labels suggest that popular narratives about him were in circulation, and he was a known king. Nevertheless he is given no exalted title.

A tangential echo of Aśoka comes from the post-Mauryan inscription of Khāravela from Orissa.[28] He mentions calling a council of Jaina monks of diverse views to help sort the teaching. He also refers to his respect for all sects—*sava pāsaṃḍa pūjako*.

An official record of at least one activity of Aśoka's administration is available from post-Mauryan times. Rudradāman's inscription at Girnar of AD 150 records the building of a dam at the Sudarśana Lake in Saurashtra by a governor of Chandragupta Maurya.[29] It was subsequently repaired because of heavy damage from a storm by the governor of Aśoka and yet again later by the governor of Rudradāman. A still later fifth century inscription records its repair once more during the reign of Skanda Gupta—a neat continuity from the Mauryas to the Guptas.[30] Significantly the inscriptions are on the same rock as the earlier Aśokan edicts, and this seems to have been deliberate, resulting in an impressive historical record.

The pillars of Aśoka received greater attention. There are traces of some imitation in Gupta times. However, among the re-use of objects, the most challenging is the re-inscribing and re-installing of Aśokan pillars. The best known is the one moved to the fort at Allahabad. Among its various inscriptions are the Pillar Edicts, the *praśasti* of Samudra Gupta, and a genealogy of Jahangir, each inscription from a different millennium and in a different language.[31] Could Samudra Gupta's engraver have read the earlier inscriptions? The scripts were not unrelated but not identical.

The meaning that might have been attached to the pillars becomes more problematic in later times. The engraving of medieval period inscriptions on some Aśokan pillars or segments can be noticed from the twelfth century onwards.[32] These are not tourist graffiti. They are statements from the likes of the Chauhans and Feroz Shah Tughlaq, and a few others. These pillars were also moved from their original locations, some of which had become derelict, to places of importance. As late as the sixteenth century they carry brief inscriptions of goldsmiths who were the traditional engravers. The Lauriya-Nandangarh pillar carries a Persian inscription of Aurangzeb.[33]

What did these later rulers make of the pillars? We know that the earlier inscriptions could not now be read. Surely the attraction of the pillars was not just the shine of the polished stone that led to their being hauled over long distances. The pillars were special but were not worshipped, although some thought they were talismans. They were not associated with any event, although popular legends linked them predictably to the Pāṇḍavas. The pillars were not trophies of victory easy to carry home. Among the more evocative explorations of the meaning of the pillars, which also suggests why they were appropriated, is the puzzlement expressed in the *Sirat-i-Firoz Shahi*. Firoz Shah describes the pillar as the *minar-i-zarrin*, as it has the appearance of a golden minar, reaching into the sky, and he compares it to the trees of Paradise.[34] Apart from their strikingly attractive quality, the pillars evidently evoked a historical legitimacy that later rulers were anxious to inherit. Can one in a somewhat contrary fashion suggest that perhaps they encapsulated a subterranean memory, waiting to be mined by historians?

Other rulers who marked their presence on other Aśokan pillars made different associations. The pillar at Lumbini commemorating the birthplace of the Buddha and the one at Nigliva associated with the Konakamana *stūpa*, both in the Nepali *terai*, were visited by the fourteenth century ruler of Nepal, Ripu Malla. This is recorded in a brief statement in *devanāgari* on the pillar which reads: *śri ripu malla ciram jayatu*. Above it is the formulaic Buddhist mantra—*om mane padme hun*—in Tibetan. Presumably these two inscriptions were connected and possibly the association may have been known, else the Buddhist mantra may not have found a place on the pillar. Lumbini as the birthplace of the Buddha may still have been venerated many centuries after the visit of Xuanzang. Aśoka was a familiar figure in Tibetan historical writing, as attested to in the rather fanciful version of his rule written by the Lama Tārānatha in the late fifteenth century.[35] That the inscriptions of Aśoka on these pillars could have been read is unlikely given the change in the script. It is interesting that the ruler of the Delhi Sultanate was unaware of the contents of the inscriptions, but on the frontier of his kingdom, in the *terai*, there was a likely association.

And so we come to the rediscovery of Aśoka in our times. It began with the decipherment of the *brāhmī* script in the nineteenth century using the Aśokan inscriptions as texts. The clues from the

Sri Lankan chronicles were confirmed by the reading of some of his inscriptions discovered some decades later. This led to debates on the historical assessment of Aśoka Maurya at the start of the twentieth century. And inevitably the modern context impinged on the past and the past in turn gave shape to aspects of the present. Various historians wrote monographs on the king during the early half of the twentieth century—Vincent Smith, Hem Chandra Raychaudhuri, D. R. Bhandarkar, R. K. Mookerji, Beni Madhav Barua, Nilakantha Sastri, and others.[36] Writing on Aśoka became almost a rite of passage for historians of ancient India.

Vincent Smith represented the culmination of colonial writing on ancient India just when a large body of historical writing was emerging from a nationalist ethos. Smith's assessments of early kings were peppered with references to autocracy and despotism as was common to many colonial historians invoking the theories of James Mill. Even when he was being more positive, there was the caveat of "after the Oriental manner."[37] For him Aśoka was "a masterful autocrat ruling church and state alike with a strong hand" but at the same time intermittently a monk and something of a missionary.[38] These were, in a sense, contradictory statements, and in any case they did not hold for long since there was little evidence to support them. His training in Classics led him to assert the superiority of the Greco-Roman civilization in a manner that endorsed the imperial perspective of his time. Smith was appreciated for collating the data, but his generalizations were frequently, and quite rightly, questioned.

Other contemporary European scholars had different views even if these did not take the form of monographs. Among them Etienne Lamotte attempted to view Aśoka neither from the perspective of the colonial construction of Indian history nor entirely from that of the Buddhist texts. The king was without doubt influenced by Buddhist thinking, nevertheless he had a distinctive policy as emperor.[39]

Yet other views, more central to the historiography of India and to the iconic representation of Aśoka in modern India, were those that emanated from concerns of nationalism. These widened the causal connections between the flow of history and the actions of this king. A commonly held position was that Aśoka had weakened the defenses of India by annulling the military strength of imperial Magadha through his endorsement of non-violence. In the words of H. C. Raychaudhuri, "Dark clouds were looming on the north-western horizon. India needed men of the calibre of Puru and Chandragupta to ensure her protection against the Yavana menace. She got a dreamer."[40] It was argued that Aśoka's emphasis on *ahiṃsā* opened India to invasions from the Northwest, and the fabric of power constructed by Chandragupta and Cāṇakya was allowed to collapse. The conventional image of great emperors required them to be mighty conquerors. The Mauryan inscriptions demarcated a territory covering a major part of the sub-continent. This was the closest that an earlier state had come to the boundaries of British India, which was regarded as the territorial definition of the coming Indian nation. Aśoka was accused of allowing this territory to disintegrate. This was to develop into a slogan that Buddhism had emaciated Hinduism.

Aśoka's patronage of the Buddhist Saṅgha also came in for criticism when it was said that the treasury was crippled by donations to religious institutions. That Aśoka was to Buddhism what St. Paul was to Christianity was a somewhat far-fetched analogy. Readings went in diverse ways. Some read the edicts through the lens of Buddhist texts without questioning the reasons for the Buddhist reconstructions of his reign. Others followed the prevalent view that all religions in pre-Islamic India were tangential variants of Hinduism and there was little fundamental difference between Buddhism and Hinduism. Therefore, the *dhamma* of Aśoka was in essence Hindu. The argument of Emile Durkheim, who found it problematic to define Buddhism as a religion for a variety of reasons, such as the absence of deities, found no place in this discussion.[41]

However, running counter to this there grew a gradual but increasing admiration for what was regarded as his extraordinary vision in endorsing *ahiṃsā* and the tolerance that arose from an equal respect for all religions. This was seen as an essential feature of Hindu civilization, and the Buddhist ethic was subsumed in it. It gathered even greater steam with the endorsement, albeit brief, of H. G. Wells, who wrote of Aśoka's reign as "one of the brightest interludes in the troubled history of mankind."[42] Wells, by no means a historian of substance, was nevertheless able to suggest non-colonial perspectives in surveying world history.

From the mid-twentieth century the historical treatment of Aśoka began to undergo a further change. Historians of ancient India gradually distancing themselves from Indology and, coming closer to the social sciences, introduced questions that sought to take the discussion beyond earlier studies. The interweaving of archaeological, epigraphic, and textual sources raised problems relating to the evolving of an imperial system, the governance of empire, and the reasons for the decline of the system. Historical explanations were attempts to relate the king more closely to his historical context.[43] Very different from previous approaches was the assessment of D. D. Kosambi when he writes, "The real Aśokan conversion was not merely of the king but of the whole system. State-dominated commodity production yielded place to villages supplying primarily their own internal demand for food and the few indispensable manufactures. The expensive state mechanism of force was reduced by enlisting the aid of religion."[44]

But such views were largely restricted to debates among historians of ancient history. Other perspectives that spoke to the concerns of nationalism were related to the question of the territory that had to be defended against foreign invasion, and to the endorsement of a policy of non-violence. To this was added the acceptance of the co-existence of diverse views, at least in theory. Gandhi drew on Aśoka less as a historical figure and more perhaps as an inspiration for his own methods to achieve freedom from colonial rule. Yet the *Gītā*, although not endorsing Aśoka's *dhamma,* was for Gandhi the axial text. Was it because it speaks of a just war and fighting colonialism was viewed as a just war? Was this the immediate problem rather than the debate on the use of violence *per se*? A few of the issues raised by Aśoka seemed to tie in with Gandhi's way of conducting his rather unusual anti-colonial campaign with its emphasis on *ahiṃsā* and the co-existence of diverse ideologies.

Nehru was attracted to the rejection of violence as symbolic of a civilized polity; to the plea that all sects should live in harmony despite differences; and to the propagation of a social ethic for governance that did not require adherence to a particular religion or deity. These were values pertinent to current political problems in India with the rising swell of communal ideologies, the shrill insistence of equating Indian with Hindu and the demand for a separate Islamic nation-state. History for Nehru had a special purpose, as is evident from his book *The Discovery of India.* His biographer writes of the book that, "It sought to portray an emotional comprehension of Indian nationalism and to stress the necessity of revitalizing the Indian people ... India's past could be so depicted as to draw lessons for its future."[45] Nehru's admiration for Aśoka was evident from his explanation of why the *dharma-cakra* from the Aśokan pillar at Sarnath was incorporated into the flag of independent India. This, he believed, evoked the values that India stood for both in those ancient days and throughout the ages.

The thought that the words of Aśoka need to be heard again is problematic. Giving him a voice relevant to the present would in effect be a voice-over. Historical figures are best understood as persons in their own historical context. Nevertheless it seems to me that there are some ideas implicit in the edicts that could resonate with contemporary times. (And here comes my voice-over!) I mention them not because I think Aśoka should be an exemplar for our times, but rather that in a comparison of the historical context of ideas they might provide another dimension to our analysis of the present.

The need for each sect to give space to and honour the others is a sentiment that is currently proclaimed even if not observed, especially in societies where religious factionalism has taken political forms and given direction to nationalism of an extreme kind. But equal respect, even in theory, has limitations if there are no equal rights and equal obligations. And this was so even in the time of Aśoka.

The social ethic as described in the edicts was meant to apply to any community or society. Its concern with fostering human relationships irrespective of belief systems and social status contained the seminal ideas that could have pointed modern

Indian society in what we today would call a more 'secular' direction. Such a society could be facilitated by recognizing antecedents where communities have been sympathetic to these values. This would require a rethinking of how we define what we like to call the Indian tradition, especially as constructed in the nineteenth century.

Another idea that has had some currency drew on the notion that the authority of the renouncer could be used as a challenge to political power. The duality of the world-renouncer and the world-conqueror, articulated by what is said to have been the pronouncement at the birth of the Buddha, has been examined at length in a study of Aśoka and later Buddhist polities.[46] Was Aśoka attempting to draw on this parallel power by propounding an ethic that had universal application and grew out of an association with renouncers? Gandhi was not unaware of the potential of this idea, however differently he may have used it.

The edicts were written in Prākrit, which at that time constituted a Prākrit cosmopolis, if I may borrow the term, the language that transcended political boundaries and most religious affiliations.[47] The linguistic variants in the inscriptions point to an impressive linguistic reach with the potential of large numbers of people becoming familiar with the ethic. The gods to be worshipped and the relationships among people were not invariably dictated by religious authority. This became a significant articulation of religion among many Indians, in particular among the substratum religions, as one might call them, that created their own codes and deities. They may not have been politically powerful, since they were treated as 'the Other' by those in authority. Nevertheless, they were the ones that shaped the genesis of multiple cultures that may have originated outside the mainstream but were frequently appropriated. In a sense the *dhamma* of Aśoka was at least aware of the presence of 'the Other' and the need for its inclusion. The turning to Buddhism by a few million of the socio-economic under-privileged in the mid-twentieth century may have been, apart from other things, an echo from history.

In his last edict, the Seventh Pillar Edict, Aśoka states that *dhamma* has advanced among people through two ways, through codes and rules or legislation [*niyama*] and through conviction and persuasion [*nijjhatti*].[48] Significantly he does not mention the coercion of conquest as most other kings would have done. He adds that legislating behaviour has been less effective as compared to persuasion. His belief in the effectiveness of his policies may have been in part wishful thinking. All the same, for a king of early times this is a remarkable statement. Its poignancy lies in its coming in the last of his edicts, a retrospective on his reign. We today can claim to be inheritors of his ideas only when our ideas and actions draw strength, not just from rules and legislation, but preferably from persuasion. We have a long way to go.

Notes and References

1. *'savve munisse pajā mamā'*, Jules Bloch, *Les Inscriptions d'Asoka,* 'Les Belles Lettres', Paris, 1950 : Separate Edict I, p. 137.

2. D. Schlumberger and E. Benveniste, *Epigraphia Indica,* XXXVII, 1967, pp. 193–200; D. Schlumberger *et. al.,* 'Une Bilingue Greco-Armeene d'Asoka', *Journal Asiatique,* 1958, pp. 1–48.

3. Major Rock Edict XII: Bloch, *Les Inscriptions d'Asoka*, pp.121 ff.

4. Schism Edict, Kosam-Sanchi-Sarnath: Bloch, *Les Inscriptions d'Asoka*, pp. 152–53.

5. Major Rock Edict XIII: Bloch, *Les Inscriptions d'Asoka*, pp. 125 ff; Romila Thapar, *Asoka and the Decline of the Mauryas*, Delhi, 1997, 2nd edition, pp. 167–69.

6. Thapar, *Asoka and the Decline of the Mauryas*, pp. 315–19; and Romila Thapar, *The Mauryas Revisited*, Calcutta, 1987.

7. I. Mahadevan, *Early Tamil Epigraphy*, Cambridge, 2003.

8. Bloch, *Les Inscriptions d'Asoka*, p. 146; Dinesh Chandra Sircar, *Asokan Studies*, Calcutta, 1979; see also John Strong, 'The Commingling of Gods and Human, the Unveiling of the World, and the Descent from Trayastriṃśa Heaven: An Exegetical Exploration of the Connections of Minor Rock Edict I to Buddhist Legendary Literature' in Patrick Olivelle, Himanshu Prabha Ray and Janice Leoshko (eds), *Reimagining Aśoka: Memory and History*, Delhi, 2012, pp. 342–55.

9. Major Rock Edict IV: Bloch, *Les Inscriptions d'Asoka*, p. 98.

10. Romila Thapar, 'Patronage and Community', in Barbara Stoler Miller (ed.), *The Powers of Art*, Delhi, 1992, pp. 19–34.

11. John Strong, *The Legend of Aśoka: A Study and Translation of the Aśokāvadānamālā Manuscript*, Princeton, 1983, pp. 103–13; Gregory M.

Bongard-Levin, *The Kunala Legend and an Unpublished Aśokāvadānamālā Manuscript*, Calcutta, 1965.

12. Minor Rock Inscriptions: Dinesh Chandra Sircar, *Asokan Studies*, Calcutta, 1979; Bloch, *Les Inscriptions d'Asoka*, pp. 145, 146, 151. Major Rock Edict VIII: Bloch, *Les Inscriptions d'Asoka*, p. 112. Ahraura Inscription: Sircar, *Asokan Studies*, pp. 72 ff.

13. *Milinda-pañho* (T.W. Rhys Davids trans. and ed., *Milinda-pañho*. IV. i. 47ff. Oxford, 1890.)

14. Major Rock Edict XIII: Bloch, *Les Inscriptions d'Asoka*, pp. 125 ff.

15. Two Separate Edicts: Bloch, *Les Inscriptions d'Asoka*, pp. 136-43.

16. James Legge, *Fa-Hien's Record of Buddhist Kingdoms*, Oxford, 1969.

17. Samuel Beal, *Si-yu-ki, Buddhist Records of the Western World*, Delhi, 1986.

18. Madhav M. Deshpande, 'Interpreting the Aśokan Epithet *devānaṃpiya*', in Patrick Olivelle (ed.), *Aśoka, in History and Historical Memory*, Delhi, 2009, pp. 19–44.

19. Ādiparvan, 1.61.15.

20. I. Selvanayagam, 'Aśoka and Arjuna as Counterfigures Standing on the Field of dharma: A Historical Hermeneutical Perspective', *History of Religions*, 32, 1992, pp. 59–75; N. Sutton, 'Aśoka and Yudhiṣṭhira: A Historical Setting for theTensions in the *Mahābhārata' Religion'*, 27, 1997, pp. 331–41; Alf Hiltebeitel, *Rethinking the Mahabharata: A Reader's Guide to the Education of the Dharma King*, Delhi, 2002, pp. 262–3; James L. Fitzgerald, *Mahābhārata*, Book 12, Śāntiparvan, Part 1, Chicago, 2004, pp. 98 ff.

21. Śāntiparvan 12.98.1-4.

22. K.V. Ramesh, 'The Aśokan Inscriptions at Sannathi', *Indian Historical Review*, XIV, 1987–88, pp. 36–42; K.R. Norman, 'Aśokan Inscriptions from Sannati', *South Asian Studies*, 7, 1991, pp. 101–10.

23. Harry Falk, *Aśokan Sites and Artefacts*, Mainz, 2006.

24. *Rājataraṅgiṇī*, I. 104–107.

25. F.E. Pargiter, *The Purāna Text of the Dynasties of the Kali Age*, Delhi, 1975, p. 53.

26. Romila Thapar, 'Raya Asoko from Kanaganahalli: Some Thoughts', in *Airavati*, Chennai, pp. 249–62.

27. Bhabra Edict: Bloch, *Les Inscriptions d'Asoka*, p. 154.

28. Hathigumpha Cave Inscription of Khāravela: *Epigraphia Indica*, XX, pp. 72 ff.

29. Junagarh Rock Inscription of Rudradāman I: *Epigraphia Indica*, VIII, pp. 42 ff.

30. Junagarh Rock Inscription of Skandagupta: John F. Fleet, *Corpus Inscriptionum Indicarum*, Vol. III, Inscriptions of the Early Gupta Kings, Reprint, Delhi, 1970, pp. 58 ff.

31. The Allahabad-Kosam Pillar: E. Hultzsch, *Corpus Inscriptionum Indicarum*, Vol. I, Inscriptions of Aśoka. Reprint, Delhi, 1991, pp. 155 ff.

32. Finbar B. Flood, *Objects of Translation*, Princeton, 2009, pp. 247 ff; Finbar B. Flood, 'Pillars, Palimpsests and Princely Practices: Translating the Past in Sultanate Delhi', Res 43, 2003, pp. 95–116. One is of course reminded of the Roman appropriation and transfer of some of the obelisks from the temples of the Pharaohs in Egypt after the Roman control over Egypt. A similar act was repeated by the French and the British in modern times. This seems to have been related to capturing the past of Egypt. A significant difference is that the obelisks were not re-inscribed by those that took them away nor could a claim to legitimacy be associated with the obelisks.

33. Hultzsch, *Corpus Inscriptionum Indicarum*, p. xviii.

34. Dr. Imtiaz Ahmed at the Khuda Baksh Oriental Library in Patna kindly provided me with the Persian text and the translation of the passage by Professor Syed Hasan Askari.

35. T. Chattopadhyaya, trans and ed. Lama Tāranātha, *History of Buddhism in India*, Calcutta, 1980, pp. 50–75.

36. Vincent Smith, *Early History of India*, Oxford, 1904; Hem Chandra Raychaudhuri, *Political History of Ancient India*, Calcutta, 1923; D. R. Bhandarkar, *Ashoka*, Calcutta, 1925; R.K. Mookerji, *Aśoka*, London, 1928; Beni Madhav Barua, *Ashoka and His Inscriptions*, Calcutta, 1946; K. A. Nilakantha Sastri (ed.), *The Age of the Nandas and Mauryas*, Banaras, 1952.

37. Arthur L. Basham, 'Modern Historians of Ancient India', in Cyril H. Philips ed., *Historians of India, Pakistan and Ceylon*, London, 1961.

38. Smith, *Early History of India*, pp. 168 ff, 284 ff; Vincent Smith, *Aśoka*, Oxford, 1910; Thapar, *Aśoka and the Decline of the Mauryas*, p. 148, n. 1.

39. Etienne Lamotte, *Histoire du Bouddhisme Indiens, des origins a l'ere Saka*, Louvain, 1958.

40. Raychaudhuri, *Political History of Ancient India*, p. 347.

41. Emile Durkheim, *The Elementary Forms of Religious Life*, London, 1915.

42. H. G. Wells, *A Short History of the World*, Reprint 1949, London, 1922, p. 115.

43. Damodar Dharmanand Kosambi, *An Introduction to the Study of Indian History*, Bombay, 1956; Thapar, *Aśoka and the Decline of the Mauryas*; Gregory M. Bongard-Levin, *The Kunala Legend and an Unpublished Aśokāvadānamālā Manuscript*, Calcutta, 1985; Robert Lingat, *Royautes Bouddhiques*, Paris, 1989; Raymond Allchin, *The Archaeology of Early Historic South Asia: The Emergence of Cities and States*, Cambridge, 1995; Hary Falk, *Aśokan Sites and Artefacts*, Mainz, 2006.

44. Kosambi, *An Introduction to the Study of Indian History*, p. 224.

45. Sarvepalli Gopal, *Jawaharlal Nehru*, Vol. I, London, 1975, p. 299.

46. Stanley J. Tambiah, *World Conqueror and World Renouncer*, Cambridge, 1976.

47. Sheldon Pollock, 'The Cosmopolitan Vernacular', *The Journal of Asian Studies* 57, 1998, pp. 6–37.

48. Separate Rock Inscription II, Bloch, *Les Inscriptions d'Asoka*, p. 172.

Section IV

Religion, Philosophy, and Society

CHAPTER 12

Sacrifice, Surplus, and the Soul*

The sage Yājñavalkya, discoursing on the transmigration of the soul from one body to the next, described it as analogous with the caterpillar who, when it comes to the end of a leaf, draws itself together and moves onto another leaf, or else like the goldsmith, who, taking a piece of gold, transforms it into another shape, more beautiful perhaps than the first.[1] Both analogies are actions that result in change: in the first there is movement from one object to another, and in the second there is a mutation within the same substance. These ideas are crucial to the understanding of the soul and immortality as developed in the *Upaniṣads*, the earliest recorded discourses (as they are often called) of any length in India on theories of the immortality of the soul.[2] The two analogies concretize the essence of the doctrine of transmigration, which was to become culturally hegemonic as the bedrock of religious thinking among many sects in India. It might, therefore, be worth examining more closely the initial process that enabled this doctrine to take root.

The *Upaniṣads* as a subject of scholarship have generally been left to the domain of philosophers, who see them as fundamental to many philosophical systems, and to grammarians and philologists. However, texts, and especially those with such

* This is the text of the Forster Lecture on the theme of the Immortality of the Soul, delivered at the University of California, Berkeley, on 8 April 1992. I would like to thank Frits Staal for his initial encouragement of the idea and Kunal Chakrabarti for his comments on an earlier draft. I remember with particular warmth the long discussions on this subject with the late Barbara Stoller Miller.

Published in *History of Religions*, n.s., vol. 33, no. 4, 1994, 305–24.

specific concerns, are anchored in points of time that give them a historical dimension. The historical moment is linked both to the genesis of an idea and to its reception—two aspects with which this lecture is concerned. The *Upaniṣads* are at one level philosophical speculations on an abstract theme, but at another they are embedded in the society to which they relate. They encapsulate a process that leads to the formulation of an ideology. The interaction of this ideology with its environment, its source of power, and its historical ambience need to be inquired into.[3] Ideology speaks of and from a social order and ideas can be used to justify or legitimate the particular order. This is not to suggest that there is a simplistic correlation between ideology and society, for ideology is not merely a pale reflection of reality.[4] In many early societies ideology is incorporated into religious beliefs but articulated in ritual. If ritual is tied to the social order, however, then it can also be seen as the questioning of that order. In early Indian thought ritual is viewed as *karman*/action; therefore, it has been suggested that it would be more appropriate in the case of India to speak of orthopraxy than of orthodoxy.[5]

The period of the composition of the early and major *Upaniṣads* is generally taken as from about the eighth to sixth centuries BC.[6] They emerge out of earlier compositions, stemming from the *Ṛg Veda* and the *Brāhmaṇas* in particular but deviating sufficiently from these origins to become foundational to new groups of thinkers, some of whom were to take a conservative perspective and others, such as the Buddhists, who were to be regarded as heterodox. They represent, therefore, a watershed between the Vedic corpus and the new ideologies, epitomizing features of what has often been called an 'axial age'. The earlier texts emphasize the centrality of the sacrificial ritual, whereas the new ideologies move away from this and explore alternative eschatologies with, initially at least, an absence of ritual.

The historian's concern is with why this change occurred. It has been argued that possibly the *Upaniṣads* represent an interaction between Indo-European or Aryan ideas and the belief and practices of the local non-Aryans or pre-Aryans in northern India.[7] However, once it is conceded that we cannot identify any group as specifically Aryan, it becomes difficult to support an argument that insists so precisely on the differentiation of Aryan and non-Aryan.[8] It might, therefore, be more feasible to look at other aspects of the historical background. This essay is not intended to explore all the historical changes of the time, but rather to examine more closely the relevance of a few of them.

The contribution of non-Vedic thought to the evolution of the concepts of the *Upaniṣads* remains hypothetical since there are no texts or well-articulated traditions of such thought. That some merging from such sources occurred is very likely, given that Vedic Sanskrit itself reflects non-Aryan features suggestive of bilingualism.[9] Nevertheless, the concepts of the *Upaniṣads* addressed themselves to the existing expressions of Vedic belief and ritual, and to that extent they reflect a departure from them. This was a change in the paradigm of knowledge. The nature of the change was a shift from the acceptance of the *Vedas* as revealed and as controlled by ritual to the possibility that knowledge could derive from intuition, observation, and analysis.

The *Upaniṣads* were explorations in the search for enlightenment of the human condition and release from its bonds. This was not a situation involving priest and ritual nor the regular teacher-and-pupil learning of the *Vedas*. This knowledge was part of the oral tradition but was deliberately kept to a limited audience. The teachers were unconventional and those whom they taught were specially selected.[10] The latter could, however, include those who would normally be excluded from Vedic ritual—those of uncertain social origin such as Satyakāma[11] and women such as Maitreyī, the wife of Yājñavalkya. They are included perhaps to make a point.[12] It is sometimes argued that Satyakāma was accepted not because the social status of those taught was irrelevant, but because, having spoken the truth, he was recognized as a *brāhmaṇa*. However, his uncertain origin was sufficient to suggest that the question of his being a *brāhmaṇa* was not central. Where *brāhmaṇas* were the sons of *dāsis*, they were referred to as *dāsyaḥ-putraḥ*, but nevertheless respected.[13] The legitimacy of *brāhmaṇa* teachers was sought to be established by their status in lists of succession relating to their function as priests.[14] In an otherwise patriarchal society it is curious that matronymics are so prominent in these succession lists. The *kṣatriya* teachers have no particular qualifications. They were the *rājās*, the chiefs or oligarchs, *kṣatriya* being derived from *kṣatr*, meaning power. They are not included in the succession lists nor listed separately, although on some matters they instruct the *brāhmaṇas*. The form of dialogue was new, and, in breaking away from ritual and *mantra*, it seemed to be a rationalizing movement. At the same time, however, the mysticism of the doctrine introduced other elements. The location of the discussions were frequently the residences of *kṣatriyas* or occasionally those of *brāhmaṇas*. The *pariṣads*, or assemblies of the *kṣatriyas*, mentioned as locations for these dialogues, included those of Kāśī, Videha, and the Kuru-Pañcāla. Pravahana Jaivali of the Kuru-Pañcāla taught Śvetaketu Āruneya, the son of Gautama, and his father also came to the *rājā* to be taught.[15]

It was understood that the new doctrine was concerned with knowledge not about the mundane world, but with the conceptualization of other worlds,[16] although this exploration helped systematize knowledge about the mundane world. Despite the shift of focus to new methods of attaining knowledge instead of conforming to Vedic ritual practice, sacrificial rituals were not suddenly discontinued. The deities of earlier times were not denied, but rather their role tended to fade. If the sacrificial ritual was limited in its efficacy or ineffective in its purpose, then what were the other forms that could be central to the human condition? These interests revolved around questions of mortality and immortality—the immortality of the soul, the realization of the self, and belief in rebirth and retribution. Much of this was tied into examining the nature of reality: Is reality what we perceive around us or is there a reality beyond this which becomes tangible only through new techniques of perception? These involved control over the complementary categories of body and mind (*yoga*) and meditation (*dhyāna*), both ideally requiring a form of life given to austerity if not asceticism (*tapas*). This centred on the individual 'as the seeker of immortality through his own effort. Salvation of a limited kind had been present in the ritual of sacrifice, intended, among other things, for the attainment of the heightened pleasures of the heaven of Indra. But now the concern was not for heaven, but for release or liberation, *mokṣa*. This was not initially associated with sin and redemption but was conceptualized as the liberation of the soul.

Mokṣa was seen as related to the concept of *ātman-brahman*.[17] *Brahman*, necessary to the creation of the universe that it enters, is manifest in the *ātman*, the soul, which is an essential part of every individual life. *Mokṣa* therefore lies in achieving the realization of the *ātman-brahman*, releasing it from the bonds of the body and from repeatedly having to undergo death and rebirth from body to body. The transmigration of the *ātman* must cease before *mokṣa* is possible. In other words, the caterpillar must stop moving from leaf to leaf. Perhaps because the new doctrine distanced itself from the sacrificial ritual and drew on mystic concepts, claiming almost supernatural powers, it was referred to as the secret doctrine, *guhya-adesa, rahasyam*. One statement actually equates the secret doctrine with the *Upaniṣad—iti rahasyam iti upaniṣad*. The texts tend to retain this character of closed knowledge.[18] The new doctrine questioned the sacrificial cult—it alone could not be a means of liberating the *ātman*. The *Veda*s were said to be inferior to the now more frequently discussed alternative belief systems.[19] Sarcastic references to the greedy behaviour of priests at the sacrificial ritual highlighted doubts about the ritual and its main actors.[20]

Another startling feature is that the exploration of these new ideas was often not by *brāhmaṇa*s but by *kṣatriyas*. Thus, the *rājā* of the Kuru-Pañcāla explains to Śvetaketu that his father, though learned, is not familiar with all aspects of the new teaching, and later Gautama is initiated into the teaching by the *rājā*; *brāhmaṇa*s who come to Uddālaka Aruni seeking knowledge on *ātman-brahman* are directed by him to the Kekeya *rājā*, Aśvapati; in the dialogue between Ajātaśatru the *rājā* of Kāśī and Dṛptabalaki of the Gārgya clan, it is clear that the former is the more knowledgeable.[21] The noticeably important role of the *kṣatriya*s has been commented upon both in the *Upaniṣads* and by modern scholars.[22] The *rājā* of the Pañcālas says to the learned *brāhmaṇa* Gautama, 'This knowledge has never in the past been vested in any *brāhmaṇa*, but I shall tell it to you.'[23] This is striking coming from the *rājā* of the Kuru-Pañcāla, an area noted for its learned *brāhmaṇas* and frequency of the best sacrificial rituals.[24] Those who discoursed on the doctrine taught it either to their sons or to selected pupils. These *kṣatriyas* included the *rājās* of the Uśināra and Matsya clans and of the Kekeya, Kuru-Pañcāla, Kāśī, Kośala, and above all, Janaka of Videha,[25] substantially of the western and middle Ganga plain.[26] It is impressive that this vast geographical area saw the mobility of *rājās*, *brāhmaṇas*, and ideas at so early a stage.

The interest of the *brāhmaṇas* in the new teaching may have stemmed from dissidents seeking alternative philosophies or the curious exploring new ideas. Those attracted to asceticism would have supported such discussion. However, some *brāhmaṇas* who taught the new doctrine received lavish gifts or charged huge fees,[27] and others, who were by no account ascetics, are ascribed on occasion as extremely wealthy and learned.[28] Categories of knowledge were hierarchical, reflected a spectrum of interests,[29] and incorporated what appears to be a folk or subaltern knowledge. This is suggested, for example, by the inclusion of Raikva as a teacher. He sits under his cart scratching himself and hardly behaves as would upper-caste teachers.[30] Distinctions were made between knowledge as and for ritual, as intuition, as intellectual speculation that encouraged debate and the dialectical form of argument, and as knowledge of the *ātman.* The participation of some *brāhmaṇas* may have led to the eventual inclusion of this material as part of the Vedic corpus, and it also has occasional references to other earlier Vedic compositions. But the later appropriation of the *Upaniṣads* could also have been an attempt to stem the heresies of the Buddhists and other sects by tracing the origins of their deviation to Upaniṣadic thought. Modern philosophers continue to disagree as to whether Buddhism is to be treated as a part of the spectrum of post-Vedic thought rooted in the *Upaniṣads* or as a radical departure from the *Upaniṣads.*[31]

The new teaching moved away from *brāhmaṇas* as priests to *kṣatriyas* and *brāhmaṇas* as teachers, parallel to the shift away from ritual and religious duties, which required a high degree of specialization in mantras and rites. Max Weber distinguishes between the priest, the magician, and the charismatic prophet. The priest entreats the deity via prayer and sacrifice, whereas the magician coerces the deity via ritual. The priest eventually emerges as a functionary of a social group rather than of individuals, and the office becomes hereditary.[32] The teachers of the *Upaniṣads* do not fall into any of these categories as they are distinct from the priests, and, although their teaching leads to a new belief system of a higher order, they are not prophets. Priests as mediators between men and gods were not required in this system, since in the new teaching each individual was responsible for his or her own salvation and the role of the deity could be absent. Knowledge had earlier included the kinds of questions controlled by the traditional priest, but in effect the new knowledge superseded the old.

The move away from the sacrificial ritual requires some comment. The term for sacrifice, *yajña*, means to consecrate, to worship, to convert the profane into the holy. Sacrifice as a ritual involves the one ordering the sacrifice or the patron of the ritual, the *yajamāna*; the *devatā*/gods to whom the prayer is addressed; the *brāhmaṇa* priests who act as intermediaries and mediate between the *yajamāna* and the gods; and the offering, the *dravya* or *bali*, which is transferred from the ownership of the *yajamāna* and gifted to the gods via the mediation of the priests. There is no countertransfer of any visible equivalent.[33] The concept of *tyāga*/renunciation, became increasingly important in the debate on whether there should be a renunciation of the outcome of the ritual. The sacrificial rituals were of various kinds. The smallest and most compact were the *gṛhya*, or domestic rituals, using a single priest. The *śrauta*, or traditional rituals, were more elaborate, with several priests and altars, and continued for some days.[34] To these may be added the rituals associated with the acquisition of power and fertility where the patron of the sacrifice had to be a *kṣatriya rājā*.

The *yajamāna*, or patron, had first to be changed from a profane condition to a sacralized one. This involved a lengthy purification during which all other activities were set aside, which automatically excluded as *yajamāna*s those who were essential to the daily curriculum, such as men who laboured and women.

The *yajamāna* was stripped of authority during this process and underwent a change of status through ritual cleansing. The location for the ceremony had also to be purified and demarcated, for, outside this area, all killing was not immolation but murder.[35] The offering could be first fruits, the *bali* and the *bhāga*, or could be specially selected objects, such as animals identified as the victims of the ritual. The offering was owned by the *yajamāna* and was of value, which introduced an element of renunciation. An offering implies an existing asymmetrical relationship whereas a gift creates such a relationship. Theories on the purpose and function of the sacrifice range over many explanations such as homage to and communion with the gods, catharsis, renunciation, rejuvenation, and social legitimacy. The Vedic sacrifice had many functions; what it distinctly was not, however, was a covenant between a man and his jealous God.

Ritual activity, even where it involves a simple, everyday act, must be demarcated from the mundane, sometimes by archaizing its artifacts and its articulation. The demarcation points to the ritual having a different connotation than mundane acts. Nevertheless, ritual is also social action inasmuch as it involves a performer and a professional and therefore becomes symbolic of a social statement. Such a statement has many levels of interpretation, including the religious, the philosophical, the relationship between the performer and the professional, the perception of each of these by the audience—whether physically present or not—and the material objects involved in the performing of the ritual. Rituals therefore carry multiple messages. Even when the ritual was performed by a single household it was a signal to the community. Major ritual occasions, even as early as the *Ṛg Veda*, were community occasions.

The *brāhmaṇa* as priest had a relationship of reciprocity with the *kṣatriya* embodying political power. The sacrificial ritual was an exchange in which the gods were the recipients of offerings, *bali*, the priests were the recipients of gifts and fees, *dāna* and *dakṣinā*, and the *kṣatriya* as the one who orders the ritual, was the recipient of the benevolence of the gods and of status and legitimacy among men. Reciprocity involves an offering, a giving up or 'sacrifice' of something valuable. For the *kṣatriya* this consisted of the visible *bali*, the voluntary tribute in the form of material goods as well as the acceptance of the mediation of the *brāhmaṇa* with the gods, which was to some degree an acceptance of the *kṣatriya*'s dependence on the *brāhmaṇa*. The priests were therefore deeply involved in the articulation of power in their relations with the *kṣatriya*s through the ritual of sacrifice. The new teaching, however, had little use for this particular interconnection. Admittedly, the same two social categories, the *kṣatriya* and the *brāhmaṇa*, who were the main participants in the sacrificial ritual, were now involved in the new doctrine, but their roles and purposes were different. The *brahma-kṣatra* hierarchy was reversed in the acquisition of mystical knowledge.[36]

A sacrificial ritual involves resources. It also requires the mobilizing of resources and attention to the social problems posed by the procurement of offerings. The required wealth could be a substantial portion of the *yajamāna*'s resources. Not only was the best of livestock sacrificed but the gifts to be made to the priests in terms of cattle wealth and golden objects, if taken literally, would have materially impoverished many a *yajamāna*. When something of value was offered it was in the belief and expectation of receiving in return, at a later point, something of even greater value.

The frequency of the different types of rituals—such as daily, new and full moon, and seasonal sacrifices that increased with the agricultural calendar, rites of passage, and those intended to obtain either a boon or expiation—would be in part dependent on the availability of offerings.[37] The mobilization of resources would initially be the responsibility of the family and clan members, whose resources were limited. The common sharing of offerings enhanced the unity of the participants, making the sacrifice a collective activity. Gradually, the collective element receded and the focus turned to the individual *yajamāna*. This was the price paid by the individual aspiring to status and power and using the sacrificial ritual as a means of claiming legitimacy. The power was intended to assert an authority beyond that of the ordinary authority of the chief of the clan. This authority was to increase over time and become qualitatively different in the claim, not of chiefship but of kingship, with the mutation of chiefdoms into kingdoms.

There was an element of gift exchange involved in the relationship between the *brāhmaṇa* and the *kṣatriya* through the sacrificial ritual. The participants were not of equal status and the *brāhmaṇa*s, even when consecrating a *rājā*, stated their independence by their allegiance to Soma.[38] Reciprocity was not always balanced, and the obligation to give was that of the *kṣatriya*; to receive, that of the *brāhmaṇa*. The exchange was not protected by law but was dictated by custom. The acceptance of the gift bound the two participants as partners and reiterated their bonds.

The historical context of the sacrificial ritual is first encountered in the *Ṛg Veda*. The function of the *rājā*, as the warrior chief, was to protect the *viś*, or clan, even if such protection involved skirmishes and raids against other clans, and to augment resources through cattle raids, which in a cattle-rearing culture are imperative. Raiding was a proof of manhood and a matter of honour and assumed the character almost of a ritual process. It is idealized in the heroic qualities of the lifestyle of the god Indra. A successful raid required leadership but also drew on the prayers of priests interceding with the gods. The subsequent ritual was a thanksgiving and a means of distributing the booty. This was the subject of the many *dāna-stuti*s, or hymns of praise, in which *brāhmaṇa* poets eulogized the prowess of those *rājā*s who had increased their wealth through raids.[39] Wealth was computed primarily in terms of cattle, horses, chariots, and gold. These were often listed in exaggerated amounts—sixty thousand head of cattle and a thousand horses—where the exaggeration was intended as an incentive to those *rājā*s who had heard the praise of others and, it was hoped, would emulate them. The availability of resources affected attitudes toward the offering. Because they were herders, animals were normally not killed indiscriminately for food and there was a prohibition on the eating of the animals as daily fare. They were consumed only on special occasions, when a guest visited or after a ritual.[40] This was a mechanism for conserving the herd. However, the archaeological evidence from contemporary sites suggests a larger-than-normal consumption of beef.[41] Possibly the supply of prime livestock diminished until the cow gradually was declared inviolable. The ritual conferred legitimacy on the *rājā*, and the hymns of praise articulated his power. The *rājā* bestowed *dāna*/gifts in the form of wealth on the priests and acquired status in return. This was of central importance in societies that consisted of small, highly competitive groups in which there could be a quick turnover of status, resources, and power.

Subsequently, two trends became evident. One was the concentration of power with the *rājā*, now more frequently mentioned as *kṣatriya*. This was accompanied by a change in the primary resource base from cattle herding to agriculture, and particularly to wet rice cultivation in the middle Ganga plain. The *kṣatriya* was no longer just the cattle-raiding warrior. He augmented his wealth by settling new lands and encouraging their cultivation. The territories where the clan settled, the *janapada*s, were named after the *kṣatriya* ruling clan, such as the Kuru-Pañcāla, Kosala, Videha, and so on. This did not imply their ownership of the land but is indicative of enhanced political power. Cultivation was carried out by the *viś*, or clansmen, assisted by the labour of the *śūdra*s and *dāsa*s who were outside the clan. The *kṣatriya* demanded and received prestations from them. We are told that the *kṣatriya* eats the *viś*, or the clan, as the deer eats the grain, so the *viś* is subordinate to the *kṣatriya*.[42]

The occasion for making prestations was the sacrificial ritual, and this was the second feature that had changed. There were now a variety of *yajña*s, which ranged from simple daily rituals required of heads of households to more elaborate ones.[43] The most complex were those asserting *kṣatriya* authority, often lasting many months, such as the *rājasūya* and the *aśvamedha* and the *vājapeya*, or rejuvenation ritual. The *rājasūya* involved the conquest of the four quarters and the amassing of tribute before the ritual could begin. *Kṣatriya*s who performed these rites were transformed from *rājā*s into *mahārājā*s.[44] Such rituals often incorporated the rhetoric and symbols of the raids and skirmishes of pastoral–agricultural societies, even though these were now en route to becoming established kingdoms. Simple rituals could require the gift of a cow to the priest, but elaborate rituals brought in large amounts of wealth as sacrificial fees and gifts.[45] Such rituals were in effect a display, consumption, and destruction of wealth and therefore presupposed the availability of considerable resources to the patron of the ritual.

The specific use to which the wealth was put tended to convert the sacrifice into something of a potlatch. The more the wealth expended on the ritual, the more, it was assumed, would come back to the *yajamāna* through the pleasure of the gods, the discipline of giving, successful warfare, and good harvests; but above all it further raised the status of the *yajamāna*. At the same time, however, it depleted his treasury. The competitive spirit, encouraged by the earlier eulogistic *dāna-stuti*s, still persisted and probably resulted, as far as wealth was concerned, in what has been called an 'alternating disequilibrium'.[46] Where the head of the household, the *gṛhapati*, was encouraged to perform frequent calendrical sacrifices, the voluntary tribute to the *kṣatriya* would also decrease because of the demands of these sacrifices. Given the absence of burials in the cultures of the Ganga plain, unlike most other contemporary high cultures in Asia, the utilization of wealth was concentrated on the ritual of sacrifice. The ritual, therefore, combined a testimony of religious affirmation with a claim to status on the part of the *yajamāna*, as well as a demonstration of wealth and resources.

Potlatch, it has been argued, implies maximizing net outgoings.[47] Property is distributed seemingly voluntarily but in fact under compulsion of the ritual. Ostensibly it bears no interest, although a higher return is implicit. This, however, is different from capital accumulation since it cannot be collected on demand or indeed be repaid at all. It is not a series of gifts, but a series of counter-gifts. The return gift creates a debt that has to be met in the next ritual. It is an exchange of inalienable objects between people in a state of reciprocal dependence and is particularly evident in societies with a clan structure and a strong kinship organization. The obtaining of gifts and wealth for the ritual is from the labour of the family and kinsmen. When this system changes and the labour of non-clan persons is introduced, with fresh adjustments in relationships between the clans and within the clan, then the handling of wealth also begins to change. Access to wealth begins to require coercive measures. The production of wealth draws on a different kind of impersonal relationship. In such a situation, attitudes of the major *yajamānas*/patrons toward the sacrificial ritual would presumably also change. Reciprocity was between *brāhmaṇa*s and *kṣatriya*s and the competition was among the latter, expending their wealth.

The historical background to the *Upaniṣad*s depicts a society that was no longer predominantly that of cattle-herding clans. The more common occupation was agriculture with some incipient trade. The frequent and ready violence of raids was now replaced by political control and alliances. Agricultural resources required not capturing and raiding but the availability of regular and coordinated labour. This is reflected in the intensification of the *varṇa* or status hierarchy, where the upper castes claim lineage descent, whereas the fourth caste, that of the *śūdra*s, has no lineage base. This was a method of distancing those who provided labour.[48] Claims to ownership of land still lay largely with the clan, although a slow shift is perceptible to claims by families, perhaps as a result of rights of usage.[49] In the middle Ganga region, which included Kāśī, Kosala, and Videha, marshlands and forest were cleared for settlement, assisted to some degree by new iron tools. The cultivation of wet rice led to larger yields and increased wealth. The consumption of wealth in sacrificial rituals may initially have been a stimulus to production, but perhaps when resources could not keep pace with this consumption, the ritual began to have a negative effect. Unlike the produce of herders, grain can be stored for long periods and some accumulation is possible. This may also have resulted in an upward demographic trend requiring more resources. Archaeology provides evidence of increasing numbers of settlements and larger settlements, some of which were to gradually develop into urban centres.[50] *Kṣatriya* rule over these settlements was intended to protect the settlers and maintain minimum laws. For this the *kṣatriya* received a share of the produce in the form of what began as voluntary tributes such as the *bali* and the *bhāga* from the heads of households: such tributes were eventually to evolve into taxes. This encouraged the accumulation of wealth, which ultimately provided resources for the emergence of kingdoms and states. Such wealth was necessary to the new demands of incipient state systems, such as a rudimentary administration, an army, and the expenses of kingship. In addition, the universalizing of religious belief and practice, as in Buddhism, sometimes lent ideological support to the state, as in the Mauryan period.

Let us return to the question of why the *kṣatriya*s explored the doctrines that came to be included in the *Upaniṣads*. Were they moving away from the sacrificial ritual solely because of philosophical curiosity, or was there also, perhaps subconsciously, a search for an alternative that would discourage the expending of wealth—wealth that could be eventually diverted toward maintaining a state system with enhanced powers for the *kṣatriya*s far exceeding those of the earlier chiefships? Such a shift, of course, was not seen in terms of rational well-being or economic theory. The discontinuance of the Vedic sacrificial ritual would break the nexus between the *brāhmaṇa* and the *kṣatriya* and would provide a new role for the *kṣatriya*, more in consonance with the broader changes of the time. While the *brāhmaṇa* and the *kṣatriya* were interlocked in a competition for status, the sacrificial ritual, although seemingly separating their powers, in fact made them interdependent.[51] The *kṣatriya* may have preferred to be released from this dependence. The reality of power was seen now not only as divine dispensation but also in terms of access to resources. The power of the *kṣatriya* did not need to be circumscribed by the sacrificial ritual.

The new doctrine first evolved in areas that had experienced an increase in wealth. The question of whether this wealth would be accumulated as the basis for greater power or be consumed in the sacrificial ritual may have been expressed and considered. Was the break from the prestation economy encouraged as a search for legitimation through other means? Was this tied into an interest in a wider *kṣatriya* identity in areas where there was a perceptible change toward establishing kingship?

The new doctrine required discipline, meditation, and concern with the self alone. It called for neither intermediaries nor deities, which therefore gave it a universalism in the pursuit of *mokṣa*. Whereas the sacrificial ritual required the contribution, to a greater or lesser degree, of the clan and thereby underlined clan identity, the new doctrine moved away from this identity and underlined the separation of the individual from the clan.[52] Meditation and yoga are best undertaken in isolation subsequent to the initial period of training with a teacher. The clan therefore was marginalized, and the individual emerged as the subject seeking knowledge and liberation. This placed a premium on removing oneself from one's society and renouncing social obligations, a sentiment that ran counter to involvement in clan activities required by the earlier rituals. Renunciation is also contrary to the accumulation of wealth, but the notion of such an accumulation was probably necessary for the idea of renunciation to be effective. The focus on the individual highlights the anomie of changing social relations: the breakup of clans as well as the alienation and skepticism was implicit in the new identities emerging in nascent urban centres.[53] This was to be further reinforced by the centrality of individual *nirvāṇa* in subsequent teachings, especially those of Mahāvīra and the Buddha.

If the reasons why the *kṣatriya* was supportive of this doctrine have to do with both philosophical curiosity and changes in social and political forms, these do not entirely explain its attraction for some *brāhmaṇa*s. A change in the focus of these ideas was to introduce a substantial Brahmānical concern. It is significant that not all *brāhmaṇa*s were familiar with the new doctrine: it was viewed initially as rather esoteric, meant only for the selected few. Those that supported it saw the limitations of the rituals and sought more innovative forms of liberation, even if these ultimately involved renunciation. The use of the vocabulary of release in relation to the soul may have been partially associated with release from social obligations as well. Did *brāhmaṇa*s view renunciation with a nostalgia for the nomadic life that was disappearing[54] or with a concern that radical ideas had to be introduced gradually and that renunciation would provide freedom to experiment with new ideas, a freedom not permitted by rigidly controlled rituals?

Sporadic but vague speculation on these matters has been traced to earlier Vedic compositions. The departure from them lay in the forging of a consistent theory for which the observance of the earlier rituals was not required. The construction of this theory has its own history. Shamanistic origins have been suggested[55] in references to *muni*s, *ṛṣi*s, and *késin*s,[56] the long-haired ones flying through the air, living in isolation and seeking their own forms of knowledge, which included magic and meditation. They were the forerunners of the renouncers and the ascetics. The *yātudhāna* may well have been shamans and therefore seen as sorcerers and alien by Vedic priests. The lengthy period of training under a teacher as envisaged in the *Upaniṣad*s required a desocialization from the family. Thus Śvetaketu left the home of his learned father and went elsewhere to attain knowledge.[57] Together with this, the secrecy of the doctrines is suggestive of shamanistic influence as are descriptions of the journeying of the soul.[58] The soul goes through the air, which opens out like a hole in the chariot wheel; it goes to the sun and moon; it journeys to the world of Brahmā, which is an elaborate movement through many heavens and multiple deities; it enters the clouds and then the rain, then plants and crops, which when eaten take it to the human body. The *ātman* can be larger than the universe and smaller than the mustard seed. The ecstatic state of the *ātman* when released from rebirth echoes shamanistic ecstasy when the spirit is said to be in communion with the divine.

These descriptions of the journeying of the soul and the idea of souls inhabiting plants and animals, were not, as many have pointed out, altogether alien to animistic views on the passage of the spirit.[59] If the archaeological picture of the Ganga plain provides a clue, it is that of a variety of coexisting and overlapping cultures. Fertility cults grew around the worship of trees and female deities often linked to sacred enclosures. The *stūpa* as a tumulus, perhaps with some funerary association,[60] may have drawn on ideas of a soul and an afterlife different from the Vedic. The proximity of megalithic burials in the Vindhyan region and central India indicates further the presence of non-Vedic religion. Cremation encourages a belief in an afterlife rather different from burials, which maintain greater continuity with the mundane. The reduction of the human body to a handful of ashes may have required, by way of a counterpoint, a focus on the disembodied soul and its continual reincarnation. Significantly, some *kṣatriya*s associated with the new doctrine belong to geographical areas often described as outside the boundaries of the *āryāvarta*, the land of the *ārya*s,[61] suggesting the need to incorporate other cultures.

The working out of the doctrine involved knowledge which moved from ritual to analytical and speculative argument but included meditation and contemplation.[62] Thus Sanatkumāra asks to be taught the knowledge of the *ātman*—knowledge that later was to be regarded as the higher knowledge as against the lower knowledge of the *Veda*s. The sage Uddālaka Aruni, conversing with his arrogant son, Śvetaketu, provides an explanation of *ātman* which is almost rational in its incorporation of empirical knowledge, of queries, of doubts, and of observation and in its attempts at making categories.[63]

Among the most subtle discussions of the *ātman* is the dialogue between Naciketas and Yama, the god of death.[64] The *ātman* is described as the charioteer of the body, which is the chariot, a strongly *kṣatriya* symbol.[65] *Mokṣa* was the releasing of the *ātman* from the cycle of repeated death, *punarmṛtyu*, because of being reincarnated in a body.[66] The notion of *mokṣa* as distinct from heaven introduced a change in the meaning of death in which the ideal was not a blissful life in the heaven of the heroes, but the release from being born repeatedly, a release requiring, among other things, an absence of desire. The breaking away from ritual and the search for knowledge about the soul and immortality led to other explorations of the self. But the theory was to be further formulated in a manner that linked it once more with social reality. This lay in the concept of *karma* and *saṃsara*, the actions of one's life determining the future rebirth of one's *ātman*, an idea further developed by Yājñavalkya, among others.[67]

At death, there are two possible paths that the soul can take. One is the *devayāna*, the path of the gods, taken by the soul of one who meditates, has knowledge of *brahman*, and does not have to undergo rebirth. The soul ascends by stages through the day, the bright fortnight of the month, the six-month period, the year, to the sun, the lightning, and on to *brahman*, never to return.[68] The other path, the *pitṛyāna*, the path of the ancestors, because of the ties to rituals and *karma*/actions, is a temporary residence for the soul, for, remaining on the moon until its *karma* is exhausted, the soul enters a new birth returning via the air, smoke, vapour, clouds, and rain into crops.[69] A mortal ripens like grain and like grain is born again.[70] Repeated rebirth is a form of retribution. And then comes the crucial question: What determines the rebirth of the soul in a particular body? To this the answer is that if the individual's life has been one of good actions then the soul is reborn among the higher castes—*brāhmaṇa*, *kṣatriya*, or *vaiśya*—but if the actions have been evil, then the choice of rebirth is among the lowly: the dog, the pig, or the *caṇḍāla*/the outcaste.[71] (The superiority of the *brāhmaṇa* and the *kṣatriya* and their interdependence is spoken of as epitomized in the relationship between Yājñavalkya and Janaka.)[72] There was a trace in this idea of the element of chance, since the soul entering a new body would have depended on who eats the plant, but this element of chance was denied by the increasing insistence on the ethical imperative.[73]

The answer to the next question, namely, 'Who determines good or bad conduct?' was, in later times and among some important sects, said to lie in the hands of those who prepared the norms of social behaviour—the *brāhmaṇa* authors of the *Dharmasūtras*. According to them release from rebirth was possible only by observing the *dharma* of caste. Those born among the upper castes could claim a virtuous previous life in accordance with the rules of *dharma*. The relegation of the *caṇḍāla* to the status of the despised assumed that the *caṇḍāla* was receiving the just merit of evil conduct in a previous life. *Dharma* now replaced the sacrifice as that which sustains the universe.

The explanation of social inequalities on the basis of transmigration could keep society under the control of those who pronounced on conduct. The irrelevance of *varṇa* status in the new doctrine was nullified by this explanation of social differentiation. At one level, what began as a search for an alternative path concerned with releasing the *ātman* was pursued as such. But in social practice it was also reduced to a means of controlling the less privileged and justifying their condition on ethical grounds of *karma*. Reincarnation and *karma* are logically separable since moral justice can be accorded in other ways, as the eschatology of various religions suggests. At the philosophical and religious level the theory of *karma* was to become a central marker differentiating Indian religions from Semitic religions. Much of what followed in discussions on the soul within the Indian tradition drew on this theory.

The formulation of the notion of *karma* was gradual and doubtless tapped a range of ideas emanating from the societies settled in the Ganga valley. Mention has been made of a tribal origin but this is too vague an entity.[74] The more plausible argument points toward elements of the ritual of *śrāddha*, possibly suggesting the kind of connections that became more evident in the concept of *karma*. The link with the idea of *punaramṛtyu* would have given way to that of the cycle of rebirth. The transfer of merit has also been traced to a variety of origins. Among these is the suggestion that the notion of *tyāga*, renouncing the fruits of activity, which became the essence of the sacrificial ritual, was carried over into the new teaching.[75]

These ideas also helped to marginalize another aspect of the sacrificial ritual. If transmigration included animals as possible recipients of the *ātman*, then the killing of animals in sacrificial rituals could not be approved of.[76] Although this is not made explicit, it is implied in the statements on the forms in which the *ātman* can be reborn. This established a precedent of *ahimsā* and not eating the flesh of animals.

The doctrine did not remain secret for very long. It was carried from place to place by wandering teachers, the *parivrājaka*s.[77] Inevitably, much of the post-Upaniṣadic thought traced itself to these teachers, who developed it in variant ways, some endorsing it and others opposing it. Frequently, the more prominent of the new teachers, such as Mahāvīra and the Buddha, were *kṣatriya*s, and the social aspects of the new philosophies were in part circumscribed by their caste concerns.[78] A later *Upaniṣad*, more conservative, is clear in its hostility to the contrary doctrines of those who wear the red robes and are opposed to the *Vedas*.[79] This was the birth of heterodoxy.

The theory of *ātman-brahman*, relating to the immortality of the soul and its release from the bonds of the body, was a philosophical innovation. By implication, it was a negation of the centrality of the prevalent sacrificial ritual. I have tried to argue that the search for an ideology independent of the sacrificial ritual may have had among its many interests the wish to conserve wealth. This was necessary for the transition from clan-based societies to states and kingdoms, in which the relative egalitarianism of the former gave way to social hierarchies and the enhanced power of the *kṣatriyas*. It is interesting that, in the oligarchies and in some kingdoms—the *gaṇa-rājyas*, *gaṇa-saṅghas*, and *rājyas*—of the subsequent period, where *kṣatriyas* were dominant, there is either an absence of sacrificial rituals of the Vedic variety or a decrease in their frequency. Nevertheless, the notion of transmigration as determined by the rules of caste reinstated the authority of the *brāhmaṇa*, even outside the sacrificial ritual, as pre-eminent among those determining the rules of conduct conducive to an improved rebirth. These were issues widely debated in post-Upaniṣadic times.

Arguing for a correlation between sacrifices, resources, and innovations in belief systems is not just an economic enterprise. It is an attempt to insist that ideologies are not history-free. In the complexities associated with Upaniṣadic and consequent ideas there are earlier features that were transmuted and others that were conditioned by contemporary needs. These may have coincided with the free-floating visions of the sages. Elements of embedded social contours in the sacrificial ritual should not be ignored in the larger explanation of philosophical speculations.

The universalizing of the doctrine influenced many sects and schools of thought that altered the intellectual landscape of early India. The centrality of the sacrificial ritual was displaced by the centrality of the notion of transmigration. This carried within it both the movement of the caterpillar from leaf to leaf and the mutation of the object of gold. The pursuit of comprehension of the immortality of the soul was intense. It moved from analytical arguments and discriminating discussions to a mystical idealism couched in poetically rich language. A different kind of immortality emanated from the discourses of the *Upaniṣads*, which themselves became a fountainhead for ideologies, some supportive and some dissenting, which fashioned much of subsequent Indian thought.

Notes and References

1. *Bṛhadāraṇyaka Upaniṣad* (hereafter cited as *Bṛ. Up.*), 4.4.3–4. Sarvepalli Radhakrishnan (ed.), *The Principal Upaniṣads*, London, 1953.

2. I am using the term discourse in its literal, dictionary meaning, namely, the discussion on a matter, and without reference to its extended meaning in recent works of critical theory.

3. Marc Bloch, *Ritual, History and Power*, London, 1989, pp. 113ff.

4. Jorge Larrain, *The Concept of Ideology*, London, Hutchinson, 1979, pp. 50ff; David McLellan, *Ideology*, Milton Keynes, England, 1986.

5. Frits Staal, 'The Meaninglessness of Ritual', *Numen* 26, fasc. 1 (1979), 1–22, and *Rules without Meaning*, New York, 1989, pp. 116–17.

6. For an attempted chronology of segments of the texts, see Walter Ruben, 'Die Philosophie de Upaniṣads', in *Geschicte der indischen Philosophie*, Berlin, 1954, pp. 113ff. There is a distinction between the early and the late *Upaniṣads* and the former include the ones that will be most frequently referred to here, namely, the *Bṛhadāraṇyaka* and the *Chāndogya Upaniṣads.*

7. Ruben, 'Die Philosophie de Upaniṣads'; Jan Gonda, *Change and Continuity in Indian Religion*, The Hague, 1965, p. 37; T.G. Goman and R.S. Laura, 'A Logical Treatment of Some Upaniṣadic Puzzles and Changing Conceptions of Sacrifice', *Numen* 19, no. 1 (1972), pp. 52–67.

8. Romila Thapar, 'The Study of Society' and 'Puranic Lineages and Archaeological Cultures', in *Ancient Indian Social History: Some Interpretations*, New Delhi, 1978, pp. 211ff, 240ff.

9. Madhav M. Deshpande and Peter E. Hook (eds), *Aryan and non-Aryan in India*, Ann Arbor, 1979; Murray B. Emeneau, 'Indian Linguistic Area Revisited', *International Journal of Dravidian Linguistics*, 3, no. 1 (1974), 93ff.

10. *Chāndogya Upaniṣad* (hereafter cited as *Ch. Up.*), 4.1.5.1ff.

11. Ibid., 4.4.5; *Bṛ. Up.*, 2.4.1ff, 4.5.3.

12. Only the *dvija* could perform the Vedic rituals *(Kātyāyaṇa Śrauta Sūtra*, 1.1.1ff).

13. *Bṛhaddevatā*, 4.11–15, 21–5; *Aitareya Brāhmaṇa*, 2.19; *Kauṣītaki Brāhmaṇa*, 12.3.

14. The *vaṃsa*, or succession list, was inflated to give it antiquity. Some of its members are sons, others are pupils, and sometimes the mother's name can provide an identity, as also can the social antecedents of the pupil (*Bṛ.*

Up., 2.6, 4.6.1ff). The line of teachers often traces itself from the present back to Brahmā.

15. *Bṛ. Up.*, 2.1.2, 3.1.1ff, 4.1.1, 6.2.1.7; *Ch. Up.*, 5.3.1.

16. *Muṇḍaka Up.*, 1.1.4–5.

17. *Bṛ. Up.*, 2.4.5, 4.4.7, 4.5.6ff; *Ch. Up.*, 3.14.1ff.

18. *Bṛ. Up.*, 4.4.13.

19. *Muṇḍaka Up.*, 1.1.5

20. *Ch. Up.*, 1.12.1ff; *Bṛ. Up.*, 1.5.16, 3.9.10–26; *Muṇḍaka Up.*, 1.2.9–13. Attempts have been made by modern scholars to argue that Western scholars and some Indians maintain that the *Upaniṣads* do not support the ritual of sacrifice and the worship of the Vedic deities, but that there are passages in the texts to the contrary. See B.K. Chattopadhyaya, 'Upaniṣads and Vedic Ritual', in S. *Mookerjee Felicitation Volume*, B.P. Sinha et al. (eds), Varanasi, 1969. However, such passages are few and far between.

21. *Ch. Up.*, 5.3.1–7, 5.11.1ff, 5.12.1ff; *Bṛ. Up.*, 2.1.14–15ff, 3.1.1ff.

22. *Bṛ. Up.*, 2.1.15; Paul Deussen, *The Philosophy of the Upaniṣads*, London, 1906; reprint, New York, 1966, p. 17; Arthur B. Keith, *Religion and Philosophy of the Vedas and Upaniṣads*, Harvard Oriental Series, Cambridge, 1925, p. 495.

23. *Bṛ. Up.*, 6.2.8; also *Ch. Up.*, 5.3.7.

24. *Bṛ. Up.*, 3.1.1, 3.9.19; *Śatapatha Brāhmaṇa* (hereafter cited as *Śat. Bṛ.*), 1.7.2.8, 3.2.3.15.

25. *Bṛ. Up.*, 3.1.1, 4.3.1ff, 6.2.1; *Ch. Up.*, 5.3.1.

26. Deussen, *Philosophy of the Upaniṣads*, p. 214.

27. *Bṛ. Up.*, 3.1.1ff.

28. *Mahāśālā mahā śrotriyaḥ*, *Ch. Up.*, 5.11.1ff; cf. *Dīgha Nikāya*, 1.235, Tevijjasutta.

29. *Ch. Up.*, 7.1.2.

30. Ibid., 4.1–3.

31. Buddhism, it has been argued, is a radical attack on the *ātmavāda* of the *Upaniṣads*. It opens up a new tradition by opposing theories of the unchanging, eternal soul, which lead to inaction and a refusal to better oneself. T.R.V. Murti, *The Central Philosophy of Buddhism*, 2nd ed., London, 1960; Pratap Chandra, 'Was Early Buddhism Influenced by the Upaniṣads?' *Philosophy East and West*, 21 (1971), pp. 317–24.

32. M. Beard and J. North (eds), *Pagan Priests*, London, 1990.

33. Raymond Firth, 'Offering and Sacrifice: Problems of Organisation', *Journal of the Royal Anthropological Institute*, 93, no. 1 (1963), pp. 12–24.

34. Staal, '*The Meaningless of Ritual*'.

35. Henri Hubert and Marcel Mauss, *Sacrifice: Its Nature and Function*, (trans.) W.D. Halls, London, 1964.

36. *Ch. Up.*, 5.3.7, 5.11.1ff; *Bṛ. Up.*, 2.1.15; *Śat. Bṛ.*, 11.6.2.10.

37. *Ṛg Veda*, 3.21.5; *Śat. Bṛ.*, 3.8.2.26–8; *Aitareya Brāhmaṇa*, 7.3.6.

38. *Vasiṣṭha Dharma Sūtra*, 1.45.

39. *Bṛhaddevatā*, 6.92; Romila Thapar, 'Dāna and Dakṣinā as Forms of Exchange', in *Ancient Indian Social History: An Interpretation*, pp. 105–21.

40. Yājñavalkya in *Śat. Bṛ.*, 3.1.2.21.

41. B.B. Lal, 'Excavations at Hastinapur and Other Explorations in the Upper Ganga and Satlej Basin', *Ancient India*, 10/11 (1954–55), p. 115. The formula for begetting learned sons involved eating rice cooked with veal or beef together with *ghī*. *Bṛ. Up.*, 6.4.18. One dreads to think of how few cows would survive in contemporary India should this formula have persisted!

42. *Śat. Bṛ.*, 13.2.9.8, 5.1.3.3, 12.7.3.12, 13.2.2.15. Gradually, this status came to include, although to a smaller extent, another category of *yajamānas*, namely, the *gṛhapatis*, or heads of households, who built their resources largely on the lands which they cultivated (ibid., 4.6.8.5).

43. Such as the *agrāyana-iṣṭi*, *cāturmāśa*, *piṇḍapitṛyajña*, and so on. Even more complex were the *agniṣṭoma*, *agnicāyana*, and the *sattras*.

44. *Aitareya Brāhmaṇa*, 7.34.

45. *Śat. Bṛ.*, 1.7.3.28, 4.3.4.7; *Pañcavimśa Bṛ.*, 1.8.2ff, 12.8.6; *Bṛ. Up.*, 6.2.7.

46. A.J. Strathern, *The Rope of Moka*, Cambridge, 1971, p. 11.

47. Chris A. Gregory, 'Gifts to Men and Gifts to Gods', *Man*, 15 (1980), pp. 626–52, and *Gifts and Commodities*, London, 1982.

48. Romila Thapar, *From Lineage to State*, Delhi, 1984, pp. 51ff.

49. Ibid., pp. 88–9.

50. Ibid. Earlier settlements were of the Painted Grey Ware and the Black-and-Red Ware cultures. The reaching out of the Northern Black Polished Ware, beginning in the seventh/sixth centuries BC, from its provenance between Patna and Varanasi to almost every part of the Ganga plain, suggests contacts, exchange, and increased production as compared to earlier periods. See T.N. Roy, *The Ganges Civilisation*, New Delhi, 1983; R.C. Gaur, *The Excavations at Antranjikhera*, Delhi, 1983; George Erdosy, *Urbanisation in Early Historical India*, BAR International Series, 430, Oxford, BAR, 1988.

51. *Bṛ. Up.*, 1.4.11.

52. Romila Thapar, 'Renunciation: The Making of a Counter-Culture?', in *Ancient Indian Social History: Some Interpretations*, Delhi, 1978.

53. Ibid., pp. 63ff, and 'Householders and Renouncers in the Brahmānical and Buddhist Tradition', in *Way of Life*, T.N. Madan (ed.), Delhi, 1982, pp. 273ff.

54. Frits Staal, *Exploring Mysticism*, Berkeley, 1975.

55. Walter Ruben, 'Schamanismus im alten Indien', *Acta Orientalia*, 18 (1940), pp. 164–205.

56. *Ṛg Veda*, 7.22.9, 10.14.15, 10.130, 10.136.

57. *Ch. Up.*, 6.1.1ff.

58. *Bṛ. Up.*, 5.10.

59. Erik af Edholm, 'The Colours of the Soul and the Origin of Karmic Eschatology', in S. Cederroth, C. Corlin and J. Lindstrom (eds), *On the Meaning of Death: Essays on Mortuary Rituals and Eschatological Beliefs*, Uppsala Studies in Cultural Anthropology, no. 8, Uppsala, Univ Acta Univ Uppsaliensis, Stockholm, 1988, pp. 95–111.

60. James C. Harle, *The Art and Architecture of the Indian Sub-continent*, London, 1986, p. 26.

61. *Śat. Br.*, 1.4.1.10ff.

62. Compare K.N. Jayatilleke, *Early Buddhist Theory of Knowledge*, London, 1963, p. 169.

63. *Ch. Up.*, 6.1ff.

64. *Kaṭha Up.*, 1.1.20–9.

65. *Kaṭha Up.*, 1.3.3.

66. *Bṛ. Up.*, 4.4.3–5; *Ch. Up.*, 5.10.7.

67. *Bṛ. Up.*, 3.2.13, 4.4.1ff; *Ch. Up.*, 5.3–10; *Śat. Bṛ.*, 3.7.4.4.

68. *Bṛ. Up.*, 6.2.15ff; *Ch. Up.*, 4.15.5, 5.10.1ff.

69. *Ch. Up.*, 5.10.3ff. The moon is the lord of seasons, therefore the soul goes beyond the natural rhythms. See Wilhelm Halbfass, *Tradition and Reflection*, Albany, N.Y., 1991. The distinctive symbolism of the sun and the moon was to remain dichotomous in many spheres of Indian thought.

70. *Kaṭha Up.*, 1.1.6.

71. *Ch. Up.*, 5.10.7.

72. *Bṛ. Up.*, 1.4.11, 4.1.1ff.

73. *Ch. Up.*, 5.10.7.

74. Gananath Obeyesekere, 'Theodicy, Sin and Salvation in a Sociology of Buddhism', in Edmund Leach, *Dialectic in Practical Religion*, Cambridge, 1968, pp. 7–40.

75. Frits Staal, *Agni: The Vedic Ritual of the Fire Altar*, vol. 1, Berkeley, 1980.

76. This could usefully be compared with the Greek text of Porphyry dating to the third-fourth centuries AD and the discussion of whether animals have souls, a theme and text that were suggested to me by Richard Sorabjee. See Porphyry, *On Abstinence from Animal Food*, T. Taylor (trans.), London, 1965.

77. *Bṛ. Up.*, 3.3.1.

78. Of the Buddhas who are said to have preceded Gautama, most were *kṣatriyas*.

79. *Maitrī Upaniṣad*, 7.8ff. Interestingly, elsewhere the term for a dissenter is *avaidika*.

CHAPTER 13

The Householder and the Renouncer in the Brahmanical and Buddhist Traditions*

In the discussion on the four *āśramas* as theoretical preconditions to the concept of *puruṣārtha* there has been a tendency to treat the *āśramas* as chronos-free, floating as it were in historical space. The theory has been analysed and its structure viewed essentially from the perspective of belief systems and rituals in a broadly Brahmanical context. It might, however, prove rewarding to consider that the theory has a historical specificity, and to view it as an ideology which is pertinent to and is interlinked with a historical situation; that the theory was elaborately formulated long after the idea of *āśramas* was first articulated and in its practice also, historical changes are very noticeable; and that these changes were evident particularly in the institutions which accompanied the theory.

Such an analysis requires that the *āśrama* theory be seen not as an isolate but as one segment in a larger ideological whole. A consideration of its relation to other facets of the perspective on man and his life as viewed by a variety of belief systems would not be out of place. The range of the latter is obviously vast; and two among them have been selected in terms of a methodological exercise for consideration, the Brahmanical and the Buddhist both having been major movements at the time. To see the theory only in Brahmanical terms is to leave out the context within which it developed. To separate the two

* This essay was originally published in *Contributions to Indian Sociology*, n.s., vol. 15, nos 1 & 2, 1981, pp. 272–98.

traditions in viewing the ideological concerns of the mid-first millennium BC is to pull a historiographical situation out of alignment. Historically in the initial stages, the Brahmanical and Buddhist world views presented both a dialectical and an interface relationship. Within this the notion of *āśrama* and its implications read as distinct ideological formulations relating to problems perceived in common by both. Sociological writing on India has drawn heavily on the Indological tradition which in turn has concerned itself substantially with the Brahmanical world view overlooking the fact that from the mid-first millennium BC to the mid-first millennium AD, the period when theories such as those of the *āśramas* and *puruṣārtha* were expressed and crystallized as ideals, was a period when Buddhism was, if not the dominant belief system in northern India, certainly as important as Brahmanism. The separation of the two stems in part from the decline of Buddhism in India from the second millennium AD and the tendency, therefore, to underestimate its significance for earlier times. An overly synchronic view of Indian society tends to obliterate the strands which go into the weaving of the present from the past.

The two stages of householder and renouncer have been viewed in recent writings as binary opposites.[1] It has been argued that whereas *gṛhastha* was oriented to reciprocity viewing life as a series of interactions with others, renunciation denied reciprocity and to this extent it denied a major focus in Hindu social action. Indian society, it is said, constrains the individual and renunciation alone allows the individual to be independent and liberated from the fetters of life. It is said that the renouncer was not concerned with changing the social order but being outside it. In a holistic society individualism has to be a condition of opposition to such a society.[2] It is, however, debatable whether the seeming dichotomy between householder and renouncer is as much of a binary opposition as has been made out; or whether the main thrust of the *āśrama* theory was to reduce the absolute dichotomy by introducing an interplay of the dialectic of the householder and the renouncer in each of the *āśramas* but with one being given greater prominence over the other. In other words, the binary opposition was not posed in the formulation of the theory of the *āśramas* but in the content of each of the four. Nor is the dichotomy absolute. The joining of an order by the renouncer often brought him back into performing a social role. This not only reduced the claim to individualism but also involved him in trying to change the social order. It is not accidental that socio-political reformers in India have frequently appropriated the symbols of the renouncer.[3]

The debate on renunciation, which is in many ways the focal point in both traditions, has centred on the question of whether the ideal of *saṃnyāsa* and that of the *bhikkhu* evolved independently at a particular historical conjuncture or whether the one was influenced by the other.[4] The counter-posing of the *gṛhastha*, *gahapati*/householder to the *saṃnyāsin*, *bhikkhu*/renouncer, is worked out in the form of the four *āśramas* in the Brahmanical tradition. Buddhist views pose the opposition more sharply and in essence it is reduced to two. The counter-position relates to the dialectic of attachment and non-attachment to a worldly life. In the four *āśramas*, *brahmacarya* is a stage in preparation towards the passage to the other three and swings from *gṛhastha* to *saṃnyāsa* in the symbolism of its rituals. Whereas the guru simulates the renouncer, the guru's house harks back to the setting of the householder. *Gṛhastha* is obviously the stage of the householder, but he has to aid the renouncer with alms and hospitality and is constantly aware of his obligations to the renouncer as indeed the renouncer when he intervenes in social action, as many do on occasion by demonstrating their powers, is reiterating the interplay. The location of hermitages in the vicinity of settlements points to a degree of participation in social life which cannot be taken as the renouncer making a total break from society. *Vānaprastha* is more directly a preparation for *saṃnyāsa*. It could be argued that the choice of four stages was a spelling out of the two, but that this was not entirely arbitrary. It may have been inspired by the need to conform to the four of the *varṇas* particularly useful in the model of the *varṇāśramadharma*; or perhaps that there was symbolic convenience in the number four; or that in the stretching out to four it offered choices of a kind more in keeping with the Brahmanical tradition.

Not only does the Buddhist traditions pose more sharply the dialectic of attachment and non-attachment but encourages a choice between the two, thus laying the emphasis on an implicit opposition. However, even in the Buddhist tradition the interplay is discernible. The *gahapati* has to maintain the *bhikkhu*, a relationship which is echoed in the later *Dharmaśāstras*. Even the *bhikkhu* in the monastery had eventually to choose between a greater involvement with the village or a retirement into seclusion. The *āśrama* theory seeks to ameliorate this problem of choice by converting it into a lifecycle within a lifetime, thus eliminating the need to choose at an early stage and also permitting the problem of choice to resolve itself into a given curriculum, or else occurring late in life when the extremity of the choice is less severe. The central point of the *āśramas* is not, however, the individual lifecycle so much as the concern with social obligations. The Brahmanical tradition further underlines the priority of social obligations by making *saṃnyāsa* the final stage, subsequent to the performance of social obligations. However, this does not preclude the taking up of *saṃnyāsa* at an early stage in life since this is the terminal *āśrama.*

The earliest exposition of the *āśrama* ideal as a theory is found in the *Dharmasūtras* which although they cannot be precisely dated were certainly texts of the post-Vedic period and composed in a period probably contemporary with, and in some cases subsequent to, Buddhist teaching.[5] There is no uniformity in the *Dharmasūtras* with regard to terms used for the four stages, although a broad conceptual agreement regarding three or four stages in a lifecycle is expressed. Thus Baudhāyana refers to the last two as *vānaprastha* and *parivrājaka* (II.11.14). Gautama refers to *brahmacāri*, *gṛhastha*, *bhikṣu*, and *vaikhānasa* (III.2). Āpastamba seems to suggest that after the period of *brahmacarya* it is possible to proceed to any of the following stages, *gṛhastha*, *acāryakula mauna*, *vānaprastya* (II.21.1). The early *Dharmasūtras* maintain that there is really only one *āśrama*, that of *gṛhastha.* The others are inferior to it as they do not permit the begetting of offspring.[6] The usage of describing the four *āśramas* as *brahmacarya*, *gṛhastha*, *vānaprastha*, and *saṃnyāsa* took a little time in becoming standardized. Pāṇini, generally dated to the fifth or fourth century BC, refers indirectly to the different *āśramas* but not to the theory as an entity.[7]

The notion of renunciation was however prevalent earlier than the period of the composition of the *Dharmasūtras*. It has been argued that renunciation may have been common among those not identified with Vedic society and the *yatis*, *munis*, and *śramaṇas* are quoted as among the earliest renouncers.[8] The association of renunciation with those who meditated on death and the link between repeated birth and death conditioned by attachment to desire, is a theme familiar to the *Upaniṣads*[9] although the link through the soul being reincarnated was not developed until a later period. Renunciation was seen as an important if not necessary precondition to an escape from death and rebirth. In the search for *mokśa*, the efficacy of *yajñas* was doubted, knowledge, meditation, and renunciation being seen as more viable methods. Reference is made to the three *skandhas* which may have been an early groping towards the theory of *āśramas* since they are described as *tapas*, *brahmacarya*, and absolute control over the body. Of the renouncers, the *śramaṇas* are frequently mentioned, and often they held views contrary to those of the *brāhmaṇas*. That there was intense hostility between the *brāhmaṇas* and the *śramaṇas* is reflected in the metaphor of describing them as having a natural antipathy such as between the snake and mongoose.[10] The hostility was in part due to the ideological negation of Brahmanical practices by the *śramaṇas* and their opting out of social obligations. The division is also referred to in Buddhist sources where the *brāhmaṇas* are described as being of two kinds, those who perform rites and those who meditate and are renouncers.[11] The *śramaṇas* as renouncers were also opposed to the *brāhmaṇas* as performers of the *yajña* and recipients of *dāna*. The *brāhmaṇas* were to develop the notion that in return for *dāna* they took upon themselves the sins of their *yajamānas*, thus entangling themselves further in social obligations. This was anathema to the renouncer, who even when he joined a sectarian order and thereby took upon himself at least minimal social obligations, was never as seeped as the *brāhmaṇa* in such obligations.

A suggestion of another kind, attempting to explain renunciation, has been offered in the argument that some cultures obliterate certain kinds of emotions as, for example, those of intense loneliness, by denying them public expression. It is said that the Indian environment encourages a flight from emotional involvement[12] and withdrawal from entanglements with the world. Asceticism is valued as a condition which denies the expression of passion in any form. Renunciation is born from the need to escape pain.[13] Such an explanation raises questions of a culture's articulation and would be viable in a few cases of renunciation where this specific reason is given by the individual renouncer. But it would not hold true either for *saṃnyāsa* as the final *āśrama* or for the compulsions which led *śramaṇa*s to organize themselves into sectarian orders or indeed which led to the rank and file joining such orders.

Degrees of social obligations were also written into the four *āśrama*s by the linking of this theory with that of *varṇa* and the labelling of both as *dharma*. The implication of the latter would suggest that they were regarded partially as incumbent on those *dvija*s who were concerned both with observing social obligations and attempting to attain to *mokśa*. Alternatively insofar as the *varṇa-dharma* was the theory of the ordering of society, the *āśrama-dharma* was also to be taken not literally, but as a theory towards the ordering of the individual lifecycle. However *āśrama*s and *varṇa*s do not form a vertical and horizontal grid for the entire range of society since the *āśrama* curriculum is only open to the *dvija* and consequently applies to and is the concern of a relatively smaller segment of the social whole.

Even within the *dvija* its actual applicability is limited almost to the *brāhmaṇa* caste. The *kṣatriya*s are also included within this curriculum but, in fact, the *kṣatriya* had his own *puruṣārtha* as we know from other sources. The ideal lifestyle of the *kṣatriya* falls back upon earlier heroic models of the warrior and the protector, in short the *vīra* or hero. Even when the connotation of *kṣatriya* changed from warrior to landowner and gift-giving (*dāna*) became as important as protecting, heroism remained an aspect of the ideal *kṣatriya* function. It drew on the pre-*āśrama* period of a lineage-based society in which the mores of the clan chiefs and their families were the norm and these certainly bypassed the *āśrama* theory and continued to be maintained in the widely dispersed and well-attested cult of the hero, as is evident from the numerous herostones (*vīragal*, *pāliya*, *kīrti-stamḥha*) found liberally scattered in various parts of the subcontinent from the first millennium AD. The 'good' death for the hero was that he should die defending himself, his kinsmen and their property. Such a death ensured eternal life in heaven, accompanied by his wife should she have become a *satī* on his death. In some cases the hero was deified by his kinsmen and community. So consistent is this pattern that it can legitimately be spoken of as an actual *kṣatriya āśrama* and it is curious that it was ignored in the *āśrama* model if the purpose of the model was even minimally to include varying lifestyles. This may have been due in part to the model excluding the clan-based society subscribing to heroic values, since the social milieu of the *āśrama* was that of peasant and urban society.[14]

The appeal of renunciation as envisaged in the *āśrama* theory would have been limited to the upper castes. If the texts relating to those who opted out and became renouncers, the *Upaniṣads* and the *Āranyakas*, provide any clues then clearly this option was open to *brāhmaṇas* and *kṣatriyas* in the main. The renouncers were not the sorcerers and the magic men of the earlier pastoral society but were those who had deliberately chosen to dissociate themselves from the beliefs, rituals, and social obligations of a complex society with the aim of discovering an alternate path to salvation because of disillusionment with the existing ways.

In analysing the reasons for the growth of renunciation at this time, it has been suggested that it was partially the result of the disorientation which followed on the break-up of clan-based society with the emergence of urban centres and the authority of state systems.[15] Nostalgia for the clan may have led to the particular organization of Buddhist and Jaina monasteries, where many of the ecclesiastical terms—*saṅgha*, *kula*, *gaṇa*—originate in the *gaṇa-saṅgha* chiefships of the middle Ganga valley. Alternatively, the *gaṇa-saṅgha* system provided a model for organizing such sects, especially as the founders and other important members of the *saṅgha* were from the Śakya, Jñātrika, Vajji and other such *gaṇa-saṅgha* clans. Parallels are frequently drawn between the structure of the monasteries and that of the *gaṇa-saṅgha* system.[16] The monasteries were seen ideally as egalitarian sanctuaries in an otherwise increasingly hierarchical society dominated by the monarchical state.

Urbanization in the Ganga valley in the mid-first millennium BC encouraged the growth of scepticism and sophistry among the wandering renouncers who roamed through the towns teaching their doctrines. This was, however, a later phase of an enquiry which had begun earlier in the variant ways suggested in the quest for *mokśa*. Within these suggestions can be traced an element of dissent which was crucial to the comprehension of the role of renouncers in society.

The theme of dissent originates in the questioning of revealed knowledge with a preference for perceived knowledge and in the exploration of other methods of comprehending the universe.[17] The ritual of sacrifice was found to be inadequate and was substituted by *tapas* and *dhyāna*. The change from *yajña* to *tapas* and *dhyāna* was in itself a shift from participation in a public ritual, meticulously prescribed, to a more personalized quest for an open though arduous method of individual and private articulation. But the very isolation of the renouncer from public performance imbued him with a charisma which was to be most effective in its public role. The liberty given to the renouncer to question the *Vedas* was the thin end of the wedge leading to a much wider range of questioning. The expression of dissent and protest was one element in renunciation but the joining of an order or sect could and did modify if not nullify the social content of the protest.[18] Those who joined sects and returned to preach in villages and towns had a social counterpart to their search for release from rebirth as is evident from the Buddhist view of the relationship between the householder and the renouncer. The questioning of revealed knowledge and the dependence on *yajña* for salvation coincided with the gradual erosion of the prestation economy central to the *yajña* ritual. Whereas the protagonists of the *Upaniṣads* merely opted out of the system, those who were members of what have been called the 'heterodox' sects, further threatened the slowly receding faith in the *yajña* ritual among the householders: a faith which was partially restored by the use of the Vedic sacrifice as a ritual of legitimation in the monarchical states. The householder as the performer, preserver, and guardian of the sacrificial ritual became the counterpoint to the renouncer who denied both the ritual and the social role of the one who preserved it.

The questioning of knowledge is an enterprise in which few take part. The direction of the quest was more restrictive, focus as it did on doctrines of release—these being essentially metempsychosis and rebirth. The latter is touched upon obliquely in the *Bṛhadāraṇyaka Upaniṣad* as also in references to the idea of birth and death as a repetitive cycle. The concepts of *karma* and *saṃsāra* are developed more fully in Buddhist thought and become central to the Brahmanical tradition in the period after the Buddha had taught, when expiation for the present and preparation for a new birth becomes a major concern. Nevertheless the notion of heaven and hell remain a part of the popular imagery of the after-life and become substratum ideas often interwoven into the overarching theme of *karma* and *saṃsāra.* Renunciation is never aimed at the attaining of heaven, but has as its goal release from rebirth taking the more abstract form of *mokśa.* Ultimately such an appeal could again be directed only to the limited few.

Renouncers, unconcerned with preaching their ideas to others and content either with a solitary existence or at most the company of others such as themselves, moved to forest retreats away from towns and villages, although close enough for the townsmen to know of their existence and if need be for them to supply alms. That this was not an ideal but an actuality is evident from among other sources, the descriptions of such groups met with by Greeks visiting India either in the entourage of Alexander of Macedon or as ambassadors of his successors in West Asia.[19] The hermitages referred to in Indian sources, set in forest clearings, were often the vanguard of the colonization of the area by settlers of agriculturists with or without state backing. Such hermitages were often under attack by those who claimed the forest as their territory or hunting ground.[20]

In the dialectical relationship between the householder and the renouncer a crucial question related to when a man could opt out of his social obligations as a householder and become a renouncer. Buddhist and Jaina views did not stipulate *gṛhastha* as necessary, Some among them argued that it was necessary to forego the stage of *gṛhastha* so that renunciation becomes a truly parallel stream. The authors of the *Dharmasūtra*s insisted on *gṛhastha* as a precondition arguing that this made it more difficult to renounce the worldly life.[21] In these circles the debate hinged on the individual and the problem posed for the individual in the process of renunciation. In the *Dharmasūtra*s the question of whether *brahmacārin* could proceed directly to *saṃnyāsa* and bypass the stage of *gṛhastha* was linked to the performance of one's social obligations. It may have been for this reason that there was also a difference of opinion as to whether *saṃnyāsa* should be restricted to *brāhmaṇa*s.[22] It is frequently stated that *gṛhastha* is both crucial and necessary almost to the point of suggesting that true renunciation can only be attained once one has passed through the stage of *gṛhastha*,[23] which makes renunciation all the more arduous. This insistence may have been an attempt to counteract the entry into monkhood at a young age which was being encouraged by Buddhists and Jainas. Renunciation coming after the completion of *gṛhastha*, would minimally affect the performance of social obligations. The bypassing of *gṛhastha* carried the danger of a decline in the performance of *yajña*s which would have been a serious curtailment of *dāna* for the *brāhmaṇa*s and an erosion of the status and power of the Brahmanical tradition. In terms of social dissent too it would be a muffled protest. The possibility of its encouraging an alternate form of social organization is guarded against by the insistence on celibacy. A curious reference in the *Baudhāyana Dharmasūtra*[24] states that the renunciatory stages were the creation of an *asura* who wished to annoy the gods, since if men took to renunciation the gods would lose the offerings of the *yajña*s. This would point indirectly to, perhaps, an initial disapproval of renunciation and the possibility that it had to be conceded somewhat grudgingly. However, once it was conceded, it was taken up with great eclat.

Each of the *āśrama*s is characterized by three phases which may be described as initiation, liminality, and reintegration. Initiation was into a condition different from the previous one. Liminality related to the current *āśrama* carrying traces of the earlier one and a foretaste of the later. Reintegration completed the process and provided a new context and identity to the individual.

The ritual required for the *brahmacārin* was both a preparation for *gṛhastha* but also a taste for *saṃnyāsa*, thus suggesting that the essential dichotomy was the opposition between the *gṛhastha* and the *saṃnyāsin*. The *upanayana* or initiation of the male child was his formal entry into caste status and reflects an earlier ritual of initiation into the clan. Subsequent to the *upanayana* the boy was introduced to the first *āśrama* where he was placed under the tutelage of a guru or *ācārya* symbolizing a spiritual father and reiterating his second birth and thus confirming his *dvija* status.[25] The emphasis therefore was on the transition from one status to another, non-*dvija* to *dvija*. The boy is regarded as a *śūdra* before the *upanayana*, a polluting category from which he emerges into *dvija* status. The *āśrama* theory was therefore also a social marker in which the *dvija* status was continually emphasized and a demarcation made through rituals of the separation from the *śūdra*s and others. It anticipates renunciation by removing the boy from his familiar social milieu to the hermitage of the guru. The purification required was partly to do with the fact that biological birth is polluting and the pollution can only be fully removed by a second birth, the initiation into *varṇa* status and *brahmacarya*, an initiation which affected not merely the individual boy but also his place in the social matrix, his social status. The *brahmacārin* stage is a period of preparation requiring a study of the *Veda*s (the corpus of authoritative and revealed knowledge); the precepts of moral behaviour often strikingly similar to those which governed the life of renouncers; and the practice of austerity.

The *brahmacārin*'s vows,[26] such as celibacy, tending the guru and bringing him alms daily, sleeping on the bare ground and strict dietary rules are similar to the rules for novice monks in Buddhist monasteries. Celibacy and the prohibitions regarding the guru's wife emphasize the separation from women and the domestic sphere, which of course, is reintroduced by contrast in the *gṛhastha* stage. The begging for alms (*bhikṣā*) would suggest that the guru's hermitage was in the vicinity of settlements and that the latter were in a position to support such hermitages. Evidently the forest here does not refer to the virtually inaccessible deep forest, but rather the *araṇya* or waste land on the edges of settlements. The *brahmacārin* is invested with a staff (*daṇḍa*) which becomes an essential item for both the *saṃnyāsin* and the *bhikkhu*, so essential that some renouncers are referred to as *maskarin*, the bearers of the staff.

Recognizable differences in clothing and appurtenances as well as the period of stay were stipulated on the basis of caste differencitiation.[27] To this extent there is dissimilarity with the novitiate period of monkhood. The Vedic texts studied were inevitably those of the *śākhā* to which the guru belonged, the particular *śākhā* thus receiving some secular support in terms of an investment in students who as householders would continue to be well-disposed towards their guru and his *śākhā*. The curriculum is suggestive of preparation for discourse rather than for householding and those who returned to their social obligations terminated the stage of *brahmacārin* earlier than the stipulated number of years. The highpoint of the termination ceremony was the ritual bath, hence the use of the term *snātaka*, and a mock triumphant return to the village and home from where the *brahmacārin* had originally set out. The first *āśrama* is rather like a prolonged initiation ritual with some preparation for the immediate future but with a stronger foretaste of the ultimate goal. It is characterized by separation from the social context, a period of liminality followed by a reintegration into the social context. The preparation provides an understanding of the social role of the householder in upholding the Brahmanical mores and tradition through sacrifices and the maintenance of the *brāhmaṇa*.

Marriage initiates the second *āśrama* of *gṛhastha*. Both Brahmanical and Buddhist sources continually stress the importance of this *āśrama* but for different reasons. The *Dharmasūtras* maintain that it is the most important stage because the other three are dependent on it.[28] Its prime function is the continuation of the family and the perpetuation of the *gṛhya* or domestic rituals. It is only the house-holding stage which permits of offspring and the successful householder provides material support for the others. The fire used for the marriage ritual is maintained without a break throughout the lifetime of the *gṛhastha* or as long as he remains in that condition, a custom which echoes that of the tending of the sacred fire by the kin members in clan-based societies.[29] The family fire was used for the various *yajña*s associated with rites of passage rituals, expiatory ceremonies, seasonal sacrifices, ceremonies dedicated to the ancestors, and the worship of the quarters—in short all the rituals of a temporal and spatial context. The life of the *gṛhastha* was punctuated by actions relating to social obligations and few demands of an individual nature.

The two categories of people who can always draw on the householders' respect and hospitality were the *śrotrīya brāhmaṇa* and the guest (*atithi*),[30] and often the two were identical. Generous hospitality would in such circumstances provide a means of indirect support for the *brāhmaṇa*s, as indirect but highly effective as the performance of endless daily and seasonal sacrifices. The *gṛhapati* was the mainstay of the prestation economy in a situation of sedentary agriculture and where not every *brāhmaṇa* had access to the royal court and could enjoy the *dāna* emanating from the performance of royal sacrifices. The necessity of performing the *gṛhya* rituals was emphasized doubtless in part because the system of prestations was required to be maintained since the *brāhmaṇa*s at least were dependent on it. Domestic rituals were also closely related to the household as a socio-economic unit, a self-sufficient body in terms of its daily needs since agricultural activities and minimal artisanal needs were controlled by the household. The rituals served to reiterate the status of each person in the household and more particularly, the head of the household as indeed the *āśrama* theory served to demarcate the *dvija* family from its *śūdra* servants, slaves and retainers. The *atithi*, the one who does not stay permanently, was honoured as part of the code of honouring guests, but not anyone could claim this status and it was necessary to ascertain the identity of the guest before accepting him into the household. Hospitality to the guest was part of the wider system of being able to support 'the other'.

Buddhist texts focus more closely on the *gahapati*/householder in his social milieu and the householder is perhaps given even greater importance than in the Brahmanical tradition. It often includes the *upāsaka*s or lay-followers and these are contrasted with the *bhikkhus* who are the renouncers. The householder is the source of *dāna*, the gift-giving which maintains the *saṅgha.* Since the *saṅgha* is an institutionalized body of renouncers it is dependent for its maintenance on the lay-followers. The householder and the renouncer, therefore, are counter-weights to each other in social balance and there is a clear cut distinction between the two. The institution of the *saṅgha* makes the pendant relationship much sharper than in the Brahmanical tradition. The householder is the source of recruitment to the monkhood since the monks are celibate. Support is extended by giving of alms and of donations of a material kind. This implies that it was the prime duty of the householder to ensure that he had access to wealth at all times. *Dāna* was, therefore, visualized as the giving of gifts but also the observing of certain rules of behaviour which as an ethic provided the basis of the accumulation of wealth.

Because of this it was necessary that the prestation economy in which wealth was destroyed in the rituals or else was given towards the maintenance of *brāhmaṇa*s, be substituted by a code in which wealth could be conserved if not enhanced so that it could be donated not only to individual renouncers but to the institution as well. Not only was the conservation of wealth discouraged in the Brahmanical system but commercial wealth was despised since it was based on the repeated investment of wealth. The *saṅgha* on the contrary encouraged commercial wealth and investment, the ensuing surplus being required to support the institution of monks. The *yajña*, therefore, was replaced by an ethical code encouraging austerity and ensuring the conservation of wealth. The *gṛhastha* who opted out and became a monk was in a sense terminating a source of support for the *saṅgha* and this contradiction was sought to be solved by the concession made to the *upāsaka* who could attain merit without becoming a *bhikkhu*, although in the ultimate stage renunciation would be inevitable. The Buddhist tradition demanded austerity from the *gahapati* to ensure the continuance of wealth. Although it nowhere approached the condition of *tapas* it did encourage an empathy for renunciation, since wealth was not to be enjoyed hedonistically but was to be produced in order to provide *dāna* to the *saṅgha* and to meet social obligations. Such austerity is not enjoined upon the *gṛhastha* in the Brahmanical tradition. The good householder was constantly aware of the merit of alms-giving which has priority in the list of exalted qualities.[31] The *upāsaka* is one who conforms to the five virtues and abstains from taking life, stealing, lust, lying, and intoxicants. He strives for his own welfare and that of others. The Buddha's teaching appeals to one who has few desires, is contented, secluded, energetic, composed, and wise. Gift-giving can ensure rebirth in an easier life such as that of a wealthy *kṣatriya*, *brāhmaṇa*, or *gahapati*, surrounded by luxury: or alternatively a life in heaven. The threat of rebirth in animal form or the tortures of hell are held out to those who are niggardly in their *dāna* to the *bhikkhu* or the *saṅgha.*

Dāna as virtue is clarified in the Buddha's discourse to the householder Sigāla.[32] The replacing of ritual by ethical action is clearly stated when the Buddha tells him that the worship of the quarters does not consist of prescribed rituals but the avoidance of the fourteen evils of life. These are listed as the four vices in conduct: slaughtering life, stealing, lying, and adultery; the four evil motives of action, partiality, hate, fear, and dullness; and the six channels for dissipating wealth, the taking of intoxicants, roaming the streets at unseemly hours, going to fairs and festivals, gambling, keeping evil friends, and idleness. It is significant that these are listed specifically as ways of dissipating wealth. Some of them result in harm to the family and to property and both of these have to be protected by the householder and are of course crucial to the continuity of social obligations and the maintenance of the *saṅgha.*

Family and property are again the crux of the ethic in the details of virtuous behaviour, and social obligations are spelt out in the description of what constitutes the worship of the four quarters from a non-Brahmanical perspective. The west is worshipped through the mutual concern of husbands and wives for each other and where the wife runs the daily business of the household deputizing for her husband, and she is enjoined upon in doing so to safeguard the property of her husband. The north relates to clansmen and friends who are to be treated with generosity and benevolence. The eastern quarter is reserved for parents and the wider family. The southern quarter involves the care of one's teacher through respectful behaviour and diligence in learning. The substitute for the worship of the nadir revolves around relations between the master and his servants where the humane treatment of servants encourages them to work fully and loyally. The zenith symbolizes the wider relationship between the householder and the *śramaṇa*s and *brāhmaṇa*s, where the central concern is that he is to supply their needs and they in turn will guide him towards meritorious actions and heaven. Family and property are further emphasized when the Buddha states that the amassing of wealth is required of the good layman for it is through this that he benefits his clan. The procedure for amassing wealth is described as spending a quarter of one's income on daily living, keeping another quarter in reserve, and investing the remaining half in an enterprise which will result in monetary profit. Family and private property were believed to be crucial to the evolution of human society and the state according to Buddhist theory and they emerged from a pristine utopian beginning in which both were initially absent. To the extent that the *gahapati* upholds family and property he is in a sense upholding the need for social sanctions and the authority of the state. By the same token the renouncer breaking away from family and private property represents a return to the pristine condition.

The third *āśrama*, that of *vānaprastha*, is referred to by many synonyms such as *vaikhānasa*, *parivrājakā*, and *bhikṣu* and probably included the 'hylobioi' of Megasthenes.[33] The use of a number of terms points to a wide variety of renouncers conforming to degrees of renunciation seen as part of the social scene. The differences appear to have been partly doctrinal and partly based on varied observances, both of which overlapped to a greater or lesser extent from one group to another, covering a range from gentle isolation to a fierce regime of asceticism. The category, therefore, seems to refer more to the present of 'opters out' in society than to a specific and identifiable stage in life. The *vānaprastha* is required to live in the forest but can take his wife with him. There is a heavy emphasis on dietary rules which largely confined him to what he could collect in the forest.[34] He has to avoid living in or near inhabited places except in the period of the rains thus echoing the *vassa* period of Buddhist monks who were also permitted closer contact with settled areas during this time of year. The *vānaprastha* may continue to perform, but in a modified fashion, some of the rituals of the *gṛhastha*, thus requiring in some cases that the sacrificial fire of the household be maintained even in the forest retreat. His clothing was restricted to the minimum. Nakedness or at least a change of clothing is important to all baptismal rituals. His head was shorn according to some texts or, alternatively, he refrained from cutting his hair. He prepared himself for the fourth and final stage through study and meditation, but if this was not his ambition he could terminate his life by living only on water and air and dying of slow starvation—an ideal which recalls the death enjoined upon Jaina monks.

Vānaprastha, therefore, was seen as a transition from *gṛhastha* to *saṃnyāsa* and as with all transitional stages is not very clearly defined. True renunciation was seen as *saṃnyāsa.* A distinct ceremony marked the entry into the fourth and final stage and is defined by a complete break of ties with family, property, and society and takes on the symbolic form of a death ritual. *Saṃnyāsa*, therefore, is a much more definitive action involving major changes than is *vānaprastha.* In a sense the would-be *saṃnyāsin* undergoes an ex-communication ceremony but he is not regarded as defiling because although he breaks all social taboos he does so ritually and he exiles himself not out of having sinned but voluntarily. It was regarded as a worthy end to one who had fulfilled his social obligations. He takes the vows of the ascetic, abstention from injuring the living, from lying, from stealing, and conformity to continence and to liberality. He is permitted to accept alms from either *brāhmaṇa*s or *dvija*s although in some texts even this is not permitted. That the isolation was not total in most cases is suggested by the term used by Pāṇini for ascetics. The *bhikṣu* is distinguished from the *tapasvin.*[35] Some follow the *bhikṣu-sūtras* and are differentiated from others such as the *maskari parivrājakā*.[36] The fact of renunciation did not mitigate the competition among renouncers and their claims to have discovered the true path to salvation. The distinction among ascetic orders had to do with techniques for attaining *mokṣa* and less with ritual status. The initiation of the Buddhist monk was the *pabbajja/parivrājakā* ceremony, literally the 'going out' and since it could be undertaken at any age permission was sought from kinsmen to ensure that social obligations would not preclude the opting out.[37]

In the counterposing of the householder to the renouncer the major obligations and characteristics of the one were deliberately and systematically negated by the other.[38] Initiation into *gṛhastha* was through the marriage ritual which is negated by the insistence of celibacy among renouncers. The *gṛhastha* was expected to build his life around the rearing of a family, observing the social norms required by the fact of living amidst others, worshipping his ancestors at the time of *śrāddha*, protecting and enhancing his property and labouring on his profession. The renouncer denied all this through the ritual by which he entered *saṃnyāsa* which was in effect a death rite. He was required to quench his sacrificial fire and dispose of his sacrificial implements. This is a subtle concession to the act of *yajña* being the stamp of the householder and those functioning within a temporal framework. The permission of the *vānaprastha* to perform *yajñas* indicates the degree to which he is still tied to householdership and removed from renunciation. The *saṃnyāsin* by breaking all taboos becomes ritually impure and cannot either perform the *yajña* or be a *yajamāna*. At the same time, *tapas* and *dhyāna* enable him eventually to reach a state of purity and power which supercede that of the *yajña*-performing *brāhmaṇa*. The renouncer has to foreswear any ties with property, to break any attachment to person or place and in effect take to a life which required wandering from place to place and thereby precluded working at any profession. The break with social attachments was further emphasized by his taking on the outward symbols which made him recognizably a renouncer: being naked or sparsely clothed, either removing his hair or never cutting it, carrying a staff and an alms bowl and living either in a monastery, theoretically cordoned off from secular settlements, or living isolated in a forest.

The insistence that the renouncer was dead to the world was symbolic not merely of the break with society but also because death was seen as a condition in which the social order does not prevail. Although the rituals of death serve to enforce the social order for the living, physical death releases the person from that order. *Śrāddha* rituals were a generalized worship of ancestors, reincarnation involved a fresh entry into society and heaven at least had no social ordering. The performance of death rites negated the individual identity. *Saṃnyāsa* had a character of transcendence over death. The actual death ceremonies for the renouncer had therefore to be different from those of other *dvija*s. Instead of being cremated the ascetic was buried, often bound in a sitting position and his grave became a place of worship. (Curiously burial in the earliest source was associated with *asura* customs and these were regarded as socially alien to the Aryan.) In the case of the more venerable Buddhist monks, even though the body was cremated, relics were collected and buried in the tumulus (*stūpa/caitya*) erected to their memory. Thus even the physical body of the renouncer was treated differently on death. Pollution was not associated with his corpse and bodily relics could, therefore, be preserved. The individual *saṃnyāsin* did not require his descendents or peers to observe the *śrāddha* ritual for him as he was not listed as an ancestor and no continuity was sought. But among the *bhikkhu*s and the *saṃnyāsin*s who were part of a sectarian order, continuity was maintained though the line of succession in the monastery or the institutional *āśrama*, where both the oral tradition and literate history were the means of doing this. Important as this became to institutional requirements it subtracted from one of the original purposes of *saṃnyāsa*.

Food regulations were also distinctive. In the case of the *gṛhastha* food regulations relating to caste status and purity were worked out with the same theoretical finesse as were regulations regarding marriage. The higher the caste the more restricted was access to cooked food. The Buddhist and Jaina renouncers broke this taboo by insisting that only cooked food was acceptable as alms. *Brāhmaṇa* ascetics were also permitted this concession but it was preferable that they subsist on what they could glean from the forest. Intercaste commensality, prohibited to the *gṛhastha*, was enjoined upon the monk and the ascetic, the justification for this being that neither were regarded as caste members after renunciation. Similarly, regulations regarding flesh foods observed by the *gṛhastha* were not required of the renouncers. The same held true for the consumption of alcohol and intoxicants although Buddhist ethics firmly prohibited these even to the *gṛhastha* as well and unlike the *brāhmaṇa*s made no concessions to the taking of intoxicants even on ritual occasions.

The exclusion of women is evident at the stage of initiation and in that of renunciation. Descriptions of the *gṛhastha āśrama* take women for granted speaking of them almost in the tone of sacrificial implements. The descriptions of the *gahapati* in the Buddhist sources certainly makes much more of the role of women in householding. Women *parivrājikā*s are referred to, some in their own right and some in the hermitages with their *parivrājikā* husbands. The Buddhist concession to women entering the nunnery was a major departure but its origins are concerned probably less with permitting them a search for salvation and more with the logic of permitting them an alternative life. Their necessity to the *gṛhastha* stage was doubtless sought to be reinforced by discouraging them from renunciation.

That the negation of caste implicit in all forms of renunciation raised some problems is evident from the difference of opinion in the *Dharmasūtra*s as to whether a *brāhmaṇa* alone should be permitted access to *saṃnyāsa* and, if not, whether *brāhmaṇa*s should not carry some distinguishing marks such as the *śikhā* (top-knot) to indicate their original status. Buddhist renouncers by taking on a new name when they graduated to monkhood negated or at least disguised their caste origins.

The encouragement to the *gahapati* to enhance his wealth was again in contrast to the vow of poverty which both ascetic and monk were required to observe. Eventually poverty was to be dissociated from life in the monasteries when these ascetic institutions became wealthy property owners. Inscriptions dating to the Christian era refer to extensive donations made by monks and nuns to the *saṅgha*.[38] In times when kinship was the major avenue to property rights, the property of the *saṅgha* was jointly owned. When individual property rights prevailed, members of the *saṅgha* claimed similar rights. This change grew to sizeable dimensions by the latter half of the first millennium AD when Buddhist and Jaina. monasteries competed for power and property with the *maṭhas* and *āśramas* of various Śaiva and Vaiṣṇava sects of renouncers.[39] The accumulation of such property acquired through lavish donations by lay patrons, whether privately held by monks or jointly by the institution was restricted in its ownership to the institution, although shares in the property could be held by individual renouncers who were members of the institution.[40]

This dichotomy in attitudes to property is also linked up in some ways to another dichotomy, that of the village and the forest, the *grāma* and the *vana* or *araṇya*. The word *grāma*, literally a village, refers by extension to all settlements and is, therefore, associated with the householder. By way of contrast, *araṇya* represented the waste land, the wilderness, the forest which lay between settlements. This was the great unknown with all its hazards. It was the symbol of chaos against the known order of all settled society. It would be the natural habitat of those who had broken away from society and who were confident of perceiving order in the seeming chaos which surrounded them. At another level the forest was a place of refuge where those deliberately opting out of society because of their disillusionment with its order, would go as an escape. At yet another level it was the symbol of the start of a new system of an attempt to reorder the universe which was sought to be done by setting up monasteries on the edge of settlements. The forest was the habitat of other groups segmenting off from existing settlements and creating new *janapadas*, founding new political territorial units. Interwoven with the notion of exile and of going out was that of creating or starting a new order, as is evident from the origin myths of the *kṣatriya* clans as described in Buddhist literature. But even in these new units the distinction between *grāma* and *araṇya* remained and in the history of Buddhism this was to be a dichotomy between those monks who preferred to preach in villages and remain close to the lay community and those who were concerned with the ultimate aim of monkhood, an aim which had no place for monastic property.

The argument that renunciation denied reciprocity and to this extent it denied a major focus in Hindu social action, would be tenable if renunciation did in fact remove the renouncer from social action. In effect, the monastery (whether Buddhist and Jaina to begin with and of the various Hindu sects of a later period) evolves both into an institution within which reciprocity is a fundamental need and into an institution which functions as a major social and political force and has, therefore, to maintain reciprocal relations with society. Whereas an ideal renunciation does deny reciprocity, in fact, the institutions which it spawned were deeply involved with society. The isolated renouncer remained socially marginal if not ineffective, but the image and connotation of the renouncer when it was associated with social movements became a powerful force for mobilization. The strength of such a force doubtless derived from the fact that renouncers were the only category of persons who could with impunity discard social mores.

In generalizing about the renouncer a distinction has to be made between the individual *saṃnyāsin* and the monk who joins an order. Both are concerned with individual salvation and hence remove themselves from the social group to which they belong. Remaining with the social group would involve them in having to observe the *dharma* of the group both because of social obligations and in order to acquire a better *karma. Dharma* as viewed in the Brahmanical tradition relates to the *dharma* of each caste and expressed in the interplay of the individual's *dharma* and that of his caste. The Buddhist concept of *dharma* is that of a universal category which can be subscribed to irrespective of caste. The contrast can perhaps best be seen in the discourse on the duty of the *kṣatriya* in the *Bhagvadgītā* where protection and the unholding of the *varṇāśramadharma* in its specificity is his concern, and that of the king in the Cakkavatti-sinha-nāda-sutta[41] where the *cakravartin*'s duty is to follow the precepts of the universal *dharma* applicable to all and to ensure the well-being of his people.

Renunciation in the Brahmanical tradition was restricted since it was initially open only to the *dvija*, the *śūdra*s being excluded. The non-Brahmanical sects were open to *śūdra*s as well as other castes. This in itself would require a universalistic *dharma* given the immense social divide between *dvija*s and *śūdra*s. By the time of the *Dharmaśāstra*s, *śūdra* ascetics were disallowed as this would doubtless have upset the social order and would have opened up an avenue of authority to the *śūdra* if not access to some degree of upward mobility. The possibility of renunciation being open to *śūdra*s could have been viewed with alarm since it would have resulted in materially the most productive segment in society, taking up what seemed to be materially the most counter-productive occupation. The prohibition on *śūdra* ascetics does suggest that at the ideological level renouncers were not viewed as being so far removed from society as to be ineffectual.

The monk as renouncer does raise something of a contradiction. By joining an order he subjects himself to a new set of mores and to obligations to the order which would inevitably modify his personal search for salvation even though ultimately his release from the cycle of rebirth lay in his hands alone. The Buddha tells the monks that each should live as an island unto himself guided by the *dharma* which is common for all. Monastic living would however not have allowed for the full implementation of this position. The emphasis on the individual both in *saṃnyāsa* and monkhood accounts in part for the strengthening of the notions of a person's *punya* and *pāpa* which is apparent in the texts of the time.

The contradiction is evident from the frequency with which there are debates in the *saṅgha* on the issue of whether monks should devote themselves to their own salvation or whether they should be concerned with strengthening the *saṅgha* by attending to the needs of the lay following. The distinction between the *grāma* and the *araṇya* are symbolic of this choice and these terms enter the discussion. The care of the lay following required the performing of ceremonies, particularly those associated with 'rites of passage' as these were occasions when faith would be strengthened. The dual role of the monk was kept separate in the

Brahmanical tradition by the separate functions of the *brāhmaṇa* and the *saṃnyāsin.* In the initial stages when the monks lived in rock shelters and caves the problem was marginal, but later with the establishment of large monasteries close to settlements, the problem became more complex. The solution lay either in monks breaking away and going to forest retreats or in maintaining that both meditation and preaching were required of the monk and that the two should not conflict.

Such a conflict is sought to be partially ameliorated by the emphasis of the Buddhists on the goal being more important than the method. Thus the Buddha argues that austerity for the purpose of self-mortification characteristic of some kinds of asceticism is inadequate: the fundamental question being that of the nature of the goal of self-mortification.[42] Asceticism by itself is not sufficient. It has to be accompanied by the norm, the *dharma* which ensures escape from the corruption of life and from rebirth. The discipline of living in a monastery is part of the process towards attaining salvation, since the monastic order consists of a body of people all seeking salvation.

It may legitimately be asked why some groups of renouncers sought to organize themselves into orders. This was an increasingly frequent form taken by renouncers from the late first millennium AD. 'Hindu' sects of renouncers became common after the initial organization established by Śaṅkarācārya in the ninth century AD. In subsequent centuries virtually every sect irrespective of its position in the spectrum of beliefs and forms of renunciation, was characterized by an institutional base. The search for individual salvation was not selfish and those who believed that they had found the way wished to enlighten others. The Buddhist parable of the raft where the raft symbolizes enlightenment, insists that the raft be left for the use of others. Thus the creation of a sect for preaching the message was necessary. Monkhood obviously had the advantage that it allowed those who were seeking salvation and subscribing to a particular teaching to live together and thus facilitate the search.

That a body of renouncers had to have an institutional base also has to do with the nature of a caste society. Renouncers as we have seen were required, as it were, to 'de-caste' themselves. Having broken the rules of the *dvija* code, had they remained as individuals in society, they would logically have been accorded *śūdra* status at best or been regarded as untouchables. Two *brāhmaṇa* novices wishing to become *bhikkhus* inform the Buddha that they are abused and reviled by other *brāhmaṇas* in whose eyes the novices have been lowered to *śūdra* status because of their joining the Buddhist order.[43] It was, therefore, necessary that they be organized as a group outside society and yet with some links—as a parallel group with its own norms. The *brāhmaṇas* could well regard them as outcastes and their legitimacy, therefore depended on their receiving public support in terms of recognition of their parallel or alternate system. The hierarchy of caste society was reinforced by attempting to reverse it in creating an egalitarian society of renouncers: the separation between the two societies also reiterated. If the monastery reflected a search for an ideal society, its continuation would clearly be limited since it could not reproduce itself and was dependent on fresh recruitment. An unequal, hierarchical society could not be levelled nor opposed individually, but collective retreats based on egalitarian status, in theory if not in practice, were possible. The fear of the parallel society is demonstrated in the hostility in Brahmanical sources towards the heretical sects, whereas the individual *saṃnyāsin* although breaking the same caste rules is, nevertheless, revered.

It is a moot question whether the Buddha was aware of the political potential of the *saṅgha*. Initially the harking back of the *saṅgha* to the clan-based societies may have suggested a role of opposition to the emergent monarchies which were feeling their way towards authoritarian state power at the time when Buddhism was beginning to acquire popularity. The possible opposition gave way eventually to mutual respect which may have been directed by the need to accept royal patronage. The bestowing of patronage was doubtless inspired by the personal religious proclivities of the heads of state but was combined perhaps with a political insight which saw these monastic orders as powerful networks of public opinion. Mutual respect was tempered by mutual adjustments. The monastery, although it remained a parallel society, was from time to time an accomplice of political authority in supporting the state system. The Buddha advised the monks to obey the king and agreed that royal officers and those who were under a judicial sentence should not be admitted to the *saṅgha*.[44] Bimbisara, then ruling Magadha, in turn agreed to declare monks immune from judicial punishment. Monasteries, *maṭhas* and *āśramas* in the later period, even when they were large scale property owners with judicial and fiscal rights over villages, were, nevertheless, declared immune from interference by state officials.

Buddhist historiography tends to associate major changes in the *saṅgha* with heads of state, implying thereby, that changes originated from kings who were patrons of Buddhism rather than from the internal dynamics of the *saṅgha* functioning in changing historical situations. The most obvious example of this is the attribution to Aśoka Maurya of calling the Third Council at Pāṭaliputra[45] and of acting thereby as midwife to the birth of the Therāvada sect. The association of political authority with such events could in some cases have been an after-thought on the part of the monk chroniclers who sought to integrate political authority with an event of primarily religious significance: although of course it can be argued that such events were not primarily of religious significance and did have a political repercussion even if not precisely in the manner portrayed by the chroniclers.[46] It is incorrect to maintain that the reign of Aśoka saw the earlier politicization of Buddhism[47] since this had occurred in the lifetime of the Buddha. The *saṅgha* emerged rather like 'a state within a state'. *Dāna* to the *saṅgha* meant, in addition to religious merit, support to a socio-political institution. The Buddhist network drew in a number of areas in varying stages of state formation, from the more flexible chiefships to the unified state. Where the *saṅgha* was established it rapidly became the focus of community life.

The political role of the *saṃnyāsin* is not without significance. The authority of the *saṃnyāsin* deriving from the fact of renunciation coupled with the powers of *tapas* and *dhyāna* was seen as a parallel authority to that of temporal power. With the decline of *yajña* as the sole source of sacral authority, the *saṃnyāsin* came to personify an even greater authority. The *saṃnyāsin*, if he so wished, could curb temporal power by using the energy which he had acquired through austerity and meditation. The later, didactic interpolations in the two epics raise the power of the ascetic higher than even that of the great deity of the sacrifices, Indra. Kings were fearful of the wrath of the *saṃnyāsin*. The *daṇḍa* carried by the *saṃnyāsin* was not merely a physical staff for it symbolized the power of coercion through an intangible source of strength. Far from being life-negating, the renouncer was the symbol of power and was often treated as the counter-weight to temporal authority. It may be argued that by insisting that renunciation come at the end of the lifecycle, a subtle attempt was being made to diffuse a possible concentration of authority. The encouragement of individual renunciation as distinct from joining an order was in itself a form of diffusing the political potential of the renouncer. This is demonstrated in the changed role of the renouncer in the period subsequent to the mid-first millennium AD when the *maṭhas* and *āśramas* of Vaiṣṇava and Śaiva sects were deeply involved in theories of meditation as well as problems of temporal power. The growth of these institutions changed the nature of dissent and conformity and the individual solitary renouncer tended to become a faded image. The increasing numbers of the orders of renouncers was feasible only insofar as they were permitted and protected by society.

The power of the renouncer had also to do with the fact that such groups and individuals were wrapped up in what might be called the non-orthodox understanding of knowledge. The initial absence of deities in this tradition and the break from the sacrificial ritual provided a rationalistic strain to much of their thought. There was, nevertheless, a claim to extra-sensory powers and the *saṃnyāsin* like the gods could conjure up visions of the universe and create the illusion of time, place and person. The Buddha discouraged the notion of *siddhi*, the almost magical power so deeply associated with renouncers, but the literature of Buddhism is replete with resort to such power when all else fails. Even the alchemical process was ultimately brought into such experiments with knowledge and was justified on the analogy that the process of sublimation and transmutation so central to alchemy was after all similar to that involved in the search for *mokṣa.* Besides, alchemy was centrally concerned with empirical processes of knowledge.

The more evidently rational theme was directed to the opposition of revealed knowledge and as was often the case with early civilizations,[48] to the analysis of bodily functions and experiments with the body—the foundation of *yoga* and *prāṇāyāma*—which encouraged a more empirical understanding of man. Coupled with this empirical knowledge came the notion of causation so skillfully utilized in Buddhist thought. The somewhat primitive magic associated with the performance of *yajña* and the correct recitation of the *mantra*s had to make space for the more sophisticated idea of controlling the body and the mind through *tapas*, *yoga*, *prāṇāyāma*, *dhyāna* and other such techniques with the ultimate aim of using this control if need be to perform superhuman feats. The emphasis shifts from man supplicating the gods and the supernatural to man generating the power to comprehend the universe and the supernatural from within himself.

The trend of investigating empirical knowledge received something of a setback in the post-first millennium AD when monastic centres as the nuclei of renouncers became economically self-sufficient through grants and endowments. The initiates, or at least those who were not involved in the arduous task of managing and administering the property owned by the institution and the villages over which it had authority, spent their time in writing scholarly commentaries and treatises on existing philosophical and theological texts. The empiricism of perceived knowledge gave way to hours of scholarly debate. The monastic system of encouraging literacy which was on occasion used by monks of low status to aspire to high positions was now reinforced by the vogue for scholasticism. The plethora of manuscripts which are a hallmark of these times came frequently from monastic or near-monastic centres of various ideological persuasions. As renouncers such groups had moved a long way from the genesis of the *saṃnyāsa āśrama* or *bhikkhu saṅgha.*

Seen from a diachronic perspective the *āśrama* theory was generated from an interaction of social needs, historical processes, and ideological concerns. The historical background to the dichotomy of householder and renouncer suggests an initial situation where renunciation was not at the forefront of social consciousness in that the early lineage-based society of Vedic times seemed to accept the prestation system centring on the sacrificial ritual. The renouncers were few and were concerned with the quest for comprehending the universe. Thus dissent from the existing systems was essentially an intellectual dissent and a search for alternatives or the articulation of a private world view and did not impinge on the householding society of the majority. Stratification in such a system was lest marked since clan and kinship connections were the determinants of status.

The dichotomy of householder and renouncer assumed more serious proportions in the subsequent period when, as a result of various historical changes, sects of renouncers not only became more numerous but began to organize themselves on an institutional basis. The opting out into the forest and the cutting away from society was among many such groups purely symbolic, since the sects remained in the purview of settlements and lived off them. The renouncer had now to seek the aid of the householder and was dependent on the latter. The giving of aid not only encouraged the questioning of the Brahmanical tradition in terms of the inadequacy of *yajñas* but also threatened the very system of ritual and symbol on which the Brahmanical tradition was based. Such a questioning also had a theme of social protest which was not appreciated by those who regarded themselves as the inheritors of the tradition. There was a need, therefore, to clarify the dichotomous relationship by defining its relative functions and by setting limits to the social impact of renouncers. Thus whereas the Buddhist and the Jaina traditions, for example, encouraged the dichotomous categories in the role of the *gahapati* and the *bhikkhu*, the Brahmanical tradition sought to weaken it by weaving it into a single lifecycle.

Within this definition the *āśramas* were linked to the *varṇas* so that caste functions could be continued and dissent made less apparent. The exclusion of *śūdras* from this curriculum was important and telling since it acted not only as a social marker but also guaranteed a marginal change from renunciatory groups who would have to be drawn from the *dvijas*. It also prevented the *śūdra* from having access to the kind of powers associated with renouncers. This was further reinforced by encouraging the notion that ideally only *brāhmaṇas* should be permitted renunciation. It is significant that those who did not conform to the *āśrama* theory opposed all these attempts at circumvention. The actual formulation of the idea of *āśramas* into a theory dates to a period when the strength of renunciatory groups had become noticeable. The linking of the *āśrama* theory to that of *varṇa* ensured that *varṇa* functions would not be neglected. Those who were reluctant to accept or could not accept the *āśrama* ideal could function at least with the *varṇa-dharma*. Thus *śūdras* were required to observe the *varṇa-dharma*. This was in turn subjected to the individual measure of merit and demerit in action leading to the centrality of the notions of *punya* and *pāpa*.

The Brahmanical insistence, in the early historical period, that the individual *saṃnyāsin* alone could be regarded as a renouncer was not only an attempt to reiterate the earlier model but also to hold back the tide of the various orders of renouncers who were looked upon by the *brāhmaṇas* as heretics (*pāṣaṇḍas*). What were once marginal dissenters were by now taking on the dimensions of a serious opposition to the Brahmanical world view. Earlier, individual renouncers had not only been accommodated in the Brahmanical tradition but their charismatic power had been accepted as a legitimate source of authority. This concession was born out of a genuine fear that *yoga*, *tapas*, and *dhyāna* enabled the renouncer to control the natural and the supernatural worlds, as well as from the reassuring belief that the impact of this power on society has perforce to be limited and cannot undermine the existing system. However, the rapid growth of organized groups of renouncers brought about a qualitative change in the perception of the role of the renouncer. The individual *saṃnyāsin*, although still the ideal, was hedged in by the influence on society by the sects of renouncers. Ultimately the emergence of a Śankarācārya and the organization of Brahmanical ascetic orders was a logical outcome of this situation. But prior to this, in an atmosphere of a more generalized discussion on the interplay of householder and renouncer and the social obligations of each, the Brahmanical tradition passed through a period of anxiety. The *āśrama* theory may have been less of an idealist abstraction projecting an ordering of the ideal lifecycle for the *dvija* and particularly for the *brāhmaṇa*, and more of the ventriloquism of a Brahmanical perception of a time of troubles.

Notes and References

1. L. Dumont, 'World Renunciation in Indian Religions', *Contributions to Indian Sociology*, vol. 4, 1960, pp. 33–62.

2. L. Dumont, 'A Modified View of Our Origins: The Christian Beginning of Modern Civilisation', Deneke Lecture, Lady Margaret Hall, Oxford (unpublished), 1980.

3. R. Thapar, 'Dissent and Protest in the Early Indian Tradition', *Studies in History*, 1(2), 1979, pp. 177–96.

4. H. Jacobi, *Jaina Sutras*, Oxford, 1895. V.P. Varma, *Early Buddhism and Its Origins*, Delhi, 1972. S. Dutt, *Early Buddhist Monachism*, London, 1924. D. Bhargava, *Jaina Ethics*, Delhi, 1968.

5. S.C. Banerji, *Dharmasūtras*, Calcutta, 1962. R. Lingat, *The Classical Law of India*, Berkeley, 1973.

6. P.V. Kane, *History of Dharmaśāstra*, vol. II, Poona, 1941, p. 1.

7. V.S. Agrawal, *India as Known to Pāṇini*, Varanasi, 1963, p. 83.

8. G.C. Pande, *Studies in the Origins of Buddhism*, Allahabad, 1957, pp. 251–61.

9. For example, *Bṛhadāraṇyaka* IV.3.2.2–10. *The Principal Upaniṣads*, Radhakrishnan, S. (trans.), London, 1953.

10. *Yeśam ca virodhaḥ śāśvatikaḥ*. Patañjali *Vyākarana mahābhāśyam*, I. p. 474, on Pāṇini, II.4.9. Other sources also refer to the dichotomy between *brāhmaṇa*s and *śramaṇa*s such as *Anguttaranikāya*, IV.35; Strabo, XV.1.59 in McCrindle. The etymology of *brāhmaṇa* indicates one imbued with divine knowledge which linked to Vedic knowledge. The terms *śramaṇa* and *āśrama* in both cases derive from the root *śram*, to labour or make an effort. The *śramaṇa*, therefore, is one who labours towards an objective and *āśrama* was the process of doing so. Eventually the place where the *śramaṇa*s gathered was also called the *āśrama*. The differentiation between the *brāhmaṇa* and the *śramaṇa* was, therefore, clear and unambiguous.

11. *Dīghanikāya* III.94, T.W. Rhys Davids and J.E. Carpentier (trans.), London, 1890–1911.

12. By way of an aside one might consider in this context, the centrality of tragic plays in Greek culture. Did the public expression of emotions of

sorrow and loneliness through the performance of such plays and through the cathartic experience of the audience prevent the obliteration of such emotions? The essence of Greek tragedy lay in forcing the audience to face emotional situations of a kind which in other cultures may have been treated as personal and private. And curiously the Greeks were not given to renunciation. But such an argument can perhaps be too simplistic.

13. J. Moussaieff Masson, *The Oceanic Feeling*, Leiden, 1980.

14. The epic heroes of the *Mahābhārata* and the *Rāmāyaṇa* were, in the interpolated later sections of the text, supporters of the *gṛhastha-āśrama.* They do not contemplate *saṃnyāsa* as a possible condition for themselves. When in exile they come into contact with renouncers and on occasion have to protect the renouncers against their enemies although the renouncers are frequently forest hermits still maintaining the sacrificial ritual and suggesting thereby that they were not *saṃnyāsins*. Only in one version of the *Rāmāyaṇa*, the mid-first millennium AD composition of the Jaina adaptation in the *Paumacariyam*, does Rama renounce his kingdom in his later years and becomes a Jaina ascetic—and the *Paumacariyam* is already far removed from a heroic ethos.

15. A.K. Warder, 'Early Buddhism and other contemporary systems', *Bulletin of the School of Oriental and African Studies*, 18(1), 1956, 43ff.

16. *Aṅguttaranikāya* IV.17, R. Morris, and E. Hardy (eds), London, 1885–1900; *Dīghanikāya* II.72ff.

17. K.N. Jayatillake, *Early Buddhist Theory of Knowledge*, London, 1963.

18. R. Thapar, 'Dissent and Protest in the Early Indian Tradition'.

19. J.W. McCrindle, *Ancient India as Described by Megasthenes and Arrian*, London, 1877.

20. Romila Thapar, *Exile and the Kingdom: Some Thoughts on the Ramayana*, Bangalore, 1978.

21. *Baudhāyana Dharmasūtra* (*Baudhāyana*) II.10.17.2–5, G. Bühler, Oxford, 1882; *Āpastamba Dharmasūtra* (*Āpastamba*) II.9.21, G. Bühler (trans.), Oxford, 1879.

22. *The Laws of Manu* (*Manu*), VI.1–38. G. Bühler (trans.), Oxford, Clarendon Press, 1886.

23. *Manu* VI.87ff.

24. *Baudhāyana* II.6.11.28.

25. *Āpastamba* I.1.1.16–18; *Vasiṣtha Dharmasūtra* (*Vasiṣtha*) II.6, G. Bühler (trans.), Oxford, Clarendon Press, 1882.

26. *Baudhāyana* I.2.3.7ff; I.2.4.7ff; I.3.5.1ff.

27. V.M. Apte, *Social and Religious Life in the Grihya Sutras*, Bombay, 1954, pp. 170ff, 182ff.

28. *Baudhāyana* II.11.27; *Vasiṣṭha* VIII.14; *Gautama Dharmasūtra (Gautama)* III.3, G. Bühler (trans.), Oxford, 1879.

29. One is here reminded of the discussion in Fustel de Coulanges (1864) on the significance of the sacred fire in claims to kinship and in family cults associated with it.

30. *Āpastamba* II.4.8.1ff; 4.9.1ff; *Gautama* V.43.5.

31. Gahapati vagga, *Aṅguttaranikāya* VIII.3.21–30; X.30ff.

32. Sigālovadasutta, *Dīghanikāya* XXXI.4.

33. McCrindle, *Ancient India.*

34. *Baudhāyana* II.6.11.12ff; III.3.13ff; *Āpastamba* II.9.23.2

35. *Aṣṭādhyāyi* III.22.155, 168; V.2.102ff.

36. *Aṣṭādhyāyi* IV.3.110ff; VI.l.

37. *Jātaka* IV.119, V. Fausboll (ed.), London, 1877–97; *Vinaya Piṭaka* I.82, H. Oldenberg (ed.), London, 1879–83.

38. *Epigraphia Indica* X. Nos. 1016, 1020, 1041, 1089

39. D. Lorenzen, *The Kapalikas and the Kalamukhas*, New Delhi, 1971. R.N. Nandi, R.N., *Religious Institutions and Cults in the Deccan*, Varanasi, 1973. S.N. Sarma, *The Neo-vaisnavite Movement and the Sattra Institution of Assam*, Gauhati, 1966.

40. R.A.L.H. Gunawardana, 1979, *Robe and Plough*, Arizona, 1979.

41. *Dīghanikāya* III.58.

42. *Dīghanikāya* III.2.25.

43. *Dīghanikāya* III.81.

44. *Vinaya Piṭaka* I: 73–6.

45. R. Thapar, *Aśoka and the Decline of the Mauryas*, London, 1961, pp. 41–5.

46. The relationship between the Buddhist *saṅgha* and the political state has been analysed in considerable detail with reference to the situation in early historical Sri Lanka. The Ceylon chronicles, especially the *Dīpavaṃsa* and the *Mahāvaṃsa*, are an invaluable source for indicating this relationship and a number of studies have been based on this (Geiger 1908; Perera 1976; Bechert 1978). Another study treats of this relationship with reference to Thailand (Tambiah 1976). There is undoubtedly a strong tradition in Sri Lanka of associating major changes in the *saṅgha* with political events. Recent attempts to suggest that reforms within the *saṅgha* in the last two centuries were motivated by internal developments within the *saṅgha* and did not seek external legitimisation, fail to explain the departure from tradition and in themselves are not very convincingly argued (see Carrithers 1979).

47. M. Weber, *The Religion of India*, New York, 1967.

48. G.E.R. Lloyd, *Magic, Reason and Experience*, Cambridge, 1979, pp. 37ff.

CHAPTER 14

Patronage and the Community*

The concept of patronage is usually restricted to the relationship between the patron and the recipient of patronage—often visualized for early times as the king and the artist who works for him. But the relationship created through the act of patronage can vary considerably according to the form of patronage. The patron, the artist, and the object are pointers to each other and are deeply interlinked. Art historians of India generally looked for an individual patron and this in part explains the frequency with which monuments are labelled by dynasty and rarely by the name of the architect even when this is known. Further, the recipient is often regarded as subservient to the patron since the former is dependent for his livelihood on the latter. This focus obstructs the consideration of what the patron receives in return for extending patronage.

The act of patronage is initially an exchange. Over time, the categories of persons involved in this exchange as well as the objects may change. Often the exchange involves intangibles such as status and legitimation or the acquisition of merit, in return for tangible wealth. The activity involved in patronage includes a number of concerns, such as the occasion, the formal relationship by which it is recognized, the patron, the recipient, the object which encapsulates the acts, and the function of the act. Among these the relationship between the patron and the recipient sets the tone as it were, for acts of patronage. Such a relationship

* This essay was originally published in B. Stoler Miller (ed.), *The Powers of Art*, Delhi, Oxford University Press, 1992, pp. 1–34.

can perhaps be categorized into at least four significant forms.[1] Firstly, patronage which is embedded in a society and where the patron and recipient are built into the system as it were, as for example, the chief and the bard in chiefdoms or early forms of kingship. Secondly, patronage as a deliberate act of choice can be seen when a community decides to donate wealth and labour towards the building of a monument which encapsulates its religious beliefs, social values and activities, and where the patron is not a single person but a recognizable group. Thirdly, the most familiar form of patronage is where it becomes a service, where the recipient is either a retainer or is commissioned by a patron and this form is frequently found in the relations between a court, a religious institution, or a powerful household, each of which may commission an individual or a group to produce an object generally of religious and artistic value. Finally, in more recent times, patronage can be seen as a public activity where, for the world of art, the object becomes an investment and artists are more evidently changing style and aesthetics but the material value of the object is still determined by the patrons.

This essay is concerned primarily with the second form of patronage, namely, that which involves a community donating wealth towards the building of monuments and their adornment as acts of piety. However, since the first of the four categories listed above, that of embedded patronage, contains elements of community patronage, although not particularized as such, it might be useful to consider the difference between the first and the second forms if only to focus on their social concerns.

Embedded patronage can be of at least two varieties. One is the relationship of the bard to the *rājā*/chief and the other is that of the *yajamāna*—the one ordering a sacrifice to the priests. The first can be relatively more focused on social and political relationships or on occasion tied to a ritual but where the ritual aspect is not dominant. The occasion for the second has to be a ritual. The bard performing multiple roles acted as the legitimizer of power, the moral conscience of those in power and the 'historian'. This is demonstrated in the *dāna-stuti* hymns (in praise of gift-giving) of the *Ṛg Veda*[2] where the bard composes eulogies on the prowess of the *rājā* in cattle raids and skirmishes with other chiefs and in return for his compositions receives cattle, horses, chariots, and gold as wealth. The occasion could be the *vidatha* or any other clan assembly with some degree of ritual connotation, the patron was the *rājā*, the recipient was the bard or the *brāhmaṇa* hymnodist, the object was the gift given by the *rājā* and the purpose or function of this exchange was the eulogizing of the *rājā* which acted as a form of validation and of historical memory. This form of patronage is more commonly found in lineage-based societies prior to the emergence of the state or in what are sometimes called early states.[3] However it does not die down completely with the establishing of the monarchical state. At least one aspect continues into the new system. Poets attached to a court and composing eulogies on the king were in a sense continuing this tradition. Thus, much of the *carita* literature of later times, where it relates to royal biographies, such as the *Harṣacarita* of Bāna-bhaṭṭa or the *Vikramānkadevacarita* of Bilhaṇa were, as literary forms, descendants of the *dāna-stutis*.

The *yajamāna* on a ritual occasion is also performing an act of patronage and to that extent Vedic texts as ritual texts are also, in certain passages, manuals of patronage. The word *śilpa* in the Vedic context meant a skill and even the performance of a *yajña* could be seen as a *śilpa*. The occasions are the major ritual sacrifices, such as the *cāturmāsya* and the seasonal sacrifices, as well as the *mahāyajñas* linked to the status and power of the *rājā*, such as the *abhiṣeka*, *rājasūya*, *aśvamedha*, and *vājapeya*. The seasonal rituals held in households were essentially domestic where the *gṛhapati* or the head of the household was the patron and the *brāhmaṇa* performing the ritual was the recipient. The object encapsulating patronage was the cow or the gold given by the *gṛhapati* to the *brāhmaṇa* and the exchange ensured the well-being of the *gṛhapati* and his family and reiterated his status.

In the case of royal rituals, the *yajña* itself constituted the form with the *rājā* as patron, the categories of priests—*hotṛ*, *adhvaryu*, *netṛ*, *brāhmaṇa*, and so on—as recipients; material wealth such as cattle, horses, and gold was the tangible exchange for ensuring the well-being of the clan and the power of the *rājā* and of intervening with the gods to make certain of this function. Gift-giving, together with the display and destruction of wealth became a means of claiming status and marginally redistributing wealth.

The system as such continued into later periods with some adaptations. The *mahārājādhirājas* of the centuries AD performed the *mahāyajñas*, the elaborate, large-scale sacrificial rituals. This was particularly the case where there might have been a disputed succession or where a family of obscure origin aspired to dynastic status, claimed to be *kṣatriyas* and established kingdoms, practices which are more easily recognized from the post-Gupta period. It is not altogether unexpected that when later the *jajmāni* system of service relationships came into being in some areas, the pattern was similar. The occasion was calendrical services in the form of routine functions, the patron was the *jajmān/yajamāna* or landowner, the recipients were those who performed largely routine services for him, the object was payment in kind and the function was production and consumption. When the pattern of the latter was altered, the system also changed. The *jajmān* could be an individual landowner or a temple or institution holding property in land. *Jajmāni* also referred to a method of organizing skills, relationships and wealth. The skills would centre around services, the relationship around protection by the *jajmān* and the legitimizing of the *jajmān* by the recipients. The term *jajmān* evokes the flavour of ritual which is extended to the notion of service, the interdependence of patron and recipient, the perception among his peers of the recipient being a model, the possible exploitation of the recipient by the patron, and the occasional manipulating of the patron by the recipients as innovators and conservers of skill.

In all these situations the act of patronage not only creates a new (often tangible) object, but it also creates an institution, irrespective of whether it is minuscule or on a grand scale. The legitimation of political authority, for example, also gives rise to the question of politically acceptable channels of dissent and political opposition. Thus in the second millennium AD, the bard in Rajasthan was also the articulator of political protest against the *rājā*. This was expressed in a *dharnā*, in this case a fast unto death. The guilt associated with the death of the bard would be so extreme that kings tended to negotiate an agreement before this could happen.[4]

Embedded patronage therefore has a further life in various forms, some overt and some subordinated. As such it constitutes a counterpart to the more apparent community patronage which becomes evident at the turn of the Christian era in some parts of the subcontinent. Here, the act of patronage is a freshly thought-out, conscious act, initially regarded as extraneous to other social and religious activities. There is nevertheless a link between the two which lies in the act of making a gift—*dāna*—although the context of the gift is very different in each case. *Dāna* in the earlier system is a gift made from one person to another, not necessarily in a personal capacity since it was often determined by the status of the two persons and the occasion when it was given.

Community patronage in the early period took the form of *dāna* given by a group of people who came together primarily because of a common and closely defined religious identity and a more loosely defined social identity. That the social identity could assume an importance was always possible and in some cases evident, especially where it coincided with particular religious manifestations. The gift was, therefore, initially made for personal reasons and because of requirements of status or function. Once the institution emanating from this form of patronage was established and began to indicate a social role, at that later stage the making of donations may have taken on the function of a social statement. The *dāna* given by the *yajamāna* was an individual's gift but not necessarily personalized. With community patronage, the gift is neither destroyed in a potlatch type of ritual nor does it go directly towards enhancing the personal wealth of the religious intermediary. The gift in the system under discussion here is appropriated by the *saṅgha*. Another major difference is that in the earlier system the patron and the recipient were in a condition of reciprocal dependence and the objects exchanged tended to be inalienable.[5] In the case of *dāna* to the *saṅgha*, the gift took the form of money or labour, both of which were alienable and the relation between the donor and the *saṅgha* was voluntary.

Community patronage involves social relations and a conscious act of exchange. The act of patronage asserts the status of the patrons and in addition articulates the cohesion of the community making the donation. Examples of this category of patronage become evident during the period from the second century BC to the fourth century AD in the patronage extended to the building of *stūpa*s such as those at Sanchi, Bharhut and Amaravati and the rock-cut caves of the western Deccan, all of which had at source donations to the Buddhist *saṅgha*.[6] The donations came substantially from artisans, guilds of craftsmen, traders, monks and nuns, small-scale landowners and to a lesser extent from royalty and families in high political and administrative office. In some cases this form of patronage becomes unique, where the craftsmen who actually work on the object of patronage are themselves the patrons, as in the case of the ivory-carvers' guild from Vidiśā who sculpted a part of the gateway at Sanchi.[7] Such monuments stand in contrast to many of the *stūpa*s of northwestern India of approximately the same period which were more frequently built with royal patronage.

Artisans as patrons indicate social mobilization in a period of social change with possibilities of upward mobility. Such patronage reflects the respect meted out to artisans who were wealthy as is also indicated in Buddhist texts where a *gṛhapati/gahapati* even in an artisanal profession would be given the status of *ucchakula*, or high family.[8] This, notwithstanding that in contemporary Brahmanical *Dharmaśāstra*s they are ranked low.[9] Weavers, for example in later texts, were regarded as *antyaja*s, lower than the *śūdra*.[10] Is this to be explained by the argument that when weaving declined as a trade, the impoverishment of weavers led to a lowering of their status, or, was the lowering of the status due to the weavers supporting religious sects which the *brāhmaṇa*s regarded as heretical?

The establishment of artisan guilds becomes a noticeable feature of urban life from the Mauryan period onwards. The evolution of guilds/*śreṇi*s can be traced to settlements in the proximity of raw materials and villages of craftsmen concerned with a specific craft such as weaving or carpentry, some of which villages grew into *nigama*s or market centres. Specialized areas demarcated for particular crafts remained the norm in urban settlements as well. The structure of the guild as it gained importance was further emphasized by its increasingly hereditary nature. Where endogamous marriage was encouraged it led ultimately to the *śreṇi* taking on some of the functions of caste and some *śreṇi*s came to be viewed as *jāti*s in the first millennium AD. Guild donations were, therefore, up to a point caste donations as well, and the *jāti*s which collectively donated to the building of a monument did not see themselves as sharply differentiated in social terms.

Patronage is indicated either directly through votive inscriptions which identify the donor and his or her contribution or indirectly in the sculptured panels of donors as, for example, the *daṃpati* groups at Karle. Buddhist monuments, be they *caitya*-hall, *stūpa*, cave or cistern at a monastery site, are the objects of patronage. The patrons consist substantially of the *gahapati/gṛhapati* and the *seṭṭhi/śreṣṭhin* (families of wealthy landowners and traders), of artisans, of the guilds or *śreṇi*s and just occasionally a *rājā* or his wife and a high-status officer and/or his wife. Apart from this there is also a large body of monks and nuns. The recipient is the Buddhist *saṅgha.* The medium is presumably a monetary contribution or a voluntary contribution in labour which helped in the making of the monument as the object encapsulating the act of patronage. The function is the acquisition of merit or *punya* which helped to bring individuals closer to *nirvāṇa.*

The purpose of gift-giving was in part concerned with personal salvation and not altogether uninfluenced by material benefits.[11] *Dāna* is referred to as the most meritorious act, the other two being *sila* and *bhāvanā. Dāna* is particularly meritorious when given to a *bhikkhu* or to the *saṅgha.* Ideally *dāna* consisted of those items of food, clothing, and daily life which would meet the *bhikkhu*'s minimum requirements.[12] The act of gift-giving therefore was imbued with a sacred quality in addition to its function in maintaining *bhikkhus.* When the act of *dāna* consisted of money or labour to embellish a *stūpa*, then obviously it underwent a change from its earlier function and became less an act of maintaining a monk and more that of faith in the *saṅgha*, for the *stūpa* was seen as one of the physical symbols of the *saṅgha.*

The *stūpa* becomes the symbol of the power of the *saṅgha* in relation to the patron. It emerges as a major symbol when the worship of sacred sites *per se* gives way to monuments as the physical manifestation of the *saṅgha* as an institution. Whereas in the early Pāli canon the *vīhara*s or monasteries are more frequently mentioned, the archaeology of the post-Mauryan period refers to the *stūpa* and the *caitya* as the major edifices. The *vīhara*s which have survived from these times tend to be rock-cut monasteries. Here the *caitya*-halls are the most spectacular expression of patronage often surrounded by clusters of contrastingly bare rock-cut cells and the occasional water cisterns. The free-standing *stūpa* becomes a focal monument which is adorned and enclosed within a railing demarcating the sacred from the profane. There is a distinction between those objects of patronage which are intended to benefit both monks and nuns and the laity and those intended only for the former. Contributions towards the construction of the railings and the adorning of the gateways and pillars of the *stūpa*, was an act of piety involving the entire community of believers. The rock-cut *vīhara* intended only for monks was a particularized act of piety. The patrons, both in the *Jātaka* stories and in the votive inscriptions, tend to come from the same social groups and there is, therefore, a considerable reinforcing of the identification of these patrons.

The location and symbolism of the *stūpa* has its own importance. There has been some debate on the question of whether the *stūpa* was worshipped as a symbol of the *mahāparinirvāṇa* or whether it was the *nirvāṇa* body of the Buddha. The cult of the *stūpa* came into prominence after the death of the Buddha and it has been argued that this was more conducive to Mahāyāna than to Hīnayāna Buddhism.[13] The early tradition suggests a funerary connection, the location being marked by a man-made tumulus. In peninsular India Buddhist sites often occur on or near megalithic burials as at Amaravati, pointing to continuity in areas regarded as sacred and associated with the dead. This sense of continuity also extended to the community which in the first instance built the megalithic structure and later to the Buddhist religious community. This might be a clue to the origin of the inexplicable word *eḍuka/eluka* believed to be of Dravidian etymology and used for *stūpa* in some Sanskrit and Pāli sources.[14] The association of the *stūpa* as a symbol of the Buddha when he is described as a *cakkavati* provides yet another level of meaning. Possibly the *stūpa* also symbolized an alternative source or centre of power. Thus when those in political authority were patrons of the building of a *stūpa* they would be subsuming this alternative power; and when the community as such helped build the *stūpa* it would be calling on this alternative source of power for protection. Implicit in the gift, therefore, is not only the seeking of merit which is the more obvious reciprocation but also the calling upon the Buddha for protection.

The intention of the patrons is at one level clearly stated. The contribution was an exchange of *dāna* for *punya*, a gift for the acquisition of merit. This could be either individual or collective as in the case of the guild and ultimately a collaborative act if the end result was the building of a *stūpa* or *caitya*-hall. There were also a variety of subsumed intentions and some degree of social mobilization can be inferred. Here local chiefs were involved, such as the Mahābhoja or the Mahatalāvara; these were also persons who occur in the Sātavāhana inscriptions as high-ranking officers suggesting a transfer of chiefly authority to administrative purposes.[15] The most frequently mentioned groups are of course the *seṭṭhi-gahapati* families obviously of some standing as landowners and traders. The emphasis in some cases on the donation of a family where the kin relations are specifically stated as in some Amaravati inscriptions is of interest. Does this reflect the reinforcing of the family as a relatively new unit of social identity in areas of erstwhile clan domination? Equally important are the contributions of monks and nuns mentioned by name. This is surprising in a community where monastic rules tended to blur individual identities and where monks and nuns were not expected to have access to wealth. Was this the wealth which accompanied them on entry into the monastery and which they donated to the *saṅgha*? Or did they continue to hold shares in family property and were, therefore, permitted to maintain a private income? Or did they invest this income in the trade which passed along the routes on which their monasteries were situated arguing that the profits from such investments would be donated to the *saṅgha*?

The identification of the donor is not necessary to an act of piety or of worship. It becomes necessary when such an act is a public declaration of belief and incidentally also a statement on wealth and status. Were votive inscriptions also inspired by a desire to be known to posterity particularly in a culture which did not commemorate the ordinary mortal through grave-stones or memorial stones? This is in part suggested not only by the close association of some Buddhist sites with megalithic burial sites but also by certain aspects of the Buddhist sites as well. For instance there is a burial gallery at Kanheri where small votive *stūpa*s were built to commemorate dead *thera*s believed to have achieved a high state of realization.[16] Even for the living, votive inscriptions were advertisements of the status of individuals and families or the status of professions when guilds were constituted, drawing attention to the skills and the quality of craftsmanship. Urban professionals such as ivory-carvers, weavers, potters, perfumers, bead-makers, and garland makers are often mentioned. More specifically Ānanda, the foreman of the artisans of Siri Satakani, the Sātavāhana king, states that he carved the top architrave of the south gate at Sanchi[17] or the *rūpakara* Buddharakhita of Bharhut[18] or the *vadhaki* Svamin of Dhenukākaṭa.[19] In parallel situations mention is made of an actor's sons, the Candaka brothers, involved in the temple of Dadhikarna Nāga.[20] Even better known is the reference from Mathura to Gomataka a pupil of Kunika, the sculptor of the famous Parkham *yakṣa* image.[21] This might also signify a break away from the guild to the setting up of a family identity of craftsmen or at least a *guru-śiṣya paramparā* which possibly evolved from the guild and was the dominant institution in the artistic achievements of a later period. The inscriptions are not limited to recording donations by *gahapati*s, *seṭṭhi*s and artisans, but the broad social stratum of the donors was largely that of individuals belonging to these categories.

The inscriptions also provide evidence on the networks of geographical contacts providing yet another dimension to the concept of community. Traders from Dhenukākata made donations at Karle and other caves of the western Deccan.[22] Traders and artisans from elsewhere in the Deccan and western India made gifts at places in the western coast such as at Kanheri.[23] The incidence of donors from clearly identifiable towns is smaller in number and the majority may have come from *nigamas* or market centres and villages linked to them. The location of the monuments on trade routes would point to market connections such as the *nigama* of Karahakata.[24]

Inscriptions from Bharhut included donations from persons residing in Vidiśā, Pātaliputra, Bhojakaṭa, Bhogavardhana, and Nasik,[25] indicating an extensive geographical reach. A text of the period refers to merchants and artisans from Bactria, China, and Alexandria.[26] Yavana donors are referred to in cave inscriptions such as the one at Nasik which mentions Indrāgnidatta, the son of Dhammadeva *yavana*,[27] the northerner from Dattamitri, believed to be the town of Demetrias sometimes indentified with Kandahar although the identification is not certain.[28] Yavana donors also identify themselves with Gata/s which has been taken as a reference to Trigarta in northern India but would perhaps make greater sense if identified with Coptos near Alexandria in Egypt.[29]

That Yavanas did take to indigenous Indian religions is attested to not only in these inscriptions but also in the well-known Heliodorus column at Besnagar where the Yavana ambassador from Taxila declares his faith in the cult of Vasudeva.[30] In the neighbourhood of this inscription monks are recorded as gifting pillars and railings to a Buddhist monument.[31] Buddhism in any case had by now spread way beyond the Indian heartland. As for Yavana traders who claimed to be Buddhists, a common Buddhist identity with local traders would have been of immense help in trade relations.

The reference to *nigamas* raises the question of whether ceremonial centres led to the growth of market activities or vice versa. In cases where a *stūpa* was built over a locally venerated megalithic site, there Buddhist ritual may have assimilated the local cult. There are other settlements such as Veerapuram and

Kaserpalle which are not associated with Buddhist monuments. The building of a *stūpa* requires raw materials, financial resources, commissariat arrangements for the builders and co-ordination between architects, builders, masons, and so on. That there was an existing lay community which supported the activity is evident from references in the inscriptions to members of the *goṣṭhi* and *nigama*.[32] Did this community become established after the site acquired importance? It is more likely that sites acquired sanctity (perhaps inherited in some cases) and as the community in the area grew and prospered, it began to contribute towards the building of a monument at the site. This would have brought both pilgrims and traders to the settlement. The geographical location of the *stūpa*s was often on trade routes which may earlier have been used in local circuits of exchange by the people of the Megalithic settlements.

The patrons see themselves in various ways: as individual donors, as families making donations, or as a community of donors, whether as groups of *seṭṭhi-gahapati*s or *śreṇi*s or even members of a village, as for instance Kalavaira-gāma: as a community of worshippers but differentiating between *bhikkhus* (monks), *bhikkhuni*s (nuns) and *upāsaka*s and *upāsika*s (lay-followers), which would seem to cut across social identities or at any rate not make sharp distinctions: as a community of monks and nuns who have renounced social ties but whose donations still link them to such ties. This is particularly noticeable in the donations recorded from sites in the Ganges plain which follow a somewhat different pattern. Inscriptions at Sarnath and at Saheth-Maheth of the time of Kaniṣka record gifts made by a monk together with his parents, pupils, companions and teachers, suggesting a cooperative donation.[33] Probably the monk in question, Bala, was a particularly important member of the *saṅgha*. A somewhat unusual inscription at Bedsa in the western Deccan records the gift of a pupil in honour of his teacher who is described as a hermit at the site.[34]

Social distinctions among the donors are not reflected in the location of the inscription on the monument, where the visually more dramatic parts of the *stūpa* could have been reserved for those of high status. Thus, a *torana* or gateway at Bharhut carries an inscription from a family of chiefs—Dhanabhūti Vācchiputa, the grandson of Visadeva Gāgīputa, dating to the Śunga dynasty,[35] but other inscriptions on the same *torana* are of lesser persons. Donations for pillars, coping-stones and parts of railings come from *nigamas*, *seṭṭhis*, lay-women, nuns, *gahapatis*, and preachers.[36] Similarly, at Bedsa the gifts of *seṭṭhis*, *mahārathinīs* (women of chiefly families), and pupils of monks are juxtaposed.[37]

A more direct form of patronage points to other links. Members of the royal family were known to invest money in guilds, the interest from which went towards financing some aspect of the functioning of the Buddhist *saṅgha.* For example, Usavadāta of the Kṣaharata Kṣatrapa family gave a permanent endowment of three thousand *kahapaṇas* to be invested in two weavers' guilds dwelling in Govardhana. The interest from the larger investment was to be used for purchasing the cloth for the robes of the monks.[38] Here a different kind of nexus is established which still draws on patronage but of a less obvious kind. It is also a nexus which brings together royalty, commercial interest, and the *saṅgha.* The status of a weaver's guild was clearly high at this time. Elsewhere an official of the Kuṣāṇa government made an endowment to a guild of flour millers, the interest from which was to be used to feed a hundred *brāhmaṇas* per day.[39] Investments in guilds are also referred to in inscriptions from Nagarjunakonda where *akṣaya-nīvi* or permanent endowments are made of as much as a hundred denarii.[40] Four guilds were involved in this transaction. Perhaps some of these endowments are actualized in the hoards of Roman coins from this area. Gift systems can co-exist with commerce, the gift economy and the market economy not necessarily being in conflict but juxtaposed. The gift can play a dual role of a donation as well as an investment. The geographical network may not be an arbitrary one and can constitute a network of markets and trade as well.

A striking aspect of these donations is the number of women donors. Donations from queens and women of the royal families are, of course, known from Buddhist sites. Aśoka Maurya orders the recording of the donations of his queen Kāruvāki.[41] Sātavāhana and Ikṣvāku inscriptions also record such donations. Royal patronage was generally extended to more than a single religious sect since in theory at least it was expected not to be partisan. The political and social dimensions of royal power often made it necessary for there to be a range of patronage and this could be more easily handled along gender lines, although it may not have originated in this form. Thus the Ikṣvāku and Sātavāhana rulers presided over Brahmanical *yajña*s whilst their wives and sisters made donations to Buddhist monuments.[42] This was one way of balancing socio-political factions and pressures. Within this category may also be recorded the donations of the wives of local chiefs in the western Deccan. This is not to preclude the importance of the wishes of individual women making donations to particular religious sects, but rather to suggest that the support given to religious sects may also have been encouraged by other considerations, however conscious or subconscious.

What is more striking however are the donations of ordinary women contributing to the building and adornment of *stūpa*s and *caitya*s and the cutting of cells and cisterns in the rock monasteries. These come in larger numbers from the *seṭṭhi-gahapati* and artisanal families. This is in conformity with the Pāli canon where women from wealthy *gahapati* families are listed as donors. There is also a close relation between the *saṅgha* and women donors at *stūpa* sites where many such donations come from nuns. This may have been because such donations were small. Generally the contributions are linked to individual names. However in the case of a land donation, the names are often mentioned as part of a family. In family donations women are given equal importance with men. Frequently the donations are made by a husband and wife. This raises the question of whether women in the *gahapati* group shared in rights to their husbands' property. In some cases the donations are from widows together with their sons. The recording of such joint donations may be due to Buddhist women having a better status or else, local inheritance systems being different from those described in the *Dharmaśāstra*s.

These inscriptions are in sharp contrast to the statements of the Manu *Dharmaśāstra* on the position of women.[43] Where the donation is by a single woman there it could be argued that it was part of her *strī-dhana*, the wealth given to a woman by her parents, more specifically by her mother, over which the woman theoretically had complete rights of disposal. However, it does remain curious that such records are more frequent in Buddhist and Jaina contexts than those of other religious sects. Devotion to the Buddhist teaching on the part of women from royal families and those of merchants and financiers, is not unknown in Mahāyāna texts of this period, some of which are thought to have been compiled in the eastern Deccan. A well-known section of the *Prajñāpāramitā* narrates in detail the story of the daughter of the merchant who assisted the *bodhisattva* Sadāprarudita to realize the *dhamma* (*Aṣṭasāhasrikā-prajñāpāramitā-sūtram*).[44]

As an economic activity patronage can be seen as the redistribution of wealth, in this case from the individual or the family to the *saṅgha*, or from one group of professionals to another as, for instance, in the donation made by the guild of corn dealers which doubtless went to finance the guild of stone-carvers working on the monument. The ivory-workers' guild have not told us in their inscription whether they worked on the *stūpa* in their spare time or whether they dedicated their time as wealth. Possibly the idea of time as wealth was not one readily recognized by that society. The overlap of patron and craftsman or artist in this situation enhanced the status of the craftsman. This overlap is an inversion of the pattern of patronage as it is generally defined where the patron is distinct from the artist and of a higher social status. The patron as the donor is materially richer than the recipient, but in this case the recipient is the *saṅgha* whose wealth theoretically is non-existent since the monks and nuns have renounced wealth. Nevertheless the *saṅgha* even as recipient has a higher moral authority than the patron. This may point to a characteristic of at least some other patterns of patronage as well. In the embedded patronage of the lineage-based societies (or what have more commonly been called 'tribal' societies), the bard as the genealogist of the chief had in some respects an authority higher than the chief even though the chief was his patron. The legitimation by descent of the chief so crucial to such societies lay in the hands of the genealogist. This relationship has been characteristic even of later-day smaller kingdoms until recent times.[45]

The economic structure of patronage to the *saṅgha* did not remain the same over time. Contributions to the building of *stūpa*s changed from a larger number of small donations to a fewer number of large donations. This may have had to do with a greater economic consolidation of traders and prosperous artisans.[46] Inscriptions refer to a variety of professions which earlier were regarded as not very lucrative such as timber merchants, cloak-makers, blacksmiths, masons, and builders. Contributions to the cutting of caves come less often from professional groups and more frequently from rich donors, specifically *seṭṭhi*s, apart from royalty and high status officers.

The actual process of collecting contributions in money or in kind was probably through itinerant monks doing the rounds of their 'parish', demarcated by the boundary of each monastic institution. Alternatively, donations could be collected when lay followers and others came on pilgrimage at special calendrical events. The urban organization of guilds and the concept of shares in a guild may have been the prototype for such a collection. This probably also led to monks taking on a supervisory role in the construction of the monument which may gradually have included the more technical aspects of architecture and sculpture; hence the references to the *navakamika*/builder, Damaguta, the pupil of Aya Pasanaka.[47] Another inscription[48] refers to a monk, Saṅgharakhita, who was also a pupil or *atevāsin* of Aya Pasanaka. If pupilage here referred merely to Buddhist teaching from a monk, then the word *śiṣya* is more likely to have been used. The term *atevāsin* is often used for apprenticeship. A large-scale monument would obviously require planning, phasing, and over-seeing which may originally have been left to the guild of builders but which eventually went into the making of the profession of *sūtradhāra*s so central to the architecture of the post-Gupta period.

Community patronage of this kind began to decline from the mid-first millennium AD with the increase in royal patronage and still later that of wealthy landowners. Some of this had to do with the decline of Buddhism in northern and western India when with the slowing down of trade, the usual patronage to Buddhist monasteries also decreased. Decline in trade meant the decline of the guild as an important urban unit. The guild sometimes evolved into a *jāti*, functioning therefore both as a guild and as a caste, but its economic power is likely to have been curtailed or diffused. Where the patronage to the *saṅgha* came from royalty as in the case of some Kuṣāṇa rulers its demise accompanied that of the dynasty. The rise to power of the Gupta dynasty supporting Vaiṣṇava worship diverted royal patronage. Increasing royal patronage to monuments dedicated to Purāṇic deities, which monuments grew from small shrine rooms to complex cosmic representations on a grand scale, further eroded the earlier pattern. The survival of Jainism in India continued the tradition of community patronage in areas where commerce flourished although some of the more spectacular monuments were funded by royalty.

There are, however, some examples of the continuation of community patronage in the idiom of Purāṇic Hindu religious sects. Among these is that of the guild of silk weavers who migrated from the district of Lāṭa in western India to the town of Daśapura (Mandasor) in Malwā in AD 436 and financed the building of a temple to Sūrya, the sun god.[49] Only some members of the guild continued as silk weavers whereas others took to a variety of professions such as archery and astrology and some became *kathākāras* and so on. Yet they retained their earlier identity as members of a guild and jointly financed the temple.

The migration was doubtless necessitated by the gradual fall in the silk trade between western India and the eastern Mediterranean. Earlier the routes from northern India passing through Taxila, Mathura, and Ujjain and terminating at Barbaricum and Barygaza/Bhṛgukaccha were the conduits of Chinese silk being taken to Alexandria and the eastern Roman empire. The Parthians had obstructed the overland route between Palmyra and Central Asia. Both Chinese silk routed through India and Indian silk were prized items in the Roman trade with India.[50] The Sino-Indian trade reflected an intermeshing of some varieties of Buddhist ritual with commercial commodities.[51] However, by the mid-first millennium AD not only had the Huns begun to threaten the availability of Chinese silk in northern India but Roman trade itself had declined and what remained of it had moved further east. This shift would also have affected the production of silk in western India.

There are some noticeable differences in guild patronage to the *stūpa* and to the Sūrya temple. The inscription recording the latter is more than just a statement of fact. In commissioning the poet Vatsabhaṭṭi to compose the inscription commemorating the temple and the guild, the guild was performing a further act of patronage. Vatsabhaṭṭi, as has been pointed out, was a hack poet who plagiarized liberally from the *Meghadūta* and the *Ṛtusaṃhāra* of Kālidāsa and who used, predictably, all the conventions of Sanskrit poetics.[52] He gives precise dates for both the building of the temple and its renovation thirty-seven years later, mentioning the *tithi*, *pakṣa*, season and era, in this case the Mālava era of *c.* 58 BC. Such precise dating is more often associated with the inscriptions recording grants of land, which, being legal charters of ownership had to be carefully dated. The details of the date may also have been linked to the notion of choosing the most auspicious moment for commencing the building of the temple. It forms an interesting contrast to the votive inscriptions from Buddhist monuments which are generally not dated although Buddhist textual sources more conscious of chronology than those of a Purāṇic provenance, date major events in years from the death of the Buddha. That the same guild members repaired the temple after thirty-seven years points to their continuing identity and to their economic prosperity in spite of their varying professions.

Brahmanism established status through the ritual of sacrifice, the *yajña* (among other things) which was tangible in performance but its tangibility evaporated after the ritual was completed. In Purāṇic Hinduism, which increased in popularity from the Christian era, the temple housing an image came to symbolize the sacred place and worship, and these in turn were the manifestation of the religion initially at elite levels. The sculpting of images and the building of temples initiated a new pattern of patronage. Gradually the donation came to include not only the concept of *dāna* or gift offered to the deity through the representative of the deity, but also that of *bhakti* or devotion to the deity which was essentially a relationship between the worshipper and the deity.

The act of patronage, seemingly isolated, in fact links up many facets of society. It can be functional in as much as, in one of the aspects under discussion, it makes possible the construction or the embellishment of a monument such as the *stūpa*. As an object of worship the *stūpa* carries a magico-religious meaning which is extended by some of the forms of embellishment as for example, the *yakṣīs* and the *śāla-bhañjikās*. In the making of the object there is also the aesthetic consideration which draws upon both local perception as well as more universally established aesthetic norms as is so evident in the differing styles of Sanchi and Amaravati. Both social relationships and notions of aesthetics are embodied in the *stūpa* and to that extent it becomes a cultural symbol.

Community patronage raises the question of the definition of the community. There are no tangible boundaries which define a community. Often the bonds are of various kinds—language, religion, observance of social customs, acceptance of political authority—and these would constitute intersecting communities. The definition of community in the context of the discussion in this essay, identified by religious observances and language, cuts across geographical regions. In the case of the silk weavers' guild making donations towards a Sūrya temple, the sense of community was narrower and largely coincided with the identity of a particular guild excluding other silk weavers' guilds or any guilds for that matter, as also other worshippers of Sūrya, not to mention such categories of people settled in more distant regions.

Community patronage as discussed here points to a cultural and social innovation for that period. It indicates the emergence of new social groups which, apart from other features, also identify themselves with a particular kind of patronage and with new aesthetic forms. The later association with a temple to Sūrya is a redefinition of the same social category but with enough flexibility to identify with a new idiom. In both cases the act of patronage introduces changes in cultural forms. The object chosen is associated with worship and it is curious that this new social group made no apparent attempt to contribute towards the construction of a secular building, or perhaps such attempts have not survived. One expects that there might have been an impressive meeting hall for the guilds. This absence has often been explained as deriving from the essentially religious nature of Indian society. It would be equally valid, however, to turn the argument inside out as it were and suggest that the nature of early Indian religion in the context as discussed here was closely tied to social identity and perhaps more so than to individual worship. In such a situation a religious movement tends to become a cultural signal with an extensive social dimension.

Notes and References

1. These categories are in part based on those discussed by Raymond Williams in *Culture*, London, 1984.

2. For example, 6.63; 5.27; 5.30; 8.5; 8.6.

3. R. Thapar, *Ancient Indian Social History: Some Interpretations*, New Delhi, 1978, pp. 105ff. R. Thapar, *From Lineage to State*, New Delhi, 1984.

4. N. Zeigler, 1976, 'Marwari Historical Chronicles', *Indian Economic and Social History Review*, vol. XIII, April–June 1976, pp. 219ff.

5. C.A. Gregory, *Gifts and Commodities*, London, 1982.

6. The basic archaeological and epigraphic data has been gathered from the following sources: J. Burgess, *Report on the Buddhist Cave Temples and their Inscriptions*, ASWI, IV, Varanasi, 1964 (reprint); J. Burgess and Bhagwanlal Indraji, *Inscriptions from the Cave Temples of Western India*, ASWI, X, 1881; A. Cunningham, *The Stūpa of Bharhut*, London, 1879; A. Cunningham, *Bhilsa Topes*, Varanasi, 1960 (reprint); H. Luders, *Bharhut Inscriptions*, CII, vol. II, Ootacammund, 1963 (reprint); J. Marshall and A. Foucher, *Monuments of Sanchi*, Calcutta, 1940; M.K. Dhavalikar, *Sanchi—A Cultural Study*, Poona, 1965; V. Dehejia, *Early Buddhist Rock Temples*, London, 1972; *Epigraphia Indica*, vols II, V, X, IX–XII; S.B. Deo and J.P. Joshi, *Pauni Excavation 1969–70*, Nagpur, 1972; S.B. Deo and M.K. Dhavalikar, *Paunar Excavation (1967)*, Nagpur, 1968; S.B. Deo and R.S. Gupte, *Excavation at Bhokardan*, Nagpur, 1974.

7. *Epigraphia Indica* (*Ep. Ind.*), New Delhi, II, p. 378, no. 200.

8. *Aṅguttara Nikāya*, III, 363, R. Morris and E. Hardy (eds), PTS, London, 1885–1900.

9. *Gautama Dharmaśāstra*, X.60, trans. G. Buhler, Sacred Books of the East, II, Oxford, 1879; *Manava Dharmaśāstra/Manu Dharmaśāstra*, X.99–100, J.R. Gharpure (ed.), Bombay, 1922; or even the *Kauṭilya Arthaśāstra*, 1.3.8, R.P. Kangle (ed.), Bombay, 1965.

10. Alberuni, E.C. Sachau, *Alberuni's India*, Delhi, 1964 (reprint), vol 1, pp. 101–2.

11. *Mahāvastu*, II, 363–97, (trans.) J. Jones, PTS, London, 1973.

12. *Dīgha Nikāya*, 3.218, T.W. Rhys Davids and J.E. Charpentier (eds), PTS, London, 1890–1911. *Aṅguttara Nikāya*, 4.239, 246.

13. J. Ebert, 1980, 'Parinirvāṇa and Stūpa', in A.L. Dallapiccola *et al.*, *The Stūpa, Its Religious, Historical and Architectural Significance*, Heidelberg, Band, 55, 1980, pp. 219–28.

14. Discussion by Goswamy in A.L. Dallapiccola *et al.*, *The Stūpa*.

15. H.P. Ray, *Monastery and Guild*, Delhi, 1986.

16. S. Gokhale, 'Recent Epigraphical Discoveries at Kanheri', in S.B. Deo and K. Paddayya (eds), *Recent Advances in Indian Archaeology*, Poona, 1985

17. Lüder's List 346. These numbers refer to Lüders' List in *Epigraphia Indica*, vol. x. A. Cunningham, *Bhilsa Topes*, Varanasi (reprint), 1960, p. 264, no. 190.

18. Lüders' List 857.

19. J. Burgess and Bhagwanlal Indraji, *Inscriptions from the Cave Temples of Western India*, ASWI, x, 1881, Varanasi, 1976 (reprint), p. 30, no. 6.

20. *Ep. Ind.* I, p. 390, no. 18

21. Lüders' List 150.

22. Burgess and Indraji, *Inscriptions from the Cave Temples*, p. 29 no. 4, p. 30 no. 6, p. 31 no. 7, p. 32ff no. 11; Luders List 1020, 1121.

23. Lüders' List 986, 988, 995, 998, 1000, 1001, 1005, 1013, 1014.

24. Lüders' List 705.

25. Lüders' List 712, 719, 723, 797, 799.

26. *Milindapañha*, 4.8.88, 5.4, 6.21, (trans.) T.W. Rhys Davids, New York, 1963 (reprint).

27. *Ep. Ind.* VIII, p. 90, no. 17.

28. P.M. Fraser, 'The Son of Aristonax at Kandahar', *Afghan Studies*, 1979, vol. 2, 1980, pp. 9–21.

29. Trigarta, identified in the past with the region of Kangra or of Jallandhar was not an important enough trading centre at this time to attract traders from West Asia although it lay along the Himalayan route. On the analogy of Sandracottos being equated linguistically with Candragupta, Coptos or even Aegyptos could have been rendered as Gutas or Gatas in Prākṛit. Admittedly this is not a definitive reading, but given the references to trade between western India and Egypt via the Red Sea during this period such an identification of Gatas is at least plausible. For references to Gatas see Burgess and Indraji, *Inscriptions from the Cave Temples*, Junnar inscriptions, nos 5 and 33, pp. 43, 55; Lüders' List, 1154, 1182.

30. D.C. Sircar, *Select Inscriptions . . .*, Calcutta, 1965, I, pp. 100ff.

31. Lüders' List 671–4.

32. Bhattiprolu Casket Inscriptions, *Ep. Ind.* II, 327–8, nos 3,5,6.

33. *Ep. Ind.* VIII, pp. 179–81; VIII, pp. 173ff, No. 3; IX, p. 241; IX, pp. 290–1.

34. Burgess and Indraji, *Inscriptions from the Cave Temples*, p. 26, no.1.

35. E.A. Hultzsch, 'Bharhut Buddhist Pillar Inscription', *Indian Antiquary, vol.* XIV, 1985, pp. 138ff; and 'Bharhut Buddhist Pillar Inscription', *Indian Antiquary*, vol. XXI, 1892, p. 227.

36. Hultzsch, 'Bharhut Buddhist Pillar Inscription', 1892, pp. 225, 228, no. 16; p. 229, nos 22, 27, 28, 31; p. 230, nos 33, 36; p. 232, no. 67. Luders' List 705, 712, 718, 719, 723, 725, 728, 763, 804, 812.

37. Burgess and Indraji, *Inscriptions from the Cave Temples*, p. 26, nos 1, 2; p. 27, no. 3; Lüders' List 1109, 1110, 1111.

38. Nasik Cave Inscription No. 10, *Ep. Ind.* VIH, pp. 78ff.

39. *Ep. Ind.* XXI, p. 60.

40. *Ep. Ind.* XX, pp. 16ff.

41 Bloch p. 159.

42. *Ep. Ind.* XX, pp. 1ff; Rosen in Dallapiccola *et al.*, *The Stūpa.*

43. *Manu Dharmaśāstra, 5.148–5.156; 9.2–9.7.*

44. *Quoted in D. Paul, 1984, Women in Buddhism*, Berkeley, 1984, pp. 115ff.

45. This continues to be true even in this century as is evidenced by the relationship of the Pardhans to their patrons, the Thakurs, in the upper Narmada. S.R. Hivale, *The Pardhans of the Upper Narmada Valley*, Bombay, 1946.

46. *Dīgha Nikāya* 1.51; *Majjhima Nikāya* 1.85; *Mahāvastu* 3.113.443; *Milindapañha* 5.4.331.

47. Lüders' List 154.

48. Lüders' List 155.

49. *Mandasor Inscription in* J.F. Fleet, *Inscriptions of the Early Gupta Kings and Their Successors*, Corpus Inscriptionum Indicarum, III, Varanasi (reprint), 1970.

50. M.G. Raschke, 'New Studies in Roman Commerce with the East', in H. Temporim and W. Haase (eds), *Aufstieg und Niedergang der Romischen Welt*, Berlin, 1978.

51. X. Liu, *Ancient India and Ancient China*, Delhi, 1987.

52. A.L. Basham, 'The Mandasor Inscription of the Silk Weavers', in B.L. Smith (ed.), *Essays on Gupta Culture*, Delhi, 1983, pp. 93–105.

Section V

Towards Further Change

CHAPTER 15

Śakuntalā

*Histories of a Narrative**

The manner in which we construct the past is now acknowledged as an important process in the writing of history. This involves appropriating the past, an act in which the concerns of the present are apparent. Historical sources are used to construct a link between an event in the past and how we view it today. I would like to argue that there are in addition many representations of an event between the point at which it happened and the present, and that these representations are significant to the eventual understanding of the past. Such representations in the form of a narrative may either be fictional or may claim to embody an event, but in both cases they address themselves to a historical moment. This brings the relationship between narrative and history to the forefront.

In this essay, I will be looking at this relationship through the different versions of a fictionalized narrative, illustrating my argument with the story of Śakuntalā in its variant forms. Does the retelling of the same narrative help our understanding of historical change in as much as the retelling reflects change in both society and ideology? Can we treat the act of narrativization or the making of a narrative, as constituting an event? Every narrative has a context which is consciously or subconsciously derived from a world view and an ideology. Let me hastily add, however, that this is not to authenticate a story as history, for a story remains fictional. But it can reveal perspectives of a time and a society. I am suggesting that it be analysed as representing such a perspective,

* This chapter was first published in *Narratives and the Making of History: Two Lectures*, New Delhi, Oxford University Press, 2000, pp. 1–23.

which emerges all the more clearly through a comparison of its retellings. A fictionalized narrative cannot be treated as history but it can be an indicator of a past condition. What I am arguing for is the analysis of narratives which become constituents of a historical perception and have, therefore, a contextual location.

A narrative can have its own biography and the changes it manifests can provide us with a view of historical change. By historical change I do not mean just chronology but rather, the manifold dimensions of the historical context. A narrative frequently recreated over time becomes multi-layered like a palimpsest. One can attempt to reveal the many pasts which went into the making of its present. Where the retellings of a narrative or where narratives implying an event, become contesting versions, the differing perspectives also provide evidence for historical constructions. In my next essay (Chapter 16) I shall be discussing the many representations of a well-known event—the raid of Maḥmūd of Ghazni on the temple of Somānatha in 1026—to see how the event is viewed from various perspectives. The next essay is therefore in some ways an inversion of this one. The subject matter of the two essays is not linked, but there is a methodological link in seeing the relationship of narrative to history.

This relationship has been the subject of lively discussion among historians. Best known perhaps was the discussion between Lawrence Stone on the revival of narrative in history and its critique by Eric Hobsbawm, published in the 1980s in the British historical journal, *Past and Present*. The discussions focused largely on whether there was a shift away from social and economic history, drawing on the disciplines of the social sciences, towards directing attention to language, culture, and ideas and a focus on micro-events. Was this a new way of viewing the structures of the story and of society? The suggested duality was found to be untenable since there was a considerable overlap in both sources and interpretations. Even narrative history as it has developed in recent times, was not just a bald telling of a story. The new use of narrative incorporated analytical history and the analyses of the micro-event illumined the macro-generalization.

The discussion has taken a different form in this decade with the introduction of what has been termed 'the linguistic turn'.[1] Some have stated that history as a discipline has no future given the kind of analyses of narrative which are possible. History in this argument becomes a kind of *pointillist* history—rather like the style of painting—a collection of unconnected dots which taken together compose a picture. Historians have reacted with the logical argument that even these dots have to be contextualized as indeed does the picture itself. However significant the understanding of the fragments may be, history attempts to look at the larger whole. What 'the linguistic turn' has done is to make historians more aware of the nuances of language and words, which far from terminating historical investigation, have added to its precision.

The writing of history has had a continuous interface with literature. Historians have culled literature for information on what may have happened in the past, the statements being juxtaposed with other kinds of evidence. This is a legitimate activity. I would, however, suggest a sharpening of this interface by changing the focus somewhat, by searching for the historical perspectives which this interface provides, through examining the representations present in the narrative. The same narrative or approximately the same, can occur in variant forms as different genres of literature—in this case, the story of Śakuntalā in the *Mahābhārata*, the play of Kālidāsa, the prose-poem in *Braja-bhāṣā*. From a different perspective but with a bearing on the narrative, are the many translations of the Kālidāsa play where the act of translation in itself becomes a cultural negotiation, and there is also the commentary in the form of an essay by Rabindranath Tagore. These are significant moments in the biography of a narrative.

But there is more that just an interface between literature and history. The narrative of Śakuntalā, highlights the gender perspective. The same character is depicted differently in the variant forms. Does this reflect different social perceptions, the understanding of which requires some familiarity with the historical context? The form which the variants take—epic fragment, drama, poetry—and the cultural interpretations which they encourage, makes the narrative an item in cultural history.

Choosing a particular item from the past and recreating it as a variant is in part, an act of historical significance. The past is viewed from the present, wherever the present may be located, and that which is selected from the past goes into constructing a tradition or constructing a history. A tradition is never handed down intact from generation to generation, however appealing this idea may seem. Innovation is what gives it vitality. The items selected from the past are often so chosen as to legitimize the values and codes of the present. In selecting and recasting cultural items we highlight some and marginalize others. The act of selection becomes a dialogue with the past.

The point in time at which the selection is being made gives a different value to the selection as a cultural symbol, as an idiom, as an icon. This has happened throughout our cultural history, although our awareness of this process is perhaps more apparent now. Where the narrative is culturally central to our own present today, we have also to see it as a part of the intervention of the colonial period and recognize the disjunctive this may produce.

The concept of culture in relation to the early past, implies an intersecting of disciplines of which history, it seems to me is foundational. This involves the original text and its historical contexts, as also frequently the Orientalist reading of it and equally frequently, the internalizing of this reading by commentators of the last century or two. And more recently, the questioning of this reading. Inevitably there is a contextualizing of the Orientalist representation and European perspectives brought to bear on the reading. A single item can therefore have multiple identities which change at historical moments. Understanding a cultural item historically requires some comprehension of the world view which it represented. Each version has some relation with those which preceded it: a relation ranging from endorsement to contestation of earlier versions.

I would like to touch on some of these ideas using the narrative of Śakuntalā. My focus, therefore, is not on the Kālidāsa play, but on the treatment of the central figure which transforms the narrative in its variant versions; and on the possible historical explanations for the variants and the commentaries.

Let me now turn to the narrative.

The *ākhyāna* or narrative of Śakuntalā as given in the Ādiparvan of the *Mahābhārata*[2] is one among the many bardic fragments which were stitched together in the making of the epic. In many of these fragments the morphology of the folk tale is evident. There are other sections of the *Mahābhārata*, such as the Śānti parvan, which have been labelled as didactic. These have less to do with the story and more with theories of the ideal society, of social obligations—*dharma*, of government—*rāja-dharma*, of ideas about the liberation of the soul—*mokṣa-dharma*, and such like. The Śakuntalā story occurs in the narrative section.[3]

Rājā Duḥṣanta, with the title of *goptā*, a protector of cows, has conquered widely. One day he goes on a hunt accompanied by a large entourage of soldiers. The hunt turns into a fierce killing of tigers and deer, the wounding of elephants, the uprooting of trees and a general devastation of nature. Duḥṣanta follows a deer deep into the forest which brings him to the secluded *āśrama* of Kaṇva. On calling out, a young woman answers and performs the ritual of welcome for the guest. She introduces herself as Śakuntalā, the daughter of the *ṛṣi* Kaṇva. On Duḥṣanta asking her how a *ṛṣi* could have daughter, she explains her parentage in detail. Indra, disturbed by the powers which the *ṛṣi* Viśvāmitra was accumulating through *tapasya*, sent the *apsarā* Menakā to seduce him. Śakuntalā was born but discarded by Menakā and brought up as a foundling by Kaṇva in his *āśrama.*

Duḥṣanta, deeply attracted by what he calls 'the flawless girl of the beautiful hips', proposes a *gāndharva* marriage. This was a marriage by mutual consent, appropriate it is said, to *kṣatriya*s. Śakuntalā agrees but sets a condition that she will only marry him if the son born of this marriage is declared his successor. After a three-year pregnancy she gives birth to a boy, Bharata. She takes him at a young age to Hastināpura from where Duḥṣanta rules, and demands that Duḥṣanta recognize him as his heir. Duḥṣanta pretends not to recognize her and rejects them both. Śakuntalā in extreme anger, explains why a wife and son are necessary to him, particularly a son to continue the lineage. The exchange is heated with much down-to-earth abuse. Menakā is called a slut. Viśvāmitra a lecher and Śakuntalā a whore. Śakuntalā stands her ground and insists that the boy be given his status and to that end she decides to leave him with Duḥṣanta. As she is about to return to the *āśrama*, a disembodied celestial voice proclaims that the boy is indeed Duḥṣanta's son. Duḥṣanta explains that he had remembered his meeting with her and had no doubt about the veracity of Śakuntalā's claim, but was waiting for this public legitimation of the relationship. Subsequently he accepts them both. Bharata, when he comes to rule is acclaimed as a great ruler.

The story in the epic is the origin myth of Bharata and therefore also tied into the ancestry of the Kauravas and the Pāṇḍavas, central to the events in the *Mahābhārata*. Divine proclamation establishes status and legitimacy because the relationship has also to be accepted by the clansmen. It is a society of clans and heroes, a lineage-based society, where ancestry, genealogy, and origins are vital.[4] It is also a cattle-keeping society requiring extensive grazing grounds. Hence the respect for the title of *goptā*. The clearing of land and of forest for agriculture was recognized as a source of wealth. The hunt is a surrogate raid, a war against nature but also a means of establishing claims to territory. So dominance over the forest is beginning to assume importance.

The depiction of Śakuntalā is central to the story. She is forthright, free, high-spirited and assertive. She makes her marriage conditional and then demands that the promise be honoured. She accuses Duḥṣanta of behaving unrighteously. She is the reverse of the *pativratā*, the ideal wife as described in the didactic sections of the epic. The dispute is clearly over the paternity of the child. The condition she imposed at the time of the *gāndharva* marriage hinged on the status of her son, characteristic of a patriarchal society. This was also crucial to the status of the woman in such a society even if it was a clan-based society: she was the link to kinship and alliances, and her son ensured her membership of the clan. The celestial voice describes the mother as the receptacle, for it is the father who begets the son, and the son frees the father from the abode of the dead. Implicit in this utterance is the statement that Duḥṣanta accept responsibility for the child.

The period of the composition of the epic remains controversial but generally it is thought that the composition and the interpolations can be placed between 400 BC and AD 400, the narrative sections possibly being earlier than the didactic sections.[5] The epic continues to have an audience well into the centuries AD. It is part of ancestral mythology and provides links with the heroes of old. The epic was added to often enough, and presumably when it was converted to sacred literature it became part of Brahmanical high culture. However, the hierarchy in this high culture would have placed the epics and *Purāṇa*s in what some regarded as the not-so-high culture, perhaps because of their links with folk culture.

I would now like to turn to the play, the *Abhijñāna-śākuntalam* of Kālidāsa.[6] It reflects a different historical scene. It was written subsequent to the story in the epic and is generally dated to about the fourth century AD although the date is controversial. Kālidāsa selects a fragment from the epic, converts the narrative into a *nāṭaka*/play, which is a different genre of literature from the poetry of the epic. To the original narrative he adds other sub-themes. One is the story of the ring as a token of recognition which seems to have come from the Buddhist *Kaṭṭahāri Jātaka*.[7] The other is the theme of the curse which is frequent in folk literature. There is, as a result, the creating of a new tradition. An item, selected from the past, is moulded to suit the cultural expression of the later time. It could be seen almost as a contestation with the epic version, the norms of which undergo changes in the play.

The play is no longer concerned with lineage-based societies and clans but carries the rhetoric of the political power of monarchical states. These were well established, legitimizing the concentration of power in a single family and the authority of upper-caste society. The state had its appurtenances of administration, revenue, coercive agencies, and such like. There is also the visibility of Brahmanical high culture which was dominant in the construction of classicism and therefore familiar to Kālidāsa. It is evident in the use of language and in the nuanced relationship between the characters. Kingship is approximate to deity and kings and gods intermingle. The *āśrama* of the Kaṇvas carries traces of a new incipient institution which was to develop into the *agrahāras* of post-Gupta times, institutions which changed the socio-economic landscape. Tax-free land was donated by the king for settlement by *brāhmaṇas* which could be in areas already under cultivation or newly opened to cultivation. These were to become powerful nuclei and networks of Brahmanical culture.

The play itself is intended for performance at the court before a small, sophisticated, urban audience, and not as part of a popular recitation. It reflects the values of upper-caste society although there may implicitly on occasion be some questioning of these. Intended as entertainment, the theme was inevitably romantic.

The changes introduced by Kālidāsa are significant to more than just the story-line. Duḥṣanta/Duṣyanta leaves his ring with Śakuntalā as a token of his promise to send for her on his return to Hastināpura. Deep in thought one day, Śakuntalā neglects to receive with appropriate ceremony an irascible *ṛṣi* Durvāsas who therefore spews out his curse that the person she is thinking of will not remember her. Her friends plead for at least a modification of the curse and the *ṛṣi* then says that the ring will provide the remembrance. Śakuntalā leaves for the court and on the way loses the ring. On arriving there, she is not recognized by Duṣyanta and no amount of persuasion convinces him that she is his legally wedded wife bearing his son. Śakuntalā in despair calls upon Mother Earth and there is a flash of lightning and she is whisked away to the *āśrama* of Mārīca. Here she gives birth to her son Bharata. Meanwhile the ring is found in the belly of a fish, and since it is his signet ring, it is brought to Duṣyanta. On seeing it he recollects his relationship with Śakuntalā. He is now full of remorse at having lost both a wife and a son. The eventual happy outcome occurs when the king is called to Indra's aid in a campaign against the demons. On his return he stops at the *āśrama* of Mārīca where he is united with his wife and son.

The story of the play is an elaboration of the skeletal story in the epic. Courtly drama requires a romantic mood and dramatic effects. The teasing out of the narrative is done through the subplots of the curse and the ring. There is a contrapuntal relationship between the two; the curse impedes action and is a barrier, the ring resolves the barrier so that the action can move.

The curse and the ring gloss over the tension between Duṣyanta and Śakuntalā, both over the paternity of the child and the responsibility of the father. But Śakuntalā in the play cannot defend the right of her son because the flow of events is beyond human control and she had made no conditions to the marriage. Duṣyanta cannot be blamed for rejecting her as he is under a spell. Is Kālidāsa therefore avoiding the moral issue of condemning Duṣyanta's action in rejecting Śakuntalā? Or would this not have been regarded as irresponsible in those times and in that society? The epic version does at least raise the issue through the celestial voice.

The structure of the play seems to be based on a duality which comes to be associated with an increasingly common view of the world. It is expressed in terms of the dichotomy of the *grāma* and the *araṇya* or the *kṣetra* and the *vana*—the settlement and the forest.[8] It is generic to the epic where the broader action moves back and forth from settlement to forest. But it is strongly indented in the play as well. One of the reasons for this may be that by the Gupta period attitudes towards the forest were beginning to change. Whereas earlier the settlement was the ordered society and the forest the habitat of the unknown, and the wild, now the forest was beginning to be seen differently: as a source of revenue through its natural products of timber and elephants; its potential as agricultural land after clearing; and as the location of *brāhmaṇa* settlements, in the form of *agrahāra*s. The society of the forest was no longer entirely unknown, but it was still different from village settlements and the difference continued to be emphasized.

The dichotomy is highlighted in the play between the *āśrama* of Kaṇva and the court at Hastināpura. It is further underlined in the depiction of Śakuntalā as the woman of the *āśrama* and Duḥṣanta as the man of the court. The *āśrama* in the play is the liminal area, the threshold between the settlement and the forest, for although it is set deep in the forest, the people who live there attuned to nature, are nevertheless also aware of the mores and customs of the settled society, from where they have come. They are not *aṭavikas*, forest-dwellers, in origin.

Kālidāsa seems to use this duality to reverse the activities associated with each. The *āśrama* becomes the location for what has been called love-in-union—*saṃbhoga śṛṅgāra*, generally not associated with *āśramas*. The court is the location for love-in-separation—*vipralamba śṛṅgāra*, where she is rejected and leaves, although most romances achieve fruition at the court.[9]

From the epic narrative to the play there is a change in the conceptualizing of the woman. Śakuntalā is now the child of nature and identifies with plants and animals. She dresses in bark clothes, adorns herself with flowers which miraculously turn into jewels at the time of her departure. Nature weeps at her going away. Her innocence is heightened by her grappling with the emotions of romantic love, leading her to the *gāndharva* marriage. She is shy, retiring, modest, and generally submissive. In the last act she excuses Duṣyanta's action because of his being under a spell, and instead explains to herself that she is reaping the consequences of some wrongdoing on her part in a previous birth.

If Śakuntalā claims to be the wife of Duṣyanta she has to conform to the *pativratā* ideal. Although both Kaṇva and Duṣyanta refer to her as the lawfully wedded wife, one of Kaṇva's disciples hints at the *gāndharva* marriage being a seduction. One wonders whether this is resentment against a woman's transgression of patriarchy and her taking an independent decision, for he insists that she must suffer the consequences of such a decision. She is told that she cannot return to the *āśrama* and has to remain at the court because the husband's authority over the wife is unlimited. He has the right to accept her or abandon her. It is better that a wife be a servant in her husband's home than live away from him.

The epic version had underlined the centrality of the son and the empowerment of the woman, both in herself and as the mother of a son. In the play romantic love seems to supersede this, and the question of empowerment fades away. The king does not taunt her for her illegitimacy but is uncomplimentary about women in general. Eventually the desire for an heir drives the king to as much grief as the disappearance of his beloved.

Subsequent to the Kālidāsa play there were now two versions of the story in circulation. Briefly narrated in the *Purāṇas* as an ancestral myth of the Pūrus it was important to the legitimation of dynasties of the post-Gupta period.[10] The recitations of the *paurānikas* and the *kāthakāras* kept these stories alive among audiences more comfortable with the oral tradition. That it became something of a folk stereotype is evident from the *Kathāsarītasagāra* which includes a charming story using the same theme but replete with folk motifs.[11] Interpretations of visual forms as pictorial representations of the story have also been suggested.[12]

At a somewhat later period the play becomes an item for discussion in a variety of theoretical works on literature and aesthetics. Taking off from the *Nātyaśāstra*, there were wide-ranging views on what constitutes good poetry and drama, discussed in the works of theoreticians such as Abhinavagupta and Ānanadavardhana at the end of the first millennium AD. More specific to the Kālidāsa play is the commentary of Rāghavabhaṭṭa in the sixteenth century. Much of the discussion was in the context of the evolving theories of *rasa*, central to Indian aesthetics. Gradually the Kālidāsa play became central to analysing both poetry and drama and was judged as the exemplar in the Sanskrit *nāṭaka* tradition.

It was doubtless both its reputation as the finest Sanskrit play and the popularity of the story, that led to its being adapted to yet another literary form which was to reach a still wider audience. In 1716, the Mughal emperor Farrukh Siyar bestowed a title on a nobleman at the court. To celebrate this, the court poet, Navāz Kavisvara, was asked to render—not to translate—the story of Śakuntalā from Sanskrit into Braj-*bhāṣā*, the language of much of the Hindi poetry at the time. The story now becomes a *kathā* in verse. The theme of love and separation and the style of the rendering, gives it a quality which recalls the dominant form in Braj poetry at that time—the *bārahmāsā*. This is not to suggest that it was actually a *bārahmāsā*, but shorn of the borrowings from the play, it was a *kathā* concerned with lovers, partings and reunions, characteristic of this kind of Braj poetry.[13] The language is earthy, the poetry sounds like doggerel verse at times. Śakuntalā emerges as less given to romanticism and more down-to-earth, a distinct echo of the Śakuntalā of the epic. In some ways this is a mediation between the epic version and the play.

In 1806, the Braj-*kathā* was translated into an Urdu prose-poem, *Shakuntala*, by Mirza Qasim Ali Dehlavi, a poet teaching at the recently established Fort William College at Calcutta. This brings an infusion of the Persian *dāstān* style with its world of fables and exaggerated emotions. Śakuntalā, in embarrassment, constantly hides behind her *ghunghat*, and the king in true Majnu or Farhad style, swoons almost every time he sees her. But the dialogue remains earthy and the exchanges between the king and Śakuntalā make for racy reading. The narrative moves away from being a court play and its more accessible language gives it a greater universality. Presumably its performance was accompanied by music, dance, and mime. The feel of eighteenth-century late Mughal society pervades this version.

At this point, the biography of this narrative takes another turn. There are no further literary genres for the retellings, but it entered the world stage through translations. And translation changes the cultural role of the narrative, for it introduces into the play, the culture and the world views of the society using the language of the translation and of its ideologies.

William Jones, often described as the father of British Indology, was an officer of the East India Company at Calcutta, and spent much time in reading and translating Sanskrit texts. He was enthused by the play, and translated it, first into Latin which was linguistically closer to Sanskrit, and then from Latin into English. In 1789 it was published as *Shakoontala or the Fatal Ring.*[14] He gave currency to the phrase that Kālidāsa was the Indian Shakespeare. He maintained that the play demonstrates the height of Indian civilization, all the more remarkable because it was written at a time when the Britons were as unpolished and unlettered as the army of Hanuman. His more significant comment was that he had been disturbed by some of the more erotic passages which would be unacceptable to European taste. And for the first time, the erotic in the play became a matter for debate.

Nevertheless, the play took Europe by storm. It was translated into German and acclaimed by the German poet Goethe in a verse which has since been repeated *ad nauseum.* There followed a succession of ballets and operas on the theme, including an incomplete attempt by Franz Schubert. In each decade of the nineteenth century there was yet another translation in yet another language, even Icelandic. The experimental theatre of Tairoff in Moscow made it the opening presentation with an enthusiastic reception from the Symbolist poets, just prior to the Bolshevik revolution.

Throughout the nineteenth century in European literary circles, and most particularly in the German Romantic Movement, Śakuntalā was projected as the child of nature and the ideal Indian woman encapsulating the beauty of womankind.[15] Her closeness to nature was particularly important to literary Romanticism distancing itself from the formalism of neo-classicism. This was also in part a response to what was referred to as the 'discovery' of the orient or the Oriental Renaissance. European Romanticism was intertwined with Orientalism. To understand the construction of Orientalism and its fusion with European Romanticism, requires a familiarity with the images, created as part of the intellectual history of Europe in the nineteenth century, and the politics of these images. The Oriental Renaissance it was believed, would provide new visions of how man should perceive the world.[16] But the images were what Europe projected onto the Orient. These were crystallized as the duality of the Orient and of Europe as expressed in the preference of Romanticism for the less orderly aspect of the past and its search for the exotic, the irrational, and the imaginative as against the rational and the real, thought to be typical of European classicism.

The creation of what has been called the ideal of India in German Romanticism was also conditioned by early Greek stories of Alexander of Macedon's meetings with Indian philosophers. This was said to explain the presence in substratum European thought of ideas on metempsychosis, the unity of man and nature, and the meaning of renunciation. These were central to the theories of the Neo-Platonists who believed that much of the philosophy alternative to the Judaeo-Christian tradition in Europe, came from Indian sources. Romanticism, therefore, was also questioning the theories of the European mainstream.

With the growth of notions of race and the wide acceptance of what came to be called 'race science' in the later nineteenth century, a touch of racism entered the idyllic picture of a closeness to nature.[17] The children of nature were the primitive peoples, at the foot of the evolutionary ladder. Eroticism, therefore, was an aspect of their unawareness of the need for moral laws.

But the not-so-idyllic relationship between colonizers and the colonized in the nineteenth century contributed to a fading out of the enthusiasm for Romanticism. If in the early nineteenth century there was a concern to reform the native to the ways of the colonizer, by the latter part of the century this was seen as an impossibility because the native was believed to be racially inferior. By the end of the nineteenth century, Śakuntalā had become a collector's item in Europe.

Not so in India. It was in the nineteenth century that the play became important both to debates on colonial cultural policy and to the self-definition of the Indian middle-class. James Mill, writing as a liberal utilitarian, in the early nineteenth century, saw little that was worthwhile in Indian culture, opposed Orientalism, and argued that Sanskrit literature was the literature of a self-indulgent society. It is only nations in their infancy who produce literature which is in praise of the pastoral, for such societies are fettered by despots and they can only indulge in light romances, rather than analysing their condition. The *gāndharva* marriage, the curse, the authority of the *brāhmaṇas*, were for him, signs of Indian degradation.[18]

But there was a tradition among British administrators with a bent for scholarship and working in India, of a more ambiguous view. They felt that those who governed India had to be familiar with its culture and this coincided with forms of exercising power. The so-called 'rediscovery' of the Indian past was in part directed towards this end. But it was also an attempt to revive Indian culture in the format of Orientalist scholarship. This is perhaps best stated in the introduction to yet another translation of the play, published by Monier-Williams in 1855, which superseded the translation of Jones. Where Jones in his writing was representing India both to the Indians and to Europe, now there was a subordination of cultural representation to the politics of governance. The attempt was to mould the Indian understanding of its cultural past in the way in which the colonizer intended.[19]

Monier-Williams states in the Introduction to the eighth edition of his translation published in 1898, that it was intended for a variety, of purposes. It would enable the British to familiarize themselves with the life of the Hindus. It was also part of British policy to rediscover the Indian past for the Indian, to revive Indian culture as defined by Orientalist scholarship, to make the Indian middle class aware of this culture and to imprint on the mind of the Indian middle class, the interpretation given to the culture by Orientalist scholarship. The impression conveyed is that the acclamation for the play should be attributed to Orientalist scholarship, thus forgetting or ignoring, the extensive analyses of earlier literary theorists who wrote some centuries before.

There was now a shift of emphasis and the play was viewed as an item of Hindu culture, explaining the condition of the Hindu subjects of the empire. The reading of the play was moving from Śakuntalā being the child of nature to her being what Monier-Williams calls, the 'rustic maiden'. Nature and culture were no longer juxtaposed for nature had receded and the mores of 'civilization' had become essential to assessing the actions of the play. Initially the play was not selected as a text for the teaching of Sanskrit at college level because it was said to support immorality. Eventually the supposedly erotic passages were deleted and it came to be prescribed. Implicit in this argument is the question of morality—but it is not a comment on the moral decision on which the earlier tradition had focused, that of Duṣyanta's rejection of Śakuntalā. The question of morality as related to eroticism, which had not been a concern earlier, was now made the central issue and impinged on the projection of Śakuntalā.

These ideas had an influence on the emerging Indian middle class. Nineteenth-century nationalism in India is thought to have fostered a conservative attitude towards tradition, because to question it was a concession to Western ideas.[20] The broader middle-class codes were also being forged with the emergence of a new class, associated with the upper castes. These drew from both the new historical situation of colonialism and what was described as the Indian tradition. But in relation to the perspective on women in society, the particular conservatism of Victorian morals had also entered Indian society. There was an appropriation of some of the attitudes of the Judaeo-Christian tradition, attitudes generally absent in early Indian texts. Gradually, the definition of womanly virtues focused on modesty, chastity, self-sacrifice, devotion, and patience. These were the virtues recognized in the Śakuntalā of the play but these would have been unfamiliar to the Śakuntalā of the epic.

In a later phase of nationalism, a certain liberalism towards women was encouraged and women began to tentatively assert what they saw as their rights. Participation in the national movement was not intended to emancipate women but to encourage a sense of partnership. With rare exceptions, most women remained the subordinate partners. Victorian attitudes and social conservatism could not be set aside so easily.

It was only a matter of time, therefore, before someone would declare Śakuntalā's actions as 'the fall of Śakuntalā'. What is surprising is that this comment comes from Rabindranath Tagore. In 1907 he published an essay in Bengali which was later translated into English with the title, 'Śakuntalā: Its Inner Meaning'.[21] He takes Goethe's verse on Śakuntalā as his starting point and argues that the play is a series of developments from the lesser to the finer, from the flower to the fruit, earth to heaven and matter to spirit. From a young, passionate woman Śakuntalā becomes the model of a devoted wife with qualities of reserve, endurance of sorrow, rigid discipline, and piety. According to him, the play focuses on two unions: one is the gross, earthy, physical union with desire contributing to the fall of Śakuntalā—and he uses the words *patana* and *patita* in association with her actions; and the other is the moral union when both Duṣyanta and Śakuntalā have been cleansed through a long period of separation. Their *tapasya* takes the form of grief, remorse, and penance and is necessary to a true and eternal union. Love is not its own highest glory, for goodness is the final goal of love.

This is Tagore's reading of the inner meaning of the play and he sees it as an allegory. Tagore's reading reflects the moral concerns of his time, influenced it would seem by the perspectives of Indian nationalism and also Orientalism. In this reading the empowerment of a woman through the birth of her son, which was significant to the epic story, now becomes unimportant. The woman's morality is the central question.

Let me return to the relationship of narrative and history. If I am reading history into the context of the different versions and commentaries, it is because they are distinct in form and ideology, and when seen in sequence, represent historical changes. I have tried to demonstrate the interface between literature and history not by limiting myself to garnering historical information from the texts but by trying to see the texts as representing historical contexts. I have tried to show that the narrative of Śakuntalā changes, either in itself, or through the many translations of one version, and it becomes an icon of varying concerns. Underlying the sequence is what seems to me to be a transformation of these concerns from earlier times to colonial times: a transformation which shifts the focus quite strikingly. Its visibility is clearest in the treatment of gender.

This is evident in the portrayal of Śakuntalā. She is ostensibly the same character in the variant versions but is in effect, perceived differently in each. The perception is not unrelated to a shifting social and moral focus of the story, shifting in accordance with historical demands. She is the mother of an epic hero in the *Mahābhārata* where the main issue is the paternity of her child and the father's responsibility in recognizing this. In the play she is the romantic ideal of upper-caste high culture, where moral responsibility is misted over by the introduction of the extraneous factors of the curse and the ring. In the Braj-*bhāṣā kathā*, she is not cowed down by the king—if anything it may be the reverse—and insists on his behaving in a just manner. German Romanticism sees her as the child of nature, the personification of innocence and pays little attention to problems of paternity and responsibility. The 'rustic maiden' from the colonial perspective, becomes enmeshed in colonial readings of the erotic in the culture of the colonized. The ideal wife within a nationalism reaching back to what it sees as tradition, raises the question of morality but the problem now devolves around the woman always having to exercise restraint. This is a middle-class perspective since subaltern perspectives remain outside the picture.

I have tried to show that each version comes out of a process of selection and implicit in this is the contemporizing of the icon. We select from the past those images which we want for the present. These contribute to the construction of the self-image of our contemporary culture and its projection back into what is believed to be 'tradition'. From the gender perspective we have in the last two centuries, ignored the Śakuntalā of the *Mahābhārata*, the liberated woman demanding to be justly treated, and have endorsed the Śakuntalā of Kālidāsa, the woman waiting patiently for a recognition of her virtue.

Notes and References

1. R.J. Evans, *In Defence of History*, London, 1997.
2. Ādi *parvan*, 62–9.
3. V.S. Sukthankar, *On the Meaning of the Mahābhārata*, Bombay, 1964.
4. Romila Thapar, *From Lineage to State*, Delhi, 1984.
5. Sukthankar, *On the Meaning of the Mahābhārata.*
6. M.R. Kale, The *Abhijñāna-śākuntalam* of Kālidāsa, Bombay, 1961. A discussion and translation of the play is included in B. Stoler Miller (ed.), *Theater of Memory*, New York, 1984.
7. E.B. Cowell (ed.), *The Jātakas*, vol. I, no. 7, London, 1969 (repr.) See also Stoler Miller, *Theater of Memory.*
8. C. Malamoud, *Cooking the World*, Delhi, 1996, 87–8; 'Village et Foret dans l'Ideologie de l'Inde Brahmanique', *Archives Sociologie Européene*, July 1976.
9. B. Stoler Miller, *Theater of Memory.*
10. For example, *Bhāgavata Purāṇa*, 9.20.7–32; *Matsya Purāṇa*, 49, 11–15.
11. C.H. Tawney, (ed. and tr.), 1968 (repr.), *The Kathāsarītasāgara*, Ch. XXXII, pp. 306–90.
12. V.S. Agrawala, 'Vāsavadattā and Śakuntalā: Scenes in the Ranigumpha Cave in Orissa', *Journal of the Indian Society of Oriental Art*, 14, 1946, pp. 102–9; C. Rapin, *Indian Art from Afghanistan*, Delhi, 1996; J.H. Marshall, 'Excavations at Bhita', *ASIAR*, 1911–12, Calcutta, 1915, pp. 29–49, Plates XXIII–XXIV, No. 17.
13. C. Vaudville, *Bārahmāsā in Indian Literature*, Delhi, 1986; 'A Note on the *Ghataparkara* and the *Meghaduta*', JOI(B), 1959, 9, 2, 129–34.
14. G. Canon and S. Pandey, 'Sir William Jones Revisited: On His Translation of the Śakuntalā', *JAOS*, 1976, 96, 4, pp. 530–37; G. Canon, *The Lift and Mind of Oriental Jones*, Cambridge, 1977; S.N. Mukherjee, *Sir William Jones*, Delhi, 1987 (2nd edn).

15. A. Leslie Willson, *A Mythical Image: The Ideal of India in German Romanticism*, Durham, 1964; J. Sedlar, *India in the Mind of Germany*, Washington, 1982; H. Drew, *India and the Romantic Imagination*, Delhi, 1987.

16. R. Schwab, *The Oriental Renaissance: Europe's Rediscovery of India and the East, 1680–1880*, New York, 1984 (trans.).

17. T.B. Hanson, 'Inside the Romanticist Episteme', *Thesis Eleven*, 1997, 48, pp. 21–41.

18. J. Mill, 1823, *History of British India*, London, II. 2. 111.

19. G. Visvanathan, 1989, *Mask of Conquest*, New York, 121ff.

20. P. Chatterjee, 'The Nationalist Resolution of the Women's Question', in Kumkum Sangari and Sudesh Vaid (eds), *Recasting Women*, Delhi, 1993; 'Colonialism, Nationalism and Coloured Women: The Contest in India', *American Ethnologist*, 1989, 16, 4, pp. 622–33; K. Jayawardena, *The White Woman's Other Burden*, London, 1995.

21. *Modern Review*, 1911, IX, 171ff.

CHAPTER 16

Somanātha

*Narratives of a History**

In the previous chapter, I discussed a narrative and how its retellings as well as the commentaries on it, can be used to illumine the historical times when these were written; and the historical context in turn can illumine the retelling or the commentary. In this essay I shall start with a well-known event, and discuss the diverse narratives which contribute to constructing its representations in history. This theme is in some senses an inversion of the earlier one. It is the use of narrative in history, but in a different way, although the focus is again on retellings or alternative tellings around an event, and therefore, of a different kind from those which I discussed in the previous essay.

In 1026, Maḥmūd of Ghazni raided the temple of Somanātha and broke the idol. Reference is made to this in various sources, or, reference is omitted where one expects to find it. Some of the references contradict each other. Some lead to our asking questions which do not conform to what we have accepted so far in terms of the meaning and the aftermath of the event. An event can get encrusted with interpretations from century to century and this changes the perception of the event. As historians therefore, we have to be aware not just of the event and how we look upon it today, but also the ways in which the event was interpreted through the intervening centuries. The analysis of these sources and the priorities in explanation stem of course from the historian's interpretation.

* This chapter was first published in Narratives and the Making of History: Two Lectures, New Delhi, Oxford University Press, 2000, pp. 25–50.

I would like to place before you five representations of this and other events at Somanātha, keeping in mind the historical question of how Maḥmūd's raid was viewed. They cover a wide span and are major representations. The five are the accounts originating from Turko-Persian concerns, Jaina texts of the period, Sanskrit inscriptions from Somanātha, the debate in the British House of Commons and what is often described as a nationalist reading of the event.

Let me begin with a brief background to Somanātha itself. It is referred to in the *Mahābharāta* as Prabhās, and although it had no temple until later, it was a place of pilgrimage, a *tīrtha*—also associated with Kṛṣṇa and the Pāṇḍavas.[1] As was common to many parts of the subcontinent there were a variety of religious sects established in the area—Buddhist, Jaina, Śaiva, and Muslim. Some existed in succession and some conjointly. The Śaiva temple, known as the Somanātha temple at Prabhās, dates to about the ninth or tenth century AD.[2] The Caulukyas or Solankis were the ruling dynasty in Gujarat during the eleventh to thirteenth centuries. Kathiawar was administered by lesser *rājā*s some of whom were subordinates of the Caulukyas.

Saurashtra was agriculturally fertile, but even more than that, its prosperity came from trade, particularly maritime trade. The port at Somanātha, known as Veraval, was one of the three major ports of Gujarat. During this period western India had a conspicuously wealthy trade with ports along the Arabian peninsula and the Persian Gulf.[3] The antecedents of this trade go back many centuries. The Arab conquest of Sind was less indelible than the more permanent contacts based on trade. Arab traders and shippers settled along the west coast, married locally and were ancestors to many communities existing to the present. Some Arabs took employment with local rulers and Rāṣṭrakūta inscriptions speak of Tajika administrators and governors in the coastal areas.[4] The counterparts to these Arab traders were Indian merchants based at Hormuz and at Ghazni, who, even after the eleventh century, are described as extremely prosperous.[5]

The trade focused on the importing of horses from West Asia and also included wine, metal, textiles, and spices. The most lucrative was the trade in horses.[6] Funds from temples formed a sizeable investment according to some sources.[7] Port towns such as Somanātha-Veraval and Cambay derived a handsome income from this trade, much of it doubtless being ploughed back to enlarge the profits. Apart from trade, another source of local income were the large sums of money collected in pilgrim taxes by the administration in Somanātha. This was a fairly common source of revenue for the same is mentioned in connection with the temple at Multan.[8] We are also told that the local *rājās*—the Cūḍasamas, Ābhiras, Yādavas and others—attacked the pilgrims and looted them of their donations intended for the Somanātha temple. In addition there was heavy piracy in the coastal areas indulged in by the local Chāvḍa *rājā*s and a variety of sea brigands referred to as the Bawarij.[9] As with many areas generating wealth in earlier times, this part of Gujarat was also subject to unrest and the Caulukya administration spent much time and energy policing attacks on pilgrims and traders.

Despite all this, trade flourished. Gujarat in this period experienced what can perhaps be called a renaissance culture of the Jaina mercantile community. Rich merchant families were in political office, controlled state finance, were patrons of culture, were scholars of the highest order, were liberal donors to the Jaina *saṅgha* and builders of magnificent temples.

This is the backdrop as it were, to the Somanātha temple which by many accounts suffered a raid by Maḥmūd in 1026. There is one sober, contemporary reference and this comes not surprisingly, from Alberuni, a Central Asian scholar deeply interested in India, writing extensively on what he observed and learnt. He tells us that there was a stone fortress built about a hundred years before Maḥmūd's raid, within which the *liṅgam* was located—presumably to safeguard the wealth of the temple. The idol was especially venerated by sailors and traders, not surprising considering the importance of the port at Veraval, trading as far as Zanzibar and China. He comments in a general way on the economic devastation caused by the many raids of Maḥmūd. Alberuni also mentions that Durlabha Multan, presumably a mathematician, used a roundabout way involving various eras, to compute the year of the raid on Somanātha as Śaka 947 (equivalent to AD 1025–6).[10] The raid therefore was known to local sources.

Not unexpectedly, the Turko-Persian chronicles indulge in elaborate myth-making around the event, some of which I shall now relate. A major poet of the eastern Islamic world, Farrukhī Sīstānī, who claims that he accompanied Maḥmūd to Somanātha, provides a fascinating explanation for the breaking of the idol.[11] This explanation has been largely dismissed by modern historians as too fanciful, but it has a significance for the assessment of iconoclasm. According to him the idol at Somanātha was not of a Hindu deity but of a pre-Islamic Arabian goddess. He tells us that the name Somnat (as it was often written in Persian) is actually, Su-manat—the place of Manāt. We know from the *Qur'ān* that Lāt, Uzza, and Manāt were the three pre-Islamic goddesses widely worshipped,[12] and the destruction of their shrines and images it was said, had been ordered by the prophet Mohammad. Two were destroyed, but Manāt was believed to have been secreted away to Gujarat and installed in a place of worship. According to some descriptions Manāt was an aniconic block of black stone, so the form could be similar to a *liṅgam*. This story hovers over many of the Turko-Persian accounts, some taking it seriously, others being less emphatic and insisting instead that the icon was of a Hindu deity.

In the thirteenth century, the famous Persian poet Sa'dī provides a garbled description.[13] He claims to have visited the Somanātha temple, although there is no other mention of this. According to him the idol was of ivory and decorated like the idol of Manāt—a faultless, female form. Its hands moved magically, but when he secretly investigated this, it turned out that they were attached by string to the hands of a person standing behind the idol who worked their movements. According to him the rituals were conducted by priests who came from Iran. This is obviously the fantasy of a poet who has combined the story of Manāt, information on string puppets and rumours of some *brāhmaṇas* having associations with Iran and with the worship of the sun, perhaps confusing Somanātha with the sun-temple at Multan.

The identification of the Somanātha idol with that of Manāt has little historical credibility. There is no evidence to suggest that the temple housed an image of Manāt. Nevertheless the story is significant to the reconstruction of the aftermath of the event, since it is closely tied to the kind of legitimation which was being projected for Maḥmūd.

The link with Manāt added to the acclaim for Maḥmūd. Not only was he the prize iconoclast in breaking Hindu idols, but, in destroying Manāt, he had carried out what were said to be the very orders of the Prophet. He was therefore doubly a champion of Islam.[14] Other temples are raided by him and their idols broken, but Somanātha receives special attention in all the accounts of his activities. Writing of his victories to the Caliphate, Maḥmūd presents them as major accomplishments in the cause of Islam. And not surprisingly Maḥmūd becomes the recipient of grandiose titles. This establishes his legitimacy in the politics of the Islamic world, a dimension which is overlooked by those who see his activities only in the context of northern India.

But his legitimacy also derives from the fact that he was a Sunni and he attacked Ismā'īlīs and Shias whom the Sunnis regarded as heretics.[15] It was ironic that the Ismā'īlīs attacked the temple of Multan and were in turn attacked by Maḥmūd in the eleventh century and their mosque was shut down. The fear of the heretic was due to the popularity of heresies against orthodox Islam and political hostility to the Caliphate in the previous couple of centuries, none of which would be surprising given that Islam in these areas was a relatively new religion. Maḥmūd is said to have desecrated their places of worship at Multan and Manṣūra. His claims to having killed fifty thousand *kāfirs*—infidels—is matched by similar claims to his having killed fifty thousand Muslim heretics. The figure appears to be notional. Maḥmūd's attacks on the Hindus and on the Shias and Ismā'īlīs, was a religious crusade against the infidel and the heretic. But interestingly, these were also the places and peoples involved in the highly profitable horse trade with the Arabs and the Gulf. Both the Muslim heretics of Multan and the Hindu traders of Somanātha had substantial commercial investments. Is it possible then that Maḥmūd, in addition to religious iconoclasm, was also trying to terminate the import of horses into India via Sind and Gujarat? This would have curtailed the Arab monopoly over the trade. Given the fact that there was a competitive horse trade with Afghanistan through northwestern India, which was crucial to the wealth of the state of Ghazni, Maḥmūd may well have been combining iconoclasm with trying to obtain a commercial advantage.[16]

In the subsequent and multiple accounts—and there are many in each century—the contradictions and exaggerations increase. There is no agreement on the form of the image. Some say that it is a *liṅgam*, others reverse this and describe it as anthropomorphic—a human form.[17] But even with this there is no consistency as to whether it is a female Manāt or a male Śiva. There seems to have been almost a lingering wish that it might be Manāt. Was the icon, if identified with Manāt, more important perhaps to Muslim sentiment?

The anthropomorphic form encouraged stories of the nose being knocked off and the piercing of the belly from which jewels poured forth.[18] Fantasizing on the wealth of the temples evoked a vision of immense opulence, and this could suggest that the Turkish invasions were a veritable 'gold-rush'.[19] One account states that the image contained twenty *man* of jewels—one *man* weighing several kilograms; another, that a gold chain weighing two hundred *man* kept the image in place. Yet another describes the icon as made of iron with a magnet placed above it, so that it would be suspended in space, an awesome sight for the worshipper.[20] The age of the temple is taken further and further back in time until it is described as thirty thousand years old. One wonders if the Somanātha idol was not becoming something of a fantasy in such accounts.

More purposive writing of the fourteenth century are the chronicles of Baranī and Isāmi. Both were poets, one associated with the Delhi Sultanate and the other with the Bahmani kingdom of the Deccan. Both project Maḥmūd as the ideal Muslim hero, but somewhat differently. Baranī states that his writing is intended to educate Muslim rulers in their duties towards Islam.[21] For him, religion and kingship are twins and the ruler needs to know the religious ideals of kingship if he claims to be ruling on behalf of

God. Sultans must protect Islam through the *sharī'a* and destroy both Muslim heretics and infidels. Maḥmūd is said to be the ideal ruler because he did both.

Isāmi composes what he regards as an epic poem on the Muslim rulers of India, on the lines of the famous Persian poet Firdausī's earlier epic on the Persian kings, the *Shāh-nāma.* Isāmi argues that kingship descended from God, first to the pre-Islamic rulers of Persia—in which he includes Alexander of Macedon and the Sassanid kings, and subsequently to the Sultans of India, with Maḥmūd establishing Muslim rule in India.[22] Interestingly the Arabs, who had both a political and economic presence in the subcontinent prior to Maḥmūd, hardly figure in this history. That there is a difference of perception in these narratives, is important to a historical assessment and requires further investigation.

The role of Maḥmūd it would seem, was also undergoing a change from being viewed merely as an iconoclast to also being projected as the founder of an Islamic state in India, even if the latter statement was not historically accurate. Presumably given his status in Islamic historiography, this was a form of indirectly legitimizing the Sultans in India. The appropriation of the pre-Islamic Persian rulers for purposes of legitimacy, suggests that there may have been an element of doubt about the accepted role-models of Muslim rulers. The Sultans in India were not only ruling a society substantially of non-Muslims, but even those who had converted to Islam were in large part following the customary practices of their *zāt*, their erstwhile caste, which were often not in conformity with the *sharī'a.* Is there then a hint of an underlying uncertainty, of a lack of confidence, in the insistence on taking Islamic rule back to Maḥmūd, a champion of the Islamic world? Can we say that these accounts had converted the event itself at Somanātha, into what some today would call, an icon?

In the post-fourteenth century, narratives of the event continue with still greater embellishments and these are perhaps what we would see as a cloud of hype. Of the actual temple the impression sought to be created is that it never recovered from the raid and ceased to be important. Yet every few decades some Sultan is said to have attacked the Somanātha temple and converted it into a mosque.[23] Logically therefore, and logic is not at a premium in these accounts, they would, after the first attack, be attacking a mosque. In a sense the claim ceases to be history and becomes rhetoric. Nor does this stop Sanskrit texts from continuing to refer to it as a temple, a holy city, a second Kailāśa.[24] Was this a parallel situation to the mosque-church toggle-switching at places such as Cordoba in Spain and Santa Sophia in Istanbul, each time the area changed rulers or a religion receded?

Let me turn now to the Jaina texts of this period. These, not unexpectedly, associate a different set of concerns with the event, or else they ignore it. The eleventh-century Jaina poet from the Paramāra court in Malwa, Dhanapāla, a contemporary of Maḥmūd, briefly mentions Maḥmūd's campaign in Gujarat and his raids on various places including Somanātha.[25] He comments however, at much greater length on Maḥmūd's inability to damage the icons of Mahāvīra in Jaina temples for, as he puts it, snakes cannot swallow Garuda nor can stars dim the light of the sun. This for him is proof of the superior power of the Jaina images as compared to the Śaiva, the latter having been descecrated.

In the early twelfth century, another Jaina text informs us that the Caulukya king, angered by the *rākṣasa*s, the *daitya*s, and the *asura*s who were destroying temples and disturbing the *ṛṣi*s and *brāhmaṇa*s, campaigned against them.[26] One expects the list to include the Turuṣkas as the Turks were called, but instead mention is made of the local *rājā*s. The king is said to have made a pilgrimage to Somanātha and found that the temple was old and was disintegrating. He is said to have stated that it was a disgrace that the local *rājā*s were plundering the pilgrims to Somanātha but could not keep the temple in good repair. This is the same king who built a mosque at Cambay, which mosque was later destroyed in a campaign against the Caulukyas of Gujarat by the Paramāras of Malwa. But the Paramāra king also looted the Jaina and other temples built under the patronage of the Caulukyas.[27] It would seem that when the temple was seen as a statement of power, it could become a target of attack, irrespective of religious affiliations.

In the late twelfth century during the reign of the famous Caulukya king, Kumārapāla, there is much activity around the

Somanātha temple. Among the ministers of Kumārapāla was Hemacandra, a respected and erudite scholar of Jaina religious history, and incidentally a rival of the Śaiva Pāśupata chief priest of the Somanātha temple, Bhāva Bṛhaspati. Such Śaiva–Jaina rivalry was known to other parts of the subcontinent as well. There is therefore some discrepancy between the statements of the minister and the chief priest.

Various Jaina texts, giving the history of Kumārapāla mention his connection with Somanātha. It is stated that he wished to be immortalized.[28] So Hemacandra persuaded the king to replace the dilapidated temple at Somanātha with a new stone temple. The temple is clearly described as dilapidated and not destroyed. When the new temple on the location of the old had been completed, both Kumārapāla and Hemacandra took part in the ritual of consecration. Hemacandra wished to impress the king with the spiritual powers of a Jaina *ācārya*, so on his bidding Śiva, the deity of the temple, appeared before the king. Kumārapāla was so overcome by this miracle that he converted to the Jaina faith. The focus again is on the superior power of Jainism over Śaivism. The renovating of the temple which is also important, takes on the symbolism of political legitimation for the king. It does seem curious that these activities focused on the Somanātha temple, yet no mention is made of Maḥmūd, in spite of the raid having occurred in the previous couple of centuries. The miracle is the central point in the connection with Somanātha in these accounts.

Some suggestion of an anguish over what may be indirect references to the raids of Maḥmūd come from quite other Jaina sources and interestingly, these relate to the merchant community. In an anthology of stories, one refers to the merchant Jāvadī, who quickly makes a fortune in trade and then goes in search of a Jaina icon which had been taken away to the land called Gajjana.[29] This is clearly Ghazna. The ruler of Gajjana was a Yavana—a term by now used for those coming from the west. The Yavana ruler was easily won over by the wealth presented to him by Jāvadī. He allowed Jāvadī to search for the icon and when it was found, gave him permission to take it back. Not only that but the Yavana worshipped the icon prior to its departure. The second part of the narrative deals with the vicissitudes of having the icon installed in Gujarat, but that is another story.

This is a reconciliation story with a certain element of wishful thinking. The initial removal of the icon is hurtful and creates anguish. Its return should ideally be through reconciling iconoclasts to the worship of icons. There are other touching stories in which the ruler of Gajjana or other Yavana kings are persuaded not to attack Gujarat. But such stories are generally related as a demonstration of the power of the Jaina *ācāryas*.

The Jaina sources therefore underline their own ideology. Jaina temples survive, Śaiva temples get destroyed. Śiva has abandoned his icons unlike Mahāvīra who still resides in his icons and protects them. Attacks are to be expected in the Kaliyuga—the present age—since it is an age of evil. Icons will be broken but wealthy Jaina merchants will restore the temple and the icons will invariably and miraculously, mend themselves.

The argument about Kaliyuga and iconoclasm also occurs in the *Purāṇas*, where an increasing decline in *dharma* accompanies the passing of the cycle of time. Deities desert their icons in the Kaliyuga especially if kings are not attentive enough to them.[30] Sometimes there is a mention of temples being destroyed but generally they are said to have been dilapidated and neglected—as would be expected in an age of declining virtue—and therefore requiring repair. The association with Kaliyuga gives the situation a feeling of infallibility. Kaliyuga is therefore a partial but generalized reference to the vulnerability of the practice and symbol of *dharma*. What remains curious is the lack of specific mention about Maḥmūd's raid on Somanātha, which in the Turko-Persian chronicles is so central.

The third category of major narratives is constituted by the inscriptions in Sanskrit from Somanātha itself, focusing on the temple and its vicinity. The perspectives which these point to are again very different from the earlier two. In the twelfth century the Caulukya king, Kumārapāla, issues an inscription. He appoints a governor to protect Somanātha and the protection is against the piracy and the looting by the local *rājās*.[31] A century later, the Caulukyas are again protecting the site, this time from attacks by the Malwa *rājās*.[32] The regular complaint about local *rājās* looting pilgrims at Somanātha becomes a continuing refrain in many inscriptions.

In 1169, an inscription records the appointment of the chief priest of the Somanātha temple, Bhāva Bṛhaspati.[33] He claims to have come from Kannauj, from a family of Pāśupata Śaiva *brāhmaṇas* and, as the inscriptions show, initiated a succession of powerful priests at the Somanātha temple. He states that he was sent by Śiva himself to rehabilitate the temple. This was required because it was an old structure, much neglected by the officers and because temples in any case deteriorate in the Kaliyuga. Bhāva Bṛhaspati claims that it was he who persuaded Kumārapāla to replace the older wooden temple with a stone temple.

Again no mention is made of the raid of Maḥmūd. Was this out of embarrassment, that a powerful icon of Śiva had been desecrated? Or was the looting of a temple not such an extraordinary event? The Turko-Persian chronicles may well have been indulging in exaggeration. Yet the looting of the pilgrims by the local *rājās* is repeatedly mentioned. Was Kumārapāla's renovation both an act of veneration of Śiva but also a seeking of legitimation? Was this in a sense an inversion of Maḥmūd seeking legitimation through raiding the temple? Are these then counter-points of legitimation in viewing the past?

In 1264, a long legal document was issued in the form of an inscription with both a Sanskrit and an Arabic version and concerns the acquisition of land and the building of a mosque by a trader from Hormuz.[34] Being a legal document it was dated in four current dating systems—Hijrī, Saṁvat, Siṁha, and Valabhī. The Sanskrit version begins with the usual formulaic symbol—the *siddham*—and continues with invoking Viśvanātha, a name for Śiva. But there is also a suggestion that it was a rendering into Sanskrit of Allah, the Lord of the Universe. The parallelism is striking at more than one place in the inscription and can be viewed as yet another example of cultural translation. We are told that Khoja Noradina Piroja/Nuruddin Feruz, the son of Khoja Nau Abu Brahima of Hurmujadeśa/Hormuz, a *nakhuda* or commander of a ship, a *sadr*/chief and evidently a respected trader—as his title Khoja/Khwajah, would indicate—acquired land in

Mahājanapālī on the outskirts of the town of Somanātha, to build a mosque, which is referred to as a *mijigiti/masjid*, and described as a *dharmasthāna*. The land was acquired from the local *rājā*, Srī Chāḍā, son of Nānasiṁha, and reference is also made to the governor of Kathiawar, the *mahāmātya* Māladeva, and the Caulukya–Vaghela king, Arjunadeva.

The acquisition of this land has the approval of two local bodies—the *pañcakula* and the association of the *jamātha*. The *pañcakula*s were powerful administrative and local committees, well-established by this period, consisting of recognized authorities such as priests, officers, merchants, local dignitaries. This particular *pañcakula* was headed by the Para/*purohita* Vīrabadhra, the Śaiva Pāśupata *ācārya* most likely of the Somanātha temple, and among its members was the merchant Abhyasiṁha. From other inscriptions it would seem that Para Vīrabadhra was related to Bhāva Bṛhaspati in a line of succession. The witnesses to this agreement of granting land for the building of the mosque are mentioned by name and described as the *bṛhat-puruṣa*, literally 'the big men'. They were the *Ṭhakkura*s, *Rāṇaka*s, *Rājā*s and merchants, many from the Mahājanapālī. Some of these dignitaries were functionaries of the estates of the Somanātha and other temples. The land given for the mosque in Mahājanapālī was part of these estates.

The other committee endorsing the agreement was the *jamātha*, consisting of ship-owners, artisans, sailors, and religious teachers, probably from Hormuz. Also mentioned are the oil-millers, masons, and Musalman horse-handlers, all referred to by what appear to be occupational or caste names, such as *cūnākāra* and *ghamcika*. Were these local converts to Islam? Since the *jamātha* was to ensure these endowments for the maintenance of the mosque, it was necessary to indicate its membership.

The inscription lists the endowments for the mosque. These included two large measures of land which were part of the temple property from adjoining temples situated in Somanātha-pattana; land from a *maṭha*; income from two shops in the vicinity, and an oil mill. The measures of land were bought from the *purohita* and the chief priests of the temples and the sales were attested by the men of rank. The shops and the oil-mill were purchased from the local people. One of the chief priests, Tripurāntaka, seems to appear again, twenty-three years later, in a number of inscriptions as a wealthy and powerful Pāśupata Śaiva priest who built many temples in the vicinity.[35] As with many Sanskirt votive inscriptions, it ends with the hope that the terms and conditions of the agreement may last as long as the moon and sun endure.

The tone and sentiment of the inscription is amicable and clearly the settlement had been agreed to on all sides. The building of a substantial mosque in association with some of the properties of the Somanātha temple, not by a conqueror but by a trader through a legal agreement, was obviously not objected to, neither by the local governor and dignitaries nor by the priests, all of whom were party to the decision. The mosque is thus closely linked to the erstwhile properties and the functionaries of the Somanātha temple.

This raises many questions. Did this transaction, two hundred or so years after the raid of Maḥmūd, not interfere with the remembrance of the raid as handed down, in the minds of the priests and the local 'big men'? Were memories short or was the event relatively unimportant?

Nuruddin Feroz used Sanskrit and Arabic for the agreement, Sanskrit as the local formal language and Arabic probably as the language of incoming traders. The two texts are by and large similar but not identical. The Arabic version carries the hope that the people of Somanātha will convert to Islam—a statement which is wisely deleted in the Sanskrit version. The use of Arabic points to a specific identity distinct from the use of Persian in connection with Maḥmūd. Did the local people make a distinction between the Arab and West Asian traders on the one hand—often referred to as Tājikas, and Turks or Turuṣkas on the other? And were the former acceptable and the Turks much less so? Clearly they were not all homogenized and identified as 'Muslims', as we would do today. Should we not sift the reactions to the event by examining the responses of particular social groups and situations? Hormuz was crucial to the horse trade, therefore Nuruddin was welcomed. Did the profits of trade overrule other considerations? Were the temples and their administrators also investing in horse-trading and making handsome profits?

In the fifteenth century a number of short inscriptions from Gujarat refer to the battles against the Turks. One very moving inscription in Sanskrit comes from Somanātha itself.[36] Although written in Sanskrit, it begins with the Islamic formulaic blessing—*bismillah rahman-i-rahim.* It gives details of the family of the Vohara/Bohra Farīd and the Bohras were of Arab descent. We are told that the town of Somanātha was attacked by the Turuṣkas, the Turks, and Vohara Farīd who was the son of Vohara Muhammad, joined in the defence of the town, fighting against the Turuṣkas on behalf of the local ruler Brahmadeva. Farīd was killed and the inscription is a memorial to him.

It would seem from the sources that I have tried to place before you, that the aftermath of the raid of Maḥmūd on the temple of Somanātha took the form of varying perceptions of the event, and different from what we have assumed. There are no simplistic explanations that would emerge from any or all of these narratives. How then have we arrived today at the rather simplistic historical theory that the raid of Maḥmūd created a trauma in the Hindu consciousness which has been at the root of Hindu–Muslim relations ever since. Or to put it in the words of K.M. Munshi, 'For a thousand years Maḥmūd's destruction of the shrine has been burnt into the collective subconscious of the [Hindu] race as an unforgettable national disaster'.[37]

Interestingly, what appears to be the earliest mention of a 'Hindu trauma' in connection with Maḥmūd's raid on Somanātha, comes from the debate in the House of Commons in London in 1843, on the question of the gates of the Somanātha temple.[38] In 1842, Lord Ellenborough issued his famous 'Proclamation of the Gates' in which he ordered General Nott, in charge of the British Army in Afghanistan, to return via Ghazni and bring back to India the sandalwood gates from the tomb of Maḥmūd. They were believed to have been looted by Maḥmūd from Somanātha. It was claimed that the intention was to return what was looted from India, an act which would symbolize British control over Afghanistan despite their poor showing in the Anglo–Afghan wars.

It was also presented as an attempt to reverse Indian subjugation to Afghanistan in the pre-British period. Was this an appeal to Hindu sentiment, as some maintained?

The Proclamation raised a storm in the House of Commons and became a major issue in the cross-fire between the government and the opposition. The question was asked whether Ellenborough was catering to religious prejudices by appeasing the Hindus or was he appealing to national sympathies. It was defended by those who maintained that the gates were a 'national trophy' and not a religious icon. In this connection the request of Ranjit Singh, the ruler of the Punjab, to the king of Afghanistan, Shah Shujah, for the return of the gates, was quoted. But on examining the letter making this request, it was discovered that Ranjit Singh had confused the Somanātha temple with the Jagannātha temple. It was also argued that no historian mentions the gates in the various accounts of Maḥmūd's raid, therefore the story of the gates could only be an invention of folk tradition.

The historians referred to were Gibbon who wrote on the Roman empire, Firdausī and Sa'dī—both Persian poets, and Firishta. The last of these was the only one who, in the seventeenth century had written on Indian history. Firishta was well known because Alexander Dow had translated his history into English in the late eighteenth century. Firishta's account of the sack of Somanātha was as fanciful as the earlier accounts, with obvious exaggerations such as the huge size of the idol and the quantity of jewels that poured out when Maḥmūd pierced its belly. Members of the House of Commons were using their perceptions of Indian history as ammunition in their own political and party hostilities.

Those critical of Ellenborough were fearful of the consequences; they saw the fetching of the gates as supporting a native religion, and that too, the monstrous 'Linga-ism' as they called it; and they felt that its political consequences would be violent indignation among the Mohammadans. Those supporting Ellenborough, in the House of Commons, argued equally vehemently, that he was removing the feeling of degradation from the minds of the Hindus. It would '. . . relieve that country, which had been overrun by the Mohammadan conqueror, from the painful feelings which had been rankling amongst the people for nearly a thousand years'. And that '. . . the memory of the gates [has been] preserved by the Hindus as a painful memorial of the most devastating invasions that had ever desolated Hindustan.'

Ellenborough saw Maḥmūd's raid on Somanātha as embedded in the Hindu psyche and the return of the gates he felt would avenge the insult of eight hundred years.[39] Did this debate fan an anti-Muslim Hindu sentiment among Hindus in India, which, judging from the earlier sources, had either not existed, or been marginal and localized? The absence in earlier times of an articulation of a trauma, remains enigmatic.

The gates were uprooted and brought back in triumph. But on arrival they were found to be of Egyptian workmanship and not associated in any way with India. So they were placed in a storeroom in the Agra Fort and possibly by now have been eaten by white ants.

From this point on, the arguments of the debate in the House of Commons come to be reflected in the writing on Somanātha. Maḥmūd's raid was made into the central point in Hindu–Muslim relations. K.M. Munshi led the demand for the restoration of the Somanātha temple. His obsession with restoring the glories of Hindu history, began in a general way with his writing historical novels, inspired by reading Walter Scott. But the deeper imprint came from his familiarity with Bankim Chandra Chatterji's sentiments in *Ānandamaṭha*,[40] as is evident from his novel, *Jaya Somanatha*, published in 1927. And as one historian, R.C. Majumdar, puts it, Bankim Chandra's nationalism was Hindu rather than Indian. This is made crystal clear from his other writings which contain passionate outbursts against the subjugation of India by the Muslims'.[41] Bankim Chandra was not alone in being hostile to both British and Muslim rule. Munshi was concerned with restoring the Hindu Aryan glory of the pre-Islamic past. Muslim rule was viewed as the major disjuncture in Indian history. Munshi's comments often echo the statements made in the House of Commons debate as is evident from his book, *Somanatha—The Shrine Eternal*.

His insistence that the temple be restored led to the excavation of the site in 1950, the results of which contradicted much of what he maintained. The reconstruction through archaeology and architectural history indicated an original temple of the ninth or tenth century, more likely the latter, with some signs of desecration.[42] An eleventh-century temple was rebuilt on the earlier plan and this structure was replaced in about the twelfth century. There is little evidence of later structures of importance or major reconstructions.

Munshi made the Somanātha temple into the most important symbol of Muslim iconoclasm in India. But prior to this, its significance appears to have been largely regional. Consistent references to it as a symbol of Muslim iconoclasm are to be found largely only in the Turko-Persian chronicles. Possibly the fact that Munshi was himself from Gujarat may have had some role in his projection of Somanātha. In other parts of the country the symbols of iconoclasm, where they existed, were places of local importance and knowledge of the raid on Somanātha was of marginal interest.

On the rebuilding of the Somanātha temple in 1951, Munshi, by then a minister of the central government had this to say. '... the collective subconscious of India today is happier with the scheme of the reconstruction of Somanātha, sponsored by the Government of India, than with many other things we have done or are doing.'[43] Nehru objected strongly to the Government of India being associated with the project and insisted on its being restored as a private venture.[44] That the President of India, Rajendra Prasad was to perform the consecration ceremony was even more unacceptable to him. He was further irritated by Munshi writing to Indian ambassadors in various parts of the world, asking for jars of water from the rivers of the countries to which they were accredited as also a variety of plants, to be sent to India—presumably via the diplomatic bag—and all of which were said to be necessary to the consecration ceremony of the reconstructed temple. The ceremony itself was attended by a few stalwart nationalists some associated with the government, thus providing a hint of some of their substratum concerns. This introduces a further dimension to the reading of the event, involving the secular credentials of society and state.

The received opinion is that events such as the raid on Somanātha created what has been called, two antagonistic categories of epic: the 'epic of conquest' and the 'counter-epic of resistance'.[45] It has also been thought of as epitomizing in later Turko-Persian narratives 'the archetypal encounter of Islam with Hindu idolatry'.[46] We may well ask how and when did this dichotomy crystallize? Did it emerge with modern historians reading too literally from just one set of narratives, without juxtaposing these with the other narratives? If narratives are read without being placed in a historiographical context, the reading is, to put it mildly, incomplete and therefore distorted. Firishta's version for example, was repeated endlessly in recent times, without considering its historiography: neither was this done within the tradition of the Turko-Persian chronicles nor in the context of other narratives which can be said to impinge on the same event. Or, has the dichotomy becomes such a mind-set that we are unable to comprehend the complexities and nuances of the representations of an event, and its aftermath, however familiar they may be?

We continue to see such situations as a binary projection of Hindu and Muslim. Yet what should be evident from the sources which I have discussed is that there are multiple groups with varying agendas, involved in the way in which the event and Somanātha are represented. There are differentiations in the attitudes of the Persian chronicles towards the Arabs and the Turks. Within the Persian sources, the earlier fantasy of Manāt gradually gives way to a more political concern with the legitimacy of Islamic rule in India through the Sultans. Was there, on the part of the Persian chroniclers, a deliberate down-playing of the Arab intervention in India? Were the politics of heresy and revolt in the history of Islam at this period, linked to these attitudes? The hostility between the Bohras and the Turks, technically both Muslims, may have also been part of this confrontation since the Bohras had some Arab ancestry and probably saw themselves as among the settled communities of Gujarat and saw the Turks as invaders.

Biographies and histories from Jaina authors, discussing matters pertaining to the royal court and to the religion of the elite, focus on attempts to show Mahāvīra in a better light than Śiva and the agenda becomes that of the competing rivalry between the Jainas and the Śaivas. But the sources which focus on a different social group, that of the Jaina merchants, seem to be conciliatory towards the confrontation with Maḥmūd, perhaps because the trading community would have suffered heavy disruptions in periods of raids and campaigns.

From the Veraval inscription of 1264, co-operation in the building of the mosque came from a range of social groups, from the most orthodox ritual specialists to those wielding secular authority and from the highest property holders to those with lesser property. Interestingly, the local members of the *jamātha*, if they were all Muslims—as is likely—were largely from occupations at the lower end of the social scale. As such, their responsibility for the maintenance of the mosque would have required the goodwill of the Somanātha elite. Did the elite see themselves as patrons of a new kind of control over property?

These relationships were not determined by the general category of what have been called Hindu interests and Muslim interests. They varied in accordance with more particular interests and these drew on identities of ethnicity, economic concerns, religious sectarianism, and social status.

Let me conclude by briefly returning to my initial comments on narrative and history. There are those who argue that narrative speaks for itself and does not require historians to interpret it. But narrative does not speak, it is spoken. The historian in giving a voice to the narrative invests it with nuances, emphases, and interpretations. This is inevitably a different voice from that of the poet, the dramatist, the chronicler, although there may be points of fusion. The recognition of differences, it seems to me enriches the reading. We need to understand why there are variants and what is their individual agenda. Even in fictionalized accounts there is a politics in the telling and the retelling, as I have tried to show in the first essay. This becomes more evident where diverse narratives are wrapped around what might relate to the same event.

Different narratives reconstitute events in different ways. Narratives involve an interface with the historical moment and encapsulate ideological structures. All narrative representations do not have an equal validity even if a single, authentic, foundational narrative cannot be identified. Merely to analyse fragments cannot be the end purpose of writing history. The priorities used by the historian in explaining the narratives becomes relevant and can suggest the interlinks and patterns emerging from the fragments. The narrative can also stretch its presuppositions over a long duration of time and move across this duration; as indeed each narrative can present a different image.

In the retelling of an event, there may be a claim that it encapsulates memory or a succession of memories: so too the question of whether or why there may be an amnesia. Memory is sometimes claimed in order to create an identity, and history based on such claims is used to legitimize the identity. Establishing a fuller understanding of the event is crucial in both instances, for otherwise the identity and its legitimation, can be historically invalid.

I have tried to show how each set of narratives turn the focus of what Somanātha symbolizes: the occasion for the projection of an iconoclast and champion of Islam; the assertion of the superiority of Jainism over Śaivism; the inequities of the Kaliyuga; the centrality of the profits of trade subordinating other considerations; colonial perceptions of Indian society as having always been an antagonistic duality of Hindu and Muslim; Hindu nationalism and the restoration of a particular view of the past contesting the secularizing of modern Indian society. But these are not discrete foci. Even when juxtaposed, a pattern emerges; a pattern which requires that the understanding of the event should be historically contextual, multi-faceted, and aware of the ideological structures implicit in the narratives.

I would argue that Maḥmūd of Ghazni's raid on the Somanātha temple, did not create a dichotomy, because each of the many facets involved in the perception of the event, consciously or subconsciously, was enveloped in a multiplicity of other contexts as well. These direct our attention to varying representations, both overt and hidden, and lead us to explore the statements implicit in these representations. The assessment of these facets may provide us with more sensitive insights into our past.

NOTES AND REFERENCES

1. *Vana parvan* 13. 14: 80. 78; 86. 18–19; 119. 1.

2. B.K. Thapar, 'The Temple at Somanātha: History by Excavations', in K.M. Munshi, *Somnath: The Shrine Eternal*, Bombay, 1951, pp. 105–33; M.A. Dhaky and H.P. Sastri, *The Riddle of the Temple at Somanātha*, Varanasi, 1974.

3. V.K. Jain, *Trade and Traders in Western India*, Delhi, 1990.

4. *Epigraphia Indica*, XXXII, 47ff.

5. Muhammad Ulfi, *Jami-ul-Hikayat*, in Eliot and Dowson, *The History of India as Told by Its Own Historians*, II, 201. Wasa Ābhīra from Anahilvada had property worth ten lakhs in Ghazni: impressive, even if exaggerated.

6. Abdullah Wassaf, *Tazjiyat-ul-Amsar*, in Eliot and Dowson, *The History of India as Told by Its Own Historians*, III, 31ff. Marco Polo also comments on the wealth involved in the horse trade especially with southern India. *Prabandha-cintamani*, p. 14; Rajasekhara, *Prabandhakosa*, Santiniketan, 1935, p. 121.

7. Abdullah Wassaf, Eliot and Dowson, *The History of India*, I, 69; Pehoa Inscription, *Epigraphia Indica*, 1, 18Aff.

8. A. Wink, *Al-Hind*, vol. 1, Delhi, 1990, 173ff; 184ff; 187ff.

9. Alberuni in E.C. Sachau, *Alberuni's India*, New Delhi, 1964 (reprint), I.208.

10. Ibid., II.9–10, 54.

11. F. Sīstānī in M. Nazim, *The Life and Times of Sultan Maḥmūd of Ghazni*, Cambridge, 1931.

12. *Qur'ān*, 53. 19–20. G. Ryckmans, *Les Religions Arabes Pre-Islamique*, Louvain, 1951.

13. Sa'dī, *Bustan* in A.H. Edwards, *The Bustan of Sadi*, London, 1911, p. 109. Quoted in R.H. Davis, *Lives of Indian Images*, New Jersey, 1997, 100ff, Delhi 1971.

14. Muhammad Nazim, *Life and Times of Sultan Maḥmūd.*

15. André Wink, *Al-Hind*, Leiden, 2002. 184–9; pp. 217–18.

16. Cf. Mohammad Habib, *Sultan Maḥmūd of Ghazni*, Delhi, 1967.

17. Ibn Attar quoted in Nazim, op. cit.; Ibn Asir in *Gazetteer of the Bombay Presidency*, I, 523; Eliot and Dowson, II, 248 ff; 468 ff. Al Kazwini, Eliot and Dowson, I 97 ff. Abdullah Wassaf, Eliot and Dowson, III, 44 ff; IV. 181.

18. Attar quoted in Nazim, *Life and Times of Sultan Maḥmūd*, 221; Firishta in J. Briggs, *History of the Rise of the Mohammadan Power in India*, Calcutta, 1966 (reprint).

19. A. Wink, *Al-Hind*, volume II, 124ff.

20. Zakariya al Kazvini, *Asarul-bilad*, Eliot and Dowson, *The History of India*, I, 97ff.

21. *Fatāwa-yi-Jahāndārī* discussed in P. Hardy, *Historians of Medieval India*, Delhi, 1997 (repr.), 25ff; 107ff.

22. *Futūḥ-al-Salāṭīn* discussed in Hardy, *Historians*, pp. 107–8.

23. M.A. Dhaky and H.P. Sastri, *The Riddle of the Temple*, Varanasi, 1974.

24. Ibid.

25. *Satyapurīya-Mahāvīra-utsaha*, III.2. D. Sharma, 'Some New Light on the Route of Maḥmūd of Ghazni's Raid on Somanātha: Multan to Somanātha and Somanātha to Multan', in B.P. Sinha (ed.), *Dr Satkari Mookerji Felicitation Volume*, Varanasi, 1969, pp. 165–8.

26. Hemacandra, *Dvyāśraya-kāvya*, in *Indian Antiquary* 1875, 4, 72ff, 110ff, 232ff; 265ff, Ibid.; J. Klatt, 'Extracts from the Historical Records of the Jainas', *Indian Antiquary*, 1882, 11, pp. 245–56.

27. P. Bhatia, *The Paramaras*, Delhi, 1970, 141.

28. Merutunga, *Prabandha-cintāmani*, C.H. Tawney (trans.), Calcutta, 1899, vol. IV, p. 129ff. G. Bühler, *The Life of Hemacandracarya*, Shantiniketan, 1936.

29. *Nābhinandanoddhāra*, discussed in P. Granoff, 'The Householder as Shaman: Jaina Biographies of Temple Builders', *East and West*, 42, 1992, 2–4, 301–17.

30. P. Granoff, 'Tales of Broken Limbs and Bleeding Wounds: Responses to Muslim Iconoclasm in Medieval India', *East and West*, 41, 1991, 1–4, 182–203. *Vāyu Purāṇa*, I. 58. 31–74; II. 36, pp. 115–25.

31. Praci Inscription, *Poona Orienalist*, 1937, 1.4. 39–46.

32. *Epigraphia Indica*, II, 437ff.

33. Prabhāspattana Inscription, *Bhavnagar, Prakrit and Sanskrit Inscriptions* (BPSI), 186.

34. Somanāthapattana Veraval Inscription, *Epigraphia Indica*, XXXIV, 141ff.

35. The Cintra *Praśasti*, *Epigraphia Indica*, I, 271ff.

36. D.B. Disalkar, 'Inscriptions of Kathiawad', *New Indian Antiquary*, 1939, 1, p. 591.

37. K.M. Munshi (ed.), *Somnath: The Eternal Shrine*, Bombay, 1951, p. 89.

38. *The United Kingdom House of Commons Debate, March 9, 1943*, on, The Somnath [Prabhās Patan] Proclamation, Junagadh 1948, pp. 584–602, 620, 630–2,656, 674.

39. R.H. Davis, *Lives of Indian Images*, p. 202.

40. Pers. com. U. Joshi

41. R.C. Majumdar, *British Paramountcy and Indian Renaissance*, Part II, History and Culture of the Indian People, 1965, Bombay, p. 478.

42. B.K. Thapar, 'Temple at Somnatha: History by Excavations', in Munshi (ed.), *Somnath*, pp. 105–33.

43. Munshi (ed.), *Somnath*, p. 184.

44. S. Gopal (ed.), *Selected Works of Jawaharlal Nehru*, vol. 16, part I, Delhi, 1994, 270ff.

45. Aziz Ahmed, 'Epic and Counter-Epic in Medieval India', *Journal of the American Oriental Society*, 83, 1963, pp. 470–6.

46. Richard H. Davis, *Lives of Indian Images*, Princeton, 1999, p. 93.

Index

About the Author

Romila Thapar is Professor Emeritus of History at Jawaharlal Nehru University, New Delhi. She is a Corresponding Fellow of the British Academy and an Honorary Fellow of Lady Margaret Hall, Oxford, as well as the School of Oriental and African Studies, University of London. She was elected General President of the Indian History Congress in 1983.

She has researched and written extensively on early Indian history and on its historiography, both of earlier and modern times. She was awarded the John W. Kluge Prize for Lifetime Achievement in the Study of Humanity in 2008, administered by the John W. Kluge Center at the Library of Congress. She has also received honorary doctorates from a number of universities including Chicago, Oxford, Edinburgh, Peradeniya, Calcutta, and Panjab. Her publications include *Aśoka and the Decline of the Mauryas* (1961/Third Edition 2012); *A History of India, Vol. I* (1966/1990); *Ancient Indian Social History: Some Interpretations* (1978/Second Edition 2010); *From Lineage to State: Social Formations in the Mid-first Millennium B.C. in the Ganga Valley* (1984/1999); *Śakuntalā: Texts, Readings, Histories* (1999/2010); *Cultural Pasts: Essays in Early Indian History* (2000); *Early India: From the Origins to AD 1300* (2002); *Somnatha: The Many Voices of a History* (2004); *The Aryan: Recasting Constructs* (2008); and *The Past before Us: Historical Traditions of Early North India* (2013).